HBJ

HARCOURT BRACE JOVANOVICH, PUBLISHERS

San Diego   New York   Chicago   Austin   Washington, D.C.
London   Sydney   Tokyo   Toronto

Richard M. Hodgetts
Florida International University

Donald F. Kuratko
Ball State University

MANAGEMENT

THIRD EDITION

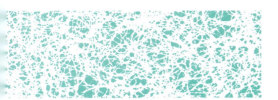

PREFACE

*E*very enterprise, regardless of size, faces the challenge of managing operations effectively. In fact, effective management is an objective that organizations have been pursuing for thousands of years, and there is no evidence that this pursuit will cease in the near future. No matter how well a manager carries out his or her job, there are always ways of doing at last part of the task more effectively. Fortunately, over the last half-century, practitioners of management have come to realize that this process of getting things done through others requires more than just experience, intuition, and a genuine concern for the well-being of the workers. It also requires a basic understanding of management fundamentals that is often more efficiently achieved through some formal study than through on-the-job experience exclusively. The purpose of this book is to identify, examine, and explain these fundamentals, or principles, of management. In doing so, we have employed a number of special features.

SPECIAL FEATURES

The special features are designed to make this book interesting, useful, and challenging. They have been developed to provide ease of reading and clarity of ideas and to make the book "user friendly."

Overall Model

Managers do many different things throughout their work day. The many tasks can be placed in an overall context of planning, organizing, staffing, leading, influencing, and controlling. That is the general model for this book.

Managerial Environment

Management involves more than just a series of functions and does not take place in a vacuum. The manager needs to understand the environment in which he or she operates. For that reason, this book opens with four chapters that examine the nature of management and closes by reviewing the value of management education to the reader. We begin our study of management by looking at the manager's job and the environment in which organizations function and conclude by putting all this information into a meaningful and applied perspective.

Objectives and Review Questions

Each chapter begins with a set of objectives and closes with a series of questions for analysis and discussion. The text material is tied directly to these objectives and questions. At the beginning of the chapter there is a preliminary introduction of what will be covered, and at the end there are follow-up questions that can be used to measure reader understanding and progress.

Margin Notes

In each chapter we have written a series of comments that appear alongside the text material. The purpose of these margin comments is to provide a brief summary of, or reference to, the material that is presented there. For readers who like to make notes as they go along, the comments can be complemented by written personal remarks and summaries that can be used in referring to the text material or studying its contents.

Figures, Exhibits, Charts

Every textbook writer faces the challenge of making the material interesting without sacrificing content. One way in which this can be done is through the use of figures, exhibits, charts, and other materials that enhance the readability and flow of the book. In this text, we have used these tools to present information in an interesting, informative, and entertaining style.

Photographs

Chapter opening photographs have been added throughout the book. In addition, Chapter 2, which presents the history of management thought, contains photographs of famous management personalities, making it easier for the reader to associate names, faces and contributions.

Chapter Summaries

At the end of each chapter, we have written a brief summary of the major points that were presented. The purpose of these summaries is to provide a quick refresher for study and review purposes.

Glossaries

At the end of each chapter there is a glossary of the important terms presented in that chapter. These chapter glossaries allow the reader to quickly review the most important terms associated with the material.

End-of-Chapter Cases

Two cases appear at the end of each chapter. The first is a short one that provides the opportunity to apply some of the major ideas in the chapter to a real-life situation. The second is longer and gives the reader a chance to gather together most of the material in the chapter and apply it to a detailed and involved situation. We have called these longer cases "You Be the Consultant." This type of case allows the reader to assume the role of managerial decision maker and apply chapter materials to lifelike situations. We believe this type of case to be unique.

Integrative Cases

Each major part of the text concludes with a comprehensive, integrative case study that incorporates numerous factors. These cases were professionally prepared, presented, and refereed by professors who are members of the Midwest Society for Case Research. We gratefully acknowledge the following authors for their work: James W. Camerius, Northern Michigan University; Charles F. Douds, DePaul University; Lynda L. Goulet, University of Northern Iowa; Walter E. Greene, Pan American University; Cyril C. Ling, University of Wisconsin — Whitewater; Monty L. Lynn, Abilene Christian University.

These authors have developed these cases as a basis for class discussion through analysis of the material found in the chapters. Each case applies and integrates material from the entire section.

At first, these cases may prove challenging to some readers. By carefully reading each one, making notes, and then rereading it, however, the reader will grasp the critical issues and topics. A review of the chapter material will help establish the link between the text material and the case data. Finally, recommendations and answers to the questions at the end of the case can be formulated. The important thing to remember when working with these cases is that analytical ability will improve with experience. Most readers will find the case analysis approach to be an interesting growth process and one of the most valuable aspects of this text.

SUPPLEMENTARY MATERIALS

While *Management* is a detailed text and is able to stand by itself, supplementary materials have been designed for use by students and teachers.

Study Guide

A Study Guide accompanies this text. It was written by Douglas W. Naffziger, Ball State University. The purpose of the manual is twofold: to reinforce the concepts presented in *Management* and to complement the coverage in the text. Concepts are reinforced by the use of true-false, multiple choice, and matching exercises. The text coverage is complemented by the inclusion of additional problems and application exercises for each part of the text.

Instructional Aids

In addition to the Study Guide, an extensive package of instructional aids accompanies *Management*.

Instructor's Resource Manual

The Instructor's Resource Manual was prepared by Donald F. Kuratko and contains the following features:

(1) Lecture Review and Organization. For each chapter in *Management,* the Instructor's Resource Manual provides (a) learning objectives, (b) a brief summary of the chapter, (c) a chapter outline, (d) a set of comprehensive lecture notes, and (e) suggestions on how to teach the chapter.

(2) Class Discussion and Case Analysis. The questions at the end of the chapter are designed for analysis and discussion. The cases have been developed as a means of reinforcing the important concepts in the chapter. The Instructor's Resource Manual provides recommended answers to all the questions at the end of the chapter as well as the questions that follow the cases. Suggested answers and strategies for using the comprehensive cases are also provided.

(3) Integrative Cases – Teaching Notes. The integrative, comprehensive cases that appear at the conclusion of each major part in the text are designed to provide a basis for class discussion. The Instructor's Resource Manual provides the case author's teaching notes containing suggested strategies and answers

for using the particular case. These are especially helpful in guiding the instructor through the major points of each case.

Testbook

A Testbook of true–false and multiple-choice questions has been developed for use with *Management*. For each chapter in the book, there are 25 true–false and 75 multiple-choice questions.

Transparencies

Approximately 125 2-color and 4-color transparency acetates are available to the instructor. Chosen for their pedagogical value, these transparencies are designed to complement the lectures and provide a basis for discussion of key concepts in the book.

Computerized Test Service

A computerized version of the Testbook is available to adopters. Besides allowing microcomputer test generating, this service also provides options for random question selection and for the inclusion of your own test questions.

ACKNOWLEDGEMENTS

Many people played an important role in helping us refine and improve this edition of *Management*. As always, our families, from whom we take so much time, deserve our love and appreciation — Sally, Steven, and Jennifer Hodgetts, and Debbie, Christina, and Kellie Kuratko.

We would also like to express our appreciation to the staff of Harcourt Brace Jovanovich who worked closely with us on this project, in particular, Scott Isenberg, acquisitions editor; David Watt, manuscript editor; Judi McClellan, production editor; Mandy Van Dusen, production manager; Cheryl Solheid and Linda Harper, designers; and Karen DeLeo, art editor.

For their particular contributions to the development of the present edition, we wish to thank James D. Brodzinski, Salisbury State University, and Monico L. Cisneros, Austin Community College. In addition, we want to express again our appreciation to the following, who aided in the development of previous editions: Robert Findley, Northwest Missouri State University; Robert Gatewood, University of Georgia; Joseph Gray, Nassau Community College; Ki Hee Kim, William Patterson College; Arthur La Capria, Jr., El Paso Community College; James McElroy, Iowa State University; Coenraad Mohr, Illinois State University; and Richard Shapiro, Cuyahoga Community College.

We also would like to express our appreciation to our colleagues at Florida International University, Ball State University, and elsewhere, in particular, Dana Farrow, chairperson of the Management Department, Florida International University, and Jane Gibson, Nova University, for their continued support of our efforts; Jatinder N. D. Gupta, Ball State University, for his advice and direction on the productions and operations research segments; and Marilyn White, Ball State University, for her continued assistance in typing the manuscript. Finally, thanks to Neil A. Palomba, dean of the College of Business at Ball State University, for his enthusiastic support.

Richard M. Hodgetts
Donald F. Kuratko

CONTENTS

THE CHANGING ENVIRONMENT OF MODERN ENTERPRISES   65

INTERNATIONAL MANAGEMENT   91

PART TWO

PLANNING THE
ENTERPRISE'S DIRECTION   129

5

DECISION MAKING IN ACTION   131

6

THE FUNDAMENTALS OF PLANNING   161

7

STRATEGIC PLANNING IN ACTION   191

PART THREE

ORGANIZING THE ENTERPRISE'S STRUCTURE   235

8

DESIGNING THE OVERALL STRUCTURE   237

9

COORDINATION AND DESIGN OF JOBS   271

10

THE HUMAN RESOURCE MANAGEMENT PROCESS   311

PART FOUR

LEADING AND MOTIVATING THE ENTERPRISE 367

11

MANAGERIAL COMMUNICATION 369

12

THE MOTIVATION PROCESS AT WORK 405

13

GROUP BEHAVIOR AND DYNAMICS 439

16

PRODUCTION AND OPERATIONS MANAGEMENT   563

17

PERFORMANCE APPRAISAL AND ORGANIZATIONAL DEVELOPMENT   601

PART SIX

MANAGING THE ENTERPRISE IN A CONTEMPORARY ENVIRONMENT   655

18

ETHICAL STANDARDS AND SOCIAL RESPONSIBILITY   657

19

CORPORATE ENTREPRENEURSHIP: MANAGING INNOVATION   683

20

MANAGEMENT IN THE FUTURE   703

21

MANAGEMENT CAREER PLANNING AND YOU   739

A MANAGEMENT OVERVIEW

The purpose of Part I of this book is to introduce you to the field of management by providing a general overview of the subject. Some of the specific questions answered in this section include: What is management? How do managers spend their time? How did modern management emerge from the contributions of earlier theorists in the field? How does the external environment affect organizations?

Chapter 1 focuses on management and the manager's job. In addition to learning what the term *management* means, you will learn about the various types of managers and the skills required for success in management's ranks. You will also study the four major management functions and learn how together they enable the manager to get things done through other people.

Chapter 2 discusses the evolution of management thought and the people who have contributed the most important ideas to our developing knowledge of management. How do we currently know so much about management? The answer is that both the art and science of management were learned over thousands of years. The Egyptians provided contributions, as did the Greeks, the Chinese, and the people of virtually every other major civilization. Yet it was not until the rise of the Industrial Revolution that a systematic study of management was undertaken on a large scale.

Chapter 3 then examines the environment of modern organizations, considering the external factors with which enterprises today must contend. The chapter identifies, describes, and analyzes these factors, paying particular attention to such environmental forces as the economy, competitors, customers, suppliers, technology, political–legal issues, customs/culture, and international developments.

Chapter 4 describes the international environment that managers must confront. The concepts of international management are discussed, along with the challenges that arise from multinational corporations (MNCs). A final look at the functions of management focuses on their role in the international arena.

When you have finished studying the material in these first four chapters, you will have a basic understanding of what management involves. You will also be aware of some of management's challenges, opportunities, and environments.

1

The Nature and Role of Management

The success of every organization depends heavily on the ability of its managers. This chapter examines the nature of management and the manager's job. It answers questions such as: What is management? What skills are needed by managers? How do managers spend their time? What functions do managers perform? When you have finished studying the material in this chapter, you will know what management entails and how the modern manager carries out his or her job. You will be able to·

1. Define the term *management.*
2. Explain why management is both an art and a science.
3. Describe the criteria of a profession.
4. Compare and contrast the three different types of managers.
5. Describe the three skills of a manager and discuss the difference between efficiency and effectiveness.
6. Tell how managers spend their time.
7. Describe the four basic functional areas of management.
8. Explain the importance of the systems concept to the study of modern management.

THE NATURE OF MANAGEMENT

Management is a universal consideration. Almost every problem faced by organizations or nations can be at least partially solved through effective and efficient management practices. Firms in the private sector continually strive to increase their managerial efficiency and effectiveness, as do organizations in the public sector. Both can profit from the ideas and concepts described in this book. In beginning our discussion of modern management, let us start with a consideration of the nature of management. The following material addresses six major topics that help describe what management is all about.

What is Management?

Management defined

Management has been defined in many different ways. In this book we shall be using the following operational definition: **management** is the process of setting objectives and coordinating the efforts of personnel in order to attain them. Note that by its very definition, management involves getting things done through other people. The manager must be a planner, communicator, coordinator, leader, and controller; and most of all the manager must be a facilitator. He or she must smooth the way for subordinate performance.

The material in this book is designed both to explain and to teach effective and efficient management practices and principles. Before we begin our discussion, we should point out that not every person who carries the title of manager actually is a manager. Some "managers" have so little authority—for example, managers who have to check everything with the boss—that they are little more than managerial assistants. Others really do not want to manage. Preferring to let subordinates be in control, they delegate virtually all of the authority to lower-level people who, then, are responsible for seeing that things get done.

Still others who are called managers only manage some of the time. Consider the following:

> Tim Carver is a sales manager. He was promoted to this position four months ago. Tim spends four days a week on the road calling on customers and helping his people sell. During this time his secretary runs the office. On Friday Tim returns and together the two work on problems that have come up during the week.

Is Tim a manager? Yes, but not all of the time. He spends some of the week getting things done through others and the rest of the time doing things himself. In fact, unless it is company policy, he should not be out selling. He should be in the office handling administrative work or helping the salespeople sell. Now consider the following:

Mary Carren is an associate administrator at a local hospital. Mary spends approximately 20 percent of her day working with the administrator, 40 percent handling administrative paperwork, and 40 percent meeting with department heads to discuss operational problems and ways of dealing with them. Except for the occasional times when she attends national professional meetings or training programs, Mary's time is spent at the hospital.

Is Mary a manager? Indeed, yes. She spends a great deal of her time getting things done through others. In fact, assuming that both she and Tim are doing their jobs properly, Mary has the greater need for management expertise because her job is more managerial in nature.

Management as an Art and a Science

Is management an art or a science? This question is often asked by both practitioners and students of management. The answer is that management is *both* an art *and* a science.

Management requires the use of behavioral and judgmental skills . . .

As an art, management requires the use of behavioral and judgmental skills that cannot be quantified or categorized the way scientific information in the fields of chemistry, biology, and physics can be. For example, management involves communicating, motivating people, leading, and using qualitative judgment, intuition, gut feeling, and other nonquantifiable abilities. In this respect, management is similar to another art, the art of acting. Who can say precisely why one actor is a great Richard II and another is merely good? Although theater critics attempt to describe differences in style, interpretation, and movement, their evaluations are subjective and open to dispute. Critics cannot quantify the qualities of a performance.

A manager can be described as an actor in an organizational setting. Just as the actor tries to sway the audience, the manager tries to influence those with whom he or she comes into contact in the enterprise. Both have objectives, both strive to plan and execute their strategies, and both are judged by a group of critics. A major difference, however, is that the actor can go home after a poor performance with the resolve of doing better the next day. The manager often finds that yesterday's mistakes remain and have to be dealt with today and tomorrow.

as well as the use of computers and quantitative formulas

Management is a science, as well as an art, in that it requires the use of logic and analysis. The manager arrives at a solution by systematically observing, classifying, and studying facts in relation to the problem at hand. The scientific aspects of management have been greatly advanced by the development of computers and applicable mathematical formulas. Today there are quantitative techniques that can be used for dealing with a variety of management-related problems, ranging from the control of inventory to the reduction of customer waiting time. These techniques can also answer such questions as when to repair or replace machine parts and what combination of product lines to manufacture for maximum profits.

When dealing with people, managers approach management as an art; when dealing with material things, they approach it as a science. The approach used most often varies at different levels of the organizational hierarchy. At the lower levels of an organization, managers most often face problems that can be resolved using scientific techniques, for example, problems in work flow, machine replacement, and overall efficiency. At the upper levels, managers most often solve problems using judgment, reflection, thought, and intuition. Successful managers at *all* levels of the hierarchy, however, need to employ both the art and science of management. They also need to be tough (see "Management in Practice: The Toughest Bosses in America").

Management as a Profession

Profession defined

In addition to being an art and a science, management is a **profession**. By definition, "a profession is a vocation whose practice is founded upon an understanding of the theoretical structure of some department of learning or science, and upon the abilities accompanying such understanding." [1] To qualify as a profession, an occupation must meet five major criteria. It must accumulate knowledge about the field and require competent application of that knowledge. It must also accept social responsibility, exercise self-control, and receive community sanction. [2] In ways that vary according to the kind of business, management meets all of these criteria.

Knowledge

Management knowledge has accumulated rapidly during the past ten years

Management meets the first criterion because a large fund of information has been accumulated on the subject. Particularly during the last ten years, the amount of management-related research and writing has risen dramatically. Articles, books, college courses, and degree programs all make this information available to managers.

Competent Application

Competent application occurs on the job

Management encourages competent application of knowledge, using a system of on-the-job controls. Other professions such as medicine and law ensure competent application by certifying people for practice. Management provides no such preliminary screening process. Screening occurs on the job and those who are unable to measure up are replaced by others who can.

---

[1] Cited by Morris L. Cogan in Howard W. Vollmer and Donald L. Mills, *Professionalization* (Englewood Cliffs, NJ: Prentice-Hall, 1966), 10.
[2] Kenneth R. Andrews, "Toward Professionalism in Business Management," *Harvard Business Review* (March–April 1969):50–51.

Social Responsibility

Business assumes social obligations

Today, more than ever, business is aware of its social role. Without neglecting obligations to stockholders, companies are trying to be good citizens. They demonstrate this intent in various ways, for example, by contributing time and money to charitable organizations, by creating programs to train the hard-core unemployed, by developing voluntary ecological programs to protect the environment, and by setting up consumer clinics to help customers understand how to use the company's products and services better.

Self-Control/Ethics

It employs self-control . . .

Business exercises self-control through both industry codes of conduct and the ethical codes of managers. Industry codes are developed by industry representatives to protect the image and reputation of all the industry's firms. Managers' ethical codes depend on their personal standards, and, according to research, most executives believe that their ethical standards are higher than ever before. Of course, many people argue that managers try to get away with as much unethical conduct as they can. Managers, however, are quick to point out that with today's media coverage and the ever-present possibility of public disclosure, they are not likely to resort to unethical conduct, even if they are tempted to do so. Self-control is now a prerequisite for effective management.[3]

Community Sanction

and has community sanction

Management is now widely recognized as a profession. The public knows of business's contributions to social programs. More generally, it knows how important effective management is to our free enterprise system.

Types of Managers

For classification purposes, there are three types of managers: first-line, middle, and top. These managers have different titles depending on the field or department in which they work. Table 1-1 provides some examples of the titles commonly found at each hierarchical level.

First-Line Managers

Many **first-line managers** are called supervisors, although, depending on their specific jobs, they may instead have other titles such as foreman in a production plant, ward nurse in a hospital, or department chairperson in a

---

[3] Kenneth R. Andrews, "Ethics in Practice," *Harvard Business Review* (September–October 1989):99–104.

The Toughest Bosses in America

*T*he fury of a tough boss has been experienced by many of us at one time or another. Toughness can be good or bad depending on how it is used and, more importantly, how it is perceived. *Fortune* magazine recently surveyed executive search firms, consultants, academics, financial analysts, and corporate executives, in order to find the toughest bosses in America. The most interesting aspect of the "winners" is not the names but rather the feature of how others see them vis-à-vis how they see themselves.

Name	How Others See Him	How He Sees Himself
Francisco A. Lorenzo Chairman, Texas Air	He thinks he's a great manager, but he's not . . . incredibly impulsive . . . not trusted inside or outside the organization . . . good dealmaker though.	I have to be tough but fair. We built this company from businesses that were failing. We didn't just take over a big company and blow out the cobwebs.
Hugh L. McColl, Jr. Chairman, NCNB Corp.	We sit on the edge of our chairs . . . he manages with aggressiveness and perfectionism, and he expects us to cope with the tension.	I expect the Herculean. There's no golf in the middle of the day, no coasting to retirement. If you're not leading, you're out of here.
Carl E. Reichardt Chairman, Wells Fargo & Company	Carl's bag is execution, not talk . . . he's blunt . . . don't make mistakes around him . . . his narrow focus may be limiting middle management, a lot are leaving.	Good operations succeed with a minimum of foolishness and glitter. Maybe I am tough. But my 80-year-old mother will be shocked to learn of it.
Harry E. Figgie, Jr. Chairman, Figgie International	From horrendous to delightful, from idiotic to brilliant . . . working with him was a nightmare . . . really abusive . . . the Steinbrenner of industry.	You don't build a company like this with lace on your underwear. We bought small companies with no management depth. There's no room for error.

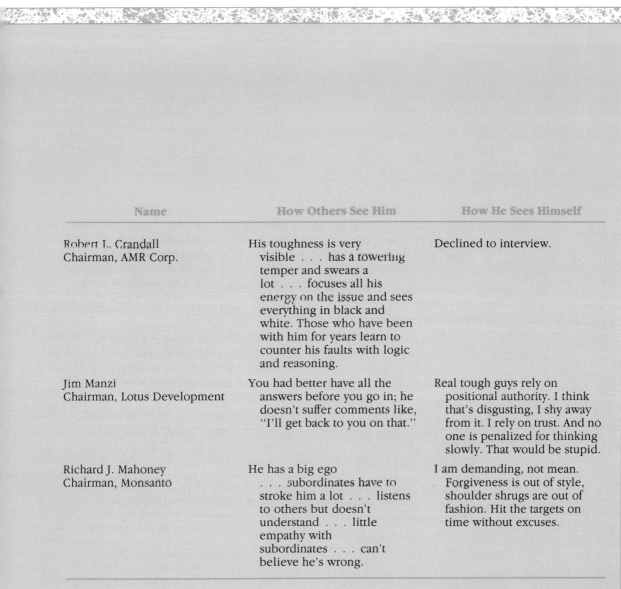

Name	How Others See Him	How He Sees Himself
Robert L. Crandall Chairman, AMR Corp.	His toughness is very visible . . . has a towering temper and swears a lot . . . focuses all his energy on the issue and sees everything in black and white. Those who have been with him for years learn to counter his faults with logic and reasoning.	Declined to interview.
Jim Manzi Chairman, Lotus Development	You had better have all the answers before you go in; he doesn't suffer comments like, "I'll get back to you on that."	Real tough guys rely on positional authority. I think that's disgusting, I shy away from it. I rely on trust. And no one is penalized for thinking slowly. That would be stupid.
Richard J. Mahoney Chairman, Monsanto	He has a big ego . . . subordinates have to stroke him a lot . . . listens to others but doesn't understand . . . little empathy with subordinates . . . can't believe he's wrong.	I am demanding, not mean. Forgiveness is out of style, shoulder shrugs are out of fashion. Hit the targets on time without excuses.

Adapted from: Peter Nulty, "America's Toughest Bosses," *Fortune* (February 27, 1989):40–54.

TABLE 1-1 **Job Titles in Different Departments and at Various Hierarchical Levels**					
Organizational Level	*Marketing*	*Production*	*Finance*	*Accounting*	*Personnel*
Top	Vice President	Vice President	Vice President	Comptroller	Vice President
Middle	Division Sales Manager	Purchasing Manager	Credit Manager	Internal Auditor	Director of Training
First-line	Unit Sales Manager	Foreman	Unit Supervisor	Accounting Supervisor	Training Supervisor

university. First-line managers supervise employees and resources at the lowest levels of the organizational hierarchy (see Figure 1-1). Much of their concern is with seeing that specific work assignments are carried out on time.

Most first-line managers find their days continually interrupted by workers who need their assistance and problems that require immediate solutions. These managers spend very little time with superiors or outsiders; instead they concentrate on technical details, work quality, work quantity, employee job performance, and employee coaching and counseling.

One recent study concluded that although the position of first-line manager will remain important, there will be fewer positions for them in organizations. The reason is that future activities of first-line managers will center around external representation and internal human relations.[4]

> . . . these changes probably will require organizations to refine their selection techniques for new supervisors and their training methods for incumbents. Tomorrow's first-line supervisors will have to be more technically proficient, as well as more highly skilled in human relations than their predecessors. Also, such individuals probably will expect compensation levels that match these increased skill levels. This will help to position the first-line supervisor closer to the ranks of lower level management and further from their subordinates.[5]

Middle Managers

Middle managers function between first-line and top managers (see Figure 1-1). Their jobs vary according to their positions in the middle management ranks. For example, those who directly supervise first-line managers are more concerned with day-to-day activities than are those who report directly to a top manager. The latter middle managers, in fact, often spend as much as 25 percent

---

[4] Steven Kerr, Kenneth D. Hill, and Laurie Broedling, "The Line Supervisor: Phasing Out or How to Stay," *Academy of Management Review* (January 1986):103–117.
[5] Ibid., p. 115.

FIGURE 1-1   Management Levels in the Hierarchy

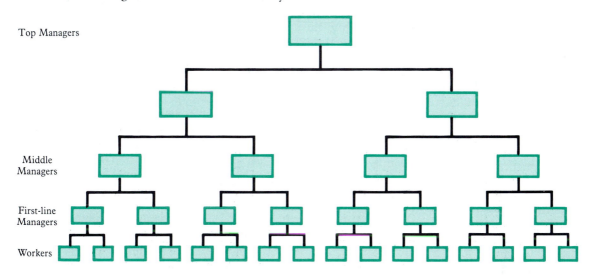

of their time away from the office working with clients, customers, and other key groups. In this regard, their work is very similar to that of the top manager.

In contrast to the hectic life of the first-line manager, the life of the typical middle manager is slower and more carefully planned. Commenting on the way middle managers see themselves, Lyman Porter and Edward Ghiselli have written that "they seem to describe themselves as stable and dependable individuals who try to avoid making mistakes on the job or elsewhere." [6]

The middle manager coordinates organizational activities

Much of the activity of middle managers is related to organizing and controlling resources. Middle managers participate in meetings with superiors and other managers, handle paperwork, write reports, and carry out other activities designed to keep the organizational machine moving smoothly. J. H. Horne and Tom Lupton have found that middle managers spend more than half their time giving and seeking information (42 percent) and seeking and preparing explanations (15 percent).[7] These managers concentrate on coordinating organizational activities.

It is important to recognize that today's major enterprises are operating on efficiency and productivity. Thus, a flatter and more market-driven organizational structure is being sought after as a means to greater competitiveness, which means layers of middle management are being eliminated as companies "downsize" their workforces. It has been estimated that over 500,000 managers

[6] Lyman Porter and Edwin Ghiselli, "The Self-Perceptions of Top and Middle Management Personnel," *Personnel Psychology* (1957):402.

[7] J. H. Horne and Tom Lupton, "The Work Activities of Middle Managers: An Exploratory Study," *Journal of Management Studies* (February 1965):26.

in 300 corporations have been eliminated since 1984.[8] However, some experts predict that the pressures to find well-qualified middle managers will cause a "major shortage" during the 1990's.[9] Credibility, sensitivity, confidence, and the capacity to think analogically will be essential qualities that organizations need to nurture in their current managerial levels.[10]

Top Managers

Top managers have many different titles. Some of the most common include chairman of the board, chief executive officer, president and vice president in business firms; administrator and director in government and hospital organizations; and academic vice president and dean in academic organizations. These individuals are the chief policymaking people in their organizations.

Top managers are planners

Planning is an important part of every top manager's job. In fact, it usually takes more of the manager's time than any other function. Top managers chart the overall course of action; the other managers follow through by organizing and coordinating the necessary activities (middle managers) and seeing that the final output is produced (first-line managers).

Individuals who make it to the top usually do so because they have been successful at the middle levels. Do these individuals have any characteristics in common? A *Fortune* magazine survey found that they do.[11] After surveying the chief executive officers of the 500 largest industrials, the magazine reported that sixty-five percent continued their studies beyond the bachelor's degree. Almost 75 percent had majored in business, engineering, or economics in undergraduate school while over 70 percent reported their graduate degrees in those fields. Most executives (90 percent) reported their backgrounds as middle class or wealthy and over 50 percent had fathers who were executives, managers, or small business owners. Finally, the study reported that there was no one road to the top in terms of functional area, however, experience in their current company was an overwhelming factor (72.5 percent). Sixty-three percent indicated they had worked for their company ten years or more before becoming CEO.

Management Skills

Success at the lower levels of management does not require the same combination of managerial skills as does success at the upper levels. Robert Katz has

---

[8] Rod Willis, "What's Happening to America's Middle Management," *Management Review* (January 1987):24–33.

[9] Ibid., p. 24.

[10] Thomas V. Bonoma and Joseph C. Lawler, "Chutes and Ladders: Growing the General Manager," *Sloan Management Review* (Spring 1989):27–37.

[11] Maggie McComas, "Atop the Fortune 500: A Survey of the CEOs," *Fortune* (April 28, 1986):26–31.

FIGURE 1-2
Relative Amounts
of Conceptual,
Human, and
Technical Skills
Needed for
Effectiveness at
Various Levels of
the Management
Hierarchy

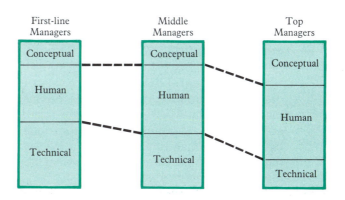

identified three different kinds of managerial skills: technical, human, and conceptual. As seen in Figure 1-2, the requisite degree of each kind of skill varies, depending on the manager's level in the management hierarchy.[12]

Technical skill is the ability to use the techniques, procedures, and tools of a specific field. This skill is particularly important at the lower levels of the organization where the manager needs to know how the work is done. Only in this way can the manager direct subordinates effectively and assist them when they have problems. Many times, in fact, lower-level managers are given their positions because of their ability to do technical work well. Management reasons that if these workers know how to do the job, they will also do well in supervising the work of others. After all, at this level of the hierarchy, the main concern of the manager is to get the work out.

> Technical skill is the ability to use the techniques, procedures, and tools of a specific field

Human skill is the ability to communicate, motivate, and lead individuals and groups. An understanding of human relations and organizational behavior is most important to managers in the middle ranks of the management hierarchy. Because these managers are concerned with directing lower-level supervisors and other middle managers, their jobs are more human than technical in nature. The ability to persuade, negotiate with, and coordinate the activities of others is the key to their success.

> Human skill is the ability to communicate, motivate, and lead

Many people like to describe the middle manager as a kind of politician. Situated between upper- and lower-level management, this individual takes top-management directives, turns them into operational plans, and passes them on to the lower management for action. The middle manager must have all the human skills of a politician who is trying to balance the various needs or concerns of groups with different interests. No wonder one researcher has reported that some of the things middle managers want to learn more about include (1) how to relate to people in higher-level positions; (2) how to acquire communication skills on a one-to-one basis, in oral presentations, in

---

[12] Robert L. Katz, "Skills of an Effective Administrator," *Harvard Business Review* (September–October 1974):90–102.

listening, and in obtaining information; (3) how to improve their skills in sizing up employees; (4) how to use time more efficiently; (5) how to become results oriented rather than activity oriented; and (6) how to deal with organizational policies.[13]

Conceptual skill is the ability to plan, coordinate, and integrate activities

Conceptual skill is the ability to plan, coordinate, and integrate all of the organization's interests and activities. It is most important at the upper levels of the organization where long-range forecasting and planning are the principal activities.[14] To chart the organization's course, the top manager must be able to balance the demands of the organization's various departments and units with the demands of the external environment. Some other characteristics of the top manager include:

1. The capacity to abstract, to conceptualize, to organize, and to integrate different ideas into a coherent frame of reference.
2. Tolerance for ambiguity—the ability to withstand confusion until things become clear.
3. Intelligence—the capacity not only to abstract but also to be practical.
4. Judgment—the ability to know when to act.[15]

Notice in Figure 1-2 that as a manager progresses up the hierarchy, the importance of technical skill decreases while the importance first of human skill and then of conceptual skill increases. The lower-level manager must be a technician who knows a great deal about one area of operations; the top manager must be a generalist who knows a little bit about many areas of organizational activity. The former has to take a narrow view of things, while the latter takes a broad view.

Efficiency and Effectiveness

Although often used interchangeably, the terms *efficiency* and *effectiveness* have different meanings. The distinction is important because successful managers tend to be *both* efficient and effective.[16]

Efficiency is measured by output/input

Efficiency is measured by dividing output by input. It is an economic concept. A manager who initiates a cost-cutting program that reduces overall departmental expenses by 10 percent is being efficient. The amount of work being done (output) remains the same while the cost of producing this output

---

[13] Peter D. Couch, "Learning To Be a Middle Manager," *Business Horizons* (February 1979):37.
[14] Shu-hsiun Chen and Ernest C. Miller, "Conceptual Ability: A Critical Skill of Management," *Industrial Management* (August 1988):23–26.
[15] Harry Levinson, "Criteria for Choosing Chief Executives," *Harvard Business Review* (July–August 1980):114–16.
[16] Fred Luthans, "Successful vs. Effective Real Managers," *Academy of Management Executive* (May 1988):127–32.

FIGURE 1-3
Efficiency and
Effectiveness in the
Automobile
Industry in the
Early 1980s

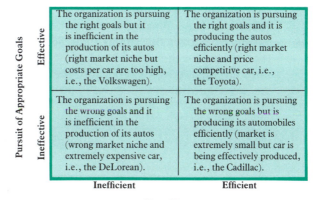

		Inefficient	Efficient
Pursuit of Appropriate Goals	Effective	The organization is pursuing the right goals but it is inefficient in the production of its autos (right market niche but costs per car are too high, i.e., the Volkswagen).	The organization is pursuing the right goals and it is producing the autos efficiently (right market niche and price competitive car, i.e., the Toyota).
	Ineffective	The organization is pursuing the wrong goals and it is inefficient in the production of its autos (wrong market niche and extremely expensive car, i.e., the DeLorean).	The organization is pursuing the wrong goals but is producing its automobiles efficiently (market is extremely small but car is being effectively produced, i.e., the Cadillac).

Use of Resources

(input) declines. Another efficient manager is the one who has new machinery installed so that the number of units produced per hour (output) increases while the amount of material and labor (input) remains the same.

Effectiveness means doing the right things

Effectiveness pertains to the manager's ability to choose appropriate objectives and the means for achieving them. While efficiency means doing things right, effectiveness means doing the right things. Of the two, effectiveness is more important. The reason is perhaps best explained by Peter Drucker, the well-known management writer and consultant, who has noted that, "The pertinent question is not how to do things right but how to find the right things to do, and to concentrate resources and efforts on them." [17]

It does no good to attain an objective efficiently if the objective is wrong. For example, organizations that produce goods and services for which there is a limited market do not realize high profits. Their major problem is not cost or price; it is market demand. Regardless of price, does anyone but a barber really want to buy a straightedge razor? Is there much demand for shirts that have been out of fashion for five years? Are many people interested in buying an inexpensive, inefficient air conditioner when utility prices are so high? Products such as these have very limited markets no matter how efficiently they can be produced.

Figure 1-3 shows how efficiency or inefficiency and effectiveness or ineffectiveness have been combined in the automobile industry. Notice that efficiency and effectiveness are *independent* factors in that one does not affect the other. A manager can be high in both, low in both, or high in one and low in the other.

A manager who is high in both sets appropriate objectives and is efficient in attaining them. A manager who is low in both sets inappropriate objectives and is inefficient in attaining them. A manager who is effective – inefficient sets

---

[17] Peter F. Drucker, *Managing for Results* (New York: Harper & Row, 1964), 5.

appropriate objectives but spends too much time and uses too many resources attaining them. Finally, a manager who is ineffective–efficient pursues the wrong objectives but attains them at a very reasonable cost. Of the latter two combinations, the second is less desirable. More organizations fail because they are ineffective than because they are inefficient.

HOW MANAGERS SPEND THEIR TIME

Over the years a number of researchers have sought to expand our understanding of management by answering the questions: How do managers spend their time? What do they do during their work day?[18]

The Mahoney Study

In one study, Thomas Mahoney and his associates studied managers operating at all levels of the hierarchy, from supervisor to president.[19] Their research involved 452 managers from 13 companies. They found that lower-level managers did less planning than their upper-level counterparts. Planning took up only 15 percent of the lower-level manager's time compared with 28 percent of the upper-level manager's. They also found that the need for the conceptual skills of the generalist was much higher at the upper levels than at the lower levels, while the middle manager has to be a coordinator and negotiator. The Mahoney study supports our comments on the skills needed by managers at the various levels of the hierarchy.

The Mintzberg Study

More recently, studies have focused on determining whether managers really behave as they are said to by literature in the field. Henry Mintzberg followed five top managers for one week, analyzing their behavior and attempting to categorize the functions they performed.[20] Basically he found that these managers did not perform *all* of the traditional functions described in the literature.

---

[18] William Oncken, Jr. and Donald L. Wass, "Management Time: Who's Got the Monkey?" *Harvard Business Review* (November–December, 1974):75–80. See also: Ford S. Worthy, "How CEOs Manage Their Time," *Fortune* (January 18, 1988):88–97.

[19] Thomas A. Mahoney, Thomas H. Jerdee, and Stephen J. Carroll, "The Job(s) of Management," *Industrial Relations* (February 1965):97–110.

[20] Henry Mintzberg, "The Manager's Job: Folklore and Fact," *Harvard Business Review* (July–August 1975):49–61; and Henry Mintzberg, *The Nature of Managerial Work* (Englewood Cliffs, NJ: Prentice Hall Inc., 1973).

Managers keep the organization running smoothly

However, he did find that their work activities could be classified into three categories representing types of roles: interpersonal, informational, and decisional. In an *interpersonal role* the manager serves as a figurehead, leader, and liaison with others. In an *informational role* the manager monitors information, disseminates data to others, and serves as a spokesperson both within and outside of the department. In the *decisional role* the manager acts as an entrepreneur, handles disturbances, allocates resources, and negotiates.

Every manager performs these ten roles. Some, however, will be more important to the individual manager than others. For example, sales managers spend the largest percentage of their time in interpersonal roles. Staff managers spend most of their time in informational roles since they are experts who manage departments that advise other parts of the organization. Production managers most often assume decisional roles.[21]

The Luthans-Hodgetts-Rosenkrantz Study

The latest, and certainly most comprehensive study of managers in action was conducted by Luthans, Hodgetts, and Rosenkrantz.[22] Over a four-year period, the researchers gathered data from 457 real managers (RMs) in numerous organizations. They found that managers performed four basic types of activities: (a) routine communication such as exchanging information and handling paperwork; (b) traditional management activities such as planning, decision making, and controlling; (c) networking such as interacting with outsiders, socializing, and politicking; and (d) human resource management activities such as motivating, disciplining, managing conflict, staffing, training, and developing.[23] The researchers then sought to identify whether certain managers performed some of these functions more than they did other functions. This was particularly clear when the activities of two groups of RMs were examined: successful RMs and effective RMs. Successful RMs were those who were promoted most frequently. Effective RMs were those who had: (a) high quality and quantity of performance and (b) satisfied and organizationally committed subordinates. Some managers fit into both of these categories, but most did not. This allowed the researchers to create three distinct groups of RMs and to analyze the breakdown of time associated with each of their major activities. These are presented in Figure 1-4. The findings show that there are distinct differences between the way successful, effective, and RMs in general behave. In particular, successful managers spend a great deal of time networking, while effective managers spend a lot of time engaged in routine communication.

---

[21] Mintzberg, ''Manager's Job,'' 59.
[22] Fred Luthans, Richard M. Hodgetts, and Stuart Rosenkrantz, *Real Managers* (New York: Ballinger Publishing Company, 1988).
[23] Ibid., p. 12.

FIGURE 1-4 Activities of Real Managers

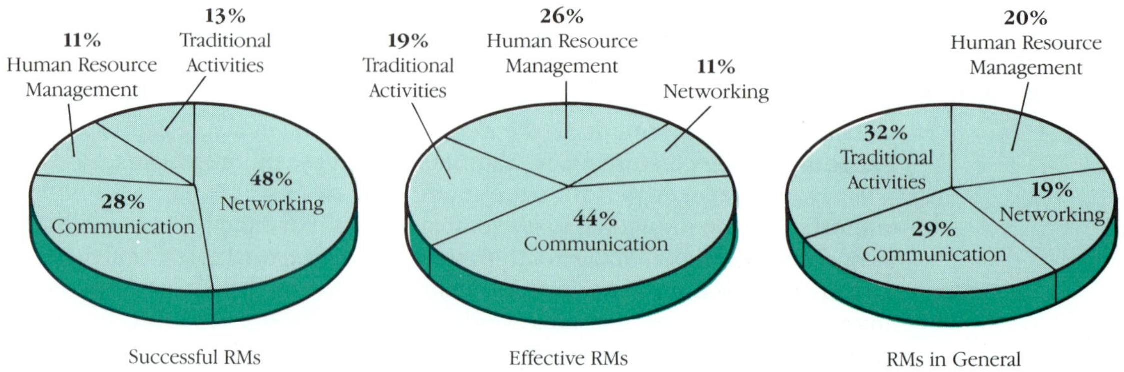

Successful RMs

Effective RMs

RMs in General

Source: Fred Luthans, Richard M. Hodgetts, and Stuart Rosenkrantz, *Real Managers* (New York: Ballinger, 1988).

MANAGEMENT FUNCTIONS

The roles described by Mahoney, Mintzberg, and other researchers provide a basis for the study of management in that they allow the formation of a *functional framework.* This framework helps us to identify and analyze each of the management functions. It shows the component parts of the manager's job.

In this book we will examine four basic functional areas of management: (1) planning and enterprise's direction, (2) organizing and staffing the structure, (3) leading and influencing the personnel, and (4) controlling organizational operations and resources. Before we begin, however, a few introductory remarks are in order. First, some people might argue with our choice of these four specific functional areas, suggesting, for example, that planning and decision making should be considered separately. We realize that arguments can be made for other categories because the four functional areas encompass many managerial duties. For purposes of analysis, however, we have grouped similar duties together.

Second, there is no universal agreement regarding the management functions that every manager performs. If we looked into a large enough number of organizations, we would indeed find some managers who had very little staffing responsibilities and some who were greatly limited in their decision-making power. The four functional areas we have identified, however, are both encompassing and representative of the modern manager's job.

Finally, these functions will be studied in sequence, beginning with planning and ending with controlling, although in practice the manager does not perform them in this way. He or she actually may begin with influencing, go on to planning, then to organizing, and then to controlling. The manager's schedule depends on the problems or issues that arise day to day and hour to hour. It is important to understand that the managerial functions are interrelated.[24]

Planning the Enterprise's Direction

Planning defined

Planning is the process of setting objectives and then determining the steps needed to attain them. In carrying out this process, organizations often rely on many different types of plans, such as purposes or missions, objectives, strategies, policies, procedures, rules, programs, and budgets. These types of plans vary in nature and scope, with some being developed at one level of the hierarchy exclusively while others are developed at every level. The planning process itself consists of five steps: (1) awareness of the opportunity, (2) establishment of objectives, (3) determination and choice of alternative courses of action, (4) formulation of derivative plans, and (5) budgeting of the plan.

In large companies the planning process is called strategic planning. The four elements of a strategic plan include the formulation of the basic mission, the setting of long-range objectives, the determination of strategy, and the management of the organization's product lines. Having determined its strategic plan, the organization then begins developing an operational plan that breaks the strategic plan into its component parts, delegates responsibility to the various departments or units, and helps bring the strategic plan to fruition.

Decision making involves choosing from among alternatives

Decision making is the process of choosing from among alternatives. Decisions are made under one of three conditions: certainty, risk, and uncertainty. The manager must know under which condition the decision is being made in order to understand how to make the choice. The manager also needs to know what steps form the decision-making process and how this process is affected by behavorial factors such as simplification, subjective rationality, and rationalization. Finally, the manager needs to know how decision making can be improved through the use of management science tools and techniques, through creativity, and through matching decision-making situations with leadership styles.

Planning and decision making are covered in depth in Chapters 5–7. Also see "Management in Practice: Pepsi Makes a Move."

Organizing and Staffing the Structure

Organizing is the process of assigning duties to personnel and coordinating employee efforts in order to ensure maximum efficiency. Organizing is a

---

[24] Stephen J. Carroll and Dennis J. Gillen, "The Classical Management Functions: Are They Really Outdated?" *Proceedings of the Academy of Management,* 44th meeting (August 1984):132–36.

Pepsi Makes a Move

Planning and decision making are critical to management success, especially in the international arena where business firms are finding that failure to take advantage of growing markets can leave them vulnerable to strong competition. In an effort to increase its European foothold and take advantage of the European Common Market's economic growth, Pepsico Inc. recently paid $1.35 billion for Walkers Crisps and Smith Crisps, two major snack food firms. Walkers is the market leader for potato chips in Britain, holding approximately one-third of the national market. Smiths is the leader for "extruded" snacks such as wheat puffs, and it also holds around one-third of the market.

These latest acquisitions by Pepsico put it in an important competitive position in Europe and strengthened the firm's overall world market potential. Throughout the 1980s the firm had expanded its share of the international snack market in Mexico, Latin America, Australia,

Brazil, South Korea, and Thailand. What makes Europe, and England in particular, so attractive is that the per capita consumption of snack foods is well below that in the United States. The average American eats almost 13 pounds of salted snack foods a year, in contrast to less than 8 pounds per person in England. The situation is even more promising worldwide, where the average person eats less than one pound per year. Over the last four years Pepsico's international sales have risen dramatically. In 1985 the company had less than $1 billion (12 percent of company sales) in overseas sales. By 1988 the figure was close to $2.5 billion (19 percent of overall sales), and during the 1990s Pepsico believes that these sales figures will continue to rise. Quite obviously careful planning and decision making are paying off for the firm.

Source: Douglas C. McGill, "Pepsico Buys Two Snack Units in Britain," *New York Times,* July 4, 1989, p. 29.

natural outgrowth of planning and decision making. Once the organization knows what goals it wants to achieve, it can organize to achieve them.

Organizing is concerned with both structure and people

To organize, the manager must consider both structure and people. In dealing with structure, the manager's primary concerns are departmentalization, job descriptions, organizational charts and manuals, and organizational design. In organizing people, the manager works on the delegation and decentralization of authority, job design, coordination, and overall people–structure fit. The purpose is to meld the structure and the people.

Staffing involves recruiting, selecting, training, and developing personnel

Staffing is the process of recruiting, selecting, training, and developing organizational personnel. This process begins with a forecast of the organization's staffing needs. The manager, for example, may try to determine how many people the organization should hire during a six-month period and what skills these people should have. The next steps are recruitment and selection, orientation of the new employees, and then training and development. At this stage, the new personnel who are workers receive technical training, while the new managers receive training that is behaviorally oriented. After the initial training period, some of the new personnel are let go, following performance appraisals; others receive additional training. The manager then starts to fill the empty positions by beginning the staffing process over again.

Staffing considerations are discussed further in Chapter 10.

Leading and Influencing the Personnel

As soon as an organization knows what its goals are and has the necessary people to achieve them, leading becomes the manager's most important function. **Leadership** is the process of influencing people to direct their efforts toward the achievement of some particular goal. To be good leaders, managers must be knowledgeable about human behavior, the concept of leadership, and communication.

The study of human behavior is important . . .

More specifically, managers must understand the behavior both of individuals and of groups. Personality, attitudes, learning, values, interpersonal relations, and motivation all are important aspects of the individual's behavior. To understand the group, managers should have knowledge of group characteristics, intragroup behavior, intergroup behavior, and the informal organization. With regard to leadership, managers should study both leadership behavior and contingency leadership theory. They must also understand interpersonal and organizational communication. Because **communication** is the process of transferring meanings from sender to receiver, they need to know about communication flows, communication barriers, and ways to develop communication effectiveness.

as is the study of leadership . . .

and the study of communication

In Chapters 11–14 you will learn how modern managers lead and influence their personnel.

Controlling Organizational Operations and Resources

The **controlling** process consists of three steps: (1) establishment of standards, (2) comparison of results against standards, and (3) correction of deviations. Every organization needs to control both operations and people.

Operations can be controlled . . .

Techniques for controlling operations vary, depending on what needs to be controlled. The budget and the break-even point are particularly useful for handling departmental and divisional control problems. For control of the entire organization, many enterprises have developed key result area control systems. By monitoring performance on these key result areas, they ensure that everything is going according to plan. Additionally, expanding organizations are often turning to operations management tools and techniques and computerized information systems.

as can organizational performance

Yet control is more than a mechanical process for analyzing quantitative results. Managers must also know how to control people. They must meet the challenge of managing conflict and change, inevitable events in every organization.

The way in which modern managers go about controlling organizational operations and resources is the focus of attention in Chapters 15–17.

MANAGEMENT AND THE SYSTEMS CONCEPT

Managers do not operate in a vacuum. They are continually being influenced by their environment and, in turn, trying to influence it. For example, consider the manager who at noon receives an order from the boss to prepare a special report by 3 P.M. When the manager drops everything and immediately starts working on the report, he or she is being influenced by the environment. When the manager realizes that the report cannot be completed without assistance and orders two subordinates to help, he or she is influencing and leading others. This example shows that the organization is made up of many different interrelated individuals, groups, and forces. These forces can be thought of as systems that affect organizational output.

The Nature of Systems

A **system** is defined in the *Oxford English Dictionary* as a "set or assemblage of things connected, or interdependent, so as to form a complex unit; a whole composed of parts in orderly arrangement according to some scheme or plan." Within every organization there are many systems, from the company at large to the various departments and units within. Each influences the others and, in turn, is influenced by them. Some of the key concepts of systems theory include the following:

Key concepts of systems theory

1. A system, such as an organization, is more than the sum of its parts. It has to be viewed as a whole.
2. Systems can be either closed or open. When the system has no interaction with its environment, it is closed. When the system receives information, energy, or material from the outside environment in order to function more efficiently, it is open. Organizational systems are open systems since they are continually being influenced by the outside environment and adjusting to new conditions.
3. In order for a system to exist, it must have boundaries that separate it from the outside environment. An organization can be distinguished from its external environment.
4. Closed systems are subject to entropy, a process of increasing energy loss that leads eventually to the system's death. Open systems are able to overcome the effects of entropy because they are influenced by the external environment.

5. In responding to the external environment, the organization must contend with two kinds of forces. One kind encourages the organization to continue doing what it is doing and not to take in any new information or material from the outside. The other encourages the organization to change. Effective organizations try to balance the two in order to make necessary changes without creating chaos or uncertainty by changing too rapidly.

6. By using feedback from the external environment, a system is able to achieve dynamic equilibrium. Equilibrium occurs when the organization achieves a steady state and is not in danger of breaking down.

7. Every system is also a subsystem. An organization is a subsystem of the entire industry. Meanwhile, within the organization there are such subsystems as divisions, departments, units, groups, and individuals (see Figure 1-5).

FIGURE 1-5

Relationship of General and Task Environments to the Organizational System

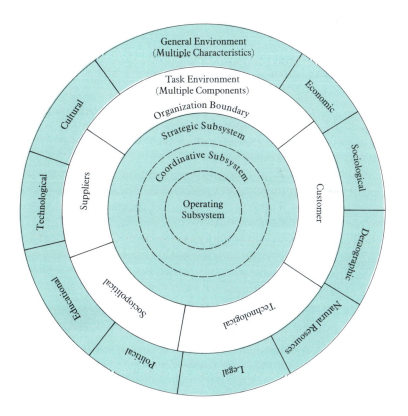

Source: Fremont E. Kast and James E. Rosenzweig, *Organization and Management: A Systems and Contingency Approach,* 3rd ed. (New York: McGraw-Hill, 1979), 134. Reprinted by permission.

8. Open systems tend to become more specialized as they grow larger. For example, as an organization increases in size, specialized departments will spring up, the organization will expand its product line, and new offices or districts will be created.
9. Open systems may grow in different ways. For example, one large manufacturing company may produce moderate-price, moderate-quality goods while another turns out high-price, high-quality goods. (As applied to the automobile market, the first organization could be Chevrolet and the second could be Rolls Royce.)

Systems and the Management Job

The systems concept is useful to managers because it helps them understand how their organizations function. Organizations and organizational units continually interact with the external environment. The organization and the external environment are interdependent, and the larger or more powerful the organization, the greater their reciprocal influence. Units within the organization are interdependent, too. Divisions, departments, and individuals all influence each other.

The manager's job is systems oriented

The manager's job by it's very nature is systems oriented. Managers oversee the **transformation process** through which inputs are transformed into outputs (see Figure 1-6). For example, they supervise new employees (inputs) who produce a certain number of units per hour (outputs). Managers are responsible for planning, organizing, staffing, influencing, leading, and controlling. To carry out these responsibilities efficiently and effectively, they must understand how the organization interacts with the external environment and how the different parts of the organization work together.

Figure 1-7 completes this chapter's brief discussion of management. In graphic form, it summarizes the material covered throughout the book. As later chapters present the manager's role in more detail, you will learn how to make the process depicted in this figure work well.

SUMMARY

1. Management is the process of setting objectives and coordinating the efforts of personnel in order to attain them. Some managers have a greater need for management training and expertise than do others.

FIGURE 1-6
Basic Input-Output Process

FIGURE 1-7   Management as a Transformation Process

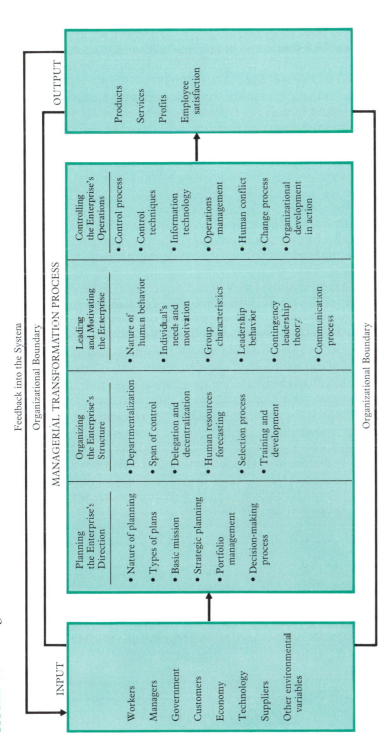

Feedback into the System

Organizational Boundary

INPUT

Workers

Managers

Government

Customers

Economy

Technology

Suppliers

Other environmental
variables

MANAGERIAL TRANSFORMATION PROCESS

Planning
the Enterprise's
Direction

• Nature of planning

• Types of plans

• Basic mission

• Strategic planning

• Portfolio
management

• Decision-making
process

Organizing
the Enterprise's
Structure

• Departmentalization

• Span of control

• Delegation and
decentralization

• Human resources
forecasting

• Selection process

• Training and
development

Leading
and Motivating
the Enterprise

• Nature of
human behavior

• Individual's
needs and
motivation

• Group
characteristics

• Leadership
behavior

• Contingency
leadership
theory

• Communication
process

Controlling
the Enterprise's
Operations

• Control process

• Control
techniques

• Information
technology

• Operations
management

• Human conflict

• Change process

• Organizational
development
in action

OUTPUT

Products

Services

Profits

Employee
satisfaction

Organizational Boundary

2. Management is both an art and a science. As an art it requires the manager to use behavioral and judgmental skills. As a science it calls for the manager systematically to observe, classify, and study facts in relation to the problem at hand. Management is also a profession because it meets the five requisite criteria: it has accumulated knowledge about the field and requires competent application of that knowledge; it also accepts social responsibility, exercises self-control, and receives community sanction.

3. There are three types of managers. First-line managers supervise workers directly. They are greatly concerned with work quantity, work quality, and employee job performance. Middle managers function between first-line and top managers. They are concerned with organizing and controlling resources and seeing that the organizational machine moves along smoothly. Top managers function at the highest levels of the hierarchy. They are most concerned with charting the overall course of the enterprise.

4. Every manager needs three kinds of skills: technical, human, and conceptual. Technical skill is the ability to use the techniques, procedures, or tools of a specific field and is most important at the lower levels of the hierarchy. Human skill is the ability to communicate, motivate, and lead individuals and groups. It is most important at the middle levels of the hierarchy. Conceptual skill is the ability to plan, coordinate, and integrate all of the organization's interests and activities. It is most important at the upper levels of the hierarchy. In using these three kinds of skills the manager must be both efficient and effective. Efficiency refers to doing things right and is measured by the equation "output/input." Effectiveness means doing the right thing and is measured by market demand considerations such as market share and growth rate.

5. First-line managers spend most of their day supervising, while top managers spend more time planning than anything else. Mintzberg found that managers perform three different types of roles: interpersonal, informational, and decisional. Luthans and his associates found that successful managers spend a great deal of time networking while effective managers spend a large amount of their time in routine communication.

6. The management process can be broken down into four basic functional areas. The first is planning the enterprise's direction. The second is organizing and staffing the structure. The third is leading and influencing personnel. The fourth is controlling organizational operations and resources.

7. Managers do not operate in a vacuum. They are continually being influenced by their environment and, in turn, trying to influence it. The organization itself is made up of many different divisions, departments, and individuals. These different units can be thought of as

interdependent systems, and the way they work together affects organizational output. The manager who works efficiently and effectively understands how the organization interacts with the external environment and how the different parts of the organization work together.

KEY TERMS

Communication   The process of transferring meanings from sender to receiver.

Conceptual skill   The ability to plan, coordinate, and integrate all of the organization's interests and activities.

Controlling   The process of establishing standards, comparing results against these standards, and correcting deviations.

Decisional roles   The manager's roles as entrepreneur, disturbance handler, resource allocator, and negotiator.

Decision making   The process of choosing from among alternatives.

Effectiveness   Doing the right thing. It is often measured by market demand considerations such as market share or growth rate.

Efficiency   Doing things right. It is often measured by the equation "output/input."

First-line manager   The lowest level manager in the hierarchy; this individual directly supervises workers.

Human skill   The ability to communicate, motivate, and lead individuals and groups.

Informational roles   The roles a manager plays when he or she monitors information, disseminates it, or acts as a spokesperson.

Interpersonal roles   The manager's roles as figurehead, leader, and liaison person.

Leadership   The process of influencing people to direct their efforts toward the achievement of some particular goal.

Management   The process of setting objectives and coordinating the efforts of personnel in order to attain them.

Middle manager   This individual, who functions between a first-line manager and a top manager, is most concerned with organizing and controlling resources and seeing that the organizational machine moves smoothly.

Organizing   The process of assigning duties to personnel and coordinating employee efforts in order to ensure maximum efficiency.

Planning   The process of setting objectives and then determining the steps needed to attain them.

Profession   A vocation whose practice is founded upon an understanding of the theoretical structure of some department of learning or science, and upon the abilities accompanying such understanding.

Staffing   The process of recruiting, selecting, training, and developing organizational personnel.

System   A set or assemblage of things connected, or interdependent, so as to form a complex unit; a whole composed of parts in orderly arrangement according to some scheme or plan.

Technical skill   The ability to use the techniques, procedures, and tools of a specific field.

Top manager   This person, who functions at the highest levels of the organization, is most concerned with charting the overall course of the enterprise.

Transformation process   The process by which inputs become outputs.

QUESTIONS FOR ANALYSIS AND DISCUSSION

1. In your own words, define the term *management.* Illustrate your definition by using an example of a manager and a nonmanager.
2. In what way is management an art? A science? Is it also a profession? Be as complete as possible in your answer.
3. How do the following differ from each other: first-line manager, middle manager, top manager? Compare and contrast the three.
4. What is meant by each of the following terms: *technical skill, human skill, conceptual skill?* Who would profit most from each? Integrate a discussion of the three types of managers into your answer.
5. How does management efficiency differ from management effectiveness? Be sure to define the terms in your answer. Then compare and contrast them.
6. Using Mintzberg's research as your guide, what roles do modern managers perform?
7. Drawing upon the research of Luthans and his associates, what activities are performed by managers? Do all managers perform these activities to the same degree? Explain.
8. What does the manager do in each of the following four functional areas: (1) planning and decision making, (2) organizing and staffing the structure, (3) leading and influencing the personnel, and (4) controlling organizational operations and resources? Describe each area.
9. How is the systems concept of value to the modern manager? Include in your answer a discussion of the key concepts of systems theory and then relate the use of systems thinking to the use of effective management.

CASE

A Great Worker But . . .

In the insurance company where she works, Rosemarie Carillo is considered very efficient. In fact, three months ago she was chosen over 11 others for a promotion to the supervisory level. Rosemarie's performance had been exceptional and, since this is the primary criterion used by management for promotion to the supervisory level, she was the overwhelming choice of the management committee that made the final decision.

Rosemarie initially was overjoyed with the news. However, this is no longer the case. During the last three weeks she had indicated to some of her fellow supervisors that she does not care very much for her job. One of the primary reasons appears to be her inability to get along well with the members of her unit. Rosemarie supervises seven workers, and while she appeared to be establishing a rapport with them soon after her promotion, that is no longer so. Two of the seven have asked for transfers to other units and another has submitted her resignation effective next Friday.

In an effort to understand the problem, Rosemarie's boss has had her in for a talk. He has also talked to three of the people in the unit. Here are their viewpoints:

Rosemarie: I don't really care to supervise these people. They are not very hard working and they resent being shown the proper way to do their job. They seem to think they know it all—but they don't. We could do 25 percent more work if they would just do things the way I show them.

Workers: In the beginning we got along just fine with Rosemarie. However, our feelings have changed. She may have been a great worker but she's a lousy boss. She has very little human relations skill. She tells us what to do, gets angry if we don't do things her way, and is critical of anything less than perfect performance. It's no fun working for her.

1. In terms of the skills of a manager, which one does Rosemarie have in abundance? Explain.
2. What exactly seems to be Rosemarie's problem? Why is she having trouble with her work group? Why do they dislike her management style?
3. If you were Rosemarie's boss, what would you tell her? How would you attempt to help her? Be complete in your answer.

YOU BE THE CONSULTANT

Work, Work, Work

Roberta Sanchez started her own catering service five years ago. At that time she had only two part-time employees. These women worked on weekends only and Roberta accepted only three types of jobs: birthday parties, weddings, and small dinners.

In the beginning, most of Roberta's week was spent planning the menu for each event and getting the food together. After a couple of months, however, she was able to provide the customer with a description of a typical menu and quote a price as soon as she had a basic idea of what the person wanted.

Roberta's good reputation soon began to spread. There were two reasons for her success. First, her prices were at least 10 percent lower than those of the competition. Second, she was an excellent cook and, with her assistants, could provide fast, efficient service. She seemed to have a knack for the catering business.

A year ago Roberta began expanding her schedule and taking jobs for the middle of the week as well. Since the two women who were working for her had families of their own and could not get away, she hired two other part-time people for this time period. It took a couple of months for them to adjust, but these individuals also began to do their jobs extremely well.

When Roberta realized that she could expand her business still further, she decided to hire full-time people and try to generate as much business as possible. She made the decision just four months ago. Since then she has hired five full-timers to supplement the four part-time people. These new people do the same work as the others: they help her prepare the food, purchase any party favors or miscellaneous items that will be needed, transport the food and sundry items to the party's locale, serve the food, clean up afterwards, and return everything to the small store out of which Roberta operates.

Since her decision to go into the business on a full-time basis, Roberta's income has tripled. However, she is not sure the decision was a good one. One of her biggest concerns is that she is now working harder than ever. In the beginning she could set up the menu, order the food, and get everything arranged for that weekend's parties in perhaps five hours. Now she gets up first thing in the morning, begins working, and does not stop until late in the evening. Most of her time is spent seeing that the food is being cooked properly, that nothing is being omitted, and that everyone knows what he or she is supposed to be doing.

Yesterday she mentioned to her husband that she might have overextended herself. "Maybe I should cut back and just handle a small number of parties and dinners each week like I used to do," she said. Her husband disagreed, presenting her with some surprising arguments. The gist of his conversation was as follows:

> You don't need to cut back on the overall business work load. You need to cut down on your own personal work time. You are doing too much. You have to turn more things over to the employees. You supervise and direct everything, yet most of them know almost as much as you do about running this business. You should spend more time planning the operation, talking to customers on the phone, and ordering the food and other things you will need for the party. Turn the busy work over to these other people. Quit killing yourself. You're supposed to be the owner, not one of the workers.

Your Consultation

Assume that you are Roberta's personal friend and that after looking over her operation you find her husband's comments to be accurate. What would you recommend that Roberta do? What skills must she develop? Which does she already have in abundance? Using Figure 1-2 of the text, tell her about the manager's job and where she might be falling down in getting it done. Be as complete as possible in your answer, and be sure that your advice is of a practical (as opposed to theoretical) nature.

2

Foundations of Modern Management

OBJECTIVES

The purpose of this chapter is to study the foundations of modern management. Since the first foundations were laid thousands of years ago, many dramatic changes have occurred. Basically, however, there were three main branches of early management thought: (1) scientific management theory, which sought to increase work efficiency at the lower levels of the organization and served as a forerunner of modern management science; (2) administrative theory, which helped pave the way for modern management theory and the process approach to management; and (3) behaviorism, which helped set the stage for modern behavioral science approaches to management. This chapter explains the emergence, development, and importance of these three sets of ideas. When you have finished reading and studying this material, you will be able to:

1. Provide a brief review of early management thought for the purpose of illustrating management practices and interests.
2. Explain the effect of the Industrial Revolution on the rise of the factory system and the emergence of the scientific management movement.
3. List the contributions of leading scientific managers to American industry.
4. Describe the current interests and scope of concern of modern management scientists.
5. Explain the contributions of early administrative theorists to management thought and discuss the current interests of these administrative scientists.

6. Describe the work of early behaviorists and the emergence of modern behavioral science.
7. Place all three major branches of early management theory in perspective by discussing modern management thought.

EARLY MANAGEMENT THOUGHT

Management has been practiced for thousands of years. All early civilizations that rose to prominence and power employed management tools and techniques effectively. The Egyptians and Greeks provide representative examples.

The Egyptians

The Egyptians are best known for their construction of the pyramids, a massive engineering *and* management feat. From an engineering viewpoint, the largest of these structures, the Great Pyramid in Giza, is almost perfectly square. When intact, it covered an area slightly over 13 acres and was approximately 147 meters high. The sides were accurately oriented to the four cardinal points and, according to modern engineers, the inside is so vast that the Cathedral of Florence, the Cathedral of Milan, St. Paul's in London, Westminster Abbey, and St. Peter's in Rome could all be grouped within it.

The Egyptians had important managerial insights

To accomplish this engineering feat, the Egyptians had to have important managerial insights into planning, organizing, staffing, leading, and controlling people at work. Stones had to be precut at the quarries, numbered, floated downriver, taken from the raft, dragged to the construction site, and hoisted into place. Much of what is currently known about construction management was undoubtedly known, if only in rudimentary fashion, to the management team that constructed the Great Pyramid.

The Greeks

The Greeks also had a working knowledge of effective management practices. For example, they were aware that maximum work output could be attained most easily by using uniform methods at a set work tempo. They found this principle to be especially true in the case of monotonous, repetitive, or difficult tasks, and they set the pace with music. This latter approach is still used today, in firms that pipe soft music into their work surroundings to make the environ-

The Greeks
knew about
specialization of
labor

ment more pleasant. The Greeks also employed specialization of labor. They realized that great efficiency could be attained if each worker concentrated on just one job or task. In his *Republic,* Plato stated the idea this way:

> Which would be better—that each should try several trades, or that he should confine himself to his own? He should confine himself to his own. More is done, and done better and more easily when one man does one thing according to his capacity and at the right moment. We need not be surprised to find that articles are made better in big cities than in small. In small cities the same workman makes a bed, a door, a plow, a table, and often he builds a house too. . . . Now it is impossible that a workman who does so many things should be equally successful in all. In the big cities, on the other hand . . . a man can live by one single trade. Sometimes he practices only a special branch of a trade. One makes men's shoes, another women's, one lives entirely by the stitching of the shoe, another by cutting the leather. . . . A man whose work is confined to such a limited task must necessarily excel at it.[1]

While history indicates that early civilizations had already developed important knowledge of management techniques, the writings of select individuals reveal that management philosophy and leadership have been subjects of concern for many centuries. These subjects are studied, for example, in the works of Sun Tzu and Niccolò Machiavelli.

Sun Tzu

The oldest military treatise in the world is the *Art of War* written by Sun Tzu, a Chinese military writer, around 500 B.C. This treatise illustrates that strategy, planning, leadership, and the effective management of people were all basic areas of interest to early military leaders. Commenting on two of these areas, Sun Tzu wrote:

Directing and
planning were
areas of interest to
ancient military
leaders

> *On directing:* If the words of command are not clear and distinct, if orders are not thoroughly understood, the general is to blame. But if his orders are clear, and the soldiers nevertheless disobey, then it is the fault of their officers.
>
> *On planning:* Now the general who wins a battle makes many calculations in his temple ere the battle is fought. The general who loses a battle makes few calculations beforehand. It is by attention to this point that I can see who is likely to win or lose.[2]

These basic guidelines are of value to military leaders even today.

---

[1] Francis Cornford, *The Republic of Plato* (New York: Oxford University Press, 1959), 165–67.
[2] Thomas P. Phillips, *Roots of Strategy* (Harrisburg, PA: Military Service Publishing, 1955), 23, 75.

Niccolò Machiavelli

Niccolò Machiavelli was born in Florence and obtained employment there at the age of 29, eventually serving as an unofficial emissary to every important city-state in Italy, as well as to several outside countries. When the Medici family returned to power in 1512, however, Machiavelli lost his job and was exiled.

During his time in exile, Machiavelli wrote extensively. His most famous book is *The Prince,* which presents broad management principles to which he believed all leaders should subscribe.[3] In particular, Machiavelli set forth four principles of leadership. The first principle was *mass consent.* Every leader should realize that authority emanates from the bottom and that no one is a leader unless the followers agree. Second, a leader must *strive for cohesiveness* in the organization by rewarding friends and supporters, thus maintaining their allegiance. Leaders must also have a *will to survive* to keep them alert and ever-prepared to protect their position should danger strike. Finally, the leader has to *set an example* for the followers so that they can identify with him or her.

Machiavelli made a systematic analysis of the leader's job and from it derived practical principles that are as useful today as they were 500 years ago. No wonder that one writer has described Machiavelli's works as "bursting with urgent advice and acute observations for top management of the great private and public corporations all over the world."[4]

Machiavelli's four principles of leadership

THE INDUSTRIAL REVOLUTION

The earliest management practices developed in relation to the needs of specific civilizations and countries. When the Industrial Revolution took place in the eighteenth century, however, it affected management practices throughout the entire world. Nowhere was it more fully felt than in Great Britain, where the factory system was in full swing by 1750.

Some of the major developments the Industrial Revolution brought about included (1) a rising per capita income, (2) economic growth, (3) reduced dependence on agriculture, (4) a high degree of specialization of labor, and (5) a widespread integration of markets.[5] These developments occurred in conjunction with the invention of new machinery and the scientific application of job specialization in the workplace. The result was the emergence of the factory system.

---

[3] Niccolò Machiavelli, *The Prince* (New York: The Modern Library, 1940).

[4] Antony Jay, *Management and Machiavelli* (New York: Holt, Rinehart and Winston, 1967), 4.

[5] Phyllis Deane, *The First Industrial Revolution* (London: Cambridge University Press, 1965), 5–19.

The Factory System

Before the Industrial Revolution began, many people were employed within their own homes, spinning and weaving textiles. The demand for this output was very high. As a result, attention was directed to finding faster and cheaper methods of production. As technical inventions emerged,[6] the entire textile industry became mechanized.

Technology revolutionized business practices

This same pattern occurred in other industries, and as it did, many small entrepreneurs were gradually forced out of business. The owner-managers lacked the capital to purchase the new, efficient machinery and they could not compete for long with firms that could produce much greater output at a much lower price than they could. When the owners of the new machines realized that it was more efficient to place all of them in one locale and hire a workforce to come to this site to work, the factory system came into being.

The factory system was characterized by strict control of operations. The owners were intent on making the greatest profit possible. Therefore, they focused their attention on streamlining operations, eliminating waste, and increasing output. Their two main areas of concern were production power and standardization of operation.

Power and Standardization

Arnold Toynbee, the great historian, has credited the rise of industrialism to two individuals: James Watt and Adam Smith. Watt provided the power and Smith popularized standardization.

James Watt developed the steam engine

The power James Watt provided was the steam engine. In 1781, he made his greatest breakthrough in technology with the development of an engine with a rotary, as opposed to an up-and-down, movement. This invention made the machine more adaptable to factory use.[7]

Adam Smith popularized the concept of division of labor

Adam Smith popularized the concept of **division of labor** in his book *An Inquiry Into the Nature and Causes of the Wealth of Nations* (1776). Using the manufacture of pins as an example, he explained how a group of individuals who specialized their efforts, with one drawing out the wire, a second straightening it, a third cutting it, and so on, could make 12 pounds of pins in a day while one of them working alone could not make 20 pins.[8]

While Watt's invention and Smith's concept helped factories increase their output, there was still interest in developing other labor-saving

---

[6] Some of the most important were John Kay's flying shuttle (1733), James Hargreave's spinning jenny (1765), Richard Arkwright's water frame (1769), Samuel Crompton's "mule" (1779), and Edmund Cartwright's power loom (1785).

[7] Daniel A. Wren, *The Evolution of Management Thought,* 2nd ed. (New York: John Wiley, 1979), 45.

[8] Adam Smith, *The Wealth of Nations* (New York: The Modern Library, 1937), 7.

techniques and devices that could further increase productivity. The individuals who helped discover and perfect these techniques have come to be known as scientific managers.

SCIENTIFIC MANAGEMENT

Scientific management was a natural outgrowth of the Industrial Revolution. As the factory system emerged, more and more attention was directed toward increasing output. Managers studied many possible ways to achieve this goal. For example, they looked for ways to feed work into a machine at a faster rate, to increase the speed of the machine, and to determine the most efficient flow of materials through the workplace. In every instance, the objective was the same: increased efficiency.

By the middle of the nineteenth century, "efficiency experts" could be found in all large industrial complexes, not only in England, but also in the United States, which was emerging as a giant industrial power. While some of these efficiency experts learned their business through trial and error and on-the-job experience, many of them were trained mechanical engineers. These individuals ushered in the era of scientific management that dominated management thinking until well into the twentieth century. **Scientific management** was a system that attempted to develop ways of increasing productivity and to formulate methods of motivating workers to take advantage of these labor-saving techniques. While many people made contributions to this field, three of the most important American scientific managers were Frederick Taylor, Frank Gilbreth, and Henry L. Gantt.

Frederick Taylor (1856–1915)

A mechanical engineer by training, Taylor contributed to the field of scientific management by conducting time-and-motion study experiments and by recording his knowledge of management. Taylor's primary objective was to discover the most efficient way of doing a job and then to train the workers to do it that way. Relying heavily on time-and-motion study, Taylor and his associates approached management by breaking a job down into its fundamental operations, determining how each operation could be done quickly and efficiently, and establishing a work quota for the job.

During his career, Taylor conducted many important time-and-motion study experiments. In one case he redesigned the work of individuals who were loading "pigs" of iron (blocks or ingots weighing about 92 pounds each) into an open railroad car. Before Taylor's experiments, the average worker loaded 12½ long tons (2,240 pounds per long ton) a day. After Taylor completed his

Frederick Taylor gained fame through his experiments and writings.

work, the average individual loaded 47½ long tons a day. In another case Taylor studied the amount of coal a worker shoveled in a day. His experiments led him to conclude that an average scoop load of 21 pounds would result in maximum output. By matching the scoop size and the weight of the coal, Taylor was able to increase the daily number of tons loaded from 16 to 59 and to reduce the average cost of handling a ton of coal from 7.2 cents to 3.3 cents.

In addition to his experiments, Taylor also published articles and wrote books on scientific management. In his best known work, *Principles of Scientific Management,* he set forth what he felt were the four basic **principles of scientific management**:

1. Management should develop a science for each element of the work to be done.
2. Management should scientifically select, train, teach, and develop each worker.
3. Management should cooperate with the worker in ensuring that all of the work is done in accordance with the principles of scientific management.
4. Management should divide work responsibilities between management and the workers with the former studying jobs and determining how they should be done and the latter carrying them out.[9]

The four basic principles of scientific management

By the time he died, Frederick Taylor was already being referred to as the "Father of Scientific Management."

Frank Gilbreth (1868–1924)

Frank Gilbreth passed up the opportunity to attend the Massachusetts Institute of Technology, deciding instead to go into the contracting business. Starting as an apprentice bricklayer, he quickly realized that much of the work was performed inefficiently at best. This realization eventually led him into the area of time-and-motion study.

During his long career Gilbreth made so many contributions to the field that today he is known as the "Father of Motion Study." One of his most significant studies was in bricklaying where, after much experimentation, he was able to increase the number of bricks a man could lay in an hour from 120 to 350. He also pioneered the use of the movie camera for scientific management purposes, filming people in the workplace and then playing back the film to see how the work could be streamlined by eliminating extraneous time and motion. So detailed was his approach to the area that he developed a categorization

Frank Gilbreth developed a categorization of basic hand motions.

---

[9] Frederick Taylor, *Principles of Scientific Management* (New York: Harper & Brothers, Publishers, 1911), 36–37.

FIGURE 2-1
A Gantt Chart

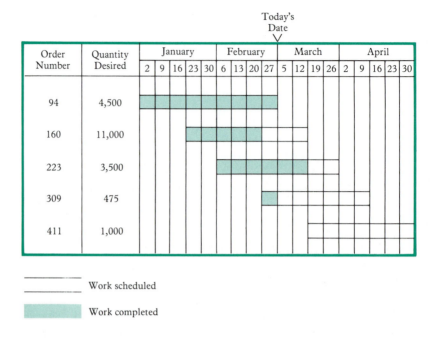

Order Number	Quantity Desired	January 2	9	16	23	30	February 6	13	20	27	March 5	12	19	26	April 2	9	16	23	30
94	4,500																		
160	11,000																		
223	3,500																		
309	475																		
411	1,000																		

Today's Date ∨

——— Work scheduled

▓▓▓ Work completed

of basic hand motions (grasp, hold, position) that could be used in analyzing the work. Today these motions are called **therbligs** (Gilbreth spelled backwards with the *t* and *h* transposed).[10]

Henry L. Gantt (1861–1919)

Henry L. Gantt was Frederick Taylor's protegé. His most significant contribution was the chart (Figure 2-1) he developed in 1917. Known today as the **Gantt chart**, it shows that scientific managers were not confined to time-and-motion study in their quest to improve worker efficiency. Along the horizontal axis of the chart, work scheduled and work completed are measured. Along the vertical axis are the jobs to be done. In the example given in Figure 2-1, there are five jobs scheduled. The first, order number 94, calls for the production of 4,500 units. The job was begun on January 2 and is scheduled for completion on March 2. The second job, order number 160, was begun on January 23 and is scheduled to be finished on March 16. The *V* at the top of the chart after the week of February 27 indicates the current date, namely March 2. Progress on each order is designated by the dark line bar that extends throughout the bar line. A visual examination of the chart reveals the following:

Henry L. Gantt developed a planning and control chart.

---

[10] For additional insights, see J. Michael Gotcher, "Assisting the Handicapped: The Efforts of Frank and Lillian Gilbreth," *Academy of Management Proceedings* (1989):143–46.

- Order 94: finished on time
- Order 160: currently one week late
- Order 223: currently two weeks ahead of schedule
- Order 309: currently on time
- Order 411: scheduled to begin March 19

MANAGEMENT SCIENCE

The proponents of scientific management made important contributions to the management of work. Their time-and-motion study experiments resulted in dramatic increases in efficiency, and this quantitative orientation continues to the present day. Along the way, however, their work has been complemented by that of other quantitatively oriented people whose interests extend beyond time-and-motion study to encompass linear programming, inventory control, work flow, production planning, purchasing, quality control, quantitative decision making, computers, and systems theory.[11] Today these areas are collectively grouped under the title of **management science**, and modern scientific managers and others with an interest in improving work quantity or efficiency are referred to as *management scientists.*[12] They practice the scientific method, use mathematical tools and techniques, and have a high regard for systems theory.

Scientific Method

As will be seen throughout this chapter, one of the major characteristics of the group that helped establish the foundations of modern management was their interest in the **scientific method**. Today, management scientists emphasize the use of this method because of their interest in solving mathematical or quantitatively oriented problems. The steps they follow in this scientific process are the following:

Steps in the scientific method

1. *Identifying the problem.* Here the emphasis is on clearly stating the issue under study. What roadblock or hurdle needs to be overcome? Does the organization need a more efficient purchasing system? An inventory reorder point for certain products? A better work flow design? In other words, what is the purpose of the study?

---

[11] Norman Gaither, "Historical Development of Operations Research," *Papers Dedicated to the Development of Modern Management,* 50th Anniversary of the Academy of Management (August 1986):71–77.

[12] James R. Miller and Howard Feldman, "Management Science—Theory, Relevance, and Practice in the 80s," *Interfaces,* (October 1983):56–60.

2. *Obtaining preliminary information.* In this step the management scientist gathers as much available data on the problem as possible. Some of the questions that are addressed include: What is currently known about the situation? What other types of information would be helpful? In this way a link is established between current information and the information needed to solve the problem under study.

3. *Posing a tentative solution to the problem.* In this step the management scientist states a tentative hypothesis that can be tested and proved to be either right or wrong. The individual, drawing on knowledge of the problem and preliminary information, establishes a problem-solving direction.

4. *Investigating the problem area.* Using currently available data and any other information that can be gathered, the management scientist now examines the problem in its entirety. He or she conducts research, obtains more data, and secures all necessary inputs needed to solve the problem.

5. *Classifying the information.* The management scientist now takes all of the data and puts it into an order that will expedite its use and help establish a relationship with the hypothesis. During this step, he or she analyzes the information and gains insight into how it can be used to solve the problem.

6. *Stating a tentative answer to the problem.* The management scientist now draws a conclusion regarding the "right" answer to the problem. He or she may develop a mathematical formula, set forth a new work flow design, or simply provide a reorder point level for inventory. In any event, a specific recommendation for action is forthcoming.

7. *Testing the answer.* Now the answer or proposed solution is tested. If it works, the problem is solved. If it does not work, the management scientist goes back to Step 3 and continues through the process again, reworking the solution based upon these latest results.

Use of Mathematical Tools and Techniques

A second major characteristic of management science is its reliance on mathematical tools and techniques for decision making and problem solving. Many of these tools and techniques have been developed and need merely to be modified to meet the particular situation. In some cases, however, the management scientist has to develop a new formula or model that can be tested and modified for use in a specific situation. In using all of these tools and techniques, management scientists often rely upon computers. They have found these machines to be extremely efficient and cost effective in handling the quantitative computations and analyses required for solving modern management problems. (See "Management in Practice: Pick a Winner.")

Pick a Winner

*I*s it necessary to use sophisticated mathematical tools and techniques to make important business decisions? It can help, but in many matters business people use simple tools or basic rules of thumb and they end up with good choices. For example, will next year be a good year in which to float a new stock issue in the market? One way of answering this question is to predict whether the market will go up or down and then float the issue if it appears that the market will go up. How can this be determined? Some people have suggested a rather simple approach: Forecast who will win the Super Bowl. If it is an NFC team, float the issue because the market is likely to go up; if it is an AFC team, do not float the issue because the market is going down. This does not sound like a very sophisticated approach, but history is on the side of this theory. Consider the results of all previous Super Bowl winners, as shown below, and not that only twice in 22 years was the theory wrong.

SUPER BOWL FORECAST RESULTS

Year	Winner	League	Change in the Market
1967	Green Bay Packers	NFC	+20.09%
1968	Green Bay Packers	NFC	+ 7.66
1969	New York Jets	AFC	−11.42
1970	Kansas City Chiefs	AFC	+ 0.16*
1971	Baltimore Colts	NFC	+10.79
1972	Dallas Cowboys	NFC	+15.63
1973	Miami Dolphins	AFC	−17.37
1974	Miami Dolphins	AFC	−29.72
1975	Pittsburgh Steelers	NFC	+31.55
1976	Pittsburgh Steelers	NFC	+19.15
1977	Oakland Raiders	AFC	−11.50
1978	Dallas Cowboys	NFC	+ 1.06
1979	Pittsburgh Steelers	NFC	+12.31
1980	Pittsburgh Steelers	NFC	+25.77
1981	Oakland Raiders	AFC	− 9.72
1982	San Francisco 49ers	NFC	+14.76
1983	Washington Redskins	NFC	+17.27
1984	Los Angeles Raiders	AFC	+ 1.39*
1985	San Francisco 49ers	NFC	+26.34
1986	Chicago Bears	NFC	+14.33
1987	New York Giants	NFC	+ 2.03
1988	Washington Redskins	NFC	+12.58
1989	San Francisco 49ers	NFC	+21.54
1990	San Francisco 49ers	NFC	+26.96

* Shows incorrect forecast.

The Systems Approach

Management scientists also have a high regard for the systems approach. This regard is undoubtedly a reflection of their need to understand how decisions affect more than one part of the organization. For example, if they design a more effective inventory control system, they also may have to design a new purchasing system. Of course, the systems concept is not restricted to management scientists. However, they do employ it in their day-to-day operations.

ADMINISTRATIVE MANAGEMENT

The early scientific managers had great success at the lower levels of the organizations. As output increased and operations grew, however, organizations began to be confronted with new management problems. Planning and coordinating operations became much more important than ever before, and the organization of people in the workplace became a focal point for consideration. The individuals who were interested in dealing with these problems began to formulate theories of administration. Four of the most famous were Henri Fayol, Mary Parker Follett, James D. Mooney, and Lyndall F. Urwick.[13]

Henri Fayol (1842 – 1925)

Henri Fayol, a Frenchman, spent his entire career working for a mining combine. By the age of 46 he was president of the organization and remained so for 30 years.

Fayol's interest was in the administrative side of operations. In particular he was concerned about the fact that different abilities were needed as one moved up the management ranks. At the lower levels an individual required greater technical skill in order to supervise workers effectively. At the upper levels the individual required administrative ability in order to get things done through other people. This idea is illustrated in Figure 2-2.

Fayol's experience led him to conclude that there were five basic functions of administration: planning, organizing, commanding, coordinating, and controlling. *Planning* called for the formulation of objectives and an operating program. *Organizing* entailed the effective coordination of resources for accomplishing the predetermined objectives. *Commanding* was the art of effective leadership. *Coordinating,* the orderly arrangement of group efforts to provide unity of action, ensured the harmony necessary for a smoothly functioning

Henri Fayol identified five basic functions: planning, organizing, commanding, coordinating, and controlling.

---

[13] David D. Van Fleet and Gary A. Yukl, "A Century of Leadership Research," *Papers Dedicated to the Development of Modern Management,* 50th Anniversary of the Academy of Management (August 1986):12–23.

FIGURE 2-2
Managerial Skills

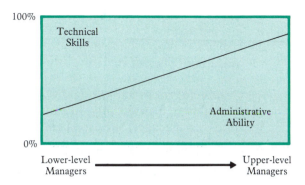

organization. *Controlling* involved seeing that everything was done according to the adopted plan.

Fayol also set forth a series of administrative principles. These principles were intended as flexible guidelines for managing both people and work. The 14 principles Fayol felt he used more frequently were:

1. *Division of labor.* Efficiency can be increased through work specialization.
2. *Authority and responsibility.* Authority, which is the right to command, should always be equal to responsibility, which is the obligation or duty to carry out assigned tasks.

Fayol's administrative principles

3. *Discipline.* In its essence, discipline requires obedience, diligence, and a proper attitude on the part of employees and effective leadership on the part of managers.
4. *Unity of command.* Everyone should have one and only one boss.
5. *Unity of management.* For every plan there should be an objective and a manager who is responsible for overall direction.
6. *Subordination of individual interests to the common good.* The goals of the organization and the department must take precedence over the personal goals of individual employees.
7. *Remuneration of the staff.* All staff members should receive compensation that is fair and motivates them to do good work.
8. *Centralization.* Organizations tend to confine too much decision making to the upper levels. Instead, they should seek that balance of centralization-decentralization that provides the greatest overall efficiency.
9. *The hierarchy.* There should be a clear-cut chain of command running from the top of the organization to the bottom.
10. *Order.* A place should exist for everything, and everything should be in its place.
11. *Equity.* Everyone in the organization should be treated fairly and justly.
12. *Stability of staff.* Since it takes time for people to learn their jobs and function at the highest level of efficiency, the long-term commitment of the staff should be a primary concern of management.

13. *Initiative.* Managers need the power both to conceive and to execute a plan of action.
14. *Esprit de corps.* Morale depends heavily on harmony and unity of the organization's staff.[14]

These functions and principles provide an important framework for the study of modern management. In particular, they illustrate that by studying the functions of a manager, one can obtain a high degree of administrative training and insight. Fayol's contributions to the field were so significant that today he is known as the "Father of Modern Management Theory."

Mary Parker Follett (1868–1933)

Mary Parker Follett was trained in philosophy and political science and from this background made a series of important contributions in the administrative management field. One idea for which she has become well known is the **law of the situation**. Follett pointed out in her writings that the situation itself, not the hierarchical chain, should dictate who has authority. The person giving the orders should be the one who knows the most about the situation and is best able to get the job done, not necessarily the one who is highest in the hierarchy. This philosophy was a result of her belief that people should cooperate with each other for the overall good of the group instead of allowing personal interests to dominate the situation. Follett also believed that if people examined each situation closely they could work out a solution that would be beneficial to all parties involved. This concept, often known as *conflict resolution,* was her second important contribution to the field of administrative management. The third was her writing on the value and importance of *coordination.* Only through effective coordination, she argued, could unity, control, and efficiency be attained. Finally, her philosophy of *community service* by administrators showed that she was aware of the importance of management's social role. She put her belief this way:

We work for profit, for service, for our own development, for the love of creating something. At any one moment, indeed, most of us are not working directly or immediately for any of these things, but to put through the job in hand in the best possible manner. . . . To come back to the professions: Can we not learn a lesson from them on this very point? The professions have not given up the money motive. I do not care how often you see it stated that they have. . . . Professional men are eager enough for large

Mary Parker Follett emphasized the importance of conflict resolution.

---

[14] Henri Fayol, *Industrial and General Administration,* tr. J. A. Coubrough (Geneva: International Management Institute, 1930), 19–33. See also: Stephen J. Carroll and Dennis J. Gillen, "Are the Classical Managerial Functions Useful in Describing Managerial Work?" *Academy of Management Review* (January 1987):38–51.

incomes; but they have other motives as well, and they are often willing to sacrifice a good slice of income for the sake of these other things. We all want the richness of life in terms of our deepest desire. We can purify and evaluate our desires, we can add to them, but there is no individual or social progress in curtailment of desires.[15]

In retrospect, we can see that Follett was a management philosopher. She was also ahead of her time. Over the last three decades, her ideas have gained in importance as executives have come to realize the value of conflict resolution, coordination, and the need to temper a concern for efficiency and profit with concern for social responsibility.

James D. Mooney (1884–1957)

James D. Mooney was a General Motors executive. In 1931, with a coauthor,[16] he wrote a book entitled *Onward Industry!*[17] This book analyzed the organizing function in detail, drawing heavily from Mooney's business experience and studies of military, government, church, and industry patterns. Mooney concluded that the first principle of organizing was coordination, which is the orderly arrangement of group efforts to provide unity of action in the pursuit of a common objective.

While the book was difficult to read and overly complex in presentation, it was an important effort toward uncovering principles of organizing. Most significantly it provided additional insights into administrative theory and helped advance the growing body of knowledge in the field.

James D. Mooney uncovered principles of organizing.

Lyndall F. Urwick (1894–1983)

Lyndall Urwick was educated at Oxford and from 1928 to 1933 was director of the International Management Institute in Geneva. Until his retirement, he was also chairman of Urwick, Orr and Partners Ltd., a management consulting firm located in London.

Urwick was familiar with management theory literature on both sides of the Atlantic. This knowledge enabled him to write a book entitled *The Elements of Administration,* which integrated the theories of Taylor, Fayol, Mooney, and other early management writers.[18] In synthesizing the major ideas of these

Lyndall F. Urwick undertook a synthesis of management theory.

---

[15] Henry C. Metcalf and Lyndall F. Urwick, eds., *Dynamic Administration: The Collected Papers of Mary Parker Follett* (New York: Harper and Row, 1940), 145.

[16] The coauthor was Alan C. Reiley. It is widely accepted that Mooney provided the framework for the book while Reiley contributed primarily to the historical analyses of the organizations that were presented.

[17] James D. Mooney and Alan C. Reiley, *Onward Industry!* (New York: Harper & Brothers, Publishers, 1931).

[18] L. Urwick, *The Elements of Administration* (New York: Harper & Brothers, Publishers, 1943).

theorists, Urwick discovered that they agreed about many administrative principles. Commenting on their agreement, he wrote:

> The main point [of the book] is that it focuses in a logical scheme various "Principles of Administration" formulated by different authorities. The fact that such "Principles"—worked out by persons of different nationalities, widely varying experience and, in the majority of cases, no knowledge of each other's work—were susceptible to such logical arrangement, is in itself highly significant.[19]

As a result of Urwick's writings, it became evident by the early 1940s that administrative theory was far more scientific, better researched, and more clearly understood than had previously been believed.

ADMINISTRATIVE SCIENCE

The contributions of these early administrative theorists helped develop a framework for the study of modern management. The outcome of their efforts, as complemented by current writers and researchers, is known as the **administrative science** or **management process** approach. This approach is similar to the one suggested by Fayol when he set forth the functions of a manager. First, a list of management functions is developed. Then each is studied in detail. A typical list of such functions might include planning, organizing, staffing, leading, and controlling. This approach offers a number of important advantages in the study of modern management.

An Enduring Framework

A framework for the study of management emerges

One of the primary advantages of a process approach is the enduring framework it provides. Anything new in management can be integrated into this framework. For example, a new development in strategic planning can be made part of the planning material; new contingency organization design research can be added to the organizing material; and a newly developed information system approach can be made part of the controlling material. In this way the process approach offers a lasting framework for the study of management.

Management functions can be systematically studied

In contrast to management scientists, *management theorists* are not as interested in providing tools and techniques for decision making as they are in developing a model for the systematic study of management. Like the management scientists, however, they recognize the value of a systems approach. For

---

[19] Urwick, *Elements,* 7.

FIGURE 2-3
Interrelationship
of Management
Functions

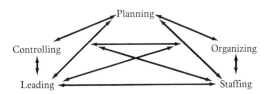

example, while they study functions in a sequential order, they also recognize the functions' interrelationships. Planning affects organizing, staffing, leading, and controlling; the same is true, in turn, for the other functions. This idea is illustrated in Figure 2-3.

A Focal Point for Study

A second major benefit of the process approach is that it provides focal points for the study of management. The identification of functions helps make possible their systematic study. Individuals interested in becoming more effective managers can determine those functions about which they have insufficient information and can work on improving their understanding of them.

Research findings developed over a period of time can provide additional insights into the way to carry out these functions. Sometimes these insights are provided in the form of management principles, which are general guidelines for understanding and implementing the functions. An example is the exception principle of control, which holds that managers should concern themselves with controlling exceptional cases and not with routine results.

A Generalist Viewpoint

Management theorists have a generalist point of view

Modern management theorists have a generalist point of view. They are most concerned with studying how organizations function in general and how managers should carry out their jobs. Management scientists, on the other hand, are interested in quantitative tools and techniques. Administrative science, management theory, or management process people are more concerned with macro-oriented topics such as strategic planning, organizational design, and the formulation of key areas of control for the organization at large. Management scientists are empirical in their approach to the field; they want to use the scientific method to formulate problems and obtain results. Administrative scientists are happier using a general approach; and while they respect the need for empirical research, they also place great value on intuition, gut feeling, and the importance of past experience. Many practicing managers like this general approach because they are uneasy dealing with management science techniques. Nevertheless, both are important to the study of modern management. Behavioral orientation, which will now be the focus of our attention, is important as well. (See "Management in Practice: Here Comes Japan.")

Here Comes Japan*

Past experience can be a very useful tool in helping identify the strategic moves of competitors. Quite often, people's past strategies help dictate their future moves. The Japanese are a good example. During the 1970s and 1980s Japanese firms began to push in, and in some cases dominate, certain industries including automobiles, televisions, radios, and computers. What will the future see? The answer is: More of the same and some new products as well. A recent forecast of new Japanese products for the 1990s included the following:

1. Tape recorders the size of a matchbox, without cassettes or moving parts.
2. High-definition televisions with 21-foot screens that have movie theater clarity.
3. Flat TV screens that can be hung on the wall.
4. Translation telephones, with simple vocabularies at first, that handle multilingual conversations almost instantaneously.
5. Semiconductor chips the size of silver dollars that act as electrical transformers.
6. Air conditioners that use a third less power than today's models.
7. Microminiaturized personal computers a

fraction the size of the IBM PS/2 and Apple Macintosh.
8. Robots that sew, smooth concrete floors, hoist slabs into place, or wash windows better and faster than people do.
9. Sports cars that can compete head-to-head with Ferraris and Lamborghinis but which cost only about half as much.

These new products have a number of common characteristics. They are high technology based; they are a result of improvements of goods that were already on the market; they work faster or better than their predecessors; they provide more performance for the dollar than the latter. How can American firms compete effectively with the Japanese? One way is by realizing the past strategies of the Japanese and using this historical base to predict what they are likely to do in the future. An understanding of business history and strategy can be very helpful in doing so.

* Gene Bylinsky, "Where Japan Will Strike Next," *Fortune* (September 25, 1989):42–50.

HUMAN BEHAVIOR

At the same time that the early administrative theorists were concerning themselves with the management of organizations, other people were arriving on the business scene who were concerned with human behavior at work. Some of their work was heavily psychological in nature; some of it was sociological. In either case, these early behaviorists made the first contributions to out understanding of human behavior in organizations. Four of the major contributors during the pre-World War II period were Hugo Munsterberg, Lillian M. Gilbreth, Elton Mayo, and Chester Barnard.

Hugo Munsterberg (1863–1916)

Hugo Munsterberg, born in Prussia, received his Ph.D. from Leipzig where he studied under Wilhelm Wundt, the "Father of Modern Psychology." Two years later he was awarded his M.D. from Heidelberg University. In 1892 he came to Harvard University as a visiting professor and five years later returned to direct Harvard's Psychological Laboratory.[20]

Munsterberg's major contribution to management came in the field of industrial psychology. Determined to strengthen the bridge between scientific management and industrial efficiency, he wanted to find out why some workers did well on the job and others did not.[21] He was convinced that the scientific managers spent too much time trying to match the physical skills of the worker with those required by the job, and that in the process they overlooked psychological or mental skills. This interest led him into the area of vocational testing.

Munsterberg believed that he could develop tests that would help screen out unfit job applicants and workers. His most famous experiment was conducted among trolley car operators, but he also developed screening tests for other work groups, including ship's officers and telephone operators. Always the central objective was to determine whether or not the person was psychologically fit for the job. Did the individual have the requisite mental skills? Munsterberg was convinced that psychological testing could be valuable in screening people at *all levels* of an organization:

> The results of experimental psychology will have to be introduced systematically into the study of the fitness of the personality, from the lowest to the highest technical activity and from the simplest sensory function to the most complex mental achievement.[22]

Munsterberg popularized psychology by showing how it could be of value in many fields, and heralded the advent of psychologists into industry. He also showed how a scientific approach to the study of human behavior at work could bring forth effective results. Today Munsterberg is known as the "Father of Industrial Psychology."

Lillian M. Gilbreth (1878–1972)

Dr. Lillian Moller Gilbreth, the wife of Frank Gilbreth, not only played an important role in her husband's work but earned a significant reputation of her own. After they married, she changed her academic interests to psychology. A detailed thesis at the University of California was turned into a book, *The Psychology of Management*[23] and stands in the literature as one of the earliest

Hugo Munsterberg developed screening tests.

---

[20] *Encyclopaedia Britannica,* 1982 ed., vol. 7, 104.

[21] Hugo Munsterberg, *Psychology and Industrial Efficiency* (Boston: Houghton Mifflin, 1913).

[22] Munsterberg, *Industrial Efficiency,* 96.

[23] L. M. Gilbreth, *The Psychology of Management: The Function of the Mind in Determining, Teaching and Installing Methods of Least Waste* (New York: Sturgis and Walton, 1914).

Lillian Gilbreth focused on individual behavior.

contributions to understanding the human factor in industry. Later, in 1915 she received a Ph.D. from Brown University. She also played an important role in bringing to scientific management an understanding of the role and importance of psychology. Prior to her time, much of the concern of psychologists was with crowd behavior. Lillian Gilbreth, in contrast, focused on individual behavior. She also examined management styles and concluded that there were three: traditional, transitory, and scientific. The traditional style was typified by the hard-driving manager who believed in unity of command and employed centralized authority. The transitory style fell between traditional and scientific. The scientific style depended on the careful selection of personnel, the use of incentives, and an overall consideration of worker welfare. Each employee was to be developed to the fullest degree possible. These ideas were advanced for their time. Not until the 1970s did the behavioral field turn toward a human resources philosophy in which concern for the development of the employee's total potential became a focal point of interest. Lillian Gilbreth had already presented many of these ideas 50 years earlier. By the time she died in 1972, she was known throughout the world for her contributions to the field of management psychology, earning the title "First Lady of Management."

Elton Mayo (1880–1949)

Elton Mayo was an Australian who taught ethics, philosophy, and logic at the Queensland University and later studied medicine in Edinburgh, Scotland. He then became a research associate in the study of psychopathology and eventually came to America. By 1926 he was an associate professor of industrial relations at Harvard University.

During his early work in American industry, Mayo seemed to have more understanding of scientific management principles than of behavior at work. He gradually came to recognize, however, that output often increased when work patterns and procedures were changed not because the new arrangement was more efficient but because the workers liked it better. Morale and attitude were often more important than work flow and efficiency procedures.[24]

Mayo is best remembered for coordinating the writing and reporting of the **Hawthorne studies**. Today these behavioral studies are regarded as the single most important historical foundation for the behavioral approach to management.[25]

Elton Mayo coordinated the Hawthorne studies.

---

[24] For other examples of early behavioral work see Charles D. Wrege and Ronald G. Greenwood, "Applying Psychiatry to the 'Brains of Industry': The Pioneer Work of Dr. Jau Don Ball," *Academy of Management Proceedings* (1989):147–51.

[25] For more on this see Fred Luthans, *Organizational Behavior*, 5th ed. (New York: McGraw-Hill, 1989), 28–30; and Ronald G. Greenwood and Charles D. Wrege, "The Hawthorne Studies" in Daniel A. Wren, ed. *Papers Dedicated to the Development of Modern Management,* Academy of Management, 1986, pp. 24–35.

Hawthorne Studies

The initial purpose of the Hawthorne studies (1924–1932) was to determine the effect of illumination on output. The studies, sponsored by the National Research Council, were started in late 1924 at the Hawthorne Works of the Western Electric Company near Cicero, Illinois. Before the studies were completed, they passed through four major phases: the illumination experiments, the relay assembly test room experiments, the interview program, and the bank wiring observation room study.[26]

The illumination experiments determined that lighting was only one factor affecting output

ILLUMINATION EXPERIMENTS   These initial experiments, designed to study the effect of illumination on output, lasted two-and-one-half years. During this time, numerous experiments were conducted. They were all inconclusive and the researchers were unable to determine the relationship between illumination and output. Two conclusions were reached, however: lighting was found to be only one factor affecting output and also there were too many variables present to allow the researchers to isolate illumination as a casual factor. Greater control of the experiment was needed.

In the relay assembly test room experiments, output went up and stayed up

RELAY ASSEMBLY TEST ROOM   To obtain this control, the researchers decided to isolate a small group of employees from the regular work force and study their behavior. Six women were placed in a room by themselves. After allowing some time to study the effect of the new environment, the experimenters began introducing changes such as rest pauses, shorter work days, and shorter work weeks. Output went up. When these changes were taken away, however, output still remained high. Why were the women doing more work than ever before? The researchers concluded that changes in their social conditions and the method of supervision were bringing about improved attitudes and increased productivity. To gain more information, management decided to investigate employee attitudes through an interviewing program.[27]

The interviewing program provided a wealth of information about employee attitudes

INTERVIEWING PROGRAM   During this third phase of the studies, more than 20,000 interviews were conducted. The interviewers asked questions regarding supervision and the work environment. They found, however, that the employees gave guarded and stereotyped answers. They therefore switched to a nondirect method of questioning, allowing each employee to choose his or her own topic. The outcome was a wealth of information about employee attitudes.

---

[26] For a complete description of these studies, see F. J. Roethlisberger and William J. Dickson, *Management and the Worker* (Cambridge, MA: Harvard University Press, 1939). See also: Ronald G. Greenwood and Charles D. Wrege, "The Hawthorne Studies," *Papers Dedicated to the Development of Modern Management,* 50th Anniversary of the Academy of Management (August 1986):24–35.

[27] Ronald G. Greenwood, Alfred A. Bolton, and Regina A. Greenwood, "Hawthorne a Half Century Later: Relay Assembly Participants Remember" *Journal of Management,* (Fall/Winter 1983):217–21.

The researchers realized that a person's work performance, position, and status in the organization were determined not only by the individual personally, but by the group members as well. This insight led to a decision to study group behavior at work more systematically.

BANK WIRING OBSERVATION ROOM   The researchers then decided to study a small group at work, and they chose to study the bank wiring room, where workers were wiring and soldering bank terminals. After studying behavior in the room for an extended period of time, the investigators realized that many behavioral norms affected the workers' actions. Some of these norms were related to the amount of work the workers did, the individuals with whom they traded jobs or to whom they offered assistance, and the way in which they treated the various managers who came by. As a result of this phase of the study, the researchers were able to identify a series of behavioral norms, some of which included: You should not do too much work. You should not do too little work. You should not squeal to a supervisor about a fellow employee.

The Hawthorne studies had a significant impact. In particular, they uncovered important insights into individual and group behavior and focused attention on supervisory climate and leadership research. The studies heralded the advent of the behaviorists into industry. Much of the behavioral work that was to follow had its beginnings here.

The bank wiring observation room experiments uncovered a series of behavioral norms

Chester I. Barnard (1886 – 1961)

Chester Barnard was president of New Jersey Bell from 1927 until his retirement. A practicing manager, he found much of the management writing of the day to be incomplete, misleading, or superficial. In 1938 he wrote *The Functions of the Executive.*[28] This book has proven so influential to the study of management that one writer has credited Barnard with having had "a more profound impact on the thinking about the complex subject matter of human organization than has any other contributor to the continuum of management thought." [29]

Barnard's behavioral contributions fall into two major areas. First, he identified and described the functions of the executive. These he found to be (a) the establishment and maintenance of a communication system throughout the organization; (b) the promotion and acquisition of essential effort by recruiting the best people and rewarding them appropriately; and (c) the formulation of the purpose and objectives of the organization.

Chester Barnard identified and described executive functions.

---

[28] Chester I. Barnard, *The Functions of the Executive* (Cambridge, MA: Harvard University Press, 1938).

[29] Claude S. George, Jr., *The History of Management Thought,* 2nd ed. (Englewood Cliffs, NJ: Prentice-Hall, 1972), 140.

Barnard formulated
the acceptance
theory of authority

Second, Barnard set forth a theory of authority. As a behaviorist, he realized the importance of educating people to cooperate. Giving someone an order is insufficient, he said, for the person might well refuse to carry it out. When will the individual not refuse? Barnard answered the question this way:

> A person can and will accept a communication as authoritative only when four conditions simultaneously obtain: (a) he can and does understand the communication; (b) *at the time of his decision,* he believes it is not inconsistent with the purpose of the organization; (c) *at the time of his decision,* he believes it to be compatible with his personal interest as a whole; and (d) he is able mentally and physically to comply with it.[30]

Today this view is known as the **acceptance theory of authority**, which holds that the ultimate source of authority is the individual who chooses either to accept orders or to refuse to follow them. Of course, as a practicing manager Barnard realized that there were few times when people would refuse to follow orders deliberately. In explaining why, he introduced the concept of the *zone of indifference.* Orders falling within this zone are accepted without question. Other orders either fall on a neutral line or are considered unacceptable. The zone of indifference is either wide or narrow, depending on the incentives management provides for employees and the sacrifices employees have to make on behalf of the organization. The effective executive makes sure that the employees feel they are getting more from the organization than they are giving to it. In this case the indifference zone is wide and they are likely to accept orders. Barnard also hastened to point out that even when one person does not want to follow orders, the other members of the group will pressure that person to comply, if they are satisfied with the organization.

Barnard is important to the study of management because he was one of the first people to describe executive functions in analytical and dynamic terms. He stimulated an interest in behavioral topics, especially communications, decision making, and authority–responsibility relationships. Many behaviorists who came later considered Barnard to be the "Father of Modern Behavioral Science" because of the contributions of his early writing.

BEHAVIORAL SCIENCE

The work begun by Munsterberg, Gilbreth, Mayo, and Barnard continues today. Thousands of psychologists, sociologists, anthropologists, and social and industrial psychologists are employed in both industry and academia. Their area

---

[30] George, *Management Thought,* 165.

of interest is now called **behavioral science** and its focus extends from the study of individual behavior, on the one hand, to the study of large groups and organizations on the other. Three of the broadly based areas of interest for behavioral scientists today are individual behavior, group behavior, and organizational development.[31]

Individual Behavior

Some behavioral scientists focus on the individual as a sociopsychological being

Some behavioral scientists are most interested in individual behavior. These people tend to be psychologists and their focus is on the individual's motivation as a sociopsychological being. What motivates the worker? How does motivation work? Why are some people more motivated by a particular reward than others? These are the kinds of questions that intrigue this kind of behavioral scientist.

Group Behavior

Others study individuals as parts of a social system

Other behavioral scientists are concerned with studying people as parts of a social system or collection of cultural interrelationships. They see an organized enterprise as a social organism which, in turn, is made up of many social suborganisms. They are interested in studying such subjects as attitudes, habits, and the effects of pressure and conflict within the cultural environment. They are also concerned with the effect that personnel have on organizations and the countereffect of organizations on the personnel. To what degree do people make the organization and vice versa?

Organizational Development

Still others help managers understand and cope with change

In recent years some behavioral scientists have begun calling themselves *organizational development experts* or *change agents*. These people typically work for large organizations or are brought into companies as consultants. Their objective is to help managers and employees both understand and cope with change. They are also useful in helping employees understand interpersonal and intraorganizational behavioral problems and in developing behavioral change strategies for dealing with them.

MODERN MANAGEMENT THOUGHT

In this chapter we have examined the three basic foundations of modern management: management science, administrative science, and behavioral science.

---

[31] Lee E. Preston, "Social Issues in Management: An Evolutionary Perspective," *Papers Dedicated to the Development of Modern Management,* 50th Anniversary of the Academy of Management (August 1986):52–57.

As seen in Figure 2-4, each of these three approaches has been seriously modified since its beginning. The scientific managers were interested in the efficiency of operations. Today management science is concerned with the management of work. The administrative theorists were interested in the nature of
management and organizations. Today the management process or administrative science people concern themselves with the management of organizations.
Finally, the human relations orientation of the early behaviorists has given way
to a behavioral science approach that is concerned with the management of
people.

The management science and behavioral science approaches are much
more empirically based than is the approach of the administrative science or
management theory group, and this is the way it should be. The first two provide
specific information that helps us understand such important management
topics as decision making, work flow, inventory control (management
science), individual behavior, group behavior, and organizational behavior
(behavioral science). The management theory group shows how to use this
information in a comprehensive framework for studying management.

All three approaches are important in the study of modern management,
and you will see that they are intertwined. For example, decision-making techniques are an important area of concern in management science. In studying
them, however, we must also be interested in the way decisions affect organizations and people. The three developments illustrated in Figure 2-4 actually
overlap. For this reason, many modern management scholars and practitioners
like to think of management in *contingency* terms: The manager must make
those decisions and take those actions that will produce the desired results.
Fulfilling this responsibility sometimes requires a quantitative orientation; at

FIGURE 2-4
The Emergence of
Modern Manage-
ment Thought

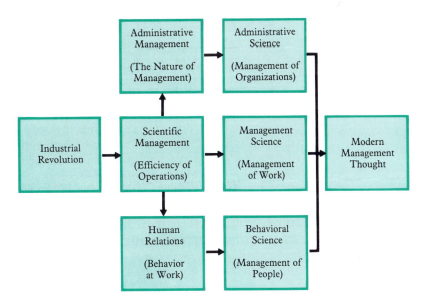

other times it demands a qualitative approach. To cover both kinds of managerial responsibilities, this book attempts to provide the comprehensive framework of the management process approach while studying too the information provided by both management science and behavioral science.

SUMMARY

1. Management has been practiced for thousands of years. The Egyptians and Greeks employed many of the ideas known to us today, and selected writings of historical figures such as Sun Tzu and Niccolò Machiavelli are as useful now as they were when originally written.
2. The Industrial Revolution brought about the factory system. Two of the men who contributed most to the rise of industrialism were James Watt, who invented the rotary steam engine, and Adam Smith, who popularized the division of labor concept.
3. Factory managers sought to increase efficiency, and this resulted in the scientific management movement. Many of the scientific managers were mechanical engineers who used time-and-motion study to analyze and redesign jobs so they could be carried out more quickly and efficiently. Frederick Taylor's experiments, Frank Gilbreth's studies, and Henry Gantt's chart all contributed to attaining these objectives.
4. The work of the scientific managers has been complemented by the work of other quantitatively oriented researchers. Today these researchers are known collectively as management scientists. Their interests include not only time-and-motion study but inventory control, linear programming, work flow, production planning, computers, and systems theory. They also make extensive use of the scientific method.
5. The success of the scientific managers at the lower levels of the organization resulted in a need to understand more about the overall administration of the enterprise. Four of the people who provided early administrative theory insights were Henri Fayol, Mary Parker Follett, James Mooney, and Lyndall Urwick. Fayol set forth a series of management functions and principles that would eventually serve as a framework for the study of modern management. Follett contributed a philosophy of management that emphasized organizational needs vis-à-vis the individual and the larger community. Mooney made a systematic study of the organizing function. Urwick synthesized the work of early contributors and provided a basis for understanding the current state of knowledge.
6. The contributions of the early administrative theorists helped develop a framework for the study of modern management. Today these administrative scientists use a process framework in studying and

analyzing the subject. Their generalist approach is very popular with practicing managers.

7. At the same time that the early administrative theorists were doing their work, behaviorists were arriving on the business scene. Hugo Munsterberg developed personnel screening tests; Lillian Gilbreth was a pioneer in management psychology; Elton Mayo participated in the Hawthorne studies; and Chester Barnard wrote about the functions of the executive and set forth the acceptance theory of authority. The work begun by these four individuals continues today, carried on by psychologists, sociologists, and other behavioral scientists. Three of the latter's primary areas of concern include individual behavior, group behavior, and organizational development.

8. Modern management is an integration of all three approaches: management science, administrative science, and behavioral science. Each plays an important role in helping explain how to manage people.

KEY TERMS

Acceptance theory of authority   A theory, popularized by Chester Barnard, which holds that the ultimate source of authority is the individual who chooses either to accept orders or to refuse to follow them.

Administrative science   *See* Management process.

Behavioral science   The study of human behavior in organizations, including individual behavior, group behavior, and organizational development.

Division of labor   Dividing work into small components so that the workers become specialists in their tasks.

Gantt chart   A chart used for scheduling jobs and measuring work progress.

Hawthorne studies   Early behavioral studies (1924–1932) that are regarded today as the single most important historical foundation for the behavioral approach to management.

Law of the situation   A law of management that holds that the situation itself should dictate who has authority. This law argues against the idea of a hierarchical chain in which the superior always gives orders to the subordinate.

Management process   (also known as administrative science) An approach to the study of management that involves the identification and systematic analysis of management functions. Modern management theorists support this approach.

Management science   A quantitatively oriented discipline, studying such topics as time-and-motion experiments, linear programming, inventory control, work flow, computers, and systems theory.

Principles of scientific management   As set forth by Frederick Taylor, they were that (1) management should develop a science for each element of the work to be done; (2) management should scientifically select, train, teach, and develop each worker; (3) management should cooperate with the worker in ensuring that all of the work is done in accordance with the principles of scientific management; and (4) management should divide work responsibilities between management and the workers, with the former studying jobs and determining how they should be done and the latter carrying them out.

Scientific management   An approach to management concerned with (1) studying work methods and processes for the purpose of determining how to increase work efficiency, and (2) developing ways of motivating the worker to use these methods and processes.

Scientific method   A logical approach to problem solving that contains seven steps: (1) identifying the problem, (2) obtaining preliminary information, (3) posing a tentative solution to the problem, (4) investigating the problem area, (5) classifying the information, (6) stating a tentative answer to the problem, and (7) testing the answer.

Therblig   A basic hand motion (grasp, hold, position) used in analyzing work.

QUESTIONS FOR ANALYSIS AND DISCUSSION

1. The Egyptians who supervised the building of the Pyramids had the greatest understanding of management in which of the following three areas: management science, management process, or behavioral science? In which one of these three areas did the Greeks show an understanding of management when they established uniform work methods and used music to set the work tempo?

2. Can the writings of Sun Tzu be of any value to the modern manager? What about those of Niccolò Machiavelli? Explain.

3. How did the Industrial Revolution bring about the emergence of the factory system? How did James Watt and Adam Smith contribute to this development?

4. In what way was scientific management a natural outgrowth of the Industrial Revolution? Explain.

5. Specifically, what contributions did each of the following make to the scientific management movement: Frederick Taylor, Frank Gilbreth, Henry Gantt?

6. Modern management scientists have an interest in the scientific method, the use of mathematical tools and techniques, and a systems approach. What is meant by this statement? Be sure to include in your answer a description of the steps in the scientific method.

7. How did the following individuals contribute to the emergence of

modern management thought: Henri Fayol, Mary Parker Follett, James Mooney, Lyndall Urwick?

8. What is the management process approach and what are some of the advantages it offers in the study of modern management?

9. How did the following people contribute to the early study of human behavior at work: Hugo Munsterberg, Lillian Gilbreth, Elton Mayo, Chester Barnard?

10. What are the three broadly based areas of interest for modern behavioral scientists? Describe each.

11. The three basic foundations of modern management are management science, administrative science, and behavioral science. What is meant by this statement? Be complete in your answer.

CASE

Quality Efficiency

The Quality Wholesale Company distributes its products to more than 500 retailers in a six-state area. One primary profit factor in wholesaling is rapid order filling. Retailers need to have their orders filled as quickly as possible and, should there be a breakdown in delivery time, they are likely to turn to other wholesale sources.

The owner of Quality Wholesale, Bert Wilson, finished revamping his facilities last month. A number of major changes have been introduced. First, all merchandise has been rearranged so that the fastest moving items are located closest to the loading dock. Second, a new inventory control system has been installed. Third, all major record keeping has been computerized. Fourth, the main office has been rearranged, new fixtures and equipment have been installed, and music is being piped into the workplace.

Since making these changes, Bert has been keeping close tabs on operating performance. Records show that delivery time has been reduced from four to three days and profitability is up 27 percent. Of course, it is still too early to tell whether this is the beginning of a long-term trend or just a temporary development. Bert believes, however, that much of this efficiency can be tied directly to the changes he introduced in the work environment.

1. Which of the major approaches to management did Bert employ: management science, administrative science, or behavioral science? Defend your answer.

2. Did these work changes have any effect on work behavior? Explain.

3. An understanding of the management process helped Bert make these work changes. In what other ways can it help him be an effective

manager? Which of the functions in this process would Bert rely on in determining whether current profitability is a long-term trend or a temporary development? Be complete in your answer.

YOU BE THE CONSULTANT

An In-House Program

A few months ago the president of a large multiline corporation made two major decisions. First, he announced that the company would begin recruiting and hiring graduates from both business and nonbusiness colleges. In the past the corporation had concentrated its efforts almost exclusively on business graduates. Second, he informed the Training and Development Department that he wanted a basic management course offered to all new personnel. He explained his reasoning this way:

> My daughter was graduated from a top-flight liberal arts college last year and immediately came to work for us. Since then she has taken a number of management training programs. All she has gotten, however, is a series of tools and techniques related to subjects such as decision making, communication leadership, time management, and stress management. How do these different training programs make her an effective manager? What she needs is a basic course that will familiarize her with the general field of management. Then she can take training programs to supplement her knowledge of basic concepts.

The head of the Training and Development Department has been working on developing such a basic, in-house course. He has asked for input from a number of people throughout the company. So far, however, he feels he has not gotten what he needs. All the people who responded to his request for training ideas stressed the importance of their own areas. The people in sales want everyone to have a sales-management orientation. Those in production feel newcomers to the firm should know about production planning, layout, and inventory control. Those in personnel want the training to emphasize communication, small group behavior, and behavioral techniques. Two of the top managers who responded noted the importance of overall planning and control techniques.

The outcome, so far, is a mixture of suggestions lacking a common unifying theme. The training and development director thinks that all of the ideas are good but that they are still too technique oriented and that there is no broadly based management approach that can pull all of them together. For this reason, he has decided to have someone from outside the organization integrate the ideas of the various in-house people and formulate a well-balanced basic course that will meet with the approval of the president.

Your Consultation

Assume that you have been called in as a consultant to the training and development director. Drawing upon your knowledge of the material in this chapter, broadly outline the types of topics that should be included in a basic management course. Use Figure 2-4 to help you in this process. Be as specific as possible, but remember that the in-house director will refine your answers to comply with the request of the president.

3

The Changing Environment of Modern Enterprises

Every enterprise operates within a changing environment. The external environment consists of forces outside the organization's direct control. These outside forces are major sources of **change** that impact on today's enterprises. This chapter examines these forces within the context of changing conditions.

The first objective of this chapter is to examine the changing forces that exist in the external environment. These forces can be divided into two groups: first tier and second tier. First-tier forces create the general environment in which enterprises operate; second-tier forces make up the specific environment in which enterprises function.

The second objective of this chapter is to examine the change process, that is, how modern management perspectives have impacted upon management thought in this changing environment

When you have finished studying the material in this chapter, you will be able to:

1. Identify the four major first-tier environmental forces and describe each in depth.
2. Identify the four major second-tier environmental forces and describe each in depth.

3. Describe the factors involved in the challenge of productivity facing managers.
4. Identify the three phases of the change process.
5. Examine the manager as a change agent and explain the six major approaches used in dealing with resistance to change.
6. Describe the eight key attributes exhibited by "excellent" companies.
7. Identify the ten major trends that are reshaping the environment of management.

THE EXTERNAL ENVIRONMENT (SOURCES OF CHANGE)

The external environment consists of forces outside the direct control of the organization. These forces stand as sources of change that managers must deal with. These forces are of two types: first tier and second tier (see Figure 3-1). The following sections examine both tiers.

First Tier

First-tier forces affect virtually every organization

First-tier forces make up the *general environment* in which organizations operate. Included in this group are the general economy, technology, and international and political-legal forces. An enterprise may not be influenced by

FIGURE 3-1
First- and Second-Tier Environmental Forces

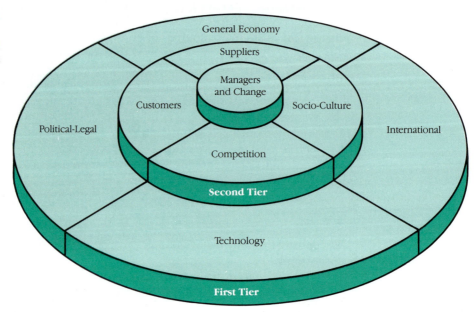

all of these forces, nor is it always able to respond to every one of them. It is important to remember, however, that these forces are usually *dependent* on each other, even though they can act independently.

The General Economy

The most dominant first-tier force is the general economy, which affects organizations both directly and indirectly. Automakers such as General Motors (GM) are directly affected when customers either stop buying or start purchasing from competitors. Smaller businesses that supply firms like GM with parts or equipment are indirectly affected by the economy when the corporate giant cancels or cuts back sales orders. However, all industries in the United States economy do not move in the same direction at the same time. Some may do well while others are doing poorly. For an example, we can look at some key U.S. industries during the 1980s.

The economy affects organizations both directly and indirectly

At that time the apparel, shoe, and textile industry was having a very difficult time. Heavy imports and overly optimistic sales forecasts had resulted in a retail glut, greatly affecting industry profitability.

The air transport industry was also having a difficult time. A decline in fuel prices and labor costs were more than offset by industry-wide price cutting and lower-than-anticipated traffic growth. As a result, profits were much lower than had been anticipated and some airlines were operating in the red.

The tire and rubber industry was another industry that was doing poorly. Demand was down and most firms were cutting back on capacity while attempting to diversify outside of the industry.

On the other hand, some industries were doing quite well. The soft drink industry was a winner with PepsiCo and Coca-Cola, in particular, doing very well.

Communication was also faring well. The industry's earnings growth and return on equity and sales growth were high. The major networks (ABC, CBS, NBC) were prospering although Fox and Turner were making strong inroads. Finally thanks to regulated price decreases, AT&T's share of the long distance market was growing while MCI and Sprint appeared ready to offer long-term competition.

As economic developments like these filter through the overall economy, some organizations benefit while others suffer. In one way or another, all feel some impact. For this reason, in recent years, large companies have begun maintaining a full staff of economists who specialize in many different areas.[1] As seen in Figure 3-2, these areas include economic forecasting, international trade, industrial organization, and political economy. Such a staff helps the corporation deal with many first- and second-tier forces.

---

[1] Thomas G. Marx, ''The Corporate Economics Staff: Challenges and Opportunities for the '80s,'' *Business Horizons* (April 1980):55–18.

FIGURE 3-2
The Corporate
Economics Staff

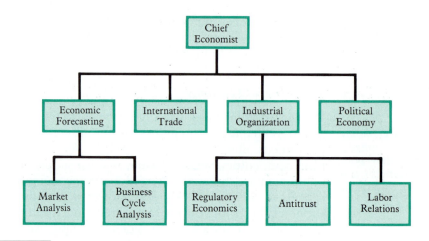

Source: Thomas G. Marx, "The Corporate Economics Staff: Challenges and Opportunities for the '80s," *Business Horizons* (April 1980):17. Reprinted with permission.

Political – Legal Forces

Political – legal
forces
constrain and
direct activity

One of the most common second-tier forces is the political – legal force. Political – legal forces consist of those laws and regulations that constrain and direct organizational activity. Laws that constrain activity set forth those things organizations are prohibited from doing. Examples include laws that prohibit an organization from engaging in unfair labor practices, from discriminating against employees on the basis of race, color, creed, sex, or national origin, and from disposing of hazardous wastes in a dangerous manner. Laws that direct organizational activity set forth those things which must be done. Examples include laws that require organizations to withhold taxes from employee paychecks, ensure safe working conditions for all personnel, and abide by all legal contracts that they have entered into.

During the last 50 years, thousands of new laws have been enacted. Table 3-1 provides a select sample. Most of these laws both constrain and direct organizational activity.

Over the years, legislative emphasis changes. In 1935 Congress passed the National Labor Relations Act, a prounion law prohibiting management from carrying out certain unfair labor practices. In 1947 Congress passed an amendment to this act, the Taft – Hartley Act, prohibiting unfair labor practices by unions. The legislative pendulum had swung from prolabor to promanagement.

As laws change, organizations must adjust to the new political – legal environment. In most cases this means following the change, not leading it. Even when organizations expect a change in legislation, they should not take early action. For example, years ago the automakers knew that safety equipment such as passive restraints would be advantageous to the consumer. However, such

TABLE 3-1   Government Regulation: Selected Examples

Year	Act	
1932	Federal Home Loan Bank	Regulated home financing institutions for the first time
1935	National Labor Relations	Promoted collective bargaining and prohibited unfair labor practices by employers
1947	Taft–Hartley	Extended the National Labor Relations Act to cover prohibition of unfair labor practices by unions
1954	Atomic Energy	Opened nuclear technology, under regulation, to private industry
1964	Civil Rights	Prohibited discrimination in private employment because of race, color, creed, sex, or national origin
1972	Consumer Product Safety	Provided for mandatory product safety standards and for the banning of hazardous substances
1978	Airline Deregulation	Loosened control over airline routes and rates—the first major deregulation step

equipment would also add a few hundred dollars to the price of a car, making it less price competitive. As a result, no one automaker wanted to start adding these safety features independently. As legislation calling for more safety was passed, they all began to do so at the same time. The changes became "safe" for the industry.

Organizations should try to anticipate the impact of laws already in effect. For example, large companies are always trying to evaluate the likelihood of antitrust action. In the mid-1960s when GM was dominant in the auto industry, it was concerned that the government would try to break it up. More recently, American Telephone & Telegraph (AT&T) was required to divest itself of its operating companies, a move occasioned by government action.[2]

Technology

Technology is a key environmental variable for many firms, especially those in industries such as manufacturing, chemicals, and information processing. If a competitor produces a superior product, the other manufacturers may face a dramatic loss of business. On the other hand, the company with the latest development may not be able to cash in on it, especially if competing companies can improve their products quickly. By using a follow-the-leader strategy, some firms have managed to be second or third in the market with a product and still acquire a very large share of the sales and profits. Others, especially small enterprises, cannot afford to lead. The costs of this strategy are too high. They must be content with a follow-the-leader approach.

Sometimes a follow-the-leader strategy is best

[2] For more on this challenge, see Joel Bleeke, "Deregulation: Riding the Rapids," *Business Horizon* (May–June 1983):15–25.

Technology must be developed in conjunction with the resources needed for capturing and maintaining the customer. Companies usually have to develop effective marketing plans and provide adequate product service in order to sell their technological advances. When Texas Instruments (TI) improved digital technology during the mid-1970s, it was able to reduce the price of digital watches greatly. Japanese manufacturers, however, were able to follow suit quickly. When the competition for customers came to depend on low-cost production and marketing effectiveness, TI lost sales. By the late 1980s Japanese and Hong Kong manufacturers dominated the digital watch market. The Swiss were in third place, and the Americans were far behind them all.

Other firms have been more successful in blending technology with marketing expertise. General Motors and Ford Motor Co. are betting that machines capable of mimicking human beings will give them a competitive edge in automobile manufacturing of the future. The automakers are further betting that the key to the future is to move rapidly growing artificial intelligence technology onto factory floors. Included in the artificial intelligence family are: machine vision technology which emulates human sight; robotics technology that imitates human movement; and expert systems, also known as knowledge engineering—a technology that emulates the human ability to reason. Artificial intelligence, the auto companies believe, is the key to gaining a competitive advantage, or eliminating its competitive disadvantage, with the Japanese. It is the key to higher productivity, improved quality, enhanced manufacturing flexibility, and better use of resources, company officials say.[3]

International Forces

International forces are a consideration for firms doing business in other countries. Companies known as **multinational corporations (MNCs)** or transnational firms have their headquarters in one country but operate in many different nations. Management views the entire organization as one giant, interdependent system, and the relationships between headquarters and the various subsidiaries are collaborative. Communication flows in two directions. Top management sets directions for the whole organization. Subsidiary managers carry out these plans at their particular locale and report the results to the top. Two-way planning discussions then lead to follow-through activity.[4]

MNCs operate worldwide

Some of the best-known MNCs in the United States include IBM, Exxon, General Electric, Ford Motor, and National Cash Register. Some of the primary advantages of multinationals include their access to natural resources and mate-

---

[3] Michelle Krebs, "GM–Ford Bet on *Human Machines*," *Automotive News* (February 17, 1986):1–43. For more on technology, see Alan L. Frohman, "Putting Technology into Strategic Planning," *California Management Review* (Winter 1985):48–59.

[4] Mark Fitzpatrick, "The Definition and Assessment of Political Risk in International Business: A Review of the Literature," *Academy of Management Review* (April 1983):249–54.

rials not available to domestic firms, their capacity to recruit and train personnel from a worldwide labor pool, and their ability to capitalize on world markets.

CUSTOMS/CULTURE   In every country of the world there is an established way of doing business. Business customs often reflect the culture or values of the society. For example, in many Latin American countries a manager from the United States finds that 2 P.M. meetings do not get started until well past the hour. On the other hand, in western European countries punctuality is expected. Or consider the entertainment of business executives. In the United States a top manager might take a visiting overseas customer to his house for a home-cooked meal and feel proud when the customer tells his spouse, "You're a terrific cook." However, this scenario would not be reenacted worldwide. In Japan business entertaining is usually done outside the home, while in Latin America, the U.S. manager might be invited to a home-cooked meal but should not praise the wife's cooking. Such praise might be interpreted as a comment on the Latin executive's financial status because it suggests that the wife actually had to prepare the meal herself.

Customs and culture affect organizational activity

Customs and culture also affect the way organizations are run. German managers expect obedience from their subordinates. On the other hand, labor does participate in the decision-making process because it is represented on supervisory boards in executive committees of large organizations. In Japan many employees (about 35 percent) spend an entire working life with a single organization. Among the large firms, lifelong employment is virtually guaranteed, and a seniority system provides privileges for older workers. At the same time there is a great deal of participative decision making. Many changes are initiated by lower-level employees, presented to the supervisor, discussed, analyzed, clarified, and, after a complete review and approval, sent back for implementation.

Business firms wishing to operate in industrial nations such as Germany and Japan must be aware of their customs and cultures. These businesses must also know how the different countries conduct their economic planning.[5]

ECONOMIC PLANNING   Some nations of the world employ an economic planning process similar to that of the United States. Others use a much more centralized approach.

Some planning is heavily market oriented

Like the government in the United States, the German government pursues a steady, anti-inflationary, macroeconomic policy. The objective of this policy is to create a climate of investor confidence. Corporate managers are free to decide how and where to invest company resources. In other words, the Germans employ the market concept, in which customer demand is allowed to determine which goods and services to produce.

In France the situation is different. The French government sets industrial

[5] For more on this see Richard M. Hodgetts and Fred Luthans, *International Management* (New York: McGraw-Hill Book Company, 1991), Chapter 2.

objectives and encourages businesses to pursue them. It indicates industrial areas, for example, that it feels are promising and offers incentives to firms that develop them. During the 1980s, the government has set an objective for the electronic office equipment industry, asking it to acquire 20 to 25 percent of the world market and to eliminate trade deficits. The government has also established an objective for the consumer electronics industry, asking it to create a world-scale groups of manufacturers including TV-set and tube makers who will each rank among the top three globally. The government is prepared to negotiate contracts and set specific goals for sales, exports, and jobs with firms that are willing to pursue these objectives. These companies will qualify for tax incentives, subsidized loans, and other official aid.

Some is moderately government influenced

Japan employs even more control over the economy with its national industrial plan. The strategy is quite simple. The government supports industries that seem likely to develop new technologies and exploit world market opportunities. Conversely, it takes both financial support and workers away from industries that are declining. During the 1980s the Japanese focused on new products such as optical fibers, ceramics, solar energy, nuclear power, aircraft, ocean development, and ultra-high-speed computers. During the 1990s most of these will continue to be areas of focus, especially such high tech areas as computers, aircraft, and consumer electronics. The Japanese are working to develop supercomputers and become the number one country of the world in this market niche. They are also examining the feasibility of producing a 10,000 mph airplane and have developed such high tech expertise that the U.S. government has subcontracted work to them for a new American jet fighter.[6]

Some is heavily government influenced

Second-Tier

Second-tier forces make up the *specific environment* in which organizations operate. These forces, also sources of change, more heavily affect large organizations than they do small ones. Included in this group are suppliers, customers, competition, and sociocultural forces although this is certainly not an exhaustive list. In contrast to first-tier forces, second-tier forces influence an enterprise directly. There is no sidestepping or avoiding them. Their impact on operations is so important that the organization must develop ways of accommodating them.

Second-tier forces greatly affect large organizations

Suppliers

Suppliers provide an organization with those materials it needs for turning out goods and services. Examples include raw materials, parts, equipment, ma-

Suppliers provide important materials

---

[6] Gene Bylinsky, "Where Japan Will Strike Next," *Fortune* (September 25, 1989):42–50.

chinery, energy, and labor. Most organizations, realizing their dependence on suppliers, try to maintain multiple sources. If the needed materials or parts cannot be obtained from one supplier, the organization can quickly turn to another. This strategy is particularly important when there is a shortage of materials or when one supplier cannot provide everything the organization needs.

Sometimes business can turn the tables on suppliers and put the latter in a weak position. The metal container industry provides an excellent example. Because of the overcapacity for production in this industry, those who sell metal containers are at a disadvantage. Buyers can demand the lowest possible prices and concessions and get them. If they do not they will simply stop doing business with one container manufacturer and start doing business with another. The threat of the buyer's going to the competition is sufficient to keep each container manufacturer responsive. In most cases, however, this situation does not develop. An organization has to cultivate sources of material supply.

The labor market, meanwhile, is most influenced by the economy in general and business conditions in particular. When the economy is flourishing and businesses are expanding, there is a good chance that workers can get higher salaries and greater fringe benefits. In a tight market, however, firms find it necessary to maintain wages and benefits at a fixed level.

The economic status of a particular company also affects labor. For example, when business was good at the Chrysler Corporation, the unions were able to obtain increased wages and benefits. When the corporation began to run into trouble in the late 1970s, the union went along with the company's request to hold its demands to a minimum. Suppliers of labor want higher salaries, but not at the price of organizational bankruptcy. As the company turned around in the early 1980s, the union again started demanding more wages and benefits. In the late 1980s the company again started trimming costs and labor began hedging its aggressiveness.

Customers

The customer is still king

Ultimately, it is the customers who dictate the success of organizations. If no one needs the services of a particular governmental agency, it will go out of existence. A hospital without patients will soon close its doors. A business without customers will be forced to declare bankruptcy. Customers create the demand for goods and services. America is still a market economy. The customer is king.

Many illustrations can be cited to support this statement. One of the most interesting is Wal-Mart, the giant retail chain that increased annual sales at a +30% rate during the 1980s. The company built a series of huge stores called hypermarts, as well as opening over one new store a week during the decade. Result: By the end of the 1980s Wal-Mart had sales in excess of $25 billion and was forecasting $50 billion before the end of the 1990s along with a work force of 800,000 people. In the process, the company had closed much of the sales gap between itself and K-Mart and, if the current trend continues, will be the number two retail store in the U.S. by the turn of the century. Wal-Mart also forced Sears to rethink its retail strategy, as that retail giant continued to have sluggish sales and slipping market share. How did Wal-Mart achieve such success? One way was by making the customer the focal point of its sales effort. The firm introduced and operationalized strategies that were geared to provide the highest quality goods at the lowest price. The company also introduced a "no hassles" campaign, whereby it encouraged customers to return any merchandise for a full refund. In fact, the company began accepting merchandise from other stores because it realized that if people bought something at, say, Sears but returned it to Wal-Mart, the next time they went shopping they would come to Wal-Mart. It was a small price to pay to win over a new customer. The company also began putting "greeters" at the front door to say hello to people and to offer initial assistance.

By the end of the decade, Wal-Mart was being hailed as one of the major success stories of the decade. Its founder, Sam Walton, was the richest man in America and many of the store managers who had joined Mr. Sam back in the early 1970s when the company first went public were now millionaires. The lesson was simple—the customer is still king.[7]

Competition

Every organization faces competition

Virtually every organization has to be concerned with competition. Governmental agencies scramble to beat out other agencies for a bigger piece of the budget. Hospitals and other medical facilities attempt to justify current services and to add new ones, objectives which can often be attained only at the expense of other institutions in the field. The business arena provides an even clearer example. Business managers are paid for their ability to compete effectively with other organizations. During the late 1980s such efforts seemed to be reaching new heights. General Motors was closing plants and relying on its remaining factories to generate lower costs and higher profits, which was exactly what happened as the firm's annual sales topped $120 billion and profits reached new heights. Meanwhile, in the airline industry, mergers and acquisitions were taking place as the number of carriers was reduced and companies worked to increase efficiency and cut overall operating costs. In the computer industry IBM saw its market share decline as competitors, especially in the microcomputer market, began to introduce more powerful models with lower prices than those of "Big Blue." In other cases firms retreated from an industry so as to return to what they did best. Zenith, for example, sold its microcomputer business to Groupe Bulle of France, the giant international computer firm

---

[7] For other examples of how businesses are changing to accommodate the customer see, Zachary Schiller, "Stalking the New Consumer," *Business Week* (August 28, 1989):54–62.

FIGURE 3-3
Forces That Govern
Competition in an
Industry

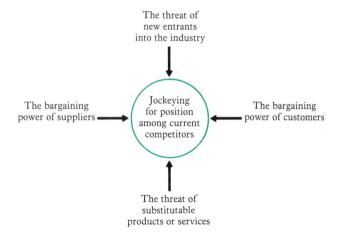

so that it could concentrate on its main business, televisions.[8] In a similar move, Harcourt Brace Jovanovich, the giant publishing firm, sold its theme parks (Sea World, etc.) to Anheuser-Busch, so that it could focus more heavily on its publishing business. Conversely, Anheuser-Busch bought these parks so that it could expand, supplement its beer business, and diversify its overall holdings.

Some industries, of course, are more competitive than others. (See "Management in Practice: An Industry Under Siege.") However, only in those cases where profits or return on investment are low does competition diminish. Conversely, the greater the available profit or return on investment, the more intense the competition. In fact, some researchers seem to feel that competition combines many of the other forces described here and helps shape the organization's strategy.[9] Figure 3-3 illustrates this idea.

Sociocultural Forces

Sociocultural forces are in a state of flux

Sociocultural forces consist of the attitudes, beliefs, and values of individuals and groups in society. These forces have been in a state of flux since the end of World War II. Values have been changing, largely as a result of changes in the economic environment. Young Americans have grown up in a more affluent environment than their parents did. They have also been exposed to television, movies, and a faster pace of life. As a result, young people today are apt to question authority, to want immediate satisfaction of needs, and to feel that more should be done to help the poor and disadvantaged. Their values have helped to promote the practice of social responsibility. Many people feel that business should become actively involved in the social arena.

---

[8] Steven Greenhouse, "Bull to Buy Zenith PC Subsidiary," *New York Times,* October 3, 1989, pp. 27, 31.
[9] For more on this topic, see Michael E. Porter, "How Competitive Forces Shape Strategy," *Harvard Business Review* (March–April 1979):137–45.

An Industry Under Siege

The once-tranquil world of insurance is in turmoil. Once the most ignored industry in America, it has now become one of the most reviled. Consumers, corporate executives, and lawmakers are lambasting insurers for everything from profiteering to an unseemly attitude of arrogance and insensitivity. "We're being besieged. It's a holocaust that's going on," complains Robert E. Vagley, president of the American Insurance Association, the most prominent commercial insurance trade group. Adds chief executive John J. Byrne of Fireman's Fund Insurance Co., "We're at the bottom of everyone's list. Our name is mud."

A muddy image is only the most obvious sign of a far-reaching deterioration in the industry's well-being. Everywhere they look today, insurance executives see their power eroding, their markets contracting, and their profits evaporating. "They're in a state of panic," says J. Robert Hunter, president of the National Insurance Consumer Organization and the industry's best-known critic. Consumers and other insurance buyers are benefiting from these developments, which are producing better insurance services at more competitive prices. The insurance industry, however, may end up losing its status as the chief provider of these services. "It is threatened," says consultant Orin S. Kramer, "by a period of long term decline." This reversal of fortunes would be among the most dramatic for a major industry in American business history.

Insurers are suffering from many forces beyond their control, notably surging liability damages that have beset property-casualty companies and high interest rates that have squeezed life insurers.

In addition, the industry is also facing additional changes.

- customer revolt—consumers are rebelling against higher rates.
- adversarial political environment—legislators are currently working to answer the customer complaints.
- threat of government takeover—the auto and health markets pose this threat.
- financial problems—there is a significant downsizing of companies and shrinkage of profits.

Overall, there isn't much insurers can do to prevent the changes but pray. There is a lot they can do to arrest their slow slide into a permanent eclipse. It would require a heavy dose of enterprise, imagination, and hustle—in short, a cultural revolution. But if insurers are to regain anything close to their former power and glory, they have no other choice.

* *Source:* "Insurers Under Siege," *Business Week* (August 21, 1989):72–79.

THE PRODUCTIVITY CHALLENGE

One of the great challenges confronting contemporary managers is the responsibility to improve productivity.

The challenge is neither easy nor simple. A White House conference on productivity brought together 750 experts from business, government, educa-

TABLE 3-2   Potential Barriers to Productivity Growth in the United States

1. The comparatively low savings rate that decreases capital spending.
2. The violent economic swings from recession to inflation-induced prosperity which handicap long-range planning and weaken financial structures.
3. The shift from a manufacturing oriented economy to a service economy, in which it may be argued that productivity gains are more difficult to achieve, or at least to measure.
4. The mandatory capital spending for environmental protection, which has no accompanying, measurable growth in goods and services.
5. The OPEC oil price hikes—tariff-like actions which idle much of our energy-intensive productive capital.
6. The antagonistic relationship between labor and management and government, which results in large business expenditures, unlikely to improve productivity.
7. Our litigious society, with its tremendous cost in time and money, which is not only nonproductive, but is counterproductive.
8. New government regulatory laws in a number of areas, such as consumer protection and safety, which increase costs without increasing products.
9. A tax system which not only promotes spending rather than saving, but also curbs investment, innovation, and entrepreneurship.
10. A social security system which deters saving for one's old age, a historic source of saving for capital investment.
11. Huge federal deficits caused by runaway government spending which preempts productive private-sector capital and uses it for "Robin Hood"-like transfer payments.
12. The short-term outlook of business executives encouraged by comprehension based on current results, which promotes operating business on a near-term,
"forget the future" basis.
13. Reduced spending for product research and development which has been attributed to a number of different factors, from lack of trained scientists to administration of patent laws.
14. The declining ability of the computer to improve productivity due to the decrease in hardware costs and the increase in software costs, software being much less amenable to productivity improvement.
15. The decline in workers' desire to produce a full day's work for a full day's pay; sometimes, in part, attributed to union-dictated work practices, and other times to a general decline in the work ethic.
16. Inflation, a predominant force during recent years that eroded savings, hampered long-term planning, and produced discounted cash flows, all of which prohibit long-term investments.
17. The training given future executives by American schools of business which emphasizes graduating MBA consultants who know the financial and theoretical sides of business, but not how to be "hands-on" managers, the schools also have not produced the engineers and scientists necessary for improved business performance.
18. The alleged inefficiency of governmental operations, which take a larger share of resources, while returning a less efficient service.
19. The decline in the rigors of education at all levels resulting in lower literacy, employability, and productivity.
20. The large increase in numbers of young unskilled and untrained individuals in the work force, resulting in a lower productivity potential for a skilled work force.

Source: L. William Seidman, "The White House Conference on Productivity," *National Productivity Review*, Vol. 2, No. 4 (Autumn 1983):420–21. Reprinted by permission of the National Productivity Review. Copyright 1983, Executive Enterprises, Inc., New York, NY.

tion, and labor, and established an array of recommendations for greater productivity. Table 3-2 provides a list of barriers to productivity that were presented at the conference.

From a management standpoint, there are eight major factors that affect productivity:

1. *Management inattention.* During the past two decades, management has been accused of its lack of attention to productivity and its proper measurement. Today, productivity is high on the list of priorities.

2. *Lack of managerial focus.* In the past, many managers have not focused on the actual causes of productivity problems. Today, symptoms are being analyzed in an effort to find the cause of poor productivity.

3. *Excessive layers of management.* One of the mistakes made by management has been the constant addition of management levels. Today, those levels are being eliminated as management structures become more lean.

4. *Short-term results focus.* This focus has been the cause of improper strategic planning. This failure to be future oriented and understand that investments today will pay off in the future has led management to trade large long-term gains for small short-term profits. Today, this mistake is being corrected.

5. *Changing work force.* The make up of the work force has been changing over the last ten years. Some of the new developments include increased manual white-collar positions, more women professionals in the work force, and a demographically older population. These developments are leading to greater attention to motivating a heterogeneous work force.

6. *Measurement difficulties.* Past means for measuring productivity were ineffective. The contemporary trend is for better use of measurement techniques aimed at improved productivity.

7. *Lack of productivity goals.* Setting specific goals for management and employees alike has been ignored during the last 20 years. Organizations today are striving to carefully set out goals for productivity and to monitor performance toward these goals.

8. *Government regulation.* Government regulation has been a stumbling block to many organizations in their efforts to achieve greater productivity. However, in this first White House conference on productivity, many issues were brought out to alleviate government interference with productivity (see Table 3-2). It is hoped this is only the beginning of such efforts.

These factors present a clear challenge to managers interested in and committed to long-term improvement in productivity. Additional suggestions were recently offered by a group of productivity experts from the Massachusetts Institute of Technology. After conducting a bottom-up study of U.S. industrial performance, they found both weaknesses and strengths in U.S. industrial practices.[10] In particular, they found that successful firms emphasize *simultaneous* improvements in quality, cost, and speed of commercialization of products, in contrast to less successful counterparts who trade off one of these dimensions against another. The commission also reported that successful firms developed

---

[10] Suzanne Berger *et al.,* "Toward a New Industrial America," *Scientific American* (June 1989):39–47.

closer ties to their customers and had less bureaucratic red tape with which to contend. While these are only a few of the findings, they illustrate how important the issue of productivity has become for the United States and why it will continue to be a focal point for action during the 1990s.

MANAGEMENT AND CHANGE

There is increasing evidence that the environment within which managers must operate is becoming more dynamic and uncertain every year. Change is becoming a predominant factor in the management of organizations. As Alvin Toffler, the reknowned futurist, has noted, "Change is increasing at a geometric rate. Every day that we live the pace accelerates and experience becomes less reliable. Each passing year demands more emphasis upon analysis of the situation and less attention to how it worked last time." [11] As a result, understanding change and developing strategies for dealing with goals is a major challenge for today's manager.[12]

Managing Change

Change is an alteration of the status quo. Since change often scares people, it is important that this process be carefully managed. Kurt Lewin, the noted psychologist, has described a planned-change effort as a three-phased process. This process is illustrated in Figure 3-4.

1. *The unfreezing phase.* **Unfreezing** is the stage of preparing a situation for change. It involves creating dissatisfaction with existing attitudes and behaviors and creating a conscious need for something new. Conflict is an important unfreezing force in organizations. It often helps people break old habits and recognize alternative ways of thinking about or doing things.
2. *The changing phase.* The **changing** phase involves the actual modification in organizational targets for change, including purpose, strategy, people, task, structure, and/or technology. When managers implement change before felt needs exist in the minds of the people involved, there is an increased likelihood that the change attempts will fail.
3. *The refreezing phase.* The final stage in the planned-change process is

---

[11] Alvin Toffler, *The Third Wave* (New York: William Morrow Co., 1980).
[12] J. Fred Bateman, "The Unending Revolution," *Business Horizons* (July–August 1986):2–8. *See also:* Frances J. Milliken, "Three Types of Uncertainty About the Environment: State, Effect and Response Uncertainty," *Academy of Management Review* (January 1987):133–43.

FIGURE 3-4
The Change Process

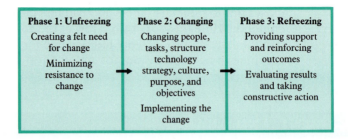

Phase 1: Unfreezing	Phase 2: Changing	Phase 3: Refreezing
Creating a felt need for change	Changing people, tasks, structure technology strategy, culture, purpose, and objectives	Providing support and reinforcing outcomes
Minimizing resistance to change	Implementing the change	Evaluating results and taking constructive action

refreezing. This phase is designed to maintain the momentum of the change. Refreezing efforts include positively reinforcing desired outcomes and extra emotional and resource support when difficulties are encountered. Evaluation and feedback are key elements in this final step.

TABLE 3-3   Methods for Dealing with Resistance to Change

Approach	Commonly Used in Situations	Advantages	Drawbacks
Education and communication	Where there is lack of information or inaccurate information and analysis	Once persuaded, people will often help with the implementation of the change	Can be very time consuming if many people are involved
Participation and involvement	Where the initiators do not have all the information they need to design the change, and where others have considerable power to resist	People who participate will be committed to implementing change, and any relevant information they have will be integrated into the change plan	Can be very time consuming if participants design an inappropriate change
Facilitation and support	Where people are resisting because of adjustment problems	No other approach works as well with adjustment problems	Can be time consuming, expensive, and still fail
Negotiation and agreement	Where someone or some group will clearly lose out in a change, and where that group has considerable power to resist	Sometimes it is a relatively easy way to avoid a major resistance	Can be too expensive in many cases if it alerts others to negotiate for compliance
Manipulation and cooptation	Where other tactics will not work, or are too expensive	It can be a relatively quick and inexpensive solution to resistance problems	Can lead to future problems if people feel manipulated
Explicit and implicit coercion	Where speed is essential, and the change initiators possess considerable power	It is speedy, and can overcome any kind of resistance	Can be risky if it leaves people mad at the initiators

Source: John P. Kotter and Leonard A. Schlesinger, "Choosing Strategies for Change," *Harvard Business Review* (March–April 1979):111. Reprinted by permisson of the Harvard Business Review. Copyright © 1979 by the President and Fellows of Harvard College; all rights reserved.

FIGURE 3-5   A Model for Effective Organizational Change

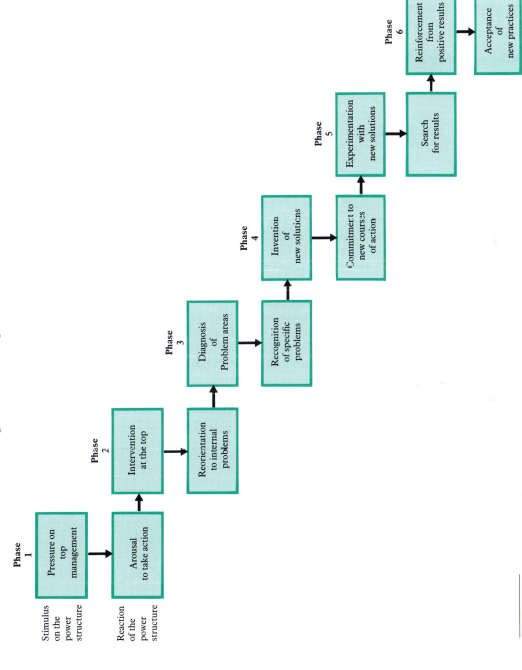

Source: Larry E. Greiner, "Patterns of Organization Change," *Harvard Business Review* (May–June 1967) in *Organizational Change and Development,* eds., G. W. Dalton, P. R. Lawrence, and L. E. Greiner (Homewood, IL, Richard D. Irwin, Inc., 1970):222. Reprinted by permission. All rights reserved.

The Manager as an Agent for Change

One of the manager's jobs is that of a change agent. This is an important responsibility that requires managers who are open to new ideas, responsive to the needs of others, and supportive in the implementation of innovative changes. The overall organizational change process has a number of phases. Figure 3-5 illustrates these.

As a facilitator, and sometimes an initiator of change, the manager often targets specific areas for change. Sometimes those changes bring about resistance, but there are ways of dealing with this. Table 3-3 provides some examples.

THE MODERN PERSPECTIVE: A SEARCH FOR EXCELLENCE

In 1982, Thomas Peters and Robert Waterman published their bestselling book, *In Search of Excellence: Lessons from America's Best–Run Companies.* The authors identified eight key attributes exhibited by "excellent" companies based upon a set of 36 companies screened through a criteria of subjective and objective items. (See Figure 3-6 for a summary of these key attributes.)[13]

While some management scholars have criticized the book's simplistic approach, the fact remains that over one million hardcover copies were sold and the book initiated discussion of management principles at every level of the organization. One major thrust of the book was that today's successful companies may not be the excellent companies of tomorrow. The changing environment surrounding enterprises demands a more flexible, innovative style of management in order to achieve the desired level of performance and productivity. The keys to this modern management approach are innovation and entrepreneurship.

Innovation and Entrepreneurship

The innovation process extends from the development of a new idea to its practical implementation. Systematically, the process can be described as a step-by-step diagram (see Figure 3-7). The enterprise needs to maintain a continuing flow of new ideas from its members. More importantly, these ideas must be modified to fit the needs and objectives of the enterprise. Finally, certain new ideas, those that are feasible and appropriate for the enterprise, must be implemented in order to reinforce the innovative process as part of the enterprise's operations. In accomplishing this, an enterprise begins to develop

---

[13] *See also:* Michael A. Hitt and R. Duane Ireland, "Peters and Waterman Revisited: The Unending Quest for Excellence," *Academy of Management Executive* (May 1987):91–98.

FIGURE 3-6
Key Attributes of
Excellent Firms

1. A bias for action.
2. Close to the customer.
3. Autonomy and entrepreneurship.
4. Productivity through people.
5. Hands-on, value driven.
6. Stick to the knitting.
7. Simple form, lean staff.
8. Simultaneous loose-tight properties.

Source: List of ''The Eight Basic Attributes of Excellence'' from Thomas J. Peters and Robert H. Waterman, *In Search of Excellence: Lessons From America's Best-Run Companies* (New York: Harper & Row Publishers, Inc., 1982). Copyright © 1982 by Thomas J. Peters and Robert H. Waterman, Jr. Reprinted by permission of Harper & Row Publishers, Inc.

a dynamic, risk-taking, creative group of managers and, in the process, promotes entrepreneurial habits among them.

The concept of entrepreneurship is commonly used to describe those starting and/or owning their own business. However, during the last few years a growing trend has evolved that applies the idea of entrepreneuring inside the structure of an established firm. *Intrapreneurship* is the process of nurturing entrepreneurs within their own organizations. More on this topic will be covered in Chapter 19. (See ''Management in Practice: Innovation Is the Name of the Game.'')

MEGATRENDS: THE GENERAL SHAPE OF THINGS TO COME

Another important recent development has been the identification and analysis of major trends in the general environment, for trends will affect an organization's specific environment. John Naisbitt is most closely associated with the identification of these ''megatrends.'' The ten megatrends he and his colleagues have identified promise to reshape the environment of management significantly. He and his team of researchers conducted an extensive content analysis of 6,000 local newspapers every month. The following describe the ten megatrends they discovered:

FIGURE 3-7
The Innovation
Process

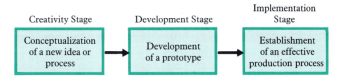

MANAGEMENT IN PRACTICE

*Innovation is the Name of the Game**

*I*nnovation and change are proving to be critical factors in the success of many companies. The creation of new products, and the redesign of old ones so that they can be produced more efficiently, are proving to be highly profitable steps. Some of the successes businesses have had in these efforts are worth highlighting:

■ At General Electric researchers have developed a durable, heat-resistant plastic that can be used in everything from circuit boards to auto parts. Sales are expected to be over $100 million by the early 1990s.
■ At Corning Glass a glass has been invented that has a porous surface. The product has proven to be a very effective anchor for various coatings including Teflon. As a result, the firm has been able to develop nonstick skillets that dominate the market today.

■ At Procter & Gamble's research lab scientists developed polymers that are able to hold 1,000 times their own weight in water. As a result, the company has now developed a highly absorbent and sleeker looking baby diaper and managed to capture over 50% of this market.

Moreover, technology will continue to play a major role in the development of new products, so those companies that are unable to adapt to innovation and change are going to find themselves unable to keep up. Simply put, during the 1990s innovation is going to be the name of the game.

* Kenneth Labich, "The Innovators," *Fortune* (June 6, 1988): 49–64; and Gene Bylinsky, "Technology in the Year 2000," *Fortune* (July 18, 1988): 92–98.

1. *Industrial society – Information society.* Our industrial society is being replaced by an **information society.** Over 60 percent of today's employees in America's service-oriented economy have jobs involving the creation, processing, and distribution of information. The economic value of information needs to be more widely recognized because of the computer revolution and robotics. Generalists who have the ability to adapt will replace specialists who will tend to become obsolete.
2. *Forced technology – High tech/High touch.* Society is searching for a workable balance between impersonal technology and the need for meaningful human interaction. In the workplace, increased use of "high-tech" robots is being accompanied by "high-touch" quality control circles (small problem-solving groups who work to improve quality). Employees will continue to strive for a new balance between work and leisure.
3. *National economy – World economy.* There actually are two distinct economies in the United States. In the emerging "sunrise economy," opportunities are exploding in the fields of telecommunications, biotechnology, electronics, alternative energy, and health-care. In the

"sunset economy," opportunities are being lost to foreign competitors in smokestack industries such as automobiles and steel. The U.S. economy is no longer self-sufficient; it is part of a highly interdependent global economy.

4. *Short term – Long term.* Management's preoccupation with short-term profitability is giving way to preparations for long-term survival. Businesses are redefining their purposes more broadly. People are realizing that although pollution is expedient in the short-term, it erodes the long-term quality of life.

5. *Centralization – Decentralization.* A fundamental distrust of centralized power in the United States has paved the way for proportionately more state and local power. A growing number of city dwellers are moving back to the country; small towns and rural areas grew nearly 16 percent faster than cities during the 1970s. Companies are building facilities away from big cities in response to employees' quality-of-life needs.

6. *Institutional help – Self help.* A growing disenchantment with institutional help has prompted a return to the traditional value of self-reliance. People are discovering that disease prevention through wellness and exercise is cheaper than hospitalization and cure. There also has been an entrepreneurial explosion in the United States: 600,000 new businesses were formed in 1980 versus 93,000 in 1950.

7. *Representative democracy – Participative democracy.* People are increasingly demanding a direct say in the decisions that affect their lives, both in government and on the job. Worker participation schemes are growing in popularity. The new leader is a facilitator, not just an order giver.

8. *Hierarchies – Networking.* The predominantly vertical orientation of traditional bureaucracies is giving way to horizontal linkages based on convenience and need. Minorities and women have learned the value of networks. The new networks are more egalitarian than the traditional "good old boy" networks.

9. *North – South.* According to the 1980 census, more Americans lived in the South and West than in the North and East for the first time in history. Sunbelt states are stealing people away from Frostbelt companies. Florida, Texas, and California are largely responsible for what Naisbitt calls the Sunbelt mystique.

10. *Either/Or – Multiple Option.* New options are opening up regarding how we work, live, and play. Gender barriers are breaking down as more women join the work force. As a sign of how much things have changed, only 7 percent of American families fit the traditional pattern (i.e., father as sole breadwinner, housewife/mother, and two children). More choices in life, work, and play mean challenging new responsibilities.[14]

---

[14] For the latest update on Megatrends, see: John Naisbitt, *Megatrends 2000* (New York: William Morrow CO., 1990).

SUMMARY

1. The external environment consists of forces outside the direct control of the organization. These forces can be divided into two groups: first tier and second tier. First-tier forces affect virtually every organization. Second-tier forces are of more importance to large organizations than to small ones.

2. The most dominant first-tier force is the economy. The economy affects organizations both directly and indirectly. However, not all industries are affected in the same way at the same time. In an economic slump, some industries are affected earlier than others. Moreover, some are hard hit while others do not show much of a downturn.

3. Suppliers provide an organization with the materials it needs for turning out goods and services. In order to avoid shortages, most organizations cultivate two or more suppliers.

4. Customers, ultimately, dictate the success of organizations. The competition attempts to steal customers away.

5. Political–legal forces consist of laws and regulations that constrain and direct organizational activity. As laws change, organizations must adjust to the new political–legal environment. In most cases this means following the change, not leading it.

6. Technology is an important variable for many large firms. Some, such as GE, must maintain a high technological base because it provides the input for new product development. Smaller firms are often more content to adopt a follow-the-leader strategy.

7. International forces are a consideration for firms doing business in other countries. These multinational corporations (MNCs) must be concerned with two major environmental challenges: customs/culture and economic planning.

8. Sociocultural forces consist of the attitudes, beliefs, and values of individuals and groups in society. These forces are currently in a state of flux.

9. The productivity challenge is one of the greatest responsibilities facing contemporary managers. There are major forces that have inhibited productivity including: management inattention, lack of managerial focus, excessive layers of management, short-term results focus, changing work force, measurement difficulties, lack of productivity goals, and government regulation.

10. Change is a predominant factor in managing an enterprise. The planned-change process includes three phases: unfreezing, changing, and refreezing.

11. The major methods for dealing with resistance to change include: education and communication, participation and involvement, facilitation and support, negotiation and agreement, manipulation and cooperation, and explicit and implicit coercion.

12. In the modern perspective of management, certain key attributes were identified in Peters and Waterman's bestselling book, *In Search of Excellence,* including a bias for action, sticking close to the customer, developing autonomy and entrepreneurship, realizing that people are the key to productivity, building on strength, keeping the organization lean and simple; and using loose-tight properties so as to maintain control but not to suffocate the personnel.

13. Ten "megatrends" identified by John Naisbitt, promise to reshape the environment of management. These include moves toward an information society, a high-tech/high-touch society, a world economy, long-term strategies, decentralized organizations, self-help and self-reliance, participative democracy, networking, southern/western population growth, and the emergence of a multiple-option society.

KEY TERMS

Change   An alteration of the status quo.

First-tier forces   External environmental forces that affect virtually all organizations. These forces include the economy, technology, international, and political-legal forces.

Information society   A service-oriented economy that involves the creation, processing, and distribution of information.

Multinational corporations (MNCs)   Firms that have their headquarters in one country but operate in many different nations.

Refreezing   The momentum of the change is reinforced.

Second-tier forces   Specific environmental forces that more heavily affect large organizations than small organizations. They include suppliers, customers, competition, and sociocultural forces.

Unfreezing   A phase of the change process during which creating a felt need for change is developed.

QUESTIONS FOR ANALYSIS AND DISCUSSION

1. The economy affects organizations both directly and indirectly. What is meant by this statement?
2. What types of materials do suppliers provide to an organization? Be complete in you answer.
3. In what way are customers and competitors environmental forces with which an organization must deal? Give an example of each.
4. Why are second-tier forces of more importance to large organizations than to small ones? Defend your answer.
5. In what way do political–legal and technological forces affect an organization? Which is more important? Why?

6. In dealing with international forces, the organization must take two things into account: customs/culture and economic planning. What is meant by this statement? Be complete in your answer.

7. How do sociocultural forces affect the organization? Explain. Do these forces have a greater or lesser effect on the organization than competition does? Than technology? Defend your answer.

8. What is the productivity challenge? In your answer discuss the eight major factors that have affected productivity growth.

9. What are the three phases involved in the planned-change process? Describe each.

10. How can managers be change agents in an enterprise? Identify the methods for dealing with resistance to change and explain the advantages and drawbacks of each method.

11. What are the eight key attributes of excellent firms? Explain each one.

12. Megatrends has identified ten major trends reshaping the environment of management. What are these? List and explain each.

CASE

Work Philosophy and Values

The backlog of orders at the Shellett Company has been increasing month by month. Six months ago it was $95,000. Three months ago it was $240,000. Currently it is $460,000. In an effort to reduce this backlog, the company president devised an incentive payment scheme. The plan is tied to the hourly wage rate and rewards workers for overtime and Saturday and Sunday work. Overtime pays 150 percent of the hourly rate. Saturday work pays double time. Sunday work pays triple time. In order to qualify for Sunday work, and individual also has to work Saturday.

The average employee at Shellett makes $6.75 an hour plus fringe benefits. The person willing to work an extra two hours a day, all day Saturday and all day Sunday would make $641.25 for the week. The total is computed this way:

Regular 40 hours (40 × 6.75)	$270.00
Weekly overtime (10 × 6.75 × 1.5)	101.25
Saturday work (8 × 6.75 × 2.0)	108.00
Sunday work (8 × 6.75 × 3.0)	162.00
	$641.25

The president feels that this is quite an incentive for those willing to help reduce the backlog. Surprisingly, however, only 35 percent of the workforce takes weekly overtime. Just under 15 percent work Saturdays and 10 percent work Sundays. The president cannot understand it. "These guys are downright lazy," he has complained to his senior vice president. "The work ethic in America must be dead."

The vice president agrees, but many of the managers do not. One of them put it this way, "Why do the workers want to knock themselves out with weekend work? Life is too short. The president should realize this. In fact, he himself ought to take more time off. There's a lot more to running a company than just maximizing profits. Quality of life should be a major consideration. I know it is with a lot of us managers."

1. How would you describe the workers' philosophy of work? Use Figure 3-4 in answering this question.
2. How would you describe the president's work philosophy? Explain.

YOU BE THE CONSULTANT

Managing for Excellence

Each year the Belcar Corporation, an engineering company, enlists the help of various consultants to present programs to the managers. In the last five years, topics have ranged from budgeting, planning and controlling, to communications and group dynamics. As part of this managerial development program, Belcar Corp. conducts an evaluation and follow-up of these programs to find out if there has been any impact on the organization. To date, the results have been lukewarm at best. The managers have not been exposed to contemporary principles of management that could be applied to their particular situations. Many have heard or read about "excellent" companies in the U.S. that are continually applying effective techniques that drive their companies toward high achievement. The Belcar executives believe that an "excellence" approach to management should be taken in this year's development program.

With that in mind, you have been contacted as the management consultant to prepare a program for the Belcar Corporation. There are 35 managers that will take part in this year's program. The expectations are simple and yet, complex—to understand the contemporary methods of management in the "excellence" companies across America.

The president of Belcar has agreed to be flexible with the dates, times, and length of the seminars. Your major goal is relating the attributes needed by contemporary managers to excel in a competitive economy. Your program proposal must be submitted in 10 days.

Your Consultation

Outline the type of program you would present to the managerial staff at Belcar Corporation. What specific contemporary attributes would be included for an "excellent" company and how would you introduce and develop an understanding of change in the managerial environment?

4

International Management

Many businesses have found that it pays to "go international." This chapter examines the international environment of business and the operations of the multinational corporations (MNCs) that do business there.

The first objective of this chapter is to present the reasons why firms go international and to discuss the most common forms of international involvement. The second objective is to examine the impact of MNCs on the home country as well as the host country. The final objective of this chapter is to discuss the challenges confronting firms that go international, including philosophical attitudes, economics, politics, culture, and the use of management functions. When you have finished studying the material in this chapter, you will be able to:

1. Identify the reasons for an enterprise going international.
2. Discuss the various forms of international involvement.
3. Describe the impact that MNCs have on both the home and the host country.
4. Identify the challenges of international management, including philosophical attitudes, economic differences, political differences, and cultural differences.
5. Discuss the managerial functions: planning, organizing leading, and controlling in the international environment.

INTRODUCTION

Today, more than ever, managers have to be concerned with international business. Effective management entails the ability to foster and develop global markets. Thus, managers are confronting a borderless world and a thorough understanding of international management is essential.[1]

International management is the setting of objectives and how businesses conduct operations in foreign countries. Many American firms have "gone international." General Motors, Ford, and Chrysler, for example, do business in many countries. Exxon, Phillips Petroleum, and Texaco also have customers worldwide. So do IBM, ITT, General Electric, Dow Chemical, and Honeywell. In fact, American firms export over $70 billion of goods every year and the percentage of foreign profits and assets in relation to the totals is illustrative of the growth of multinationals. (See "The One Hundred Largest Multinationals.")

At the same time that American firms are exporting goods, the United States is importing from other countries, including Mexico, Canada, Germany, England, and Japan, to name but five. The latter, in particular, has been the focus of much attention recently because of the large trade surpluses it has been having with the U.S. However, in all fairness, it should be noted that there is some degree of reciprocity. Many American firms are finding Japan to be a receptive market for their goods:

> More than 50,000 U.S. products are being sold in Japan. U.S. companies are represented in more than 85 percent of Japan's 126 industrial sectors, and at least 12 hold the number one market position in their fields. In the soft-drink market, Coca-Cola has a 60 percent share; Warner-Lambert's Schick razors hold 71 percent of the safety-razor market; and McDonald's is the top fast-food chain in Japan.
>
> American high-technology companies have come on strong, including IBM with 1985 sales of $3.5 billion; Digital Equipment, whose Japanese sales have grown 10 times in the last seven years; and Polaroid, with 66 percent of the Japanese instant-camera market.
>
> Since 1982, U.S. computer sales to Japan have increased by 48 percent; telecommunications equipment, by 38 percent; pharmaceutical products, by 41 percent; and electronic parts, by 63 percent.[2]

International management is the setting of objectives and how businesses conduct operations in foreign countries

---

[1] Kenichi Ohmae, "Managing in a Borderless World" *Harvard Business Review* (May–June 1989):152–61.

[2] Vernon R. Alden, "Who Says You Can't Crack Japanese Markets?" *Harvard Business Review* (January–February 1987):52–56.

The 100 Largest U.S. Multinationals

*T*he list below of America's 100 largest multinationals is a good reminder of how extensive U.S. overseas investments are. These companies' foreign operations booked sales of $506 billion last year. The figure represents a 15% increase over 1987.

    Unless protectionism catches hold, foreign sales should continue to increase. For example, the free trade pact with Canada—our largest trading partner by far—will go along way toward boosting two-way trade and

also increase direct investment by U.S. multinationals north of the border. The multinationals' Canadian divisions, like Canadian companies, want to be able to sell their output freely to the U.S. market. Deborah Kuenstner, an international investing strategist will Merrill Lynch, predicts that future foreign investments will emphasize acquisitions and improving distribution networks over new bricks and mortar.

1988 Rank	Company	Foreign Revenue (mil)	Total Revenue (mil)	Foreign Revenue as % of Total	Foreign Net Profit[1] (mil)	Total Net Profit[1] (mil)	Foreign Net Profit as % of Total[1]	Foreign Assets (mil)	Total Assets (mil)	Foreign Assets as % of Total
1	Exxon	$48,192	$67,292	71.6%	$3,910	$5,360	72.9%	$30,740	$74,293	41.4%
2	Ford Motor	41,842	92,446	45.3	2,285	5,300	43.1	35,912	143,367	25.0
3	IBM	34,361	59,681	57.6	4,071	5,491	74.1	35,293	73,037	48.3
4	Mobil	33,039[2]	49,237[2]	67.1	1,517[3]	2,514[3]	60.3	19,424	38,820	50.0
5	General Motors	29,128	120,388	24.2	3,070	4,856	63.2	34,424	163,820	21.0
6	Citicorp	16,451	32,024	51.4	977	1,698	57.5	87,723[4]	207,106[4]	42.4
7	Texaco	16,325	33,544	48.7	1,336	1,304	102.5	8,358	26,337	31.7
8	EI du Pont de Nemours	12,896[5]	32,917[5]	39.2	847[6]	2,454[6]	34.5	9,019	30,719	29.4
9	ITT[7]	10,419	24,239	43.0	618[3]	1,533[3]	40.3	7,983	41,941	19.0
10	Dow Chemical	9,185	16,682	55.1	1,189	2,410	49.3	8,682	16,239	53.5
11	Procter & Gamble	7,294	19,336	37.7	241	1,020	23.6	4,751	14,820	32.1
12	Eastman Kodak	7,010	17,034	41.2	639	1,397	45.7	6,201	22,964	27.0
13	Chase Manhattan	6,080	12,365	49.2	339	1,059	32.0	31,880	97,455	32.7
14	Xerox	5,739	16,441	34.9	211	388	54.4	6,735	26,441	25.5
15	Digital Equipment	5,665	11,475	49.4	1,160[3]	1,741[3]	66.6	4,388	10,112	43.4
16	United Technologies	5,279	18,518	28.5	249[8]	705[8]	35.3	3,776	12,748	29.6
17	Chevron	5,264	25,196	20.9	898	1,768	50.8	6,680	33,968	19.7
18	Philip Morris	5,258	25,920	20.3	226	2,064	10.9	7,458	36,960	20.2
19	Hewlett-Packard	5,068	9,831	51.6	315	816	38.6	2,984	7,497	39.8
20	American Intl Group	4,979[9]	13,613	36.6	631[3]	1,425[3]	44.3	13,932[9]	37,409	37.2

[1] From continuing operations. [2] Includes other income. [3] Operating profit. [4] Average assets. [5] Includes excise taxes. [6] Operating income after taxes. [7] Includes proportionate interest in unconsolidated subsidiaries and affiliates. [8] Net income before minority interest. [9] Excludes Canadian operations. [10] Net income before corporate expense. [11] Pretax income. D-P: Deficit over profit. P-D: Profit over deficit. NA: Not available.

Source: "The *Forbes* Foreign Rankings," *Forbes* (July 24, 1989): 320.

The 100 Largest Foreign Investments In The U.S.

*F*oreign capital again flooded into the U.S. in record amounts. U.S. Commerce Department figures show that in 1988, foreigners spent $219 billion on American assets. This exceeds the 1987's revised figure by $8 billion. Of the total, $161 billion was invested in financial assets such as bank deposits and U.S. government securities, including U.S. Treasurys.

Rank	Foreign Investor	Country	US Investment
1	Seagram Co Ltd*	Canada	EI du Pont de Nemours* Joseph E Seagram & Sons Tropicana Products
2	Royal Dutch/Shell Group*	Netherlands/UK	Shell Oil
3	British Petroleum Plc*	UK	BP America
4	B.A.T Industries Plc*	UK	BATUS
	*Imasco Ltd**	Canada	Farmers Group Peoples Drug Stores Imasco USA
5	Tengelmann Group	Germany	Great A&P Tea*
6	Grand Metropolitan Plc*	UK	Pillsbury Grand Metropolitan USA
7	Campeau	Canada	Federated Dept Stores Allied Stores Ralphs Grocery
8	Nestlé SA*	Switzerland	Nestlé Enterprises Alcon Laboratories
9	Hanson Plc*	UK	Hanson Industries
10	Pechiney	France	American National Can Pechiney
11	Petróleos de Venezuela, SA	Venezuela	Citgo Petroleum Champlin Refining
12	Unilever NV* Unilever Plc*	Netherlands UK	Unilever United States

* Publicly traded in the U.S. in shares or ADRs. E: Estimate. NA: Not available. Note: Some foreign investors on the list own U.S. companies indirectly through companies in italics.
Source: "The *Forbes* Foreign Rankings," *Forbes* (July 24, 1989):313.

Total direct investment by foreigners in U.S. property, plant, equipment and services advanced to a record $58 billion.

% Owned	Industry	Revenue (mil)	Net Income (mil)	Assets (mil)
23%	chemicals, energy	$32,657	$2,190.0	$30,719
100	alcoholic beverages	2,540	495.6	7,946
100	beverages	741	NA	NA
		35,938		
100	energy, chemicals	21,070	1,204.0	27,169
100	energy	14,378	NA	22,452
100	multicompany	6,251	535.3	3,788
100	insurance	1,191	292.8	7,704
100	drugstores	1,498	NA	NA
100	fast food	1,431	NA	NA
		10,371		
53	supermarkets	10,068	127.6	2,640
100	food processors	6,191	69.3	3,840
100	beverages, retailing	2,700	NA	NA
		8,891		
100	retailing	6,220	NA	10,784
100	retailing			
100	supermarkets	1,842	NA	1,112
		8,062		
100	food processing	6,089	NA	4,863
100	optical products	500E	NA	NA
		6,589		
100	multicompany	6,030	300.3	5,772
100	packaging	4,320	NA	3,120
100	metal castings	1,398	NA	1,228
		5,718		
50	refining, marketing	4,110	165.6	1,343
100	refining, marketing	1,600E	NA	550E
		5,710		
100	food processing	5,688	133.2	6,449

GOING INTERNATIONAL

There are a number of reasons why firms choose to go international.[3] Quite often the final choice is a result of three or four overriding reasons rather than just one. Having made the decision to enter a foreign market, the company will then decide the form of involvement it wishes to make. In some cases, the enterprise will simply export to the market. In other cases, the firm will become more deeply involved by entering into a joint venture with foreign partners. In still other cases, the firm will become heavily involved by setting up manufacturing facilities in the other country and making a large financial commitment to the project.[4] This development has gone so far that many international firms see themselves as global enterprises and not dependent on the economy of their home country.[5]

Reasons for Going International

Some major reasons for going international

There are many reasons for going international or at least being involved in international activities. Some of the most common are the following:

1. *Opportunity for expanded or new markets.* Increased sales activity in new countries offers the opportunity to increase market share and/or create new markets as well.
2. *Opportunity for greater profits.* Initiation of international activities offers enterprises the opportunity to increase profits.
3. *Opportunity to access raw materials.* The operation of an enterprise in various countries sometimes allows the opportunity to gain access (and perhaps control) to larger supplies of needed raw materials.
4. *Opportunity to increase financial resources.* The various types of international operations allow different types of capital and financial arrangements to be established. Each nation has financial resources that may be utilized.
5. *Opportunity for decreased labor costs.* Labor-intensive enterprises seek foreign labor supplies that operate under a lower wage scale, thus offering the opportunity to cut costs in that realm.
6. *Opportunity to acquire new technology.* An enterprise may seek to acquire foreign-based technology or at least have easier access to it by locating in that country.

---

[3] See Michael E. Porter, "Changing Patterns of International Competition," *California Management Review* (Winter 1986):9–40.
[4] *See also:* Jeremy Main, "How To Go Global–And Why?" *Fortune* (August 28, 1989):70–76.
[5] Louis Uchitelle, "U.S. Businesses Loosen Link To Mother Country," *New York Times* (May 31, 1989):1, 12.

FIGURE 4-1
Forms of
International
Involvement

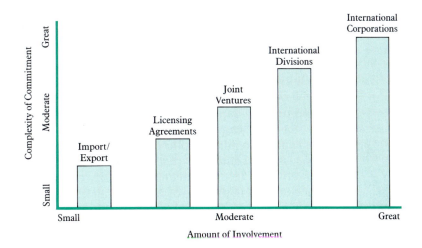

7. *Opportunity to geographically move toward customers.* Some enterprises seek to physically move closer to their customers and to employ workers from those countries in order to demonstrate a commitment to them.

These reasons help to explain why American firms enter foreign markets. They also help to explain why foreign firms enter the U.S. market. As the most affluent nation in the world, the United States offers excellent opportunities for overseas companies. In some cases, these firms will go so far as to set up operations in the U.S. However, it is more common for them to purchase, or invest in, an existing American firm and thus more quickly gain a foothold.[6] "The 100 Largest Foreign Investments in the U.S." reports some of the latest U.S. acquisitions that have been made by foreign firms that are following this strategy.

Forms of International Involvement

When entering a foreign market, a company must decide on the amount of involvement it wishes to make. Figure 4-1 depicts the five most common forms of international involvement.

The simplest form of international involvement is exporting or importing   The simplest form of international involvement is exporting or importing. In the case of exporting, for example, a company will find someone in a foreign country to either purchase its goods directly or act as a selling agent. In the first case, the company has very little responsibility—it merely produces the goods

---

[6] Jonathan P. Hicks, "The Takeover of American Industry," *New York Times* (May 28, 1989) Section 3: 1, 8; and "John Markoff, "Gould Being Acquired by Nippon Mining," *New York Times* (August 31, 1988):25–26.

and ships them to the foreign customer. In the second case, the company typically is responsible for the costs of warehousing the goods until they are sold and paying all the costs associated with insuring the goods, shipping them to the customer, and so on. While this arrangement is more costly than merely selling directly to a foreign customer, it can be more profitable if the market for the product is good. This is because the company will pay the agent only a salary (and perhaps commission) and can keep the rest of the sales revenue.

Under a licensing arrangement, one firm allows another to use its patents, production processes, trademarks, or company name

A **licensing arrangement** is an agreement in which one firm (the licensor) agrees to allow another firm (the licensee) to use its patents, production processes, trademarks, or company name in return for the payment of an agreed-upon fee. The licensor typically controls the agreement very closely. For example, in the case of an American licensor that allows an overseas firm to produce and market its products in Europe, the licensee will be required to manufacture the product to precise specifications. The licensee cannot make changes in the production process or modify the product without specific approval. The licensor receives either a fixed fee or a percentage of the gross revenues from the sale of the product. In most cases, the latter arrangement is used. If the agreement gives the licensee the exclusive right to produce and sell the product in a geographic area, such as Europe, the percentage of gross revenues is usually larger (often 10 percent) than in the case where there are three to four licensees and they are restricted in terms of geographic area. An example would be when one company has the exclusive rights to Great Britain only, another has France, and a third has Germany, and so on. Most licensing agreements are for the production of manufactured goods such as industrial motors or equipment. However, these agreements are not limited to these areas. For example, the Southland Corporation's 7-Eleven chain has licensed its stores in London, and *Playboy* has licensed both British and Chinese-language editions of its magazine.

A joint venture is a partnership agreement in which two or more firms or investors undertake a project for a specific length of time

A **joint venture** is a partnership agreement in which two or more firms or investors undertake a project for a specific length of time. Many joint ventures are a matter of necessity. Quite often, neither firm has enough capital, or is willing to risk this total amount, to undertake the project alone. In some cases, a joint venture is used because the overseas partner wants to get a foothold in a foreign market and realizes that by teaming up with a company in that geographic locale, a great deal of time and effort can be saved. For example, in doing business in Japan, many firms have found that it is most profitable to get a Japanese partner. The latter knows the customs and culture of the country and is aware of how business should be transacted. In recent years, Johnson and Johnson has entered into a joint venture with dong Ah Pharmaceutical Company to produce baby-care items for the Korean market. Similarly, IBM has teamed up with Matsushita Electric Industrial Company to produce and market a personal computer in Japan. There are also many joint ventures in the U.S. market. For example, Honeywell and L. M. Ericsson of Sweden are manufacturing PBX systems in the U.S., and General Motors and Toyota are producing a

Joint Ventures are Slowing

Joint ventures were supposed to be a quick and cheaper way for U.S. parts suppliers to get in on the Japanese gravy train—the $6.6 billion investment in auto output. But it's not working that way. Of the 126 U.S. auto suppliers that entered into joint ventures to supply Honda, Nissan, and Mazda—as well as General Motors and Ford Motor—almost all are losing money. The number of new joint ventures is falling; and Japanese suppliers hold about 20 percent of the $40 billion U.S. auto parts market.

Underlying the failures are problems of divergent management styles, inflated expectations, disputes over quality and labor practices, and in some cases, bad luck. More important, the two sides often entered into such ventures with very different agendas. American suppliers wanted access to the Japanese automakers. But Japanese suppliers were looking further ahead, using their partners to gain footholds in the U.S. market. Now, as many of the ventures prove unworkable, the Japanese partners are beginning to strike out on their own.

It is the well-known story of the Japanese slowly and deliberately gaining ground in the U.S.—in consumer electronics, autos, and now auto parts.

What's more, U.S. suppliers are facing declining auto production levels in the U.S. For those that had high hopes of increasing their business, the souring ventures are likely to accelerate a shakeout already in progress in the auto parts industry. According to the Automotive Parts of Accessories Association, there are 2,225 parts suppliers, about 500 fewer than a decade ago. The odds are that more and more of the survivors will be Japanese.

Mixing Japanese production methods and American work styles has been difficult at many ventures. Workers grumble about daily calisthenics and the dedication ceremonies Japanese seem to love. And managers can't understand Japanese frugality. At one plant, the size of memo paper caused a 40-minute debate.

For the Japanese, working with Americans has been no picnic, either. Japanese executives complain that they must hire up to one-fifth more employees at a U.S. plant than at a similar one in Japan. "In Japan, we talk about just-in-time delivery in terms of minutes," says Norio Kikuchi, general manager of Nova Steel Processing, a joint venture between Armco Inc. and C. Itoh & Co. to process steel for Armco. "Here in the U.S., the time reference is in days."

If Americans had understood Japanese strategy better from the beginning, there might have been something in joint ventures for both sides.

Source: Stephen Phillips, "When U.S. Joint Ventures with Japan Go Sour," *Business Week* (July 24, 1989):30–31.

An international division is often established when a firm sets up manufacturing plants overseas

Toyota-designed subcompact for the American market.[7] (See "Management in Practice: Joint Ventures are Slowing.")

When a company decides to set up an international division, it accepts a large amount of involvement in the overseas market. This typically involves the

---

[7] For more on this subject, see Kathryn Rudie Harrigan, "Joint Ventures and Global Strategies," *Columbia Journal of World Business* (Summer 1984):7–16.

establishment of manufacturing plants in one or more countries. These plants may range from assembly plants to full-scale operations. When this happens, the company's domestic operations are often separated from the overseas operations and an international division is established.

An international corporation views overseas operations as a full-fledged part of the business

The last step in international involvement is the emergence of an international corporation. Under this form of involvement, the overseas operation is viewed as a full-fledged part of the business rather than just an overseas branch or foreign sales arm. The company's strategic plan reflects this change in thinking by viewing the firm's markets as worldwide. It is also common to find international corporations with boards of directors whose members come from many different nations. This helps the company develop and maintain an international focus. IBM, with its U.S. headquarters in Armonk, New York and its overseas headquarters in Paris, France, is an excellent example of an international corporation. The firm views its markets in global terms rather than in terms of just the U.S. and Europe.

As companies become more and more involved in the international arena, a number of factors change. For example, they become more active in the overseas market and their locus of operations expands from domestic to domestic and international. The orientation, type of international activity, and organizational structure also change. Table 4-1 illustrates these developments.

TABLE 4-1   Degrees of Internationalization

	First-Degree Internationalization	Second-Degree Internationalization	Third-Degree Internationalization	Fourth Degree Internationalization
Nature of contact with foreign markets	Indirect, passive	Direct, active	Direct, active	Direct, active
Locus of international operations	Domestic	Domestic	Domestic and international	Domestic and international
Orientation of company	Domestic	Domestic	Primarily domestic	Multinational (domestic operations viewed as part of the whole), foreign trade, foreign assistance contracts, foreign direct investment, global structures
Type of international activity	Foreign trade of goods and services	Foreign trade of goods and services	Foreign trade, foreign assistance contracts, foreign direct investment	
Organizational structure	Traditional domestic	International department	International division	

Source: Christopher M. Korth, International Business, Environment, and Management, 2nd ed., 7. Copyright 1985. Reprinted by permission of Prentice-Hall, Inc., Englewood Cliffs, NJ.

TABLE 4-2   Ten Large U.S. and Foreign Industrial Multinational Corporations

Rank	Company
U.S.	
1	General Motors
2	Ford
3	Exxon
4	IBM
5	General Electric
6	Mobil
7	Chrysler
8	Texaco
9	DuPont
10	Philip Morris
Foreign	
1	Royal Dutch/Shell Group
2	Toyota
3	British Petroleum
4	IRI
5	Daimler-Benz
6	Hitachi
7	Siemens
8	Fiat
9	Matsushita Electric
10	Volkswagen

Source: Fortune, April 24, 1989 and July 31, 1989.

A multinational corporation is a business enterprise with extensive international operations in more than one country

Firms that progress to the third or fourth degree of internationalization (see Table 4-1) are often referred to as **multinational corporations** (MNCs) or **transnational enterprises** (TNEs). A multinational corporation is a business enterprise with extensive international operations in more than one country. There are many of these enterprises. Table 4-2 lists the 10 largest U.S. and foreign MNCs. These firms play a major role in the international business arena.

THE IMPACT OF MNC OPERATIONS

MNCs have had both positive and negative impacts on the host countries where they reside. In most cases, the net impact has been positive although it would be erroneous to conclude that the host country has not paid some costs associated with allowing the MNC to operate within its borders.

Impact on Host Country

There are a number of benefits that can accrue to a host country in which an MNC operates. Five of these include:

Benefits that accrue to the host country

- Transfer of capital, technology, and entrepreneurship to the host country.
- Improvement of the host country's balance of payments.
- Creation of local job and career opportunities.
- Improved competition in the local economy.
- Greater availability of products for local customers.

On the other hand, there are also some costs associated with an MNC operation in a host country. Four of the most common are:

Costs associated with allowing an MNC into the country

- Interference with the local political structure.
- Ignorance of local customs and needs.
- Social and/or cultural disruptions caused by dominance of the local economy.
- Anger or mistrust caused by a refusal to transfer advanced technology into local hands.

In most cases, the benefits have outweighed the costs and, particularly in recent years, MNCs have been training their people to stay out of local politics and to learn local customs and mores.[8] As a result, it is common to find foreign governments actually seeking out MNCs to operate in their country. The government feels that the MNC has something to offer to the nation, and the MNC, in turn, seeks important economic advantages to be gained by setting up operations there. This is known as **multinational reciprocity,** which is the mutual exchange of benefits between a host country and a multinational corporation.

Impact on Home Country

In weighing the benefits of multinational operations it is also important to examine the impact on the home country. This is the nation where the MNC originates. If the company has a number of different worldwide headquarters, the home country is the locale where the chief executive officer and senior managers reside. In the case of IBM, for example, it is the United States.

There are a number of potential benefits that can be realized by a home country. Five of these include:

---

[8] For interesting research, see Mack P. Krieger, "Creating Strategic Windows: The Increasing Role of Subsidiary Boards in Japanese, European, and North American MNCs," *Proceedings of the Academy of Management,* 46th Annual meeting, (Chicago, IL 1986):91–96.

Benefits that
accrue to the home
country

- The acquisition of raw materials from abroad, often at a better price than can be purchased domestically.
- Technology and expertise acquired from competing in foreign markets.
- The export of components and finished goods for assembly and/or distribution in foreign markets.
- An inflow of income from overseas profits, licensing fees, and management contracts.
- Job and career opportunities at home and abroad in connection with overseas operations.

There are also drawbacks that can result from MNC operations. Four of these are:

Costs the home
country may end
up paying

- A weakening of the balance of payments due to the outflow of capital.
- A possible loss of technological advantage at home.
- The loss of domestic jobs.
- An acceptance of dual ethical standards: one for doing business at home and one for doing business abroad where different standards are employed.[9]

CHALLENGES OF INTERNATIONAL MANAGEMENT

Quite often MNCs find they cannot do business overseas the way they do in their home country. Different economic and cultural conditions prevail and the company must adjust to this environment. In doing so, there are four major kinds of challenges: philosophical attitudes, economic differences, political differences, and cultural differences.

Philosophical Attitudes

Three possible
attitudes
management can
have toward its
overseas operation

When a company goes international, there are three possible attitudes that management can have toward this new operation. (See Table 4-3.) One is an **ethnocentric attitude,** which means that the home country's ideas and policies are viewed as superior to those in the foreign market. When this attitude dictates management direction, home country policies are applied to all operations without any consideration for the cultures or customs of the foreign countries in which the MNC is operating.

---

[9] John L. Graham, ''Foreign Corrupt Practices: A Manager's Guide,'' *Columbia Journal of World Business* (Fall 1986):89–94.

TABLE 4-3	Three Different Attitudes Toward International Operations		
Organization Design	**Ethnocentric**	**Polycentric**	**Geocentric**
Complexity of organization	Complex in home country, simple in subsidiaries	Varied and independent	Increasingly complex and interdependent
Authority, decision making	High in headquarters	Relatively low in headquarters	Aim for a collaborative approach between headquarters and subsidiaries
Evaluation and control	Home standards applied for persons and performance	Determined locally	Find standards which are universal and local
Rewards and punishments (incentives)	High in headquarters, low in subsidiaries	Wide variation: can be high or low rewards for subsidiary performance	International and local executives rewarded for reaching local and worldwide objectives
Communication, information	High volume to subsidiaries: orders, commands, advice	Little to and from headquarters, little between subsidiaries	Both ways and between subsidiaries: heads of subsidiaries part of management team
Identification	Nationality of owner	Nationality of host country	Truly international company but identifying with national interests
Perpetuation (recruiting, staffing, development)	Recruit and develop people of home country for key positions everywhere in the world	Develop people of local nationality for key positions in their own country	Develop best people everywhere in the world for key positions everywhere in the world

Source: Howard V. Perlmutter, "The Tortuous Evolution of the Multinational Corporation," *Columbia Journal of World Business,* (January–February 1969):12.

A second is the **polycentric attitude,** which is the assumption that local managers know what is best for their operations since they are familiar with the culture. Under this attitude, the overseas operations are given greater day-to-day control over policies, procedures, rules, and operating tactics.

The third is the **geocentric attitude,** which is a worldwide view of operations. Under this philosophy, the objective of international and local operations is balanced and the company views its markets as both national and international in scope. Successful MNCs have a geocentric attitude.

Economic Differences

Although many countries share similar concerns over economic growth, capital investments, and trade factors, there are aspects of the economic environment that differ between nations. One of these is the nature of the economic system itself. World economies operate on a continuum of systems from free market — those based upon a free-market method of supply and demand and competition as a driving force — to government-planned economies — those that require a control government to supervise most economic decisions.

Other economic differences typically include:

Common economic differences that exist between countries

1. *Import/Export controls.* Each nation generally has a variety of different tariffs and/or quotas.
2. *Foreign exchange rate.* The value of each country's currency is different.
3. *Quality of life.* The standard of living of each is different.
4. *Technology.* Lesser-developed countries having little modern technological capability while highly developed firms have a great deal.
5. *Investment.* Sources of available capital for investment and growth in foreign countries vary from nation to nation.

Political Differences

The type of government also affects MNC operations

The type of government — democratic, socialistic, or communistic — will be a major factor in the commercial and legal affairs of a country. In democratic countries, the marketplace will greatly influence the free economic environment. In socialistic countries, central planning is done in free elections for the concern of the country as a whole. Primary industries will be carried out by the government in addition to market forces. In communistic countries, strong central planning in all industries will dictate commercial and legal affairs.

The political system sets the stage for a variety of environmental forces that may differ substantially from those in the home country. The magnitude of differences in taxation, trade tariffs, copyright laws, exchange regulations, and business practices can increase the risk of an enterprise conducting business in a foreign country.[10]

Cultural Differences

To be successful in international operations, a multinational enterprise needs to be aware of, and many times must adapt to, the cultural differences of the foreign country.[11] **Culture** is defined as socially transmitted behavior patterns, such as the values, mores, and customs of a society. When managers deal with the culture of a foreign nation, they must avoid stereotypes and myths and develop systematic guidelines for understanding these differences. One international researcher, Geert Hofstede, conducted a study of personnel in U.S.-based companies operating in 40 countries. From this study, he developed four dimensions of national culture (see Table 4-4). These four dimensions are:

---

[10] Sakash P. Sethi and K. A. Luther, "Political Risk Analysis and Direct Foreign Investment: Some Problems of Definition and Measurement," *California Management Review* (Winter 1986):57–68.
[11] Vern Terpstra, *The Cultural Environment of International Business* (Cincinnati: South-Western, 1978).

TABLE 4-4   Examples of Four Dimensions of National Culture

Power-Distance Dimension

Small Power-Distance	*Large Power-Distance*
All people should be independent	A few people should be independent; most should be dependent
Superiors are accessible	Superiors are inaccessible
All should have equal rights	Power holders are entitled to privileges

Uncertainty-Avoidance Dimension

Weak Uncertainty-Avoidance	*Strong Uncertainty-Avoidance*
Hard work, as such, is not a virtue	There is an inner urge to work hard
More willing to take risks in life	There is great concern with security in life
There should be as few rules as possible	There is a need for written rules and regulations

Individualism-Collectivism Dimension

Collectivist	*Individualist*
"We" consciousness holds sway	"I" consciousness holds sway
The emphasis is on belonging to organizations; membership is the ideal	The emphasis is on individual initiative and achievement; leadership is the ideal
Belief is placed in group decisions	Belief is placed in individual decisions

Masculinity Dimension

Feminine	*Masculine*
There should be equality between the sexes	Men should dominate in society
One sympathizes with the unfortunate	One admires the successful achiever
Small and slow are beautiful	Big and fast are beautiful

Source: Adapted from Geert Hofstede, "Motivation, Leadership, and Organization: Do American Theories Apply Abroad? *Organizational Dynamics* (Summer 1980):46–49. Reprinted by permission of the author and copyright holder.

The four dimensions of national culture greatly influence the climate in which an MNC will operate

1. *Power–Distance.* The degree to which a society accepts a hierarchical or unequal distribution of power in organizations.
2. *Uncertainty–Avoidance.* The degree to which a society perceives ambiguous and uncertain situations as threatening and as things to be avoided.
3. *Individualism–Collectivism.* The degree to which a society focuses on individuals or groups as resources for work and social problem solving.
4. *Masculinity.* The degree to which a society emphasizes often

TABLE 4-5   What Americans Are Like: Cultural Differences

- Citizens of the United States call themselves "Americans." Other "Americans"—citizens of Mexico, Central and South America—often find the term inappropriate.

- Americans are very informal. They like to dress informally, entertain informally and they treat each other in a very informal way, even when there is a great difference in age or social standing. Foreigners often consider this informality disrespectful and even rude.

- Americans are generally competitive. The American style of friendly joking or banter, of "getting the last word in," and the quick, witty reply are subtle forms of competition. Although such behavior is natural to Americans, many foreigners find it to be overbearing or disagreeable behavior.

- Americans are achievers. They are obsessed with records of achievement in sports, and they keep business achievement charts on their office walls and sports awards displayed in their homes. Many foreign cultures emphasize group achievement, not individual achievement.

- Americans ask a lot of questions, some of which seem to be pointless, uninformed, or elementary. No impertinence is intended; the questions usually grow out of genuine interest. Many foreigners are taught not to ask a lot of questions.

- Americans value punctuality. They keep appointment calenders and live according to schedules. To most foreigners, Americans seem "always in a hurry," and this often makes the Americans appear brusque. In truth, most are simply trying to be efficient and get a great many things done by rushing around. Foreigners tend to move at a much slower pace.

- Silence makes Americans nervous. They would rather talk about the weather than deal with silence in a conversation. Just the opposite is true for many foreigners.

Source: Excerpts from Margo Ernest, ed., *Predeparture Orientation Handbook: For Foreign Students and Scholars Planning to Study in the United States* (Washington, D.C.; U.S. Information Agency, Bureau of Educational and Cultural Affairs, 1984):103–05, as cited in "What Americans Are Like," *New York Times* (April 16, 1985).

stereotyped "masculine" traits, such as assertiveness, independence, and insensitivity to feelings, as dominant values.

From this study, Hofstede concluded that management must tailor its practices and policies to fit the local cultures.[12] These should not be directly transferred from one country to another without careful analysis of the cultural impact.

Other differences in culture include such factors as:

1. *Education.* The level and quality of educational systems vary from one country to another. As a result, literacy and technical understanding can be a major factor in doing business in either country.
2. *Language.* Languages vary from country to country if only in terms of cultural variations. For example, a new product that does not do well in

---

[12] For more on this subject see Richard M. Hodgetts and Fred Luthans, *International Management* (New York: McGraw-Hill Book Company, 1991), Chapter 2.

the U.S. is often said to "have bombed." In England this term means the product was a big success.

3. *Customs.* Local customs and habits create important differences between people. Table 4-5 offers some examples. The way people behave can be difficult to understand and it is easy to insult innocently. (See "Management in Practice: Going Global By Acting Local.")

MANAGEMENT IN PRACTICE

Going Global by Acting Local

Procter & Gamble (PNG) has learned a lot about marketing overseas.

P&G wasn't always too nimble abroad. For years, it was something of an "ugly American," taking products developed for the U.S. market and trying to push them into foreign markets with American-style marketing and ads. Such efforts to standardize worldwide marketing techniques were fashionable in the early 1980s, under the banner of "global marketing." But P&G has learned that the trick to going global is acting like a local.

Take P&G's experiences in Japan. A homogeneous society, Japan remains in many ways a classic mass market. Still, for P&G, it is a fragment of the worldwide market, and one for which it has carefully tailored its marketing. But it learned to do so only after some bitter lessons—and more than $200 million in losses from its arrival in 1971 to 1987. "P&G has a very hard time accepting that Japan was not going to be like the U.S.," says an American marketing executive in Tokyo.

P&G won an early lead in disposable diapers after introducing Pampers in Japan in 1977, for example. But it quickly lost a market share when competitors Unki-Charm Corp. and Kao Corp. introduced fitted, thin diapers that won over mothers who had resisted disposables. "We really didn't understand the consumer," says Edwin L. Artzt, P&G's vice-chairman, who acknowledges that P&G was slow to improve its bulky, rectangular Pampers.

Now, things have turned around dramatically. P&G's sales in Japan grew 40 percent, to $1 billion, in the latest fiscal year. Overall international profits increased by 37 percent to $417 million.

Says P&G's Artzt: "We want to be the No. 1 consumer-products company in Japan." To reach that goal, P&G has hired more Japanese staff and attuned its ways to local styles. "It's more Japanese than some Japanese companies," says Noriko Sakoh, an analyst at SBCI Securities (Asia) Ltd.

Worldwide, P&G is rolling out new products more quickly, partly because it has built strong local operations that are closer to the market. "P&G used to be bloody slow," says Michael R. Angus, chairman of Unilever PLC, P&G's global archrival. "They were so thorough, the world changed between the origination of an idea and the product actually appearing on shelves."

P&G now tries to develop what Artzt calls "big edge" products, with a technology that can be applied worldwide but in forms tailored to local needs.

Source: Zachary Schiller, Ted Holden, and Mark Maremont, "P&G Goes Global by Acting Like a Local," *Business Week* (August 28, 1989):58.

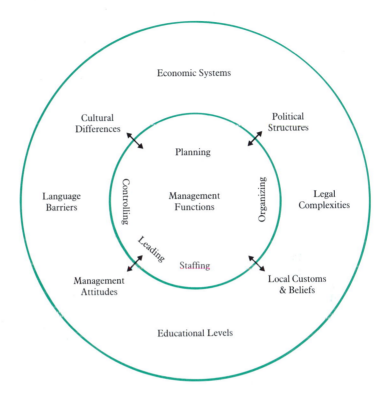

FIGURE 4-2
The International
Environment
of MNCs

THE MANAGEMENT FUNCTIONS IN THE INTERNATIONAL ENVIRONMENT

The international environment affects the ways in which the basic management functions of planning, organizing, staffing, leading, and controlling are implemented (see Figure 4-2). The challenges discussed earlier obviously influence each of the functions due to differences in economics, political structure, culture, language, and customs.

The Planning Function

The differences and challenges of the international environment make planning vital.[13] As an example, note the difference in scope, distance, and efficiency that increase the challenge of strategic planning:

---

[13] Balaji S. Chakravarthy and Howard V. Perlmutter, "Strategic Planning for a Global Business," *Columbia Journal of World Business* (Summer 1985):3–10. See also: Edward R. Koepfler, "Strategic Options for Global Market Players," *Journal of Business Strategy* (July/August 1989):46–50.

FIGURE 4-3
Product
Departmentalization
for Multinationals

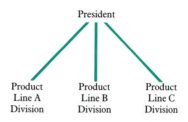

- Scope: multinational and global in nature
- Distance: enterprises' operations are distant and often different from each other
- Efficiency: due to the larger scope, greater distances of locations, and varied competition, there is a stronger need for overall coordination and efficiency

The global nature of the MNC directly affects its planning

Moreover, rather than merely supplementing their domestic strategy with a separate international one, MNCs are likely to adopt a global strategic plan that incorporates both areas. The result is a multitiered plan that balances the autonomy and initiative of individual subsidiaries with the necessary consistency and predictability of the total system.[14]

The Organizing Function

The organizational structure must strike a balance between efficiency and coordination

The same factors that challenged the planning function (see Figure 4-2) also influence the basic organizing function. It is especially important for a multinational corporation to find the optimum balance between the most efficient form of organization (type of structure) and the coordination of tasks within that framework.

The structure must provide clear delineation of jobs and the authority granted to accomplish them.[15] The choice of structure may follow the product, geographic, or functional departmentalization concept.

Product departmentalization for a multinational firm is widely used when there are diverse product lines being developed for different geographic areas. (See Figure 4-3.)

Geographic departmentalization is used by a multinational firm when product lines are not very diversified. An example is when vice presidents are assigned all operations within a geographic region, such as in the U.S., Canada, Europe, and so on. (See Figure 4-4.)

The functional structure assigns the authority to plan and control all global

[14] Gary Hamel and C. K. Prahalad, "Do You Really Have A Global Strategy?" *Harvard Business Review* (July–August 1985):139–48.
[15] Theodore Herbert, "Strategy and Multinational Organization Structure: An Interorganizational Relationship Perspective," *Academy of Management Review* (April 1984):259–70.

FIGURE 4-4
Geographic
Departmentalization
for Multinationals

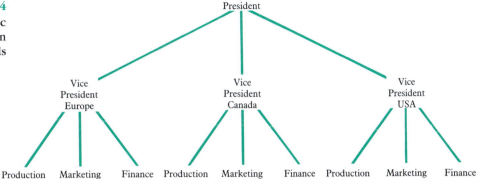

operations of the multinational firm within a specific function (for example, marketing, finance, production). All vice presidents report to the president and have their offices located at domestic corporate headquarters. (See Figure 4-5.)

The organizational structure of multinational enterprises tends to evolve as the firm's global orientation and strategy begin to take shape. Thus, no single structure mentioned is suitable for all companies. As enterprises balance their strategies and capabilities with the foreign environments, continual reorganization may be appropriate. Another factor that affects the multinational's structure is its home country and host country relationships, which were discussed earlier. Thus, the different foreign environments and the relationships developed in these environments will ultimately dictate the type of structure employed.

The Staffing Function

Staffing also
presents a series
of important
challenges to the
MNC

The staffing function for MNCs offers both advantages and disadvantages. The advantages include the talent of various foreign nations that can be drawn upon, as well as the particular knowledge and skills that these personnel possess. The disadvantages center around the proper selection and/or training that is needed

FIGURE 4-5
Functional
Departmentalization
for Multinationals

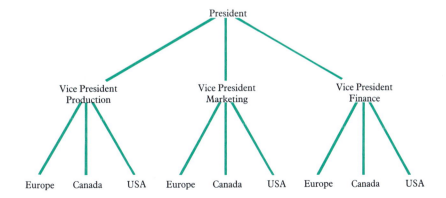

to effectively staff the foreign operations.[16] Training may be of particular importance for any personnel who will have a high level of international involvement, either by being stationed abroad or by interacting frequently with managers and other individuals from overseas. Another area of concern is international compensation. Often there are conflicts within the organization regarding attempts to adapt to differences among countries and pressures to maintain uniform compensation policies throughout the organization as a whole. If an organization adopts inconsistent salary scales, it will probably have difficulty in moving managers from high-paying countries to low-paying ones. Yet if companywide uniform pay scales are used, the MNC may find itself paying well above the market level in some countries, while in other countries, salary scales may be below the country's norm, and the MNE may have trouble attracting and retaining skilled managers. From the enterprise's point of view, the staffing function must be carefully implemented for effective operations in all international divisions.[17]

The Leading Function

As we have already studied, good management implies and involves good leadership. How effective leadership applies across different cultures is under constant debate. Since the environmental differences of various foreign nations affect the planning, organizing, and staffing functions, it seems obvious that leadership is also contingent upon certain differences. However, what about the current theories of leadership, motivation, and group behavior when applied to foreign operations? Do the theories apply in a global sense or must they be developed in each specific culture? It appears that the latter is true, making leadership an ongoing challenge in international operations.[18]

Leadership practices must be adapted to fit the environment

The Controlling Function

There must be a balance between the need for control and the need for operating autonomy

Effective global performance is partially a result of the basic control process implemented by the MNC. Establishing standards, comparing performance to those standards, evaluating results, and taking direct action (feedback) are all important concepts that were examined under the basic control process. These steps do not change for a multinational firm. However, foreign environments (culture, customs, language, politics) do result in special considerations to the implementation of the control process. In deciding the appropriate manner in which to establish an effective control process over international operations,

[16] Sally Solo, "Japan Discovers Woman Power," *Fortune* (June 19, 1989):153–58.
[17] See Edwin L. Miller et al., "The Relationship between Global Strategic Planning Process and Human Resource Management Function," *Human Resources Planning* (Fall 1986):9–23.
[18] F. T. Murray and Alice Haller, "Global Managers for Global Businesses," *Sloan Management Review* (Winter 1986):75–80.

the gamut of choices ranges from total centralization of decisions—where all operating decisions are made at corporate headquarters–to high decentralization of decisions—where international headquarters are greatly independent and autonomous. Some of the factors that influence the range of decision-making control include the following:

1. The size of the MNC and its length of time in the international arena.
2. The proficiency of overseas management and the degree of reliance on that management at corporate headquarters.
3. The need to motivate management through involvement in the decision-making process.

Even with these factors influencing the control decisions, however, in the majority of cases, most actions are taken by international managers with specific guidelines from corporate headquarters. Effective managerial control of a global enterprise is extremely complex yet vital to the firm's survival.

SUMMARY

1. International management is the setting of objectives and the conduct of business operations in foreign countries. Many firms have gone international as seen by the direct investment made by U.S. companies overseas and by foreign firms in America.
2. There are a number of reasons for going international. Some of the most common include the opportunity for (a) expanded or new markets, (b) greater profits, (c) access to raw materials, (d) increased financial resources, (e) decreased labor costs, (f) acquisition of new technology, and (g) geographic relocation in relation to customers.
3. When entering a foreign market, a company must decide on the amount of involvement it wishes to make. The five most common forms of international involvement are export/import, licensing agreements, joint ventures, the creation of international divisions, and the formation of an international corporation.
4. MNCs can have both a positive and a negative impact on the host country. Similarly, these firms can have a positive and negative impact on their home country.
5. There are many different challenges that MNCs face in the international arena. Four of the major ones are philosophical attitudes, economic differences, political differences, and cultural differences.
6. The international environment also affects the ways in which the basic management functions of planning, organizing, staffing, leading, and controlling are implemented. Although the basic processes remain the

same, the steps used in carrying them out are modified in order to adapt to the overseas environment.

KEY TERMS

Culture   Socially transmitted behavior patterns, such as the values, mores, and customs of a society.

Ethnocentric attitude   An attitude under which the management of an MNC views home country ideas and policies as superior to those in the foreign market.

Geocentric attitude   An attitude under which the management of an MNC views both local and international operations in worldwide terms and attempts to balance a concern for both in its overall plan.

International management   The setting of objectives and the conduct of business operations in foreign countries.

Joint venture   A partnership agreement in which two or more firms or investors undertake a project for a specific length of time.

Licensing arrangement   An agreement in which one firm (the licensor) agrees to allow another firm (the licensee) to use its patents, production processes, trademarks, or company name in return for the payment of an agreed-upon fee.

Multinational corporation   A business enterprise with extensive international operations in more than one country.

Multinational reciprocity   The mutual exchange of benefits between a host country and a multinational corporation.

Polycentric attitude   An attitude under which the management of an MNC feels that local managers know what is best for their operations since they are familiar with the culture and so allows the overseas unit a great deal of control over day-to-day matters.

Transnational enterprise   See Multinational corporation.

QUESTIONS FOR ANALYSIS AND DISCUSSION

1. Why are many firms beginning to set up international operations? What are the benefits they hope to attain? Explain.
2. What is the simplest way for an American firm to go international?
3. How does a licensing agreement work? Why would a company be willing to become a licensor? Why would a company be willing to become a licensee? Explain.
4. How does a joint venture work? Include a specific example in your answer.
5. When is a firm likely to set up an international division? Give an example.

6. How does an international corporation's view of its operations differ from that of a company that is exporting goods to another country? Explain.
7. In your own words, define a multinational corporation.
8. What benefits does an MNC offer to a host country? What drawbacks are there for the host country when allowing an MNC to set up operations within its borders? Cite at least three benefits and drawbacks in your answer.
9. What benefits does an MNC offer to a home country? What drawbacks might a home country suffer as a result of its MNCs? Cite at least three benefits and drawbacks in your answer.
10. In managing its overseas operations, some managements have an ethnocentric attitude, some have a polycentric attitude, and some have a geocentric attitude. What does this statement mean? In your answer, be sure to define or describe the three types of attitudes.
11. How can economic differences affect firms doing business overseas? How can political differences affect these firms? Explain.
12. What are the four dimensions of national culture? What effect do these dimensions have on businesses setting up operations in overseas locations?
13. In carrying out the management processes of planning, organizing, staffing, leading, and controlling, would there be any differences in implementation between that used in the U.S. and that used in other countries? Be complete in your answer.

CASE

Going International

The Lengler Corporation is a medium-sized, highly profitable corporation that manufactures a wide range of industrial products. Most of its output is sold directly to other production firms or to contracting firms.

Last month the president of Lengler, Earl Carthall, received a visit from a Japanese businessman. The visitor was a representative of one of the largest industrial firms in Japan. The company was seeking to expand its markets by establishing a worldwide sales force. It was also looking to increase its product offerings. One of the easiest ways of accomplishing the latter objective was to enter into contractual arrangements with companies that have successful products that are not for sale in the international arena and who would be agreeable to allowing someone else to produce and/or market them in overseas locations.

Earl likes the idea and is willing to enter into a contract with the Japanese firm. The two basic routes that he feels are available to his firm are exporting or a licensing arrangement. Although they only discussed the arrangement in general terms, the Japanese businessman explained to Earl that his company would be willing to buy approximately $1 million of merchandise. The price would be

10 percent above Earl's production cost and the buyer would assume all costs associated with shipping the goods to Japan or some other overseas market. On the other hand, if Earl would like to enter into a joint venture with the firm, the company would be willing to pay 10 percent of all revenues received from merchandise produced under this arrangement. The firm also would be prepared to absorb all expenses associated with buying the necessary machinery and equipment and training the workers. Earl has promised to get back in touch with the businessman within 30 days. In the interim he wants to talk the proposal over with the board of directors.

1. How would an export arrangement work? What would Earl do? What would the Japanese firm do? Explain.
2. How does a license arrangement work? What would Earl's firm be required to do? What would the Japanese firm have to do?
3. Which of the two approaches would you recommend to Earl? Why? Explain.

YOU BE THE CONSULTANT

A Change in Philosophy

When the Carter Brothers set up their first hotel in San Antonio, they hoped to make enough money to buy two more over the next 10 years. In this way, all three of the brothers would have a hotel of his own to manage.

Within two years the brothers made enough money to buy a second hotel and during each of the next five years they purchased an additional one. Within 10 years the brothers had bought, or built, a total of 27 hotels and motor inns. The next five years saw the company expand to 110 units in a 27-state area. At the same time the Carters began to realize that the hotel business had its limits. There were many strong competitors on both a regional and national basis and it would be very difficult to go on expanding at the current rate unless they decided to enter the international market.

Six months ago the brothers were contacted by the chief financial officer of a major European conglomerate. Among other things, the conglomerate owns a large hotel chain with units in England, France, West Germany, Switzerland, Italy, and Spain. The conglomerate has made a lot of money from this chain but feels that this is a good time to sell the chain. In particular, the conglomerate wants to get more into the computer and high-technology fields. With the $100 million it could get from the hotel chain, the firm can expand the operations of its computer company, thus becoming one of the largest high-tech firms in Europe.

The Carters have looked over the hotel chain's financial records and believe that $100 million is a fair price. However, they are concerned about buying out an existing chain. They always assumed that if they were going to go international, it would be best if they set up, or bought, one hotel and then began to move on from there. In this way they would be able to keep their feet on the ground and, slowly but surely, get into the European market. The brothers know nothing about European customs and culture. They are novices when it comes to understanding what Europeans want in hotel service and how to price these services. On the other hand, they realize that the hotels already have personnel who understand many of these things and they could rely on these people to keep the operation doing well.

The other major problem the brothers have relates to overall company planning. With the addition of a hotel chain that is 50 percent the size of the one they have in the states, management is going to have to take a different view of its overall operations. It will have to think of the business in worldwide terms rather than just national terms.

"Are we getting in over our heads?" the oldest of the brothers recently asked. "Or are we looking at the greatest opportunity that will ever come our way?" Before doing anything, the brothers have decided to bring in a consultant who can advise them on the benefits and drawbacks associated with going international and how their approach to planning and implementing strategy will have to change if the overseas purchase is made.

Your Consultation

Assume you are the consultant brought in by the brothers. What do you see as the advantages and disadvantages of their going international? How can they handle the problem of taking a worldwide view of operations rather than just a national view? Additionally, what other challenges do the brothers have to be concerned with? Write your answer in the form of a letter to the three brothers.

Integrative Case Study
ATARI CORPORATION

Phase I: The Bushnell Era (1971–1977)

Founded with $250 in 1971, Atari was the first successful producer of a video arcade game ("Pong"). At age 28, Nolan Bushnell, a recent graduate of the University of Utah, founded Atari and profoundly affected its initial structure, culture, strategy, and performance.[1]

When Bushnell introduced Pong, it competed only with pinball manufacturers. But arcade video games caught on fast and demand quickly exceeded supply. Atari produced as many games as they could but growth was limited by their small manufacturing capacity.

New game developers, licensees, and illegal copiers flooded into the market, easily selling what they produced. To protect sales, Atari took legal action against copiers and set license fees without knowing how popular a game might become. Nevertheless, by 1974, Atari could claim only one-tenth of the 100,000 Pong-type video games operating in arcades.[2]

Industry turbulence was heightened by the short, two- to four-year product life cycle of video games. Consumers rapidly changed their preferences, losing interest as new games were introduced and as old ones were mastered. To be maximally successful, new games had to reach full production as quickly as possible.

During the 1973–1974 fiscal year, Atari's payroll was cut in half because production delays on a new game slashed expected revenues.[3] Success in the early 1970s demanded that research and development be active and production be flexible.

The dynamic nature of this new high-tech market helped shape Atari's casual atmosphere and loose structure. But the company also reflected Bushnell's personality. "There's a difference between having fun and running a company," reported one insider. "Nolan [Bushnell] is a creator, a dreamer, a pie-in-the-sky thinker, but he operated in a 'hey, man' kind of way."[4]

Bushnell and his engineers would periodically spend two to three days in brainstorming sessions at Pajaro Dunes, a resort on the California coast. "It was

This case was prepared by Monty L. Lynn of Abilene Christian University and is intended to be used as a basis for class discussion rather than to illustrate either effective or ineffective handling of the situation. Appreciation is expressed to Philip Ganezer, Anek Nuntapreda, and John Zumbrennen who assisted in writing the case.

Presented and accepted by the refereed Midwest Society for Case Research. All rights reserved to the author and the MSCR. Copyrighted © 1988 by Monty L. Lynn.

[1] "Atari Sells Itself to Survive Success," *Business Week* (November 15, 1976):120.
[2] "Atari and the Video Game Explosion," *Fortune* (July 27, 1981):42.
[3] "Atari Sells Itself," p. 120.
[4] "From Atari to Androbot," p. 123.

like having a meeting at a fraternity house with everybody trying to get their ideas on the board at the same time."[5] Employees wore T-shirts to the meetings — as they did to work — and there was plenty of marijuana and beer for those in attendance.[6]

Although Bushnell looked more like a group facilitator than a CEO, he was the hub of communication at Atari and a major source for new product ideas. Only after the 1973–1974 production crisis did Bushnell relinquish operational control to a subsidiary president.[7]

Although information channels, marketing, and manufacturing were quite inefficient, Atari was able to achieve significant growth during these early years. To expand their product line and keep up with competition, the company focused their attention on new game research and development. One of the products of Atari's research was a game attachment for home television sets which allowed the company to grow tenfold from 1973–1976.[8]

Cash was Atari's main financial problem during its early years. The market for television-adapted video games was embryonic. Atari had the talent and ideas but lacked capital for growth. To remedy this limitation, Bushnell began looking for a buyer. MCA and Disney investigated Atari but did not initiate an acquisition. Atari appeared to be a favorable purchase for Warner Communications, however, partly because of declines in Warner's record and tape sales. They purchased Atari in 1977.

The six-year-old game manufacturer cost Warner $28 million, $15 million of which went to Bushnell. In exchange, he signed a noncompetition agreement and agreed to stay on as Atari's president . . . for a while.

Bushnell's style and ideas differed from that of Warner's top management. Conflict was inevitable and frequent. In one incident, the vice president who acquired Atari for Warner was reported to have said to Bushnell, "you [can] no longer expect to rule Atari by the divine right of kings."[9]

Bushnell himself confessed, "I'm not a very good chief executive officer. I like to develop the strategy, not to work it."[10] In his typically unstructured way, Nolan Bushnell announced that he would resign during a lunch meeting.[11] He left Atari to develop a high-tech restaurant chain named Pizza Time Theatre.

Phase II: The Kassar Era (1977–1983)

Home video and arcade games continued to grow in popularity. Demand was so great that almost anything would sell. Total expenditures for video games in

---

[5] "Atari and the Video Game," p. 42.
[6] *Ibid.,* p. 42.
[7] "Atari Sells Itself," p. 120.
[8] *Ibid.*
[9] "Atari and the Video Game," p. 42.
[10] *Ibid.*
[11] *Ibid.,* p. 45.

1982 were approximately equal to the combined expenditures for prerecorded music and movie theatre admissions.

At the peak of its operations, Atari held the majority of the video game cartridge market share and accounted for 70 percent of Warner's total operating earnings.[12] One contributing success during this time was the introduction of the arcade and television video game, "PacMan."

The number of industry competitors increased fivefold (from six to thirty) between 1977 and 1983. To secure a solid industry position, it was critical that companies develop and market new products frequently. Atari did so and also continued to protect games from copyright infringement through the courts.

As competitors filled the market in 1983, severe price competition forced some manufacturers out. Failing companies liquidated their inventories of games at a loss, putting more downward pressure on prices. Demand started to wane and inventories stacked up.

Atari's loose organizational structure might have been functional when the company was smaller, but it resulted in turmoil as Atari expanded. The company had fewer than 3,000 employees in 1981 but expanded worldwide employment to 10,000 by the end of 1982.[13] The administrative and communication problems which developed during this time were tremendous. The company desperately needed restructuring.

Warner Communications chose Raymond Kassar to be Bushnell's replacement. Although he knew little about the video game business—he was hired out of the textile industry—Kassar was a meticulous man with a passion for discipline.

At the time Kassar took the helm, the company was in a state of chaos. Several of the original top executives left when Bushnell stepped down. Kassar quickly hired top and mid-level managers and gave them huge budgets. He allowed the executives to build their own divisions; administrative ranks grew rapidly. But the highly paid professional managers proved to be incapable of working together. Kassar fired several of them before their contracts expired.

Kassar kept relations with most staff members cool and distant. "Things were kind of casual here," he recalled, "People didn't work very hard."[14] Some have suggested that the lackadaisical attitude may have been due to large salaries awarded to managers and engineers, sometimes without clear reason or performance to show for it.[15] But part of the cooler "culture" probably also was due to Kassar's style and his expectations.

Kassar generated considerable resentment as he initiated formal reporting procedures, tightened financial controls, set specific sales and marketing goals, and tightened security measures to protect confidential information. He

[12] "Atari's Struggle to Stay Ahead," *Business Week* (September 13, 1982):56.
[13] *Warner Communications 10k SEC Report, 1981.*
[14] "Atari and the Video Game," p. 45.
[15] Anne B. Fisher, "Glamour: Getting it or Getting it Back," *Fortune* (May 12, 1986):20-21.

expected employees to be at work at 8:00 a.m. sharp, answer the phone promptly, and wear ties and jackets instead of T-shirts.

Many who remembered the company's earlier days didn't like the fact that Kassar dressed in expensive clothes, was chauffeured to work, gave six-figure bonuses to executives, and opened an opulent dining room in the company's headquarters.[16]

Some engineers who had been treated royally under Bushnell felt antagonized by Kassar. "After a newspaper story quoted Kassar comparing engineers to operatic divas, T-shirts with the words 'I'm just another high-strung prima donna from Atari' became popular attire in the company's research labs."[17]

Employees became frustrated by the way Kassar clung to the controls when he should have delegated. One employee reported, "Atari is run by telling people what to do and giving them almost no responsibility, that's why many of us just think of this as a great training ground and don't plan to stay."[18] Morale suffered. Trust and job security were at an all-time low. The entrepreneurial zest which epitomized Bushnell's Atari was gone.

In line with the parent company's expectations, Kassar shifted Atari's emphasis from research and development to marketing.[19] Atari developed an understanding for consumer merchandising, whereas its early competitors in the video game business — RCA, Fairchild, and Magnavox — were not so capable at marketing and distribution.

Atari's sales were often fairly flat until the fourth quarter of each year when Christmas sales skyrocketed the company's earnings. Kassar launched a $6 million advertising campaign—which Atari had resisted before—and introduced four new game cartridges in late January. This strategy changed Atari's games from being Christmas items to year-round products. Atari rose from relative obscurity to the 37th largest advertiser in the country, spending $159 million on advertisements in 1981. (In comparison, IBM ranked 98th, spending only $40 million.)[20]

While its advertising was strong, Atari's marketing forte was distribution. The company always had sold games exclusively through retail stores, giving them a tremendous base from which to sell.[21] Kassar added to that base seven hundred factory-trained and authorized service centers throughout the U.S.

Through the Kassar years, Atari held its strong commitment to long-term internal software development. They kept close to the customer by allowing youngsters to develop new video games at Atari facilities. Through this innovative effort, Atari hoped to get the first shot at marketing games developed by computer whiz kids.

---

[16] Gary Hector, "The Big Shrink is on at Atari," *Fortune* (July 9, 1984):28.
[17] "Atari and the Video Game," p. 45.
[18] "Atari's Struggle," p. 56.
[19] *Ibid.*
[20] "Atari: Playing with House Money," *Datamation* (December 1982):90.
[21] *Ibid.*

Atari's experience in arcade games provided a distinct advantage for expanding into the personal computer field. Under Kassar's leadership, Atari began developing and marketing low-priced (under $500) home computers.

In the early 1980s, foreign competitors began eroding Atari's and other U.S.-based manufacturers' market share in the game industry. Atari's 80 percent plus share of the 1977 video cartridge market dropped to 41 percent in 1983. Its 70 percent share of the 1981 game machine market fell to 50 percent by 1983.[22]

Atari had overflowing inventories by the end of 1982. The company increased its production abroad in a drastic measure to boost profit margins; many viewed this as a symptom of faltering management. "We thought we had a monopoly, but now people are passing us up."[23] While they had excelled in other ways, the company had not concentrated on forecasting broad industry trends.

Added to the turmoil inside Atari and among domestic game producers, in early 1982, charges were brought against Kassar for insider trading.

Phase III: The Morgan Era (1983–1984)

Atari reported record total sales of $2 billion and a profit of $323 million in 1982. Unfortunately, those sales included millions of video game cartridges that never sold and were returned by retailers, cutting 1982 net sales to $1 billion.[24]

By the summer of 1983, Atari was clearly out of control. James J. Morgan, Executive Vice President of Philip Morris, was brought in to replace Kassar. (Kassar was informed of the change after the new president has been hired.) Morgan was 42.

Jim Morgan had been a successful marketing executive rising quickly through the ranks. He was lured to Atari by two things—the chance to turn around a faltering company and a multi-million dollar contract. He occasionally compared his job to that of Lee Iacocca, believing he was capable of reorganizing and revitalizing Atari.[25] Morgan looked to be a breath of fresh air for Atari employees. Although Atari had several serious problems, Morgan took a two-month vacation before reporting as president.

During Morgan's early months at Atari, the video game market continued to decline. Most of the games on the market were low quality products. A cutthroat price war forced Timex, Mattel, and Texas Instruments out of the video game business.[26]

The glut of video game cartridges drove games which once sold for $40 down to $4. Even Atari's arcade games were losing money.[27] Both markets were

---

[22] "What Sent Atari Overseas," *Business Week* (March 14, 1983):102.
[23] *Ibid.*
[24] "The Big Shrink," p. 23.
[25] *Ibid.*
[26] "How Jack Tramiel Hopes to Turn Atari Around," *Business Week* (July 16, 1984):30.
[27] "Jim Morgan's Unhappy 10 Months at Atari," *Business Week* (July 23, 1984):90.

saturated. Demand also fell because more parents were concerned about the amount of time their children spent playing video games. Home computers were decreasing in price and within reach of many families.

Morgan's first move when he reached Atari in September 1983 was to initiate a 30-day freeze on new product development. Although Kassar had succeeded in making Atari's products purchasable year-round, the Christmas season still provided the company's biggest sales period.[28]

Morgan's freeze resulted in not getting a new IBM-compatible computer ready for Christmas shoppers. This was a major disappointment to many but not to Morgan since his strategy was to continue to compete with Commodore in the less than $500 computer market rather than move to the more expensive computer line. Atari was already being significantly undercut in price by Commodore, however.[29] Defective product returns in 1983 exceeded $100 million.

Even if they had been able to get the new computer out, Atari's image was troublesome. How could a children's game manufacturer be taken seriously in the sophisticated computer market? An Atari marketing executive reflected that "the need to make a statement about what Atari was and what it stood for . . . was ignored."[30]

Morgan tried to keep communication channels open with employees. He often met with the press and with large staff groups and was committed to making Atari's working environment positive. But some claimed that Morgan listened only to optimists. "In the beginning Morgan didn't want to hear any bad news, and he wanted desperately to believe the good news."[31]

In a painful effort to cut costs, Morgan laid off 4,500 of Atari's 7,000 employees and closed plants in Hong Kong and Puerto Rico. Other layoffs and plant closings were scheduled to be made if necessary.[32]

Employees under Morgan were dissatisfied with his attempts to increase morale because everyone knew that the problem was much deeper than that. At the same time, it was difficult for people to work under a constant threat of layoffs. Although drastic cuts were made, some believed Morgan was too slow in making decisions about layoffs and product development; many felt uncertain about their job tasks and security.

Sales volume continued to decline during the fourth quarter of 1983 as did Morgan's support. Top managers were more unified than in earlier years. Still, executives battled and some ignored Morgan's decisions.[33]

The company's collection policy and practice was weak; Atari's accounts receivable included more than $100 million overdue by three months or more;

---

[28] *Ibid.*

[29] *Ibid.*

[30] Richard Arroyo, "A Postmortem on Atari," *Advertising Age* (April 22, 1985):28.

[31] *Ibid.,* p. 29.

[32] "A Game Plan for Survival at Atari," *Business Week* (April 9, 1984):32.

[33] Hector, p. 28.

some debts dated back to 1981. This problem was so severe that in 1984, the company stopped sending salespeople to overdue retailers and distributors. Instead, the finance staff was sent out to collect bills.[34]

Atari's sales force was using dubious tactics. Former Atari executives said sales teams shuffled merchandise among dealers to keep stores from returning unsold goods. It was originally Atari's practice to take back retailers' unsold games. The sales force began to retreat from that practice as early as 1981, agreeing to accept returns in some cases only if the merchant would take a consignment of other merchandise.

This shuffling kept returns from deflating revenues in the short run, but it also irritated retailers and delayed the resolution of accounts.[35] By 1983, Atari's strength in distribution had deteriorated. A discouraged Morgan left Atari after only ten months.

Phase IV: The Tramiel Era (1984–Present)

In July 1984, Jack Tramiel, former CEO of Commodore International, bought Atari from Warner Communications. The deal cost Tramiel $240 million, $7 million of which was his own money. The buy-out was a complete surprise on Wall Street and its purchase price prompted one analyst to call it "the most embarrassing" takeover of 1984. Another said Warner had "given away" Atari.[36]

Tramiel's reputation—with his slogan "Business is War"—is that of a hard-nosed, experienced leader in the computer industry. Tramiel signed papers Sunday evening for the takeover and then flew from New York to California during the night so he could be at corporate headquarters for the start of the work week.

Immediately after arriving in Sunnyvale, Tramiel claimed that Atari would have new products on the market by January 1985. He also predicted that his company would "be in the whole spectrum of the [home computer] market," presumably starting at the lower-price end and working up.[37] For Tramiel, low-cost production and trim operations were the strategies which would help him achieve his goals.[38]

Tramiel quickly reduced Atari's 2,500 employees to 1,500, declared he would sign all company checks, fired almost all marketing and research personnel, and placed three of his sons—Sam, Garry, and Leonard—in top management positions.[39]

---

[34] "A Game Plan for Survival," p. 32.

[35] Ibid., p. 29.

[36] David Pauly, "A Tough Man for a Tough Job," Newsweek (July 16, 1984):50.

[37] "How Jack Tramiel," p. 30.

[38] Cleveland Horton, "'New' Atari Tries to Bring Back Old Growth," Advertising Age (April 22, 1985):4.

[39] Ibid.

EXHIBIT 1 Market Share in the Home and Personal Computer Markets

Company	Market Share (%)		
	'83	'84	'87
Apple	18	29	9
Atari	6	5	—
Commodore	23	19	—
Compaq	—	—	7
IBM	12	18	23
Radio Shack/Tandy	8	7	—
Texas Instruments	9	0	—
All Others	24	23	61

Sources: 1983–1984: Cleveland Horton, " 'New Atari' Tries to Bring Back Old Growth," *Advertising Age,* April 22, 1985, p. 4; 1987: "Confusing Days for Personal Computers," *The Wall Street Journal,* September 13, 1988, p. 41.

Note: Double-dashes indicate unknown percentages.

Tramiel also broke advertising contracts with the Men's Professional Tennis Tour ($1 million), actor Alan Alda ($10 million), and the Olympics ($6 million).[40] The perspective of one Atari insider was that "the company is almost being run as a startup."[41] Others thought differently—"Tramiel is a boss, not a manager."[42]

Although severe cutbacks might have improved Atari's competitive position, Tramiel's reputation did not help sales. As CEO of Commodore, Tramiel shifted sales from outlet stores to mass merchandisers, undercutting the Commodore outlets. Because of this action, many top retail companies (e.g., ComputerLand) refused to sell Atari computers.[43]

In 1985, Atari's biggest competitors in home computers were IBM (in the $2,000 price range), Apple (in the $1,000 price range), and Commodore (in the $500 price range). Atari held only 5 percent of this market, a far distance behind some strong competitors (see Exhibit 1).

In 1985, Atari introduced its 520ST computer which was nicknamed the "Jackintosh." The 520ST is as powerful as Apple's MacIntosh but cost less than half the price (about $800 compared to $1800 for the Mac). Perhaps the introduction was not a moment too soon. The $500 computer market began drying

---

[40] "Atari Wants Out of Tennis Tie," *Advertising Age* (August 6, 1984):64.

[41] Pauly, p. 50.

[42] "Jim Morgan's Unhappy," p. 91.

[43] Geoff Lewis, "Atari and Commodore Want to Get on Your Gift List," *Business Week''* (June 10, 1985):49–50.

EXHIBIT 2   Atari's Yearly Net Sales and Income ($thousand)

Year	Net Sales	Net Income (Loss)
1987	493,172	57,429
1986	258,131	44,516
1985	141,987	(14,314)
1984	110,680	(62,758)
1983	540,000	(539,000)
1982	1,070,000	504,000
1981	740,000	281,000
1980	270,000	40,000
1979	110,000	10,000
1974	—	(500)
1973	3,200	500

Sources: 1984–1987: Atari annual reports; 1983–1979: Estimated from Peter Petre, "Jack Tramiel is Back on the Warpath," *Fortune,* March 4, 1985, p. 48 and "Atari's Struggle to Stay Ahead," *Business Week,* September 13, 1982, p. 56; 1974–1973: "Atari Sells Itself to Survive Success," *Business Week,* November 15, 1976, p. 120.

up in 1985 as consumer interest turned to the more powerful Apple and IBM lines.[44]

Atari's financial picture improved under Tramiel but the company has room for growth (see Exhibit 2). The same year the 520ST was released, Tramiel announced that Atari would go public. These two events provided the company with needed cash to pay off its $36 million debt to Warner Communications. An additional $18 million from the public offering is earmarked for the development of several new products. The Tramiel family retained slightly more than 50 percent of Atari's stock, with father Jack holding about 45 percent of that.[45]

By Christmas of 1986, video games were on the comeback. The resurrection of video games was both a curse and a blessing for Atari since customer interest in computers waned somewhat as a result.[46] Atari, however, welcomed the revival of games and planned on selling two million game machines in 1987. Hasbro, Mattel, and some Japanese firms also had games on the market by the 1987 holiday season.[47]

In October 1987, Atari acquired the Federated Group, Inc., a chain of 68 electronic retail stores located in the Western United States. These stores had been operating in the red two years prior to the acquisition. Atari is looking in

---

[44] "Between a Rock and a Hard Place," *Financial World* (February 6, 1985):100–101.
[45] Katherine M. Hafner, "Father Knows Best—Just Ask the Tramiel Boys," *Business Week* (December 15, 1986):106.
[46] Brian Moran, "New Home Videogames Posed for Comeback," *Advertising Age* (June 9, 1986):4.
[47] Neil Gross and Geoff Levine, "Here Come the Super Mario Brothers," *Business Week* (November 9, 1987):138.

the future toward acquiring or forming an alliance with a semiconductor manufacturing plant. There is no doubt that computers are Atari's present and future focal point; games play a minor role in company operations today.

Tramiel takes business seriously. He taught his sons about business from "day one." "Business isn't taught at Harvard. It's taught at home," he believes. His philosophy is just as serious with employees. Garry Tramiel describes it as a "kiss and kick" management philosophy: Jack "wants to make sure people understand they have to work hard and that at the same time he cares about them."[48]

Tramiel has experienced some success with Atari in the computer industry. Whether he can continue to do so has drawn no small amount of speculation. Whether the video game industry should become a major focus of the company is also a question which will have to be answered in the future. But one thing is certain — like his predecessors, Jack Tramiel and Atari have quite a challenge ahead of them.

One final twist brings the story full circle. A summer 1988 *Fortune* article reported that Nolan Bushnell was back working for Atari. His software development company, Axlon, is scheduled to produce about twenty video games for Atari. "Says Bushnell: 'I always knew, even when I was at the bottom, that I could pick myself up and make it all back again.'[49]

---

48 "Father Knows Best," p. 108.
49 Jaclyn Fierman, "Great Fortunes Lost," *Fortune* (July 18, 1988):84.

TWO

PLANNING THE ENTERPRISE'S DIRECTION

This part of the book begins our systematic study of the manager's functions. Planning is a good topic to begin with because until an organization has a plan, there is really no basis for organizing, staffing, and influencing or controlling operations.

Chapter 5 is about decision making in action. Actually, planning and decision making are intertwined. When an organization formulates its strategic plan, it also chooses objectives; and this is what decision making is —the process of choosing from among two or more alternatives. In this chapter, you will learn the nature of decision making. You will also see how the typical rational decision-making process, often used when people try to describe how decisions are made, differs from what is called the bounded rationality model, which takes into account such considerations as simplification, subjectivity, and rationalization. You will also learn how managers attempt to improve their decision-making effectiveness through the use of mathematical tools and techniques, creativity, and a matching of decision-making styles with leadership situations.

Chapter 6 is devoted to an examination of planning fundamentals. It attempts to answer the question: What is planning all about? In this chapter, you will learn about planning horizons, types of plans, the planning process, and management by objectives. These fundamentals are building blocks that can be used in any planning activity. They are the basics found in both the least sophisticated and most complex projects.

In Chapter 7, the topic of strategic planning is presented. In this chapter you will learn the characteristics of a strategic plan. You will also study the four basic elements of strategic plans: the basic mission, strategic objectives, strategy determination, and portfolio planning. The last part of the chapter pulls together these diverse ideas and discusses how to put a strategic plan into operation.

When you have finished reading the three chapters in this part of the book, you will know how modern managers actually formulate plans and make decisions. You will also have a basic appreciation of both the objective and subjective sides of this process. The material you read in Chapter 1, where management was described as both an art and a science, will become more meaningful.

5

Decision Making in Action

Planning and decision making are related in that plans are brought to fruition through decisions. In this chapter we will examine how decision making is carried out. Particular attention will be given to studying both rational and bounded rationality decision-making models. Consideration will also be given to the conditions under which decisions are made and to ways in which decision-making effectiveness can be improved. By the time you have finished studying all of the material in this chapter, you will be able to:

1. Define the term decision making and explain how the manager should go about reviewing decision-making situations.
2. Compare and contrast programmed and nonprogrammed decisions.
3. Describe the three conditions under which decisions are made and explain how these decisions are implemented.
4. Set forth some of the steps a manager can follow in improving decision-making effectiveness.
5. Compare and contrast the rational decision-making process with the bounded rationality process.
6. Explain how each of the following affects decision making: satisficing behavior, simplification, subjective rationality, and rationalization.
7. Explain how the following can be of value in improving decision-making effectiveness: use of management science tools and techniques, creativity, and the matching of decision-making situations with leadership styles.

THE NATURE OF DECISION MAKING

As we saw in Chapter 2, *decision making* is the process of choosing from among alternatives. Sometimes this process is a simple one. In making the final choice the manager can rely on simple guidelines and techniques such as rules, policies, procedures, or basic quantitative analysis. At other times the process is a complex one. In these cases the manager must draw on intuition, judgment, gut feeling, and highly mathematical tools and techniques. Table 5-1 illustrates these ideas. Also see "Management in Practice: The Jury Is Still Out."

In deciding how to approach each particular situation, the manager needs an understanding of the basic nature of decision making. Specifically, this requirement involves (1) knowing how to review the situation properly, (2) understanding the types of decisions that will be involved, (3) determining the conditions under which the decision will be made, and (4) having a fundamental grasp of the techniques involved in making effective decisions. The following section examines each of these kinds of knowledge.

Reviewing the Situation

The first thing a manager facing a decision needs to do is review the situation. He or she must answer three key questions. The first two are designed to help the manager sidestep personal action. The third is designed to help the manager formulate a response.

Will the problem resolve itself?

The first question is: Will the problem resolve itself? If nothing is done, will the matter go away? If the answer is yes, the manager can ignore the problem. A classic example is found in the case of managers who receive reports, memos, and other written communiqués that are labeled "for your attention and action." In most cases the manager does not have to read this material or do anything with it. The material is simply informational. It can be glanced at and then filed.

Is a personal decision required?

The second question is: Does the issue require a personal decision? Many times the matter can be delegated to a subordinate. It is not important enough to warrant personal consideration.

How should the problem be handled?

If the issue does require a personal decision, the third question is: How should the problem be handled? Having determined that the issue cannot be sidestepped, the manager must develop a plan of action. Managers who review

TABLE 5-1 Decision-Making Continuum	
Simple Problems	**Complex Problems**
Rules, policies, procedures, basic quantitative analysis	Intuition, judgment, gut feeling, highly mathematical tools and techniques

At Sears, The Jury Is Still Out

*U*ncertainty is the word for 520,000 employees of Sears, the retail giant. Edward A. Brennan, chairman of the board recently announced a completely new strategy called "A New Beginning." Restructuring the distribution system and pushing Sears into an "everyday low priced strategy," Brennan is attempting to regain the 15 percent of market lost to the major competitors. In July 1989, Sears placed brand-name appliances (such as G.E. and Amana) in their stores along with the traditional Kenmore name and called the addition "Brand Central." The strategy is to compete with the "superstore" concept developed by Highland Superstores, Inc. in the area of appliances.

Sears overall profit growth has remained stagnant for five years and the retail group's

earnings have fallen at an annual rate of 7.7 percent during this time period. In 1987, 9,230 jobs were slashed in an attempt to streamline the distribution system, but this has not been enough.

With a sagging performance level and the internal anxiety now apparent at Sears, other steps were necessary. Yet, analysts question the direction and focus of Brennan's strategy of a "new beginning." Will it be the step that vaults Sears into the next century or one that confuses and frustrates those involved? For the moment, the jury is still out.

Source: Bryan Bremner and Michael Oneal, "The Big Store's Big Trauma," *Business Week* (July 10, 1989):50–53.

decision-making situations by asking these three questions in the order in which we have presented them find they can greatly reduce the amount of time and effort expended in choosing from among alternatives.[1]

Types of Decisions

The manager needs to have a fundamental grasp of the various types of decisions. Table 5-2 provides one framework for categorizing them. Notice from the table that there are two basic types of decisions: programmed and nonprogrammed.

Programmed decisions use well-defined methods

Programmed decisions are those that are traditionally made using standard operating procedures or other well-defined methods. Some standard modern techniques include the use of operations research, mathematical analysis, and computer simulation. Programmed decisions are the easiest for managers to make because they can rely on preestablished patterns or programs to provide an answer.

---

[1] Jugoslav S. Milutinovich, "Business Facts for Decision-Makers: Where to Find Them," *Business Horizons,* (March–April 1985):63–80. *See also:* Daniel J. Isenberg, "Thinking and Managing: A Verbal Protocol Analysis of Managerial Problem Solving," *Academy of Management Journal* (December 1986):775–88.

	TABLE 5-2 Traditional and Modern Techniques of Decision Making	
	Decision-Making Technique	
Types of Decisions	*Traditional*	*Modern*

Programmed:
Routine, repetitive decisions
Organization develops specific
  processes for handling them
	1. Habit
	2. Clerical routine:
	  Standard operating procedures
	3. Organizational structure:
	  Common expectations
	  A system of subgoals
	  Well-defined informational
	    channels
		1. Operations research:
		  Mathematical analysis
		  Models
		  Computer simulation
		2. Electronic data processing

Nonprogrammed:
One-shot, ill-structured, novel policy
  decisions
Handled by general problem-solving
  processes
	1. Judgment, intuition, and creativity
	2. Rules of thumb
	3. Selection and training of
	  executives
		Heuristic problem-solving
		  technique applied to:
		  a. Training human decision
		    makers
		  b. Constructing heuristic
		    computer programs.

Source: Herbert A. Simon. *The New Science of Management Decision,* rev. ed.(Englewood Cliffs, NJ: Prentice-Hall, 1977), 48. © 1977. Reprinted by permission of Prentice-Hall, Inc.

Nonprogrammed decisions are ill structured

Nonprogrammed decisions are unique or out of the ordinary. They are often ill-structured, one-shot decisions. Traditionally they have been handled by techniques such as judgment, intuition, and creativity. More recently decision makers have turned to heuristic problem-solving approaches in which logic, common sense, and trial and error are used to deal with problems that are too large or too complex to be solved through quantitative or computerized approaches. In this area of nonprogrammed decision making managers have the opportunity to prove themselves. In fact, many management training programs on decision making are designed to help managers think through problems using a logical, nonprogrammed approach. In this way they learn how to deal with extraordinary, unexpected, and unique problems.

Decision-Making Conditions

Decisions are made under one of three possible conditions: certainty, risk, and uncertainty. As seen in Figure 5-1, these conditions are based on the amount of knowledge the decision maker has regarding the final outcome of the decision.

FIGURE 5-1
Decision-Making
Conditions

The amount of knowledge the decision maker has regarding the outcome of the decision determines the decision-making condition.

Certainty

Under conditions of **certainty** the manager has enough information to know the outcome of the decision before it is made. For example, a company president has just put aside a fund of $50,000 to cover the renovation of all executive offices. This money is in a savings account at a local savings and loan (S&L) association that pays 5.25 percent. Half will be drawn out next month and the rest when the job is completed in 90 days. Can the president determine today how much interest will be earned on the money over the next 90 days? Given the fact that the president knows how much is being invested, the length of investment time, and the interest rate, the answer is yes. Investing the funds in an S&L is a decision made under conditions of certainty. The ultimate outcome in terms of interest is known today.

Another example of decision making under certainty is found in the case of an organization with a warehouse full of machine parts. Assume that these parts can be used to produce any one of three machine models: A, B, or C. Each model requires a different combination of parts and has a different profit level. For example, model A is the simplest, uses the fewest parts, and has the lowest profit. Model C is the most complex, uses the greatest number of parts, and returns the highest profit. Given the fact that the parts are all on hand, the company can make any model or combination of models it wants. If we assume the firm wants to maximize profit, the only question that needs to be answered is: Which model or models should be assembled in order to reach this objective? This question may be difficult to answer through visual analysis of the inventory report, but it can be answered by using mathematical decision-making tools. The company can determine with certainty the outcome of its decision.

Risk

Most managerial decisions are made under conditions of risk.[2] **Risk** exists when the individual has some information regarding the outcome of the decision but does not know everything. When making decisions under conditions of risk, the manager may find it helpful to use probabilities. To the degree that probability assignment is accurate, he or she can make a good decision.

Consider the case of a company that has four contract proposals it is interested in bidding on. If the firm obtains any one of these contracts, it will make a profit on the undertaking. However, because only a limited number of personnel can devote their time to putting bids together, the firm has decided to bid on one proposal only—the one that offers the best combination of profit and probability that the bid will be successful. This combination is known as the *expected value*. The profit associated with each of these four contract

---

[2] David B. Hertz and Howard Thomas, ''Decision and Risk Analysis in a New Product and Facilities Planning Problem,'' *Sloan Management Review* (Winter 1983):17–31.

TABLE 5-3	Computation of Expected Values		
Contract Proposal	Profit	Probability of Getting the Contract	Expected Value
1	$100,000	.6	$ 60,000
2	200,000	.5	100,000
3	300,000	.4	120,000
4	400,000	.2	80,000

proposals, as presented in Table 5-3, varies from $100,000 to $400,000. Notice that the contract offering $400,000 is the least likely to be awarded to the company. Conversely, the first contract is much more likely to be awarded to the company, but it offers the smallest profit of the four. On which of the proposals should the firm bid? As the table shows, the answer is number three. It offers the greatest expected value.

This example illustrates the importance of probability assignment when decisions are made under risk. If we reversed the probabilities so that proposal #1 had a 20 percent success factor and proposal #4 had a 60 percent success factor, the manager would opt for the latter proposal. The effective manager must investigate each alternative in order to be as accurate as possible in making probability assignments.

Uncertainty

At still other times the outcome is unknown

Uncertainty exists when the probabilities of the various outcomes are not known. The manager feels unable to assign estimates to any of the alternatives. While the situation may seem hopeless, mathematical techniques have been developed to help decision makers deal with uncertainty. Some of these are heavily quantitative in nature and are outside the scope of our present consideration.[3] Some nonmathematical approaches have been developed to supplement these techniques, however, and they do warrant brief discussion. One is simply to avoid situations of uncertainty. A second is to assume that the future will be like the past and assign probabilities based on previous experiences. A third is to gather as much information as possible on each of the alternatives, assume that the decision-making condition is one of risk, and assign probabilities accordingly.

[3] J. F. Preble and Pradeep A. Rav, "Combining Delphi and Multiple Scenario Analysis for Planning Purposes," *Journal of Business Strategies* (Fall 1986):12–21; see also Richard M. Hodgetts, *Management: Theory, Process, and Practice,* 5th ed. (San Diego: Harcourt Brace Jovanovich, 1990): 278–288.

Using these approaches actually requires sidestepping the uncertainty factor. It is assumed not to exist; and this can be a wise philosophy. After all, by definition, uncertainty throws a monkey wrench into decision making. The manager's best approach is to draw back from this condition either by gathering data on the alternatives or by making assumptions that allow the decision to be made under the condition of risk.[4]

Making Effective Decisions

When a manager does have to make a decision, he or she should strive to be as effective as possible. One way of ensuring effectiveness is to follow the steps in the decision-making process. These will be discussed shortly. A second way is to use guidelines that help carry out this process. While many guidelines can be of help, the following seven, set forth by Irving Janis and Leo Mann, have been found to be of particular value:

Effective decision-making guidelines

1. Thoroughly canvas a wide range of alternative courses of action.
2. Survey the full range of objectives to be fulfilled and the values that are implied in the choice.
3. Carefully weigh whatever is known about the costs and risks of negative consequences as well as the positive consequences that can flow from each alternative.
4. Intensively search for new information relevant to the further evaluation of the alternatives.
5. Correctly assimilate and take into account any new information or expert judgment to which one is exposed, even when the information or judgment does not support the course of action initially preferred.
6. Reexamine the positive and negative consequences of all known alternatives, including those originally regarded as unacceptable, before making a final choice.
7. Make detailed provisions for implementing or executing the chosen course of action, with special attention to contingency plans that might be required if various known risks were to materialize.[5]

These guidelines are somewhat utopian. The manager does not always have either the time or the resources for carrying out all of them. They do serve, however, as a basis for rational decision making.

---

[4] Paul Shrivastava and Ian I. Mitroff, "Enhancing Operational Research Utilization: The Role of Decision Makers' Assumptions," *Academy of Management Review* (January 1984):18–26.
[5] Irving Janis and Leo Mann, *Decision Making* (New York: Free Press, 1977), 11.

RATIONAL DECISION-MAKING PROCESS

The **rational decision-making process** describes how decisions are made in the ideal.[6] As we shall see shortly, most decisions are not made in quite this way. Some of the steps are either shortcircuited or bypassed entirely. Nevertheless, when the problem or issue is a simple one that is addressed in logical fashion, the steps as outlined in Figure 5-2 do describe how decisions are made.

Uncover the Symptoms

The first step in rational decision making is to uncover the symptoms of the problem.[7] The company that produces an outmoded product will find its market share slipping away. The manager who fails to obtain average raises for personnel will find an increase in absenteeism and tardiness among the workers. In each case the problem presents itself through its symptoms.

Identify the Problem or Define the Goal

Having uncovered the symptom, the manager must identify the problem or the desired goal. In other words, he or she must answer the question: Why did the symptom arise? More specifically, the question might be: Why is the company's product outmoded, or why are worker absenteeism and tardiness increasing?

Develop Decision Criteria

The next step is to develop criteria for evaluating the alternative courses of action. In the case of the outmoded product, the objective might be to recapture the old market share. The manager who failed to get average raises for the personnel might compare the cost of these raises with the expenses associated with the lost work output.

Develop Alternative Solutions

At this point the decision maker lists all of the possible solutions to the problem. Some may be very unlikely; others may border on the absurd. In rational decision making all are listed. Not all of the solutions are explained in detail, however. The decision maker focuses on the ones that seem most likely to solve the problem.

---

[6] Noreen M. Klein, "Utility and Decision Strategies: A Second Look At The Rational Decision Maker," *Organizational Behavior and Human Performance* (February 1983):1–25.

[7] Gerald F. Smith, "Defining Managerial Problems," *Management Science* (August 1989):964–80.

FIGURE 5-2   Steps Involved in the Rational Decision-Making Process

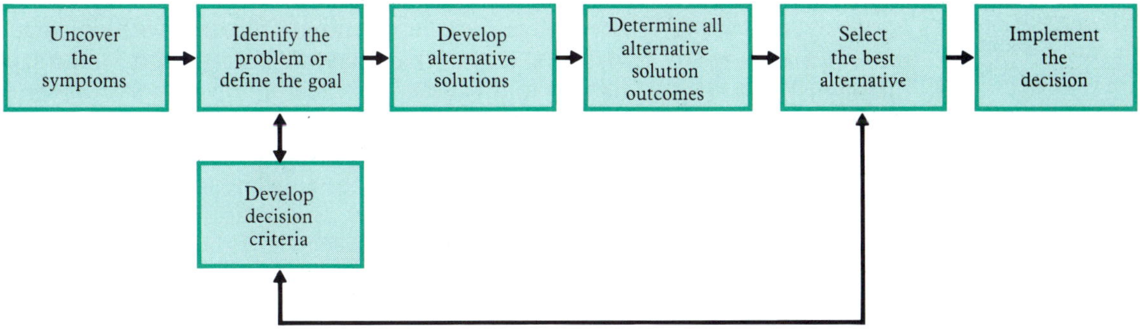

Determine All Alternative Solution Outcomes

All of the alternative solutions are then examined in terms of outcome. What will happen if each is implemented? Whenever possible the manager attempts to quantify the answer.

Select the Best Alternative

After determining the probable outcomes of alternative solutions, the manager evaluates them using the decision criteria. Which one best meets the criteria that have been established? At this point, selection of the best alternative is a fairly simple matter.

Implement the Decision

The final step in decision making is to carry out the decision. The solution is put into effect. If the decision has been well thought out and there are no problems in communicating what is to be done, this step should be fairly easy.

BOUNDED RATIONALITY CONSIDERATIONS

The rational decision-making process is an ideal approach. Unfortunately, in practice decision making is not often carried out this way. The manager's knowledge may be limited or bounded in a number of ways. The following discussion examines four of the most important kinds of limitations and then describes the bounded rationality process.

Satisficing Behavior

Rational decision making assumes that the manager will choose the alternative that offers the greatest return or benefit. This kind of manager, often referred to

To most managers
many choices are
merely "good
enough"

as **economic man**, always strives for the maximum payoff. In contrast, **administrative man** exhibits **satisficing behavior**, choosing a course of action that is merely satisfactory. Most managers are happy most of the time with a satisfactory return. They are "satisficers" rather than maximizers. Herbert Simon has distinguished between the two in this way:

> Whereas economic man maximizes—selects the best alternative from among all those available to him—his cousin, administrative man, satisfices—looks for a course of action that is satisfactory or "good enough." Examples of satisficing criteria, familiar enough to businessmen if unfamiliar to most economists, are "share of the market," "adequate profit," "fair price." [8]

The decision maker, in many cases, is content with a satisfactory solution. This statement is particularly true when such a solution is easy to implement. Why spend 100 hours of work to get a 20 percent return on a project investment when for 10 hours of work an 18 percent return can be obtained?

Simplification

Simplified models
of reality are often
employed

A great deal of empirical evidence shows that many decision makers employ a simplified model of reality. If the manager has made a successful decision concerning a similar problem in the past, he or she quickly opts for the same type of decision again. The manager molds the problem to the solution instead of molding the solution to the problem.

If the situation is new, the manager may gather information about the problem. He or she is likely, however, to try to formulate an answer quickly. As a result, the first pieces of data uncovered are used as a foundation for the solution even when the information they present is inconclusive or incomplete. Managers may become overly concerned with making these data fit into a total composite solution. Unfortunately, such attempts at an early and simple answer often result in the screening out of all new incoming information, especially when this information challenges some of the initial input or indicates that the early solution may be wrong. Realizing that any acceptance of new information will require a reformulation of the entire answer, the manager ignores this input. The result is a simple, but erroneous, solution.[9]

Subjective Rationality

In determining the possible outcomes of alternative solutions, the manager is sometimes forced to assign probabilities subjectively. In this process, known as

---

[8] Herbert A. Simon, *Administrative Behavior,* 3rd ed. (New York: Free Press, 1976), xxix.

[9] For more on this, see Steven Altman, Enzo Valenzi, and Richard M. Hodgetts, *Organizational Behavior: Theory and Practice* (Orlando: Academic Press, 1985), 493–95.

Sometimes managers make subjective probability assignments

subjective rationality, probabilities are assigned based on personal judgment. Research shows that most people are ineffective when making such subjective assignments. They simply do not know how to determine the likelihood of a particular outcome, so they guess—and they do so incorrectly.[10] Moreover, as the complexity of the decision-making situation increases, most people become more and more conservative. As a result they become increasingly inaccurate in assigning probabilities. Others stop trying to obtain additional information, even when it can be secured easily and inexpensively, and start relying more heavily on personal judgment. Still others fall prey to one of the biggest problems of subjective probability assignment: they overestimate the likelihood of rare events and underestimate the likelihood of common events.

What accounts for such behavior? Numerous personality traits can be cited, including aggression, autonomy, intelligence, and fear of failure. Whatever the reason, subjective rationality leads to erroneous decision making.

Rationalization

Many decision makers rationalize their choice

Empirical evidence also shows that many decision makers are rationalizers.[11] They go further than just choosing satisficing solutions: they choose those they can justify.

If time is short, the first feasible solution often is implemented. The decision maker rationalizes this choice by noting that there was no time for considering other possible solutions.

Even when a great deal of time is available, decision makers often make a final choice before examining all alternatives. As soon as this choice is made, all other alternatives are found to have some problem or shortcoming. As a result, the early choice becomes the final alternative. The decision maker defends or rationalizes this choice against all others. In the process the objectivity of rational decision making is replaced by the subjectivity of **bounded rationality**.

Bounded Rationality Process

As seen in Figure 5-3, eight steps are involved in bounded rationality. Notice that after the problem is identified or the goal is defined, a minimum level of acceptability is established. This is the satisficing factor at work. After a decision

---

[10] Cameron L. Peterson and Lee Roy Beach, ''Man as an Intuitive Statistician,'' *Psychological Bulletin* (July 1967):29–46. *See also:* Herbert A. Simon, ''Making Management Decisions: The Role of Intuition and Emotion,'' *Academy of Management Executive* (January 1987):57–64.
[11] Roger Hagafors and Berndt Brehmer, ''Does Having to Justify One's Judgments Change the Nature of the Judgment Process?'' *Organizational Behavior and Human Performance* (April 1983):223–32.

FIGURE 5-3   Bounded Rationality Model

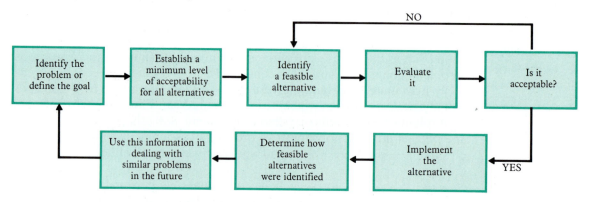

is implemented, it serves as a basis for dealing with similar problems in the future.

A close analysis of Figure 5-3 reveals that the bounded rationality model can save the manager a lot of time. It is also a more behaviorally acceptable approach for dealing with difficult or complex problems. So instead of comparing it with the rational decision-making model to determine which is better, let us simply say that the bounded rationality model shows more accurately how decision making is actually carried out.

IMPROVING DECISION-MAKING EFFECTIVENESS

The major concern of American industry today is increasing productivity (output/input). This concern is being addressed through improved decision-making effectiveness. Whether a manager follows the rational decision-making model or the bounded rationality model, he or she can improve decision-making effectiveness in several ways.[12] Depending on the particular situation, these include (1) the use of management science tools and techniques, (2) creativity, and (3) the matching of decision-making situations and leadership styles. The following discussion examines these three approaches to decision-making effectiveness.

Use of Management Science Tools and Techniques

In some cases more effective decisions can be made through the use of management science tools or techniques.[13] Commonly referred to as *operations re-*

---

[12] Herbert E. Kindler, "Decisions, Decisions: Which Approach To Take?" *Personnel* (January 1985):47–51. *See also:* Hillel J. Einhorn and Robin M. Hogarth, "Decision Making: Going Forward in Reverse," *Harvard Business Review* (January–February 1987):66–70.
[13] Jacob W. Ulvila and Rex V. Brown, "Decision Analysis Comes of Age," *Harvard Business Review* (September–October 1982):130–41.

search (OR), management science tools have four basic features: (1) they emphasize gathering and using information that helps the manager make a useful decision; (2) they try to determine the highest profit/lowest cost decision commensurate with the end results; (3) they employ mathematical models; and (4) they rely on the computer to perform the necessary mathematical calculations.

Quite often an organization will develop a specific OR tool or technique to help it solve a particular problem. In other cases there is already a prepackaged program for dealing with the problem. In either event, OR techniques have been used frequently to solve many different types of problems. Five of the most common techniques are described in the following discussion. In all but the last case, only a qualitative description of the technique is provided. There are two reasons for treating the subject in this way. First, our objective is to show how management science techniques can be of value in decision making, not how to perform quantitative analysis. Second, modern managers need to know what these tools can do, but they themselves do not need to know the specific mathematical mechanics except in the case of such "hands on" tools as decision trees, the last technique to be examined.

Inventory Problems

No firm wants to have too much inventory on hand. The greater the amount of inventory, the higher the cost of storage and insurance as well as the possibility that the goods will become obsolete or that demand for them will decline. On the other hand, if there is too little inventory on hand the organization will be continually running out of stock, the costs of ordering inventory will rise, and customers may soon turn to more reliable suppliers.

Balancing demand and carrying costs

How can inventory be balanced so that these problems do not occur? The answer is found in an OR program known as the **economic order quantity (EOQ) formula**. By taking the costs associated with carrying inventory and balancing them against annual demand for the product, an organization can determine an ideal inventory level. The formula tells how much to reorder each time.

The formula is

$$\sqrt{\frac{2(D)(F)}{(P)(C)}}$$

where D = expected annual demand

F = fixed cost associated with placing and receiving a single order

P = price per unit

C = carrying costs associated with storage, insurance, taxes, spoilage, etc., as a percentage of inventory value

To see how this formula works, assume that a manager has a product line with an expected annual demand of 500,000 units, a reorder cost of $10, a price of $100, and a carrying cost of 10 percent. Putting these values into the formula results in the following:

$$\sqrt{\frac{2(500,000)(\$10)}{(\$100)(.10)}} = \sqrt{\frac{10,000,000}{10}}$$
$$= \sqrt{1,000,000}$$
$$= 1,000$$

The manager should reorder 1,000 units every time. Ordering more units a lesser number of times drives up the carrying costs; ordering fewer units a greater number of times drives up the reordering costs. The EOQ formula helps the manager balance these two costs.

Of course, the manager does not actually compute the formula and place the order. Firms using the EOQ have their decision making computerized, so the computer tells the purchasing manager what to reorder and how many items to request. This determination is based on the current depletion of inventory, the EOQ, and the amount of time between when an order is placed and when it is filled. For example, if the current depletion of inventory is 10 units a day, the EOQ is 100 units, and delivery takes three days, the 100 units must be ordered at least three days before they are needed. Otherwise there will be a shortage of this good. The EOQ formula helps the organization manage its inventory problems.

Allocation Problems

Many times an organization finds that it has a large number of parts or materials to use for producing its products. If the organization has two or more product lines, however, it has to decide whether to put all the resources into one product line or to produce some of each. This is an allocation problem because the manager must determine how to allocate or assign parts for production.

One way of solving the problem is to produce as many units as possible of the most profitable product and allocate the remaining parts to the next most successful lines in the order of profitability. The most profitable product may take three times as many parts as the next most profitable line, however, thereby severely limiting the number that can be produced. So this is not always the best strategy for maximizing profit. In fact, sometimes the answer is to make a combination of product lines such as 500 units of product A, 350 units of product B, and 200 units of product C. The answer is determined by finding the ideal mix or the combination of products that will yield the highest profit. When the number of parts and product lines is more than a handful, this answer can be difficult to work out in one's head. In this case, OR can help. Linear program-

Ideal allocation of resources

ming formulas can quickly and easily determine the best mix. What is a difficult problem to work out mentally can be resolved via a mathematical approach.

Queuing Problems

Balancing
customer waiting
time and service

Queuing problems are waiting-line problems. These arise any time there is a need to balance service with waiting time. Numerous examples can be cited, from the time it takes to be served at the local supermarket to the time it takes to load a truck at the warehouse and send it on its way. The longer the waiting time, the greater the loss of business. Since many purchasers will not return to the store if they have to wait one hour in a supermarket line, the store needs to look into opening more checkout lines. In the case of the warehouse, the firm needs to examine the payoff from increasing the number of people loading the trucks as well as the cost of building more loading stations.

Of course, there is a limit to the amount of service the organization should provide. If service is too great, customers may be very happy and trucks may be loaded quickly but the business will lose money because the cost of the service more than outweighs any benefits. The cost curve associated with service is illustrated in Figure 5-4.

Using an OR approach known as the *queuing theory,* the organization can balance waiting lines and service. In this way waiting is reduced to an acceptable level while profit is maximized.

FIGURE 5-4
Cost and Service

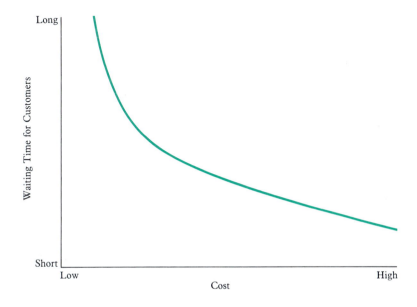

Replacement Problems

Over time every organization has to replace obsolete or worn-out machinery and equipment. If kept too long these assets become inefficient and increasingly expensive to operate. The question for the manager is: When should replacement take place?

There are OR programs that can answer this question, depending on its exact nature. For example, consider a large factory floor where there are thousands of overhead lights. When should each be replaced? There are basically two answers: as each goes out or all at once. An OR program for dealing with this problem can help compare the cost of replacing each light as it goes out with the cost of changing all of them at the same time. In most cases the company will replace all of the lights at a predetermined time because that is more cost effective.

Another typical replacement problem is determining when to fix worn or used machinery. By keeping a log on machine breakdown, the company can forecast the number of hours before the next breakdown will occur. Then it can decide whether to do preventive maintenance first or to go ahead with the next job. By simulating machine breakdown, OR can help the manager decide the best time for conducting preventive maintenance. Once again, an OR approach can produce an efficient answer.

Decision Trees

A **decision tree** is a graphic illustration of a management decision in which those aspects of a decision that are often implicit are made explicit. In constructing such a tree the manager begins by setting forth all of the alternative approaches to the problem, the payoffs associated with each, and the probability of success for each. From this information an expected value is then computed and the path with the greatest expected value is chosen for implementation. Figure 5-5 shows a decision tree for plant expansion.

In this decision tree, the manager is confronted with three alternatives for dealing with current production facilities: building a new plant, expanding the current one, or modernizing present facilities. The decision maker has determined that one of these alternatives must be implemented. The decision tree can help the manager make the choice. To see how it can help, let us first examine the tree in greater depth.

Note that the tree is constructed from left to right. The decision maker first identifies the alternatives under consideration. Next he or she determines the conditional value of each outcome. This is the value or benefit the firm will obtain under each of three possible economic states. For example, if the firm builds a new plant and the economy is strong, the company will make $3 million. If the economy is weak, the company will make only $400,000. Third, the decision maker determines the probability of each of these economic states. Notice that the likelihood of a strong economy is 0.25 while the likelihood of a

FIGURE 5-5   Decision Tree for Plant Expansion

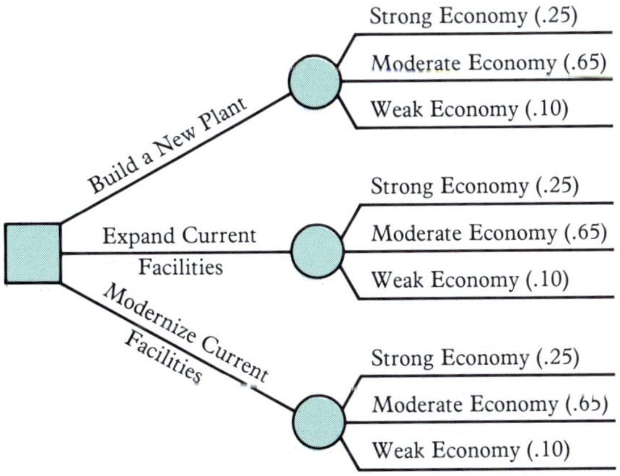

	Conditional Value for Each Outcome	Probability of Each Outcome	Expected Value of Each Outcome	Expected Value of Each Decision Alternative
Build a New Plant				
Strong Economy (.25)	$3,000,000	.25	$750,000	
Moderate Economy (.65)	1,000,000	.65	650,000	
Weak Economy (.10)	400,000	.10	40,000	$1,440,000
Expand Current Facilities				
Strong Economy (.25)	2,000,000	.25	500,000	
Moderate Economy (.65)	1,500,000	.65	975,000	
Weak Economy (.10)	100,000	.10	10,000	1,485,000*
Modernize Current Facilities				
Strong Economy (.25)	1,000,000	.25	250,000	
Moderate Economy (.65)	500,000	.65	325,000	
Weak Economy (.10)	300,000	.10	30,000	605,000

*Alternative to implement.

The expected value for each decision alternative is determined

moderate economy is 0.65 and the likelihood of a weak economy is 0.10. Fourth, he or she computes the expected value of each outcome by multiplying the conditional value by the probability of its occurrence. Finally, the decision maker computes the expected values of each decision alternative by adding up the expected values for each of its outcomes. In Figure 5-5 the highest expected value is associated with expanding current facilities, so that is the alternative the manager should implement.

Decision trees are useful for nonrecurring events

Decision trees are very useful in helping managers deal with nonrecurring events. They help decision makers see clearly the alternatives and the likely outcomes of each. Two points of clarification are in order, however. First, once the manager has constructed the decision tree, assigned the probabilities, and computed the expected values of each alternative, he or she must choose the one with the highest expected value. The manager cannot go back and say, "Oh, I've always wanted to build a new plant so let's do that." If this is what the manager wanted all along, why did he or she waste time with decision-tree analysis? Decision trees help the manager analyze alternatives objectively, and the answer they point to should be implemented, not altered. Second, in interpreting decision trees, the manager must remember that the expected values are only relative measures of values used to compare one alternative with another. For example, if the firm expands current facilities and the economy is

From King of Beers to King of Theme Parks?

Anheuser-Busch (A-B) has been working aggressively during the last decade to dominate the U.S. beer market. The results are apparent as A-B has increased its market share from 28 percent in 1980 to 41 percent in 1989 with the Budweiser brand controlling 27 percent of the total market. Profits have grown at a compound annual rate of 19 percent during the decade of the 80s while national per capita beer consumption has decreased almost 4 percent during the same period.

In the midst of a turbulent environment facing the beer industry, A-B has diversified into a number of other businesses including food, transportation, real estate, professional baseball, and theme parks, and it is the theme park business that Chairman August A. Busch III has the most interest in. Already owning four theme parks, including two Busch Gardens, late in 1989 A-B purchased five theme parks owned by Harcourt Brace Jovanovich, Inc. (HBJ): three Sea Worlds, Boardwalk & Baseball, and Cypress Gardens.

Until the purchase, the theme park business had accounted for only 2 percent of Anheuser-Busch's sales. However, the acquisition of HBJ's parks more than doubled A-B's sales to $490 million. In addition, August A. Busch III is planning to open a $300 million theme park in Spain on the Mediterranean coast. The 2,000 acre park will represent what Busch calls "Anheuser-Busch's Footprint in Europe." Since Anheuser-Busch witnessed a 31 percent increase in profits in their four initial theme parks, the strategy looks promising indeed!

* *Source:* Julia Flynn Silver, "Even August Busch Can Only Handle So Much Beer," *Business Week* (September 25, 1989):182–87.

strong, the company will make $2 million. It will not earn the expected value of $1,485,000. Depending on the state of the economy, the firm will earn $2 million, $1.5 million, or $100,000.[14]

Creativity and Group Decision Making

In some cases decision making can be improved through the use of creativity or group decision analysis or both. This is particularly true when the problem requires an innovative or unique approach as illustrated by Anheuser-Busch (see "Management in Practice: From King of Beers to King of Theme Parks?").

---

[14] For more on decision-tree analysis, see Efrain Turban and Jack R. Meredith, *Fundamentals of Management Science,* 3rd ed. (Dallas, TX: Business Publications, Inc., 1985), Chapter 4.

Creative Thinking Process

Creative thinking and decision making actually go hand in hand. In particular, creative thinking can help generate alternative solutions to the problem under review.[15] The **creative thinking process** involves four steps: preparation, incubation, illumination, and verification.

First comes mental readiness . . .

Preparation is the stage in which the decision maker gets ready mentally. During this period he or she gathers all of the available information on the problem. This stage involves problem definition and analysis. At this time the decision maker becomes saturated with data.

then subconscious analysis . . .

After gathering data the decision maker sits back and lets his or her subconscious mind work on the problem. This is the *incubation* period. During this time the brain analyzes and rearranges information, often presenting it in a new or innovative way. At this stage the decision maker also develops alternative solutions to problems. Of course, if no solution is forthcoming after a period of time, such as 10 days, the decision maker is wise to go back to the preparation stage and review the data again.

followed by an answer . . .

In the *illumination* stage the decision maker realizes the answer to the problem. The answer usually does not come like a bolt out of the blue. More commonly it comes in bits and pieces, revealing itself slowly. This characteristic of illumination is particularly true in the case of complex problems. As the decision maker works out parts of the problem, he or she writes them down until the entire solution has been determined.

which is then refined and used

Verification is the last stage of creative thinking and involves testing the answer. In most cases there is a need to refine or rethink some part of it. For example, an inventor usually has to do some trial-and-error work to eliminate minor bugs. Modification and improvement smooths the way for implementing the solution.

Brainstorming

Sometimes creative thinking is an individual process but groups can use it as well. In fact, groups are often superior to individuals when it comes to generating creative ideas. One of the most popular approaches to group creative thinking is brainstorming.[16]

Brainstorming encourages imaginative, creative solutions

Brainstorming was developed by Alex F. Osborn as a method of encouraging creative thinking in an advertising agency. Since then the technique has been applied in many situations where the objective is to obtain a large number of ideas for solving a problem. A brainstorming session begins with the group

---

[15] Charles E. Wilson, "Managerial Mind Sets and the Structural Side of Managing," *Business Horizons* (November–December 1983):21–27. Also, see Timothy A. Matherly and Ronald E. Goldsmith, "The Two Faces of Creativity," *Business Horizons* (September–October 1985):8–11.
[16] Joseph H. Boyett, "The Creative Force," *Entrepreneur* (July 1989):55–64.

leader telling the members the problem under analysis and encouraging them to be as imaginative and creative as possible in their recommended solutions. During the session criticism is forbidden, and group members can say what they want. Emphasis is placed on quantity, and as one group member calls out ideas, other group members are allowed to combine some of them or improve them in any way they see fit.

These sessions usually last from 40 to 60 minutes and involve six to nine participants. The members sit around a table, so that they are able to communicate quickly and easily. As ideas are called out, a secretary or recording machine keeps track of what is said. In some cases ideas are written down on a blackboard so that group members can expand or piggyback on them more easily.

Of course, many of the ideas thrown out may be of little value. Some are superficial, others too imaginative to be workable. To the extent that brainstorming helps generate plausible solutions that could not be obtained in routine ways, however, it is a valuable decision-making technique.

Gordon Technique

Another group participation, problem-solving technique has been developed by William J. Gordon. It is used for handling technical problems.[17] Commonly referred to as the **Gordon technique**, it is similar to brainstorming in that it employs free association. When this approach is used, however, only the group leader knows the problem under consideration. He or she gives a hint or a stimulus to the other group members, and the discussion begins.

The Gordon technique addresses technical problems

> For example, if the group leader wanted the participants to come up with ideas on auto engine designs that might lead to better mileage, the key phrase might be "better mileage." From here the members would toss out all sorts of ideas. Some ideas might be valuable in redesigning current engines, while others might be more useful on some other project in the future. In any event, the Gordon technique is an excellent method for obtaining creative ideas for solving technical problems.[18]

In most cases the group sessions last from two to three hours. The members often come from diverse backgrounds, although all are capable of understanding and responding to the technical problem. As with brainstorming, in most cases group size is six to nine people. With this technique a blackboard is always used so that ideas can be written down and seen by all.

When creative solutions for technical problems are needed, the Gordon

---

[17] Charles S. Whiting, "Operational Techniques of Creative Thinking," *Advanced Management Journal* (October 1955):28.
[18] Richard M. Hodgetts, *Introduction to Business,* 3rd ed. (Reading, MA: Addison-Wesley Publishing, 1984):471.

technique can be very useful. In particular it provides an approach for generating innovative solutions to what is often a mechanistic, engineering oriented challenge. The result can be a solution superior to that obtained by typical individual or group decision-making processes.[19]

Matching Decision-Making Situations and Leadership Styles

Some researchers have noted that decision-making effectiveness can also be improved by matching leadership styles and problem situations. In illustrating how this can be done, let us first identify five types of management decision styles:

There are five types of management decision styles

1. The manager can solve the problem or make the decision personally by using the information that is available at that point in time.
2. The manager can obtain the necessary information from the subordinates, and then decide on the solution to the problem. In obtaining the information the manager may or may not tell the subordinates what the problem is. Their role in making the decision is confined solely to providing the necessary information rather than generating or evaluating alternative solutions.
3. The manager can share the problem with relevant subordinates on an individual basis, obtaining their ideas and suggestions without bringing them together as a group. Then a decision, which may or may not represent the views of the subordinates, can be made.
4. The manager can share the problem with the subordinates as a group, collectively obtain their ideas and suggestions, and then make a decision that may or may not reflect the subordinates' influence.
5. The manager can share the problem with the subordinates as a group. Together all can generate and evaluate alternatives and try to reach a consensus on a solution. The manager's role here is one of a chairperson. The manager does not try to influence the group to adopt his or her solution, and he or she is willing to accept and implement any solution that has the support of the entire group.[20]

Using diagnostic questions to choose decision styles

In deciding which of these decision styles to use, the manager asks a series of diagnostic questions. The answers to these questions help the individual decide what to do. These seven questions are presented in Figure 5-6. A close examination of the figure reveals that the questions at the top (A through G) help dictate which of the five decision styles to use. For example, if the manager

---

[19] Frank J. Sabatine, "Rediscovering Creativity: Unlocking Old Habits," *Mid-American Journal of Business* (Fall 1989):11–13.
[20] Victor H. Vroom, "A New Look at Managerial Decision Making," *Organizational Dynamics* (January 1973):67.

FIGURE 5-6   A Decision Process Flow Chart

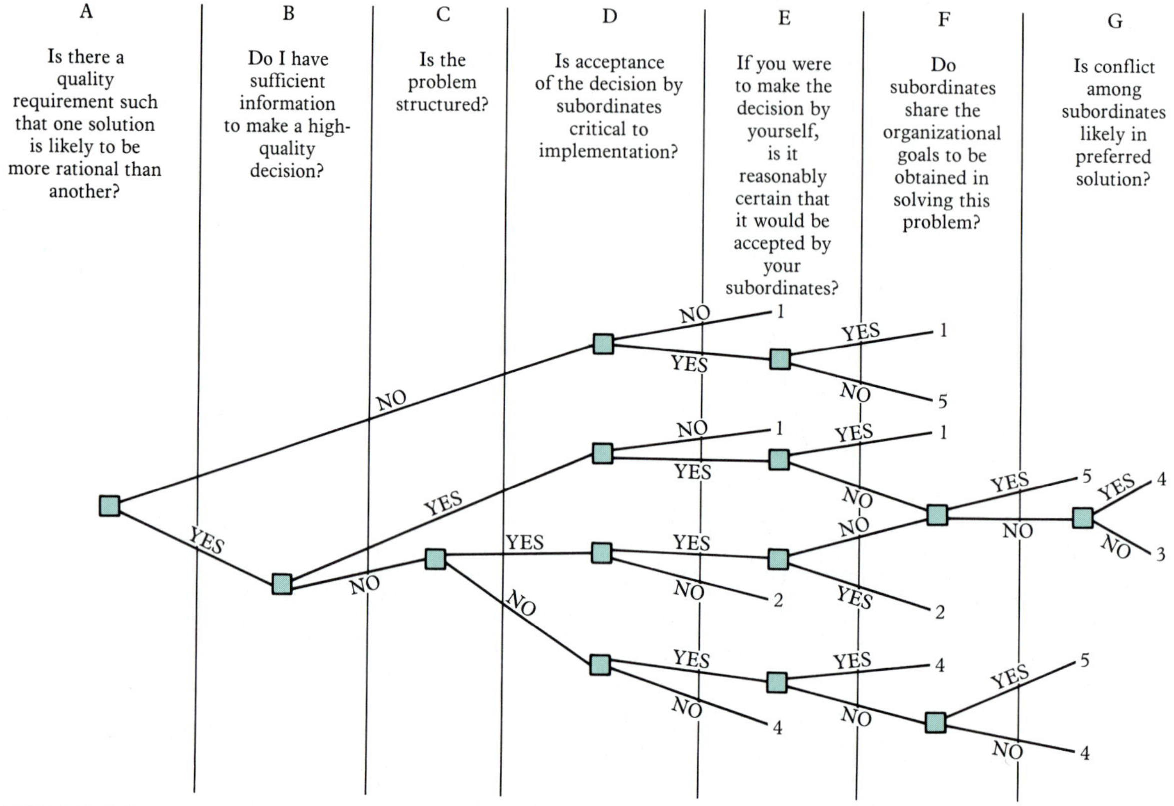

A	B	C	D	E	F	G
Is there a quality requirement such that one solution is likely to be more rational than another?	Do I have sufficient information to make a high-quality decision?	Is the problem structured?	Is acceptance of the decision by subordinates critical to implementation?	If you were to make the decision by yourself, is it reasonably certain that it would be accepted by your subordinates?	Do subordinates share the organizational goals to be obtained in solving this problem?	Is conflict among subordinates likely in preferred solution?

feels that there is a quality requirement such that one solution is likely to be more rational than another (question A) and acceptance of the decision by subordinates is not critical to implementation (question D), then management decision style #1 should be used. The manager can solve the problem or make the decision personally by using the information that is available at that point in time. The same logic can be used in going through all of the other paths in the flow chart.

This framework for analyzing decision making is very useful. It helps the manager identify the various approaches that can be employed in making decisions. At the same time it offers flexibility. For example, if the manager has a group problem, he or she can share it with subordinates on an individual basis (management decision style #3) or in a group (management decision style #5). There is no one set way of handling everything. As Victor Vroom, one of the individuals who helped develop Figure 5-6, has noted, however, when several management styles are possible, the manager should select the one that will cost the least in terms of time or resources. Thus some judgment on the manager's part is involved in the process. The decision process flow chart is only a recommended guideline for improving decision making; it is not a mechanistic approach for solving all problems.

SUMMARY

1. Decision making is the process of choosing from among alternatives. Sometimes this process is a simple one and rules, policies, procedures, or basic quantitative analysis can be used in making the decision. At other times the process is a complex one and requires the manager to draw on intuition, judgment, gut feeling, and highly mathematical tools and techniques.

2. In understanding the basic nature of decision making, the manager needs to know four things. The first is how to review the situation properly. In doing so, there are three questions the manager must answer: Will the problem resolve itself? Does the issue require a personal decision? How should the problem be handled? The second thing the manager should know is the difference between programmed and nonprogrammed decisions. The third is the conditions under which decision making is carried out: certainty, risk, and uncertainty. The fourth is the guidelines for making effective decisions.

3. When making decisions under risk conditions, the manager needs to make probability assignments. These allow him or her to determine what combination of profit and probability of success each alternative offers. The result is known as the expected value. By comparing the expected values of all alternatives, the manager can opt for the alternative with the greatest expected value.

4. When making decisions under conditions of uncertainty, the manager feels unable to assign probability estimates to any of the alternatives. As a result, he or she may use the mathematical techniques that have been developed to help deal with this problem. Other suggestions include simply avoiding situations of uncertainty, assuming that the future will be like the past and assigning probabilities based on previous experiences, and gathering as much information as possible about each alternative while assuming that the decision is being made under a condition of risk and assigning probabilities accordingly.

5. Rational decision making consists of seven basic steps: (1) uncovering the symptoms, (2) identifying the problem or defining the goal, (3) developing decision criteria, (4) developing alternative solutions, (5)

determining all alternative solution outcomes, (6) selecting the best alternative, and (7) implementing the decision.

6. Bounded rationality considerations refine the rational decision-making model. These considerations include satisficing behavior, simplification, subjective rationality, and rationalization. The result is a bounded rationality model consisting of the following steps: (1) identifying the problem or defining the goals; (2) establishing a minimum level of acceptability for all alternatives; (3) identifying a feasible alternative; (4) evaluating it; (5) determining whether it is acceptable; (6) if it is not, going back to step three — if it is, implementing the alternative; (7) determining how feasible alternatives were discovered; and (8) using this information in dealing with similar problems in the future.

7. Decision making can be improved in a number of different ways. One is by using management science tools and techniques. Some of the most helpful include those that solve inventory, allocation, and replacement problems. Another important tool is the decision tree. By determining the alternatives, the conditional values for each outcome, the probability of each outcome, and the expected value of each outcome, the decision maker can determine the expected value of each decision alternative. The decision alternative with the largest expected value is then chosen for implementation.

8. Creative thinking involves four steps: preparation, incubation, illumination, and verification. During the preparation stage the decision maker gets ready mentally. During incubation he or she sits back and lets the subconscious mind work on the problem. During the illumination period the solution comes to the decision maker. During the verification period the answer is tested, and modified if necessary, to smooth the way for implementation.

9. Brainstorming is a group approach to creative thinking. The group leader tells the group members the problem under analysis and encourages them to be as imaginative and creative as possible. Criticism is forbidden; freewheeling is encouraged; and individuals are allowed to combine ideas or piggyback on them in an effort to improve them. The Gordon Technique is another group creative thinking approach. However, it is used only to deal with technical problems. The group leader does not spell out the problem but rather gives the participants only a hint or stimulus before the discussion begins.

10. Some researchers have noted that decision-making effectiveness can also be improved by matching styles and problem situations. The five styles described in the latter part of the chapter are combined with the problem situations presented in Figure 5-6 to illustrate this idea. Managers who want to improve their decision making can use this type of approach to help them make more effective decisions.

KEY TERMS

Administrative man   An individual who looks for a course of action that is satisfactory or good enough.

Bounded rationality   A model of decision making that illustrates how most managers make decisions by requiring minimum levels of acceptability and using "satisficing" criteria.

Brainstorming   A group creative-thinking technique. It involves telling the group members what the problem is and then encouraging them to be as imaginative as possible, allowing each to expand and piggyback on the ideas of others in the group in an effort to improve earlier suggestions.

Certainty   A decision-making condition under which the manager has enough information to know the outcome of the decision before it is made.

Creative thinking process   A process used for generating innovative or unique approaches to problem solving. It consists of four steps: preparation, incubation, illumination, and verification.

Decision tree   A graphic illustration of a management decision that shows the various alternatives, the conditional values of each outcome, the probabilities of each outcome, the expected value of each outcome, and the expected value of each decision alternative.

Economic man   An individual who always strives to implement the decision that will provide the maximum payoff.

Economic order quantity (EOQ) formula   An inventory control formula. The purpose of the EOQ is to balance demand for a product against the costs associated with carrying the inventory.

Gordon technique   A group participation, group problem-solving technique that is commonly used for handling technical problems. The group leader gives the group members a hint or stimulus about the problem and encourages them to be as creative as possible in arriving at suggested solutions.

Nonprogrammed decisions   Decisions that are unique or out of the ordinary. They are often ill structured and are handled by judgment, intuition, and creativity.

Programmed decisions   Decisions that rely upon habit, routine, standard operating procedures, or some other well-defined method.

Rational decision-making process   A process that describes how decisions are made in the ideal. It involves the following steps: (1) uncovering the symptoms, (2) identifying the problem or defining the goal, (3) developing decision criteria, (4) developing alternative solutions, (5) determining all alternative solution outcomes, (6) selecting the best alternative, and (7) implementing the decision.

Risk   A decision-making condition under which the manager has some information regarding the outcome of the decision but does not know everything.

Satisficing behavior   Decision-making behavior in which the individual chooses a course of action that is merely satisfactory or good enough.

Subjective rationality   The assignment of probabilities based on personal judgment.

Uncertainty   A decision-making condition under which the manager feels incapable of assigning probabilities to the various outcomes.

QUESTIONS FOR ANALYSIS AND DISCUSSION

1. In handling simple problems, a decision maker often relies on rules, policies, procedures, and basic quantitative analysis. In handling complex problems, a decision maker employs intuition, judgment, gut feeling, and highly mathematical tools and techniques. Are these two statements accurate? Explain.

2. What are the three questions a manager should ask when reviewing a decision-making situation? Briefly discuss each.

3. How do programmed decisions differ from nonprogrammed decisions? Compare and contrast the two.

4. Decisions are made under one of three possible conditions: certainty, risk, and uncertainty. What does this statement mean? Be complete in your answer.

5. Are there any guidelines that can help a manager improve his or her effectiveness? State and explain at least five.

6. How does the rational decision-making process work? Describe each of the steps. Then compare it with the bounded rationality model. How are the two similar? How do they differ?

7. What is meant by the term "satisficing behavior"? How does it help describe decision-making behavior?

8. In what way do the following characteristics describe decision making in action: simplification, subjective rationality, and rationalization? Explain.

9. How can management science tools and techniques be of value in dealing with problems in these areas: inventory, allocation, and replacement? Explain each.

10. In your own words, what is a decision tree? How can a decision tree help the manager make effective decisions? Be complete in your answer.

11. How can leadership styles be tied together with decision-making situations? Explain, being sure to include the steps in Figure 5-6 in your answer.

CASE

One, Two, or Three

For the last six months Chuck Beatty, a product development manager, has been engaged in the design and market testing of three new electronic games. Chuck's company has five product development managers. Each is responsible for working with the design, engineering, and manufacturing departments to produce one electronic game every six months. Each is also responsible for working with three marketing people to market-test the product. Since the company puts such an emphasis on turning out a winner each time, it is typical for each product development manager to start with three to five games and, for either technical or marketing reasons, to reduce the final choice to one. Over the last two years Chuck has had the best-selling game each time. The other product development managers admit Chuck is the best. He would like to keep it this way.

  The next new electronic game is to be presented by the product development managers to the manufacturing and marketing executives in six days. Right now Chuck is in the throes of making a final decision. He has taken all of the manufacturing data he has available and constructed the decision tree in Exhibit 1.

EXHIBIT 1   Decision Tree

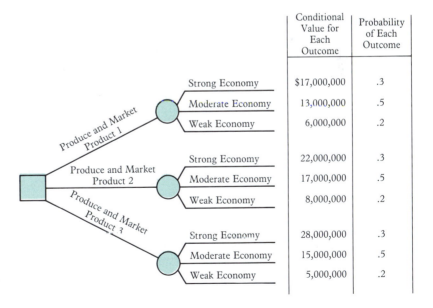

	Conditional Value for Each Outcome	Probability of Each Outcome
Produce and Market Product 1		
Strong Economy	$17,000,000	.3
Moderate Economy	13,000,000	.5
Weak Economy	6,000,000	.2
Produce and Market Product 2		
Strong Economy	22,000,000	.3
Moderate Economy	17,000,000	.5
Weak Economy	8,000,000	.2
Produce and Market Product 3		
Strong Economy	28,000,000	.3
Moderate Economy	15,000,000	.5
Weak Economy	5,000,000	.2

To the best of his knowledge, this tree is accurate. The marketing people on the project have told him, however, that a new survey they conducted last week shows that forecasted profits for product 1 may be 35 to 50 percent higher than initial estimates suggested. Chuck is unsure whether to include this information or go with what he has currently. Time is short, and he must make a final decision soon.

1. Describe Chuck's decision-making process. Is it closer to the rational or bounded rationality process? Explain in detail.
2. Is Chuck making a decision under conditions of certainty, risk, or uncertainty? Defend your answer.
3. Drawing upon the information in the decision tree, decide which product Chuck should opt for. Would your answer change if the conditional profits for product 1 were increased by 40 percent? Explain.

YOU BE THE CONSULTANT

The $10 Million Project

Memorial Hospital has been in existence for more than 80 years. Built just after the turn of the century, Memorial has expanded its facilities three times. Today the hospital has 575 beds and offers a wide range of health services. In fact, a large portion of the institution's budget is spent for medical equipment and research.

A recent survey conducted in the local community reveals that Memorial Hospital is considered to be the best health care facility in the city. In an effort to keep this reputation, Mary McKenna, the hospital administrator, is planning a $10 million capital expenditure proposal designed to increase the number of beds, the overall facilities, and the health care services. At the present time she has a report put together by an outside consulting group that shows that the local population will grow by 44 percent during the next 10 years. A large percentage of this growth will be among the elderly (60 years and older), which is not surprising since Memorial is located in a major southeastern city famous for its mild winters.

Based on an analysis of this consulting report, Mary's initial conclusion is that the hospital will need to increase the number of beds by 75 and expand its emergency room and outpatient services to approximately double their present size. By coupling these demands with the other changes needed to modernize the facilities, Mary has arrived at an initial estimate of $10 million. Before taking this proposal to the board of trustees, however, she wants to work up the report in depth so that every part of it is clear and can be justified.

Mary believes that the best way to do this is to call together her immediate subordinates and discuss the proposal with them. In analyzing the decision process, she has concluded that (1) there is not a quality requirement such that one solution is likely to be more rational than another; (2) acceptance of the decision by the subordinates is critical to implementation; and (3) the subordinates do indeed share the organizational goals to be obtained in solving this problem. Mary also believes that a creative approach to writing and presenting the report might be helpful. It would help pull together all of the data in a unique way and might go a long way toward selling the trustees on the proposal.

Over the last five years, under Mary's direction, Memorial has made money each year. Prior to her arrival, however, the hospital head managed finances poorly, and Mary knows that many of the board members are fiscally conservative. She is going to have to do a good selling job to get them to go along with her proposal. Among other things, she will have to show the board how the expenditure will result in increased revenue and maintenance of the hospital's current reputation. Some of the board's biggest arguments are going to be: "Why do we need to spend all of this money? What are we going to get for this? Is this really a wise decision? Can't we accomplish almost the same thing for a lot less?"

Mary has decided to use the next six months getting everything in order. Then she will give the board members a copy of her report, ask them to read it over and note their questions, and schedule a day for intensive discussion. Mary is convinced that this selling job will take almost six months, but she can do it if she lays the proper groundwork now.

Your Consultation

Assume that you are Mary's personal consultant. Help her better understand how to put this report together and present it. First, explain the decision-making process she should use. Second, help her match this decision-making situation with her leadership style in dealing with subordinates. (Use Figure 5-6 to assist you.) Third, describe to her how creativity in decision making can be promoted and tell whether such an approach would have any value. Fourth, drawing upon your study of the material in this chapter, tell her anything else you believe would be helpful to her. Be as complete as possible in your recommendations.

6

The
Fundamentals
of Planning

This chapter examines the fundamentals of planning—the ideas and concepts that every manager should know. Its subject matter extends from the nature of planning to the planning process to the methods and techniques that can be used in putting the process into operation. When you have completed your reading and study of the material in this chapter, you will be able to:

1. Define the term planning and discuss key factors that influence planning time horizons.
2. Explain what is meant by a purpose or mission statement and describe its value to a modern organization.
3. List some of the major types of goals pursued by modern organizations and state four general conclusions that can be drawn about these organizations.
4. Explain how a strategy differs from an objective and how such approaches as gap analysis and a strategic issues orientation can be of value in strategy formulation.
5. Compare and contrast policies, procedures, rules, programs, and budgets, and explain how each can be of value to the modern manager in planning.
6. Describe the planning process in detail, including in your description a comparison of strategic, intermediate, and operational plans, a

description of forecasting techniques, an explanation of how alternative courses of action are chosen, and a discussion of the value of budgeting.

7. Discuss how management by objectives can be of value in carrying out the planning process.

THE NATURE OF PLANNING

Planning is the process of setting objectives and then determining the steps needed to attain them. Of course, planning actually begins before objectives are set; it starts with an analysis of the environment for the purpose of determining which objectives to pursue. Then when the analysis has been completed, objectives are set, and the organization has the direction it needs for developing a plan of action.[1]

Planning Horizons

There are three time horizons: long-, intermediate-, and short-range

Specific instances of planning can be categorized according to their *time horizons:* **long-range planning** covers more than five years, **intermediate-range planning** covers one to five years, and **short-range planning** covers less than one year. Top managers are typically responsible for drawing up the long-range plan, while middle managers develop the intermediate-range plan, and lower-level managers work up the short-range plan. Figure 6-1 describes the planning horizons of a typical medium-sized firm. For a large firm these horizons would extend farther into the future, while for a small organization they would move closer to the present.

Many factors affect these time horizons

Time horizons are affected by a number of factors. In many business firms, one of the most common is the *length of time required to recover capital funds* invested in plant and equipment. For example, if a company buys $5 million worth of new machinery, it should have a plan showing how this money will be recovered. A second factor is the *lead time* for the products or the industry at large. Many firms engaging in research and development (R&D) have five- to ten-year plans, while many retail organizations get by with much shorter time horizons. The R&D company has to take a product through a very long cycle before it gets to the customer, while a retailer is most concerned with seasonal sales and some general long-range planning. A third factor is *competitiveness* in the industry. The greater this competitiveness, the more likely it is that management will emphasize the short- and intermediate-range plans that will

---

[1]*See:* Vasudevan Ramujam and N. Venkatraman, "Planning and Performance: A New Look at an Old Question," *Business Horizons* (May–June 1987): 19–25.

FIGURE 6-1   Planning Horizons at Different Hierarchical Levels

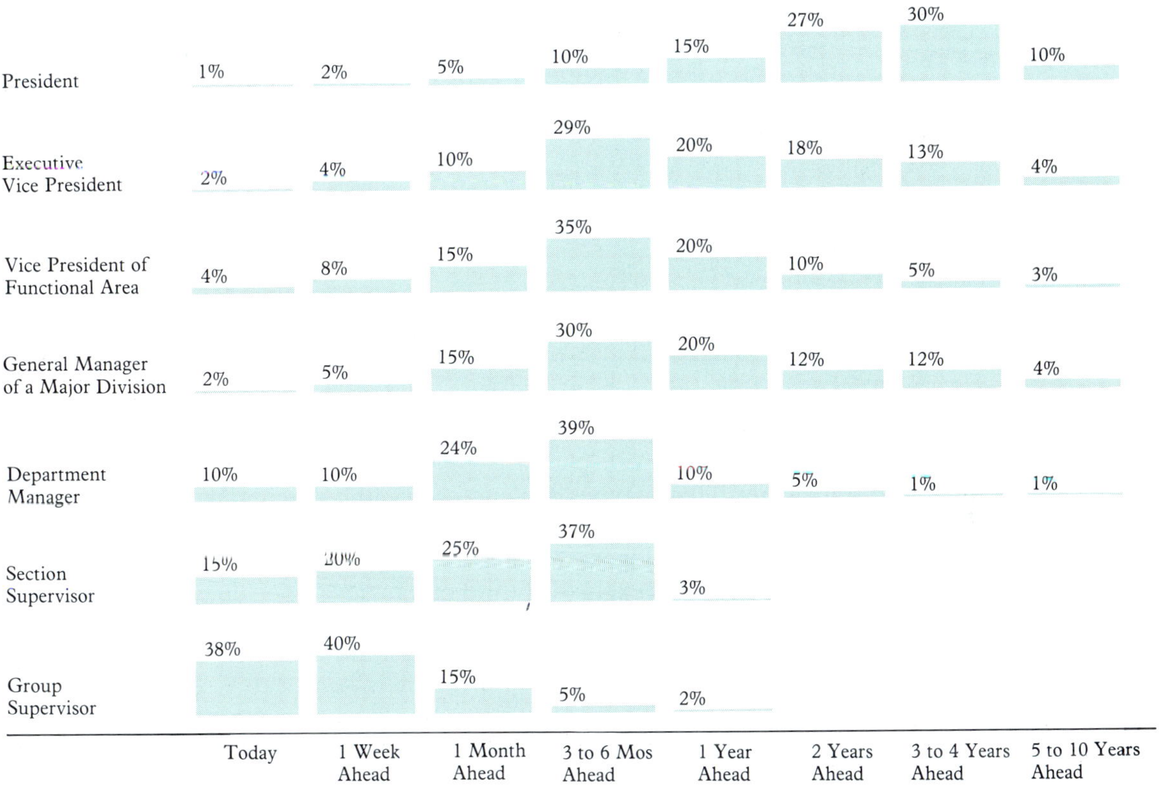

	Today	1 Week Ahead	1 Month Ahead	3 to 6 Mos Ahead	1 Year Ahead	2 Years Ahead	3 to 4 Years Ahead	5 to 10 Years Ahead
President	1%	2%	5%	10%	15%	27%	30%	10%
Executive Vice President	2%	4%	10%	29%	20%	18%	13%	4%
Vice President of Functional Area	4%	8%	15%	35%	20%	10%	5%	3%
General Manager of a Major Division	2%	5%	15%	30%	20%	12%	12%	4%
Department Manager	10%	10%	24%	39%	10%	5%	1%	1%
Section Supervisor	15%	30%	25%	37%	3%			
Group Supervisor	38%	40%	15%	5%	2%			

Source: Reprinted with permission of *Business Month* magazine (April 1957). Copyright © 1957 by Business Magazine Corporation, 38 Commercial Wharf, Boston, MA 02110.

help it respond to changing events. A fourth factor is organizational *size relative to others* in the industry. The larger the firm, the more likely it is that the company will have longer planning horizons.[2]

Given the varying nature of organizations and their environments, it is impossible to establish rigid time-horizon guidelines. Except for the very smallest organizations, however, all prepare short-range plans. Many small and medium-sized firms and virtually all large enterprises have intermediate-range plans. Many medium-sized and large organizations have all three time-horizon plans: short-, intermediate-, and long-range.[3]

[2] Philip H. Thurston, "Should Smaller Companies Make Plans?" *Harvard Business Review* (September–October 1983):162–63+.
[3] Ronald D. Michman, "Why Forecast for the Long Term?" *Journal of Business Strategy* (September-October 1989):36–41. *See also:* John G. Keane, "Focusing on the Future: Not a Trivial Pursuit," *Business Horizons* (January–February 1987):25–33.

TABLE 6-1 Types of Plans Developed at Different Hierarchical Levels			
	Top Management	Middle Management	Lower-Level Management
Purposes or Missions	X		
Objectives	X	X	X
Strategies	X		
Policies	X	X	
Procedures		X	X
Rules		X	X
Programs	X	X	X
Budgets	X	X	X

Types of Plans

There are many different types of plans, each with a different purpose. The most common are purposes or missions, objectives, strategies, policies, procedures, rules, programs, and budgets. These plans very in nature and scope, with some developed at one level exclusively and others developed at every level. Table 6-1 shows the level(s) at which each type of plan commonly is prepared.

Purposes or Missions

The **purpose or mission** of an organization is its underlying aim or thrust. Large firms often express their aims in the form of mission statements. Small firms do not, although the mission is known to the owner-manager and is often a reflection of the individual's personal values and philosophy.

Missions are usually stated in product or market terms. The following are general examples for different types of organizations:

Type of Firm	Basic Mission
Insurance Firm	To provide personal financial planning and protection
Airline	To provide fast, efficient, and economic air transportation for people and freight.
Oil Company	To meet the energy needs of an increasing population.
Fertilizer Manufacturer	To improve food production throughout the world through the manufacture of multipurpose fertilizers.
Compact Car Manufacturer	To provide economical, efficient automobiles.

Mission statements are often broadly based and very encompassing. A bronze plaque on the Lever House in London reads as follows: "The mission of our company, as William Hasketh Lever saw it, is to make cleanliness common-place, to lessen work for women, to foster health, and to contribute to personal attractiveness that life may be more enjoyable for the people who use our products." Other statements are multidirectional in nature.

> Hallmark is on a diversification drive into specialty publishing, broadcast-ing, and crayons—and may eventually embrace such far-flung industries as insurance and computer software.[4]

Mission statements set the stage for planning. They determine the com-petitive arena in which the business will operate and how resources will be allocated. George Steiner, a leading authority on planning, notes that such statements

Missions are usually stated in market or product terms

> . . . make much easier the task of identifying the opportunities and threats that must be addressed in the planning process. They open up new opportu-nities, as well as new threats, when changed. They prevent people from "spinning their wheels" in working on strategies and plans that may be considered completely inappropriate by top management.[5]

Objectives

Objectives, often called goals, are the ends toward which activity is aimed. In planning, objectives flow from the purpose or mission statement but are much more specific. Most organizations have multiple objectives. Table 6-2 provides an example.

Although business organizations pursue many different kinds of objec-tives, economic goals tend to predominate. The most common include profit-ability, growth, and market share. Table 6-3 shows the range of corporate goals in 82 firms in four basic industries. The table reveals that after these three economic objectives, several noneconomic goals, including social responsibil-ity and employee welfare, are the most popular. Then come goals that emerged during the last decade, including maintenance of financial stability, conserva-tion of resources, multinational expansion, and consolidation.

Profitability, growth, and market share are common objectives

What must be remembered is that these goals vary in accordance with both industrial group and company size (see Tables 6-4 and 6-5). Some general conclusions can be drawn, however, regarding corporate objectives during the 1980s. After conducting an interindustry analysis of firms in chemicals and drugs, paper and containers, electrical products and electronics, and food pro-cessing, Y. K. Shetty reports:

---

[4] Jeff Roberts, "Irv Hockaday is Leaving His Mark on Hallmark: Diversity," *Business Week* (November 12, 1984):73–76.
[5] George A. Steiner, *Strategic Planning: What Every Manager Must Know* (New York: The Free Press, 1979), 156.

TABLE 6-2   Hewlett-Packard's Corporate Objectives

Profit. To achieve sufficient profit to finance our company growth and to provide the resources we need to achieve our other corporate objectives.

Customers. To provide products and services of the greatest possible value to our customers, thereby gaining and holding their respect and loyalty.

Field of interest. To enter new fields only when the ideas we have, together with our technical, manufacturing and marketing skills, assure that we can make a needed and profitable contribution to the field.

Growth. To let our growth be limited only by our profits and our ability to develop and produce technical products that satisfy real customer needs.

People. To help our own people share in the company's success, which they make possible; to provide job security based on their performance, to recognize their individual achievements, and to help them gain a sense of satisfaction and accomplishment from their work.

Management. To foster initiative and creativity by allowing the individual great freedom of action in attaining well-defined objectives.

Citizenship. To honor our obligations to society by being an economic, intellectual and social asset to each nation and each community in which we operate.

Source: Y. K. Shetty, "New Look at Corporate Goals," *California Management Review* (Winter 1979):72, © 1979 by the Regents of the University of California. Reprinted from the *California Management Review,* Vol. 22, No. 2. By permission of The Regents.

TABLE 6-3   Range of Corporate Goals

Category	Number	Percent*
Profitability	73	89
Growth	67	82
Market Share	54	66
Social Responsibility	53	65
Employee Welfare	51	62
Product Quality and Service	49	60
Research and Development	44	54
Diversification	42	51
Efficiency	41	50
Financial Stability	40	49
Resource Conservation	32	39
Management Development	29	35
Multinational Enterprise	24	29
Consolidation	14	17
Miscellaneous Other Goals	15	18

* Adds to more than 100 percent because most companies have more than one goal.
Source: Y. K. Shetty, "New Look at Corporate Goals," *California Management Review* (Winter 1979):73. © 1979 by the Regents of the University of California. Reprinted from the *California Management Review,* Vol. 22, No. 2. By permission of The Regents.

TABLE 6-4   The Five Most Frequently Cited Goals of Corporations in Four Industrial Groups

Chemicals and Drugs ($n = 19$)		Paper and Containers ($n = 17$)		Electrical and Electronics ($n = 24$)		Food Processing ($n = 22$)	
1. Profitability	79%	Profitability	100%	Profitability	96%	Growth	91%
2. Social Responsibility	74	Growth	94	Growth	88	Profitability	86
3. Research and Development	63	Social Responsibility	59	Research and Development	83	Market Share	82
4. Growth	53	Efficiency	59	Product Quality and Service	75	Social Responsibility	73
5. Product Quality and Service	47	Resource Conservation	53	Social Responsibility	67	Product Quality and Service	68

Source: Y. K. Shetty, "New Look at Corporate Goals," *California Management Review* (Winter 1979): 76. © 1979 by the Regents of the University of California. Reprinted from the *California Management Review*, Vol. 22, No. 2. By permission of The Regents.

1. The dominant goals of corporate enterprise continue to be profitability, growth, and market share.
2. The changing economic environment and poor track record of many organizations have resulted in their moving away from diversification into unrelated industries and toward goals such as financial stability, resource conservation, and the consolidation of activities.
3. Strategic issues facing an industry help determine company goals, so that drug and electronics firms stress R&D while container and paper firms give attention to efficiency and conservation.

TABLE 6-5   The Five Most Frequently Cited Goals of Corporations with Different Amounts of Sales

Greater Than $5 Billion ($n = 19$)		$1 Billion to $5 Billion ($n = 16$)		$500 Million to $1 Billion ($n = 20$)		Less Than $500 Million ($n = 27$)	
1. Profitability	89%	Profitability	87%	Profitability	95%	Profitability	93%
2. Growth	84	Growth	75	Growth	85%	Growth	85
3. Social Responsibility	74	Research and Development	69	Market Share	75	Efficiency	67%
4. Product Quality and Service	68	Social Responsibility	63	Financial Stability	65	Market Share	63%
5. Employee Welfare	58	Market Share	56	Efficiency	55	Financial Stability	55%

Source: Y. K. Shetty, "New Look at Corporate Goals," *California Management Review* (Winter 1979): 76. © 1979 by the Regents of the University of California. Reprinted from the *California Management Review*, Vol. 22, No. 2. By permission of The Regents.

FIGURE 6-2   Hierarchy of Objectives

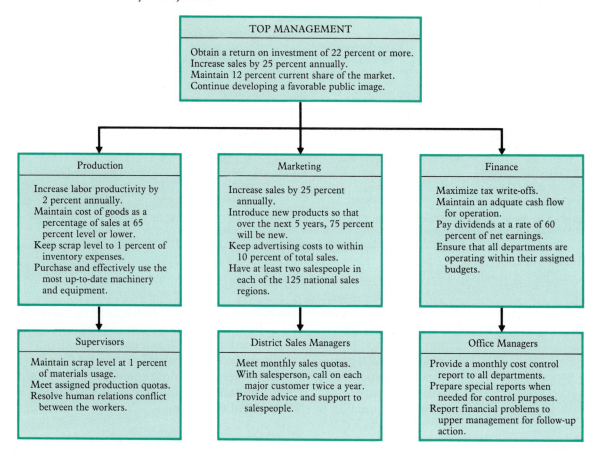

TOP MANAGEMENT

Obtain a return on investment of 22 percent or more.
Increase sales by 25 percent annually.
Maintain 12 percent current share of the market.
Continue developing a favorable public image.

Production

Increase labor productivity by
2 percent annually.
Maintain cost of goods as a
percentage of sales at 65
percent level or lower.
Keep scrap level to 1 percent of
inventory expenses.
Purchase and effectively use the
most up-to-date machinery
and equipment.

Marketing

Increase sales by 25 percent
annually.
Introduce new products so that
over the next 5 years, 75 percent
will be new.
Keep advertising costs to within
10 percent of total sales.
Have at least two salespeople in
each of the 125 national sales
regions.

Finance

Maximize tax write-offs.
Maintain an adquate cash flow
for operation.
Pay dividends at a rate of 60
percent of net earnings.
Ensure that all departments are
operating within their assigned
budgets.

Supervisors

Maintain scrap level at 1 percent
of materials usage.
Meet assigned production quotas.
Resolve human relations conflict
between the workers.

District Sales Managers

Meet monthly sales quotas.
With salesperson, call on each
major customer twice a year.
Provide advice and support to
salespeople.

Office Managers

Provide a monthly cost control
report to all departments.
Prepare special reports when
needed for control purposes.
Report financial problems to
upper management for follow-up
action.

4. Large firms give relatively more attention to socially oriented goals
   while small companies focus on economic objectives.[6]

A hierarchy of objectives

After the overall objectives are determined, they are broken down into more specific goals. This is done on a hierarchical basis, with each level translating the objectives of the one above it into more concrete end points. The result is a **hierarchy of objectives** from the top of the organization to the bottom. Such a hierarchy is illustrated in Figure 6-2. The long-range strategic objectives are thus translated into short-range objectives which serve as the basis for day-to-day, operational plans.

---

[6] Y. K. Shetty, "New Look at Corporate Goals," *California Management Review* (Winter 1979):78.

MANAGEMENT IN PRACTICE

"Barbie Stabilizes Mattel"

*A*fter launching Masters of the Universe toy figures followed by the Captain Power electronic game, Mattel, Inc. was left with $20 million of unsold products. In 1986 and 1987 the firm lost $121.5 million. John W. Amerman, chairman of the large toy making company, began taking action. He reduced headquarters payroll by 22 percent and proceeded to close 10 company plants around the world.

What has kept Mattel alive during this period? Barbie. Yes, the ageless queen of American dolls has been the top selling toy for Mattel over the last two years. In fact, the Barbie line of toys has grown at an annual rate of 12.5 percent and has accounted for 45 percent of Mattel's total revenue since 1985.

Admitting they overdiversified into too many types of toys, Mattel is now nurturing Barbie and introducing "Beach Blast Barbie," "Animal-Loving Barbie," and "57 Chevy-Driving Barbie," as well as new Barbie friends Teresa (an Hispanic), and Christie and Steven (a Black couple). All of this is planned in order to boost sales 25 percent annually.

Mattel has reached a six-year high in its stock price and most experts agree that the Barbie line has kept them going. Some industry observers believe that she may also be their key to future growth.

* *Source:* Patrick E. Cole, "Mattel is Putting Its Dollhouse in Order," *Business Week* (August 28, 1989):66–67.

Strategies

As used by the military, a **strategy** is a grand plan that is drawn up to reflect the results the unit would like to achieve in dealing with its adversaries.[7] In nonmilitary organizations the term strategy still carries this competitive implication. More important, a strategy sets forth "a general program of action and an implied deployment of emphasis and resources to attain comprehensive objectives."[8] (See "Management in Practice: 'Barbie Stabilizes Mattel.' ")

Strategies flow from objectives

Strategies flow from objectives. The organization first decides its goals and then formulates a plan of action to attain them. In practice, however, there is often a give-and-take between objectives and strategies. The organization sometimes finds it necessary to modify one or more major objectives in formulating strategy. In recent years, for example, some American auto manufacturers have had to alter their market share objectives to more accurately reflect the competitive nature of foreign imports and the need to revise and reallocate resources

---

[7] J. Scott Armstrong, "The Value of Formal Planning for Strategic Decisions," *Strategic Management Journal* (March–April 1986):183–185.

[8] Harold Koontz, Cyril O'Donnell, and Heinz Weihrich, *Management,* 8th ed. (New York: McGraw-Hill, 1984), 107.

FIGURE 6-3   A Gap Analysis Approach to Strategy

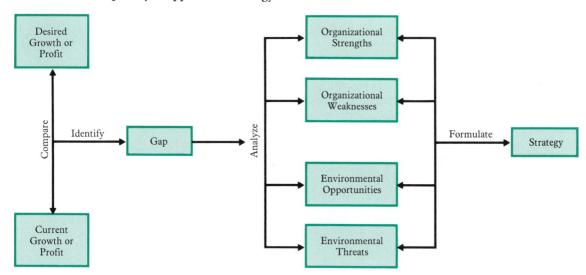

Regardless of the way strategies are actually tied to objectives, two differ-

Some strategies are formulated by using gap analysis

ent approaches are popular today. One is called **gap analysis**. Using this approach, the organization compares current performance with desired performance. With knowledge of the gap between the two, the organization analyzes its strengths, weaknesses, environmental opportunities, and threats and then formulates a strategy for closing this gap. (See Figure 6-3.)

The other approach is a **strategic issues orientation**. In this case the organization examines its current strategic profile (where it is now) and reviews developments occurring in the external and internal environments. It

FIGURE 6-4

A Strategic Issues Approach to Strategy

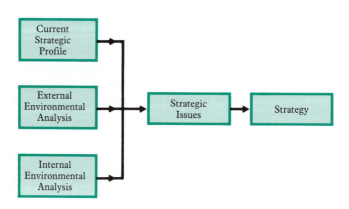

FIGURE 6-5
Policy and Hierar-
chical Level

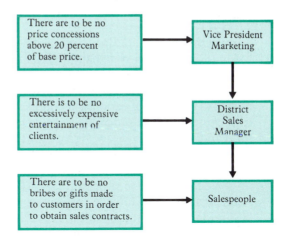

then identifies the major issues to be dealt with and addresses them via specific strategies. (See Figure 6-4.)

Policies

Policies are
guidelines to
thinking and action

Policies are guidelines to thinking and action. They delimit the area within which a decision is made and ensure that the decision is consistent with objectives. There are many types of policies. Some are used to channel decision making at the upper levels, others at the middle ranks, and still others at the lower levels. Figure 6-5 depicts a hierarchy of policies related to the ways in which personnel may go about marketing the firm's products. Notice that in each case the policy provides a guideline both to thinking and to action. The respective manager or salesperson's authority is limited, but within given parameters he or she is free to make decisions. The vice president, for example, can approve price concessions up to 20 percent. The district sales manager can entertain in any manner that is not "excessive." The salesperson can entertain and attempt to influence customers as long as no bribes or gifts are given. There is clearly a hierarchy of policies just as there is a hierarchy of objectives. The organization develops policies for objectives at each level of the hierarchy.

The purpose of a policy is to provide direction. In implementing policy, however, personnel may sometimes use either too much discretion or too much initiative. To reduce the likelihood of such an occurrence, many organizations encourage managers to talk to their subordinates and discuss how they can stay within bounds. This practice does not always eliminate policy violations, but it can help in reducing the number of flagrant cases.[9]

---

[9] Wayne Earley et al., "Avoiding Planning Backlash," *Journal of Business Strategy* (Fall 1983):93–96.

Procedures

Procedures are
guidelines to action

A **procedure** is a guideline to action that sets forth a list of chronological steps for employees to follow in handling a particular activity. In contrast to a policy, a procedure allows no room for interpretation.

Numerous examples can be cited. One of the most typical procedures relates to the filing of expense accounts when someone returns from a business trip. Quite often the procedure is to attach all receipts to a completed expense form and send them to a designated individual in the accounting department. This person then checks the form over for accuracy and completeness and authorizes payment if everything is in order.

A second typical procedure explains how to deal with merchandise refunds. If a customer returns defective goods to a retailer, the store usually has a policy for handling the situation. For example, employees may be authorized to give a credit refund in the department where the defective merchandise was purchased. They would also be required to record the transaction and report it directly to the computer. For cash refunds, procedures vary. In some cases the money is returned in the department, while in others the buyer is given a receipt and sent to the business office for the money.

Procedures serve a double purpose. First, they provide an orderly system for handling specific types of situations. Second, they establish controls to ensure that money, merchandise, and other assets are accounted for.

Rules

Rules are inflexible
plans requiring
specific, definite
action

A **rule** is an inflexible plan that requires specific, definite action. Rules are the simplest form of plans and are used by modern organizations in a variety of situations. Typical examples include the following: "No smoking." "Safety glasses must be worn in this area." "Only authorized personnel are allowed beyond this point."

Rules, unlike policies, do not allow for interpretation. In practice managers and other employees often misuse the terms, saying, for example, "It is our policy not to give cash discounts." Since this is a hard-and-fast statement, it is actually a rule, not a policy.

Rules are useful plans because they severely limit action and help personnel decide how to handle specific situations. Of course, if there are too many rules, personnel may have trouble remembering them all. However, to the extent that rules are limited in number and carefully formulated, they can be very valuable in the planning process.

Programs

A **program** is a complex of objectives, policies, procedures, rules, resources, job assignments, and other elements necessary to carry out a given plan of action. Programs typically are supported by the necessary capital and operating budgets.

Primary programs are often accompanied by derivative programs

A primary program is often accompanied by a series of derivative programs. For example, a primary program to replace half of a manufacturing firm's plant and equipment would have derivative programs for maintenance, personnel training, cost and quality control, financing, and insurance. In the case of a private university with a $50 million building program, there would be derivative programs for maintenance, facilities usage, financing, and insurance.

The larger the organization, the greater the likelihood that it has a number of primary programs. Each program has to be monitored carefully because of internal complexity and external interdependence. Within each program there are many activities that must be carried out. At the same time, it is often necessary to coordinate programs since each may influence or affect the others.

Budgets

Budgets are statements of expected results expressed in numerical terms

A **budget** is a statement of expected results expressed in numerical terms. While often thought of as a control technique, a budget is also a plan since it sets forth objectives to be attained. For this reason, the financial operating budget is commonly referred to as a profit plan. Typical objectives expressed in a budget relate to profit, cost, units of production, labor hours, advertising, promotion, and other measurable goals.

A discussion of many of the specific techniques of budgeting is best left for the chapters devoted to controlling. It should be noted, however, that the construction of a budget is clearly a planning activity. In fact, in many organizations it is the primary planning instrument. A budget forces an organization to think through its goals; the budget is an effective control tool only if it reflects the organization's goals accurately.

THE PLANNING PROCESS

The three planning horizons noted earlier (long, intermediate, and short range) provide the basis for the planning process itself. The long-range plan is the *strategic plan*. The medium-range plan is the *intermediate plan*. The short-range plan is the *operational plan*.[10] Figure 6-6 provides an illustration of this model. Note that planning begins before the strategic plan is constructed and continues through tactical planning to the review and evaluation of results. Throughout the entire planning process, feedback and monitoring keep the

---

[10] C. Aaron Kelley, "The Three Planning Questions: A Fable," *Business Horizons* (March–April 1983):46–48.

FIGURE 6-6   Overall Planning Model for a Large Organization

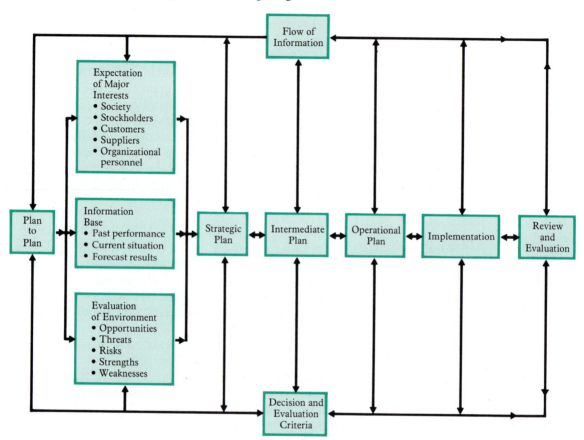

plan on track. Keep in mind as this process is discussed, however, that Figure 6-6 presents a planning model for a large organization. This is the entire process. It will be reduced or shortcircuited in smaller organizations.

Regardless of planning detail there are five basic steps in the planning process, as shown in Figure 6-7. Some of these have already been discussed in detail, while others have not. The five basic steps, in sequence, are (1) awareness of the opportunity, (2) establishment of objectives, (3) determination and

FIGURE 6-7
Steps in the Planning Process

choice of alternative courses of action, (4) formulation of derivative plans, and (5) budgeting of the plan.

Awareness of Opportunity

The real starting point for planning is an awareness of opportunity. For this reason, an organization should maintain a continual surveillance of the environment to detect changes in the market and the competition and to determine its own current strengths and weaknesses. In conducting such an analysis, the organization evaluates the external environmental forces discussed in Chapter 3. It also evaluates its internal capabilities. What can it do well? What does it do poorly?

Based on an awareness of opportunity and the organization's ability to capitalize on it, a general plan of direction starts to emerge. The company knows what it should do and how to proceed.

Forecasting

The most common way to identify opportunities is to conduct external forecasts and then decide on the best course of action. Many different kinds of forecasts can be conducted. Four of the most important are economic, technological, social–political, and sales. The first three kinds of forecasts address the general environment while the fourth helps the organization translate its findings into a plan of action.

ECONOMIC FORECASTING   There are two basic kinds of economic forecasts. One, which is quite simple, is known as **extrapolation**. This kind of forecast assumes that the economy will continue to develop predictably and that the future will follow the pattern of the past. Using extrapolation, an organization that has had sales of $2.5, $2.6, and $2.7 million, respectively, during the last three years would forecast $2.8 million for the coming year. Small businesses often use extrapolation or some similar approach because it is both easy and inexpensive.

Extrapolation is a simple kind of economic forecasting

Larger organizations are more sophisticated in their approach. Some use **econometric models**, which are mathematical models designed to represent either the economy at large or a select part of the economy that affects the company specifically. By testing various economic scenarios in the model, the company can determine their effect on operations.

Econometric models are very sophisticated

Most firms choose a way of forecasting that lies between the two extremes of simple extrapolation and sophisticated econometric models. They examine economic conditions in the general environment and attempt to predict how these conditions will affect their industry and their share of the market. If the firm is large, some of these calculations are done in-house. In many cases, however, companies rely on studies available through either industry or governmental sources. Most federal government departments with a business interest publish economic material that is useful for forecasting. The same is true of trade associations, trade publications, banks, private research organizations, and professional associations.[11]

TECHNOLOGICAL FORECASTING   In many industries technology is changing rapidly. Comparing the typical business office of today with that of 10 years ago reveals changes in typewriting equipment, photocopying processes, communication systems, and the range of computer uses. Products being offered for sale to the general public have also changed dramatically. A look around an average home or a large department store reveals that the number of electronic and computerized products is larger than ever before. As a result, technologically based companies such as Texas Instruments, IBM, and Honeywell need to forecast changes in their environment continually. (See: "Management in Practice: A Solid Steel Strategy That Worked.") A failure to predict developments in the market accurately can result in a severe financial setback, and, in some cases, bankruptcy.

While there are a number of ways to carry out a technological forecast, currently the most popular method is the **Delphi technique**. Assume that a high-technology consumer goods manufacturer is in the process of developing a minitelevision set that can be carried around in a person's pocket. The company expects to have a model ready for the market by 1996, but wants to know when the competition will have a similar product. To answer this question it might use the Delphi technique. The first step in using this technique is to assemble a panel of experts who are knowledgeable about the product and the market. Each is asked to forecast the time when the competition will have a competitive product. The answers are then compiled and the results are fed back to the panel members. Throughout this process all members of the panel remain anonymous to avoid the possibility that they will be influenced by an expert with a prestigious reputation. Finally, based on the answers to the first round, everyone is asked to give a second answer. At the same time those who intend to give answers that are outside of the interquartile range of the previous quarter (the range of answers where 50 percent of all the responses fall) are asked to explain their answers. In this way, those who predict earlier or later developmental times than the majority have to defend their responses.

After four or five rounds, responses tend to converge around a central range which becomes the acceptable forecast. In the case in question, for example, the forecast might be that the competition will have a similar product ready between 1995 and 1996.

Not every firm uses the Delphi. Some prefer alternative approaches. One is simply to extrapolate from the present and ask the question: If technology

Steps in the Delphi process

Exploratory forecasting uses simple extrapolation

---

[11] John J. Casson, "The Contribution of the Economic Forecast to the Business Plan," *Business Economics* (April 1989):14–18.

MANAGEMENT IN PRACTICE

A Solid Steel Strategy that Worked

*I*n 1982 the entire U.S. steel industry was shocked by the worst recession in 40 years. An influx of low cost, high quality imports from Japan resulted in the once-secure American steel producers suddenly facing dramatic challenges.

In this environment Bethlehem Steel Corporation was hampered with inefficient production, shoddy quality, and late deliveries. Major customers such as Firestone, Caterpillar, and Campbell Soup Co. abandoned Bethlehem and turned to other steel producers. The slide was beginning. Bethlehem slashed 39,000 jobs, shut down mills, and spent several billion dollars in upgrading existing facilities.

Walter F. Williams became CEO in 1986 and instituted a new strategy called "Operation Bootstrap." With the company's stock price at an all-time low of $4, Williams mounted a campaign to boost productivity and improve quality. He sold off unrelated assets (16 operations, including a plastics company and a steel distributor), worked on improving customer relations and supply coordination, granted some wage concessions to labor, persuaded the banks to stay with Bethlehem,

and paid down debt and pension liabilities by $1.7 billion.

The results have been remarkable. In 1988 Bethlehem Steel Corporation posted earnings of $403 million on $5.5 billion in revenues (a 131% increase), reduced debt from 67 percent of capital to 31 percent, and increased the stock price fivefold to $24. After purchasing more than $800 million worth of state-of-the-art equipment, quality is on the rise. As an example, the amount of sheet steel rejected by Ford Motor Company has been reduced from 8% in 1982 to less than 1% today.

Analysts predict "The New Bethlehem" will continue to rise. Compared to 1981, which was the last peak year for Bethlehem, in this past year Bethlehem made 25 percent less raw steel and prices did not rise a penny. Yet profits per employee increased fivefold and sales per employee doubled. "Operation Bootstrap" has brought the company back as a world power in steel production, a solid steel strategy that worked.

Source: Gregory L. Miles, "Forging The New Bethlehem," *Business Week* (June 5, 1989):108–110.

continues to develop at its present rate, what new products can we expect to be produced in this industry by 1996? This is known as an **exploratory forecast.**

Another approach is to select a future technological development and then determine how long it will take to attain it. For example, how long will it take our firm to develop a miniature portable TV set? In this case the company works from the future back to the present, identifying obstacles that will have to be surmounted along the way. This type of forecast is known as a **normative forecast**.

Normative forecasting works from the future to the present

Regardless of the approach used by the firm, the results of technological forecasting are estimates regarding future developments. Companies use these estimates to formulate objectives and draw up plans.

Social forecasting involves the prediction of changing values

SOCIAL–POLITICAL FORECASTING   Social forecasting involves the prediction of social values and their impact on business operations. How will changing values affect business results? Because this question is so difficult to answer, many companies simply wait for values to change and then try to address them. However, the large retailing and consumer product firms have tried to keep up with changing values by providing the new goods and services demanded by today's customers.

Political forecasting is done by governmental agencies

Political forecasting has not received a great deal of attention from firms operating solely in the United States. Usually these companies wait until a development occurs and then adjust for it, although in some cases they do draw up a series of forecasts on the amount and type of spending they believe will be done at the local, state, or federal level. The election of George Bush as President in 1988 was undoubtedly forecast by some businesses which then proceeded to act on the basis of this forecast. Firms in military production keep a close eye on political developments, as do governmental agencies whose budgets can be expanded or contracted, depending on who is elected.

SALES FORECASTING   Just about every business firm conducts a sales forecast. Some of these are quite simple while others are very sophisticated. In any case, these forecasts often serve as the primary basis for annual planning. Operations are tied to the sales forecast. The most common types of sales forecasting include (1) the jury of executive opinion, (2) the sales force composite method, (3) the users' expectation method, and (4) statistical and deductive methods.

Sometimes executives make the sales forecast

The **jury of executive opinion** method combines the views of top managers to arrive at a sales forecast. This method typically entails having the executives give their opinions about future sales and then having the result modified by the president. This approach can be useful if the executives have a basic grasp of marketing and are knowledgeable about customer demand.

At other times salespeople have primary input; in other cases a marketing survey is employed

The **sales force composite method** relies upon the salespeople to provide a forecast for sales. When an organization uses this method, salespeople in each district make forecasts which are reviewed by the regional sales manager and then forwarded to headquarters. Many people feel that since the salespeople are out in the field every day they should have a very good idea of what will sell. It is common, however, to find these sales force forecasts being modified by top executives, in which case the organization actually combines the jury of executive opinion method and the sales force composite method.

The **users' expectation method** requires the company to poll customers and find out their demand for the firm's goods and services. This approach is widely employed among companies that sell industrial goods, although marketers of consumer products also employ such sales or marketing surveys. If a random sample of the market can be obtained, the results can be extremely accurate.

All three of these approaches can profit from the use of *statistical or deductive methods* or both. Statistical methods include trend analysis, sampling, correlation analysis, and other mathematical techniques that can help refine the sales forecast and increase its validity. Deductive methods use judgment, intuition, gut feeling, and experience to modify and adjust the final forecast. Most firms use both of these approaches, objective and subjective, so that the final sales forecast is actually the result of a combination of forecasting methods.

Usually companies use a combination of forecasting methods

Establishment of Objectives

The first formal step in planning is to establish objectives. We discussed the value of objectives earlier in the chapter, but you should note again that objectives are established at all levels of the structure, beginning at the top and cascading downward. The hierarchy of objectives begins at the strategic planning level and ends at the operational planning level.

Strategic objectives are effectiveness oriented; operational objectives are efficiency oriented

The difference between strategic and operational objectives is very important. **Strategic objectives** are *effectiveness oriented*. They help the organization compare itself with the competition. Typical strategic objectives state what the company would like to accomplish in terms of return on investment (profit/assets), market share, and growth. Operational objectives are *efficiency oriented*. They help the organization control internal resources. Typical operational objectives include plans for cost control, output, and employee turnover.[12]

Strategic objectives help the organization operate in an environment in which it has minimal control. Most of these objectives concern marketing and finance. **Operational objectives** help the organization operate in an environment in which it has a great deal of control. Most of these objectives concern production and personnel.

Determination and Choice of Alternative Courses of Action

Having set objectives, the organization must identify alternative courses of action for reaching its goals. Actually in most instances the challenge is not to find alternative courses but to determine which ones are best. This decision requires an evaluation process.

Acceptable criteria must be developed to evaluate alternative courses of action

The most effective way to evaluate alternative courses is to establish acceptable criteria. If the organization wants profit above all else, the choice may be quite easy. However, if the firm wants to minimize its outflow of cash, it may have to accept a lower level of profit. For example, a company whose objective is to enter a new industry usually determines the maximum loss it is willing to sustain during the entry period. Entry strategies must balance market share against operating loss. Firms leaving an industry or abandoning a product line

---

[12] See, for example, Noel M. Tichy, David L. Dotlich, and Dale C. Lake, "Revitalization: The Honeywell Information Systems Story," *Journal of Business Strategy* (Winter 1986):70–81.

FIGURE 6-8   Development of Operating Budgets

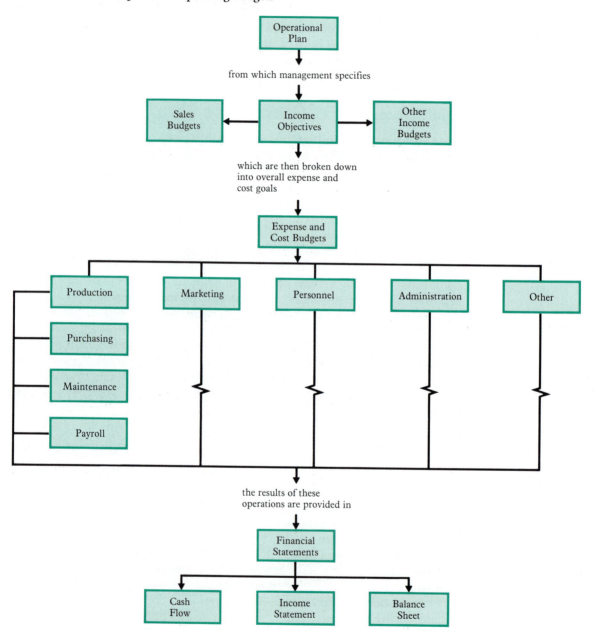

follow the opposite strategy, choosing a course of action that minimizes expenses and maximizes profit. On the way out they do little advertising or promotion, keep costs down, and sell to people who still want the product. The first example describes a firm that is trying to develop a stronghold in the market and is willing to pay for it. The second describes a company that has developed a foothold and wants to milk this share for all it is worth.

Formulation of Derivative Plans

After the organization has chosen alternative courses of action, it can formulate derivative plans. These plans are particularly important in the case of major programs.

Derivative plans help companies breach the gap between where they are and where they want to go

Derivative plans help the organization breach the gap between where it wants to go and where it is currently. In the case of a strategic plan, derivative plans take the form of intermediate and operational plans. In this way the organization forges a link between long-range and short-range objectives. Part of this process was illustrated in Figure 6-2 which presented the hierarchy of objectives concept.

Budgeting the Plan

The budget activates the plan

The last step in the planning process is to budget the plan. Budgeting serves to activate the plan while setting forth numerical targets that can be used for control purposes. Figure 6-8 shows how operating budgets are put together from the operational plan. Notice the flow from income objectives to expense/ cost budgets to the financial statements that report operating results. Based on these results, the organization can begin the planning process anew. In this way planning becomes a closed cycle in which current results help to shape future actions.

MANAGEMENT BY OBJECTIVES

Regardless of their size, many organizations have found they need a simple, easy-to-understand approach for carrying out the planning process. **Management by objectives** (MBO) has proven very useful in this regard. Figure 6-9 shows the sequence of steps used in managing by objectives.

Everything Flows from Objectives

Identifying key result areas

Starting at the top of the organization, each manager reviews the objectives for his or her department. These objectives are then translated into key result areas in which specific performance must be attained, for example, a 25 percent

FIGURE 6-9
The MBO Process

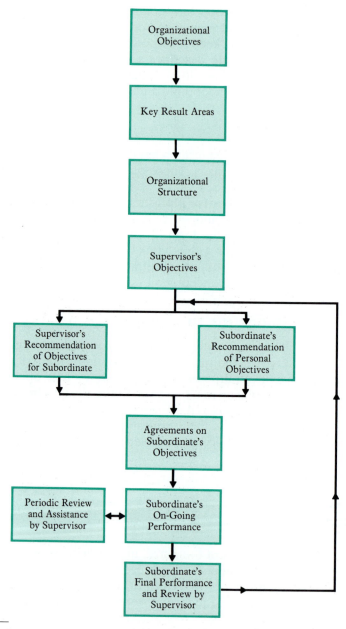

Source: Ralph M. Beese, "Company Planning Must Be Planned." Reprinted with the special permission of *Dun's Review* (April 1957):48. Copyright 1957, Dun & Bradstreet Publications Corporation.

return on investment, a 6 percent market share, an 18 percent increase in sales, a 4 percent reduction on scrap, a 10 percent reduction in turnover.

Then the manager reviews the organizational structure. What is everyone in the department or unit doing? Will their current responsibilities, if carried out properly, result in the desired performance? If not, what changes in structure need to be made?

Setting Objectives

Once the supervisor has the organizational structure in order, he or she can turn to the setting of objectives. The first step is to determine how departmental or unit objectives can be broken down into subobjectives and delegated to subordinates. This step is carried out through a mutual goal-setting process.

Goal setting is a mutual process

The supervisor sets preliminary objectives for each subordinate, and the subordinate is asked to do the same for himself or herself. Then the two meet, discuss their respective lists, and agree on a final set of objectives for the subordinate. This list usually contains no more than five or six objectives, which are specific and tied to a time frame. For example, it might cite the following goals: (1) to reduce personnel turnover by 6 percent by June 30; (2) to increase work output by 9 percent by August 31; (3) to maintain the current level of productivity for the entire year; (4) to increase the sales force by 20 percent by December 15; and (5) to complete all initial supervisory training by March 30.

As soon as the supervisor and subordinate agree on the goals the latter will pursue, they are written down. Both the supervisor and the subordinate then get a copy. The supervisor uses the list for performance review and to provide assistance. The subordinate uses the list as a guide to developing an action plan for accomplishing the goals.

Review and Performance

Throughout the MBO cycle (often quarterly), the supervisor and subordinate sit down, discuss the latter's ongoing performance, and determine how any problems can be resolved. At the end of the entire cycle, the results of these evaluations are used as a basis for rewards and for setting future objectives for the subordinate.[13]

MBO: An Evaluation

MBO has its strong points . . .

MBO has been used effectively by many organizations.[14] On the positive side, employees often like the participation they are given in setting objectives and

---

[13] For an excellent review and description of MBO, see Mark L. McConkie, "A Clarification of the Goal Setting and Appraisal Processes in MBO," *Academy of Management Review* (January 1979):29–40.

[14] Jack N. Kondrasuk, "Studies in MBO Effectiveness," *Academy of Management Review* (July 1981):419–30.

developing a commitment to them. The communication system that is established between supervisor and subordinate also helps to ensure that people know what they are to do, by when, and how they are going to be evaluated. In fact, by clarifying expected results, the manager often reduces employee anxiety and helps build high achievement drive.

and its limitations   Problems can occur, however, that if not corrected, can result in the failure of the total program.[15] One such problem often develops when subordinates fail to get top management support at the beginning. Without such support, most programs are doomed. Another common problem results from an inadequate explanation of how the program works. If the personnel do not understand the total MBO process, they may not fully support it. A third problem is a failure on the part of some managers to set clearly defined, measurable objectives with the subordinates. A fourth problem is personality conflicts between superiors and subordinates during the joint development of objectives. A fifth is an overemphasis on paperwork, which can turn MBO into a costly, technique-oriented exercise in filling out forms. Finally, some managers fail to tie rewards to the attainment of objectives.

Overall, it has   Studying both the benefits of MBO and its potential problems reveals that
great potential   the process can be time consuming and demands a commitment on the part of all involved. If the organization is devoted to planning effectiveness, however, the approach can be profitable for the organization and rewarding for participants.

SUMMARY

1. Planning is the process of setting objectives and then determining the steps needed to attain them. In planning there are three time horizons: long-range (more than five years), intermediate-range (one to five years), and short-range (less than one year).
2. There are many different types of plans. The purpose or mission of an organization is its underlying aim or thrust. Missions are usually stated in product or market terms.
3. Objectives are the ends toward which planning activity is aimed, with long-range objectives serving as a basis for strategic planning and short-range objectives serving as the basis for operational planning. In the process, a hierarchy of objectives is created. The most common business goals are profitability, growth, and market share.
4. Strategies set forth general programs of action that are used in deploying resources for the attainment of comprehensive objectives. One way of formulating strategy is to use gap analysis, which involves comparing current and desired performance for the purpose of determining a plan of action. Another way is to employ a strategic issues orientation in

---

[15] Charles M. Kelly, "Remedial MBO," *Business Horizons* (September–October 1983):62–67.

which the current strategic profile is examined in light of environmental analysis, and major strategic issues are identified and addressed via specific strategies.

5. Policies are guidelines to thinking and action. They delimit the area within which a decision is made and ensure that the decision is consistent with objectives. Just as there is a hierarchy of objectives, there is a hierarchy of policies that runs throughout the organizational structure.

6. Procedures are guidelines to action. They set forth a list of chronological steps that employees must follow in handling a particular activity. Procedures are not open to interpretation. Rules are inflexible plans that require specific, definite action. They are the simplest form of plans.

7. Programs are a complex of objectives, policies, procedures, rules, resources, job assignments, and other elements necessary to carry out a given plan of action. Primary programs are often accompanied by a series of derivative programs.

8. Budgets are statements of expected results expressed in numerical terms. In many organizations they are the primary planning instrument.

9. The planning process begins with awareness of opportunity. This awareness is often achieved through forecasting. Some of the most common types of forecasting include economic, technological, social–political, and sales. Sales forecasting often uses the jury of executive opinion, the sales force composite method, the users' expectation method, statistical methods, and deductive methods.

10. The first formal step in the planning process is the establishment of objectives. There are two basic types of objectives: strategic and operational. Strategic objectives help the organization compare itself with the competition. They address marketing and finance. Operational objectives help the organization control internal resources. They address production and personnel.

11. The next step in the planning process is the determination and choice of alternative courses of action. The most effective way to evaluate alternative courses is to establish acceptable criteria.

12. The next step in the planning process is the formulation of derivative plans. These plans help the organization breach the gap between where it wants to go and where it is.

13. The last step in the planning process is to budget the plan. This serves to put the plan into action.

14. Some organizations have turned to management by objectives (MBO) to help them implement the planning process. In MBO, the first step is to review the organizational objectives of the department or unit and determine key result areas. Then the organization structure is reviewed. Next the supervisor sits down with the subordinate and together the two establish objectives for the latter. Finally, periodic reviews and assistance are provided by the supervisor, who also conducts a final performance review. Based on the results, the process then starts anew.

KEY TERMS

Budget   A statement of expected results expressed in numerical terms.

Delphi technique   A technological forecasting technique.

Derivative plans   Plans that help the organization translate long-range goals into shorter-range ones.

Econometric model   A quantitative economic forecasting model.

Exploratory forecast   A technological forecast based on the idea that technology will continue to develop at its present rate.

Extrapolation   A forecast that assumes that the future will follow the trend of the past.

Gap analysis   An approach to strategy formulation that involves comparing current and desired performance to determine a plan of action.

Hierarchy of objectives   A chain of objectives beginning with long-range ones and cascading downward, with shorter-range and more specific goals being formulated from those directly above them.

Intermediate-range planning   Planning that covers a time period of 1–5 years.

Jury of executive opinion   A sales forecast based on the expectations of managers.

Long-range planning   Planning that covers a time period of more than five years.

Management by objectives (MBO)   A planning approach that involves (a) identification of organizational objectives and key result areas, (b) a review of the organizational structure, (c) a mutual goal-setting process in which supervisor and subordinate agree on objectives for the latter, and (d) a review of subordinate performance by the supervisor followed by the setting of new objectives for the subordinate.

Normative forecast   A technological forecast that identifies a future technological development and then determines how long it will take to attain it.

Objectives   Ends toward which planning activity is aimed.

Operational objectives   Objectives that help an organization control its internal resources. Examples include plans for cost control, output, and employee turnover.

Planning   The process of setting objectives and then determining the steps needed to attain them.

Policy   A guideline to thinking and action.

Procedure   A guideline to action.

Programs   A complex of objectives, policies, procedures, rules, resources, and other elements necessary to carry out a general plan of action.

Purpose or mission   The underlying aim or thrust of an organization. It is usually stated in product or market terms.

Rule   An inflexible plan that requires specific, definite action.

Sales force composite   A sales forecast that is put together with input solely from the salespeople.

Short-range planning   Planning that covers a time period of less than one year.

Strategic issues orientation   An approach to strategy in which the current strategic profile is examined in light of environmental analysis, and major strategic issues are identified and addressed via specific strategies.

Strategic objectives   Objectives that help an organization compare itself with the competition. Examples include the company's objectives for return on investment, market share, and growth.

Strategy   A general program of action used in deploying resources for the attainment of comprehensive objectives.

Users' expectation method   A sales forecast constructed on the basis of customer surveys and/or marketing polls.

QUESTIONS FOR ANALYSIS AND DISCUSSION

1. What is meant by the term planning? Do all organizations have a need to plan? Explain.
2. Planning time horizons are affected by a number of factors. What are some of those factors? Identify and describe three.
3. How can a definition of purpose or a mission statement help an organization? Cite two examples and explain each.
4. What are some of the major types of goals pursued by modern corporations? Identify and describe five. Then set forth four general conclusions that can be drawn regarding corporate objectives during the 1980s. How can an understanding of the concept of hierarchy of objectives be of value to managers interested in understanding the role and importance of objectives?
5. How does a strategy differ from an objective? How can gap analysis be of value in strategy formulation? How can a strategic issues orientation be of value?
6. How does a policy differ from a procedure? How does a rule differ from a policy? How does a program differ from a procedure? In your comparison, be sure to cite an example of each. Then explain how policies, procedures, rules, and programs help modern managers.
7. In what way is a budget a type of plan? Why do some organizations use it as the primary planning instrument? Explain.
8. How does the strategic plan differ from the intermediate plan? How does the intermediate plan differ from the operational plan? In your answer be sure to include a discussion of Figure 6-6.
9. How are each of the following types of forecasting conducted: extrapolation, technological forecasting (specifically the Delphi technique), social–political forecasting, and sales forecasting (specifically the jury of executive opinion, sales force composite, and users' expectation method)? Which of these is most valuable to a small

retailer? A research and development firm? A large consumer products manufacturer?

10. How do strategic objectives differ from operational objectives? Compare and contrast the two.

11. How should an organization go about determining and choosing alternative courses of action? What is the process? Additionally, how can the formulation of derivative plans be of value in the planning process? How does the budgeting of the plan fit into this process? Explain.

12. How does management by objectives (MBO) work? What are the key steps in the process? Use Figure 6-9 to help you formulate an answer. Then, after comparing the advantages and problems of MBO, write a brief answer to the question: How valuable is MBO to modern organizations?

CASE

And Then Things Changed

Things had been very good at Harper Manufacturing. For seven years sales had risen by an average of 26 percent annually. Last year, however, the company encountered a severe slump. Sales dropped 18 percent, and this year, unless there is a dramatic turnaround, sales will decline another 12 percent.

The reason for the sales drop-off is no secret. Harper has had three basic products that accounted for 40 percent of total sales. Two of these products were manufactured under a subcontract with a national retailer. The third was developed in-house and sold to wholesalers under a competitive bidding process. A year ago all three began to nose-dive. The national retailer witnessed a decline in some of its own major products so it canceled a portion of the subcontracting agreement with Harper and began producing these products with its own available machinery and equipment. At about the same time three competitors began selling products similar to the ones Harper had developed and was providing to wholesalers. Since the new products were less expensive, wholesalers began canceling their orders to Harper.

Harper has conducted an analysis of these developments and reached four conclusions. First, the company failed to do substantive forecasting. It assumed that things would continue as before; this was a major mistake. Second, most of its efforts went into production with little attention given to the development of marketing objectives. Third, no contingency plan was developed regarding what the company would *do* if one of its major markets dried up. Fourth, it did not identify new market opportunities and ways to pursue them. As one manager put it, "We were basically concerned with the here and now."

1. In terms of time horizons, what kind of planning did Harper Manufacturing do?

2. Using the information in the case, identify the kinds of forecasting Harper did. What kinds should it have done?
3. Using the planning process as your guide, develop a general plan of action to take Harper Manufacturing through the next three years. What should the firm do? Be as complete as possible in your answer.

YOU BE THE CONSULTANT

A New Acquisition

John L. Barndt, branch manager of Johnston Distributors, has a relatively young and inexperienced salesforce. Barndt believes that the salesforce needs more experience and leadership, and has concluded that there are two ways in which this can be accomplished. First, he can hire experienced salespeople away from the competition. However, this could prove difficult since Johnston Distributors has tried this before under different management and was unsuccessful. Second, he can purchase a small, profitable, independent dealership, S&S Inc. Barndt believes that this is the best plan.

After several meetings with Steve Miller, owner and sole sales representative of S&S, Inc., an agreement was reached for the purchase. Mr. Barndt could hardly wait to tell his branch employees of this new acquisition. However, the information was not well-received by Johnston's salespeople or inside staff. The agreement with S&S, Inc. had allowed Steve Miller to keep his current customer list intact. It allowed for his inside staff to keep their current positions and pay as part of Johnston Distributors. The inside staff of S&S would directly overlap the functions performed by the inside staff of Johnston. Also, Mr. Miller calls on several of the same accounts as do the Johnston sales representatives. The agreement allows Steve Miller to keep his customers, forcing the Johnston sales representatives to give up that business.

Everyone understands that the acquisition has been good from the standpoint of the company. However, they see their customers being taken away, and in the process, personal incomes will decrease due to lost commissions.

Johnston representatives have argued that although Steve Miller did write a lot of business with his customers, he had been calling on them for years. Their sales reports show that they have steadily been increasing their business with these same customers. Given time, they argue, they too will be selling as much or more than Mr. Miller to these same accounts. Why should they not be allowed to keep these accounts?

Your Consultation

Assume that you are a consultant for Barndt. How would you advise him regarding the course he is taking? Outline a plan that you would have him follow.

7

Strategic Planning in Action

The previous chapter examined the planning process. Now we want to study this process in more depth by looking at the area of strategic planning. Virtually every modern organization uses strategic planning to some degree. The first objective of this chapter is to study the nature of strategic planning and learn its value for modern organizations. In examining the uses of strategic planning, we will use specific illustrations from industrial settings. The second objective of this chapter is to study the elements of strategic planning, giving particular emphasis to basic mission, strategic objectives, strategy determination, and portfolio planning. At this point we will consider various ways of handling both successful and unsuccessful product lines. When you have finished studying the material in this chapter, you should be able to:

1. Identify the major characteristics of a strategic plan.
2. Discuss the overall importance of strategic planning.
3. Tell who needs strategic planning.
4. Describe in depth the four elements of strategic planning: basic mission, strategic objectives, strategy determination, and portfolio management.
5. Describe how modern organizations use portfolio management to handle stars, cash cows, question marks, and cash traps.
6. Explain how strategic planning is put into operation.

191

THE NATURE OF STRATEGIC PLANNING

Strategic planning draws heavily on many of the ideas discussed in the previous chapter. However, two major characteristics differentiate strategic planning from planning in general.

Characteristics of Strategic Planning

One of the major characteristics of strategic planning is the value system it promotes. When an organization carries out only operational planning, it emphasizes *meeting the budget.* As the organization grows and gives more attention to planning, its value system becomes concerned with *predicting the future.* As the organization grows still larger, it begins to focus on external developments and ways of responding to them. Its value system becomes

Changes in an organization's value system

concerned with *thinking strategically.* A final shift in orientation usually occurs only among companies that have grown extremely large. These companies attempt to manage all resources in such a way as to create competitive advantages. At this stage their value systems are concerned with *creating the future.* So, as an organization moves more and more toward a strategic planning posture, passivity gives way to activity, and the desire to respond to the environment is replaced by a plan to control it.

A philosophy of planning

A second major characteristic of strategic planning is the philosophy behind the process. In many organizations when managers have completed a general plan they breathe a sigh of relief and note, "Thank heaven that's over. Now let's get back to work." In contrast, strategic planning fosters a philosophy of "plan now, plan later." Planning becomes a regular part of organizational activity. It is not added on to the top of managers' activities; it becomes an integral part of their job.[1]

Elements of Strategic Planning

As seen in Figure 7-1, there are four elements in strategic planning: formulation of the basic mission, setting of objectives, determination of strategy, and the use of portfolio planning. Each of these elements is briefly described and then elaborated upon later in the chapter.

The basic mission

The basic mission was discussed in the previous chapter. However, organizations that engage in strategic planning examine this mission in much greater depth than do organizations that are merely interested in general planning.

---

[1] Daniel H. Gray, "Uses and Misuses of Strategic Planning," *Harvard Business Review* (January–February 1986):89–97.

FIGURE 7-1
Elements of
Strategic Planning

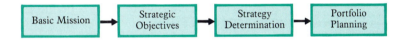

Setting strategic
objectives

The setting of strategic objectives was also covered in Chapter 6. However, it is important to realize that in setting strategic objectives management carries its philosophy down the line, influencing the rewards, leadership, and problem-solving approaches that are used.

Formulating
strategy

Strategy determination involves decisions regarding how to attain strategic objectives. Strategy depends heavily on the industry or environment in which the organization operates. Companies that are dominant have different strategies from companies that "follow the leader"; companies that serve the entire market have different strategies from those that appeal only to a specific portion of it; companies that are interested in building market share have different strategies from those interested in maintaining theirs.

Portfolio
management

Finally, organizations with a number of product lines are now turning to what is called portfolio planning. This entails an evaluation of product lines on the basis of the profit or return on investment they earn currently and what can be expected of them in the future. Based on the results, top management allocates resources.

Before turning to a more detailed discussion of these major elements of strategic planning, let us address two preliminary subjects. The first is the importance of strategic planning; the second is the kind of company that needs it.

THE IMPORTANCE OF STRATEGIC PLANNING

Strategic planning is important for two reasons. First, it helps organizations cope with their external environment. Second, it assists them in redefining or reformulating their strategies or both.

Coping with the External Environment

Most organizations operate in a dynamic environment. In the world of business, a firm is either moving forward or it is falling behind; and this statement is more than just a cliché. Research shows that on a year-to-year basis among even the largest industrials, some firms always are improving their position at the expense of others.

One way to obtain a closer look at this situation is to take the 100 largest industrials and examine their relative sales positions at the end of different decades. How many industrials that were among the largest in terms of sales at the beginning of the 1980s were still maintaining their positions at the beginning of the 1990s? Year after year, the results are the same. Approximately eight out of ten remain in the top ten and six out of ten are in the next group of ten. All others are either moving up or down, and this volatility increases as one moves farther down the last of 100 industrials.

In an effort to cope with this kind of external environment, many firms are turning to strategic planning. In fact, William Lindsay and Leslie Rue, after conducting a two-stage survey of 199 corporations in 15 industrial classifications, have reported that firms tend to adopt more complete, formal, long-range planning processes as the complexity and instability of their environment increase.[2]

Obtaining an Adequate Payoff

Strategic planning helps to improve financial performance

The second major reason why strategic planning is important to modern organizations is that it pays off. Many studies support this statement. Hans Ansoff and his associates have found that firms that conducted formal planning outperformed those that did not on almost every one of 21 different financial criteria.[3] More recently, Lawrence C. Rhyne examined the impact of strategic planning on performance among large firms. He reported the following:

> *The relationship between financial performance and characteristics of corporate planning systems was investigated. Planning systems that combined an external focus with a long-term perspective were found to be associated with superior 10-year total return to stockholders. A lagged relationship between such systems and 4-year average annual returns to investors also was identified.[4]*

In another application, Jeffrey S. Bracker and John N. Pearson studied planning and financial performance of 265 small, mature firms. Their study found that firms which conformed to structural strategic planning outperformed all others in regards to overall financial performance.[5] In a later study conducted by Bracker, Pearson, and Keats, similar financial performance results among firms that used sophisticated strategic plans were found.[6]

---

[2] William M. Lindsay and Leslie W. Rue, "Impact of the Organization Environment on the Long-Range Planning Process: A Contingency View," *Academy of Management Journal* (September 1980):385–404.

[3] H. I. Ansoff, et al., "Does Planning Pay? The Effect of Planning on Success of Acquisitions in American Firms," *Long Range Planning* (December 1970):2–7.

[4] Lawrence C. Rhyne, "The Relationship of Strategic Planning to Financial Performance," *Strategic Management Journal* vol. 7 (1986):423–36.

[5] Jeffrey S. Bracker and John N. Pearson, "Planning and Financial Performance of Small Mature Firms," *Strategic Management Journal* vol. 7 (1986):503–22.

[6] Jeffrey S. Bracker, Barbara W. Keats, and John N. Pearson, "Planning and Performance Among Small Firms in a Growth Industry," *Strategic Management Journal* vol. 9 (1988):591–603.

Keep in mind that strategic planning does not guarantee success. Nor is there a direct relationship between strategic planning and organizational results; the companies that do the most planning do not always have the best performance. However, strategic planning generally does pay off.

WHO NEEDS STRATEGIC PLANNING?

As organizations grow, their need for strategic planning increases. For this reason, all industries can profit from such planning, as can specific companies that are concerned with redefining or reformulating their strategies. The following discussion examines five firms that can benefit from strategic planning. Keep in mind, however, that this discussion is not meant to provide a comprehensive answer to the above question; it is merely designed to illustrate strategic planning's value.

Large Businesses in Particular

Many large businesses find that they can profit from strategic planning.[7] Quite often these firms need to redefine their strategy because (1) they are not having a great deal of success with their current one, (2) they have sold away some of their product lines and have to decide what to do next, or (3) they feel they have moved too far in one direction and want to realign their strategy with what they do best. In any event, these companies can find a strategic plan helpful. In the following cases, notice that a great deal of emphasis is given to the success or failure of strategic planning. Thus, the identification of specific target markets, coupled with a decision about which product lines to keep and which either to sell away or to stop producing, is one of the primary considerations.

Playboy Enterprises: The Party Is Over

For Playboy Enterprises, the party is clearly over. Its empire has shrunk almost to the vanishing point; the magazine has lost readers and is down to 3.4 million from an all-time high of 7.2 million in 1972; its publishing and video enterprises have become the targets of radical feminists, antiporn fundamentalists, and even a government commission; and its stock has dropped to approximately $7 a share from a high of $30.25 in 1978. Whether or not Playboy Enterprises, Inc. can weather the storm is of some concern.

In 1981, Playboy lost its British gambling license, and with it an operation

---

[7] Kenichi Ohmae, ''Getting Back to Strategy,'' *Harvard Business Review* (November–December 1988):149–56.

TABLE 7-1   Playboy's Turbulent Markets

Casinos. Four in England hit big until licenses were lost in 1981. In Atlantic City: No license, no dice.

Clubs and Resorts. One million keyholders to 22 clubs in 1972. All are gone today.

Publications. *Oui Magazine.* It was sold in 1981.

Games. Didn't fit into the product mix.

Cable. In 1985, 753,000 subscribed to the Playboy Channel. In 1986, 650,000; it has now been dropped.

Merchandising. Sells $18 million a year worth of clothes, accessories, and home fashions with the bunny logo.

The Magazine. Top circulation, 7 million in 1972, 1988, 3.4 million.

Source: Adapted from Charles Leerhsen et al., "Aging Playboy," *Newsweek* (August 4, 1986):50 and Claudia H. Deutsch, "Playboy Takes Off Its Ears," *New York Times* (October 22, 1989): F4.

that accounted for 85 percent of its pretax profits. It seemed that Playboy executives had reacted too soon in firing Victor Lownes, head of their England-based subsidiary and perhaps the only man who could have successfully negotiated with the British government. Partly because Playboy lost its British license, the company was denied a gambling permit by New Jersey authorities in 1983 for the Atlantic City hotel it opened shortly before. With no casinos to keep the empire afloat, the company reported losses of $51.7 million in 1983.

Playboy desperately needs advertising growth to balance its weakened circulation. A full 58 percent of the magazine's circulation comes from subscriptions, and 61 percent of the new subscriptions were discounted. In sharp contrast, *Penthouse* logs 95 percent of its circulation from more profitable newsstand sales.

President Christie A. Hefner is quietly, but radically, trying to remold Playboy into what she hopes will be a smaller, but more profitable, leisure company attuned to the tastes and values of the 1990s. In determining what kind of man *does* read *Playboy* in the 1990s, she is faced not only with turning around the company's operations but also with redefining Playboy and the "Entertainment for Men" credo it espouses.

Hugh Hefner started Playboy in 1953 with only $600, and it quickly became more than just a magazine. At its height in 1981, Playboy Enterprises, Inc. earned a profit of $13.7 million on revenues of $221.5 million. (Table 7-1 provides a brief description of the rise and fall of the Playboy Empire.) Today it is scurrying to stay profitable. The company obviously needs to rethink its strategy.[8]

Playboy needs to rethink its strategy

[8] Charles Leerhsen et al., "Aging Playboy," *Newsweek* (August 4, 1986):50–56; and Claudia H. Deutsch, "Playboy Takes Off Its Ears," *New York Times* (October 22, 1989):F4.

Hasbro: King of the Toymakers

Despite predictions that the toy industry sales would be flat in 1987, chief executive officer Stephen Hassenfeld told the directors at Hasbro that company sales should jump impressively. Just eight years previously, Hasbro, dubbed "Hasbeen" by industry cynics, was losing money. In 1985, Hasbro passed Mattel, Inc. to become the number 1 toy company in the world. In 1988 sales were $1.4 billion with profits of almost $100 million.

In the notoriously difficult toy business, Hasbro is a phenomenon. "No toy company has been able to string together a series of ups in profits and revenues the way Hasbro has," says David S. Leibouritz, senior vice president for New York Investment Banker American Securities Corporation. With a stream of megahits, Hasbro has defied the industry's boom-and-bust cycle. There are toys for tots and games for grown-ups. Hasbro's success hinges on its ability to specialize in creating big-selling toys with staying power, and it follows with debt promotion. In 1985, Hasbro captured 15 percent of the U.S. toy market and by 1989 Alan G. Hassenfeld (Stephen's brother) had taken over the helm and boosted international sales to $433 million.

Hasbro likes to get a head start in selling toys. "We want to reach mothers from the time of their child's birth," notes a senior vice president for corporate development. As children grow up they encounter Hasbro toys at every stage of their lives. To its base in preschool toys, Hasbro added action toys in 1982 and stuffed animals in 1983. With the acquisition of the Milton Bradley Company in 1984, it entered the stable and profitable niche of games and puzzles. Since then it has acquired other firms, including Ideal (preschool toys) and Coleco (Cabbage Patch, Scrabble, and Parcheesi).

Hasbro combines its idea people and development people

Unlike some toymakers, Hasbro doesn't separate its idea people from its development people. Everybody in the research group does both, and they don't rely just on homegrown products. Hasbro has bought the rights to an electronic toy and first rights to other concepts developed over the next three years by the Axlon Corporation.

Children's clothing and children's publishing are two related areas the company is considering. For a company trying to achieve staying power in a volatile industry further diversification may be unavoidable. However, one thing is certain, Hasbro strategy is paying off.[9]

Avon's New Formula

Over 52 percent of women are now working, which means they are not home when an Avon representative rings the doorbell. Hicks B. Waldron, president of

---

[9] Louis Therrien, "How Hasbro Became King of the Toymakers," *Business Week* (September 22, 1986):90–92. Also, Laura Jereski, "It's Kid Brother's Turn to Keep Hasbro Hot," *Business Week* (June 26, 1989):154–55.

Avon Products, Inc. since 1983, has attempted to explore new avenues for reaching the career woman market.

Avon is exploring direct mail and telephone sales

Waldron has redefined the company's goals by exploring direct mail and telephone sales. Waldron also established a long-term strategic plan for the entire company. One of his goals has been to change Avon from a distribution company to a brand marketer emphasizing the value and quality of the Avon name and de-emphasizing jewelry and gifts. Yet Waldron admits, "Our future is still in direct selling. That's the goose that laid the golden egg." [10]

GM Repositions Itself in Recent Years

GM is repositioning itself through product changes

GM marketing and strategic planning executives have revealed that their divisions are now fleshing out plans for fewer, more distinctive models. Very simply, the company is repositioning itself through product changes. These changes are designed to reduce overlap and duplication. The company's 1984 reorganization, which fundamentally shifted GM from a manufacturing-oriented, selling-what-you-make-best company, to a marketing-oriented, make-what-you-sell-best operation, is also part of this strategy. By building on the traditional strengths of its division, GM intends to reduce the risk inherent in image reshaping and to recapture its previous market dominance. While industry experts doubt whether GM can do this, its repositioning strategy is bound to help the firm maintain more market share than would otherwise be the case.[11]

Alcoa: Recycling the Company

Alcoa is developing space-age materials to replace aluminum

The Aluminum Corporation of America (Alcoa) once held 90 percent of the American primary aluminum market. However, in the last couple of years the company has been forced to face one important fact: aluminum is on its way out. Just as steel production peaked in the mid-1970s and has been on its way down ever since, aluminum peaked in the early 1980s and is unlikely to see a revival. For Alcoa the two most important questions are: What will replace aluminum? Will we be the ones to develop these new products? The answer to the first question is still unclear, but Alcoa is working hard to ensure that the answer to the second question is "Yes." At the present time it has over 1,200 researchers working on developing new materials to replace aluminum. This is part of the company's current strategy of transforming itself from a 100-year-old metals firm into the leading space-age materials producer of the twenty-first century. The firm predicts that by 1995 it will be getting 50 percent of its sales from new,

---

[10] Terry Hourigan, "Avon Tries a New Formula to Restore Its Glow," *Business Week* (July 2, 1984):46–47.

[11] Jesse Snyder, "4 GM Car Divisions are Repositioned in Effort to Help Sales," *Automotive News* (September 15, 1986):1–49; James B. Treece and John Hoerr, "Shaking Up Detroit," (August 14, 1989):74–80.

nonaluminum businesses. The company realizes that in order to do this it must reformulate its strategy and start changing product line emphasis. Alcoa does not want to end up in the same position as the steel companies who, for a long time, formed one of the country's premier industries. However, they spent too long following a strategy of "business as usual." Alcoa knows that it is time for a change and is actively engaged in altering its strategy so that it is back on top again within a decade.[12] See also "Management in Action: Forging a Successful Strategic Alliance."

STRATEGIC PLANNING ELEMENTS

As seen in Figure 7-1, there are four major elements in strategic planning. The first two, basic mission and strategic objectives, were discussed in some detail in Chapter 6. At this point only key elaborations will be made. The last two elements, strategy determination and portfolio planning, will be examined in detail.

Basic Mission

In determining the basic mission of the organization, top management must ask itself: What business are we in? What business should we be in? Will we need to change this mission over the next five years? Ralston Purina is a good example. Starting out as an animal feed store on the St. Louis riverfront, it began diversifying during the 1970s. By the end of the decade, it was breeding shrimps in Panama, growing mushrooms from Connecticut to California, fishing for tuna in the Atlantic and Pacific oceans, selling cat and dog food in Europe, and operating the Jack in the Box fast-food chain, in addition to buying the St. Louis Blues hockey team. A few years later the tuna-catching, mushroom-raising, and European-based pet foods were gone and the hockey team was for sale. The company had gone back to its basic markets of agricultural and grocery products. Many firms today are finding themselves returning to their primary lines of business, although many others are expanding. Sears, for example, has recently expanded into real estate and financial services.

When it comes to basic mission, however, companies that are interested in strategic planning must go beyond a simple definition or identification of the basic business. They must examine the relationship between mission and corporate culture.[13]

---

[12] Gregory L. Miles and Matt Rothman, "Alcoa: Recycling Itself to Become a Pioneer in New Materials," *Business Week* (February 9, 1987):56–58.
[13] David C. Shanks, "The Role of Leadership In Strategy Development," *Journal of Business Strategy* (January–February 1989):32–36.

Forging a Successful Strategic Alliance

*S*trategic alliances may be the rage among high-technology companies these days, but MIPS Computer Systems must surely be the first one to base an entire corporate strategy on them. And a winning strategy at that. The company, which has used some two dozen partnerships with semiconductor and computer companies to become a major competitor in the fast-growing workstation market, is being touted as Silicon Valley's next superstar.

In high technology, as in any other industry, a successful strategic alliance is a long-term relationship that will produce more benefits for both partners than either could achieve on its own. By breeding a mutual sense of ownership, says Robert Miller, CEO of MIPS Computer Systems, "you're building strength on strength and getting better results." But it takes careful preparation and procedures to make an alliance work. Here are six key tips:

- Bear in mind that strategic alliances—which are, after all, partnerships—entail dependency and some loss of control. The partners have to agree on what is a reasonable price to pay for the expected benefits. Even technology giants such as IBM no longer have the resources to develop everything in-house.
- In the same vein, it takes diplomacy, trust, and personal chemistry to make a partnership work. Before a deal is consummated, each company must know exactly what it is—and is not—getting from the arrangement. And it must be clear that the relationship is mutually profitable. "The deal must be structured in a way that you could put it on the table, have

the two parties trade places, and each would be happy," says Charles Boesenberg, MIP's marketing chief.

- Make sure that managers throughout each company have ample autonomy. This is important, because they have to communicate regularly with the partner's managers, and decisions cannot be reached quickly if they lack authority.
- As in a marriage, both partners must work on the relationship every day. Engineers from both companies must sit at their counterparts' desks as a matter of course, and the CEOs should meet regularly. "Companies are fundamentally motivated by their own needs," notes Michael Murphy, editor of the *California Technology Stock Letter,* "so to keep the alliance alive, they have to be careful that their needs continue to overlap."
- New small companies should not seek partnerships with bigger companies mainly for an infusion of capital. Such a relationship is too one-sided. There also should be an exchange of technology. "Two companies can't build a long-term relationship simply around a bagful of money," Boesenberg says.
- Do not attempt to form a strategic partnership with a head-to-head competitor. Despite the best intentions, something will invariably go wrong when companies are vying for the same business.

* *Source:* "Sharing the Wealth," *Business Month* (September 1989):52–54, and Gary Hamel, Yves L. Doz, and C. K. Prahalad, "Collaborate With Your Competitors—And Win," *Harvard Business Review* (January–February 1989):133–39.

Corporate culture relates to the values such as defensiveness or agressiveness that set a pattern for a company's activities, opinions, and actions. This pattern is instilled in the employees by the examples of the managers and is passed down to succeeding generations of employees. The chief executive officer's words and actions, as well as those of the other managers, create this culture, and it may last for years before it is effectively changed by managers with a different culture.[14] When this culture is consistent with strategy, the firm can develop an effective game plan. The following are examples:

> International Business Machines Corp., where marketing drives a service philosophy that is almost unparalleled. The company keeps a hot line open 24 hours a day, seven days a week, to service IBM products.

> Digital Equipment Corp., where an emphasis on innovation creates freedom with responsibility. Employees can set their own hours and working style, but they are expected to articulate and support their activities with evidence of progress.

> Delta Airlines Inc., where a focus on customer service produces a high degree of teamwork. Employees will substitute in other jobs to keep planes flying and baggage moving.[15]

> Tektronix Manufacturing Operations, where the company is reeducating a work force accustomed to a culture where rigid rules were thought antithetical to creativity. Now manufacturing efficiency is as important as creativity.[16]

> Chase Manhattan, where executives encourage their employees to renew their commitment to treating customers like human beings instead of numbers. As one manager put it, "We have to start looking at what the customer wants. The customer is always right." [17]

Corporate culture can help the organization adapt to its changing environment or it can prevent the company from meeting competitive threats, thereby leading to stagnation and ultimately to failure.[18] In recent years many firms have worked to change their corporate culture and become more aggressive. For example, Pepsico moved from being a company that was content to being number two to a firm that was willing to take on Coca Cola and try to beat it out for the number one slot. Another successful corporate culture is promoted by J. C. Penney, although it is quite different from that of Pepsi. At Penney's the

---

[14] Robert C. Ernest, "Corporate Cultures and Effective Planning," *Personnel Administrator* (March 1985):49–60. See also: Cass Bettinger, "Use Corporate Culture to Trigger High Performance," *Journal of Business Strategy* (January-February 1989):32–36.
[15] "Corporate Culture," *Business Week* (October 27, 1980):148.
[16] Kathleen K. Weigner, "Manufacturing Was an Afterthought," *Forbes* (January 27, 1986):34.
[17] Howard Gold, "Can the Performance Match the Promise?" *Forbes* (January 27, 1986):87.
[18] John J. Sherwood, "Creating Work Cultures with Competitive Advantage," *Organizational Dynamics* (Winter 1988):4–27.

MANAGEMENT IN PRACTICE

Betting on the Future Through R&D

Monsanto Co., the $8.3 billion chemical company giant, recently increased its research and development budget 78 percent to $470 million per year. More importantly, 44 percent of those dollars are being reserved for new business development.

This type of strategy has its risks. Since these research funds are being concentrated on the life and food science areas such as drugs, herbicides, and animal growth stimulants, rigorous testing procedures and government regulations can cause long delays in establishing products. For example, Monsanto has already spent $150 million in developing disease-resistant plants, yet the commercial prospects will not be seen until the mid-1990s. However, the firm's R&D strategy is surging ahead in every division. For example, in agricultural chemicals (a $1.4 billion unit) thirteen new agricultural products are being developed for the mid-1990s with fourteen more in the early research stages.

While the strategy is time-consuming and costly, Monsanto believes it is the greatest investment for the 1990s and beyond. Says Richard J. Mahoney, CEO, "We commit to see a project through to the end. . . . This is a rigorous process, but it is also the guts of the company's future. R&D isn't part of our strategy. R&D *is* the strategy."

Source: James E. Ellis, "Why Monsanto Is Plunking Down Its Chips on R&D," *Business Week* (August 21, 1989): 66–67.

aggressiveness that is so evident in Pepsi's culture is discouraged. Penney's believes that building long-term customer loyalty is the most important objective. It tries to do this by ensuring that customers "know they can return merchandise with no questions asked; suppliers know that Penney's will not haggle over terms; and employees are comfortable in their jobs knowing that Penney's will avoid layoffs at all costs and will find jobs for those who cannot handle more demanding ones.[19] No wonder that the average tenure of executives at Penney's is 33 years! Meanwhile, at Monsanto the focus is now on R&D for new product development. (See "Management in Action: Betting on the Future Through R&D.")

A company's basic mission is affected by its corporate culture. Organizations that have encouraged a competitive culture formulate strategies markedly different from those that have encouraged a more relaxed approach. Depending on the industry and degree of competitiveness, either kind of culture can result in the formulation of an ideal basic mission.[20]

---

[19] "Corporate Culture," *Business Week,* 148.

[20] Rohit Deshpandé and A. Parasuraman, "Linking Corporate Culture to Strategic Planning," *Business Horizons* (May–June 1986):28–37.

Strategic Objectives

The strategic objectives that an organization formulates are external in orientation. They attempt to provide the firm with a means for comparing its performance with that of the competition. As noted in Chapter 6, typical examples of strategic objectives include return on investment, growth, and market share while examples of short-range, operational objectives include profit, productivity, and cost containment. Strategic objectives set overall direction; operational objectives provide a basis for short-run progress and control.

Strategic objectives are future oriented

The focus and problem-solving styles required for strategic planning are quite different from those used for operational planning. For example, strategic objectives are directed toward future profits, while operational objectives are concerned with present profits. Strategic objectives help determine future opportunities and call for a flexible/entrepreneurial leadership style that is willing to accept moderate to high risk; operational objectives are concerned with current opportunities and call for a stable/adaptive leadership style that is willing to accept only low to moderate risk.

Strategic objectives are formulated to help the organization attain its basic mission. Like the latter, they are directional in nature.

Strategy Determination

Over the past two decades there has been a dramatic change in the way strategy is determined. For many firms diversification is now giving way to integration. More important, strategic planning is being used to tailor-make a "fit" between the organization and its environment.

Strategic Planning: Past, Present, and Future

Investment planning is declining

While more and more businesses are now employing strategic planning, many are changing their approach. During the 1960s, for example, the term strategic planning often meant investment planning. The conglomerates attempted to buy diverse firms and parlay these portfolios into high profits the way an individual investor seeks to buy the most profitable stocks in a number of different industries. In the case of the conglomerates, however, quite often the acquisition did not meld with or complement the business's line, and the company had trouble managing the operation. As a result, profits lagged and real growth declined. These firms soon learned that investment planning was not a substitute for strategic planning.

Compatibility of basic mission and synergy is sought

During the 1970s many firms turned away from the investment planning approach and toward growth opportunities within the company itself. Strategies for cost reduction were initiated, reviews of the firm's marketing strategy were undertaken, and efforts were made to develop innovative research and development. At the same time, acquisitions and mergers were examined from the standpoint of compatibility of business missions and synergistic effect. One of the best examples is Pepsico, which acquired Pizza Hut and Taco Bell, two firms that tied in well with Pepsico's rapidly growing soft drink division and helped serve the same group of consumers.

During the 1980s and into the 1990's there has been continued emphasis on strategies designed to help organizations build on what they do best. However, since there is the danger of antitrust action from the federal government should a firm begin acquiring or merging with other companies in its own industry, we are likely to see many companies seeking a balance between growth and market share in the industry. This will be done through what is called **concentric diversification**, which is a combination of integration and diversification. Concentric diversification requires a firm to "develop or acquire new products which have marketing and/or technological synergies with its current products but which are normally not intended for sale to the company's present markets." [21] In this way the firm gains the benefits of its experience and knowledge while avoiding the dangers of antitrust action. An example is found in the case of Philip Morris, which bought Miller Brewing. At first blush, an acquisition like this appears to be a simple conglomerate diversification. However, beer and cigarettes are distributed through many of the same retail outlets, and many of the same people who drink beer also smoke. So Philip Morris really knew a great deal about marketing to Miller beer drinkers when it entered this market. Hence, the purchase of Miller Brewing is actually an illustration of concentric diversification. Another example is found in the case of Texas Instruments (TI), which has relied heavily on internal concentric diversification, with technological expertise providing the major thread binding its diversity. As the 1980s began, the firm's sales were spread over five market segments: digital products, components, metallurgy, government electronics, and services. TI has avoided inordinately high shares in any of these segments while remaining a growth-oriented and integrated single technology firm, concentrating on what it does best.

Some firms employ concentric diversification

Tailor-Making Strategies

Today strategic planning is tailor-made to meet the needs of the organization. Keeping in mind that there are far too many situations to address all of them in just a few pages, let us look at three typical strategic planning concerns: (1) building market share, (2) maintaining market share, and (3) surviving in a hostile environment. Each requires a tailor-made strategic plan.[22]

---

[21] William L. Shanklin, "Strategic Business Planning: Yesterday, Today, and Tomorrow," *Business Horizons* (October 1979):13. Also, see Richard Reed and George A. Luffman, "Diversification: The Growing Confusion," *Strategic Management Journal* (January–March 1986):29–35, and Clark E. Chastain, "Divestiture: Antidote to Merger Mania," *Business Horizons* (November–December 1987):43–49.
[22] For one not covered here, see Kathryn Rudie Harrigan and Michael E. Porter, "End-Game Strategies for Declining Industries," *Harvard Business Review* (July–August 1983): 111–20.

BUILDING MARKET SHARE   The Strategic Planning Institute has been sponsoring the Profit Impact of Marketing Strategies (PIMS) since the mid-1970s. Drawing upon information from almost 2,000 businesses, PIMS has found that high-share businesses enjoy above-average profit margins and rates of return on investment, while most small-share businesses have below-average margins and returns.[23]

Strategic factors for increasing market share

How can a company plan strategically for higher market share? What does it need to do? Research to date reveals that the strategic factors generally involved in market share gains include the following: (1) the development and introduction of new products, (2) increases in relative product quality, and (3) increases in the marketing budget for such things as the sales force, advertising, and sales promotion relative to the growth rate of the particular market. When these factors are employed in combination, the result is a balanced marketing program.

> A classic illustration of the effectiveness of a balanced marketing program is evident in the experience of L'eggs pantyhose. The Hanes Corporation introduced L'eggs in 1971 with a marketing strategy that included several novel elements: a one-size product to fit most users, a new system of direct-to-the-store distribution, and heavy introductory advertising and promotion. By 1974, L'eggs was the leading brand in the pantyhose market. While each component of the strategy undoubtedly contributed to the product's success, it also seems clear that the components reinforced each other. For example, heavy advertising and promotion speeded up consumer trial; that facilitated acceptance by retailers; and the system of direct distribution ensured that L'eggs would seldom be out of stock, allowing satisfied buyers to develop steady repeat buying routines.[24]

Most successful share-building strategies are based on the idea that a company should focus on a limited number of segments within a particular market. Most successful firms have achieved their success by concentrating their efforts on selected market segments. Often these segments are relatively small at first. Philip Morris provides an example. The company was successful in promoting Merit, a low-tar cigarette with special appeal for health-conscious smokers, and Miller "Lite," a beer aimed at diet-conscious drinkers. In building market share, a business must select its markets and then work to cultivate and expand them.

MAINTAINING MARKET SHARE   Some companies do not want to increase their market share. They are interested in maximizing their return on invested capital by maintaining the share of the market that provides them the highest

---

[23] Robert D. Buzzell and Frederik D. Wiersema, "Successful Share-Building Strategies," *Harvard Business Review* (January–February 1981):135.
[24] Buzzell and Wiersema, "Successful Strategies," 143.

return. Research has shown that a strategic plan for maintaining market share consists of four basic elements.[25]

Segment the market

The first element is for the company to compete in a limited number of market segments within the industry. The company should focus on market segments in which its own strength will be most highly valued and in which its major competitors will be most unlikely to compete. This type of plan was adopted by Crown Cork & Seal, a company that concentrated on two products: metal cans for hard-to-hold products such as beer and soft drinks, and aerosol cans. By building small single-product plants close to the customers, the company managed to secure a much higher return on investment than the competitors who made a broad assault on the metal container market and built large, multiproduct plants at some distance from the customers.

Use R&D efficiently

The second element of this strategy is to use R&D (research and development) efficiently. Successful firms spend their money on applied, as opposed to basic, research. If a competitor produces a good product, they try to copy it. If they must do basic R&D, they try to be innovative or unique in some way. Crown Cork & Seal, for example, worked very closely with large breweries in developing drawn-and-ironed cans for the beverage industry. As a result, the firm beat all three of its major competitors in equipment conversion for the introduction of this new product.

Think small

The third element is to think small. Companies that are successful in maintaining market share limit their growth. Consider the case of Burroughs, a mainframe computer manufacturer that limited its growth to 15 percent per year because its president said that fast growth would not allow for proper employee training or for proper development of the management structure. When successful firms interested in maintaining market share do diversify, they diversify cautiously.

Have an influential chief executive

The final element of a successful plan for maintaining market share is the strong influence of the chief executive. Influential chief executives often view obstacles as challenges and enjoy competing in unorthodox ways to beat the odds. They also work closely with teams of other senior managers and limit their responsibilities to a few key areas. In fact, as R. G. Hamermesh and his associates have noted, "In successful low-share companies, the influence of the chief executive often extends beyond formulating and communicating an ingenious strategy to actually having a deep involvement in the daily activities of the business."[26]

SURVIVING IN A HOSTILE ENVIRONMENT   Economists and business analysts agree that, compared with the previous decades, the 1990s will be a decade of slower growth, intensified regulatory pressures on business conduct, increas-

---

[25] R. G. Hamermesh, M. H. Anderson, Jr., and J. E. Harris, "Strategies For Low Market Share Businesses," *Harvard Business Review* (May–June 1978):95–102.
[26] Hamermesh et al., "Strategies," 191.

Low cost and a differentiated position are important

ing inflation, and greater competition both at home and abroad. How can firms survive in this hostile environment? After conducting an in-depth study of 64 companies, William Hall has found that success comes to those that achieve either the lowest cost or most differentiated position:

> . . . throughout their modern history . . . leading companies have demonstrated a continuous, single-minded determination to achieve one or both of the following competitive positions within their respective industries:
>
> Achieve the lowest delivered cost position relative to competition, coupled with an acceptable delivered quality and a pricing policy to gain profitable volume and market share growth.
>
> Achieve the highest product/service quality differentiated position relative to competition, with both an acceptable delivered cost and a pricing policy to gain margins sufficient to fund reinvestment in product/service differentiation.[27]

The strategic plan should be developed with this information in mind.

Hall reports that firms that achieve both of these strategic objectives, whether by developing a full product line or by specializing in a limited number of products, have the highest growth rates and returns in the industry and are most likely to prosper. Those that achieve the next lowest costs and the next most differentiated position or both have moderate but generally acceptable growth rates and returns. As the market matures, firms that are less successful in achieving low costs and a differentiated position show little growth and small returns. They can become profitable only by discovering new market segments and focusing on them or by transferring their assets into diversified markets.[28] Finally, in hostile environments, when firms do not achieve either low costs or a differentiated position, they fail.

PORTFOLIO PLANNING

Regardless of its strategy, every organization finds that some product lines do better than predicted, some do more poorly, and the rest perform as expected. Based on its findings, the firm decides whether to invest more money in the line, reduce the investment, or do nothing.

---

[27] William K. Hall, "Survival Strategies in a Hostile Environment," *Harvard Business Review* (September–October 1980):78–79.

[28] For more on strategies in mature industries, see Donald C. Hambrick, "An Empirical Typology of Mature Industrial-Product Environments," *Academy of Management Journal* (June 1983):213–30.

In an effort to analyze product line performance systematically and develop a follow-up strategy, some companies have turned to the use of the **strategic business unit** (SBU). Popularized by General Electric in the early 1970s, the SBU concept of planning breaks the company into business units based on the following principles:

> The . . . firm should be managed as a "portfolio" of businesses, with each business unit serving a clearly defined product-market segment with a clearly defined strategy.
>
> Each business unit in the portfolio should develop a strategy tailored to its capabilities and competitive needs, but consistent with overall corporate capabilities and needs.
>
> The total portfolio of business should be managed to allocating capital and managerial resources to serve the interests of the firm as a whole—to achieve balanced growth in sales, earnings, and asset mix at an acceptable and controlled level of risk. In essence, the portfolio should be designed and managed to achieve an overall corporate strategy.[29]

Each SBU is a discrete, independent, product-market segment serviced by the firm. Some of the characteristics of an SBU include a distinct mission, its own competitors, the focus of a single business or collection of related businesses, and the ability to plan independently of the other SBUs in the organization. The SBU is a business within a business.[30] Some firms can handle their portfolio planning with two or three such units, while large corporations such as General Electric in the United States and Toshiba Corporation in Japan have more than 40.

The Portfolio Matrix

The business portfolio matrix helps the organization allocate resources among the various SBUs. This matrix is illustrated in Figure 7-2. Two major criteria determine the resource allocation: product-market attractiveness and competitive position.

The Dimensions

Market potential   The **long-term product-market attractiveness indicator** measures market potential. Two distinct philosophies have evolved about ranking SBUs on this dimension. The first advocates using the long-term projected real growth rate of the product-segment. When this method is used, the break point between

---

[29] William K. Hall, "SBUs: Hot, New Topic in Management of Diversification," *Business Horizons* (February 1978):17.

[30] For more on this, see R. G. Hamermesh and R. E. White, "Manage Beyond Portfolio Analysis," *Harvard Business Review* (January–February 1984):103–109.

FIGURE 7-2
Portfolio Matrix
Used to Evaluate
SBUs

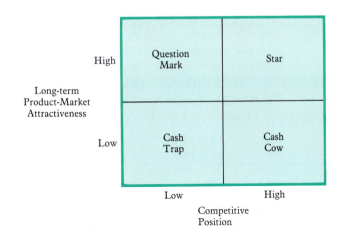

industry high and low growth rates is commonly set at 10 percent, although sometimes it is set at the level of growth for the economy as a whole or the level of growth of a particular sector of the economy. The second philosophy concerned with ranking SBUs according to market potential considers a combination of quantitative and qualitative factors. At GE these factors include segment size, segment growth rate (in units and real dollars), competitive diversity, competitive structure, segment profitability, and technological, social, environmental, legal, and human impacts.

Measuring business strength   **Competitive position** refers to the firm's business strength. Here again, two alternative philosophies have evolved for ranking SBUs. One considers a single market share relative to the competition. The other considers a combination of qualitative and quantitative factors such as segment size, SBU growth rate, share, profitability margins, technological position, skill or weaknesses, image, environmental impact, and management.

Strategic Handling

Depending on its long-term product-market attractiveness and competitive position, an SBU is either a star, a cash cow, a question mark, or a cash trap. After an SBU has been evaluated, the company can choose the appropriate strategy for handling it. This strategy is then employed until the next evaluation period (usually one year later), at which time the unit is again evaluated and a new decision is made regarding its ranking. A new product line often starts out as a question mark, grows and becomes a star, matures and becomes a cash cow, and then declines and becomes a cash trap. Of course, during this product life cycle the organization can work to move the product back to one of its previous positions, as in the case of a cash cow that, with a dynamic advertising program and some new product design, becomes a star again. Or, if a product line is on its way out, the organization can terminate it before it becomes a cash trap.

A star is to be
groomed

STAR   A star is an SBU with high long-term product-market attractiveness and a high competitive position. Star product lines are businesses that must be groomed for the long run. Right now they are cash consumers. Resources must be spent to develop their full potential. If this is done, they will grow faster than the competition in this market segment in terms of sales, profits, and cash flow. The strategy to employ with stars is one of building and investing.

A cash cow is to
be held and
milked . . .

CASH COW   A cash cow is an SBU with low long-term product-market attractiveness and a high competitive position. Since the product line is dominant in the industry, it generates a great deal of cash from operations. The strategy to employ with a cash cow is to preserve market position while generating dollars.[31] Some of the most common strategies that are employed for these product lines include targeting growth segments, stabilizing price, differentiating the product, using selective cost reduction, and employing less creative marketing.

and sometimes
harvested

If things start to turn bad, however, the organization must begin to milk the cow for all it is worth. The strategy to use with strong cash cows is to "hold," while the strategy to employ with weak ones is to "harvest." Unfortunately, there is no single indicator that points reliably to candidates for harvesting; one must rely on a multiple set of indicators. Seven of the most important are the following:

1. The business entity is in a stable or declining market.
2. The business entity has a small market share, and building it up would be too costly; or it has a respectable market that is becoming increasingly costly to defend or maintain.
3. The business entity is not producing especially good profits or may even be producing losses.
4. Sales would not decline too rapidly as a result of reduced investment.
5. The company has better uses for the freed-up resources.
6. The business entity is not a major component of the company's business portfolio.
7. The business entity does not contribute other desired features to the business portfolio, such as sales stability or prestige.[32]

The fact that a product line has begun to be harvested does not mean that the line will generate cash for only a short period of time. Some companies have found, to their surprise, that harvested products can have remarkable staying power long after their marketing support levels have been reduced or removed.

---

[31] See, for example, "Burlington Northern's Cash Cow," *Business Week* (March 8, 1982):112, 114.
[32] Philip Kotler, "Harvesting Strategies for Weak Products," *Business Horizons* (August 1978):17–18.

For example, Bristol-Myers sold its Ipana toothpaste brand rights to two small businesspeople who continued to produce it and stock distributors while stopping all advertising. Sales continued for years, and the two made a healthy profit. Lifebuoy soap's market dropped off and Lever Brothers cut most of its advertising and promotional support. Sales continued, however, and because the soap was priced higher than its leading competitors were, it produced enough profit to justify its existence. General Electric decided to harvest its artillery manufacturing division because it did not want to risk poor public relations by getting deeper into the arms business. Despite its reduction of investment, failure to maintain high R&D, and raising of prices, the company found demand for these products persisting at a high level. The result was a substantial increase in profits.

A question mark must become a star for the company to keep it

QUESTION MARK   A question mark is an SBU with high long-term product-market attractiveness and low competitiveness. This SBU poses a major problem for the firm. If its competitive position is not strengthened, its product-market segment will be attacked by the competition. Yet the costs of an effort to strengthen the SBU's position may not be justified. Some firms opt to put money behind a question mark and see what happens. If the SBU develops into a star, everything is fine. If it declines or does not improve enough to justify further support, the company divests itself of the SBU. Question marks must either get into the star category or get out of the portfolio.

A dog must be managed for short-term cash flow

CASH TRAP   A cash trap is an SBU with low long-term product-market attractiveness and a low competitive position. SBUs in this category are clearly unattractive for either the short or the long run. Additionally, even if the organization were to put more resources into the unit to improve its position, the SBU would still have low potential. This is why cash traps are commonly referred to as "dogs." The strategy here is always the same: to manage the SBU in such a way as to maximize the short-term cash flow. Sometimes this strategy is carried out by closing the SBU down or conducting a rapid divestiture. In other cases it is carried out by harvesting cash from operations through cost cutting, short-term pricing policies, and giving up market share and growth opportunities that absorb short-term cash.

Given the fact that SBUs are often changing from one quadrant of the portfolio matrix to another, management must continually assess the progress of each. Moreover, since all of them eventually will be harvested or divested, the company must always be on the lookout for new ventures that will turn into profitable SBUs of the future.[33]

---

[33] For a complementary approach to portfolio planning, see Thomas J. Cossé and John S. Swan, "Share Profit: A Planning Model for Product Managers," *Business Horizons* (July–August 1983):69–73.

FIGURE 7-3
The Relationship
Between the
Strategic Plan and
the Operational
Plan

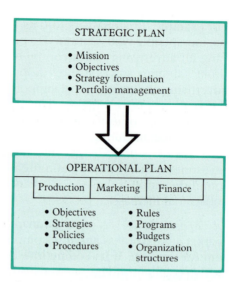

PUTTING STRATEGIC PLANNING INTO OPERATION

Once an organization has finished its portfolio management analysis, it knows which SBUs to push via further investment and which to prune via harvesting or direct divestment. It can then begin to put the plan into operation. The way this is done was explained in Chapter 6. Sometimes a firm opts for MBO; at other times it prefers a different type of approach, which helps break the overall plan into its component parts, delegating responsibility to the various departments or units. Figure 7-3 illustrates the relationship between the organization's strategic and operational plans.

Dealing with Problems

One thing that management needs to do is to deal with problems that arise.[34] Table 7-2 reports some of the major pitfalls that have to be avoided in carrying out strategic planning. These pitfalls were identified by managers themselves in a national survey.[35]

Another thing management must realize is that few plans ever work as anticipated.[36] This is why many firms have contingency plans that support their

---

[34] Donald C. Hambrick and Steven M. Schecter, "Turnaround Strategies for Mature Industrial-Product Business Units," *Academy of Management Journal* (June 1983):231–48.

[35] For more on this subject, see Alex R. Oliver and Joseph R. Garber, "Implementing Strategic Planning: Ten Sure-Fire Ways To Do It Wrong," *Business Horizons* (March–April 1983):49–51.

[36] Joseph Z. Wisenblit, "Crisis Management Planning Among U. S. Corporations: Empirical Evidence and a Proposed Framework," *SAM Advanced Management Journal* (Spring 1989):31–40.

TABLE 7-2   The Ten Most Important Pitfalls in Strategic Planning

1. Top management assumes that it can delegate the planning function to a planner.
2. Top management becomes so engrossed in current problems that it spends insufficient time on long-range planning and the process becomes discredited among other managers and staff.
3. Failure to develop company goals that are suitable as a basis for formulating long-range plans.
4. Failure to assume the necessary involvement in the planning process of major line personnel.
5. Failure to use plans as standards for measuring managerial performance.
6. Failure to create a climate in the company which is congenial and not resistant to planning.
7. Assuming that corporate comprehensive planning is something separate from the entire management process.
8. Injecting so much formality into the system that it lacks flexibility, looseness, and simplicity, and restrains creativity.
9. Failure of top management to review with departmental and divisional heads the long-range plans which they have developed.
10. Top management's consistently rejecting the formal planning mechanisms by making intuitive decisions which conflict with formal plans.

Source: George A. Steiner, *Strategic Planning: What Every Manager Must Know* (New York: The Free Press, 1979), 294. Copyright © 1979 by The Free Press. Adopted with permission of The Free Press, a Division of Macmillan, Inc.

primary ones. If something unexpected happens they switch to the contingency plan; if they had not planned for the new development in the contingency plan, they begin to do so immediately. They are flexible.

Finally, organizations must develop a monitoring system that lets them know what is going on and where progress is less than anticipated. Such a system allows them to play "catch-up ball" when necessary. Many firms have missed the boat but managed to correct their mistake. Consider McDonald's, the leading fast food franchiser. Initially it sold hamburgers and french fries, but over time the firm realized that customers wanted other fast foods, such as steak sandwiches and breakfast offerings. Eventually McDonald's added these items to its line. Examples such as this one suggest why it is important for a strategic plan to be reviewed and revised annually. In this way, the company ensures that its plan is as current as possible and takes into account the latest changes in the environment. Updating the plan involves effective decision making, a topic that will be explored in the next chapter.

SUMMARY

1. Two major characteristics differentiate strategic planning from planning in general. The first is the value system promoted by strategic planning. The second is the philosophy behind the process.

2. There are four elements in strategic planning: formulation of the basic mission, setting of strategic objectives, determination of strategy, and the use of portfolio planning.

3. Strategic planning is important for two reasons. First, it helps organizations cope with their external environment. Second, it assists them in redefining or reformulating their strategies or both.

4. Many organizations can profit from strategic planning. In particular, large businesses are finding this type of planning very helpful.

5. In determining the basic mission of the organization, top management must ask itself: What business are we in? What business should we be in? Will we need to change this mission over the next five years? Corporate culture is also important. It relates to values, such as defensiveness or aggressiveness, that set a pattern for a company's activities, opinions, and actions.

6. During the 1960s many firms used an investment planning approach as a substitute for strategic planning. Today this has changed. Organizations look for internal growth opportunities, and when they do buy other firms, they seek compatibility or a synergistic fit. Strategy is tailor-made to fit the situation.

7. Portfolio planning involves breaking the company into small business units (SBUs). Each SBU is a discrete, independent, product-market segment serviced by the firm. It is a business within a business. Those firms with a large number of SBUs have turned to the use of a portfolio matrix. This matrix measures long-term product-market attractiveness and competitive position. Based on the two measurements, an SBU can be judged to be a star, question mark, cash cow, or cash trap. There are recommended strategies for dealing with each.

8. Once the organization has finished its portfolio management analysis, it knows which SBUs to push via further investment and which to prune via harvesting or direct disinvestment. The organization can then put its strategic plan into operation.

KEY TERMS

Cash cow   An SBU with low long-term product-market attractiveness and a high competitive position. The strategy to employ with strong cash cows is to hold them, preserve market position, and generate dollars; with weak cash cows it is to harvest the unit and start moving toward divestment.

Cash trap   An SBU with low long-term product-market attractiveness and a low competitive position. The strategy to take with cash traps is to manage them so as to maximize short-term cash flow.

Competitive position   A portfolio matrix indicator that refers to the firm's business strength. Some of the factors commonly considered in measuring competitive position include growth rate, profitability, and management.

Concentric diversification   A combination of integration and diversification. It involves the development or acquisition of new products that have marketing and/or technological synergies with the company's current products but which are normally not intended for sale to its present markets.

Corporate culture   Values that set a pattern for a company's activities, opinions, and actions.

Long-term product-market attractiveness indicator   A portfolio matrix indicator that measures market potential. Some of the factors commonly considered in this measurement are segment growth rate, competitive diversity, and segment profitability.

Question mark   An SBU with high long-term product-market attractiveness and a low competitive position. The strategy to employ with these SBUs is to put some money behind them and see what happens. If the SBU develops into a star, fine; if not, the company should divest itself of the unit.

Star   An SBU with high long-term product-market attractiveness and a high competitive position. The strategy to employ with stars is one of building and investing.

Strategic business unit (SBU)   A discrete, independent, product-market segment serviced by a firm.

Strategic objectives   Return on investment, growth, market share, and other objectives that help determine future opportunities and call for a flexible/entrepreneurial leadership style that is willing to accept moderate to high risk.

QUESTIONS FOR ANALYSIS AND DISCUSSION

1. There are two major characteristics of strategic planning: the value system it promotes and the philosophy behind the process. What does this statement mean? Explain it in your own words.
2. In what way can strategic planning help an organization cope with the external environment? Be specific in your answer.
3. What does Table 7-1 illustrate about the external environment of business? What conclusions can be drawn from the findings it presents? Explain.
4. In general terms, what companies need strategic planning? Defend your answer.
5. How does an identification of the basic mission help an organization formulate a strategic plan? What role is played by corporate culture?
6. In what way has strategic planning changed between the 1960s and the 1990s? Be sure to include a discussion of investment planning in your answer.

7. How do modern firms go about building market share? Maintaining market share? Surviving in a hostile environment? In each case, give examples.

8. What is meant by portfolio planning? What is an SBU? Bring both ideas together and discuss how a portfolio matrix can help an organization manage its various business units. Be sure to include a discussion of stars, cash cows, question marks, and cash traps in your answer.

9. What are some of the most important pitfalls that must be dealt with in putting a strategic plan into operation? Identify and discuss five of them.

CASE

A Case of Portfolio Management

When the Robinson Products Company first designed its small hair blow dryer, management thought it would capture a large share of the market. Robinson's dryer was much smaller than the one sold by the competition, and it could be folded in two by swinging the handle parallel to the main blower. Robinson Products had put more than $3 million into designing and developing the dryer, but it was certain that these costs would be recovered quickly. However, that is not what happened.

When the machine was first introduced, sales were quite good. Unfortunately, one of the largest competitors came out with a similar hair dryer a month later. As a result Robinson's first-year sales were only 24 percent of forecast. Additionally, the company discovered that the competition had developed a much better advertising campaign.

Over the last three years Robinson's share of the market has fallen from 14 percent to just over 4 percent. Top management is now looking either to sell the product or simply to phase it out. The company knows that a strong advertising campaign would undoubtedly return a small profit but, as one of the top managers put it, "Why push a marginal product line? We have a lot of stars that warrant our investment." At the company's evaluation of product lines last week, the blow dryer was rated as having a low competitive position in a market segment with low long-term product-market attractiveness. Now management has to decide what to do with the product.

1. Based on the portfolio matrix in Figure 7-2, how should this product be labeled: star, cash cow, question mark, or cash trap?

2. Given your answer to the above question, what approach should the company use in handling this product line? Explain your answer.

3. If the product line had a high competitive position but had been judged to have low long-term product-market attractiveness, how would your answer to the above question be different? Explain.

A Campus of the Future?

A large regional state university is in the process of expanding into new and innovative educational opportunities. The university already has 10 colleges of various disciplines including a well-known architectural program, an industrial technology program, one of the nation's largest business schools, and a newly created Center for Information and Communication Sciences.

The new center has developed a master's degree for information and communication science, received state funding for and subsequently built a $10 million building to house the program, established a corporate fellows program that includes some of the top executives in the nation, and developed satellite capabilities in order to uplink and downlink programs, conferences, and other educational resources.

The center's goal is to create a "campus of the future" through a newly proposed partnership with a major communications corporation. The partnership idea is new but promising for the campus as a whole.

However, the president of the university is concerned with the costs, complications, and implementation of the project. The proposed networking of the campus entails a $1 million investment that would span 13 months before the project could be implemented.

The networking involves the use of voice, data, and video transmission throughout the campus, classrooms, dormitories, and offices. An installation of fiberoptics will be the major cost. Yet, a savings of thousands of dollars per year is expected due to the reduction of current activities individually performed in data, voice, or video.

The future of the university's image could be enhanced through implementation of the innovative project. Yet, the president of the university must be willing to take the risk.

Your Consultation

Assume the president has called on you for advice. What would you tell him in regard to the advantages and disadvantages of this project? What would you tell him about the risks involved in such an undertaking? What would you recommend that he do? Explain.

Integrative Case Study
Ford Motor Company — the 1980s

After Henry Ford II retired in 1979, the Ford Motor Company found itself in a challenging transitional stage. During the first three years of the 1980s, Ford lost $3.3 billion. Management blamed the loss on competition from imports, high inflation, and generally poor economic conditions worldwide.

According to industry experts, the company had also inherited morale and productivity problems which resulted in low-quality cars and unimaginative car designs.

Now, however, Ford is being cheered for superior product quality, inventive aerodynamic car designs, and a successful employee involvement program. Current president and CEO Donald Petersen was even named Man of the Year by *Motor Trend* magazine.

This decade of dramatic shifts in the company's fortunes has witnessed important strategic changes amid evolving political, social, technical, and consumption patterns.

Industry Background

The 1970s were tumultuous times for the auto industry. Oil price shocks of 1973 and 1979 reverberated throughout the economy. The American consumer, long enamored with large, powerful automobiles, began to clamor for smaller, more efficient cars. While domestic manufacturers scrambled to adjust their product lines to new consumer demands, European and Japanese manufacturers continued to provide high-quality, fuel-efficient small cars.

Foreign manufacturers, especially the Japanese, had a $1,000 to $1,500 per car cost advantage. This cost advantage can be traced to three primary causes. First, several foreign manufacturers had achieved greater productivity. The largest car importer to America, Japan, was able to use resources more effectively than Ford, General Motors, or Chrysler by using techniques such as "just-in-time" inventory. In contrast, the big three United States automobile manufacturers held costly inventories in raw materials, work-in-process, and finished goods.

The Japanese also had a labor cost advantage. The average Japanese production worker earned one-third less than his American counterpart. Finally, Japan's government and business community worked together on important issues such as trade and taxes while the United States typically had a more

This case was prepared by Cyril C. Ling of the University of Wisconsin-Whitewater with the assistance of Lynn Cohen, Roger Peterson, James Schad, and Brenda Stewart, and is intended as a basis for class discussion. Presented and accepted by the referred Midwest Society for Case Research. All rights reserved to the author and the USCR. Copyright © 1988 by Cyril C. Ling.

adversarial relationship. For example, U.S. government regulation of the auto industry occurred in several areas that made car production more costly. Emission control standards required equipment that added $600 to the retail price of a car between 1979 and 1981. Several required safety features, such as automatic restraints, were also introduced.

One of the major government requirements came in the area of fuel economy. Domestic manufacturers were required, in 1978, to raise the average level of car fuel economy from 19 mpg to 27.5 mpg by the 1985 model year. (Congress has since eased this requirement slightly.)

Double-digit inflation and high interest rates dampened the demand for domestically produced autos and raised borrowing costs for the industry, further aggravating the cost pressures of safety and emission requirements.

Ford faced some unique problems during the late 1970s and early 1980s. Henry Ford II, like his grandfather Henry Ford, liked to point out to his executives, "My name is on the building." From 1960 to 1979, Ford saw a parade of seven presidents. Lee Iacocca, now head of Chrysler, was fired by Henry Ford II in 1978 during the litigation which alleged Ford was negligent in designing the Pinto/Bobcat and was therefore responsible for several deaths.

Henry Ford II's greatest achievements while he headed Ford were building a management structure similar to General Motor's, and expanding overseas. Ford hired the "whiz kids," a team of young management experts from the Air Force, including Robert McNamara, to strengthen management though Henry was clearly the chief executive. This young team brought advanced, quantitative analytical methods, including cost benefit analysis and information systems, to the troubled company. Successful turnaround of Ford management was due to the efforts of this group and those of Ernest Breech, a lower TWA executive, selected by Henry for this task.

Perhaps his biggest mistake was Ford's failure to downsize the company's fleet as quickly as General Motors. In 1975, Lee Iacocca persuaded Ford to approve a small front-wheel-drive vehicle and have it ready for the 1978 market. Henry Ford II lobbied against then-president Lee Iacocca's plan to quickly downsize Ford offerings to have them ready for the 1978 showrooms. Ford thought that the Fiesta project started in Europe was enough of an investment in the small car future.

"I said 'It's wrong,'" Iacocca recalled, "We were drowning in cash. It was the greatest tactical error in automotive history. They get an F for management."[1]

But in the first quarter of 1975 Ford lost $11 million. Henry Ford II decided that it would be too risky to develop such an innovative car. Ford executives could only watch their market share decline as oil prices jumped, following the fall of the Shah of Iran in 1979. Iacocca's car, the Escort, would not be ready until 1980.

Along with its failure to downsize its products, Ford faced severe image and quality problems. In 1978, Ford recalled more cars than it built in the

United States. That year, the company retrofitted 1.2 million Bobcats and Pintos with fuel tank shields. "We have as much an image and perception problem as we have a product problem," explained Bennett E. Bidwell, vice-president of Ford's Car and Truck Group in 1980.[2] In April of 1979, Ford closed its Mahwah, New Jersey, assembly plant citing its poor quality record as the reason.

Ford Motor Company Management

Henry Ford II was never confronted. He handpicked a few bright managers to surround him and enact his policies and strategies. Ford's family owned 40 percent of the voting stock and he dominated the company from 1945 until his resignation as chairman in 1979.

"When you have a personality dominated company, you get a system of insiders built up around the boss. Ford has never been able to keep its first team intact," an industry analyst said.[3]

"There have been some pretty qualified people there, but they look over their shoulders a lot," said one former executive. "A system in which you occasionally shoot a lieutenant or a captain — or once in awhile a general — in front of the troops to maintain order tends to throttle initiative." [4]

Ford admits that some of its major problems were rooted in a management style dating to founder Henry Ford. Management had maintained a culture based on top-down directives and the snuffing out of any ideas that did not originate in the "Glass House" in Dearborn, Michigan.[5]

After Ford retired, the Ford Motor Company tried to break from the past management style. The new team, headed by Philip Caldwell, was made up of competent managers from Ford's European headquarters who lacked experience in product management — knowing what the American car buyer wanted and how to give it to them. He was left struggling with outdated models, a severe cash squeeze, and an image of quality so tarnished that it was feared the company's shrinking market share may continue for years.[6]

Soon after Caldwell took over, he announced that he was cutting back capital investments through 1984 to $3.5 billion a year from a planned $4 billion, and he closed two unprofitable assembly plants. Even this level of spending could strain Ford during the recessionary times ahead. "The situation is urgent," Caldwell said. "Our immediate problem is too little revenue and too much cost." [7]

Caldwell established a 1980 to 1985 plan that included production of the Ford Escort and Mercury Lynx, though he conceded that it would be difficult to make a profit on the Escort. A major component of the plan also included speeding up downsizing efforts.

"We are actually going through a real industrial revolution. Consider that every car, light truck, engine, transmission, axle and all of the smaller components will have to be retooled. Every plant that produces any of these is being redone from wall to wall," Caldwell said, adding that this was a rate of change three times faster than any Ford had experienced in the past.[8]

Caldwell reluctantly supported the Taurus project which had its inception in 1980. His okay held a caveat — he wanted reasons why this new car would be a success and he wanted to know how Ford planned to make it live up to the goal of being world-class in terms of quality and customer satisfaction. Final approval of the Taurus project came in 1982. Lewis Veraldi, then vice-president of engineering for Ford Europe, gathered the players for what would become "Team Taurus."

The team concept brought together all of the major specialties and disciplines *before* the designers began drawings and the engineers laid out production processes. "We (U.S. industry) were kind of segmented. If you were a marketer or a salesman, you did not worry about engineering. If you were a PR guy you didn't worry about manufacturing. You did not work as a group," Veraldi said. "(Team) Taurus was an example of how a group working together . . . really can address customer satisfaction better." [9]

In 1985, Ford's project Alpha, designed to reassess all aspects of car manufacturing, was instituted as a major method of improving efficiency. The Alpha team studied car manufacturing, purchasing, marketing, distribution, and all related business systems. Alpha defined 400 attributes of "world-class" cars.

In 1985, Caldwell stepped down and Donald E. Petersen took over as chairman of Ford. Petersen described Ford as a "people-centered company producing customer-centered products." Some believed Petersen was best suited by background to attack Ford's product problems. He holds a degree in mechanical engineering, has experience in product planning at Ford, and is proud of Ford products. He championed Ford's decision to adopt a boldly aerodynamic look to its newest car models.[10]

"Today, we talk about Ford people. That's all of us, and we're working together as a team. Together, we are coming up with solutions to problems that have remained intractable for decades . . . like job training, job security, job satisfaction . . . as well as productivity improvements, absentee reduction and keeping benefit costs in line," Petersen said.[11]

Petersen identified five strategies for a successful future at Ford Motor Company. First, he said that Ford must recognize that the only way to keep its North American business profitable is to produce high-quality products that provide the customer good value. Second, Ford must continue to expand product lines in markets worldwide and improve product performance with new technology and reduce cost by capitalizing on low-cost sources of production.

Third, Petersen said, Ford must expand its relationship with Mazda Corporation — a Japanese automotive manufacturer in which it has a 25 percent interest. Mazda has assisted in the design of several vehicles, among which the Probe, built in the Mazda plant at Flat Rock, Michigan, may be the best known. The fourth strategy involves improving Ford's overall strength by developing new sources of earnings and strengthening the existing non-automotive businesses. The final element of the strategy for the future is to increase shareholder value.

Labor Relations at Ford

Since 1979, Ford and the United Auto Workers have been creating joint programs that seek to create conditions which encourage employee contribution. Through these joint efforts, workers have the opportunity to participate in decisions concerning their jobs and also have access to education and training. Company and union have actively pursued cooperation rather than an adversarial relationship.

In the past, employees weren't active in decision making. As stated by Bill Skaggs, local union president at the Indianapolis plant, "Until now, the company has been putting more emphasis on maintaining a machine than on maintaining an employee." [12] Ford management and workers realized that improving the quality of work life was significant in improving the quality of products. Thus, in 1979 Ford started a program called Employee Involvement (EI). Ford and the UAW worked together to develop the program, building on employee knowledge to improve the quality of work life. EI activities started with a select pilot group and later expanded to involve groups in many departments encompassing every level of the organization.

There were three types of EI activities: (1) problem-solving groups included those involved in the same type of work; (2) quality circles used formal quality control and statistical techniques; and (3) team-building activities focused on common objectives. The UAW-Ford National Joint Committee on Employee Involvement (NJCEI) provided guidance to Ford managers and union officials. Education and training that stressed the importance of communication were provided.

In 1980, at the Ranger and Bronco II plant in Louisville, engineers sent drawings, parts, and models to the assembly division to get input from the line workers.[13] Employees were willing to share their ideas and their knowledge. EI gave workers the authority to solve mechanical problems and take an active role in increasing productivity.

With the advent of the Employee Involvement program, the 1982 labor contract expanded on employee relations. Donald F. Ephlin, former UAW director of Ford negotiations and current director of General Motors negotiations, outlined the 1982 contract, which included:[14]

- Profit sharing
- Supplemental Unemployment Benefits (SUB)
- Joint training
- Wage freeze until September 1984
- Deferred cost-of-living allowances (COLA)
- Elimination of paid personal holidays

- 24-month moratorium on plant closings resulting from outsourcing
- 2 plants under lifetime job security plans
- Guaranteed Income Stream (GIS)
- Reopener

The significance of this contract was the concessions made by both parties. Under the Guaranteed Income Stream program, workers with high seniority were guaranteed a minimum income until the age of 62 or retirement. The reopener allows the UAW to reopen the contract with the right to strike if sales increase by a specified amount. Never before had an auto maker agreed on profit sharing for line workers.

The 1982 contract also introduced the Employee Development and Training Program (EDTP), which offered assistance to active and displaced workers. Much of the training takes place at the UAW-Ford National Development and Training Center in Dearborn, MI. Employees were given opportunities to learn skills pertaining to their current position, gained expertise to help them advance, had access to education unrelated to Ford, and even education enhancing personal growth.

Philip Caldwell, former president and CEO, emphasized the importance of education: "Ford has recognized that training and education cannot be treated as expendable 'fringe benefits,' but rather they are critical elements in meeting quality and productivity goals — and in building for the future." [15]

During the period that EI was introduced, Ford underwent a drastic reduction in its labor force: 86,000 jobs were eliminated. The reduction allowed more job flexibility and emphasis on team work. The 1982 contract was designed to save existing jobs with the introduction of lifetime job security.

In October 1984, and again in 1987, the contract continued the advances produced in the earlier agreement. In 1984 there was a wage increase with 2.5 percent lump-sum increases in the second and third years and a three year moratorium on plant closings. The most significant change was the introduction of the Protected Employee Program (PEP). This program once again proved Ford's commitment to labor relations and employee involvement.

The 1987 contract expresses Ford's commitment to employee relations and to constructive joint efforts with the UAW, including:

- Guaranteed employment numbers for each plant
- Layoffs only for sales reductions, and reinstatement of those workers as sales increase
- Three percent wage increase in the first year, and three percent lump-sum bonuses for the second and third years
- Cost-of-living adjustment (COLA) maintained
- Benefit increases
- Child care assistance
- Moratorium on most plant closings

- Joint labor-management groups
- Continuation of a 1984 program to explore the creation of non-automotive businesses

Benefit increases negotiated included pensions, insurance, profit sharing, and payments to laid off workers. Joint labor-management groups were developed to examine ways to reduce job classifications and production costs, and to improve product quality. Creating non-automotive businesses as part of a risk reduction strategy was expected to absorb displaced Ford auto workers.

Experts agree that opening up of communications at Ford led to a substantial information exchange. People had better understanding of each other's problems, and more and better information was available for decision making.[16] The EI program helped employees become more aware of manufacturing "concerns"—a "concern" is a problem which can cause customer dissatisfaction. Some plants have been recorded as having as high as 700 concerns per 100 cars. At the end of 1982, the Louisville plant had a mere 198 concerns per 100 cars.[17]

Ford Products

During the 1970s, Ford cars were big, boxy, and boring—"sofas with seatbelts," according to Veraldi. Ford executives thought that they could make no mistakes by following the industry leader, General Motors. But by the end of 1980 the harsh reality of a cyclical industry arrived. Over the next two years the company lost almost $4 billion. Clearly, products were one critical element needing careful study.

Louis Lataif, a Ford vice-president, noted, "A large organization will keep right on doing whatever it's doing as long as the profits hold out. Individual buyers were telling us they didn't like the products but as an organization, we didn't hear them until the message was written in big, big numbers." [18] In the past, top management had always asked the design team to reach out and stretch the imagination. Whenever presented with unique designs, however, management always vetoed those considered to be too radical. Ford's top management wanted, and always got, a car just like last year's model.

The seed of change was planted in the 1960s as Ford started to rotate more managers to the European division. Time in Europe was an initiation. If successful in Europe, managers were brought back to corporate headquarters in Dearborn with expectations of further advancement. Donald Petersen, chairman of the board, spent time in Europe and became disenchanted after his return. "Every year we had a higher percentage of managers who had spent time in Europe and, when they came back, didn't have such built-in prejudices against functionality." [19]

Surprisingly, the background of many top executives in Detroit is in finance. Roger Smith is the latest of more than two decades of GM chief executives to rise through finance — not engineering, manufacturing, or design. Not only is Petersen's background in product-planning, he's a true "car nut." He loves talking about cars and driving cars. Ford executives now routinely go to Bob Boundurant's performance driving school in California where amateurs are taught the same driving principles used by competitive drivers the world over.

When Petersen approached Jack Telnack, Ford's top designer, in the early 1980s and asked if he was proud of his own designs Petersen received a frank reply, "No, I'm embarrassed by them." After showing Petersen designs of a radically different Thunderbird, aerodynamically smooth and European in influence, Telnack got the go-ahead for cars that take the driver seriously. Telnack brought Ford design into the future with the 1983 Thunderbird and the less-radical Tempo and Topaz compacts. However, the Ford Taurus and Mercury Sable midsize cars were designed to capture the young and prosperous buyers who were intrigued by European design and handling.

Not all Fords yet have the 'acro' look — Lincoln Town car, a very profitable model, still maintains a boxlike shape. Telnack cars have steeply angled windshields, lights that wrap around rounded corners, and integral bumpers/spoilers. Even the Town car will receive some "rounding."

Ford engineers dissected the competition. They analyzed the trunk mechanism of the Audi 5000. They studied the hood balancing mechanism on the Toyota Camry. Engineers incorporated some of the best features of competitors' automobiles into their own, so that Taurus and Sable were American-made cars worth a second look. Telnack is not remaining static in the wake of the success of Taurus and Sable; his designs for the future include shorter hoods, more glass area, and passenger compartments moved further forward.

In 1980, Ford was the nation's second largest auto maker, facing its worst year ever since the near-bankruptcy after World War II. Philip Caldwell saw many problems for Ford Motor Company and didn't expect sales to improve quickly. Many of these same problems also faced General Motors and Chrysler. Import sales continued to be strong. Caldwell and other auto executives spent a great amount of time seeking import restrictions which would effectively force the price of the popular imports up to a level that Ford could compete with. Hoping to regain market share from the fuel-efficient subcompacts from overseas, Ford introduced the Escort and Lynx in 1980. Credit buyers could take advantage of direct interest subsidies of amounts between $500 and $1,000. Ford, like other car makers, also offered rebates of up to $500 a car. While Ford only held about 17 percent of the small car market it was the leading domestic producer of small cars.

Ford finally did downsize its biggest cars — Continentals, Thunderbirds, and others — in 1981. Engine and drive-train systems were changed to allow for fuel-efficient operation but the cars still looked like "gas-guzzlers." Ford was convinced that this was what the American car buyer wanted. But, consumers continued spending their money on Japanese imports. To entice buyers, Ford continued to offer rebates in 1982, some as much as $2,000. The number two auto maker also increased warranties, offering five year/50,000 mile protection plans, low financing charges, and free maintenance, following Chrysler's lead in some of these areas.

Ford hesitated to leave the larger cars because of the larger profit margin they carried. Even though the Escort claimed the title as the best-selling small car in the United States — domestic or foreign — Ford lost $400 on every Escort it sold, according to 1984 data.[20]

Imports seem to have won over the American public on the basis of quality, reliability, and cost. The Japanese built a reputation for a quality product by keeping the assembly process uncomplicated and by offering a few basic models with extensive standard equipment and only a few options. Ford built cars to dealer orders, contending with dozens of separate options and features.

Along with product considerations, Ford was fighting an image problem. To convince the public it was changing, Ford beefed up its corporate image advertising which highlighted the company's "World Class Technology." "We're selling the competence of Ford Motor Company, the resources of the company, trying to convey to the American public this is a massive worldwide organization with the capabilities bigger than they believed and that we are right on target with today's requirements . . . for small cars," John Boweres, corporate advertising manager said.[21] At the same time, in a Ford boardroom, top managers were deciding to make the Taurus a "clean sheet" car rather than a combination of existing cars. They committed themselves to the estimated $3.25 billion project.

Ford increased prices in 1981 by 4.8 percent. Even the rebate offers didn't seem to bring in the customers. Japan had agreed to voluntarily curb auto shipments because it was afraid of possible quotas but Ford still lost $334.5 million. Caldwell blamed the loss on generally poor economic conditions, including high inflation and interest rates.

Ford began a campaign to at least get on people's shopping lists, to be considered for purchase. At the time, only 30 percent of new car shoppers considered Ford. About 25 percent of new car shoppers wouldn't give any attention to buying a Ford — most of these had been converted to imports.[22] "Have you driven a Ford lately?" became the company's new slogan. A year later Ford added a quality-oriented statement to this theme: "Best built American cars," and "Best built American trucks." Claims of high quality were backed by Rogers Research, a private industry firm and Product and Consumer Evaluations Inc., which interviewed 14,000 new car owners six months after their purchase.[23]

Recovery in the American auto industry began in 1983 as interest rates started to come down. Car and truck sales were at their highest levels in four years. Profits, also on the rise, were due partly to cost-cutting programs instituted during the recession. Imports still held a 26.5 percent market share in the U.S. and Japan extended its voluntary quota for one more year.

In late 1982, Team Taurus members were brought over from Europe.

Team Taurus, a new integrated approach to car design and manufacturing at Ford, was made up of people from styling, engineering, manufacturing, sales, marketing, legal, and other departments. Interaction between all of these departments before the product was planned helped avoid costly changes later in the process. The old approach was based on each person having sequential responsibilities to perform, like a relay race. The design was passed on to the manufacturing people and later the engineer learned that manufacturing couldn't make the design changes effectively with necessary reliability, so design changes were required—in product, process, or both. Ford estimated that it saved $400 million developing the Taurus car with the team concept. The Taurus and its sister, the Sable, were rated by many industry experts as the year's top cars and the public responded in kind. The timing was right. Total U.S. car sales in 1985 rose to a record 15.6 million units. Cut-rate financing, generally good economic conditions and a variety of new models contributed to the boom. Some say that Ford bet the company on its new "jelly bean" styling while General Motors stayed with its squarish look. Ford's new rounded look had been pioneered in the early 1980s in Europe by Audi, Opel, and other manufacturers. Mercedes, Volkswagen, and NSU had also experimented with rounded shapes in the design projects. But Louis Lataif, Ford's head of sales, believed the company had captured a "big victory" with the Taurus and Sable.

At the same time, there was a growing movement of Japanese automobile manufacturers into United States assembly operations. A new line of low-priced cars, made up entirely of imports, was established. Domestic producers feared these new low-priced cars would attract those who in the past had purchased used cars. Foreign cars posted the biggest gains in 1985, even though Japan was still restricting imports.

Ford did have two stabilizing factors throughout the 1980s. The company's truck line remained for the most part unchanged during this time. It was able to maintain a large portion of its market share and its profitability without any large expenditures for retooling. The solid image and profitability of Ford trucks contributed a great deal to the company at a time when Ford was risking so much with the broad-based changes in the car lines. Also, European operations were profitable, and permitted the company some financial success during the costly domestic restructuring.

Ford's Risk Diversification Strategy

In November 1979, Ford took a major step toward diversification from the automotive industry. It merged a subsidiary company, Ford Industries Ltd., with Toyo Kohyo Ltd. (Mazda) in exchange for 25 percent of its stock. This move allowed the company to profit, at least marginally, from the increasing sales of Japanese cars in the American market.

During the 1980s, Ford Motor Company expanded the policy of risk diversification. The most notable of many acquisitions were the purchases of First

Nationwide Financial Corporation in 1985 and the New Holland farm equipment company from Sperry Corporation in 1986. The purchase prices of these acquisitions were $493 million and $330 million, respectively. Ford President Harold Poling said in regard to the First Nationwide acquisition, "This acquisition is part of Ford's plan of adding to our present strengths by developing new sources of earning." [24]

Eventually, Ford expects 10 to 15 percent of its sales revenues in non-automotive businesses. Other major domestic automakers have expressed similar goals and have begun making acquisitions in financial services and other areas. Traditionally, Ford has earned seven to eight percent of its income from non-auto revenues. In recent years the non-automotive businesses have not been profitable, failing to even cover their operating expenses.

The First Nationwide acquisition is expected to provide steady earnings which can smooth those of the cyclical auto industry. Ford estimates First Nationwide's growth at 10 percent per year in the near future. On the negative side, Ford paid $239 million over fair market value for First Nationwide. This additional expense is denoted as goodwill in the accounting statements and will be amortized on a straight-line basis over the next 25 years.

The purchase of New Holland farm equipment from Sperry Corporation was viewed as a "natural" for Ford by many industry followers. Ford was able to add to its tractor division through the assumption of the complementary lines of New Holland. Ford intends to keep the New Holland name on its product lines, which include combines, mowers, balers, and other tractor-driven equipment. Ford was able to assume the New Holland dealerships with relatively little overlap of their current Ford dealerships.

The farm equipment industry had been sluggish throughout the 1980s and has undergone a significant amount of change. Several large firms have merged recently, including J. I. Case, International Harvester, and Duetz-Allis Chalmers. Reduction in the number of competitors and the associated reduction in production capacity is expected to make the farm implement industry more profitable in the future. New Holland generated a profit throughout the 1980s despite the adverse conditions, and at a purchase price of $330 million many analysts consider it a bargain.

Ford is also diversified internationally. International operations have contributed to Ford's profit during the 1980s at a time when the North American operations were in serious trouble. Foreign revenues have also helped smooth the cyclical nature of domestic auto industry earnings. In 1980, when Ford reported a loss of $1.5 billion, that loss would have been much greater if it wasn't for the $600 million of overseas profits that were included. Of course, the effectiveness of international diversification is heavily dependent on international exchange rates.

Another strategy for spreading risk is to become involved in joint ventures with other auto producers. Ford has continued its relationship with Mazda since the 1979 merger, and more recently has undertaken some new joint ventures. In

April 1986, Ford announced plans for Ford of Britain to begin a joint venture with Iveco, a subsidiary of Fiat S.P.A. The agreement calls for the companies to manufacture and sell heavy trucks in Britain, the vehicles produced at Ford's Langley, Berkshire plant which employs 1,700 workers. This new line of trucks will be sold and serviced through a unified network of Ford and Iveco dealers. Outside the U.K. the trucks will be marketed through current Ford dealerships.

Ford also announced in May 1987 that the company had agreed to study the possibility of a joint venture with the Nissan Motor Company to build a new multipurpose vehicle in North America. The joint study has encompassed plant sites, parts procurement procedures, and other aspects related to profitability of the venture.

A Look to the Future

When asked about Ford's future, Petersen talks about a plan to globally integrate the company around "Centers of Excellence," to carry Ford through the 1990s and beyond. He considers auto manufacturing a global industry now and plans to make Ford the first truly global auto maker.[25] Under the Centers of Excellence plan, Ford will focus the development of a specific automobile or component in the Ford technical center that has the greatest expertise in that particular area. The ultimate goal is to do each project only once for all of Ford's markets. Ford executives estimate savings in the millions of dollars by eliminating duplicative efforts and expensive retooling. This strategy has proven to be difficult to implement due to old loyalties and values, and established ways of serving automobile markets.

As the auto industry expands globally, the oligopolistic structure is changing. In addition to the "big three," the U.S. industry now includes three big Japanese companies: Toyota, Nissan, and Honda. The smaller contenders, like Mercedes, Volkswagen, Mazda, and others are strong too—not only in the U.S. but also in their home markets.[26] Joint ventures in research, development, and manufacturing and some mergers will likely describe the future of a variety of auto manufacturers.

A study conducted by the Massachusetts Institute of Technology, titled "The Future of the Automobile," produced six principal findings:

1. The auto's future as the prime means for personal transport is quite secure because of the flexibility of the basic concept and the robustness of automotive technology.
2. Recent predictions that by early in the twenty-first century there would remain only about six producers is wrong.
3. An earlier held perception that the industry's output would be a family of new "world" cars is also no longer valid.
4. The outlook for large cars is good even if energy prices rise and competition from foreigners is not expected in this area.

5. U.S. makers are continuing to refine fuel-efficient drive trains and bodies and have the ability to quickly shift the drive train mix toward increased fuel efficiency.
6. The shift by major auto makers to low-wage locations will not occur on the scale once expected—the markets of the developing countries are demanding precise high-quality production.[27]

APPENDIX A
Financial Summary

Ford Motor Company's financial records give added support to the contention that the organization has undergone a great deal of change in the 1980s. Even in late 1983, some industry analysts predicted that Ford would not survive. The large losses in the U.S. market were offset by profits from abroad and by tax credits as well as from depreciation, but the company's cash flows were quite small. Liquidity ratios fell significantly throughout 1982, adding to Ford's credit risk. This happened at the same time interest rates were reaching all-time highs. Ford needed to raise additional capital for retooling their factories and it was going to be expensive. The poor profitability, increased financial leverage, and the high level of capital spending all contributed to a much riskier position for Ford.

During this time, Ford was also criticized for maintaining a stable dividend policy despite record losses. But, Ford defended its actions by saying the dividend was necessary to protect the integrity of Ford's securities and that Ford was being socially responsible in not eliminating a source of income many people depended on. Ford treasurer John Sagan said, "You can't willy-nilly raise dividends or eliminate them. You do that, you're a schlock company. It's like your virtue. Once you lose it, it's gone forever." [28]

As discussed, the capital spending resulted in new products that enabled Ford to increase its market share in the mid-1980s and greatly improve its

TABLE 7-3   Ratio Analysis for Ford Motor Company

	1979	1980	1981	1982	1983	1984	1985	1986
Current ratio	1.2	1.0	1.0	0.8	1.0	1.1	1.1	1.2
Quick ratio	0.6	0.6	0.6	0.4	0.7	0.8	0.7	0.8
Inventory turnover	7.4	7.2	8.2	8.9	10.8	12.7	11.5	10.8
Average collection period	22.5	29.1	24.4	23.1	22.4	17.4	19.5	20.0
Fixed asset utilization	4.7	3.7	3.9	3.7	4.5	5.0	4.2	4.8
Total asset utilization	1.9	1.5	1.7	1.7	1.9	1.9	1.7	1.7
Total debt to toal assets	0.6	0.6	0.7	0.7	0.7	0.6	0.6	0.6
Long-term debt to C/S equity	0.1	0.2	0.4	0.4	0.4	0.2	0.2	0.1
Net profit margin	2.7%	−4.2%	−2.8%	−1.8%	4.2%	5.6%	1.8%	5.2%
Return on assets	5.0%	−6.3%	−4.6%	−3.0%	7.8%	10.6%	8.0%	8.7%
Return on equity	11.2%	−17.8%	−14.4%	−10.8%	24.7%	29.6%	20.5%	22.1%

TABLE 7-4   U.S. Car Market Shares

Year	U.S. Manufacturers (including imports)				
	Ford	GM	Chrysler	AMC	Total
1981	16.6%	44.6%	9.9%	2.0%	73.1%
1982	16.9%	44.2%	10.0%	1.9%	73.0%
1983	17.2%	44.3%	10.3%	2.5%	74.3%
1984	19.2%	44.5%	10.4%	2.0%	76.1%
1985	19.0%	42.7%	11.4%	1.2%	74.3%
1986	18.2%	41.1%	11.5%	0.7%	71.5%

Year	Imports by Foreign Companies		
	Japanese	All Others	Total
1981	20.4%	6.5%	26.9%
1982	21.2%	5.8%	27.0%
1983	20.2%	5.5%	25.7%
1984	18.3%	5.6%	23.9%
1985	19.7%	6.0%	25.7%
1986	20.5%	8.0%	28.5%

TABLE 7-5   U.S. Truck Market Shares

Year	U.S. Manufacturers (including imports)				
	Ford	GM	Chrysler	AMC	Other
1981	31.4%	37.1%	8.2%	2.8%	5.4%
1982	30.6%	40.2%	9.5%	2.5%	3.5%
1983	31.3%	39.5%	8.7%	2.6%	3.2%
1984	28.0%	34.5%	12.6%	3.7%	3.8%
1985	26.8%	34.9%	12.8%	3.8%	3.1%
1986	28.1%	32.4%	12.1%	4.2%	2.9%

Year	Imports by Foreign Companies		
	Japanese	All Others	Total
1981	12.8%	2.3%	15.1%
1982	12.5%	1.2%	13.7%
1983	13.9%	0.8%	14.7%
1984	16.8%	0.6%	17.4%
1985	18.0%	0.6%	18.6%
1986	19.9%	0.4%	20.3%

profitability. Ford used the cash flow from operations to fund additional capital-intensive projects, as well as repay a substantial portion of its debt.

As of May 1987, the company held more than $9 billion in cash. Plans for the future call for Ford to increase capital spending into the 1990s. Ford also intends to operate plants at near capacity and discount the risk of not being able to produce enough during industry booms. Chairman Petersen said, "We're going to be very aggressive." [29]

References

[1] Meadows, Edward, "Ford Needs Better Ideas Fast," *Fortune,* June 16, 1980, pp. 82-86.

[2] "The Massive Recall that Ford Faces," *Business Week,* December 8, 1980, pp. 31-34.

[3] Meadows, "Ford Needs," pp. 82-86.

[4] "Ford After Henry II," *Business Week,* April 30, 1979, pp. 62-72.

[5] Moskal, Brian, "Glasnost in Dearborn," *Industry Week,* September 21, 1987, pp. 53-55.

[6] Meadows, "Ford Needs," pp. 82-86.

[7] "Driving to Rebuild Ford for the Future," *Business Week,* August 4, 1980, pp. 70-71.

[8] Seidler, Edouard, "Caldwell: Man at the Helm at Ford," *Automotive News,* June 16, 1980, pp. 32-38.

[9] Ealey, Lance, "Ford's Lewis Veraldi: Man of the Year," *Automotive Industries,* February 1987, pp. 64-67.

[10] Edid, Maralyn et al., "Now That It's Cruising, Can Ford Keep Its Foot on the Gas?" *Business Week,* February 11, 1985, pp. 48-52.

[11] "Ford 'People Changes' Reviewed by Petersen," *Automotive News,* August 15, 1985, p. 53.

[12] Tavernier, Gerard, "Awakening a Sleeping Giant: Ford's Employee Involvement Program," *Management Review,* June, 1981, pp. 15-20.

[13] Main, Jeremy, "Ford's Drive for Quality," *Fortune,* April 18, 1983, pp. 62-70.

[14] Ephlin, Donald, "SMR Forum: The UAW-Ford Agreement—Joint Problem Solving," *Sloan Management Review,* Winter 1983, pp. 61-65.

[15] Caldwell, Philip, "Cultivating Human Resource Potential at Ford," *Journal of Business Strategy,* Spring 1984, pp. 74-77.

[16] Moskal, "Glasnost," pp. 53-55.

[17] Main, "Ford's Drive," pp. 62-70.

[18] Easterbrook, Gregg, "Have You Driven a Ford Lately?" *The Washington Monthly,* October 1986, pp. 23-34.

[19] Ibid.

[20] Hamilton, Kathleen, "$2.5 Billion Turnaround for Ford," *Automotive News,* February 20, 1984, p. 4.

[21] Bohn, Joseph, "Ford Ad Drive to Push Firm's Global Strengths," *Automotive News,* July 21, 1980, p. 2.

22 Bohn, Joseph, "Low-Keyed Ad Theme for 1983 Ford," *Automotive News,* October 4, 1982, p. 32.

23 Bohn, Joseph, "Ford Ads Accent Product Quality," *Automotive News,* Sept. 5, 1983, p. 7.

24 Krebs, Michelle, "Ford Spends $500 Million for S & L Firm," *Automotive News,* August 5, 1985, p. 1.

25 Treece, John, "Can Ford Stay On Top?" *Business Week,* September 28, 1987, pp. 78–86.

26 Flint, Jerry, "Best Car Wins," *Forbes,* January 27, 1986, pp. 71–77.

27 Plotkin, A. S., "MIT Dissects Future of Auto and Finds Outlook Promising," *Automotive News,* August 13, 1984, p. 2.

28 Sloan, Allan, "Generous to a Fault?" *Forbes,* April 13, 1981, pp. 31–32.

29 Versipal, Donald, "Ford to Increase Capital Spending in Next 5 Years," *Automotive News,* May 18, 1987, p. 6.

THREE

ORGANIZING THE ENTERPRISE'S STRUCTURE

This part of the book studies the ways in which managers design their organizational structures and staff the positions within the enterprise.

Chapter 8 addresses the topic of overall design. In this chapter, you will learn the three internal and three external factors that most influence organizational design. You will also study the most popular forms of departmentalization, including functional, product, territorial, and matrix. The role of job analysis, job descriptions, and job specifications in the organizing process will also be presented.

Chapter 9 is a natural follow-up to the previous chapter. Now that you know how the structure is designed, you are ready to examine the coordination and design of jobs. In this chapter, you will learn the most common types of coordination found in modern organizations and how authority is used to bring coordination about. The subject of decentralization will also be broached, and key factors that influence the degree of decentralization will be identified and studied. Attention will also be focused on such key coordination topics as delegation, the role of committees, and job design.

Chapter 10 is concerned with recruiting, selecting, training, and subsequent development of organization personnel. At this point, you will learn about human resource planning and the link between strategic planning and employment needs. You will also find out how organizations forecast employment needs and use the recruiting and selection process to obtain the necessary personnel. The subject of orientation, so valuable in retaining personnel and ensuring that their work performance is as high as possible, is also covered. Attention will be focused on both employee training and management development programs, with consideration given both to the types of programs modern enterprises use and how they measure results to evaluate the overall effectiveness of these programs.

When you have finished studying all of the material in these three chapters, you will have a sound understanding of the way managers organize and staff their structures. You will also be aware of the many pitfalls and problems that confront them as they attempt to implement these efficiency measures.

8

Designing the Overall Structure

OBJECTIVES

This chapter examines the ways in which modern enterprises organize their overall structures. This examination covers both the internal and external forces that influence organizational design, as well as the specific forms of departmentalization used in organizations. Consideration is also given to the influence of span of control on structural design and the role played by job definitions. By the time you have finished reading and studying the material in this chapter, you should be able to:

1. Define the term organizing.
2. Identify and describe the three internal and three external factors that most influence organizational design.
3. Compare and contrast mechanistic and organic structures.
4. Explain how the following major forms of departmentalization work— functional, product, territorial, and matrix.
5. Discuss the effect of span of control on organizational design and discuss how managers can determine ideal spans for their own particular departments or units.
6. Discuss the role of job analysis, job descriptions, and job specifications in the organizing process.

THE NATURE OF ORGANIZATIONAL DESIGN

Organizing defined   As we saw in an earlier chapter, organizing is the process of assigning duties and coordinating the efforts of personnel in their pursuit of the enterprise's objectives. This process has two specific facets: structure and coordination. Having identified objectives and strategy during the planning phase, the organization has to determine who will do what and how intra- and interdepartmental coordination will be attained.[1] Figure 8-1 shows how structural considerations are addressed.

STRUCTURAL CONSIDERATIONS

Strategy influences structure   Strategy influences structure. If the organization intends to sell its goods or services in the local area, the structure used will be different from that employed by an enterprise operating in a 10-state area or by one with branches in overseas locations. Moreover, as organizations change their strategies, they also modify their structures.[2] For example, a firm selling a single product or service in a stable environment usually opts for a functional organizational structure in which personnel are organized according to the activities they perform. As the company increases its offerings to several products, it may change to a product form of organization. If the firm becomes a multiline manufacturer it will typically change again, opting for a territorial or matrix structure. These four forms of organizational design will be explained later in the chapter.

Internal and external factors also help dictate the most effective structure. One internal force, for example, is the characteristics of the employees. The way the employees want to be managed influences the type of structure used. One external force is the dynamism of the external environment. Firms in a competitive environment are organized differently from those in a stable environment.

An organization's structure usually takes the form of one or more of the following four kinds of departmentalization: functional, product, geographic, or matrix (again see Figure 8-1). In creating an overall structure the organization also has to determine the specific design of each department. How many levels should each contain? What are the effects of having just a few as opposed to many? Which is most efficient and why? How can the manager determine

---

[1] Richard S. Blackburn, "Dimensions of Structure: A Review and Reappraisal," *Academy of Management Review* (January 1982):59–66; See also: Gregory K. Dow, "Configurational and Coactivational Views of Organization Structure," *Academy of Management Review* (January 1988):53–64.

[2] Ron Lachman, "Power From What? A Reexamination of its Relationship with Structural Conditions," *Administrative Science Quarterly* (June 1989):231–251.

FIGURE 8-1   Designing the Overall Structure

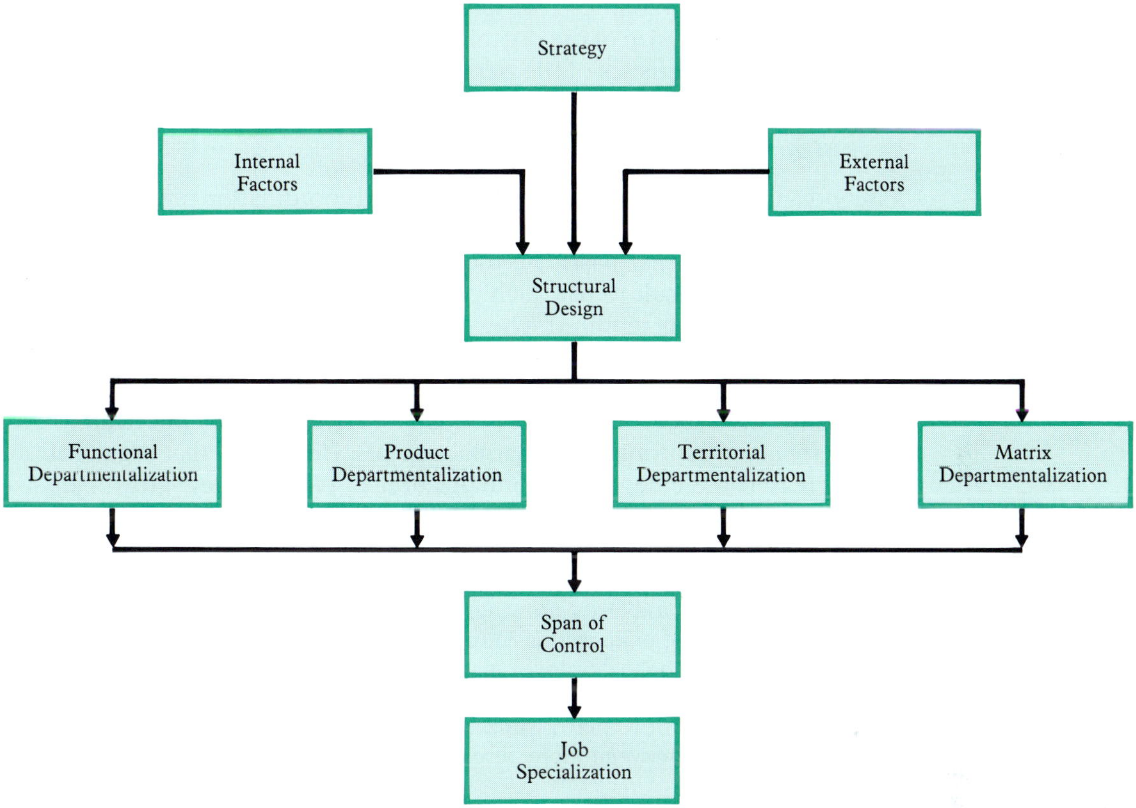

what is best for each specific department? What are the major factors to be examined? These questions are all answered in the section of the chapter that addresses the span of control concept.

Finally, each department contains personnel who carry out the necessary duties and tasks. Job descriptions are used to acquaint them with their assignments and tell them to whom they report and who reports to them.

In this chapter, the four major parts of Figure 8-1 will be studied in detail. The first area of consideration is the internal and external factors affecting structure.

INTERNAL AND EXTERNAL FACTORS

Three internal and three external factors influence organizational structure. These factors help dictate whether the structure is basically bureaucratic or highly innovative. They also influence the form of departmentalization.

Internal Factors

The three internal variables that have the greatest effect on organizational structure are (1) the size of the organization, (2) the diversity of its operations, and (3) the characteristics of the personnel.

Organization Size

As an organization increases in size, control and coordination requirements are likely to increase.[3] When an organization has 25 people, business can be carried out on a very informal basis. As the number increases to 250, however, it becomes more difficult to use such procedures, and a more formal organizational arrangement is required. These findings have been supported with empirical data, some of it collected by John Child, who conducted research involving 82 British firms selected from a series of different industries, including advertising, insurance, electronics manufacturing, newspaper publishing, confectionary manufacturing, and pharmaceuticals. He reports that organizations that increased their degree of formalization to parallel their growth in size tended to achieve higher levels of performance than those that did not.

Large organizations are usually more bureaucratic than small organizations

> Much as critics may decry bureaucracy, we found that in each industry the more profitable and faster-growing companies were those that had developed this type of organization in fuller measure with their growth in size above the 2,000-or-so employee mark. At the other end of the scale, among small firms of about 100 employees, the better performers generally managed with very little formal organization. The larger the company, the higher the correlation between more bureaucracy and superior performance.[4]

These findings do not mean, however, that all large organizations turn into huge bureaucracies. When personnel are spread out among a number of different locations, formalization at each locale is likely to be less than it would be if all personnel were located under a single roof. For this reason, we are likely to find greater bureaucracy in a large manufacturing plant than in a retail chain with stores spread over a five-state region.

Moreover, while many research studies have investigated the effect of size on structure, the relationship between the two is not totally clear.[5] Some studies have found a strong relationship and argue that it is causal, while others either

Size is a causal factor in many cases

---

[3] Robert J. Dowling, "Is the Big Corporation Its Own Worst Enemy?" *Business Week* (April 22, 1985):12, and Greg Couch, "Is Your Company Too Big?" *Business Week* (March 27, 1989):84–94.
[4] John Child, "What Determines Organization Performance? The Universals vs. the It-All-Depends," *Organizational Dynamics* (Summer 1974):13.
[5] For more information, see Jeffrey D. Ford and John W. Slocum, Jr., "Size, Technology, Environment, and the Structure of Organizations," *Academy of Management Review* (October 1977):564–66.

have found no such relationship or argue that size is a consequence rather than a cause. Yet it is safe to say that while size alone does not dictate organizational structure, it does play a role, in combination with the other internal and external factors discussed here.[6]

Diversity of Operations

Diverse organizations have complex structures

An organization that offers a wide range of products or services is organized differently from one that offers only a few. It is likely to have a series of product groups, each headed by a manager who supervises the particular line. It is also likely to have more salespeople, each specializing in certain product areas.

An organization with a narrow range of products and services can usually get by with a much less sophisticated structure. It has fewer lines to push, and its support services are much more restricted. Even if the company's volume of sales is as great as that of a large, diversified organization, a simple organizational design is sufficient. Decision making, communication, and control can be carried out without a sophisticated structure.

Characteristics of the Personnel

Some people like rules and regulations; others do not

Not everyone responds the same way to organizational rules, policies, procedures, and control methods. One reason is that young workers who have been raised in more affluent conditions than their parents usually are less willing to be subjected to bureaucratic rules. For these people, more flexible designs are needed. Conversely, older employees tend to accept restrictions more willingly.

Second, the training, education, and experience of personnel help dictate the best design. Engineers, accountants, marketing specialists, and other highly educated employees tend to work more effectively under democratic rule. They want a say in what goes on; they want to feel that they are contributing; they want the opportunity to use their training and expertise. Those with less education and training often feel comfortable in a more bureaucratic setting. In fact, many of them like the direction and guidance provided by organizational rules and policies. If placed in an environment where there is too much latitude and discretion, they often feel uncomfortable because they want more structure.

To accommodate the characteristics of the personnel, many organizations find they have to alter the degree of control/autonomy accorded to a particular department or work unit. Only by blending the organization's needs with those of the employees are they able to obtain the desired efficiency.

---

[6] Robert E. Hoskisson, "Multidivisional Structure and Performance: The Contingency of Diversification Strategy," *Academy of Management Journal* (December 1987):625–44.

External Factors

The three external factors that have the greatest effect on an organization's structure are (1) environmental stability, (2) technology, and (3) a variety of external pressures.

Environmental Stability

The nature of the external environment helps shape organizational structure. If the environment is a stable, placid one, the company generally has a formal organizational chart, well-defined jobs, and a set way of doing things. If the environment is dynamic and changing, the company tends to ignore such formalities as the personnel rely heavily on teamwork and informal relationships to meet the ever-present challenges.

Mechanistic designs are highly structured; organic designs are not

Today, in the study of organizational structure, well-defined formal structures are referred to as **mechanistic** and their informal, minimally structured counterparts are called **organic.** This mechanistic-organic framework is the result of research by Tom Burns and G. M. Stalker.[7] After investigating 20 industrial firms for the purpose of studying how the technological and market environment affected the management processes, they discovered that organizations operating in a stable environment had a much different structure from that used by companies operating in an unpredictable setting. Table 8-1 presents the essence of their findings.

The Burns and Stalker research examined the effect of the environment on overall organizational design. The external environment can also affect specific departments, however. For example, a research and development (R&D) department is likely to be interested in developments in the external environment. Has there been a new breakthrough by the competition? What new patents have been applied for at the U.S. Patent Office? Do any of them offer potential for current or future product development?

Because of its interest in the external environment and the changes taking place there, an R&D department is likely to have an organic structure. In this characteristic it differs from a manufacturing department, where the focus is usually internal and the objective is to produce the goods as efficiently as possible. The manufacturing department is likely to have a mechanistic design. So the mechanistic-organic framework developed by Burns and Stalker applies to specific departments as well as overall organizational structures.[8]

Of course, the intraorganizational mix can produce headaches for top management. Each department may develop a different kind of structure, have very different objectives, vary in terms of whether it is most concerned with

---

[7] Tom Burns and G. M. Stalker, *The Management of Innovation* (London: Tavistock Publications, 1961).
[8] Alberto A. Zanzi, "How Organic is Your Organization?" *Journal of Management Studies* (March 1987):125–42.

**TABLE 8-1   Organizational Structure
in Different Types of Environments as Reported by Burns and Stalker**

Stable Environment   **Dynamic Environment**

Rayon Mill	Electrical Engineering	Radio & TV Manufacturing	Other Electronics Firms	Electronics Development Manufacturer
■ Highly structured	■ Somewhat flexible structures	■ Relatively flexible structure	■ Flexible structure	■ Very flexible structure
■ Carefully defined roles	■ Roles somewhat defined	■ No organization chart	■ No organization charts	■ No organization charts
■ Carefully defined tasks	■ Tasks somewhat defined	■ No great degree of role or task definitions	■ Reliance on informal cooperation and teamwork	■ Emphasis on teamwork and interpersonal interaction to ensure goal attainment

short-range, medium-range, or long-range goals, and have different managerial styles. These characteristics—structure, objectives, time orientation, and management style—are often used to measure **differentiation,** the degree to which each department is developing its own specific posture with regard to its external environment. Research shows, however, that effective top managers know how to obtain the right degree of **integration,** which can be defined as the amount of collaboration that has to exist between departments in order to achieve unity of effort.[9]

Regardless of specific departmental arrangements, successful organizations have the following characteristics: (1) the individual departments effectively address their specific external environments and (2) personnel exhibit the right degree of cooperation and teamwork to ensure overall organizational effectiveness. In every industry the degree of differentiation and integration varies from firm to firm. Those enterprises having the combination that best meets the demands of their environment are the most successful.

Effective organizations address the demands of their external environments

Technology

Technology is one causal variable in organizational design

Technology consists of the equipment, computers, and other machinery that help an organization attain its objectives. Technology is employed internally, but its use is dictated by the external environment. If every other company in an industry is using computers for inventory control, the one that does not will find its profits and efficiency suffering.

[9] Paul R. Lawrence and Joy W. Lorsch, *Organization and Environment* (Homewood, IL: Richard D. Irwin, Inc., 1967).

Research shows that technology does indeed influence structure. For example, Joan Woodward surveyed 100 firms and identified differences between them in terms of structure, management operating processes, and profitability. She then grouped the firms according to the kinds of technology they used. The firms fell into three basic groups: (1) those using unit or small-batch production technology for making one-of-a-kind items or a small number of units produced to customer specifications; (2) those using assembly-line technology for large-batch and mass production; and (3) those using process production technology to produce liquids, gases, and crystalline substances. After examining the most successful firms in each category, Woodward discovered that the unit and small-batch firms used organic structures. So did the process production firms. The mass production firms, meanwhile, employed mechanistic designs. Table 8-2 provides a further comparison of the organizational characteristics that Woodward found among the successful firms in each category.[10]

Numerous external forces affect organizational design

Since Woodward's research was conducted, numerous other studies have been launched in an effort to discover exactly how much of an impact technology has on organizational design. A number of these studies support Woodward's findings that technology is one causal variable in organizational structure. It should also be realized, however, that technology is not equally influential in shaping the structure and style of all organizations or parts of them.[11] It appears to have the greatest influence in small, production-oriented units and the least influence at the upper levels of organizations and in nonproduction units such as staff service.[12] While technology is important, it is only one of a handful of key variables influencing organizational structure.

External Pressures

Every successful organization attempts to accommodate external pressures that it cannot sidestep. A typical example is government regulation, as in the case of a utility. Realizing that its rate structure, plans for expansion or replacement of current facilities, and customer service all come under the critical eye of regulatory boards, a utility typically has a department or unit addressing each of these areas. In some cases, for example to deal with rate increase requests, a com-

---

[10] Joan Woodward, *Industrial Organization: Theory and Practice* (London: Oxford University Press, 1965).

[11] Frank M. Hull and Paul D. Collins, "High Technology Batch Production Systems: Woodward's Missing Type," *Academy of Management Journal* (December 1987):786–97.

[12] For an excellent review of the literature on this subject, see Ford and Slocum, "Organizations," 562–64; David F. Gillespie and Dennis S. Mileti, "Technology and the Study of Organizations: An Overview and Appraisal," *Academy of Management Review* (January 1977):7–16; Mariann Jelinek, "Technology, Organizations, and Contingency," *Academy of Management Review* (January 1977):17–26; and Donald Gerwin, "The Comparative Analysis of Structure and Technology: A Critical Appraisal," *Academy of Management Review* (October 1979):41–51.

TABLE 8-2   Comparison of Organizational Characteristics Among the Firms in Woodward's Study

Organizational Characteristics	Unit and Small-Batch Production	Large-Batch and Mass Production	Process Production
Number of employees controlled by first-line supervisors	Small	Large	Small
Relationship between work groups and supervisor	Informal	Formal	Informal
Basic type of workers employed	Skilled	Semiskilled & unskilled	Skilled
Definition of duties	Often vague	Clear-cut	Often vague
Degree of delegation of authority	High	Low	High
Use of participative management	High	Low	High
Type of organization structure	Flexible	Rigid	Flexible

mittee consisting of personnel from the finance, operations, and legal area may be organized to write the proposal. The utility's structure is designed to meet the regulatory pressures the organization is certain to face.

Another major source of external pressure is the organization's resource suppliers. Large business firms that are unionized typically have industrial relations departments that handle contract negotiations and assist the management in resolving union grievances. The structure of the company enables it to meet the pressure of union demands. The same is true in the case of resource suppliers such as major stockholders. In organizations where one or a handful of people hold a large percentage of ownership, such as Edwin Land at Polaroid or Hugh Hefner at Playboy Enterprises, the organization is set up to accommodate their wishes.

A third major source of external pressure is generated by clients and customers who provide a sizable portion of a company's business. Aerospace contractors who obtain 70 percent of their business from federal contracts are organized in a way that obliges the government. They have at least a representative, if not an office, in Washington and are set up to respond to this very important client. A firm that sells 40 percent of its output to a national retail firm is organized to address the particular needs and wishes of this customer. It may have a local office in the same city as the retail firm's headquarters, and the manufacturing personnel are in close touch with the retail company's people regarding any changes in product line or new items to be manufactured.

A fourth major source of external pressure is competitors. If an organization is in a very competitive environment, it has to respond quickly to changes in the industry. A price cut has to be met at once; a new product line has to be matched as soon as possible. In recent years government deregulation of business has brought about an increase in the competitive nature of many industries. Airlines are one example. So is the trucking business. In fact, of all six internal and external factors examined in this section, more firms are concerned with competition than with any of the others.

Specific Influence of the Factors

If an organization is affected by only one or two of these structural factors, the effect is easy to measure. A small business that operates in a stable environment offering a service for which there is little competition may need to be concerned only with the impact of government regulation (licensing, health and safety laws, and minimum wages, for example). A large public utility has to consider at least two of these factors: government regulation and technology.

For some companies, only one factor is important

If an organization is affected by three or more factors, the effect is not as easy to measure. For example, a multinational enterprise such as IBM is affected by all six. How should these enterprises be organized? The answer depends on the specific influence of each factor. In each company, some have a minor effect while others have a major impact. In the case of IBM, technology, market stability, and size are the most crucial factors. The firm needs to offer the most efficient equipment possible (technology), keep abreast of the competition (market strategy), and have an overall organizational design for coordinating its far-flung operations (size). The next most important factors are external pressure (the specific needs of the customers) and diversity of operations (how to organize systematically and monitor the various product offerings). The least important one is the characteristics of the people in the organization, because in addressing the other factors IBM creates an organizational environment in which creative and high-achieving people can work well.

For others, all six are important

Each organization must examine its own environment to determine which variables are most important for it individually. After conducting a thorough review of research in this area, William Glueck concluded that the three most important variables for organizations in general are size, environmental stability, and diversity of operations. The second group consists solely of technology. The last group is made up of external pressures and the characteristics of the personnel.[13]

The overall effect of the variables must be weighed

In any event, if most of these six variables point toward a particular type of organizational structure, that is the one the enterprise should choose. If the variables point toward different structures, the firm must decide which variables are most important to it and select a structure that accommodates them. Finally, if the most important factors do not point to any one particular type of design (such as mechanistic or organic), management should seek a compromise or blend between the two.[14]

---

[13] William F. Glueck and Arthur G. Bedeian, *Management,* 3rd ed. (Hinsdale, IL: Dryden Press, 1983), 373.
[14] Darrell E. Owen, ''The Corporate Cube: A Managerial Perspective,'' *Managerial Planning,* (March–April 1985):31–35.

Restructuring:
Common Threads Emerging

The following statements were drawn from the annual reports of selected major corporations. These statements provide insights into some of the common threads emerging from the restructuring activities in these firms.

Kraft, Incorporated: "We put Duracell up for sale [signalling] Kraft's return to being 'all food' for the first time in over 30 years." This was in response to the company's core business after a lengthy period that incorporated growth through diversification by both merger and acquisition.

General Electric Company: "Principal unusual costs were expense provisions for corporate restructurings: $1.027 billion in 1987, $0.311 billion in 1986, and $0.447 billion in 1985." Since Jack Welch became CEO in 1981, mergers, acquisitions, divestitures, and restructurings have been a way of life as part of G.E.'s strategy to be first or second in each of the markets in which it chooses to participate. Revenue growth and financial returns have been impressive. However, critics decry "financial gamesmanship" and the enormous human toll.

Schlumberger Limited: "Nonperforming assets were sold, most notably Fairchild Semiconductor Corporation (to National Semiconductor Corporation for $122 million in common stock and warrants). We took a loss of $220 million on this transaction. This ended our eight-year diversification into the semiconductor business." The purchase of Schlumberger's Fairchild was a diversification move that failed, at least in part, because the semiconductor business was completely foreign to the new parent. Sadly, Fairchild, the early 1960s founder of the integrated circuits business, has now disappeared, having been absorbed into National Semiconductor's operations.

Penn Central Corporation: "In 1986 the company recorded a $409 million charge to earnings. $137 million reflects the write-down of certain assets and efforts to further consolidate operations and reduce costs at Sprague Electric Company."

The common threads:

- failure of a diversification strategy
- failure to understand an acquired business
- a change in corporate strategy
- corporate renewal
- technological obsolescence
- competition
- a severe economic downturn
- redundancy in operations, plants, and personnel
- corporate obesity
- stockholder pressure
- an effort to repair previous management mistakes
- survival

Source: John L. Sprague, "Restructuring and Corporate Renewal," *Management Review* (March 1989):34–36.

The decade of the 1980s witnessed a number of organizations restructuring in order to better position themselves in their environment. The "Management-In-Practice" insert provides some interesting excerpts from several corporations' annual reports. These examples of restructuring indicate certain common patterns in this increased activity within organizations.[15]

The challenges of the 1990s will bring about even more fluid structures. There is an increase today of network style organizations that interconnect individuals and groups within the enterprise in order to better adapt to volatile environments, changing technologies, and stronger competition.[16]

The important factors are reflected in the specific organizational design, which can take a number of different forms. These forms are referred to as types of departmentalization.

DEPARTMENTALIZATION

Departmentalization defined

Departmentalization is the orderly arrangement of activities and functions that must be performed by organizational personnel. The specific form of departmentalization depends on the needs of the organization. In broad terms, however, there are four major forms of departmentalization: functional, product, territorial, and matrix.

Functional Departmentalization

Functional departmentalization is very popular

Functional departmentalization is the arrangement of the enterprise around the key functions or activities that it must perform. In the case of a manufacturing firm, such major departments as production, marketing, finance, and engineering usually report directly to the chief executive officer (CEO). Figure 8-2 illustrates such a structure. In the case of a hospital (see Figure 8-3), it is common to find financial, nursing, support service, ancillary, and medical staff departments under the direct control of the administrator or CEO. In the case of a department store, typical functions include merchandising, publicity, and finance; in the case of a meat packer, typical departments are dairy and poultry, beef, lamb and veal, by-products, and agricultural research.

A functional departmentalization arrangement is the most popular of all because it is easy to understand and employ. Personnel are organized based on what they do, and if new lines or functions are added they can be accommo-

---

[15] Jean M. Bartunek and Frank J. Franzak, "The Effects of Organizational Restructuring on Frames of Reference and Cooperation," *Journal of Management* (December 1988):579–92.
[16] Neal E. Boudette, "Networks to Dismantle Old Structures," *Industry Week* (January 16, 1989):27–31.

FIGURE 8-2   Typical Functional Structure for a Manufacturing Firm

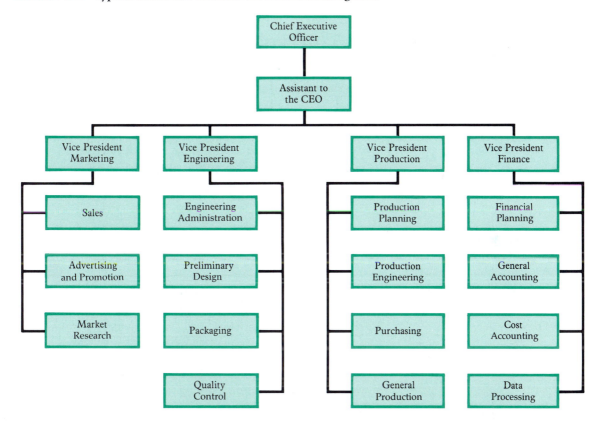

dated easily. As certain areas increase in size, *derivative departments* can be created. For example, if the marketing department becomes too large for one individual to manage, it can be broken down into two derivative departments: selling and advertising. The functional arrangement permits the organization to break large departments into smaller and more manageable subfunctional areas.

Product Departmentalization

Product depart-
mentalization
helps create profit
centers

Product departmentalization occurs when an enterprise organizes itself around product lines. Many firms, as they increase their number of product lines, find a functional structure too unwieldy. In an effort to concentrate the necessary attention on each offering, they organize around product lines. Figure 8-4 shows a typical product departmentalization structure for a manufacturing firm.

FIGURE 8-3   Typical Hospital Organizational Chart

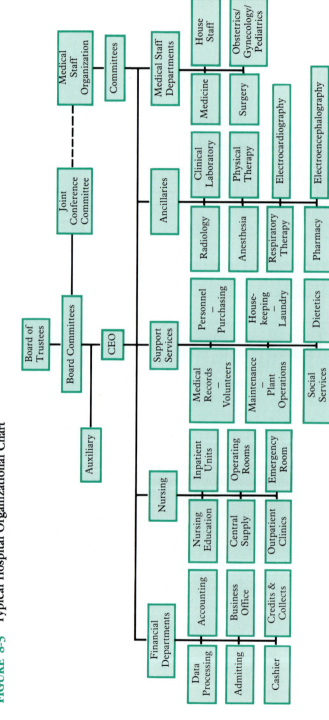

FIGURE 8-4   Product Departmentalization Arrangement for a Manufacturing Firm

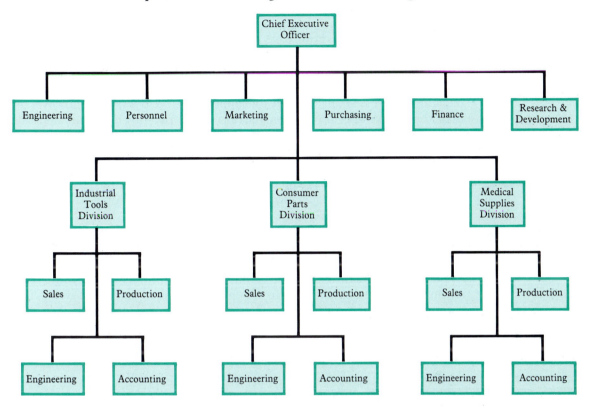

Notice how product departmentalization helps the enterprise create *profit centers*. Each product area is a semiautonomous business that has what is needed to manufacture and sell the product. Note too how the basic functions of a manufacturing firm—production, marketing, and finance—are incorporated into the product arrangement. Many large multiline corporations (General Motors, Ford, Du Pont, General Electric) employ this organizational form. The arrangement also helps the firm develop general managers who, when they eventually move into top positions, have had the requisite training needed for strategic planning.

Territorial Departmentalization

Territorial department-mentalization is used for servicing physically dispersed customers

Territorial departmentalization is employed by many organizations trying to serve customers who are physically dispersed. Retail stores are a classic example. As a retail chain begins to grow, more and more stores are opened in different locales. There may be a store downtown, one in the eastern suburbs, and another in the western suburbs. Then the organization may expand to other cities and towns so that over time there are 50 to 60 stores located throughout a five-state region. In the case of the giant retailers like Sears, J. C. Penney, and K-Mart, there are literally thousands of outlets.

Another common example is found in the case of firms that expand into foreign markets. These firms have national and international departments.

Figure 8-5 presents the organizational chart for a retail store that has expanded internationally. This chart bears some resemblance to the structure in Figure 8-2 in that there are functional departments reporting to the CEO. These departments are responsible only for supporting store operations, however. As in the case of product departmentalization, most operating decisions are made at the store level. It is also important to note that within each store there is a series of departments organized according to both function (accounting, personnel, payroll) and product (home appliances, toys, electronic products, books). The result is a mix of all three types of departmentalization: functional, product, and territorial. This mixture of different organizational arrangements is even clearer in the case of the matrix organization.

Matrix Organization

A **matrix organization** is a *blend* of functional and product (and in some cases territorial) departmentalization in which there is a dual command system that

FIGURE 8-5 A Retail Chain with International Operations

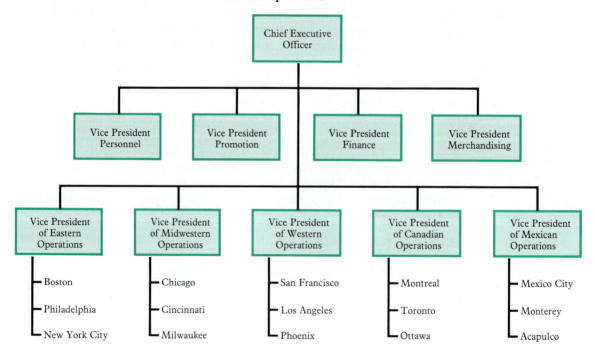

emphasizes both inputs and outputs. Allen Janger has described some of the most typical arrangements this way:

> *The product-function matrix,* which overlays a functional "resource" organization with a number of product managers who are charged with achieving "business results" and whose responsibilities cut across the functional organization.

> *The product-region matrix,* which overlays a regionally divisionalized structure with a number of product managers who are charged with achieving "business results" for their product lines and whose responsibilities cut across regional lines.

> *The multidimensional matrix,* whose regional divisions are organized into product-functional matrixes and which are, in turn, part of a product-region matrix.[17]

A matrix structure uses a *dual* command system in which personnel have two types of bosses: *resource managers* and *business managers.* Resource managers provide the personnel. In a business matrix structure these managers come from such functional areas as manufacturing, engineering, R&D, and marketing. Business managers receive the personnel from the resource managers and are charged with coordinating the employees' efforts in such a way as to ensure the profitability of the particular business or product line. The resource managers are concerned with the *inputs;* the business managers are concerned with the *outputs.* The matrix structure helps the organization balance these two concerns, something that can often be difficult when one of the other typical departmentalization arrangements is employed.[18]

Sometimes the matrix is used to accomplish a particular objective such as to build a spacecraft or a piece of hardware, and when the project is finished, the matrix is disbanded. At other times the matrix is used for ongoing operations such as managing product lines.[19] When the structure is used for handling geographically dispersed operations, a multidimensional matrix emerges. Figure 8-6 illustrates both a product-function matrix and a multidimensional matrix as used by Dow Corning.

The first matrix in Figure 8-6, the product-function matrix, was introduced by Dow Corning to handle its domestic U.S. operations. The marketing, manufacturing, technical service and development, research, and economic evaluation/controller managers provide resources for the firm's various businesses. They also provide people to serve on the business boards, which give advice

---

[17] Allen R. Janger, *Matrix Organization of Complex Businesses* (New York: The Conference Board, Inc., 1979), vii.

[18] John L. Brown and Neil McK. Agnew, "The Balance of Power in a Matrix Structure," *Business Horizons* (November–December 1982):51–54 and William F. Joyce, "Matrix Organization: A Social Experiment," *Academy of Management Journal* (September 1986):536–61.

[19] Lawton R. Burns, "Matrix Management in Hospitals: Testing Theories of Matrix Structure and Development," *Administrative Science Quarterly* (September 1989):349–68.

FIGURE 8-6   **Dow Corning's Product-Function Matrix and Multidimensional Matrix**

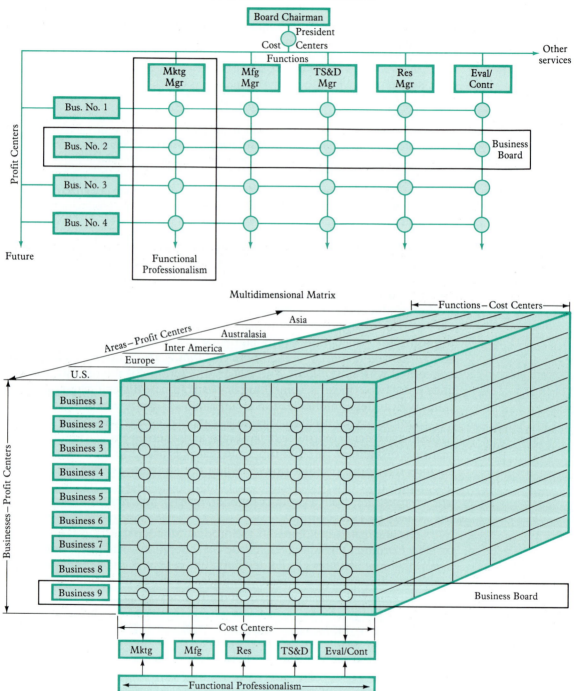

Source: Allan R. Janger, *Matrix Organization of Complex Businesses* (New York: The Conference Board, 1979), 31. Reprinted by permission.

and assistance to the business manager. In the international areas the firm eventually replicated this product-function matrix, giving the design a 3-D effect (functional-product-territorial). Each area—the United States, Europe, Inter-America, Australasia, Asia—is a regional profit center set up along matrix lines. In coordinating the business activities of these areas on a companywide basis, Dow Corning introduced a product region matrix by assigning an additional worldwide product-line "business results" role to each of the U.S. business managers. At the same time, the functional managers have responsibility for worldwide development of their functions.

The matrix design can become quite complex, creating as many problems as it solves. This is why the structure is never a first choice. It evolves gradually as the organization realizes that the other structural designs are not getting the job done. Some firms such as Skandia, the Swedish insurance company, have moved to a matrix structure and then gone back to a more classical organizational arrangement. So the matrix is not the ultimate in organization design. In some cases it proves to be only a temporary structure as the enterprise searches for some hybrid form of departmentalization that will help it operate more efficiently.[20]

Matrix is not the ultimate in organizational design

SPAN OF CONTROL

Span of control defined

Another important structural consideration is **span of control,** which refers to the number of people who report directly to a manager. This span affects organizational design. A **narrow span of control,** in which two or three people report to a superior, results in a **tall organizational structure.** Conversely, a **wide span of control,** in which as many as 10 or 15 people may report to the same person, results in a **flat organizational structure.** These two different types of structure are illustrated in Figures 8-7 and 8-8, respectively.

The Matter of Effectiveness

For many years management theorists and practitioners argued over the "ideal" span. Some people felt it should be narrow; others said it should be wide. In recent years, however, the focus of consideration has shifted from defining ideal spans to identifying factors that make one span more effective than another. This idea is illustrated in Figure 8-9, which shows that effectiveness of supervision can be influenced by the number of people managed.[21]

---

[20] Robert A. Pitts and John D. Daniels, "Aftermath of the Matrix Mania," *Columbia Journal of World Business* (Summer 1984):48–54. See also: Fred V. Guterl, "Goodbye, Old Matrix," *Business Month* (February 1989):32–38.
[21] John S. McClenahen, "Managing More People in the '90s," *Industry Week* (March 20, 1989):30–36.

FIGURE 8-7   A Tall Structure (A Span of Control of Two)

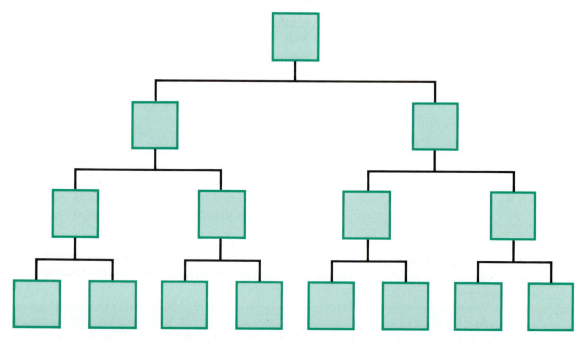

If the number of subordinates is small, the manager may spend too much time trying to control them. He or she has a great deal of available time and may use it to keep an eye of what everyone is doing. On the other hand, if the number of subordinates is too large, the manager is unable to keep track of what everyone is doing. If someone needs assistance on a project, the manager may not be able to provide it because too many people are vying for his or her time.

FIGURE 8-8   A Flat Structure (A Span of Control of Ten)

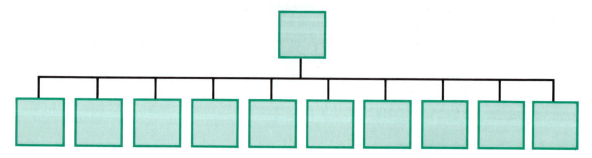

FIGURE 8-9
The "Optimum Span" Concept

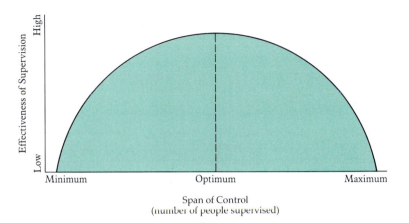

Span of Control
(number of people supervised)

Research in the Area

Some studies argue for wide spans

Research in industry shows that some organizations are very effective with a wide span while others seem to do quite well with a narrow one. For example, after making an extensive study of Sears, Roebuck and Company, James C. Worthy found that a wide span of control produced a less complex structure for the firm and tended "to create a potential for improved attitudes, more effective supervision, and greater individual responsibility and initiative among employees."[22] In more recent years management writers such as Peter Drucker have echoed support for wider spans, noting that "a basic rule of organization is to build the *least* possible number of management levels and forge the shortest possible chain of command."[23]

Others support narrow spans

On the other hand, there is also research support for narrow spans. Rocco Carzo and John Yanouzas tested the relative efficiency of the two types of structures under controlled conditions and found that, once the groups learned their tasks, those operating under a tall structure had both higher profits and higher rates of return. This finding led them to conclude that "the tall structure, with a great number of levels, allowed group members to evaluate decisions more frequently, and . . . the narrow span of supervision provided for a more orderly decision process."[24]

Still other researchers have found that the size of the firm can have an important effect on whether a flat or a tall structure is better. For example, Lyman Porter and Edward Lawler surveyed more than 1,500 managers and

[22] James C. Worthy, "Organizational Structure and Employee Morale," *American Sociological Review* (April 1950):179.

[23] Peter F. Drucker, *Management: Tasks, Responsibilities, Practices* (New York: Harper & Row, 1974), 546.

[24] Rocco Carzo, Jr. and John N. Yanouzas, "Effects of Flat and Tall Organization Structure," *Administrative Science Quarterly* (June 1969):191.

MANAGEMENT IN PRACTICE

Big Companies Structure to be Small

As smaller enterprises emerge in America as the fuel for economic resurgence, major corporations are seeking to emulate the structure that gives entrepreneurial companies their advantage. That structure is smaller, and has more autonomous units that allow flexibility and that limit bureaucratic complexity in order to compete better. Some examples include:

AT&T: Chopping up six major businesses into 19 or more smaller groups. Goals: eliminate turf wars, deemphasize management by committee, encourage individual risk-taking, improve focus on individual markets.

General Electric: Cutting management layers between factory floor to executive suite from nine to as few as four. Staff will serve in role of "facilitator, adviser, and partner," not "monitors, checkers, kibitzers, approvers."

General Motors: Stripping out layers of management; seeks ideas from customers and suppliers; is developing technological advances through acquisitions.

Hewlett-Packard: The company has 50 units with their own profit-loss, planning, and support responsibilities to give managers "self-direction and ownership."

McDonald's: Building on structure as far-flung collection of independent entrepreneurs; autonomous franchisees credited with such innovations as McDLT and Egg McMuffin.

Source: Greg Couch, "Is Your Company Too Big?" *Business Week* (March 27, 1989):84–94.

found that in firms with less than 5,000 people, managerial satisfaction was higher in flat structures, while among those with more than 5,000 people, managerial satisfaction was higher if the company had a tall structure.[25]

At the present time there is a trend toward wider spans of control and flatter structures. "Management in Practice: Big Companies Structure to be Small" explains the reason for this trend.

Current Views

At the present time the focus of attention is less on studying spans of control that exist in various organizations and more on identifying the factors that actually influence the ideal span of control.[26] One of the earliest studies was reported by

[25] Lyman W. Porter and Edward E. Lawler, III, "The Effects of 'Tall' Versus 'Flat' Organization Structures on Managerial Job Satisfaction," *Personnel Psychology* (Summer 1964):135–48.
[26] David D. Van Fleet, "Span of Management Research and Issues," *Academy of Management Journal* (September 1983):546–52.

FIGURE 8-10   Organizational View of Span Relationships

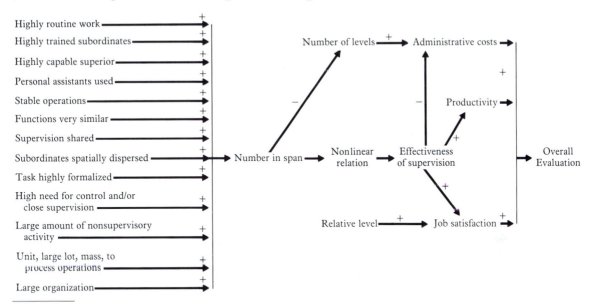

Source: Reprinted with permission from David D. Van Fleet and Arthur G. Bedeian, "A History of Span of Management," *Academy of Management Review* (July 1977):364.

Harold Stieglitz, who described how the Lockheed Corporation assigned point values to span of control factors.[27]

In the case of job functions, for example, Lockheed assigned a rating of "1" to the job if all of the functions were identical, a "2" if the functions were essentially similar, and so on, up to a "5" if the functions were fundamentally distinct. The same approach was used in handling other span of control factors such as complexity of functions, coordination, and planning time required. The higher the number of points, the lower the span of control recommended.

Although this is the best-known attempt to develop a quantified approach for dealing with span of control, there is still a great deal of interest in studying the factors that influence the ideal span of a particular job. David Van Fleet and Arthur Bedeian have pointed out that the important thing is not the specific number of subordinates supervised by a particular superior but the effect of the span on overall performance. Figure 8-10 illustrates their approach to the topic.

Notice that the factors on the left side of the figure influence the span of control number. This number, in turn, influences a series of other variables. By the end of the process, these variables have been reduced to three: administrative costs, productivity, and job satisfaction, which, in turn, influence the overall

The most important thing is how the span affects performance

---

[27] Harold Stieglitz, "Optimizing Span of Control," *Management Record* (September 1962):25–29.

effectiveness of the span. Figure 8-10 does not offer any solution to the question: What is the ideal span of control? But it does highlight the important factors that must be taken into consideration when examining span of control relationships. After conducting an exhaustive review of the literature on this subject, Van Fleet and Bedeian concluded that

> . . . there is a limit to the number of subordinates a superior can effectively supervise, manage, or control. Clearly this limit will vary depending upon the individual superior, members of his or her group, and the situation. Further, an optimum . . . may exist which is . . . different from that limit.
>
> More precise definitions need to be used in future research regarding the span of (control) concept. Future research must clearly identify not only the "factors" which may affect the span, but also the criteria upon which any value judgments of "too large" or "too small" are to be based.[28]

JOB SPECIALIZATION

The final aspect of organization design that warrants consideration is job specialization. This concept was at the heart of Frederick Taylor's task concept, described in Chapter 2. In accordance with this concept, the work of every worker was spelled out in advance so that the individual knew exactly what was expected of him or her. This basic form of specialization is still in existence today. In fact, it forms the basis for division of labor and is crucial to departmentalization. Job specialization is promoted through the use of job descriptions.

Job Descriptions

A **job description** is a written statement that sets forth the duties and responsibilities associated with a particular job. The basic purpose of any job definition is to clarify the functions to be performed by the employees, or to provide them with *role clarity.* The greater the clarity, the more likely it is that employees will perform their work in a satisfactory manner. In fact, numerous studies have found that role clarity has both a significant and a positive impact on such key organizational variables as job satisfaction, absenteeism, turnover, and effectiveness.[29]

Unfortunately, not every organization has well-developed job descriptions. The result is *role ambiguity,* a situation in which different people, all

---

[28] David D. Van Fleet and Arthur G. Bedeian, "A History of Span of Management," *Academy of Management Review* (July 1977):364.
[29] Robert H. Miles and M. M. Petty, "Relationships Between Role Clarity, Need for Clarity, and Job Tension and Satisfaction for Supervisory and Nonsupervisory Roles," *Academy of Management Journal* (December 1975):877–83; Randall S. Schuler, "Role Perceptions, Satisfaction and Performance Moderated by Organizational Level and Participation in Decision Making," *Academy of Management Journal* (March 1977):159–65.

doing the same basic job, have different understandings of their roles and responsibilities. Some see themselves as having a great deal more authority and responsibility than others do. Obviously this form of role ambiguity affects the way they do their jobs. Additionally, if their superiors all have different expectations regarding their performance, this too has an impact on the situation.

The surest way of dealing with role ambiguity problems is to determine exactly what each individual should be doing. Then a comprehensive and clear job description can be developed. The employee and the superior can discuss job expectations, and performance evaluation can be tied to them. This entire process begins with what is called job analysis. While it is easier to apply such an analysis to lower-level jobs than to upper-level ones, an organization should use it for every position in the hierarchy, if only to generate a general description of that particular job.[30]

Job Analysis

Job analysis   **Job analysis** is the process of observing, studying, and reporting pertinent information related to the nature of a specific job. This information is of three types: (1) an identification of the job, (2) a complete and accurate description of the tasks involved in the job, and (3) a specification of the requirements the job makes on the employee.

There are many ways of analyzing a job. Some of the most common methods include (1) examining previous job analyses or job descriptions of the position, (2) observing both the job and the job occupant, (3) interviewing the job occupant, (4) having the job occupant or the supervisor or both complete a questionnaire about the job, (5) having the job occupant keep a log or a diary of work activities, (6) recording job activities via film or audio techniques, and (7) analyzing equipment design information from blueprints and design data. Of these methods, numbers 1, 4, and 7 are the fastest but may also provide the least reliable data. Methods 2, 3, 5, and 6 are more accurate but also more costly.

Developing Job Descriptions

Job description   When the job analysis is complete, the job description can be prepared. One of the best sources for use in writing job descriptions is the *Dictionary of Occupational Titles.*[31] In fact, some organizations that need job descriptions for new positions simply go to this dictionary and either directly copy the descriptions they require or modify them slightly to fit the specific job. Table 8-3 provides an example of a job description prepared using the latter procedure.

---

[30] John P. Wanous, "Installing a Realistic Job Preview: Ten Tough Choices," *Personnel Psychology* (Spring 1989):117–34.

[31] See Paul D. Geyer, John Hice, John Hawk, Ronald Boese, and Yvonne Braddon, "Reliabilities of Ratings Available from the Dictionary of Occupational Titles," *Personnel Psychology* (Autumn 1989):547–60.

TABLE 8-3   Job Description for a Project Director

General Description of the Job

Plans, directs, and coordinates the activities of the designated project to ensure that the aims, goals, and/or objectives that are specified for the project are accomplished within the prescribed priorities, time limitations, and funding constraints.

Job Duties

- Reviews project proposals or plans to determine the time frame and funding limitations.
- Determines the methods and procedures for accomplishing the project, staffing requirements, and allotment of funds to the various phases of the project.
- Develops the staffing plan and establishes the work plan and schedules for each phase of the project in accord with time limitations and funding.
- Recruits personnel according to the staffing plan.

- Confers with the staff to outline project plans, designates personnel who will have responsibilities for phases of the project, and establishes the scope of authority.
- Directs and coordinates the activities of the project through delegated subordinates and establishes budgetary systems for controlling expenditures.
- Reviews the project reports on the status of each phase and modifies schedules, as required.
- Confers with project personnel to provide technical advice and to assist in solving problems.

Notice in the table that there is a general description of the job. It is followed by a list of the most important job duties to be carried out by the person occupying the position.

Developing Job Specifications

Job specification

From the job description, job specifications are prepared. A **job specification** is a written statement that describes the specific qualifications a person must have in order to carry out the job effectively. For the job of the project manager in Table 8-3, the specifications would include the type of education, experience, training, knowledge, skills, and abilities required to perform the job properly. In many situations, especially for lower- and middle-level jobs, the job specifications spell out the minimum amount of experience required (such as two years or three years) as well as the education needed (engineering degree, master of business administration, for example). Perhaps the biggest problem that modern organizations face in the use of job descriptions and job specifications is that the description is too vague and the specifications do not tie closely to the job. If a person were to pick up the job description and read it, he or she would not know exactly what the job required. The individual would have a general idea but that is all. Another problem is that the specifications often seem to have little direct relationship to the work. Why does this job

TABLE 8-4 Ambiguous and Behaviorally Defined Objectives in a Job Description	
Ambiguous Job Objectives	**Terminal Job Objectives**
1. To demonstrate satisfactory ability on the job and perform at required standards.	1. To operate the press such that a minimum of 120 pieces are produced correctly each hour, with no more than one incorrect (defective) piece produced in any hour.
2. To develop a positive attitude toward the work; to be dependable.	2. To give evidence of willingness to perform the job by not being absent from work except for those reasons and on those days specified by the union agreement; and by being at the proper work place when the shift bell sounds.
3. To be able to communicate effectively with subordinates.	3. To notify each division head of all changes in the budget by written memo to each no later than one day after notification of such change reaches your desk.

Source: Craig Eric Schneier, "Content Validity: The Necessity of a Behavioral Job Description," *Personnel Administrator* (February 1976): 42. Reprinted from the February 1976 issue of *Personnel Administrator*, Copyright 1976, The American Society for Personnel Administration, 606 North Washington Street, Alexandria, Virginia, 22314.

require a college degree in engineering? Why does this job require 10 years of actual managerial experience?

In recent years more and more attention has been called to the fact that job descriptions and job specifications are too general and too ambiguous. Researchers such as Craig Schneier have suggested tying everything to behaviorally defined objectives.[32] In this way, when people read the job description they know exactly what the job calls for and the type of education and training that is required to perform it well. Table 8-4 provides an example of ambiguous and terminal behavior in job objectives. Notice that the descriptions that are spelled out in detail are more complete and easier to understand than their less descriptive counterparts.

Behaviorally defined objectives

Well-written job descriptions and job specifications are extremely important in overcoming role ambiguity and promoting organizational efficiency. They are also important in helping ensure that the organization is not found guilty of employment discrimination because it establishes job qualifications that are not job-related or because it screens out women or minorities who apply for the position.

[32] Craig Eric Schneier, "Content Validity: The Necessity of a Behavioral Job Description," *Personnel Administration* (February 1976):38–44.

SUMMARY

1. Organizing is the process of assigning duties and coordinating the efforts of personnel in their pursuit of the enterprise's objectives.

2. Strategy influences structure. A single-product organization that is determined to penetrate the local market has a much different structure from a multiline company that wants to expand overseas.

3. The three internal factors that have the greatest influence on organizational structure are the size of the organization, the diversity of its operations, and the characteristics of the personnel. As an organization gets larger it usually becomes more formalized. As the enterprise increases the scope of its operations its structure changes to accommodate the new demands placed on the organization. If personnel want a less bureaucratic design, management is more likely to adopt it than if the employees want a more bureaucratic structure.

4. Three external factors have a great effect on organizational structure: environmental stability, technology, and various external pressures. Organizations operating in stable environments tend to use a mechanistic structure while those in dynamic environments are more likely to opt for an organic design. This principle holds true for both the organization at large and departments in particular. Technology also influences structure, especially that of small, production-oriented units. Also, organizations subject to such external pressures as government regulation, resource suppliers, clients, customers, and competitors organize to accommodate the demands of these forces.

5. In examining the overall effect of all six variables, an organization must first decide which of these has the greatest impact on operations. Then, working in descending order, it must determine the degree of importance of each variable and how each can be accommodated.

6. There are four major forms of departmentalization. One is functional departmentalization, which involves the arrangement of the enterprise around the key functions or activities that it must perform. A second is product departmentalization, which occurs when an enterprise organizes itself around its major product lines. A third is territorial departmentalization, which is employed by organizations trying to serve customers who are physically dispersed. The last is the matrix organization, in which there is a dual command system and management attempts to balance a concern for inputs with a concern for outputs.

7. Span of control refers to the number of people who report directly to a manager. If the span is narrow, the organization has a tall structure; if the span is wide, the organization has a flat structure. The ideal span depends on a number of factors. In evaluating these factors the organization should keep in mind the impact of each factor on overall effectiveness.

8. Job specialization is promoted through the use of job descriptions. A job

analysis helps to ensure that these descriptions are both complete and clear. From this analysis, a job description can be written. Then job specifications can be prepared. In recent years researchers have been encouraging organizations to tie their job descriptions to behaviorally defined objectives.

KEY TERMS

Departmentalization   The orderly arrangement of activities and functions that must be performed by the organizational personnel.

Differentiation   The degree to which each department in an organization goes about developing its own specific posture in regard to its external environment.

Flat organizational structure   An organizational structure characterized by a small number of hierarchical levels and a wide span of control.

Functional departmentalization   The organizational arrangement of the enterprise around the key functions or activities that it must perform.

Integration   The amount of collaboration that exists between the organization's departments and other units in achieving unity of effort.

Job analysis   The process of observing, studying, and reporting pertinent information related to the nature of a specific job.

Job description   A written statement that sets forth the duties and responsibilities of a job.

Job specifications   A written statement that describes the specific qualifications that a person must have in order to carry out a job effectively.

Matrix structure   A hybrid combination or blend of functional, product, and/or territorial departmentalization in which there is a dual command system that puts emphasis on both inputs and outputs.

Mechanistic structure   An organizational structure that is often effective in a stable environment. It is characterized by rules, policies, procedures, organizational charts, and other forms of structure.

Narrow span of control   A span of control in which only a small number of people, usually from two to six, report to a superior.

Organic structure   An organizational design that is often effective in a dynamic environment. It is characterized by a lack of rules, policies, procedures, organizational charts, and other forms of structure.

Product departmentalization   The organizational arrangement of an enterprise around its major product lines.

Span of control   The number of people who report to a superior.

Tall organizational structure   An organizational structure characterized by a large number of hierarchical levels and a narrow span of control.

Technology   The equipment, computers, and other machinery that help an organization attain its objectives.

Territorial departmentalization   The organizational arrangement of an enterprise along geographic lines.

Wide span of control   A span of control in which a large number of people, often between eight and fifteen, report to a superior.

QUESTIONS FOR ANALYSIS AND DISCUSSION

1. What is meant by the term organizing? State the definition in your own words.
2. How does strategy influence structure? Give an example.
3. Does an organization's size have any effect on its structure? Explain your answer.
4. In what way do diversity of operations and the characteristics of the personnel have an effect on organizational structure? Explain the impact of both factors by using examples.
5. Would a successful firm operating in a stable environment have a different type of organizational structure from one operating in a dynamic environment? Why or why not? Defend your answer.
6. Would all of the departments in a mechanistic structure by highly bureaucratized? Would all of the departments in an organic structure be highly nonbureaucratized? Explain your answer.
7. How much of an impact does technology have on organizational structure? Explain.
8. What are some of the major types of external pressures that influence an organization's structure? Identify and describe at least three.
9. How can an organization go about deciding how to address the internal and external factors that influence organizational structure? Which ones should get the most attention? Should any be ignored?
10. How does functional departmentalization work? What are some of its benefits?
11. Why have some firms opted for a product departmentalization arrangement? What benefits does it offer?
12. When is territorial departmentalization likely to be used by organizations? What kinds of firms are most likely to use it?
13. A matrix organization is a blend of functional and product (and in some cases territorial) departmentalization arrangements. What is meant by this statement?
14. In what way does span of control help determine whether an organization has a flat or a tall structure? Illustrate by using an example.
15. Using research as the basis for your answer, tell which type of span is superior: narrow or wide? Defend your choice.
16. What types of factors influence the ideal span of control? In answering this question, incorporate Figure 8-10 into your answer.
17. In what way can well-written job descriptions help an organization deal with role clarity and role ambiguity?
18. What role do job analyses and job specifications play in the organizing process? Explain.

The Newly Proposed Structure

The Philby Corporation has been in operation for six years. During this time the company has increased its product lines from one to six, and sales have climbed from just under $100,000 in the first year to more than $16 million last year. Because of this rapid sales growth, Philby has focused most of its attention on manufacturing problems. The corporation has a rule that it will not allow backlog orders to extend more than 90 days. If they do, the firm employs subcontractors to help out.

This year promises to be another big one for Philby. Management is not as concerned as usual with manufacturing problems, however. The large plant that was constructed last year went into full operation three weeks ago, and it now appears that Philby will not have to rely on subcontractors in the future. In fact, if the plant is as efficient as it seems to be, the company should be able to meet all orders within 40 days after they are received.

Having resolved this problem, management is now turning its attention to the company's organizational structure. Currently the firm is organized along functional lines. Reporting directly to the president are the vice presidents of marketing, finance, and production. The latter, of course, has been of greatest importance to the firm in past years, and any organizing concerns the firm had in the past were related to improving production operations. Now, however, the president believes a total reorganization is in order. He feels that the company has done a good job of handling product production but should focus more attention on the marketing side of operations. His idea is to redesign the structure and convert it from a functional to a product arrangement. Each product line will be given its own manager, who is to be responsible for handling the advertising, selling, and order placing for that particular line. Each manager will also be given some financial control over the operations of the product line, although there will continue to be a centralized finance department reporting directly to the president. Finally, the production department will be reorganized, with specific managers appointed to oversee the manufacture of each of the product lines. While no new production facilities will be built, the company's internal structure will be organized to help manufacturing support and respond to the various product line managers.

If this new structure works well and the firm continues to grow, the president is talking about going to territorial departmentalization. This change will not take place for at least three more years, however.

1. What does the current organizational structure look like? Draw it.
2. What will the newly proposed product organizational structure look like? Draw your version of it.
3. If the company does adopt a territorial departmentalization arrangement, how will this be integrated into the product departmentalization

structure? Be sure to draw the territorial structure in a way that makes clear how the new arrangement will work.

Organizing for Dynamic Growth

A large multiline manufacturer is located in the Midwest. The company has eight product lines. Four are consumer goods; the other four are industrial products. Figure 8-11 provides a partial illustration of the company's organizational chart.

The company had only three product lines five years ago. Because of an aggressive acquisitions program, however, it was able to buy three more. The last two were developed in-house. This rapid expansion has resulted in an

FIGURE 8-11   Partial Organizational Structure

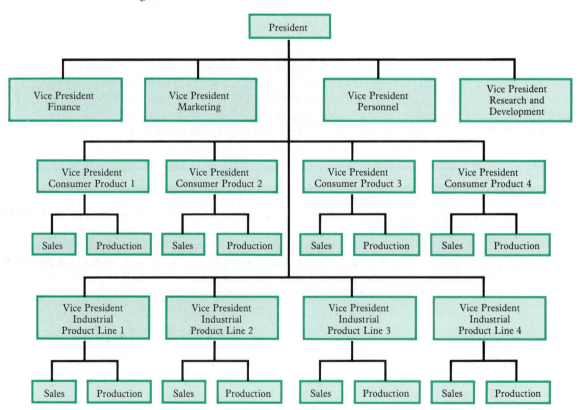

average sales increase of 38 percent annually. The board of directors would like to continue this rate of growth but realizes that there are risks associated with expanding too fast. The primary problem the board is concerned about is control. The members are convinced that when an organization grows too quickly, things start to go haywire and costs escalate dramatically. On the other hand, both the board and top management are committed to vigorous expansion.

In line with this strategy, the company has decided to expand into foreign markets. The ventures planned with be in Europe (England, France, and Germany initially), South America (Brazil, Argentina, and Chile at first, others later), and the Far East (Japan at first, China in a few years). In the European theater the concentration will be on selling all of the company's current product lines. In South America and the Far East only the industrial products will be marketed.

Management believes that a demand exists overseas for its products. Initial marketing research conducted by local research firms in all three international areas has supported this conviction. The main reason for the demand is that the company's strong research and development program has allowed it to produce industrial machinery that is superior to anything being offered by the competition.

On the negative side, while management believes that it can make a great deal of money overseas, it is concerned about the link that will exist between the American-based home office and the international offices. While the firm is expanding overseas it will also be looking for additional acquisitions in the States. Coupled with the company's vigorous marketing of current product lines is the president's desire to plan for "stable growth." He believes this can be done if the company has the "right" structure. After giving the matter a great deal of thought, he and his top management advisory staff have concluded that a matrix design would be most effective. This arrangement would allow the organization to emphasize both inputs and outputs. Of course, it is also a very sophisticated type of design and could result in "overorganization" if things are not done properly. This is why he is going to use outside consultants to help out.

Your Consultation

Assume that you have been called in by the president to serve as the consultant in designing the desired matrix structure. After carefully studying the material in this case, draw the matrix design you would propose. Then explain how it would work. Be sure to explain how your structure would increase efficiency and pull together all of the various departments and units into a working team. Also, tell the president how the structure would be of value if more product lines were added (or why the structure would be ineffective if more product lines were added, in which case tell him how the firm will then have to be reorganized to accommodate this latest growth).

9

Coordination and Design of Jobs

OBJECTIVES

This chapter studies the ways in which modern organizations coordinate their personnel and the work they do. In the previous chapter consideration was given to the "building blocks" of organizational design. This chapter examines the way in which the people and the work are brought together within this design. In essence, the enterprise needs to coordinate the efforts of its employees in such a way as to attain objectives efficiently. The ways in which this coordinative effort are carried out are the focus of attention here. By the time you have finished studying the material in this chapter, you will be able to:

1. Define the term coordination and explain some of the most common types of coordination that exist in modern organizations.
2. Describe the four most common types of authority and explain the value of each in coordinating the personnel and the work.
3. Explain how decentralization can be measured and describe four of the key factors that influence the degree of decentralization in an organization.
4. Define the term delegation, explain how this process works, and explain the ways in which managers can go about dealing with delegation-related problems.
5. Describe the three most common types of committees found in organizations, how they function, some of the basic advantages and disadvantages associated with using them, and how they can be used most effectively.

271

6. Discuss the most common approaches to job design and illustrate how each can be of value in coordinating the work and the employees.
7. List some of the most common costs and benefits associated with job design.

COORDINATION

Coordination is the synchronization of human effort

Coordination is the synchronization of the efforts of individuals and groups for the purpose of attaining organizational efficiency. The structural components that were described in the previous chapter—departmentalization, span of control, and job specialization—are useful in organizing personnel, but organization is not enough. The enterprise must also coordinate personnel's efforts. Coordination is particularly important when the work is of an interdependent nature.[1]

Interdependency

Few individuals in modern organizations work in isolation. Most must coordinate their efforts with the efforts of others. In doing so, they exhibit one or more of the following types of interdependency: pooled, sequential, and reciprocal.[2]

Pooled interdependence

The simplest form of interdependence is **pooled interdependence.** It occurs when units, departments, or divisions all pool their efforts to help the organization attain its objectives, but coordination between them is minimal. Retail chain stores are an example; for the most part they operate independently of each other.

Sequential interdependence

Sequential interdependence occurs when work units rely on other work units to get the job done. Figure 9-1 illustrates this kind of interdependence. Each group is dependent on the one behind it. A bottleneck in any link of the chain affects overall organizational performance. A bottleneck may occur in an assembly line, for example.

Reciprocal interdependence

Reciprocal interdependence occurs when the outputs of one unit become the inputs of another. Figure 9-2 illustrates this kind of interdependence. A car rental agency, for example, has its own auto maintenance facilities. As the fleet of cars is rented, the wear and tear caused by use results in the need for maintenance. So the better the personnel who rent these cars do their jobs, the more business they create for the maintenance people. The output from the

---

[1] Joseph L. C. Cheng, "Interdependence and Coordination in Organizations: A Role-System Analysis," *Academy of Management Journal* (March 1983):156–62.
[2] James D. Thompson, *Organizations in Action,* Chap. 5 (New York: McGraw-Hill, 1967).

FIGURE 9-1
Sequential
Interdependency

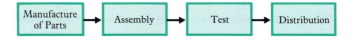

maintenance department, in turn, provides an input for the rental fleet personnel.

In every modern organization at least one of these three forms of interdependency exists. In large organizations with diversified operations, all three can be found.

Achieving Effective Coordination

There are three ways to achieve effective coordination. Two are formal in nature and one is both formal and informal.

Delegation of
authority

The first way is through the use of delegated authority. By giving managers the right to order employees to carry out certain functions or the right to combine their efforts with the efforts of other managers, formal coordination can be achieved.

Use of committees

The second way is through the use of committees. Sometimes tasks or assignments require cooperation or synchronization of effort by individuals or groups from different units or departments. In achieving this coordination, committees are formed that draw members from all of the groups involved. In the case of sequential and reciprocal interdependencies, coordination through the use of committees is quite common.

Restructuring the
work

The third way is through the use of job design in which work is restructured so as to blend personnel needs and organizational requirements. If done properly, job design can foster higher motivation and increased work quality and quantity.

In the rest of this chapter, these three ways of achieving coordination are examined in detail. The initial focus of attention is on authority.

AUTHORITY

Authority is the
right to command

As we saw earlier, **authority** is the right to command. Through the proper use of authority, formal coordination can be achieved.

FIGURE 9-2
Reciprocal
Interdependency

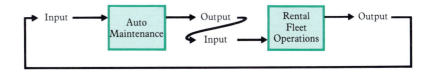

There are a number of different types of authority. Four of the most important, used in the departmentalization arrangements discussed in Chapter 8, are line, staff, functional, and project authority.

Line Authority

Line authority is direct authority

Line authority is direct authority. It is used by superiors in giving orders to their subordinates and helps establish the chain of command in an organization. Figure 9-3 illustrates line authority in action. The CEO gives orders to the vice presidents who, in turn, have authority over their respective subordinates.

Staff Authority

Staff authority is auxiliary authority

Staff authority is auxiliary authority. Those with staff authority assist, advise, recommend, and facilitate organizational activities. One of the most common examples of staff authority is the lawyer who advises the CEO. (See Figure 9-3).

Functional Authority

Functional authority is authority in a department other than one's own

Functional authority is authority in a department other than one's own. This authority is delegated to an individual or department in regard to a particular practice or process being carried out by individuals in other units. For example, the lawyer may have functional authority to demand that all public speeches by

FIGURE 9-3   Line, Staff, and Functional Authority

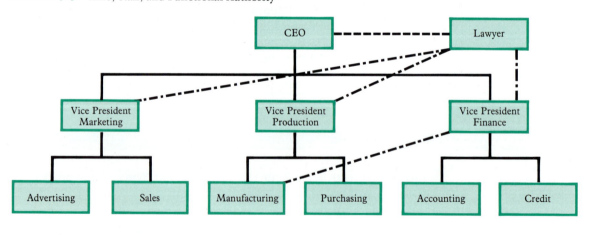

the vice presidents first be cleared by the legal department. The vice president of finance may have the right to require the head of the manufacturing department to provide cost production data on a weekly basis. (See Figure 9-3). In a manner of speaking, functional authority is a slice of line authority that can be exercised in another unit.

Line-Staff and Functional Authority Problems

When an organization is small, all coordination may be handled through the use of line authority. When staff authority is added, line-staff conflicts sometimes result. Line people may resent having staff people suggest solutions to their problems. Staff people may feel that the line personnel refuse to implement their good advice. In order to prevent such problems from undermining coordination and cooperation, four basic rules should be enforced by the organization: (1) the line people must keep the staff people aware of the kinds of problems that staff can help out with; (2) staff personnel must provide their advice and assistance in such a way as to reduce the amount of time and effort needed by line people in understanding these recommendations; (3) staff people must be prepared to sell their ideas to line people as opposed to demanding action or implementation; and (4) line people must be willing to listen to staff advice and use it in the best interests of the organization.

Resolving line-staff problems

The use of functional authority also presents problems. The major one is that it can undermine the integrity of managerial positions. After all, if the vice president of finance can give an order directly to the head of manufacturing, does he or she not undercut somewhat the authority of the production vice president? To reduce these kinds of problems, three guidelines should be followed: (1) before anyone is given functional authority, managers whose personnel will be affected should be made aware of the situation; (2) the nature and scope of the functional authority held by any manager should be spelled out precisely; and (3) whenever possible, functional authority should *not* extend more than one hierarchical level below that of the manager holding this authority.

Handling functional authority problems

Project Authority

Project authority is the authority a matrix manager has over the individuals assigned to the project. These personnel are only loaned to the matrix manager, who is more of a coordinator than anything else. He or she lacks the authority to fire, demote, promote, or raise the salary of any of these personnel. Such authority is the domain of the functional manager. Figure 9-4 provides an example. Notice how the line authority of the functional managers runs down the structure while the project authority of the matrix (project) manager runs across the structure.

The project manager is a coordinator

When the line authority of the functional manager is contrasted with the "coordinative" authority of the matrix manager, it becomes obvious that the

FIGURE 9-4   Matrix Organization

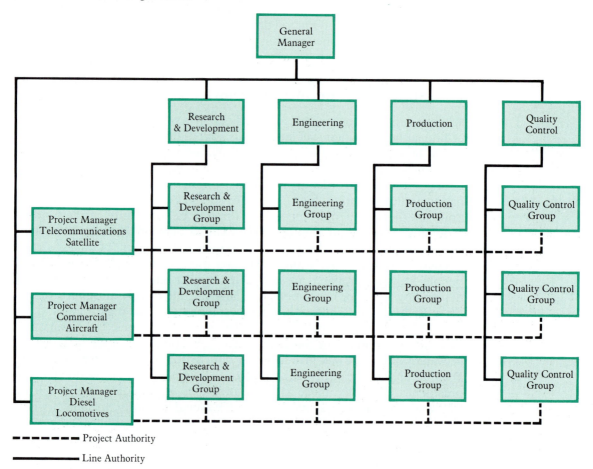

- - - - - - Project Authority

——————— Line Authority

latter has much less formal authority than the former. In fact, the matrix manager has an "authority gap." To close this gap, four techniques have been found to be of value. First, the matrix manager must be *competent* so that all the personnel involved realize that the individual knows what he or she is doing. Second, the matrix manager must be *persuasive,* able to generate the necessary support from both the functional managers and the personnel. Third, he or she must be willing to *engage in reciprocity* by trading favors with the functional managers. ("Help me out now and I'll return the favor at a later date.") Fourth, the matrix manager must be *able to live with uncertainty* as he or she tries to coordinate project efforts and get everything done within the assigned time, cost, and quality parameters.

The use of line, staff, functional, and project authority can be found in all large organizations. The degree of each, however, is affected by the amount of decentralization that exists in the structure.

Decentralization

Decentralization defined

Decentralization is a philosophy of management regarding which decisions to send down the line and which to keep near the top for purposes of organizational control. In every organization, except those owned and operated by one person, there is always some degree of decentralization and some degree of centralization. To determine whether an organization is basically decentralized or centralized, one must examine the nature and scope of its decision making. Who makes which decisions? How important are these decisions? At which level of the hierarchy is this person located? The answers to these questions help determine the degree of decentralization. In broad terms, four criteria can be employed in measuring the degree of decentralization.

Measuring Decentralization

Quantity of decisions

The first way to measure decentralization is to find out the number of decisions made at the lower levels of the management hierarchy. While this number can be quite large, even in a centralized structure, quantity is one useful initial gauge.

Quality of decisions

The second way is to find out where the important decisions are made. One of the best ways to measure importance is through cost. At what level do managers have the authority to approve expenditures of $1,000? $5,000? $10,000? The higher the amounts that managers at the middle and lower ranks have the authority to approve, the greater the degree of decentralization.

Impact of decisions

The third way is to examine the impact of decisions at lower levels in the hierarchy. Managers who make decisions that affect functional areas other than their own have more impact than those whose decisions are confined exclusively to their own functional area.

Amount of control

The fourth way is to measure the amount of control managers have over their areas of operation. An individual who can make decisions without informing his or her superior has more decentralized authority than someone who must keep the boss informed. A manager who has to consult with the superior before making a decision has even less decentralized authority. The fewer people a manager has to consult and the lower in the hierarchy the manager is located, the greater the degree of decentralized authority.

Factors Influencing Decentralization

Is decentralization superior to centralization? The answer is no. Whether an organization should be highly decentralized or basically centralized depends on its own particular environment, both internal and external. Five of the most influential factors in this area are cost, size, the employees' desire for independence, the availability of managers, and the nature of the enterprise.

Cost encourages centralization

COST   In general terms the greater the cost involved, the more likely it is that the decision will be centralized. Many organizations ensure this practice by setting financial limits that indicate when the decision must be referred to a higher authority.

Size encourages decentralization

SIZE   As an organization increases in size, it usually becomes more decentralized. Top management is unable to control personally as much as it did before. More hierarchial levels are created, and units are given increased authority over their own operations.

Desire for independence encourages decentralization

DESIRE FOR INDEPENDENCE   If the middle and lower-level managers want more authority over their areas, they are likely to get it. If they want little authority, centralization is likely to exist. The motivational effect of giving the managers what they desire is too important to be ignored. Of course, there are limits to the amount of decentralization the organization will approve, but the basic desire for independence will often, to the degree possible, be accommodated.

So does the availability of managers

AVAILABILITY OF MANAGERS   The more managers an organization has, the greater the possible extent of decentralization because managers are individuals to whom authority can be delegated. Conversely, a shortage of managerial talent means that the top managers may have to make most of the important decisions themselves. This factor illustrates the importance of managerial recruiting, selecting, and training.

Dynamic environments also lead to decentralization

NATURE OF THE ENTERPRISE   Organizations operating in a dynamic environment are often more decentralized than those functioning in a stable environment. The reason is quite simple. In a dynamic setting the top managers are being confronted continually with new problems and challenges. Realizing that they cannot handle everything themselves, they delegate much responsibility to their subordinates, thereby freeing themselves to handle the most important problems. In a stable environment the opposite often occurs. The top staff is capable of handling most things themselves.

Which is Better?

Neither centralization nor decentralization is necessarily the better choice

Is decentralization preferable to centralization? Sometimes it is; sometimes it is not. Each situation must be considered separately. Certainly decentralization seems to fit well with the American desire to democratize things. In a stable environment, however, where the middle and lower level managers prefer a centralized structure, the benefits of decentralization may well be limited. Table 9-1 sets forth some of the primary benefits of and drawbacks to centralization and decentralization. After carefully weighing these features, the organization can decide what degree of decentralization will provide it the most benefit.

TABLE 9-1   Benefits and Drawbacks to Decentralization and Centralization

	Decentralization	Centralization
Benefits	Reduces the total responsiblity to more manageable units. Encourages more involvement of the personnel in the decision-making process. Shortens lines of communication. Brings decision making closer to those affected by the decision. Disperses power and authority among many people.	Assures uniformity of standards and policies among all organization units. Allows the use of outstanding talent in managers by the whole organization rather than a single unit. Ensures uniform decisions. Helps eliminate duplication of effort and activity.
Drawbacks	Allows a lack of uniformity of standards and policies among organizational units. Necessitates making of decisions without capable managers, who may be unavailable or unwilling to participate. Can create coordination problems among the various organizational units. Can lead to interunit rivalry, which can interfere with the organization's overall effectiveness. Requires training programs which can be time-consuming and costly.	Makes great demands on a few managers instead of spreading responsibility. Forces top managers to possess a broad view, which may be beyond their ability. Gives vast amounts of authority and power to a few people. Reduces a sense of participation for all but a few.

Delegation

Delegation defined

Delegation of authority is the process of assigning duties to subordinates, giving them the authority to carry out these tasks, and creating an obligation on their part to complete the assignments in a satisfactory manner. It is the means the superior uses to ensure that all of the department or unit work is divided up among the personnel. Everyone is given something to do.[3] (See Management in Practice: Delegation Quiz.)

Boss-Related Problems

Reasons for managerial reluctance to delegate authority

Many managers are somewhat reluctant to delegate a great deal of authority to their people. Why? Perhaps the major reason is that they think they can do the job better themselves. Other typical reasons include (1) a lack of confidence in subordinates, (2) an inability to train the subordinate to do the task properly, (3) an unwillingness to let go of authority, and (4) a refusal to let others make mistakes.

---

[3] Carrie R. Leana, "Predictors and Consequences of Delegating," *Academy of Management Journal* (December 1986):754–74.

MANAGEMENT IN PRACTICE

Delegation Quiz

Take the following test to find out if you delegate effectively. For each statement, mark the answer that *most accurately describes your actual behavior or attitude and then check your score.*

1 = ALWAYS   2 = USUALLY
3 = SOMETIMES   4 = RARELY
5 = NEVER

	1	2	3	4	5
1. Delegation to me means handing over responsibility for results together with the requisite authority and decision-making power.					
2. No matter what the delegated task, I try to make it seem like a challenge.					
3. I intend to delegate to the subordinate who has the best experience with a similar task.					
4. I refrain from giving advice when delegating.					
5. I have full confidence in my subordinates' abilities to shoulder increasingly more difficult responsibilities.					
6. I make sure important decisions on delegated tasks remain with me.					
7. I insist tasks be done according to the methods I have outlined.					
8. I make sure controls are built into all tasks and projects I delegate.					
9. I am willing to admit some of my subordinates are able to do the job as well, or better, than I can.					

	1	2	3	4	5
10. I make sure to acknowledge good performance.					
11. When I have to criticize, I do it fairly, objectively, and constructively.					
12. I feel I must be in control of delegated tasks all the time.					
13. My subordinates defer all decisions on problems to me.					
14. I find work slows down when I am out of the office.					
15. I am reluctant to give feedback when a subordinate turns in poor work.					
16. Daily operations are so time consuming I have little time left over for long-range planning.					
17. I am constantly harassed by unexpected emergencies.					
18. Many of my tasks are beyond what my subordinates can handle.					
19. My subordinates are not sufficiently motivated to perform well.					
20. I am bothered by unfinished business.					
21. I have to keep close control of every detail to have a job done right.					

Subordinate-Related Problems

Reasons for subordinate reluctance to accept the delegation of authority

On the other side of the coin are subordinate-related problems. Some individuals do not want to have authority delegated to them. Some of the most common reasons are that they (1) lack self-confidence, (2) are afraid of harsh criticism, (3) perceive that inadequate rewards are associated with the increased responsibility, and (4) realize that the boss would rather not delegate authority in the first place.

Dealing with These Problems

How can a manager go about overcoming typical boss-related problems in the delegation of authority? How can he or she work with subordinates in sur-

1 = ALWAYS   2 = USUALLY
3 = SOMETIMES   4 = RARELY
5 = NEVER

	1	2	3	4	5
22. I expect perfection of myself in everything I do.	—	—	—	—	—
23. I am willing to accept complicated work that is less than perfect.	—	—	—	—	—

1 = AGREE   2 = DISAGREE

	1	2
24. I am often bogged down in endless detail.	—	—
25. I frequently put in overtime.	—	—
26. I often take work home evenings or weekends.	—	—
27. There have been times I have taken back a task midstream without explanation.	—	—
28. I work harder than most people in my department.	—	—
29. My subordinates seldom come to me to present their ideas.	—	—
30. My subordinates seldom show any initiative.	—	—
31. I seldom ask a subordinate to do something I would not be willing to do.	—	—
32. I often handle routine work in order to appear busy.	—	—
33. Some of my subordinates are out to get my job.	—	—
34. If I were promoted today and had to name a successor, I would have little trouble choosing one.	—	—
35. If I were to leave my company today, my department would continue to function properly.	—	—
36. I am often amazed at the incompetence of my subordinates.	—	—

1 2 3 4 5	17. 1 2 3 4 5
1. 6 4 2 1 0	18. 1 2 4 5 6
2. 0 1 3 4 5	19. 1 2 3 4 5
3. 1 2 3 4 5	20. 1 2 3 4 5
4. 1 2 3 4 5	21. 0 1 3 4 6
5. 6 5 3 1 0	22. 1 2 3 4 5
6. 1 2 3 4 5	23. 5 4 3 1 0
7. 0 1 3 5 6	
8. 6 5 3 1 0	1 = AGREE 2 = DISAGREE
9. 6 5 3 1 0	
10. 6 5 3 1 0	
11. 6 5 3 1 0	
12. 1 2 3 4 5	
13. 0 2 4 5 6	
14. 0 1 2 3 5	
15. 1 2 3 4 5	
16. 0 1 3 4 5	

	1 2		1 2
24.	1 4	30.	0 5
25.	2 4	31.	2 4
26.	2 4	32.	1 4
27.	3 5	33.	2 5
28.	3 5	34.	5 1
29.	1 5	35.	5 1
		36.	1 5

If you scored 136–185, congratulations, you obviously know how to effectively delegate tasks and responsibilities to your subordinates.

If you scored 74–135, you sometimes do a good job of delegating . However, some of your attitudes and behaviors are acting as barriers to consistently good delegation.

If you scored 30–73, there seem to be serious weaknesses in your delegation skills that need immediate attention.

Source: Eugene Raudsepp, "How To Delegate Effectively," *Machine Design* (April 20, 1989): 119.

mounting their resistance to its delegation? Five of the most useful recommendations are the following:

Action-oriented steps

1. Spell out all assignments in terms of the expected results. Let people know exactly what they are to accomplish.
2. Match the person with the job. Determine which subordinates are most qualified and from this pool choose the one who has the best combination of training and experience.
3. Keep all lines of communication open. In this way if there is a problem, both superior and subordinate can communicate easily with each other.
4. Set up a control procedure for seeing that the job is being done properly and provide assistance as needed. Be careful, however, not to interfere

with work progress or to give the impression of being too close-control oriented.

5. Use job performance as a basis for rewards. Those who are willing to assume responsibility and get the job done right should be placed at the head of the list when raises and promotions are given out.

COMMITTEES

Like authority, committees are important in coordinating activities. Of course, this is not all they do, but it is one of their most vital roles. In fact, the larger the number of employees, the more likely it is that an organization has formal committees.

Types of Committees

In an organizational setting, there are three common types of committees: ad hoc, standing, and plural executive.

Ad Hoc Committees

Ad hoc committees
are temporary

Ad hoc committees are those formed for a particular purpose. The words "ad hoc" in Latin mean "for this," and so it is with the committee that is formed to meet a particular objective. As soon as the objective has been accomplished, the committee is disbanded.

Ad hoc committees, often referred to as task forces or project teams, are typically formed for handling complex problems that cut across departmental or divisional lines. For example, an organization planning to install a new computer system for control purposes may form an ad hoc committee to study how the plan should be implemented. In such cases, to work through a committee is usually wiser than to order the implementation of the plan through a directive from top management. By having representatives from all of the major departments that will be affected by the installation, the organization accomplishes three objectives. First, it ensures that representatives of each unit have the opportunity to find out how the system will work and what its benefits or disadvantages will be. Second, it allows the committee to put together recommendations that will take advantage of these benefits while sidestepping or avoiding many of the drawbacks. Third, having been involved in the decision, the members of the committee can then serve as representatives to their own unit to explain why the implementation is taking place. By allowing personnel to participate in the actual decision, management gets them behind the project.

Not all ad hoc committees are interdepartmental in nature, however. Some are put together by senior executives to whom the individual members report all along. In these cases the members of the committee are usually asked to make an analysis of a particular problem or project and report their recommendations directly to the superior.

In any event, when the project group completes its recommendations, its task is over and the committee is dissolved. Ad hoc committees have no authority to order their recommendations implemented, unless such authority is expressly given to them. They are purely advisory. Of course, if they do their job well the manager who is ultimately responsible for making the decision may well implement their recommendations. This is the manager's decision, however, and not the committee's.

Standing Committees

Standing committees are permanent

Standing committees are permanent in nature. They are not disbanded. In large organizations they often take the form of finance committees and personnel committees, and there is always enough work to justify their existence. In the case of a personnel committee, for example, there are sufficient questions related to such issues as discrimination, pay, and promotion procedures to keep the group meeting on a weekly basis for an indefinite period.

Membership on these committees is usually rotated. For example, the personnel committee may consist of 10 members, each of whom is elected for five years. The terms will be staggered so that every year two members are going off and two new ones are coming on. In this way there is always a large percentage of the membership that is familiar with both the issues and the procedures.

Some standing committees spend much of their time addressing problems. Most, however, examine situations and forward their recommendations to a higher authority.

Plural Executive Committees

Plural executive committees can order implementation of recommendations

The term **plural executive** refers to a committee that has the authority to order the implementation of its own recommendations. The most common plural executive committee is the board of directors, although other standing committees can also be plural executives. In the latter cases these committees typically report directly to the CEO or the board of directors.

The biggest problem with the plural executive concept, except in the case of the board of directors, is that it is often a mistake for a committee to be given authority to make specific decisions. A well-known American Management Association study of committees in organizations reported that in some cases committees do not do a good job. Individuals are more effective. Table 9-2 presents the findings of this study. Notice from the results that only in the case of **jurisdictional question** issues — those arising between two or more departments or units regarding who has authority in a given matter — were committees considered more effective than individual managers. The study points out

TABLE 9-2   The Effectiveness of Individual and Committee Action in Carrying Out Management Functions (In Percentages)

Management Function	Can Be Effectively Exercised by a Committee	Can Be Effectively Exercised by a Committee but More Effectively by an Individual	Individual Initiative Is Essential but It Can Be Supplemented by a Committee	Individual Action Is Essential and Committee Is Ineffective
Planning	20	20	25	35
Control	25	20	25	30
Formulating Objectives	35	35	10	20
Organization	5	25	20	50
Jurisdictional Questions	90	10		
Leadership			10	90
Administration	20	25	25	30
Execution	10	15	10	65
Innovation	30	20	20	30
Communication	20	15	35	30
Advice	15	25	35	25
Decision Making	10	30	10	50

Source: Reprinted, by permission of the publisher, from *Planning and Developing the Company Structure,* Research Report #20, by Ernest Dale, p. 93, © 1952 by American Management Association, New York. All rights reserved.

the great danger of overusing committees to get things done. They should be used for promoting coordination and cooperation but seldom for actual decision making. They complement the role of the executive but should not serve as a substitute for it.

Advantages of Committees

A number of important advantages are associated with the use of committees. Most of these involve either the coordination of effort through group problem solving or the promotion of cooperation and understanding among organizational members. Four key advantages are that committees promote group judgment, representation, coordination, and motivation.

Group Judgment

Committees have wide experience

Some problems and issues are best resolved by committees. The old adage that "two heads are better than one" certainly applies here. A group of qualified people is much better able to focus its wide range of experience on an issue than is a single individual. The committee's ability to stimulate ideas and suggestions can often bring about extremely good results.

Representation

Many problems or issues facing an organization affect two or more departments or units. Committees that contain representation of such interested parties can often deal effectively with these matters. For example, the design and implementation of a new cost control report may affect both the marketing and production departments. So each may be given two representatives on the committee. If the finance department is the one that wants the new report, it is also given two representatives. At the same time, five other individuals from various departments may be assigned to round out the membership. Note that the production and marketing people may object to some of the suggestions from finance but that they do not have enough votes to force their opinion on the committee. Meanwhile, finance is put in the position of having to explain the format and logic of the report; it does not have enough votes to force its recommended report on the other two departments. The disinterested members play the crucial role of deciding what will eventually be done. While the interested groups are represented on the committee, no one group dominates it.

Interested parties are represented on committees

Coordination of Plans and Activities

Committees help coordinate organizational activities

Committees help coordinate activities between organizational units. This function is particularly important given the dynamics of modern structures, with their multilevel departments and far-reaching operations. Sometimes managers cannot pull everything together by themselves. A committee is needed:

> . . . in one study 90 percent of the respondents agreed with the statement that "committees promote coordination among departments." There was similar agreement on this point among various levels, although lower-middle management agreed slightly less (a little over 80 percent) than upper-middle and top management (about 90 percent) agreed with the statement.[4]

Motivation

Participation on committees can be motivational

Committees can also be motivational in that they provide their members an opportunity to participate and play a role. Quite often when people have a hand in fashioning a particular decision, they get behind it and work for its implementation.

---

[4] Harold Koontz, Cyril O'Donnell, and Heinz Weihrich, *Management,* 8th ed. (New York: McGraw-Hill, 1984), 338–39.

Disadvantages of Committees

Committees also have their shortcomings, however. Some of these relate to coordination per se, while others relate to inefficiency and high cost.

Indecision or Compromise

Committees often make mediocre decisions

Sometimes, rather than helping get things done, committees prove to be a source of indecision or compromise. Regardless of the number of meetings, nothing is accomplished. Either the discussions wander off to peripheral issues or the group simply "agrees that it cannot agree." In the latter case a decision is reached, but it is so watered down that the result is meaningless. This situation often occurs when one group on the committee feels that a particular line of action should be taken (develop product A), a second group supports a different line of action (develop product B), and the eventual decision is to do more marketing research on the benefits of both products. While the organization is doing this research, the competition produces a brand new product and sweeps the market.

Time and Money

Time is money

Committees can prove to be a great waste of time and money. Whether they are or not depends on their results. The important thing to keep in mind is that time is money. To determine if a committee is giving the organization its money's worth, the organization must weigh their costs and benefits. Suppose that a particular committee consisting of seven senior managers meets once a week for four weeks, three hours each time, before reaching a final decision. This decision results in an overall profit of $50,000 and 5 percent of this amount is attributed to the quality of the committee's decision. Was the committee effective from a time and cost standpoint? The following table answers this question.

Executive	Hourly Salary ×	Number of Hours	Cost
1	$50	12	$ 600
2	48	12	576
3	46	12	552
4	45	12	540
5	42	12	504
6	42	12	504
7	42	12	504
			$3,780

The committee has not been effective. The cost was $3,780 but the benefit of the committee was only $2,500 ($50,000 × 0.05). The reason for committee ineffectiveness is often found in the high cost per hour. In our example, the cost of the seven executives was $315 an hour. For the organization to benefit from such a committee, the payoffs must be extremely high. Otherwise it is best to have the decisions made by a smaller committee or a single manager.

Lack of Responsibility

When working in a group, many people make decisions that are different from those they would make if they were personally charged with the same responsibility. One reason is that in a group they feel sheltered from personal responsibility. If a decision proves to be wrong, the individual can always point out that he or she did not agree with the majority or, if the individual did agree, he or she can argue that "I'm only one of many who participated in the decision, so don't pin the blame on me." In either event, no one is personally responsible. Even if the organization wants to follow up and find out who caused the mistake, it cannot.

No one is personally responsible

Making Committees Effective

Since committees are vital to the operation of most medium-sized and large modern organizations, it is important that they be used effectively. For this objective to be accomplished, attention mut be focused on three areas.

Determine objectives and structure

First, the objectives, authority, and organization of the committee should be spelled out clearly. What is the committee to do? Does it have the authority to implement its recommendations, or are these merely forwarded to higher authority. How should the committee organize itself? Who is to do what? How often will meetings be held? When and where will the group meet?

Get good leadership . . .

Second, the committee must be led skillfully by its chairperson. This individual plays a key role in determining both the focus and the pace of committee discussions. In addition to drawing up the agenda, the chairperson must stimulate participation and encourage teamwork. Table 9-3 provides a checklist for effective meetings which can assist the manager in providing skillful leadership in committee meetings. (Also see "Management in Practice: Watching for Hidden Agendas.")

and competent members

Third, the committee members must cooperate in pursuing the group's objectives. This means that they must read the agenda, come to the meeting prepared to work, participate actively in the discussion, team up with the other members to resolve differences and deal with problems, decide what needs to be done before the next meeting, and carry out their assignments within the established time period.[5]

---

[5] For some additional ideas on using committees effectively, see Cyril O'Donnell, "Ground Rules For Using Committees," *Management Review* (October 1961):63–67 and George M. Prince, "How To Be A Better Committee Chairman," *Harvard Business Review* (January–February 1971):98–108.

TABLE 9-3 Effective Meeting Checklist

Before the Meeting

1. Explore advantages and disadvantages of meeting.
2. Plan the meeting.
3. Prepare and distribute agenda in advance.
4. Set up the meeting room.

During the Meeting

5. Start on time.
6. Explain meeting purpose.
7. Make introductions.
8. Review the agenda.
9. Set clear time limits.
10. Develop and maintain thought line.
11. Stress openness and encourage participation.
12. Involve all members.
13. Control interruptions and digressions.
14. Summarize periodically/test for understanding.
15. Establish and assign action items.
16. Evaluate the meeting.

After the Meeting

17. Close the meeting positively and on time.
18. Prepare and distribute minutes.
19. Follow up on action items.
20. Plan next meeting.

Source: Gary Ashenbrenner, "Planning Effective Meetings," *Business Credit* (July–August 1988): 44.

JOB DESIGN

A third major way of coordinating the people and the work effectively is to use job design. Over the last 10 years a great deal of attention has been directed toward the need for less job specialization. A change is being accomplished through what is called job design (or, in the case of ongoing jobs, job redesign). **Job design** is the process of introducing work changes for the purpose of increasing the quality or the quantity of work or both.[6] A close analysis of the

---

[6] T. Wall, "What's New in Job Design?" *Personnel Management* (April 1984):27–29. See also: Robert K. Kazanjian and Robert Drazin, "Implementing Internal Diversification: Contingency Factors For Organizational Design Choices," *Academy of Management Review* (April 1987): 342–54.

Watching for Hidden Agendas for Meetings

*I*f managers are going to provide effective leadership in committee meetings, then the numerous hidden reasons for meetings should be recognized in order to determine the need and direction of such get-togethers. a few of these reasons are highlighted below:

1. *Meeting as a substitute work:* Meetings may appear to offer a rest from "real" work, or at least a break from other kinds of work. People tend to avoid their own work by calling or attending meetings.
2. *The desire to share responsibility and risk:* Because decisions are difficult, it's easier to share the responsibility for making them.
3. *The desire to share gossip:* Whether it's relevant to a present task or not, people want to. And frequently, people are afraid they'll miss something someone else might say. Meetings can be valuable networking channels, but they are just as often simply gossip arenas.
4. *The need to reflect power:* Meetings are a sign of power. Appropriately or not, the person who is busy in meetings is perceived to be on the way up.
5. *People get lazy:* Particularly in respect to distributing information, some people just get lazy. Instead of taking the time to prepare written materials short enough to be read and detailed enough to be meaningful, they call a meeting and ad lib.
6. *The converted meeting:* Meetings are sometimes called for one purpose but a member attempts to convert the meeting to another use.
7. *Rushing to failure:* Some managers believe that any action is better than no action, and therefore any meeting is better than no meeting. Any meeting can be far worse than no meeting.
8. *The way it is:* The most common reason people attend meetings, particularly routine meetings, is that they simply take place, and, like robots, people attend. These are the easiest meetings to curtail once one recognizes the problem.

Source: George David Kieffer, "Meetings of the Mindless," *Across the Board* (July–August 1988). 6–8.

most common approaches to modern job design reveals that there are six very popular methods: job engineering, job rotation, job enlargement, job sharing, the sociotechnical approach, goal setting, and job enrichment. The following discussion examines each of these approaches, giving particular attention to the last four.

Job Engineering

Time and motion analysis is used

Job engineering uses time and motion analysis to achieve the most efficient interface between the worker and the machine. This approach was discussed in Chapter 2 when the scientific management movement was analyzed. Job engineering can be very important, especially in manufacturing firms, although its

FIGURE 9-5
Job Rotation in
Action

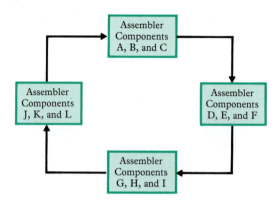

use is certainly not restricted to these industries. The biggest problem with job engineering is that the emphasis on the work may be allowed to overshadow consideration of the worker. Instead of blending the worker and the work, this approach forces the worker to adapt to the machine.

Job Rotation

Boredom can be reduced

Job rotation involves moving a worker from one job to another. The basic purpose of the approach is to reduce the boredom of the task. The technique has been used in many different types of work, particularly in assembly-line jobs, where each person does one (or a few) things. By rotating the individual worker from one job to another, as shown in Figure 9-5, management attempts to increase job interest.

Job Enlargement

Horizontal loading provides the worker with more of the same things to do

Job enlargement is a design technique that involves giving the worker more to do. When applied to the job rotation example, it would mean giving an assembler more than three components to assemble. In fact, the worker might be given all 12 so that he or she would put together the entire product. In job design terminology, job enlargement makes use of **horizontal loading:** the worker is given *more of the same things* to do. From a physical standpoint, job enlargement can bring about greater output because it reduces the amount of time spent in passing partially completed components to the next assembler. From a psychological standpoint, job enlargement can bring about greater output because it can lead to greater job satisfaction and a feeling of accomplishment on the part of the worker.[7]

Job sharing is another concept in job design that is growing in accept-

---

[7] John A. Roush, "Creating the Illusion of Indispensability," *Business Horizons* (September–October 1984):59–62.

ance as we approach the twenty-first century. This is an innovative approach to structuring and sharing responsibility for positions. Two or three employees determine with the employer how to divide the time requirements, responsibilities, needs, and benefits, for one full-time position so it can be shared by more than one employee. The benefits from this approach include greater flexibility in scheduling, retention of valued employees (that cannot devote a traditional 40-hour week to a job), recruitment from a broader labor pool, wider range of skills in one job, and options for older employees. During the last twenty years, the number of people working less than 34 hours a week has increased from 14 to 33 percent of the workforce. This steady increase has caused futurists to predict that job sharing will account for 10 percent of the workforce in the year 2000.[8]

Sociotechnical Approach

A group approach

The **sociotechnical approach** is one in which a group or team of workers is made responsible for getting the job done. This approach balances the social and technical aspects of the job. In contrast to the three previously discussed approaches, this one relies less on job design techniques and more on improving the quality of work life (QWL) and the overall work climate on the job. The sociotechnical or QWL approach is "a process of joint decision making, collaboration and building mutual respect between management and employees."[9] In recent years a number of important projects using QWL have been reported.

Over the last few years *teamwork* has become a key factor in large corporations.[10] Boeing, Catepillar, Champion International, Cummins Engine, Ford, Digital Equipment, General Electric, General Motors, Procter & Gamble, and Tektronix, are some of the companies that have reported successful results from the efforts of work teams.[11] Table 9-4 provides a summary of the evolution that worker participation has gone through in the U.S. From "problem-solving teams" through "special-purpose teams" to "self-managing teams," the results of teamwork has been favorable. In addition, Harvard University theorist Richard E. Walton has stated, "People must see the interrelationship between social performance and economic performance. To have world-class quality and costs and the ability to assimilate new technology, we must have the world's best ability to develop human capabilities."[12] Getting teams to work effectively is the challenge for managers during the 1990s.[13]

---

[8] Patricia Lee, "Job Sharing—A Concept Whose Time Has Come," *Office Administration and Automation* (April 1984):28–31.

[9] Deborah Shaw Cohen, "The Quality of Work Life Movement," *Training HRD* (January 1979):24.

[10] Bernard Portis and Neil Hill, "Improving Organization Effectiveness Through Employee Involvement," *Business Quarterly* (Winter 1989):58–61.

[11] Terry Widner, "The Payoff from Teamwork," *Business Week* (July 10, 1989):56–62.

[12] *Ibid.,* p. 62.

[13] Maurice Hardaker and Bryan K. Ward, "How to Make a Team Work," *Harvard Business Review* (November–December 1987):112–119.

TABLE 9-4   The Evolution of Worker Participation in the U.S.

	Problem-Solving Teams	Special-Purpose Teams	Self-Managing Teams
Structure and Function	Consists of 5 to 12 volunteers, hourly and salaried, drawn from different areas of a department. Meet one to two hours a week to discuss ways of improving quality, efficiency, and work environment. No power to implement ideas.	Duties may include designing and introducing work reforms and new technology, meeting with suppliers and customers, linking separate functions. In union shops, labor and management collaborate on operational decisions at all levels.	Usually 5 to 15 employees who produce an entire product instead of subunits. Members learn all tasks and rotate from job to job. Teams take over managerial duties, including work and vacations scheduling, ordering materials, etc.
Results	Can reduce costs and improve product quality, but do not organize work more efficiently or force managers to adopt a participatory style. Tend to fade away after a few years.	Involve workers and union representatives in decisions at ever-higher levels, creating atmosphere for quality and productivity improvements. Create a foundation for self-managing work teams.	Can increase productivity 30 percent or more and substantially raise quality. Fundamentally change how work is organized, giving employees control over their jobs. Create flatter organization by eliminating supervisors.
When Introduced	Small-scale efforts in 1920s and 1930s. Widespread adoption in late 1970s based on Japanese Quality Circles.	Early-to-middle 1980s, growing out of problem-solving approach. Still spreading, especially in union sectors.	Used by a few companies in 1960s and 1970s. Began rapid spread in mid-to-late 1980s, and appear to be wave of future.

Source: Terry Widner, "The Payoff From Teamwork," *Business Week* (July 10, 1989):57.

Many of the design programs used by these firms rely heavily upon worker input regarding changes that should be made. The idea has been gaining acceptance in the United States, and many people attribute this development to the success the approach has had in countries like Japan, where the **quality control circle** (or quality circle for short) has been employed profitably for years.

In Japan a quality circle typically consists of from five to 10 employees. All of the employees are assigned permanently to their circle, and their work is related in some way to that of the others. The task of each circle, headed by a foreman, is to study any problems of production or service that fall within the scope of its work. Each group meets for one to two hours each week to discuss changes and projects it wants to undertake.

A typical project may involve a problem in quality which one or more circle members have identified. . . . The group may then begin a systematic study of the problem, collecting statistics on the type and nature, perhaps even counting the number of defects per part at each of the stages in the production process covered by members of the circle. At the end of the study period . . . members meet again to analyze the data, drawing charts and graphs to determine the problem's source: Is it a defective design being supplied by engineering, a mis-designed part coming from suppliers, a machine improperly set up, or a lack of coordination among members of the circle? Once the problem is identified, circle members suggest steps that should be taken to correct it.[14]

Of course, the quality circle concept is not a panacea for organizations facing sociotechnical problems.[15] If used properly, however, it can be extremely useful in helping to meet these challenges. Some of the most important behavioral ideas that must be kept in mind when this approach is used include the following:

Quality circle guidelines

1. Quality control circles are a method of employee development as well as a means for improving organizational output and efficiency. If employee development is ignored, efficiency will suffer.
2. Membership in a quality circle should be voluntary. No one ought to be forced to join a quality circle; being forced to join may negatively affect the person's contribution to the group.
3. Participants should all be fully trained. Their training should not be only technical but also should provide them with insights regarding conference techniques and group dynamics so they will know how to work more effectively in groups.
4. Quality circles are group efforts, not individual efforts. This means that showboating and competition must be minimized and that cooperation and interdependent behavior must be encouraged.
5. The quality circle's project should be related to the members' actual job responsibilities. In this way the members are working to improve the quality of their own jobs, something in which they ought to have a high interest.
6. The quality circle program should help employees see the relationship between their work and the quality of the product or service being generated by their efforts. This quality and improvement awareness development should be used to commit the members further to quality.

---

[14] William G. Ouchi, *Theory Z: How American Business Can Meet the Japanese Challenge* (Reading, MA: Addison-Wesley, 1981), 263. Also see Jeremiah J. Sullivan, "A Critique of Theory Z," *Academy of Management Review* (January 1983):132–42.

[15] Robert P. Steel, "Factors Influencing the Success and Failure of Two Quality Circle Programs," *Journal of Management* (Spring 1985):99–119.

7. If there is a quality control department in the organization, the relationship between the department and the quality control circle should be clarified before the circle begins its job. Clarification of responsibilities prevents intergroup fights and squabbling. The best way to handle the situation usually is for the circle to complement the quality control department.

8. If the organization is just starting to use the quality control concept, a pilot study is in order. Then, if the circle produces results and wins the acceptance of managers and employees alike, its use can be expanded.

9. Management should make use of the suggestions set forth by the quality control circle. If none of the recommendations are adopted, the circle will lose its effectiveness and both membership and morale in the circle will drop off.

10. Management must be willing to grant recognition for all ideas that are set forth by the circle. If this is not done, the program is likely to backfire.[16]

Goal Setting

Challenging goals are motivational

Goal setting is a job design approach that emphasizes building goals, feedback, and incentives into the structure of the job. The logic behind the process is really quite simple. The better people understand their goals and the more challenging and interesting they are, the greater the likelihood that they will prove to be motivational. Figure 9-6 presents an integrated model of job design. Notice on the left side of the figure that task goals and enrichment are *interactive.* Goals help enrich jobs and enriched jobs have goal clarity and challenge. Because the interactive effect of goal setting and job enrichment is so strong, organizations that use a goal-setting approach are also interested in job enrichment, although the reverse is not necessarily true.

Job Enrichment

Psychological motivators are built into the job

Job enrichment is an extension of job rotation and job enlargement techniques. In essence, job enrichment is a process that attempts to build psychological motivators into the work. In particular, it often involves giving the

---

[16] The ideas in this section can be found in the following: Richard M. Hodgetts and Wendell V. Fountain, "The Defense Department Evaluates a Quality Circle Program," *Training and Development Journal* (November 1983):98–100; Edward E. Lawler, III and Susan A. Mohrman, "Quality Circles after the Fad," *Harvard Business Review* (January–February 1985):64–71; M. L. Marks et al., "Employee Participation in a Quality Circle Program: Impact on Quality Work Life, Productivity and Absenteeism," *Journal of Applied Psychology* (February 1986):61–69.

FIGURE 9-6   An Integrated Model of Job Design

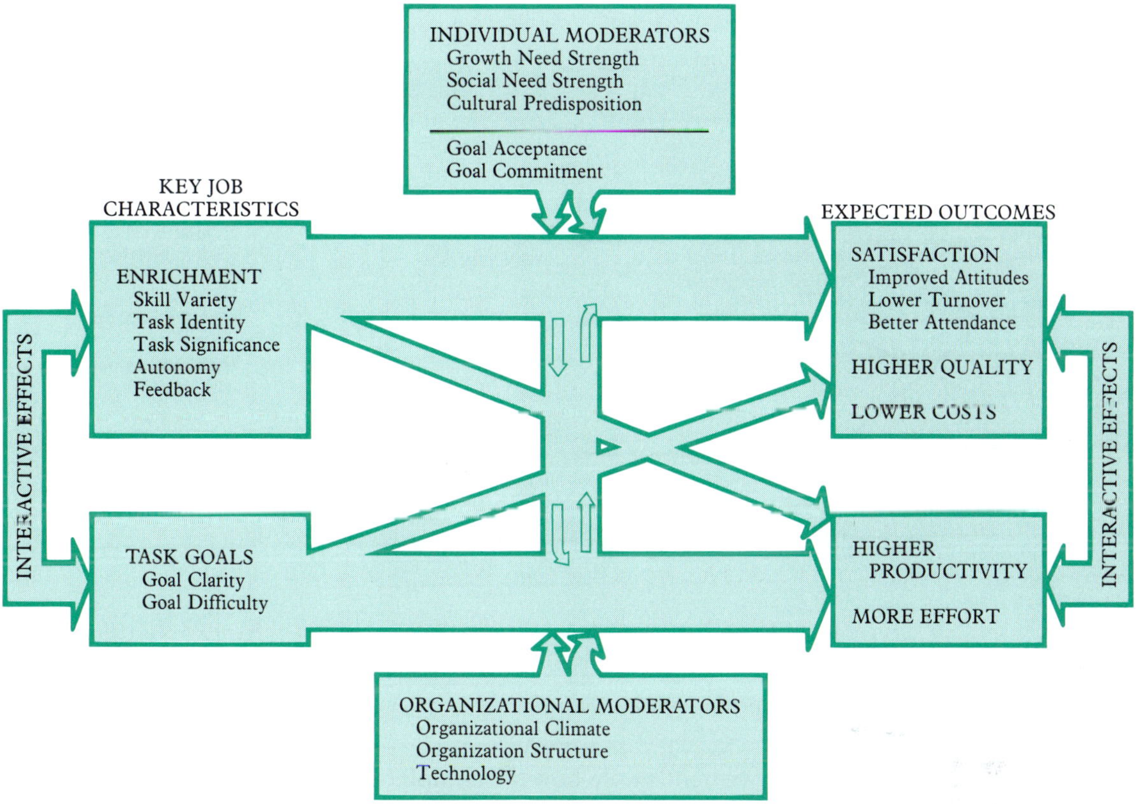

INDIVIDUAL MODERATORS
Growth Need Strength
Social Need Strength
Cultural Predisposition

Goal Acceptance
Goal Commitment

KEY JOB
CHARACTERISTICS

ENRICHMENT
Skill Variety
Task Identity
Task Significance
Autonomy
Feedback

TASK GOALS
Goal Clarity
Goal Difficulty

INTERACTIVE EFFECTS

EXPECTED OUTCOMES

SATISFACTION
Improved Attitudes
Lower Turnover
Better Attendance

HIGHER QUALITY

LOWER COSTS

HIGHER
PRODUCTIVITY

MORE EFFORT

INTERACTIVE EFFECTS

ORGANIZATIONAL MODERATORS
Organizational Climate
Organization Structure
Technology

Source: Denis D. Umstot, Terence R. Mitchell, and Cecil H. Ball, Jr., "Goal Setting and Job Enrichment: An Integrated Approach to Job Design," *Academy of Management Review* (October 1978):877. Reprinted with permission.

worker more authority both in planning the work and in controlling its pace and procedures.

There are many forms of job enrichment in organizations. Some of these include (1) giving the worker the opportunity to build an entire unit rather than just one part of that unit, (2) allowing the worker to decide when to do preventive maintenance on a machine and how to do so, and (3) letting the employee check his or her own work rather than having a supervisor or quality control person perform this function.[17] To obtain a complete grasp of job

[17] Michael A. Campion, "Ability Requirement Implications of Job Design: An Interdisciplinary Perspective," *Personnel Psychology* (Spring 1989):1–24.

FIGURE 9-7   Job Characteristics Model

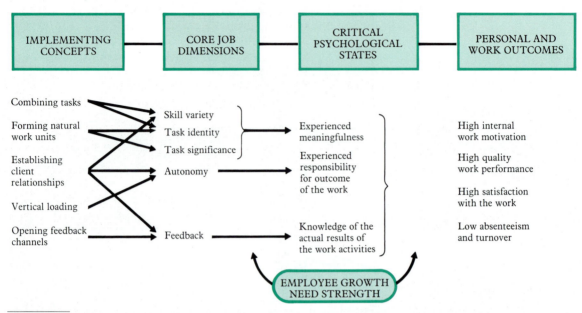

Source: R. Richard Hackman et al., "A New Strategy for Job Enrichment," *California Management Review* (Summer 1975) p. 62. © 1975 by the Regents of the Univ. of Calif. Reprinted from the *Calif. Man. Review,* Vol XVII, No. 4. By permission of the Regents.

enrichment, we need to see how the complete process works. To do so, we will analyze the job characteristics model.

Job Characteristics Model

Perhaps the most comprehensive conceptual framework for examining the effects of job enrichment on work attitudes and behavior is the **job characteristics model.**[18] This model, presented in Figure 9-7, explains the psychological impact of various job characteristics and predicts the effects that specific psychological states have on both work attitudes and performance. The most effective way to examine the model is to work backwards from work outcomes to job design concepts.

PERSONAL AND WORK OUTCOMES   Personal and work outcomes are the results that are attained from a job enrichment program. These outcomes may be

[18] J. Richard Hackman, et al., "A New Strategy For Job Enrichment," *California Management Review* (Summer 1975):57–71.

high work quantity, high work quality, high job satisfaction, and low absenteeism and turnover. Other more "psychological" behaviors include showing
initiative, cooperating with fellow workers, making creative suggestions, and
pursuing self-development and training.

CRITICAL PSYCHOLOGICAL STATES   Desired work outcomes are a result of
critical psychological states. If these states can be created, positive work

These motivators
created positive
work outcomes

outcomes may result. If the organization cannot create these states, the desired
personal and work outcomes will not materialize. As seen in Figure 9-7 there are
three such states: (1) *experienced meaningfulness of the work,* or the state in
which the worker feels that the work is important, worthwhile and valuable; (2)
experienced responsibility for work outcomes, or the state in which the worker
feels personally responsible or accountable for the results of the work; and (3)
knowledge of results of work activities, or the state in which the employee
understands, at all times, how well he or she is performing the job.

Causal factors

CORE JOB DIMENSIONS   **Core job dimensions** are the causal factors that
bring about these psychological states. There are five dimensions in all, and
their effect is illustrated in Figure 9-7. The first is *variety of skill,* or the degree to
which the job requires the person to do different things and use a number of
different skills, abilities, and talents. The second is the *identity of the task,* or
the degree to which the job allows for completion of a whole and identifiable
piece of work. The third is the *significance of the task,* or the degree to which
the job has an impact on the lives of other people, both internal and external to
the organization. These three characteristics affect the experienced meaningfulness of the work.

The fourth dimension is *autonomy,* which refers to the amount of freedom, independence, and discretion that the worker has in functions such as
scheduling work, making decisions, and determining how to do the job. This
characteristic directly affects the worker's sense of experienced responsibility
for work outcomes.

The last dimension is *feedback,* or the degree to which the job provides
the worker with clear and direct information about job outcomes and performance. This dimension directly affects the worker's knowledge of the results of
work activities.

IMPLEMENTING CONCEPTS   Core job dimensions are built into the work
through the application of job design concepts.[19] While many such concepts
can be applied, five of the most useful have been incorporated into Figure 9-7.
They include (1) *combining tasks* so as to increase both skill variety and task

---

[19] G. R. Ferris and D. C. Gilmore, "The Moderating Role of Work Context in Job Design
Research: A Test of Competing Models," *Academy of Management Journal* (December
1984):885–92.

Job enrichment techniques

identity, thereby allowing the individual to feel that he or she is doing more meaningful work; (2) *forming natural work units* by identifying basic work items and grouping them into natural categories; (3) *establishing client relationships* by allowing employees the most direct contact possible with those for whom the work is being done and setting up criteria by which the client can judge the quality of the product being received; (4) establishing **vertical loading** by giving the worker more control over both the planning and the control of work activities; and (5) *opening feedback channels* so that either the client or the employee, personally, can monitor work performance.

EMPLOYEE GROWTH NEED STRENGTH   Before ending the discussion of the job characteristics model, we need to consider the concept of employee growth need strength (see the bottom of Figure 9-7). While the model does pull together much of what is known about job enrichment and puts it into understandable form, it does not predict that all workers will have positive personal and work outcomes if their jobs are designed according to job enrichment

People must want psychological rewards

principles. The person must *want* the psychological rewards that come with the design. The need for growth must be strong. Otherwise, the employee will be just as happy if no change is made in the work.

Costs and Benefits

Over the last two decades, considerable attention has been focused on how to design enriched jobs and autonomous work groups. Only recently, however, has there been an attempt to assess the economic costs and benefits associated with job design.[20] The results of one survey, covering both business and governmental agencies, is reported in Table 9-5. The data reveal that, in general, job enrichment changes had a favorable effect on the organizations involved. This study, however, should not be allowed to overshadow a consideration of the specific costs involved.

Specific Costs

Design-related costs

A number of specific costs are associated with the implementation of job enrichment programs. Many of these are design related and include wage/salary increases, facility change costs, inventory costs, charges for implementing the new work design, and expenses incurred in training employees to carry out the newly expanded jobs.

---

[20] J. Richard Hackman, "The Design of Work in the 1980s," *Organizational Dynamics* (Summer 1978):15.

TABLE 9-5   Impact on Performance Caused by Job Enrichment Changes

Item	Number of Projects		
	Unfavorable Change	*No Change*	*Favorable Change*
Quality			
Number of items produced that were rejected for failure to meet quality standards	1	5	28
Amount of work that had to be recycled	2	3	22
Resource Utilization			
Labor force idle time	2	9	18
Production output	1	9	40
Operating Benefits			
Accident rate	1	10	4
Order expediting	1	7	8
Grievance rates	1	11	12
Absenteeism	1	11	26
Turnover	4	15	28

Source: Antone F. Alber, "The Real Cost of Job Enrichment," *Business Horizons* (February 1979):67. Reprinted with permission.

While not every job redesign results in higher wages or salaries, many do. The employees take on more work and responsibility, and many organizations feel it is only fair to give them more money. Of course, management hopes to make up these salary increases through greater efficiency and output.

In many cases job enrichment also involves changes in work procedures and work flow, particularly in assembly line or manufacturing jobs. In these cases the organization often has to expand the amount of floor space needed for the work and to purchase more tools and equipment. The result is an increase in facility costs.

An accompanying cost is that of inventory. Especially in manufacturing-related work, sequentially arranged work stations are abandoned in favor of semi-independent functioning work areas. Each person becomes more autonomous. This change requires each worker to have his or her own stockpile of inventory.

A fourth cost is that for implementation. Some organizations hire consultants to help with implementation. Others use in-house personnel. These expenses must be considered when the organization examines the costs or designs the work.

When job enrichment results in a more complex job, training of personnel is often required. The most common forms are on-the-job, although in a small percentage of cases the training is sophisticated enough to require the personnel to be trained off the job. Surprising as it may seem, researchers such as Antone Alber report that most organizations assign a very low priority to training in the overall design effort.[21] Additionally, some managers actually misread the value of job enrichment because they allow the initial increase in costs or decrease in productivity to affect their evaluation. The managers fail to realize that there is a time period during which employees are still mastering the new jobs and that efficiency is lower during this phase.

Specific Benefits

Performance-related benefits

The benefits associated with job enrichment are performance related in nature. Some of the most common include increased work quantity and quality, better use of resources, increased operating benefits, and lower absenteeism and turnover.

Many organizations that have had success with their job enrichment programs have achieved work output increases. Drawing on his own research in the field, Alber reports that

> . . . a manager in a large manufacturing company and another manager in a service-related activity of a bank both stated that a "significant improvement in supervisor/employee relations" occurs. The job utilization analyst of another bank reported better use of management time: "The supervisor's desk has been moved out of the mainstream of production and she now spends her time supervising, counseling, computing, graphing individual productivity, and approving loans."
>
> Another manager reported that organizational changes resulting from the enrichment project have eliminated unnecessary work: "The team of low-level supervisors stopped doing what they didn't have to do. For example, they reduced the amount of paperwork by one-third, and it turned out that what they eliminated wasn't being used anyway."[22]

Another benefit is higher work quality. Many times when the nature and scope of the work are increased, the job becomes more meaningful, the employees better understand the importance of the job, and the number of errors declines. Notice in Table 9-3 that the number of firms reporting improved quality was almost 30 times greater than the number reporting reduced quality!

---

[21] Antone F. Alber, "The Real Cost of Job Enrichment," *Business Horizons* (February 1979):66.
[22] Alber, "Job Enrichment," 66–67.

One of the most commonly reported benefits of job enrichment changes is increased resource use.[23] For example, the amount of labor force idle time goes down and machine use time goes up. Of course, these developments do not always occur immediately. In fact, numerous researchers have reported that output declines initially, if only because the employees lack training or are unsure of what the management is up to with its job enrichment efforts. ("Why are they redesigning this work? Why are they interested in making this job more interesting or enjoyable?")

Another payoff is the operating benefits, including improved safety features, better scheduling of work, improved labor relations, and increased levels of job satisfaction. It should be noted, however, that not everyone wants to have his or her work redesigned. Many employees admit that they like things as they are.

Still another benefit of job enrichment programs is reduced absenteeism and turnover. Sometimes, of course, these things will worsen. In most cases, however, researchers report an improvement.

Making Job Enrichment Pay Off

To make job enrichment pay off, an organization must reduce the design and performance-related costs and keep the benefits high. It can accomplish these objectives, in many cases, through the implementation of management practices such as the following:

Practical management practices

1. Find out what employee attitudes are toward job design and work to get the support of the personnel for these changes.
2. Do not underestimate the amount of time that will have to be spent on training the workers to handle these newly designed jobs.
3. Redesign the work intelligently so that there is a blend between the needs of the workers and those of the organization.
4. Emphasize the nonmonetary return to the employees by showing them how the jobs are now much more interesting and challenging than before.
5. Analyze the overall effect of the change on the organization itself. If possible use a pilot project to see how things go.
6. When one job design project proves itself, use this as a model for others; do not attempt to reinvent the wheel each time.
7. If the job enrichment program goes well, stick with it; if the program does not appear to be doing well, work to straighten out any problems

---

[23] N. Bodek, "The Unifying Theory of Productivity (UTOP): How to Manage Human Resources," *Supervisory Management* (May 1985):17–26.

that exist and wait a reasonable amount of time before throwing in the towel. Maybe the project will not work, but give it a chance.[24]

SUMMARY

1. Coordination is the synchronization of the human efforts of individuals and groups to attain organizational efficiency. Coordination is particularly important in the case of interdependent work. Interdependency can take one of three forms: pooled, sequential, and reciprocal.

2. Authority is the right to command. There are four common types of authority. Line authority is direct authority such as that which a superior has over a subordinate. Staff authority is auxiliary, as in the case of a lawyer who provides advice to a top manager. Functional authority is authority in a department other than one's own, as in the case of the finance vice president who has the authority to order the head of manufacturing to provide cost production data. Project authority is the authority a matrix manager has over the individuals assigned to the project.

3. Decentralization is a philosophy of management regarding which decisions to send down the line and which to keep near the top for purposes of organizational control. Every organization, except those owned and operated by one person, is decentralized to at least some degree. There are a number of ways of measuring decentralization, including studying the quantity of decisions made at different levels, the quality of these decisions, the impact of the decisions on lower levels, and the control the individual has in his or her own area of operation. Some of the major factors influencing decentralization include cost, size, desire for independence, availability of managers, and the nature of the enterprise.

4. Delegation of authority is the process of assigning duties to subordinates, giving them the authority to carry out tasks, and creating an obligation on their part to complete the assignments in a satisfactory manner. In the delegation of authority there are a number of boss-related and subordinate-related problems. The effective manager works to overcome these.

5. Committees are extremely valuable in coordinating activities. Basically, there are three types of committees: ad hoc, standing, and plural executive. Some of the major advantages of committees are that they

---

[24] Alber, ''Job Enrichment,'' 72.

make group judgment possible, provide for the representation of interested parties, help to coordinate plans and activities, and provide motivation. Some of the major disadvantages include their tendency toward indecision or compromise, their costs in terms of time and money, and their tendency to promote lack of responsibility. In using committees effectively, organizations must focus their attention on the objectives, authority, and organization of the committee, the leadership of the committee, and the support of the membership.

6. A third major way of effectively coordinating the people and the work is through the use of job design. Job design is the process of introducing work changes to increase work quality and quantity. Some of the most common approaches to job design include job engineering, job rotation, job enlargement, the sociotechnical approach, goal setting, and job enrichment. An examination of the job characteristics model helps us to understand the effects of job enrichment on work attitudes and behavior. This model considers personal and work outcomes, critical psychological states, core job dimensions, and implementing concepts.

7. In recent years attention has been focused on assessing the economic costs and benefits associated with job design. Some of the specific costs include wage and salary increases, facility change costs, inventory costs, charges for implementing the new work design, and expenses incurred in training employees to carry out the newly expanded jobs. Some of the benefits include increased work quality, better use of resources, increased operating benefits, and lower absenteeism and turnover.

KEY TERMS

Ad hoc committee   A committee that is formed for a particular purpose and that is disbanded upon completion of the objective.

Authority   The right to command.

Coordination   The synchronization of the human efforts of individuals and groups for the purpose of attaining organizational efficiency.

Core job dimensions   Causal factors that can bring about critical psychological states that are vital to positive work outcomes.

Critical psychological states   Psychological states, that, if created, can result in positive work outcomes such as increased quality and quantity of work and reduced absenteeism and turnover.

Decentralization   A philosophy of management regarding which decisions to send down the line and which to keep near the top for purposes of organizational control.

Delegation of authority   The process of assigning duties to subordinates, giving them the authority to carry out these tasks, and creating an obligation on their part to complete the assignments in a satisfactory manner.

Functional authority   Authority in a department other than one's own.

Goal setting   A job design approach that emphasizes building goals, feedback, and incentives into the structure of the work.

Horizontal loading   Increasing the number of tasks or activities that a worker is doing by giving him or her more of the same to do.

Job characteristics model   A comprehensive conceptual framework for examining the effects of job enrichment on work attitudes and behavior through a consideration of personal and work outcomes, critical psychological states, core job dimensions, and concepts for implementing job design.

Job design   The process of introducing work changes to increase the quality or quantity of work or both.

Job engineering   The use of time and motion analysis to achieve the most efficient interface between the worker and the machine.

Job enlargement   A job design technique that involves giving the worker more to do through the use of horizontal loading.

Job enrichment   An extension of job rotation and job enlargement that attempts to build psychological motivators into the work.

Job rotation   Moving a worker from one job to another to reduce boredom.

Jurisdictional questions   Questions or issues that arise between two or more departments or units regarding who has authority in a given matter.

Line authority   Direct authority such as that possessed by a superior over a subordinate.

Plural executive committee   A committee that has the authority to order the implementation of its recommendations.

Pooled interdependence   A form of interdependence in which all units or departments are contributing to similar objectives but the actual coordination between them is minimal.

Project authority   The authority a matrix manager has over the individuals assigned to the project.

Quality control circle   An approach to job design in which work groups meet to discuss and recommend changes in the way the jobs are being done.

Reciprocal interdependence   A form of interdependence in which the inputs of one unit become the outputs of another.

Sequential interdependence   A form of interdependence in which work units are linked together in the form of a chain and each depends on the one in front of it for inputs.

Sociotechnical approach   An approach to job design in which a group or team of workers is made responsible for getting the job done.

Staff authority   Auxiliary authority held by individuals who advise, assist, recommend, or facilitate organizational activities.

Standing committee   A committee that is permanent in nature, as in the case of the finance or personnel committees that exist in many organizations.

Vertical loading   A concept used in job design which involves giving the worker more control over both the planning and control of work activities.

QUESTIONS FOR ANALYSIS AND DISCUSSION

1. In your own words, what is meant by the term coordination? How do the following types of coordination work: pooled, sequential, and reciprocal? Explain, giving an example of each.
2. What is meant by the term authority? In your answer use examples of line, staff, functional, and project authority.
3. Numerous line-staff problems and dilemmas result from the improper use of functional authority. How can a modern organization go about dealing with typical line-staff problems? Offer at least three suggestions. How can the enterprise minimize problems in the use of functional authority? Again offer three suggestions.
4. How can a project manager deal most effectively with the "authority gap" problem? What techniques are useful? Describe at least three.
5. In your own words, what is meant by the term decentralization? How can decentralization be measured? Cite and explain three ways.
6. What are some of the factors that influence the degree of decentralization in an organization? Identify and describe three.
7. Is decentralization superior to centralization? Or is centralization superior to decentralization? Defend your answer.
8. What is meant by the term delegation of authority? What are some of the most common boss-related problems encountered with delegation of authority? What are some of the most common subordinate-related problems? How can these problems be resolved? Explain.
9. What is meant by each of the following types of committees: ad hoc, standing, and plural executive? When are committees most effective? When do they tend to be of limited value?
10. Overall, what are two of the most important advantages of committees? What are two of the most important disadvantages? Explain.
11. What can be done to improve the overall effectiveness of committees? Give at least three suggestions.
12. Some of the most popular approaches to job design include job engineering, job rotation, and job enlargement. How does each work? Be complete in your answer.
13. How does a sociotechnical approach to job design work? In what way is a quality circle an example of a sociotechnical approach?
14. How does goal setting in job design work? In what way is it related to job enrichment?
15. In your own words, what is job enrichment? How does it differ from job enlargement?

16. In what way does the job characteristics model help explain job enrichment? In your answer be sure to explain all of the major parts of the model.
17. From a cost and benefit standpoint, what are some of the typical costs associated with the implementation of job enrichment programs? What are some of the specific benefits to be derived? Overall, do you think that job enrichment has proved to be a useful tool for modern managers or is the idea basically ineffective? Defend your answer.

CASE

Ted's Idea

Last week Ted Kantor returned from a management seminar. The seminar had covered a host of different management-related topics, including job design. Ted was intrigued by some of the ideas of the trainer and is now thinking of trying to apply some of them in his own work environment.

Ted is the manager of a small (30 people) assembly-line department. The personnel assemble one product only, a small portable electric kitchen appliance. The parts are produced at another location and sent to Ted's area. His people then assemble, test, and package each unit. The process consists of the following five distinct steps:

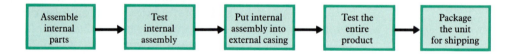

| Assemble internal parts | Test internal assembly | Put internal assembly into external casing | Test the entire product | Package the unit for shipping |

Some parts of the process take longer than others. For example, the assembly of the internal parts requires 20 minutes, while the testing of the internal assembly takes only 5 minutes. Putting the internal assembly into its casing requires 15 minutes (the assembler has to ensure a proper fit and then place three screws into the casing), while testing the entire product takes only 10 minutes (this involves a visual examination of the product as well as a test to determine whether the unit works properly). Packaging of the product requires another 10 minutes. There are three work groups in the department: one does the internal assembly; one does the internal testing and placing of the parts into the casing; the last tests the overall product and then packages it.

Ted believes that the current assembly method is good but that there is room for improvement. In particular he feels that some form of job enlargement, a sociotechnical approach (maybe some version of the quality circle), or job enrichment would be a good idea. His first step is going to be to talk to the assemblers themselves to see what ideas, if any, they might have for redesigning the work. If the response is positive, then he intends to work with them in deciding what to do.

1. If Ted does opt for job enlargement, how would this redesign work? How would each person's job change?
2. If a sociotechnical approach were used, what would it involve? Include in your answer a discussion of the quality circle.
3. Drawing upon your understanding of the job characteristics model, explain how job enrichment can be used in redesigning this work. How would it be carried out?

YOU BE THE CONSULTANT

Losing It In-House

Aldag, Inc. is a well-known national manufacturer of medical supplies and equipment. The firm sells to both hospitals and clinics as well as to doctors' offices.

At the present time Aldag estimates that its share of the medical supplies market is 12.3 percent and its share of the medical equipment market is 10.6 percent. Return on investment has declined over each of the last five years, however. This year it will be even lower: the vice president of finance has estimated a return on investment of 5.3 percent.

The chairman of the board, Ted Heckman, is not pleased with this declining ROI. He reasons that with gross sales increasing at an annual rate of 15 percent and the firm holding a large market share, returns should be much higher. His own personal evaluation is that there are too many internal inefficiencies. Specifically, organizational bottlenecks and a distinct lack of coordination are costing the firm money. "We do just fine in the external market," Ted told a few board members, "but we do not do well in-house. What's the use of beating the competition if we simply throw away our profits with inefficient organizational procedures?"

One of the things that Ted is specifically referring to is an internal report drawn up by a special organizational evaluation committee appointed by the board. The committee members were charged with making an internal analysis of company operations. When they finished their 90-day investigation, they sent their report to the board. The following is a brief summary of four of their major findings:

FIGURE 9-8 Aldag, Inc. Organizational Chart

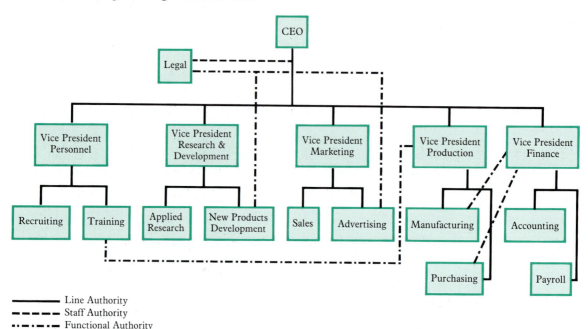

———————— Line Authority
– – – – – Staff Authority
–••–••–•• Functional Authority

1. There is an overuse of functional authority (see Figure 9-8). In particular, the legal and finance departments currently have the right to give orders in a number of other departments and this is leading to both coordination and control problems.
2. There is insufficient delegation of authority in the finance and production departments. The managers refuse to delegate authority as widely as they should. This is as true at the top levels of these departments as it is at the middle levels.
3. The R&D and personnel departments each have established committees with interdepartmental membership. The purpose of the R&D committee is to generate and discuss new product ideas. This committee was meeting weekly. Now it meets monthly and attendance is poor. The same basic situation exists for the personnel committee, which was established to review the training needs of all departments. This committee is not living up to its responsibility.
4. The manufacturing department has a series of 23 assembly line processes used for putting together medical equipment products. In most cases semifinished parts are passed from one individual to another. This is both time-consuming and, in the minds of many of the assemblers, dull work. A new approach to job design is needed.

Your Consultation

Assume that the president has provided you a copy of this in-house report and asked you to be the outside consultant. Read the case again, carefully noting the organizational problems the firm currently faces. Then give your recommendations. In those instances where you feel that a particular problem requires more information indicate (a) the type of information you would seek to gather, (b) the likely outcomes you would find, and (c) most important of all, how you would resolve the problems. Be as specific as possible in your recommendations.

10

The Human Resource Management Process

Every ongoing organization must be concerned with recruiting and selecting a workforce. Some enterprises want to expand their current operations; others want to move into totally new areas. At the same time these organizations face personnel retirements, resignations, and terminations. As a result of such developments, the typical workforce is in a state of flux. For this reason recruiting and selecting are very important to modern organizations. Unless human resource talent can be acquired and retained, the enterprise's chances of reaching its objectives are severely limited. This chapter examines the way in which the recruiting process actually works, studies the ways in which recruits are selected for positions in the workforce, and reviews the role of orientation for new employees. When you have finished studying all of the material in this chapter, you should be able to:

1. Define the term strategic human resources planning.
2. Describe the linkage between strategic planning and employment needs.
3. Tell how modern organizations go about forecasting their employment needs.
4. Explain how the recruiting process works, including both sources and methods of recruiting practices.

5. Describe the selection process, including selection criteria, specific steps that are followed in the process, and the use of assessment centers.
6. Discuss the values and benefits of orientation.
7. Define the term training, and relate the role that top management plays in the training process.
8. List the specific steps that can be used in evaluating a training program.

STRATEGIC HUMAN RESOURCES PLANNING

Strategic human resources defined

Strategic human resources planning is the process of identifying the numbers, skills, and occupational categories of personnel the organization will need in the future to ensure the attainment of its strategic objectives. At the heart of this process is the question: "What are the potential internal and external threats, opportunities, and trends taking place in human resources that may have an impact on the strategic success of the organization?"[1] Human resources planning is closely linked to the strategic planning process, which was discussed in Chapter 6. Many of the same questions that govern the establishment of strategic objectives also influence the recruiting and selecting of personnel.

Strategic and employment planning are closely linked

Human resources planning begins with the same question that strategic planning begins with: What business are we in? The remaining steps in the two kinds of planning are also parallel, as both go on to evaluate the plan and set new objectives. Human resources planning and strategic planning go hand in hand.[2] Table 10-1 illustrates this idea.

The strategic plan sets the direction in which the organization will go. The human resources plan ensures that the enterprise has the necessary people to follow the strategic plan. (See, for example, "Management in Practice: Transforming United Technologies into the 1990s.") Sometimes it calls for hiring additional personnel with particular talents. At other times it requires the organization to train and develop the current personnel.[3] In this section consideration will be focused on the first of these demands—recruiting and selecting

---

[1] Randall S. Schuler and Ian C. McMillan, "Gaining Competitive Advantage Through Human Resource Management Practices," *Human Resource Management* (Fall 1984):241–55. Also see Randall S. Schuler and S. Jackson, "Linking Competitive Strategies with Human Resource Management Practices," *Academy of Management Executive* (Spring 1987):207–20.

[2] Lloyd Baird and Ilan Meshoulam, "Managing Two Fits of Strategic Human Resource Management," *Academy of Management Review* (January 1988):116–28. See also Ellen E. Kossek, "The Acceptance of Human Resource Innovation by Multiple Constituencies," *Personnel Psychology* (Summer 1989):263–81.

[3] George S. Odiorne, "Human Resource Strategies for the 80s," *Training* (January 1985):47–51.

TABLE 10-1   The Strategic Plan — Human Resources Plan Linkage

Strategic Plan	Human Resources Plan
What business are we in?	What specific human skills are needed in this business?
What external market forces (technological, economic, social, etc.) will we have to address?	What human skills and capabilities will the personnel need in coping with these external forces?
What are the current internal resources with which we can fashion a viable strategy?	How qualified are our current personnel in helping us meet our basic mission?
In what specific markets should we concentrate our resources and what objectives should we pursue?	Are our present personnel sufficient or do we need to recruit and hire more people?
What resources do we still need to acquire in order to attain these objectives?	What kinds of additional people should we hire? What recruiting and selecting process do we need?
After the plan has been put into effect, what changes are in order?	Do we need to let anyone go? Hire more people? Train and develop any present personnel?

FIGURE 10-1
Strategic Human
Resources Planning
Process

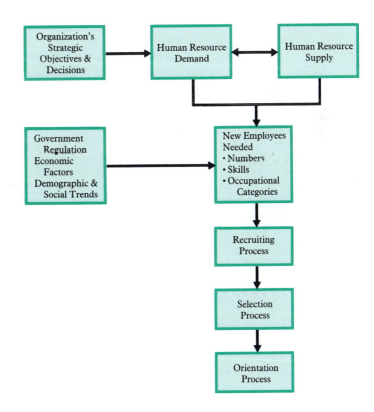

Transforming United Technologies into the 1990s

Prior to 1986, United Technologies grew into an $18 billion manufacturer of goods ranging from military helicopters to shopping mall escalators, largely through the leadership of Harry J. Gray. Gray's regime had been described as "iron-fisted," "empire-builder," and "feudal lord." However, today the company has a new leader at the helm—Robert F. Daniell. His style marks an entirely new beginning for United Technologies (UT). One of UT's major companies is Pratt & Whitney, manufacturer of jet engines. This company is the focus of Daniell's philosophical changes.

Daniell's vision includes leveling the autocratic structure of United Technologies and allowing more decision making in the hands of the 186,000 employees. Although his approach is low-key, Daniell is passionate about making his employees feel like proprietors. How can he do this? Here are a few of the points that Daniell believes executives need to "transform" the operating structure of their companies:

Flatten the hierarchy: Daniell has leveled the structure by cutting as many as eight layers of management to as few as four.

Empower the workers: Decision making has been pushed down the structure. For instance, field representatives now make multimillion-dollar decisions about reimbursing customers on warranty claims, while before they had to wait for approval from higher authority.

Get close to the customers: This is Daniell's battle cry. Worker empowerment helps, but the imperative goes even further than that. For instance, Pratt & Whitney lends some of its top engineers to customers for a year—and pays the salaries of those engineers.

Train, train, train: Training is used to revamp the corporate culture. More than 5,000 senior and middle managers are now getting at least 40 hours of classroom work per year.

Is the structure working? Orders at Pratt & Whitney have increased eight-fold to nearly $8 billion. Profits in 1989 were $675 million on sales of $20 billion with analysts expecting a 16 percent jump in 1990, and the stock price has risen 37 percent to $56 this past year. Experts say the chief competitive weapon in the 1990s will be the team approach. Robert Daniell is certainly implementing that weapon.

Source: Seth Resnick, "Where 1990s-Style Management Is Already Hard at Work," *Business Week* (October 23, 1989):92–97.

additional personnel. This specific process is outlined in Figure 10-1. Notice that three key external forces affect this process: government regulation, economic factors, and demographic and social trends.

Key External Forces

Each of the three key external forces in Figure 10-1 is important, although, depending on the specific situation, one may prove to be more important than the others. For many organizations, government regulation is at the top of the list.

Government Regulation

Many laws and executive orders prohibit discrimination in employment. The most encompassing is the *Civil Rights Act of 1964.* Title VII of this act specifically forbids employment discrimination on the basis of race, color, religion, sex, or national origin.

Another major piece of legislation is the *Equal Pay Act of 1963,* which requires equal pay for individuals doing jobs that require substantially equal skill, responsibility, and effort while working under similar working conditions. This act was amended in 1972 to include administrative, executive, and professional employees.

A third major act is the *Age Discrimination in Employment Act of 1967,* which prohibits discrimination against people between the ages of 40 and 65. This act governs all employers with 20 or more workers.

A fourth act is the *Rehabilitation Act of 1973,* which requires organizations to take affirmative action for the employment of individuals with physical or mental handicaps. Specific regulations have been developed and issued by the federal government regarding the kinds of actions that are required and the organizations that are covered.

In addition to these acts, a number of executive orders have been issued by various presidents. *Executive Order 11246,* issued by President Lyndon B. Johnson, prohibits the same actions as does Title VII of the Civil Rights Act but carries the additional requirement that contractors develop a written plan of affirmative action and establish numerical integration goals and timetables for achieving this equal opportunity objective. *Executive Order 11478,* issued by President Richard M. Nixon, forbids discrimination by the federal government on the basis of race, color, religion, sex, national origin, political affiliation, marital status, or physical handicap.

These acts and legislative orders are important to the human resources plan because they define the limits within which an organization can act. As each year goes by, they are supplemented by still other regulations. One of the more recent deals with mandatory retirement and allows people who with to continue working until age 70 to do so. This new retirement age is in marked contrast to the previous mandatory retirement age of 65 in most organizations. In an effort to deal with changing regulations, many businesses are finding that equal employment opportunity (EEO) guidelines must be developed and followed. Table 10-2 illustrates a partial framework that can serve as a guide in developing an overall affirmative action compliance strategy. Working within a framework such as this one, the organization can carry out its hiring and promotion efforts. In large enterprises, a Personnel Department is charged with staying abreast of the latest government regulations and ensuring that the firm is

TABLE 10-2   Partial Framework for an Affirmative Action Compliance Strategy

Areas for Action	Overall Objectives of Affirmative Action	Possible Tactics and Specifics
Increasing minority/female applicant flow	To insure that minorities and females are not systemically excluded from the communication of employment opportunities available in the facility; and to encourage those individuals to apply.	1. Include minority colleges and universities in campus recruitment programs 2. Personal and regular contacts with employment referral agencies, such as Job Corps or Urban League. 3. Participate in job fair or career day programs at area high schools and vocational schools. 4. Place employment advertising in minority-oriented print and broadcast media. 5. Encourage current minority/female employees to refer other minority/female individuals to the organization (for example, memo, "finder's fee"). 6. Retain applications of unhired minority/female applicants to be reviewed as vacancies occur.
Demonstrating top-management support for EEO policy	To indicate to all employees that top management considers affirmative action and equal employment opportunity to be legitimate and important activities for the organization.	1. Prepare written reports evaluating progress toward affirmative action goals as other management control reports are prepared. 2. Involve the line supervisors in the establishment of the affirmative action hiring goals. 3. Appoint an EEO coordinator who is both highly visible within the facility and from a department other than personnel.

operating within regulatory boundaries. In small organizations the top managers assume this responsibility.

Economic Factors

During the 1980s, productivity in the United States continued its slow decline. What accounts for this problem? One answer is rising labor costs. Another is that personnel are not working as efficiently or as effectively as they should be. Since labor costs, for all practical purposes, cannot be reduced very much (if at all), the best thing an organization can do is to ensure that the personnel are well trained and capable of doing their jobs. Additionally, the enterprise should

Areas for Action	Overall Objectives of Affirmative Action	Possible Tactics and Specifics
		4. Participation by the top executive in the EEO training and orientation of line supervisors.
		5. Route progress reports and related material on affirmative action through senior executives' offices.
		6. Include affirmative action issues and progress on the agenda of departmental meetings.
Keeping employees informed	To communicate to employees the specifics of the affirmative action programs, including their rights, benefits, and opportunities as organization members.	1. Discuss EEO matters, such as program success and new program efforts in internal publications (house organ, newsletter).
		2. Display EEO policy statement in work areas.
		3. Provide and publicize the availability of career development counseling.
		4. Make the affirmative action plan available for employee review.
		5. Post promotion opportunities within the work areas.
		6. Explain the EEO policy, job posting, complaint procedures, tuition refund programs, and so on, during the new employee orientation procedure.

Source: Reprinted, by permission of the publisher, from "Conducting an Internal Compliance Review of Affirmative Action," Kenneth E. Marino, *Personnel* (March–April 1980):30–32.© 1980 by American Management Association, New York. All rights reserved.

know which employees can be moved up in the case of a vacancy, which employees need further training, and which are questionable in terms of continued employment.[4]

Some companies keep an employee replacement chart

Some companies deal with these questions by keeping an **employee replacement chart.** This chart, illustrated in Figure 10-2, shows which personnel are performing extremely well, which are satisfactory, and which need to improve their performance. The chart also describes the promotion potential of each person.

[4] Robert H. Stambaugh, "HRMS: Performing a Needs Analysis," *Personnel Administrator* (March 1985):20.

FIGURE 10-2 Employee Replacement Chart

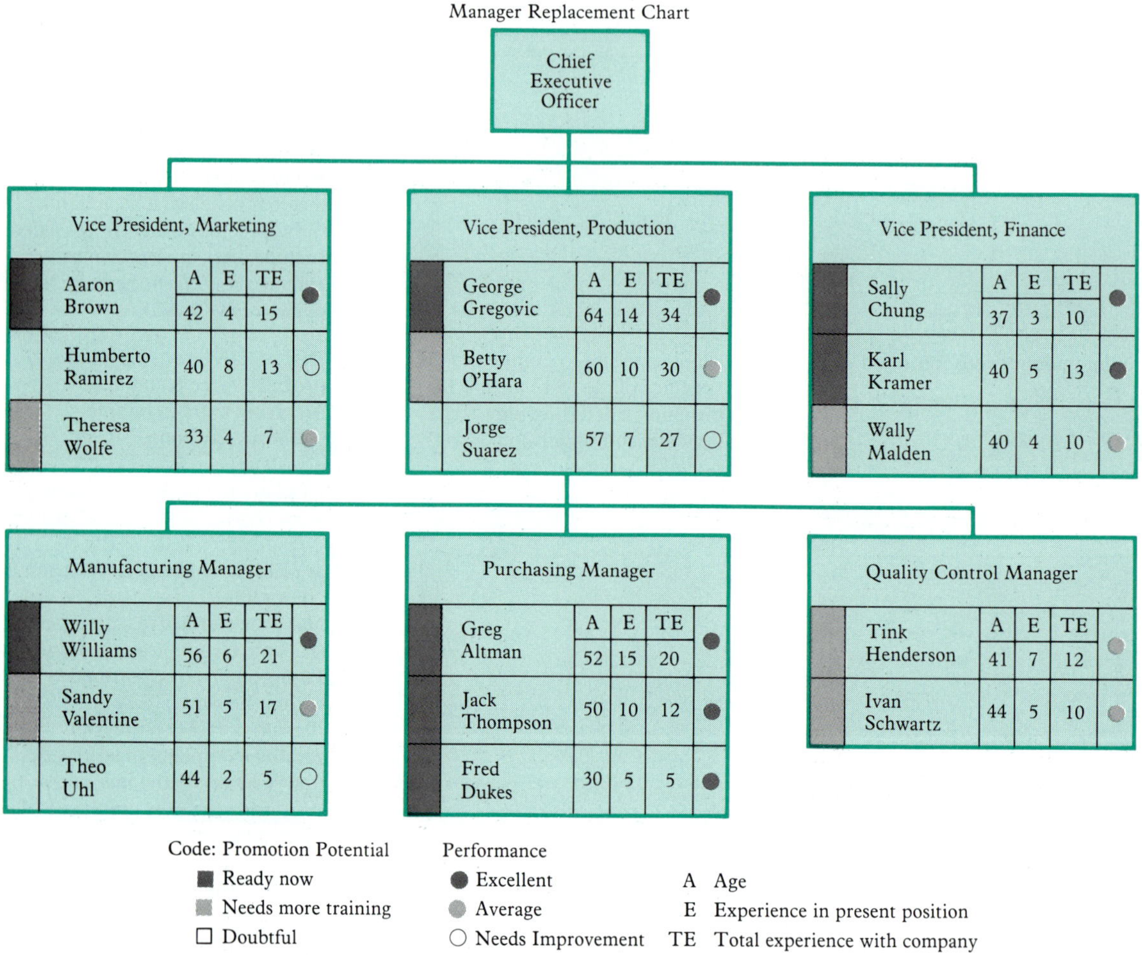

Manager Replacement Chart

Chief
Executive
Officer

Vice President, Marketing

	A	E	TE	
Aaron Brown	42	4	15	●
Humberto Ramirez	40	8	13	○
Theresa Wolfe	33	4	7	◐

Vice President, Production

	A	E	TE	
George Gregovic	64	14	34	●
Betty O'Hara	60	10	30	◐
Jorge Suarez	57	7	27	○

Vice President, Finance

	A	E	TE	
Sally Chung	37	3	10	●
Karl Kramer	40	5	13	●
Wally Malden	40	4	10	◐

Manufacturing Manager

	A	E	TE	
Willy Williams	56	6	21	●
Sandy Valentine	51	5	17	◐
Theo Uhl	44	2	5	○

Purchasing Manager

	A	E	TE	
Greg Altman	52	15	20	●
Jack Thompson	50	10	12	●
Fred Dukes	30	5	5	●

Quality Control Manager

	A	E	TE	
Tink Henderson	41	7	12	◐
Ivan Schwartz	44	5	10	◐

Code: Promotion Potential   Performance
■ Ready now   ● Excellent   A   Age
▨ Needs more training   ◐ Average   E   Experience in present position
□ Doubtful   ○ Needs Improvement   TE Total experience with company

Four common employment forecasting techniques

In dealing with economic forces, however, an organization also needs to be able to conduct employment forecasting. It must be able to project job vacancies or new positions. Basically, four methods are used in modern organizations to forecast employment needs.

The least sophisticated approach is often called the **expert-estimate technique.** It calls for knowledgeable executives to decide how many people will need to be hired during the next 6 to 12 months.

A second approach is the **trend-projection technique.** This method relies heavily on past events and tries to tie employment needs to one or more causal factors. For example, the company might say: "In the past for every increase of $100,000 in sales we have had to hire four new people. Since we project an increase in sales this year of $1 million, we will have to hire another 40 workers.''

The third forecasting method is the **unit demand forecast.** In this method a ''bottom-up'' approach is used. Each unit manager analyzes his or her unit, job by job, to determine employment needs. This information is then passed on to the superior, who carries out the same process. The data are thus passed up the line, from one level to the next, until they arrive at the top. Headquarters, in turn, sums up the estimates, and the result becomes the organization's overall employment forecast.

A fourth approach is a version of **modeling and multiple-predictive techniques** in which the organization uses mathematical models that take into account a series of employment-related data such as sales, gross national product, and discretionary income. Based on the results of the sophisticated analysis, a conclusion is reached regarding hiring needs. This approach is not very common and tends to be restricted to large, multiline corporations.

Of these four techniques, the ones most commonly used in small organizations are the expert-estimate or trend projection techniques. These are simple and do not take much time. In larger organizations the unit demand forecast is often employed.

Demographic and Social Trends

The composition of the workforce is changing

A number of important demographic and social trends have contributed to the composition of today's workforce. These trends are having a serious impact on the way organizations staff their operations. One of the most significant is the post-World War II baby boom. People born in the 1945–1955 decade began entering management positions in 1975 and will continue to move into these positions until 1990, assuming that the average person gets into middle management when he or she is between 30 and 35 years old. These people are having to fight for the limited number of management positions available. Because this trend is coupled with the extension of the mandatory retirement age from 65 to 70 and the influx of women and minorities into the labor force, human resource plans must be thought out very carefully.

In recruiting and selecting personnel, an organization also has to address the specific work demands of the personnel. These demands are being influenced by changing values. Employees are demanding, and getting, not only more enriched jobs but, in many cases, flexible work schedules as well.

More hours in fewer days

Flexible work schedules can take a number of different forms. One is the **compressed work week,** which involves fitting the normal work week (35 to 40 hours) into fewer days. For example, instead of working eight hours a day five days a week, an individual may work 10 hours a day four days a week. In some cases the individual may have a 36-hour week, working 12 hours daily three days a week.

Choosing one's hours

Another variation of flexible work schedules is flexible hours, or **flextime** for short. Under this arrangement employees are permitted to choose their own work hours. For example, the person who likes to come to work early and leave early may be given a schedule of 7 A.M. to 3 P.M. Another who likes to come in later in the morning may be given a schedule of 10 A.M. to 6 P.M. There are certain periods of the day, however, when everyone is at work. These periods are called **core hours.** Some of the benefits associated with flextime include increased job satisfaction, increased productivity, reduced commuter time, and more personal time for leisure and family activities.[5] In addressing social trends, modern organizations are finding it necessary to use techniques such as these.

THE RECRUITING PROCESS

Recruiting defined

Recruiting is carried out within the guidelines created by the key external forces discussed earlier in this chapter. **Recruiting** is the process of attracting job candidates who have the abilities and attitudes necessary to help the organization achieve its objectives.[6] Recruiting is a natural follow-up to human resource planning. As soon as the enterprise knows the number and types of individuals it needs, it can focus attention on recruiting these people.

Where to Recruit

To find job applicants, the organization must know where to recruit. Many sources are available, depending on the specific needs of the enterprise. Table 10-3 shows some of the major sources of job applicants for blue-collar, white-collar, and managerial positions.

Current personnel are tapped first

The most readily available source of job applicants is the company's current personnel. One way of tapping this source is through a job-posting system in which the organization notifies its people of openings through company publications and bulletin boards. Many firms post all permanent and transfer opportunities, giving in-house people at least one week to apply before turning to outside sources.

Many firms also encourage present employees to tell their friends and relatives about job openings. Of course, certain equal opportunity programs prohibit organizations from giving jobs to people solely on the basis of employee friendship. It is a good way to generate a pool of applicants, however.

Skills inventories help in identifying qualified candidates

Some organizations also turn to the use of **skills inventories,** employee records that contain information on each person's training and experience. Sometimes these inventories are quite simple and contain only the individual's

---

[5] Jean B. McGuire and Joseph R. Liro, "Flexible Work Schedules, Work Attitudes, and Perceptions of Productivity," *Public Personnel Management* (Spring 1986):65–73.
[6] Dan Kleinman, "What to Look For in Tomorrow's Employee," *Personnel Journal* (October 1987):102–107.

TABLE 10-3 Sources for Recruiting Personnel

Sources	Blue-Collar	White-Collar	Managerial, Technical, Professional
Internal			
Job posting and bidding	X	X	
Friends of current workers	X	X	
Skills inventories	X	X	X
External			
Walk-ins	X	X	
Agencies			
Temporary help		X	
Private employment agencies		X	
Public employment agencies	X	X	
Executive search firm			X
Educational distributions			
High school	X	X	
Vocational/technical	X	X	
Colleges and universities			X
Other			
Unions	X		
Professional associations			X
Military services	X	X	X
Former employees	X	X	X

job experience, that is, five years as a welder or four years as an advertising manager. At other times they are much more detailed and include education, training, strengths, weaknesses, present performance, and potential for promotion (ability and the possible position). By examining these skills inventories, the organization can determine the likelihood of filling current vacancies with in-house personnel. Of course, small organizations are not likely to have such records. The time and expense associated with gathering the initial information and keeping everyone's record up to date limits the use of skills inventories to larger organizations.

THE SELECTION PROCESS

Selection defined

After the firm has recruited potential personnel, it must decide which ones to hire. At this time, the selection process begins.[7] **Selection** is the process by

[7] Ann Coil, "Job Matching Brings Out the Best in Employees," *Personnel Journal* (January 1984):54–60.

which an enterprise chooses the applicants who best meet the criteria for the available positions.

Selection Criteria

In order to ensure that the best available candidates are selected, an organization must compare the applicants against the criteria established for the job. These criteria can be grouped into five basic categories: education, experience, physical characteristics, personal characteristics, and personality types. Before examining these categories, however, we must note that any criterion used for selection must be *job related.* The criterion must assist in predicting which applicants are most likely to do the best job. To make this prediction, an organization must use selection instruments that are both valid and reliable.

Validity and Reliability

Validity is vital

Validity means that a selection instrument measures what the organization wants it to measure. If the company wants to hire a typist, the test that is administered must measure typing skills and expertise. If the firm wants to hire a supervisor, the test must help in distinguishing between those with supervisory skills and those without them.

So is reliability

Reliability means that a selection instrument provides a consistent measure of something. If a typist gets a 97 on the test today, he or she should get approximately 97 tomorrow. If a supervisory applicant scores high on the test today, he or she should also do well tomorrow. The higher the reliability of the instrument, the more confidence management can place in it.

Of validity and reliability, validity is more important. For an instrument to be valid, it must also be reliable. The reverse is not necessarily true, however. In computing the validity of a selection instrument, a company may use either of two basic approaches. One is to look at current employees, find one (or more) job-related factors common to their performance, designate it as a potential predictor, and then determine if it is actually related to job performance. This approach is called *concurrent validity.* A second possibility is to use a screening test in the hiring process, see how well the hired applicants do, and correlate the test scores with their respective performances. This approach is called *predictive validity.* When attempting to screen job applicants, effective organizations all seek to develop valid predictors. Of the four criteria generally employed in the selection process, some tend to be valid while others are not.

Steps in the Selection Process

The selection process consists of six basic steps, although some organizations sidestep a few to reduce time and expense. The following discussion examines the selection process in sequential order beginning with the preliminary screening interview.

Preliminary Screening Interview

In some cases applicants apply for a job in person. They simply walk into the employment office or job location and announce that they would like to be considered for a particular position. Many times these people lack either the experience or the training to do the job effectively. This fact can be determined in just a few minutes of general interview screening. In these cases, the preliminary screening interview serves to reduce the number of applicants to be considered and the amount of organizational time expended in filling job vacancies.

Completion of Application Blank

Most firms use application blanks

If the applicant does pass the preliminary screening interview, or if the organization does not have such a process, the next step is the completion of an application blank. Almost all organizations use an application blank of some sort, although the amount of information requested varies. The application blank can help screen candidates in that the information requested may indicate clearly that they lack necessary training or experience.[8] The information also may help a company predict success on the job by allowing it to see, for instance, whether those with no background in sales do better or more poorly than those with one or two years' experience. Decisions based on application form data should also be supported by empirical evidence, however. Merely to assume that an applicant without selling experience will not do as well as one with it is insufficient justification for screening the applicant out. The company should have data on employee performance in the past to support its decision. Otherwise, a charge of discrimination can be raised.

The Employment Interview

The third step in the selection process is the employment interview. This is one of the most widely used tools in selection. In general terms, there are three types of interviews: structured, semistructured, and unstructured.[9]

Three types of interviews

In the **structured interview,** the interviewer uses a prepared list of questions and does not deviate from them. In a **semistructured interview** only the major questions to be asked have been prepared in advance and the interviewer may either expand on them or ask other questions that open new areas of discussion. The **unstructured interview** is one in which the interviewer asks whatever seems appropriate and adapts the discussion to the responses, choosing areas in which further questions appear warranted and ignoring those in which additional discussion seems fruitless.

---

[8] Richard S. Lowell and Jay A. DeLoach, "Equal Employment Opportunity: Are You Overlooking the Application Form," *Personnel* (July–August 1982):49–55.
[9] John W. Cogger, "Are You a Skilled Interviewer?" *Personnel Journal* (November 1982):840–43.

The most commonly used type of interview combines structured and unstructured approaches. It provides the interviewer general guidance while still allowing him or her to pursue subjects that warrant greater discussion.

Employment Tests

Some organizations use selection employment tests. These tests are many and varied. One of the most common is the *performance test,* in which the applicant is asked to perform a job-related task. For example, the applicant may be asked to operate a piece of machinery or make a decision regarding how to handle a disciplinary problem. Performance tests tend to have high validity and reliability because they systematically measure behavior directly related to the job.

Performance tests are many and varied

A second type of test falls under the heading of *performance simulation.* This type of test is designed to measure a person's space visualization (as in the case of a draftsman), psychomotor ability such as finger dexterity (as in the case of an assembler of components), or clerical abilities (such as the ability of a secretary to check numbers and names).

A third type of test is the *paper-and-pencil variety.* These tests often measure mental ability. Two of the most common are the Otis Quick Scoring Mental Ability Test and the Wechsler Adult Intelligence Scale. While these types of tests are still popular today, their validity and reliability are not as high as those of performance-related tests.

Another is the honesty tests which are designed to measure the level of integrity (honesty) of potential employees.

The least reliable employment tests are those used to measure *personality or temperament.* Such tests have low validity because it is too difficult to relate their findings to job-related behavior. Consequently many organizations have dropped them.

Reference Checks and Recommendation Letters

If the applicant successfully completes the steps to this point, the organization usually checks the person's references. Of greatest interest to the employer is the applicant's performance in previous jobs.[10] If the individual is applying for his or her first job, the organization relies heavily on the comments in the letters of reference regarding the applicant's overall ability, effort, initiative, and integrity. These letters are not always very reliable because the writer may be providing an evaluation based on limited input (the applicant may have been a student in one of the writer's classes, or the person writing the letter may know the applicant's family and believe that the applicant will be a good worker). Never-

---

[10] James D. Bell, James Castagnera, and Jane Patterson Young, "Employment References: Do You Know the Law?" *Personnel Journal* (February 1984):32–36. Also see "The Boom in Digging Into a Job Applicant's Past," *Business Week* (June 11, 1984):68.

theless, if the applicant seems to be qualified and the reference letters provide no information to the contrary, the firm is likely to view the applicant positively.

Physical Examination

A physical exam is often required

The last step in the selection process, before the actual hiring decision, is the physical exam. Merely because the person seems qualified to do the job does not mean he or she can do the work. Is the applicant in good health? This is an especially important question for someone who will be doing manual labor or holding a top-management position. For this reason, many firms require a physical exam.

Of course, the person may pass the physical and still develop medical problems later on. Passing the exam is no guarantee that the person will not have a heart attack within the next five years. Organizations require it, however, if only to cover themselves from liability in case the applicant's family files suit claiming that the individual had a bad heart and never should have been hired for strenuous labor. By having a physical exam report in its possession, the company is in a position to challenge the family and point out that, to the best of its knowledge, the worker was in excellent health when hired.

Assessment Centers

In selecting managers, many organizations use an assessment center. The purpose of an **assessment center** is to identify the management applicants with the greatest potential. The ultimate purpose of the center is to answer the question: Of all those who are likely to do well, which are most likely to succeed in the job?

The assessment center concept was used by German military psychologists during World War II, but the first use of the approach by industry was that by AT&T in 1956.[11] That study examined the characteristics that affected the career progress of young employees from the time they took their first job in the Bell System until they moved into middle- and upper-management levels. The results were impressive. Of the 422 people in the study, 42 percent of those who were judged to have middle-management potential achieved that level, while only 4 percent remained at their original level in the hierarchy. At the same time, of those predicted not to rise, 42 percent did not move up, while only 7 percent achieved middle-management positions.[12]

Since this original study, other firms have employed assessment centers in selecting managers. Some of the best known include IBM, Ford Motor, General

---

[11] Wayne F. Cascio, *Applied Psychology in Personnel Management,* 2nd ed. (Reston, VA: Reston Publishing Company, Inc., 1982), 243.
[12] Ron Zemke, "Using Assessment Centers to Measure Management Potential," *Training/HRD* (March 1980):26.

Electric, J. C. Penney, Merrill Lynch, and General Telephone, as well as the FBI, the Civil Service Commission, and the Social Security Administration.

How They Work

Assessment centers are designed to predict performance success more accurately than educational background, interviews, paper-and-pencil tests, and performance appraisals can. In an assessment center, a number of assessors evaluate the way the applicants perform. After watching the applicants in action for one to five days, depending on the position for which they are applying, the assessors gather, discuss the data, and agree on the evaluation of the applicants. While assessment centers may differ from organization to organization, the following six elements are considered essential to each:

Elements of assessment centers

1. A series of assessment techniques must be used. At least one of these must be a simulation or exercise in which the applicants are required to use behaviors related to dimensions of performance on the job. This simulation may be a group exercise, fact-finding exercise, interview simulation, and so on. (See Table 10-4 for an example).
2. A number of assessors must be used. These people must have had thorough training so they know exactly what to look for in the applicants.
3. The final decision regarding what to do (hire, promote, and so on) must be a result of a group decision by the assessors.
4. The simulation exercises that are used must have been developed to tap a variety of predetermined behaviors, and have been pretested prior to use to ensure that they provide reliable, objective, and relevant behavioral information.
5. The techniques used in the assessment center must be designed to provide information that can be used in evaluating the dimensions, attributes, or qualities previously determined.
6. The assessment by the evaluators must be made after the exercises are completed, not during the exercises.[13]

Overall Value

On the positive side, a number of organizations have reported great success with their assessment centers. For example, at IBM, 1,086 nonmanagement employees were classified as having either potential for successful assignment beyond the first-level management or having no potential beyond this level. Of those assessed as having such potential, 30 percent achieved second-level positions. Conversely, only 10 percent of those rated first-level were promoted beyond this level. Additionally, 20 percent of those promoted against the

[13] "When Is an Assessment Center Really an Assessment Center?" *Training HRD* (March 1980):24.

TABLE 10-4 A Typical Two-Day Assessment Center	
Day 1 Orientation Meeting	**Day 2**

Management game—"Conglomerate." Forming different types of conglomerates is the goal, with four-person teams of participants bartering companies to achieve their planned result. Teams set their own acquisition objectives and must plan and organize to meet them.

Background interview—A one-and-a-half-hour interview conducted by an assessor.

Group discussion—"Management Problems." Four short cases calling for various forms of management judgment are presented to groups of four participants. In one hour the group, acting as consultants, must resolve the cases and submit its recommendation in writing.

Individual fact-finding and decision-making exercises—"The Research Budget." Participants are told that they have just taken over as division manager. Each is given a brief description of an incident in which the predecessor has recently turned down a request for funds to continue a research project. The research director is appealing for a reversal of the decision. The participant is given fifteen minutes to ask questions to dig out the facts in the case. Following this fact-finding period, he or she must present a decision orally with supporting reasoning and defend it under challenge.

In-basket exercise—"Section Manager's In-Basket." The contents of a section manager's in-basket are simulated. Participants are instructed to go through the contents, solving problems, answering questions, delegating, organizing, scheduling and planning, just as they might do if they were promoted suddenly to the position. An assessor reviews the contents of the completed in-basket and conducts a one-hour interview with each participant to gain further information.

Assigned role leaderless group discussion—"Compensation Committee." The Compensation Committee is meeting to allocate $8000 in discretionary salary increases among six supervisory and managerial employees. Members of the committee (participants) represent departments of the company and are instructed to "do the best you can" for the employee from their department.

Analysis, presentation, and group discussion—"The Pretzel Factory." This financial analysis problem has the participant role-play a consultant called in to advise Carl Flowers of the C. F. Pretzel Company on two problems: what to do about a division of the company that has continually lost money, and whether the corporation should expand. Participants are given data on the company and are asked to recommend appropriate courses of action. They make their recommendation in a seven-minute presentation, after which they are formed into a group to come up with a single set of recommendations.

Source: William C. Byham, "The Assessment Center as an Aid in Management Development," *Training and Development Journal* (December 1971):19. Copyright 1971, *Training and Development Journal,* American Society for Training & Development. Reprinted with permission. All rights reserved.

prediction were eventually demoted. In contrast, only 9 percent of those who were promoted in accordance with the prediction were demoted.[14]

On the other hand, there is some concern about the fact that most of the validation studies to date have been restricted to large business organizations. A second concern is that unless the organization knows how to run an assessment center, the evaluators may not really know what they are doing or why they are doing it. A third area of concern is whether these assessment centers can be defended in a court of law. In one recent case an assessment center was used to select the deputy police chief of a large midwestern city. While the judge upheld the validity of the process, he questioned some of the methods used.

On an overall basis, however, assessment centers certainly do seem to be an important step toward the effective selection of managers. Commenting on this idea, Fred Luthans, a well-known behavioral scientist, has written:

> There is little question that the assessment center is a much more comprehensive and valid approach to selection than are tests and interviews. By use of the simulated exercises, the approach is much more directly related to job performance than is a question on a personality test asking whether the employee likes to sleep with a light on or off. The big companies have given a great deal of effort and financial support for relating actual job dimensions to the exercises used in their assessment centers. At this stage of the development of assessment centers, the procedures and actual conduct of the sessions in medium-sized and smaller business firms and the potential of the approach for use outside the selection process must be given further attention. Overall, the future looks bright for the use of assessment centers in the selection . . . processes of organizations.[15]

ORIENTATION

Orientation defined

Orientation is an important follow-up to selection. **Orientation** is the process of introducing new employees to the organization and to their superiors, their work groups, and their tasks. If this process is carried out properly, a number of advantages can be obtained. If it is done poorly, the enterprise will often find the new employees unsure of what they are doing or inefficient in getting it done or both.

Sufficient research in industry has been conducted to prove that some specific benefits are associated with proper orientation. One of these is a reduction in the start-up costs for new employees. Better-oriented workers reach standard performance faster than their counterparts who are not well oriented.

A second advantage is the reduction in anxiety concerning job failure. When an individual knows what is expected and how long it will take to become

---

[14] Zemke, "Assessment Centers," 30.
[15] Fred Luthans, *Organizational Behavior,* 4th ed. (New York: McGraw-Hill, 1985), 254.

proficient at the job, the nervousness that accompanies the new work is often greatly reduced.

A third benefit is reduction in employee turnover. When workers feel they are ineffective or unneeded, the tendency to quit increases.

A fourth advantage is the time saved by supervisors and coworkers. The better the individual's orientation, the less likely it is that he or she will need to seek help from others.

Finally, a well-designed orientation program helps the worker develop positive attitudes toward the employer and job satisfaction. The individual is more likely to identify with the enterprise and the work.

TRAINING

Training and learning defined

Training is the process of altering employee behavior and attitudes in a way that increases the probability of goal attainment. (See "Management in Practice: Managing the Difficult Employee.") When training is properly conducted, learning occurs. **Learning** is the acquisition of skills, knowledge, and abilities that result in a relatively permanent change in behavior.

Learning and Job Training

All people are capable of learning, although there are certainly differences in the way they learn. Some learn fastest if they are shown how to do something; others do best if they are told how to do it; still others learn fastest when they are actually allowed to carry out the task. For this reason, training methods vary, as does the locale in which the training occurs. Usually, the organization does the training using company facilities. Sometimes, however, an off-the-job location is used because it is more conducive to learning, or because the program is sponsored by a training or educational organization, such as a university, and is open to everyone on a first-come, first-served basis.

In order to ensure conditions conducive to learning, the facilities should be laid out in a way that encourages attention and ease of participation. Learning is also more likely to occur if the trainer can keep the participants alert. For this reason organizations typically use a variety of learning methods, including lectures, discussions, projects, and simulation exercises.

The company must establish a link between the training and its value to the trainee by showing the trainee the usefulness of the program. It can establish this link in two ways: by having the trainer explain and illustrate the practicality of the training and by having the superior reinforce the training by praising the subordinate for using the newly acquired methods or ideas on the job.

Depending on the nature of the material, the training sometimes can be done in a matter of hours and the trainee can master the subject quickly. At other times a longer training period is necessary. In a situation where the trainee is

Managing The Difficult Employee

*T*he following chart provides a humorous, but often realistic, illustration of difficult employees with whom managers must deal. The columns contain the nickname for the employee type, characteristics that are attributed to that type, and strategies helpful in managing them.

Employee Type	Characteristics	Strategies
"The Tank"	■ Abusive, abrupt, intimidating and overwhelming; needs to prove he or she is right. ■ Tasks seem clear, and the way to do them direct and simple. Impatient with those who don't agree.	■ Don't argue but stand your ground, look him or her in the eye, and complete what you're doing. ■ Breathe deeply. People under stress need more oxygen to think clearly and not be swept by emotion. ■ Give him or her time to run down, and interrupt if necessary, calling him or her by name. ■ Assertively "pace" or "play back" his or her comments, without defending yourself. This shows you listened and understand; it also "takes the wind out of his or her sails." ■ State your own opinions and perceptions forcefully. ■ Be ready to be friendly.
"The Sniper"	■ A "suppressed Tank" firing putdowns, digs, and the like. ■ Often snipes in a group, to undercut and make you look foolish.	■ Call immediate attention to his or her attack; ignoring it only perpetuates it. "Do I detect sarcasm?" ■ Be assertive, but don't attack. Always give him or her a way to escape. ■ Align with group intent and ask for relevancy. "I'm not sure what your comment has to do with the purpose of this meeting." ■ Probe for his or her grievance and try to solve any uncovered problems. ■ Prevent sniping by setting up regular problem-solving meetings.

Employee Type	Characteristics	Strategies
"The Balloon"	■ Seeks admiration and respect by acting like an expert when he's not. Often only partially aware of speaking beyond his or her knowledge.	■ Make sure his or her unworkable ideas are scrapped, but do it in a face-saving way that gives the individual an "out." ■ State the correct facts or alternative opinions as your own perceptions of reality. ■ It's best to cope with this person when he or she is alone.
"The Negativist"	■ "Wet blanket" who dampens any suggestion regardless of merit. Quick to point out why something won't work. ■ Like the complainer, convinced he or she has little power over life activities, but this person is more bitter, believing that those in power cannot be trusted or counted upon.	■ Maintain your optimism and avoid getting dragged into despair. ■ "Pace" this person by gathering information and asking specific questions, and use him or her as a resource. Eventually you may make a dent in the individual's self-image.
"The Clam"	■ Avoids conflict and controversy; never offers ideas or opinions or lets you know where you stand. ■ "Relator" type shuts up because he or she is afraid of confrontation. ■ "Aggressive" type shuts up because he or she wants to "get" you.	■ Help the "Clam" to open up by asking open-ended questions, ones requiring more than a yes or no reply. ■ Wait for a response, don't break the silence. ■ Plan enough time to allow waiting with composure. ■ If you get no response comment on what's happening and end with an open-ended question: "I'm still wondering how you feel . . . " If necessary, repeat the cycle. ■ Put yourself in this person's position and tell the individual you will guess how he or she is feeling, then watch for any change in expression. ■ If the "Clam" stays closed, inform him or her what you must and will do.

Source: Jim Braham, "Difficult Employees," *Industry Week* (June 19, 1989):30–35.

being taught to carry out a simple task, such as operating machinery, learning usually occurs quickly; for more complex undertakings, such as analyzing financial statements, learning may be much slower at first and may then pick up dramatically.

The Role of Top Management

Some organizations have very successful training programs while others do not. One of the primary reasons is that in some organizations management supports training while in others it does not. Unless there is a positive attitude toward training beginning at the very top, the overall impact of training is limited. Moreover, in some cases verbal support is not enough; active participation is required. Management must be prepared to (1) make it clear that training has a high priority, (2) reward those who train their people, and (3) where needed, actively participate in training programs to keep abreast of the latest developments in their own areas of expertise.

A proactive approach to training

This philosophy results in a *proactive* approach to training. Instead of waiting for training deficiencies to become apparent, the organization anticipates and plans for the types of training that will keep the workforce up-to-date. Organizations use numerous strategies to attain this objective. Eight of the most helpful are for organizations to:

Proactive strategies

1. Include human resources management and development in the strategic planning process.
2. Project important trends that will affect what management expects of the employees, including technological, social/psychological, economic, political, and intellectual trends.
3. Resist the lure of using training just to handle immediate, short-run problems.
4. Hold managers accountable for seeing the individuals in their units and departments are properly trained.
5. Set a regular, criterion-based planning and review process that can be used to build a pool of potentially promotable individuals.
6. Encourage input from those who will be trained, in designing and implementing training programs.
7. Conduct human resource audits to measure the organizational climate.
8. Review management practices and job satisfaction to measure how well things are going in the organization and to pick up early-warning signals that indicate the need for additional training and development.[16]

What specific types of training do employees need? The answer depends on the person's job. At the lower levels of the hierarchy, training is often quite

---

[16] Patricia McLagan, "How Top Executives Can Develop Training's Proactive Potential," *Training/HRD* (October 1980):43–46.

simple and learning involves memorizing procedures or operating equipment. At the upper levels training is more complex and learning involves improving interpersonal relations or developing an understanding of the way to carry out strategic planning. Before deciding on the specific type of training that is required, however, the organization must analyze its training needs.

ANALYZING TRAINING NEEDS

Some organizations, especially large ones, try to keep up-to-date records on employee training needs. Most, however, either rely on periodic assessments for discovering who needs training (and of what type) or simply depend on the individual superior to give subordinates the most effective on-the-job training possible.

Needs analysis surveys

Fortunately, there seems to be a trend, especially among the more successful enterprises, toward conducting *needs analysis surveys.* A sample questionnaire used for this purpose is provided in Figure 10-3.

Needs and Objectives

Determining training objectives

By using needs analysis questionnaires or procedures, an organization does more than simply pinpoint the types of training that are needed.[17] It also provides a basis for determining training objectives. What is the purpose of training? How can the organization know when this objective has been accomplished? To answer these questions, the organization must spell out objectives clearly and establish criteria for determining goal attainment.

While these tasks are easier to do for lower-level jobs than upper-level ones, they should be attempted for all. The following table provides some examples:

Objective	Criterion to Use in Determining When an Objective Is Met
To operate a word processor (lower-level employee)	When the trainee is able to enter a five-page report into the memory, make all typing and editorial changes, and obtain a complete and correct printout.
To discipline an employee effectively (middle-manager)	When the trainee can go through a role-playing session, using all of the steps presented in the earlier training, and explain why and how to discipline the employee while still maintaining his or her respect and trust.
To present a financial report effectively to the board of directors (upper-level manager)	When the individual is able to read, synthesize, and summarize financial data; have it worked up in the form of graphs, charts, tables, and other visual aids; present it to a group of top line managers; and be able to field questions from them.

[17] Edward H. Wolfe, "Supervisory Development: The Need for an Integrated Strategy," *Training and Development* (March 1983):28–31. Also see S. B. Wehrenberg, "How to Decide on the Best Training Approach," *Personnel Journal* (February 1983):117–18.

FIGURE 10-3   Needs Analysis Survey Form

Employee _____ Department _____ Check One   Prototype _____ Operational _____

Form Completed By _____ Title _____ Date _____

INSTRUCTIONS

This form was designed to enable you to list skills and evaluate the degree of relevancy of these skills to positions in our own department. In addition you will be asked to assess the degree of proficiency in designated skill areas distinguished by the employees occupying these positions. To accomplish this task, you are asked to follow the steps outlined below.

A) **Prototype Form**

  1) Rank the **General Job Skills** in order of your perception of their importance to successfully performing the subject job.

  2) Review the **Specific Job Skills** section; this is the preliminary listing prepared by the survey coordinator based on existing job descriptions, and add or delete skills as you feel appropriate.

  3) Rank the **Specific Job Skills** in order of your perception of their importance to successfully performing the subject job and divide into five groups as the coordinator has done for the General Skills listing (this is the skill group level).

B) **Operational Form**

  After the Prototype Form has been finalized (through rater consensus) with respect to both the type and degree of relevance of skill areas, you will be asked to evaluate each employee's degree of proficiency in each skill area. Please use the scale below.

NO PROFICIENCY   1   2   3   4   5   HIGH LEVEL OF PROFICIENCY

General Skills	General Skills in Ranked Order		Group	Place "x" on Employee Evaluation					
				1	2	3	4	5	*
Planning		1							
Controlling		2	V						
Writing Ability		3							
Oral Communications		4							
Company Credibility		5	IV						
Decision Making		6							
Creativity		7							
Initiative		8	III						
Adaptability		9							
Problem Solving		10							
People Sensitivity		11	II						
Self Evaluation		12							
Relationship to Supervisor		13							
Work Attitude		14	I						
Organizing Ability		15							
Specific Skills	Specific Skills in Ranked Order		Group	Place "x" on Employee Evaluation					
				1	2	3	4	5	*

* Check when there's a discrepancy of more than two points (employee vs. group) or when the employee is rated below 3 in Groups III and below.

Source: Reprinted from the November 1976 issue of *Personnel Administrator,* Copyright 1976, the American Society for Personnel Administration, 606 North Washington Street, Alexandria, VA 22314.

Notice that in the first case the objective can be measured objectively. The second, and more important, the third, require subjective evaluation by other people. Nevertheless, these approaches are the best that an organization can use and, if the people who are evaluating the training know what to look for, they are good enough.[18]

MANAGEMENT DEVELOPMENT

Management
development
defined

Management development is the process by which managers obtain the necessary skills, experiences, and attitudes that they need to become or remain successful leaders in their respective organizations. There are a number of specific reasons for using management development, many of which parallel the reasons for employee training. Four of the most important include (1) reducing or preventing managerial obsolescence by keeping the individual up-to-date in the field, (2) increasing the manager's overall effectiveness, (3) increasing the manager's overall satisfaction with the job, and (4) satisfying some of the requirements of equal employment opportunity by, for example, developing women and other minorities for managerial positions.

The Obsolescence Issue

Causes of
managerial
obsolescence

Modern organizations are particularly sensitive to the problem of managerial obsolescence. There are three major causes of obsolescence. One is the manager's inability to keep up with technological changes in the field. A second is the promotion of individuals to positions for which they are unqualified—for example, the Peter Principle, which holds that people rise to their level of incompetence. A third is the fact that, as managers get older, they find it difficult to keep up with the latest developments in their field.

Of course, obsolescence hits some organizations harder than others. It is most prevalent in companies in high-technology industries and those in which a large percentage of the managers are near retirement. Some researchers have reported that managerial obsolescence is highest in the over-55 age group and among engineering personnel where technical knowledge is vital. On the other hand, it has been found that those with higher levels of education and strong work ethic motivation are least likely to become obsolete.[19]

---

[18] Lawrence Olson, "Training Trends: The Corporate View," *Training and Development Journal* (September 1986):32–35.

[19] Frederick Haas, *Executive Obsolescence,* AMA Research Study 90 (New York: American Management Association, 1968); Lawrence Baughler and John Lee, "Personal Obsolescence: The Employee's Perspective," *Southern Journal of Business* (November 1971):52–61; Richard Shearer and Joseph Steger, "Manpower Obsolescence," *Academy of Management Journal* (June 1975):263–75; Frank O. Hoffman, "Is Management Development Doing the Job?" *Training and Development Journal* (January 1983):34–39.

After making an extensive review of the literature on obsolescence among professional and technical employees, Herbert Kaufman reported that the major factors causing obsolescence are limited intellectual and cognitive abilities, low motivation, low self-esteem, and personal rigidity.[20] How can this problem be addressed effectively? The alternatives are to fire the person, to move the person to another job, or to provide the person with management development programs that address the particular deficiencies. The latter is the preferable alternative. The following discussion examines how it can be implemented.

Development Methods

Smaller organizations seldom have formal development techniques; most are informal. Large enterprises, however, tend to have elaborate and formal programs which often combine on-the-job and off-the-job development. Table 10-5 illustrates the effect that organizational size can have on the specific type of program used. Some of the techniques employed in management development are the same basic ones used in employee training. The major difference is the emphasis given to certain tools and techniques.

Training often varies by hierarchical level

Table 10-6 presents some of the most common types of development programs, as reported in the recent literature. It is evident from the tables that the types of training given supervisory managers is not the same as that provided at the middle and upper levels of the hierarchy. Notice that supervisory training tends to involve more in-house workshops, coaching plus on-the-job experience, and self-study courses. At the opposite extreme, executive development consists of more external conferences and seminars, participation in university programs, association and professional conferences and workshops, and consultant programs. Middle management development is in between these two extremes, although it tends to be closer to the executive type than the supervisory type.

Development Needs and Management Level

The development needs of managers vary by hierarchical level. Lester Digman conducted a survey of the supervisory, management, and executive development practices and needs of both public and private organizations in the Midwest. The areas represented by these 84 organizations included manufacturing, wholesale/distribution, retail, finance, health care, transportation, utilities, construction, insurance, social services, schools, and federal, state, county, and city governments.[21] He found that most organizations prefer to develop their

---

[20] Herbert Kaufman, *Obsolescence and Professional Career Development* (New York: Amacon, 1974).

[21] Lester A. Digman, "Management Development: Needs and Practices," *Personnel* (July–August 1980):45–57.

TABLE 10-5 Program Type and Level Versus Organization Size

Program Level	Medium to Large: Less than 2,000 Managers	Organization Size Very Large: 2,000–8,000 Managers	Giant: over 8,000 Managers
Executive	Programs largely individualized. Primarily out-company, some internal on contract, some completely ad hoc. Oriented toward conceptual skills and strategy.	Programs divided between in-house and out-company. Oriented toward conceptual skills, strategy, and environmental understanding.	Programs largely in-house and centralized, supplemental lectures, some out-company exposure. Oriented toward interface or internal and external environment.
Middle	Programs mixed between in-house (supplemented by lecturers) and out-company. Oriented toward human and conceptual skills and analytical abilities.	Programs largely in-house, with little out-company. Conducted on centralized corporate basis. Oriented toward human and decision-making skills, geared to company policy.	Programs predominantly in-house, either corporate or division centralized. Orientation is on human, decision-making, and conceptual skills.
Supervisory	Programs on-site in division. Orientation is on basic technical and human skills, geared to company procedures.	Program on-site in division. Orientation is on basic technical and human skills, including company procedures.	Programs on-site in division. Orientation is on basic technical and human skills, including company procedures and policy. Program instructors are centrally trained.

Source: Reprinted, by permission of the publisher, from "Management Development: Needs and Practices," Lester A. Digman, *Personnel* (July–August 1980):49. © 1980 by American Management Association, New York. All rights reserved.

TABLE 10-6 Type of Development Received

Type of Development	Executive	Middle	Supervisory
External conference/seminars	27.7%	26.1%	17.3%
In-house workshops	22.9	21.6	34.7
Coaching plus on-the-job experience	13.3	29.5	33.4
Participation in university programs	10.8	10.2	4.0
Association/professional conferences and workshops	16.8	4.5	0
Consultant programs	7.2	5.7	5.3
Self-study courses	1.2	2.3	5.3

Source: Reprinted, by permission of the publisher, from "Management Development: Needs and Practices," Lester A. Digman, *Personnel* (July–August 1980):53. © 1980 by American Management Association, New York. All rights reserved.

TABLE 10-7   Most Frequent Development Needs at Each Level of Management

Executive Level	Middle Level	Supervisory Level
1. { Managing time / Team building	1. Evaluating and appraising employees	1. Motivating others
3. { Organizing and planning / Evaluating and appraising employees	2. Motivating others	2. Evaluating and appraising others
5. { Coping with stress / Understanding human behavior	3. Setting objectives and priorities	3. Leadership
7. { Self-analysis / Motivating others	4. Oral communication	4. Oral communication
9. { Financial management / Budgeting	5. Organizing and planning	5. Understanding human behavior
11. { Setting objectives and priorities / Holding effective meetings	6. Understanding human behavior	6. Developing and training subordinates
13. Oral communication	7. { Written communication / Managing time	7. { Role of the manager / Setting objectives and priorities / Written communication
14. Labor/management relations	9. Team building	10. Discipline
15. { Decision making / Developing strategies and policies	10. { Leadership / Decision making / Holding effective meetings / Delegation / Developing and training subordinates	11. { Organizing and planning / Managing time / Counseling and coaching
	15. Selecting employees	14. Selecting employees
		15. Decision making

Source: Reprinted, by permission of the publisher, from "Management Development: Needs and Practices," Lester A. Digman, *Personnel* (July–August 1980):56. © 1980 by American Management Association, New York. All rights reserved.

own managers from within. The better-managed enterprises had more advanced developmental practices and had to go outside to hire much less often than did the typical organization (71% versus 92%, respectively). In developing managers, these companies preferred on-the-job experience, aided by coaching and counseling, and in-house training. When in-house training was unavailable, the organization turned to outside sources. Professor Digman also found that well-managed firms trained their supervisors more frequently than did the average firm. The result was that their people were better prepared for higher-level positions earlier in their management careers.

Development needs vary by hierarchical levels

What kinds of development do managers need?[22] The answers is somewhat influenced by the manager's level in the hierarchy (see Table 10-7). For example, Digman reported that at the upper levels there was a decided shift

---

[22] Alan Mumford, "What's New in Management Development?" *Personnel Management* (May 1985):30–33.

toward general business areas (planning, organizing, evaluating, and appraising employees) and personal skills (time management and understanding human behavior). At the middle and lower levels the emphasis tended to be more behavioral in orientation, with evaluation, motivation, communication, and leadership holding high priorities.[23]

EVALUATING TRAINING AND DEVELOPMENT PROGRAMS

Are training and development worth the cost? Surprisingly, many firms are unable to answer this question objectively because they do not conduct any form of evaluation. They simply assume that if the training program covers areas of known deficiencies, the benefits are worth the expenses. Given the fact that many organizations are spending thousands of dollars in this area annually, a more formal evaluation process is needed. The following 10 steps can be used in evaluating training.[24]

One: Compute the Cost of Each Training Component

Direct and indirect costs are included

There are many costs involved in training and development, including trainer costs, facilities and equipment costs, materials and supplies expenses, and the salaries of the trainees. (Remember that when the trainees are not at work, output is being lost. So the salaries these people earn while being trained are part of the overall cost.)[25]

Two: Rank Each Program Based on Its Perceived Value

Programs are evaluated on the basis of importance

By drawing upon knowledgeable personnel within the enterprise, the organization must rank the relative value of each training program, from the most important to the least important. For example, the most effective training might be entry-level technical training, while the executive development program might rank second, and the orientation program last. The purpose of this type of ranking is to provide a basis for computing potential savings.

Three: Compute Potential Savings

Next to the relative value rankings of the various programs, a computation of the relative cost of each program should be made. An example is provided in Table

---

[23] H. Wayne Smith, "Implementing a Management Development Program," *Personnel Administrator* (July 1985):75–86.

[24] The data in this section can be found in Basil S. Deming, "A System for Evaluating Training Programs," *Personnel* (November–December 1979):35–41.

[25] Frank O. Hoffman, "A Responsive Training Department Cuts Cost," *Personnel Journal* (February 1984):48–51.

A "PS" rating is determined

10-8. Notice that the organization now has two ratings for each program: value and cost. The total of these two is the potential for savings, or the "PS" rank. The lower the PS number, the higher the potential savings. For example, in Table 10-8 entry-level technical training has a higher potential savings than does EEO training, and the latter has a higher potential savings than does communication skills training.

Four: Evaluate the Effect of the Training

Training objectives are reviewed

The next step is to find out whether the programs are achieving their objectives.[26] It involves (1) reviewing the training objectives and (2) asking the trainees and their superiors if the training was helpful back on the job. An overall rating of the respective programs can be done on a forced choice basis: training appears effective, training appears unclear, training is ineffective. An example is provided in column 4 of Table 10-8, where the effect of the programs has been reported.

Five: Determine Which Programs Should Be Evaluated First

Programs with the lowest "PS" factors are reviewed first

The organization now must check the PS factors of programs judged to be unclear or ineffective in regard to job performance. Those with the lowest factors are candidates for immediate evaluation. After all, they are the most expensive and most valuable; if they are also judged to have poor or uncertain effects on job performance, they should be the first to undergo the initial evaluations. In Table 10-8 the upward mobility program is most eligible for evaluation. The executive development program is second in line. Notice that while the entry-level technical training program has the highest potential for savings, it was judged to be effective, so the priority for evaluation is much lower.

Six: Establish Evaluation Objectives

Specific objectives are determined

Now managers and evaluators have to explore a number of basic questions: Are the training objectives clear? Are they acceptable to management? Can a cause-and-effect relationship be established between learning and performance? Is cost effectiveness a critical element? Should the training process be analyzed to improve instruction? Working together, managers and evaluators must determine specific objectives that can be used for evaluating the respective program.

---

[26] L. A. Tyson and H. Birnbrauer, "High Quality Evaluation," *Training and Development Journal* (September 1985):33–37.

TABLE 10-8	Program Evaluation Worksheet				
	(1)	**(2)**	**(3)**	**(4)**	**(5)**
Training Component	Relative Cost	+ Relative Value =	Potential for Savings (PS Rank)	Effect of Training	Priority for Evaluation
Executive development program	2	3	5(2)	Unclear	2
Upward mobility program	3	2	5(2)	Ineffective	1
Secretarial training	7	4	11(4)	Effective	10
EEO training	8	6	14(6)	Unclear	4
Supervisory training	4	8	12(5)	Ineffective	3
Communication skills training	11	9	20(11)	Unclear	7
Basic adult education	5	11	16(8)	Unclear	6
Technical training					
—entry-level	1	1	2(1)	Effective	9
—to improve performance	6	10	16(8)	Effective	11
—for program change	10	7	17(10)	Effective	12
Orientation training	12	12	24(12)	Unclear	8
Management intern program	9	5	14(6)	Unclear	5

Source: Reprinted, by permission of the publisher, from "A System for Evaluating Training Programs," Basil S. Deming, *Personnel* (November–December 1979):37. © 1979 by American Management Association, New York. All rights reserved.

Seven: Estimate the Cost of Evaluation

Once the basic objectives and the evaluation design are determined, an estimate of the cost of evaluating the program must be made. In many cases this is not a very difficult undertaking. The evaluator can often make an estimate or provide a reasonable cost range. The two most important things the evaluator must do are (1) to include all of the costs, both direct and indirect, that are associated with the program, and (2) to allocate the costs over the life of the program. For example, if a new executive development program is going to require three trainers and involve seven executives, the salaries of these 10 people should be allocated to the program. The total cost of the equipment should not be allocated, however, because this machinery will be used over again. A small fee of perhaps $50 can be allocated for the use of the slide projector, overhead viewgraph, film projector, and other equipment.

Evaluation costs are considered

Finally, the cost of evaluating the program must be considered. A typical rule of thumb is that evaluation costs should be no more than 10 percent of the total program cost. If the program is being run for the first time, however, and no evaluation procedures have been worked up, this 10 percent rule can be violated. As the program is run again and again, the evaluation procedures will have been established already and the costs will then be much lower than 10 percent.

Eight: Monitor the Evaluation Process

Maintenance
functions are
performed

Monitoring is the maintenance activity. Unless the organization follows up and ensures that the program continues to achieve its objectives and be worth the cost, the process may break down. The evaluator may meet resistance from the supervisors from whom the employee performance data is being collected. Or after the programs some of the evaluation forms may not be filled out in their entirety, providing only piecemeal information regarding the overall value of the program.

TABLE 10-9   Change Decision Sheet

Recommendation	Type of Change Required	Constraints	Probable Payoff	Priority of Selection	Implementation Decision
Have executive development program participants assigned to senior executives who guide them and monitor their actvities.	Evaluation of participants shifts from trainers to executives; thorough orientation needed by executives who would participate; evaluation subsystem would have to be designed	Executive might not be objective because of close working relationships developed with participants.	Regardless of some subjectivity in evaluator-participant relationship, it has strong growth potential for the participant.	1	Implement
Extend executive development program from two years to three.	Administrative	Participants are anxious to get back into regular assignments by the end of their second year; salary costs to organization is more than $140,000 per year.	The value of developmental experiences may diminish over time. Probable payoff is likely to be smaller than that of first two years.	2	Do not implement now; survey executives who served as mentors to get their opinions.

Source: Reprinted, by permission of the publisher, from "A System for Evaluating Training Programs," Basil S. Deming, *Personnel* (November – December 1979):40. © 1979 by American Management Association, New York. All rights reserved.

Nine: Study and Diagnose the Evaluation Reports

Evaluation reports are examined

The evaluation reports should be read carefully. Do they provide the kind of information that will permit the program to be judged effectively? Or are they too general or skewed toward determining whether certain ideas or concepts were presented while ignoring the value of the program to the participants? Does the evaluation need to be revised? Remember that this evaluation should relate to the original objectives so that it indicates whether these goals were or were not attained.

Ten: Make Decisions Based on the Findings

Sometimes nothing is done

The last phase of program evaluation is to decide what to do in light of the results. Sometimes nothing is done because the results are unclear or are based on faulty data collection. At other times nothing is done because the people who are empowered to make the decision are afraid of the effect change might have on the organization. At yet other times, although change appears to be warranted, nothing is done because the cost would be too great. Too much time and energy would have to be expended in redoing or revising the program.

The first rule to follow in determining what to do is to emphasize changing those programs for which the smallest investments will produce the greatest benefits. The second rule is to evaluate the magnitude of the proposed changes and balance the savings with the efforts necessary to make them and the problems that will result from implementation. The organization should begin making changes by opting for the program that provides the best cost benefit ratio. Then it is a matter of the organization's own judgment regarding how far to go in making changes in the various programs. Table 10-9 provides an example of how two proposed changes in the executive development program identified in Table 10-8 were handled. Notice that one recommendation was implemented and another was put on hold.

SUMMARY

1. Strategic human resources planning is the process of identifying the numbers, skills, and occupational categories of personnel the organization will need in the future to ensure the attainment of its strategic objectives. This process is closely linked to strategic planning.
2. Three key external forces affect human resources planning. One is government regulation, as reflected in such legislation as the Equal Pay Act of 1963, the Civil Rights Act of 1964, the Age Discrimination in Employment Act of 1967, and the Rehabilitation Act of 1973. A second is economic factors, which modern organizations address through such

means as employee replacement charts and employment forecasts. The third is demographic and social trends, which are resulting in such developments as flexible work schedules.

3. Recruiting is the process of attracting job candidates who have the abilities and aptitudes necessary to help the organization achieve its objectives. Some of the most common ways of generating job candidates internally include job posting, the contacting of friends of current workers, and the use of skills inventories.

4. Selection is the process by which an enterprise chooses those applicants who meet the criteria for the available positions. The most important characteristic of selection is that the selection techniques be both valid and reliable. Validity means that the selection instrument measures what the organization wants it to measure. Reliability means that the selection instrument provides a consistent measure of something. There are six basic steps in the selection process: (1) the preliminary screening interview, (2) the completion of an application blank, (3) the employment interview, (4) employment tests, (5) reference checks and recommendation letters, and (6) the physical exam. For screening managers, another popular approach is the assessment center.

5. Orientation is the process of introducing new employees to the organization and their superiors, their work groups, and their tasks. If this process is carried out properly, a number of important advantages can be obtained.

6. Training is the process of altering employee behavior and attitudes in a way that increases the probability of goal attainment. To ensure effective training of personnel, the support of top management is critical. Unless top management gets behind the training effort, it can prove worthless.

7. Many organizations attempt to determine training needs by carrying out what is called a needs analysis survey. This survey pinpoints areas in which training is needed. Then the training must be tied to specific, and if possible, measurable, objectives.

8. Management development is the process by which managers obtain the necessary skills, experiences, and attitudes that they need to become or remain successful leaders in their respective organizations. One of the most critical problems addressed by this training is managerial obsolescence.

9. A number of different types of management development methods are used by modern organizations. These were presented in Table 10-6. The specific choice of method tends to depend on the manager's hierarchical level.

10. In the final analysis, an organization can only determine if the training and development are worth the cost if some form of evaluation is carried out. Ten steps can be used for evaluating training. The usefulness of

each program is determined not only by its cost but by its value in helping meet the objectives of the program.

KEY TERMS

Assessment center   A method of selecting managers that involves predicting performance of candidates through the use of simulation exercises and other tools and techniques for evaluating job-related behavior.

Compressed work week   Scheduling the normal weekly hours into fewer days so that, for example, individuals work four 10-hour days rather than five 8-hour days.

Core hours   The time periods during the day when, regardless of the flexible work schedules of the various employees, everyone is at work.

Employee replacement chart   A chart that shows which personnel are performing extremely well, which are satisfactory, and which need to improve their performance, as well as the promotion potential of each person.

Expert-estimate techniques   A method of forecasting employment needs in which a knowledgeable executive, or committee, decides how many people will be needed over the next six to 12 months.

Flextime   A flexible work schedule in which employees are permitted to choose their own work hours.

Learning   The acquisition of skills, knowledge, and abilities that result in a relatively permanent change in behavior.

Management development   The process by which managers attain the necessary skills, experiences, and attitudes that they need to become or remain successful leaders in their respective organizations.

Modeling and multiple-predictive techniques   A method of forecasting employment needs that involves the use of mathematical models that take into account a series of employment-related data such as sales, gross national product, and discretionary income.

Orientation   The process of introducing new employees to the organization and to their superiors, their work groups, and their tasks.

Recruiting   The process of attracting job candidates who have the abilities and attitudes necessary to help the organization achieve its objectives.

Reliability   The degree to which a selection instrument provides a consistent measure of something.

Selection   The process by which an enterprise chooses the applicants who best meet the criteria for the available positions.

Semistructured interview   An interview in which the major questions to be asked are prepared in advance and the interviewer may expand them and ask others.

Skills inventories   Employee records that describe each person's training and experience as well as, in some cases, the person's strengths, weaknesses, present performance, and potential for promotion.

Strategic human resources planning   The process of identifying the numbers, skills, and occupational categories of personnel the organization will need in the future to ensure the attainment of its strategic objectives.

Structured interview   An interview in which the interviewer uses a prepared list of questions and does not deviate from them.

Training   The process of altering employee behavior and attitudes in a way that increases the probability of goal attainment.

Trend-projection technique   A method of forecasting employment needs that involves trying to tie employment needs to one or more causal factors.

Unit demand forecast   A method of forecasting employment needs that involves a bottom-up approach in which each unit manager analyzes the needs of his or her unit and passes the information up the line to the superior.

Unstructured interview   An interview in which the interviewer asks whatever seems appropriate and adapts the discussion to the responses, choosing those areas where further questions appear warranted and ignoring those where additional discussion seems fruitless.

Validity   The degree to which a selection instrument measures what the organization wants it to measure.

QUESTIONS FOR ANALYSIS AND DISCUSSION

1. In your own words, what is meant by the term strategic human resources planning? What is the link between strategic planning and human resources planning?
2. How does government regulation affect employment planning? In your answer be sure to discuss the following: the Civil Rights Act of 1964, the Equal Pay Act of 1963, the Age Discrimination in Employment Act of 1967, and the Rehabilitation Act of 1973.
3. How do each of the following employment forecasting techniques work: expert-estimate, trend-projection, unit demand, and modeling and multiple-predictive? Explain your answer.
4. In your own words, what is meant by recruiting?
5. In your own words, what are the six basic steps in the selection process? Briefly describe each.
6. How does the assessment center concept work? Is it of any value? When should it be used?
7. In your own words, what is meant by the term training? What role does learning play in the training process?
8. How important is the role top management plays in the organization's training effort? Explain your answer.

9. What is a needs analysis survey all about? When would an enterprise want to carry one out? Of what value would the survey be?
10. In your own words, what is meant by the term management development? Be complete in your answer.
11. How do management development needs differ by hierarchical level? Explain, incorporating the data in Table 10-7 into your answer.
12. How can an organization go about evaluating its training programs? Offer specific suggestions.

CASE

Wechsler's Training Offerings

While most of its competitors are having a difficult year, Wechsler, Inc., a midwestern manufacturing firm, is doing better than ever. Last week it received $1.2 million in new orders and it now has four-and-a-half months of backlog.

In order to fill these new orders, the company has just hired 10 new machinists. These new employees all need training in how to run the specialized machinery used in the production process. The firm has also hired three new supervisors and promoted one more from within. These four people are all scheduled for supervisory training.

Last week the organization sent around a list of the latest training courses being offered under the auspices of the Personnel Department. Six seminars are scheduled for the new three-month period: Effective Communication, Time Management, Motivation Techniques, Effective Leadership, Job Planning, and Performance Evaluation. Each of the six is fully described in a one-paragraph outline that details the specific topics to be covered and discusses what the participant will learn.

The list of courses is being circulated throughout every department in the organization. Each manager is being asked whether he or she would like to attend any of them and which subordinates, if any, would profit from attendance.

After the list has made the rounds, the head of the Personnel Department will draw up a final roster showing who will be attending each of the seminars. Inevitably, some seminars will attract 20 people while others will have more than double that number. Since the department has found the ideal number of participants per session to be between 15 and 20, management people are assigned to one session, where possible, while workers go to another. Additionally, if the number of managers is large enough to form two groups, they are divided so that no one attends a session with his or her direct superior.

In the past Wechsler, Inc. has found that its approach to training works quite well. Most of the feedback has been positive. The only real complaints have been that the number of programs offered is not large enough (some people believe the firm should offer two or three every month) and that they do not last long enough (usually a program lasts from a half day to a full day and sometimes participants argue that at least twice as much time should be allotted to the topic).

The head of the Personnel Department received back the latest list of training requests yesterday. He is now in the process of deciding how to accommodate all of them.

1. What type of training should be given to the new machinists? The new supervisors? Be complete in your answer. Also, of the six programs being offered by the firm, which ones would be of most value to the managerial people? The nonmanagerial people?
2. What types of training methods and techniques would you expect to be used in the following seminars: Effective Communication, Time Management, and Effective Leadership? Explain your answer.
3. In addition to the six programs listed in the case, what other ones would be of value to the personnel? Identify and describe three.

YOU BE THE CONSULTANT

The Leadership Development Seminar

Renée Pence, human resource director for a medium-sized but growing health care systems corporation, is trying a leadership development seminar for 125 middle managers. Realizing that the corporation is attempting to expand in an ever-changing health care market, Renée has proposed that the seminar deal with innovation and change. She has made initial contact with Steele & Associates, a management development firm that specializes in leadership and managerial seminars. Dr. Ray Steele, the firm's major partner, has convinced Renée that today's leadership development should be focused on the manager's ability to develop innovative ideas and to be adaptive to change. Renée has decided to present the proposal to her executive vice president for approval.

Alex T. Baker, the executive vice president, is reluctant to present too many new ideas to the managers. There has been a great deal of change in the company over the last two years and the managers seem to be uneasy with many of them. Mr. Baker feels that a seminar concerning new issues will only add to the confusion that many of the managers feel.

Renée knows that this proposed seminar will meet a great deal of resistance from Mr. Baker. Therefore, she wants to prepare a clear and concise proposal that will identify not only what the seminar will entail but also why the corporation needs this type of "new" material during this period of management unrest. The question remains as to how such a proposal should be written in order to sway Mr. Baker.

Renée has called Dr. Steele and discussed her dilemma. She filled him in on the expected resistance and explained the uneasy atmosphere that exists throughout the corporation. Dr. Steele listened carefully and assured Renée that he would contact her the next morning with a suggested plan for the proposal.

Your Consultation

Assume you are Dr. Steele. What exactly would you suggest to Renée? Outline the plan that you believe Renée should follow to convince her boss that this seminar is needed. Be specific in your answer. (Use the training evaluation steps from this chapter to help you.)

In January 1988, following a disappointing Christmas season, General Mills announced that it was putting its Specialty Retailing segment on the market. This segment, comprised of the Talbots and Eddie Bauer clothing retail chains and catalog sales operations, was expected by some analysts to provide the firm with $350 to $400 million, though others estimated it would yield only $200 to $250 million. The lower estimate was based on the belief by some that the historically high growth of these firms would slow in the future. Further, this prospect for slower growth, coupled with the effects of the October 1987 stock market "crash," reduced price-earnings ratios for many firms in this industry by two-thirds, from about 35 times in August 1987, to around 10–12 times in early 1988. The company announced that the proceeds from this sale would be used to finance "aggressive internal investment plans" and a significant repurchase of the company's stock.[1]

In September 1987, at the firm's annual meeting, chairman H. Brewster Atwater had announced that the retailing unit would be significantly expanded with the addition of 15–20 new Talbots stores, the introduction of new product lines for the Eddie Bauer chain, and nearly $200 million in new capital spending. However, by the end of the 1987 holiday period, security analysts were estimating that in spite of moderate increases in sales, the Specialty Retailing unit would suffer significant earnings declines in the second half of the fiscal year ending in May 1988. These forecasts followed announced operating earnings declines of 10 percent for the first half of the fiscal year, in spite of the addition of 10 stores in each chain.

Background and Recent History

General Mills began in 1928 as a combination of six large grain milling companies. In addition to their milling capacity, these mills provided the firm with the Betty Crocker brand (invented in 1921) and the Wheaties brand (1924). From 1928 to 1945 the firm relied heavily on its flour milling business. However, during that time it also expanded its breakfast cereal sales and began its entry into packaged baking mixes, acquiring Bisquick in 1931.

After World War II, in response to maturation in the flour milling business, General Mills began to concentrate its development on the production of commodity-type packaged foods such as baking mixes and cereals. During the third stage of its evolution, which lasted from 1960–1966, the firm shifted its emphasis away from a commodity product orientation to a greater emphasis on consumer packaged goods. The firm also closed half of its flour mills during this period. Following this initial period of consolidation General Mills began a decade (1967–1975) of aggressive diversification into a variety of consumer

industries including various packaged and frozen foods, toys, clothing, phila-
telic supplies, and others. In the decade from 1976–1985 the firm attempted to
rationalize these businesses and focus its attention on those with the greatest
prospects for future growth and profitability.[2]

The most recent phase of the company's history began when the board of
directors approved a corporate restructuring plan in the spring of 1985. This
plan followed General Mills's fiscal 1984 earnings decrease of 4.8 percent—

EXHIBIT 1   Financial Summary

Results Based on Continuing Operations for Businesses Owned in 1987

| | Millions of Dollars For Fiscal Years ending May 31 | | |
	1987	1986	1985
Sales	$5189.3	$4495.9	$4206.2
Cost of sales	2834.0	2497.1	2418.7
Gross profit	2355.3	1998.8	1787.5
General selling & admin. expense	1388.1	1172.7	1057.1
R&D expense	38.3	41.7	38.7
Advertising	330.0	317.0	274.3
Depr. & amort.	131.7	111.4	109.0
Operating profit	467.2	356.0	308.4
Interest expense (net)	32.9	36.7	44.8
Loss from redeployments	1.1	2.6	71.1
Earnings before tax	433.2	316.7	192.5
Income taxes	211.2	137.5	78.8
Net Income	$222.0	$179.2	$113.7
Dividends	110.8	100.9	100.4
Earnings per share	$2.50	$2.01	$1.27
Selected data:			
Total assets	$2280.4	$2086.2	$2662.6
Net property & equip.	1249.5	1084.9	956.0
Current assets	865.9	811.9	1286.6
Capital expenditures*	329.1	244.9	209.7
Current debt	923.0	772.6	1057.2
Long-term debt	285.5	458.3	449.5
Stockholders equity	730.4	682.5	1023.3
Retained earnings	924.1	812.9	1201.7
Number of employees	65,619	62,056	63,162

* Estimated 1988 expenditures = $375 million, primarily from internally generated funds.
Source: Annual Report, 1987, General Mills.

the first such decline in 22 years. As part of this restructuring plan the firm was to divest operations representing over one-quarter of total corporate sales and year-end assets. These divestitures were completed during 1985 and 1986 and involved 26 individual companies or divisions.

The most complex set of these divestitures involved the formation of two new companies whose stock was distributed to existing General Mills's shareholders in November 1985. The firm's Izod-LaCoste (Alligator brand clothing) and Ship n' Shore (women's clothing) units were combined to form Crystal Brands, Inc. The Parker and Kenner toy units were combined with a number of other consumer units to form Kenner Parker Toys, Inc. (This new firm was

EXHIBIT 2   General Mills Statement of Changes in Financial Condition

	Millions of Dollars For Fiscal Years ending May 31		
	1987	1986	1985
Cash provided: Operations	$414.2	$351.3	$64.3
Earn.: Continuing oper.	222.0	179.2	113.7
Deprec. and amort.	131.7	111.4	109.0
Other cash: Cont'g oper.*	89.2	172.1	(69.5)
Cash: Discont. oper.	(28.7)	(111.4)	(88.9)
Cash provided: Investments	($217.5)	$148.0	($188.9)
Purchase fixed assets	(329.1)	(244.9)	(209.7)
Proceeds: Dispositions	112.4	404.2	33.9
Other	(.8)	(11.3)	(13.1)
Cash: Dividends	($110.8)	($100.9)	($100.4)
Cash provided: Financing	($96.5)	($274.9)	$225.8
Reduce long-term debt	(176.5)	(144.5)	(103.2)
New debt	50.9	99.1	197.7
Current debt	(3.5)	(376.0)	129.6
Repurchase stock	(80.7)	0.0	(53.8)
Issue common stock	20.4	22.0	10.0
Tax leases	54.4	113.3	111.0
Change in treasury inv.	38.5	11.2	(65.5)
Total change in cash and short-term investments	($ 10.6)	$123.5	$ 0.8

* Includes changes in working capital, deferred taxes, and other items.
Source: Annual Report, 1987, General Mills.

subsequently acquired by Tonka for $633 million in 1987.) In the first few days after their spin-off the shares of both of these newly-formed companies fell below their respective book values. In spite of this fact it was generally believed that these units would prosper more on their own than as units of General Mills because the firm's "culture was ill-suited to the volatility of the toy and fashion industries." [3]

Other divestitures involved units in the firm's Restaurant and Specialty Retailing segments. Three small restaurant chains—Casa Gallardo, Darryl's, and The Good Earth—were sold. These units had combined sales of $152 million and operating profits of $5.5 million in fiscal 1985. The last of the divestitures involved the sale of Wallpapers To Go, Leewards, and We Are Sportswear. Finally, in 1987 the Pennsylvania House/Kittinger furniture unit of the Specialty Retailing segment was sold. This unit constituted about 2 percent of the firm's total sales and net income in fiscal 1986.

Though the major motivation for the sale of these various units was ostensibly to permit the firm to focus its attention on its core businesses, it may have also involved a desire to protect the firm from a possible takeover. At least one security analyst estimated the total value of all the firm's various businesses, valued separately, to be $97 per share (breakup value) before the divestitures began.[4] This was in contrast to a stock price at the time of about $55 per share. In early 1988, after these divestitures were completed, the stock sold in a range between $40 and $60.

The Restructured Organization

The major restructuring of 1985 resulted in a more focused firm with three major business segments: Consumer Foods, Restaurants, and Specialty Retailing. The five-year (1985 – 1990) goals for real growth (above inflation) in these segments is detailed in Table 1 along with their contribution to corporate sales.[5]

These goals may be compared to expected real growth rates in packaged foods, restaurants, and apparel of 1 percent, 3 percent, and 2 percent, respectively. In announcing these goals chairman Atwater said he believed that "the secret to getting good returns and good growth is to get yourself in the right

TABLE 1

	% 1985 Corp. Sales	Target Real Growth/Year
Consumer Foods	65%	4.0%/year
Restaurants	25	12.0
Specialty Retailing	10	10.0
	100%	6.6%/year

[market] segments."[6] The firm hoped to achieve these objectives by installing a team of new, younger managers with more entrepreneurial attitudes.

Overall, General Mills's corporate objectives emphasize maintaining a balance between good growth and high returns to provide a superior total return for its shareholders. The firm's financial objectives require its return on equity and growth in earnings per share to fall in the highest quartile of major U.S. corporations. To achieve this performance the firm feels it needs to obtain an ROE of 19 percent and growth in EPS of 6 percent above inflation for the remainder of the 1980s. In addition, the firm wishes to maintain a strong balance sheet and a bond rating of at least "A".[7]

General Mills also seeks to achieve leadership positions in highly profitable market segments within its chosen industries by entering selected new markets with innovative products and by keeping established products competitively attractive. Approximately 60 percent of the firm's total sales are from products that are ranked number one in their market segments.

Specialty Retailing Segment

By the end of fiscal 1987, with the sale of the Pennsylvania House/Kittinger furniture unit, the Specialty Retailing segment of General Mills consisted of only two units: the Talbots chain of classic women's apparel and accessories and Eddie Bauer, a leader in outdoor apparel and related products. Both units compete in the $100 billion retail apparel industry. In 1987, these companies collectively operated 148 retail stores with 933,000 square feet of floor space and three catalog outlet facilities serving over 2.5 million customers and which accounted for approximately one-third of the total sales of the segment.

Eddie Bauer

This company is a leading marketer of down-insulated apparel, sold through retail stores and a retail catalog. In fiscal 1985, Eddie Bauer reported sales growth of 19 percent, opened nine new stores (bringing the total to 39), but suffered an earnings loss resulting from an unsuccessful change in its merchandise mix. In 1985, the unit also mailed 25,000,000 catalogs in ten mailings which generated $57 million in catalog revenues, representing 55 percent of the total catalog sales of the Specialty Retailing segment in that year. As a result of this poor earnings performance, the unit narrowed its product lines, focusing primarily on outdoor products, with a greater emphasis on leisure apparel. In 1986, the unit reported a 15 percent gain in both catalog and retail sales and a return to profitability. During 1987, total sales grew by another 20 percent to slightly above $190 million, though catalog sales growth was still only 15 percent. The catalog customer base grew by 15 percent in 1986 and 20 percent in 1987. The unit exceeded performance objectives for the first time since it was acquired in 1971. The ten stores added in fiscal 1988 were the first since the 1985 expansion and brought the total to 49 stores.

During 1986 and 1987, Eddie Bauer's catalog merchandise distribution center was relocated in Columbus, Ohio (from Seattle) to improve customer service, speed order fulfillment, reduce parcel shipment fees, and increase capacity. Concurrently, a new information system was completed to improve service and responsiveness. These advances were expected to improve performance by lowering costs 20 percent in fiscal 1988. A new retail distribution center was planned for Columbus to support future store expansion plans which would double the number of stores to about 100 by the end of fiscal 1990. The unit introduced a children's apparel line in several stores and was also aggressively seeking to increase the number of catalog customers.

Talbots

By the end of fiscal 1987, the Talbots line of classic women's apparel was sold through 109 retail stores in 24 states and the District of Columbia, and through the firm's catalog. Talbots was originally concentrated in the New England states and was known for outstanding customer service and quality. By 1987, the Talbots private brand of exclusive merchandise accounted for 60 percent of its sales. The firm believed that the maturing population, the increase in the number of working women, and the growth in disposable income were all factors which would promote continued growth in this highly successful company.

In 1985, Talbots reported a record sales level of $144 million, a 44 percent increase from the previous year. These sales were achieved by a combination of record catalog sales of $47 million at an average of $100 per order (an average sales increase of 10.5 percent in its 39 established stores) and the opening of 20 new stores during the year. Average sales per square foot of selling area in the retail stores reached $550 (rising to $600 by the end of fiscal 1987). During the year the catalog and retail operations were placed under separate managements to improve the efficiency of each.

In 1986, sales at Talbots grew by 55 percent to almost $225 million, while operating earnings more than doubled. The unit's established stores posted 6 percent sales growth. Further, 25 new stores were opened and mail order sales rose over 50 percent, as catalog circulation increased over 40 percent to over 60,000,000, distributed through 20 mailings. A "Red Line" telephone system was installed in each retail store to connect customers directly with catalog sales for immediate access to catalog merchandise inventory information.

By the end of fiscal 1987, sales of the Talbots unit had almost reached $300 million from the combined effects of an 8 percent rise in the sales in established stores, the opening of another 25 stores, and continued gains of 18 percent in catalog sales. Plans were made to double the number of retail outlets, to about 220, by the end of 1990. Catalog mailings were increased through the use of eight major catalogs and fourteen smaller, focused catalogs aimed at groups such as working women. The firm's active buyer list increased over 35 percent. Direct marketing order fulfillment had increased from 9000 to 18,000 units per day since 1985. During 1987, Talbots had begun using a national advertising campaign to stimulate sales. A new distribution center was under construction, with an expected completion date in 1988.

Restaurant Segment

By the end of fiscal 1987, this segment encompassed four restaurant chains with a total of 613 company-owned units and 19 Japanese joint venture units. Table 2 illustrates the unit growth in this segment since 1984.

The restaurant segment competes in an industry which reached $112 billion in sales in 1985. During the 1980–1985 period this industry experienced 3.4 percent annual real sales growth and was expected to achieve 3 percent real growth per year for the remainder of the decade. By 1987, restaurant industry sales had reached $153 billion. This market for away-from-home eating accounted for 31 percent of all consumer food purchases and had a faster rate of growth than the market for food eaten at home. In addition to an emphasis on unit expansion, the restaurant segment of General Mills consolidated its administrative staff and functions, resulting in a 45% decrease in the average number of employees per restaurant over the past five years.

Red Lobster

When General Mills acquired Red Lobster in 1970, the chain consisted of only three units. By the end of fiscal 1985, the chain had grown to 375 units in 35 states and two foreign countries (Canada and Japan). Total domestic sales exceeded $825 million. For the ten years prior to 1986, Red Lobster's annual compound sales growth and operating profit growth had averaged 26 and 20 percent, respectively. By 1985, the chain accounted for a 13 percent share of the away-from-home seafood market and was the only national seafood dinner

TABLE 2

| | Units at End of Fiscal Years | | | | |
	1984	*1985*	*1986*	*1987*	*1988 (planned)*
Red Lobster (USA)	367	370	389	392	412
RL (Canada)	1	2	9	40	40
RL (Japan)	3	3	9	19	31
Olive Garden	4	4	14	52	92
York's	129	129	114	113	113
Leeann Chin	—	—	8	16	16
Total company-owned	501	505	534	613	673
Joint venture	3	3	9	19	31

Source: Annual Reports, 1985–1987, General Mills

EXHIBIT 3   General Mills Financial Summary by Operating Segments

Continuing Business Segments Owned in 1987*

Millions of Dollars for Fiscal Years

	Consum. Foods	Restaurants	Specl. Retail	Corp. Items	Total
Sales					
1987	$3449.9	$1249.1	$490.3	$ 0.0	$5189.3
1986	3061.3	1051.0	383.6	0.0	4495.9
1985	2771.3	1140.1	294.8	0.0	4206.2
Operating profit before asset redeployments					
1987	$ 368.6	$ 94.3	$ 31.0	($ 59.6)	$ 434.3
1986	286.1	80.8	16.5	(64.1)	319.3
1985	249.4	85.2	(13.0)	(58.0)	263.6
Operating profit after asset redeployments					
1987	$ 369.5	$ 92.5	$ 30.7	($ 59.5)	$ 433.2
1986	284.2	84.8	11.6	(63.9)	316.7
1985	245.3	45.9	(40.7)	(58.0)	192.5
Identifiable assets					
1987	$1211.7	$ 594.0	$177.8	$ 296.5	$2280.4
1986	1091.8	467.8	128.2	398.4	2086.2
1985	1008.7	424.6	204.9	1024.4	2662.6
Depreciation					
1987	$ 78.9	$ 39.4	$ 9.0	$ 1.4	$ 128.7
1986	69.2	32.7	7.2	0.7	109.8
1985	60.9	37.5	6.3	1.7	106.4
Capital spending					
1987	$ 151.5	$ 145.3	$ 30.1	$ 2.2	$ 329.1
1986	153.6	74.0	13.7	3.6	244.9
1985	103.9	40.5	27.0	39.0	209.7

* Restaurant Segment data for 1985 includes $152 million in sales and $5.5 million in operating profits for the three restaurant chains subsequently sold. The Specialty Retailing segment data for 1985 includes $13 million in sales and an operating earnings loss for a unit subsequently sold.

Source: Annual Reports, 1985 and 1987, General Mills.

chain. Pillsbury, a major General Mills rival, refers to Red Lobster as the "Goliath" of the industry and will target its own new seafood chain to serve a different, more upscale market segment.[8]

During fiscal 1986, Red Lobster USA sales grew to over $850 million, with total domestic sales exceeding $975 million in 1987. Average annual domestic unit sales for the chain were almost $2.5 million in 1987. During the mid-1980s Red Lobster began a remodeling program to create a more casual atmosphere, which included a more contemporary decor, mesquite grills, new outdoor signs, and a new menu. By October 1987, all unit remodeling was completed.

The Canadian Red Lobster chain is expanding primarily through the conversion of Ponderosa restaurants acquired in 1985. In Japan, Red Lobster operates a joint venture with Jusco, a leading Japanese retailer. Television advertising in Tokyo was initiated in 1987 with good results. These international Red Lobster units are treated as foreign investments in the firm's financial statements. Thus, the sales and operating profits of these units have been excluded from the segment results in Exhibit 3.

Olive Garden

The Olive Garden Chain features a casual, cafe-style atmosphere with a wide selection of moderately-priced Italian food. By 1986, the chain had achieved annual sales exceeding $2 million per unit. This grew to over $2.5 million per unit by 1987. This chain is in an expansion phase, with 120 new units planned for fiscal 1988–1990.

York's/York's Choices

York is a budget family steak house chain that has been undergoing a change in format since 1985 to reposition the individual units as high-quality, self-service mall restaurants. These new units are called York's Choices and offer an expanded menu, with lighter items such as deli sandwiches, fried vegetables, and broiled chicken. By the end of 1987, over half of the entrees sold in the York's Choices units were non-beef items.

Leeann Chin

This Minneapolis-based entry into Chinese cuisine was acquired in late 1985, and was being tested as either a buffet-style restaurant (4 units) or a carryout unit (12), or both. In 1987, the Leeann Chin concept was expanded to the Chicago market, where it is not performing as expected.

Consumer Foods Segment

This unit serves a market which had total sales of over $260 billion in 1985, and volume (real) growth of 1 percent per year during the first half of the 1980s. In

EXHIBIT 4   General Mills

Selected Financial Results

Millions of Dollars for Fiscal Years 1977–1987

Year	Sales	C.O.S.	R & D	Advert.	Deprec. & Amort.	E.B.T.	Net Income
1987	$5189.3	$2834.0	$38.3	$330.0	$131.7	$433.2	$222.0
1986[1]	4586.6	2563.9	41.7	317.0	113.1	326.6	183.5
1985	4285.2	2474.8	38.7	274.3	110.4	195.9	(72.9)
1984[2]	5600.8	3165.9	63.5	349.6	133.1	398.7	233.4
1983	5550.8	3123.3	60.6	336.2	127.5	409.7	245.1
1982	5312.1	3081.6	53.8	284.9	113.2	406.7	225.5
1981	4852.4	2936.9	45.4	222.0	99.5	374.4	196.6
1980	4170.3	2578.5	44.4	213.1	81.1	316.6	170.0
1979	3745.0	2347.7	37.3	188.9	73.3	263.9	147.0
1978	3243.0	2026.1	30.5	170.5	58.6	245.2	135.8
1977[3]	2909.4	1797.5	29.9	145.6	48.1	229.2	117.0

Year	Total Assets	L.T. Debt	S.H. Equity	Capital Expend.	Div'ds	E.P.S.	Aver. Price/ Share
1987	$2280.4	$285.5	$ 730.4	$329.1	$110.8	$2.50	$46.50
1986[1]	2086.2	458.3	682.5	244.9	100.9	2.06	33.00
1985	2662.6	449.5	1023.3	209.7	100.4	(0.81)	27.00
1984[2]	2858.1	362.6	1224.6	282.4	96.0	2.49	24.62
1983	2943.9	464.0	1227.4	308.0	92.7	2.45	24.00
1982	2701.7	331.9	1232.2	287.3	82.3	2.23	18.62
1981	2301.3	348.6	1145.4	246.6	72.3	1.95	14.75
1980	2012.4	377.5	1020.7	196.5	64.4	1.68	11.75
1979	1835.2	384.8	916.2	154.1	56.1	1.46	14.50
1978	1612.7	259.9	815.1	140.5	48.2	1.36	14.50
1977[3]	1447.3	276.1	724.9	117.1	39.1	1.18	15.37

[1] Discontinued furniture operations.
[2] Discontinued toy, fashion, and other operations.
[3] Discontinued chemical operations.

Stock prices and earnings per share are in dollars and adjusted to reflect stock splits prior to 1987.

Source: Annual Report, 1987, General Mills.

contrast, the Consumer Foods segment of General Mills experienced 3.2 percent annual volume growth for the same period. By 1987, the size of this market had increased to $290 billion. New products introduced by General Mills since 1980 accounted for almost 25 percent of their domestic packaged food volume. The average market share for companies or divisions within the Consumer Foods segment in established markets is over 27 percent.

Though sales from Consumer Foods increased during fiscal 1985, profits declined. Increased marketing expenditures, including a 20 percent increase in media expenses necessary to support both new and established products, was a major cause of the problem. However, programs underway to improve productivity are expected to provide savings of about $20 million for the remainder of the 1980s. General Mills's financial objectives for this segment include real profit growth of at least 4 percent annually. Its sales growth objectives are to be achieved by a combination of internal development and external acquisition. Another objective is to become the low-cost producer for consumer food products. The firm believes its success will depend on its ability to interpret demographic and lifestyle trends correctly so it may continue to develop successful new products. The firm anticipates continued consumer support for product quality, convenience, and nutrition.

Cereals

The breakfast cereal unit is General Mills's largest single business. The ready-to-eat cereal industry experienced average annual growth of 12 percent in dollar sales and 1.5 percent in real volume during the 1980–1985 period. At the same time, General Mills's cereal sales grew 13 and 3 percent, respectively. From 1986–1987 domestic Big G cereal sales grew from approximately $900 million to $1,015 million. Kellogg, General Mills, General Foods (Post), Ralston Purina, and Quaker Oats jointly control 80 percent of the cereal market. Recent cereal market trends are summarized in Table 3.

Hot cereals are experiencing revived demand, with children under 5 and adults over 65 being the chief consumers. Though the population under 5 is growing at only a 0.5 percent annual rate, the over 65 group is growing at an annual rate of 2.0 percent. Innovations such as convenient packaging in single servings, new flavors, and microwave cooking have attracted more adults to hot

TABLE 3   U.S. Cereal Consumption and Shipments

	1985	1986	1987
Per Capita Consumption (in pounds per person)	14.5	14.9	15.3
Ready-to-eat	11.0	11.3	11.7
Hot cereal	3.5	3.5	3.6
Total dollar shipments	$4.38 bil	$4.82 bil	$5.34 bil
Ready-to-eat	3.91	4.32	4.79
Hot cereal	.47	.50	.55

Source: 1988 U.S. Industrial Outlook, Department of Commerce.

cereals. The market for hot cereals continues to be dominated by the traditional leader, Quaker Oats, with a two-thirds share of the market. General Mills successfully entered this market in 1987.

Presweetened cereal demand has been under pressure from regulatory attitudes towards advertising to children and from increasing consumer health consciousness. The 5–14 age group, to which such cereals have their primary appeal, is growing at a 1.6 percent annual rate. However, the adult cereal market segment is the fastest growing market for ready-to-eat cereals. Convenience and nutrition are increasingly important to this age group, who have shown a preference for bran, fiber, multigrain, and vitamin-enriched cereals. The introduction of these new adult cereals is frequently accompanied by heavy advertising expenditures.

The strategy of the Big G cereal unit is to increase its penetration of the adult cereal market. Presently the unit has a below-average share of this market segment in which it rates at about 70 percent of the industry average. The unit intends to build on its existing strength in the children's segment where its share is 140 percent of the average and the all-family segment where it holds an average position. To accomplish this the unit has increased its advertising, reformulated and repackaged its products to sustain older brands, and increased its efforts to develop new products. Seven of the unit's top fifteen brands are over 20 years old. However, as of 1987, the unit has four cereal brands that are among the top ten in dollar sales: Cheerios, Honey-Nut Cheerios, Lucky Charms, and Total.

Flour and Mix Products

This product category includes a variety of baking products and main meal and side dish mixes, such as Hamburger Helper. The total market for retail flour, baking products, and mixes was roughly $2 billion in 1987, having experienced volume declines of 5 and 10 percent in 1986 and 1985, respectively. Though the unit's markets are relatively mature overall, certain segments are experiencing growth arising from increasing demand for high quality convenience foods. Several trends contribute to this demand growth. The primary stimulus for new product development is the microwave oven. Microwave oven penetration has increased from 10 percent of all households in 1976 to 60 percent in 1987 and is expected to reach 75 percent by the early 1990s. Further, microwave ovens are now found in about 50 percent of all workplaces. Another factor contributing to the demand for convenience foods is the increase in the number of one- and two-person households, which is expected to reach 60 percent of all households by the early 1990s. The number of working women also contributes to the rising demand for convenience foods, as two-thirds of all women are expected to be in the workforce by the early 1990s.

The retail flour market is shrinking in both dollar sales (from $420 million in 1985 to $405 million in 1986) and volume, as home baking declines. General

Mills's Gold Medal flour—over 100 years old—has increased its share (34 percent) to almost twice that of its nearest rival. Similarly, Bisquick has increased its share of the related general purpose baking mix market. In contrast, the market for commercial bakery flour, representing about 70 percent of total flour milling volume, has experienced slight growth. In addition, prepared bakery goods shipments were up from $18.3 billion in 1985 to $19.4 billion in 1987. Although per capita consumption of bread, related products, and crackers was stable, cookie consumption had increased from 17.9 pounds per person in 1985 to 18.8 pounds in 1987. General Mills's bakery flour business, the Sperry Division, has recently recorded continuing volume increases and record earnings levels, while lowering the production cost of flour 10 percent. Altogether, the U.S. milling industry had sales of $3.8 billion in 1987.

The dehydrated potato market is also experiencing dollar sales and real volume declines ($220 million in 1985 versus $205 million in 1986). However, the Betty Crocker specialty potato product line is the market leader in this category and has experienced volume gains in recent years. Main meal and side dish mixes experienced double-digit volume growth in both 1985 and 1986. Betty Crocker add-meat dinner mixes, such as the Helper lines, are leaders in this $230 million segment. Several product introductions have been made in recent years and the unit's Suddenly Salad line introduced in 1987 has rapidly become a consumer hit.

The dessert mix product market is one in which General Mills maintains a strong leadership position with its many Betty Crocker products. The unit has over a 50 percent share in the ready-to-spread frosting market and an overall 40 percent share in dessert mixes. This market has been relatively stable with sales of $1.1 billion overall in 1987. Betty Crocker has experienced 7 percent annual volume growth in the last two years, compared to a market volume growth of 1 percent.

Snack Foods

Since 1985, General Mills has significantly increased its activity in snack foods. In the market for fruit snacks ($225 million in 1985 versus $280 in 1987) General Mill's product lines have experienced volume growth of nearly 30 percent annually as a result of new product offerings. They are the market leader in this segment. The $425 million granola snack market, which Quaker Oats leads with a 43 percent share, is in decline, although General Mills has maintained its profitability in this market. In the microwave popcorn market ($190 million in 1986 versus $285 million in 1987) General Mills's Pop Secret was second after only two years.

The frozen novelties market ($1.3 billion in 1986 versus $1.5 billion in 1987) has been characterized by high levels of promotional spending and new product introductions. General Mills acquired Vroman foods, a major producer of ice cream specialties and frozen snacks, in 1985 and has been expanding its distribution of these established products. Yoplait yogurt, acquired in 1977, achieved a 22.5 percent market share by 1985 in the $880 million domestic yogurt market. This market grew at an annual compound rate in excess of 30 percent per year in the 1980–1985 period, although volume growth is now slowing. By 1987, the market had expanded to $1.1 billion and General Mills was maintaining its number two position in the market.

Seafood and Other Products

General Mills has achieved the number two position in the frozen seafood market with its Gorton's product lines. The market ($810 million in 1985 versus $955 in 1986) experienced a decline in real volume for both 1985 and 1986, but rebounded in 1987. Gorton's experienced double-digit volume increases in this period. Recent introductions have been aimed at the microwave segment of this market.

In addition to its domestic retail consumer food and bakery flour businesses, General Mills's Consumer Foods segment includes two nonfood businesses and international food operations. O-Cel-O's line of commercial and household sponges and Pioneer Product's line of cake decorations and party supplies are doing well. The segment's international businesses include a French sandwich cookie and granola bar business, a Spanish frozen precooked entree unit, a Dutch snack food unit, and other operations in Canada, Latin America, and the Far East.

Strategic Segmentation

Within each of its three operating segments General Mills's management has defined three types of product-market units: core units, established units, and major growth units. Overall these three types of units are considered strategically as distinct categories, regardless of the segment housing them. Real growth goals and capital spending plans for each category appear in Table 4.

TABLE 4

	1986 % Total Corp. Sales	1985–1990 Target Real Growth/Year	1988–1990 Planned Investment
Core units	44%	7%/year	$ 800 million
Established units	37	3	200
Major growth units	19	15	600
	100%	7%/year	$1600 million*

* includes $1.3 billion in new fixed assets.
Source: Annual Reports, 1986, 1987, General Mills.

Core Units

General Mills's core unit category is composed of one major company or division from each operating segment: Consumer Foods's Big G cereals, Restaurants's Red Lobster USA chain, and Specialty Retailing's Talbots chain. The objectives for the three core businesses are presented in Table 5. Management describes the core category and its past and planned performance as follows:

> These businesses provide both high returns and good growth, with large reinvestment opportunities. They each have a consumer franchise that is stronger than industry standards. Their size and profit contribution are substantial relative to their industry segment within General Mills.

Established Units

General Mills's established businesses include Betty Crocker desserts, Bisquick baking mix, Gold Medal flour, Helper dinner mixes, international foods, York's restaurants, and other units. According to the 1986 annual report the primary objective for each of these units in the established category is to increase market share by ". . . developing distinctive product line extensions and by finding opportunities for innovation, establishing effective cost reduction programs, and improving overall productivity." With their strong returns these businesses are expected to generate excess cash to support growth opportunities throughout the firm.

Major Growth Units

The major growth units in General Mills include businesses positioned to provide significant opportunities for future expansion. These include Yoplait yogurt, fruit snacks, Gorton's frozen seafood, Red Lobster International (as opposed to the domestic operation), the Olive Garden restaurants, Leeann Chin's restaurants, and other new food categories under development.

TABLE 5

	1986 % Total Corp. Sales	1985–1990 Target Real Growth/Year	Compound Sales Growth/Year Last Ten Years
Big G cereals	20%	6.0%/year	11%/year*
Red Lobster (USA)	19	7.0	18**
Talbots	5	15.0	33
	44%	7.5%/year	

* 1980–86 market growth = 11.8%/yr. vs. Big G, 13.7%/year.

** 1980–86 sales growth 50% above industry average.

Notes and References

[1] F. Schwadel and R. Gibson. "General Mills is Putting Up for Sale Talbots, Eddie Bauer Clothing Chains." *Wall Street Journal,* January 8, 1988, p. 4.

[2] Annual Report, 1985, General Mills.

[3] P. Houston and M. Pitzer. "Can the General Mills Babies Make It on Their Own?" *Business Week,* November 18, 1985, pp. 46–47.

[4] P. Houston and R. Aikman. "General Mills Still Needs Its Wheaties." *Business Week,* December 23, 1985, pp. 77–80.

[5] Annual Report, 1985, General Mills.

[6] P. Houston and R. Aikman, *op. cit.*

[7] Annual Reports, 1985–1987, General Mills.

[8] P. Houston and R. Aikman, *op. cit.*

In addition to these sources industry forecasts were obtained from the *1988 U.S. Industrial Outlook.*

Catalog retailing information was also obtained for 1985 from *Inside the Leading Mail-Order Houses,* 3rd edition. Colorado Springs: Maxwell Sroge, 1987.

Discussion Questions

1. Develop a table showing dollar catalog sales, dollar retail store sales, number of retail stores, number of catalog customers, average sales per store, and average sales per catalog customer for both the Talbots and Eddie Bauer chains from 1985–1987. What trends are apparent?

2. Develop a table showing dollar sales, number of units, and average sales per unit for the Red Lobster USA and the Olive Garden restaurant units. What trends are apparent? What does this imply for the two remaining domestic chains?

3. For each major business/division in General Mills identify the following: leadership position/share, recent real sales growth, relative size of the business, recent real market growth, and market size. Construct a growth-share portfolio matrix. What inferences can you make about General Mills's portfolio mix and the performance results they might expect?

4. Compare recent performance with objectives for each of the three operating segments and for the firm as a whole.

5. Consider General Mills's definitions and objectives for its core, established, and major growth categories. What role in the portfolio would you expect businesses in each of these categories to have? Do the units assigned to each of these categories match the expectations one would conclude from their position in the growth-share matrix?

6. What effect would the divestiture of the Specialty Retailing segment have on the firm's portfolio, performance, planned capital spending, and growth objectives?

FOUR

LEADING AND MOTIVATING THE ENTERPRISE

This part of the book presents some major concepts of individual and organizational behavior. It also describes some of the tools and techniques that modern managers use to influence both kinds of behavior. The chapters in this part of the book follow a natural sequence of subjects, starting with the study of interpersonal and organizational communication progressing to a consideration of motivation, group behavior at work, and culminating with an examination of managerial leadership.

Chapter 11 addresses the subject of managerial communication. Communication is vital to the leading and influencing process because unless people understand what is being communicated, they are unlikely to act in the desired manner. In this chapter, interpersonal and organizational communication processes are described in depth. Barriers to both types of communication are then identified and described and ways of dealing with these barriers are presented.

The focus in Chapter 12 is on motivation at work. In this chapter, you will find out how motivation works and become familiar with some of the most important content and process theories of motivation. These theories are extremely useful in explaining why people act as they do. Attention will also be directed to the effect of money and value on employee motivation.

Chapter 13 examines group behavior in organizations. It describes formal, informal, and combination groups and explains why people join groups. Consideration is also given to identifying and describing the most meaningful characteristics of groups, comparing and contrasting the most common types of power within groups, and discussing group dynamics in action.

Managerial leadership is discussed in Chapter 14. The chapter focuses on identifying and describing leadership styles and explaining some of the latest research in the field. Particular attention is given to the contingency and path-goal theories of leadership, the practical value of the leader-follower continuum, and the situational theory of leadership.

When you have finished studying the material in this part of the book, you will have a sound understanding of the way managers lead and influence their people.

11

Managerial Communication

OBJECTIVES

The success of every enterprise is influenced by the manner and effectiveness of organizational communication. Unless the personnel understand what they are supposed to do and the parameters within which goals are to be attained, overall efficiency and effectiveness suffer. This chapter examines the ways in which managerial communication works and the ways it can be improved. It explores intrapersonal, interpersonal, and organizational communication. When you have finished reading this chapter, you will be able to:

1. Define the term communication and describe how it works.
2. Explain the interpersonal communication process and the ways in which self, the self-concept, and intrapersonal variables influence this process.
3. Identify and describe five of the major barriers to effective interpersonal communication.
4. Discuss ways of overcoming these interpersonal organizational barriers.
5. Identify and describe five of the major barriers to effective organizational communication.
6. Discuss various ways of overcoming these organizational communication barriers.

THE BASICS OF COMMUNICATION

Communication involves the transfer of meanings

Communication is the process of transferring meanings from sender to receiver. This process is used when there is something that the sender wants the receiver to know, understand, or act upon. Given this definition, there are three important aspects of communication: (1) the sender must communicate accurately and completely; (2) the receiver must understand the message; and (3) the receiver must be willing to act on it in an appropriate manner. In this chapter, all three of these aspects of communication will be examined. We will begin by explaining how meanings are actually transferred through what is known as the communication process.

The Communication Process

The communication process has three basic elements: a source, a message, and a receiver. The message is conveyed to and interpreted by the receiver through encoding and decoding. (See Figure 11-1.)

How it works

The source is the individual or party that wants to send a communiqué or message. For some particular reason, the source wants the receiver to understand something.

The source conveys the meaning to the receiver by using the **encoding process.** In other words, the source must put the message into a form that can be understood by the receiver.

The message is the sign or symbol used to carry the meaning. Typical examples include a written letter, a telephone call, or a telegram.

The **decoding process** is carried out by the receiver, who interprets the message to determine what is being communicated. When the decoding process begins, the communication is out of the hands of the source and entirely in the hands of the receiver.

The receiver is the person or group to whom the message is communicated. If the receiver is on the same wave length as the sender, the decoding process will be accurate enough to convey the source's meaning. If not, the message will be misunderstood or not understood at all.

Communication in Action

When communication breaks down, it is usually because the receiver's understanding of the message is not the same as the sender's meaning. This problem is often overcome through the process of feedback, in which the receiver sends

FIGURE 11-1
The Communication Process

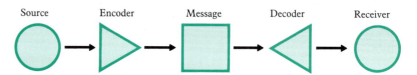

Source   Encoder   Message   Decoder   Receiver

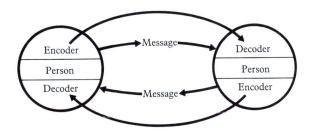

a message back to the sender. ("Is this what you meant?" "When do you need this done?" "Am I to start immediately or wait until I receive the materials you are sending?") The sender then clarifies the message through additional information. As a result, communication in action can be viewed as a series of messages flowing between the source and the receiver.[1]

When viewed in this way, communication in action can be illustrated as in Figure 11-2. Notice that the initial message sender (the encoder) is located on the left and the initial message receiver (the decoder) is located on the right. If the latter asks for further clarification of the message, these roles are reversed. The encoder becomes the decoder/interpreter and the decoder/interpreter becomes the encoder.

Of course, it is not always the receiver who has to initiate the feedback. Sometimes the sender realizes that the message is not clear or that the receiver is having trouble following what is going on. In this case, the sender may well encourage feedback by asking pertinent questions ("Would you mind telling me what you heard me say?" "I can see by the look on your face that I am confusing you; exactly what seems to be unclear?" "How are you going to carry out the order I just gave you?") As a result, feedback is promoted and the communiqué has an improved chance of being effective.

*Feedback is
essential*

Types of Communication

Managerial communication occurs in three forms. In **intrapersonal communication**, managers receive, process, and transmit information to themselves. This concept is important because unless we know how communication occurs within people, it is difficult to understand how it occurs between people. In **interpersonal communication**, meanings are transmitted directly between two or more people, on a person-to-person basis. Quite often, those involved can see each other, although, as in the case of telephone conversations, this is not always so. In **organizational communication**, finally, information is transferred formally throughout the organization, as memos, reports, and directives are sent up and down the hierarchical chain. This form of communication

---

[1] John L. DiGaetani, "A Systems Solution to Communication Problems," *Business Horizons* (September–October 1983):57–61.

is the least personal, but in large enterprises it is a vital and efficient means of conveying information throughout the structure.

INTRAPERSONAL COMMUNICATION

In studying intrapersonal communication, we have to look at the manager's self and self-concept, the intrapersonal communication process itself, and intrapersonal variables that affect this process.

The Self

Everyone has many selves

The study of intrapersonal communication begins with knowing oneself. Everyone has many selves. One is the *physical self,* which is the way the person looks (tall, short, fat, skinny). A second is the *emotional self,* which consists of conscious feelings (happiness, sadness, anger) and is accompanied by physiological changes (rapid heartbeat, tensed muscles, raised blood sugar level). A third self is characterized by *habits* and *repetitious behavior* of which the individual may be totally unaware (tapping one's fingers, scratching one's ear, biting one's lower lip). A fourth is the *public and private self,* which is illustrated in the Johari Window[2] shown in Figure 11-3.

This figure presents the public and private selves in terms of open and closed communication relationships. There are four sections to the window. The open section represents the things the manager knows about himself or herself and is willing to share with others. The hidden section represents what the individual is aware of but not willing to share. The blind section represents information of which the individual is unaware but which is known to others. The unknown section represents what is not known either to the manager or to others. Figure 11-3 presents four windows of equal size. In reality, however, these sizes require different proportions depending on the specific relationship under analysis. An open relationship with one's spouse would result in a very large open window and a quite small hidden window. Conversely, a business relationship with a subordinate whom one did not trust very much would result in a small open window and a large hidden one. Managers adjust their personal and private selves to fit the situation.

The Self-Concept

The self-concept affects intrapersonal communication

How managers feel about themselves, this feeling known as their **self-concept**, has a strong effect on their intrapersonal communication. A self-concept is developed through interactions with people and the environment. Positive past experiences encourage managers to act in certain ways; negative past experi-

---

[2] Joseph Luft, *Of Human Interaction* (Palo Alto, CA: Natural Press Books, 1969).

FIGURE 11-3
The Johari Window

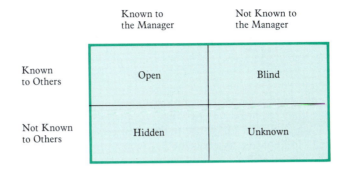

ences discourage them from acting in other ways. The result is a shaping or molding of the manager's concept of himself or herself. (See "Management in Practice: Motivating Yourself Into the Total Winner.")

Reference groups, with whom managers identify, also help establish their attitudes and values and affect the intrapersonal communication process. So, too, do the roles the manager plays in life. Some of these roles are ascribed in that the manager is expected to act in a given way. **Ascribed roles** are based heavily on sex, age, kinship, and general place in society. We see these roles reinforced when we hear people saying to others: "Act your age; you're too big to cry." "Older brothers are leaders, so take charge out there." "Women have a real chance to make something of themselves, so get on with it." **Achieved roles** are those earned through accomplishment. Depending on what a person does with life, he or she will end up with certain roles to play. An organization president, a chief financial officer, a district manager, and a union steward all have roles based on their achieved position. These roles are typically both business and social related.

The Process

Intrapersonal communication is the foundation on which interpersonal communication is based. This process is diagrammed in Figure 11-4. As the figure shows, every individual receives external stimuli that affect his or her thought and communication processes. These stimuli are of two types: overt and covert. *Overt stimuli* are received on the conscious level; *covert stimuli* are received on the subconscious level. When an individual is subjected to overt stimuli, he or she is aware of the messages being received. When subjected to covert stimuli, the individual may be unaware of the messages. A typical example occurs when one hears someone say something but it does not "register" until later on. The message was, at least originally, a covert one.

The process by which the body receives stimuli is called reception. Keep in mind, however, that the body does not accept all stimuli. A process called *Intrapersonal communication in action* **selective perception** occurs in which only certain stimuli are accepted — the ones that are most important to the individual. For example, the manager who is concerned with budget data will pick up anything related to these data

MANAGEMENT IN PRACTICE

Motivating Yourself Into the Total Winner

Dr. Denis Waitley, a noted psychologist and motivational speaker, has developed ten qualities that he believes are critical in the motivation of individuals. As a consultant to the NASA astronauts, as well as working with returning veterans from Vietnam, Waitley has developed these attitude and action qualities that individuals can use to motivate themselves. Using these qualities, he believes that people can build themselves into "total winners." Here are the qualities.

ATTITUDE QUALITIES

Positive self-expectancy. The most readily identifiable quality of a total winner is an overall attitude of personal optimism and enthusiasm. Winners understand the psychosomatic relationship—psyche and some; mind and body—that the body expresses what the mind is concerned with.

Positive self-image. Winners are especially aware of the tremendous importance of their self-image—and of the role their imagination can play in the creation and upgrading of the self-image. They know the self-image acts as a subconscious life-governing device—that if in your self-image you can't possibly see yourself doing something, achieving something, you literally cannot do it.

Positive self-esteem. Winners have a deep-down feeling of their own worth. Winners are not outer-directed. Recognizing their uniqueness, they develop and maintain their own high standards. Though they recognize the universality of fear and anxiety, winners *don't give in* to these emotions.

Positive self-awareness. Winners know who they are, what they believe, the role in life they are presently filling, their great personal potential—and the future roles and goals which will mark fulfillment of that potential.

FIGURE 11-4
Intrapersonal
Communication
Process

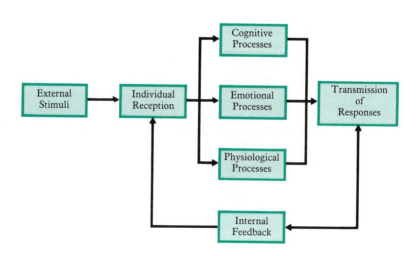

ACTION QUALITIES

Positive self-motivation. The positive self-motivation of total winners derives from two sources: (1) their self-expectant personal and world view, and (2) their awareness that, while fear and desire are among the greatest motivators, fear is destructive while desire leads to achievement, success, and happiness.

Positive self-direction. Winners in life have clearly-defined, constantly-referred-to, game plans and purposes. They know where they're going every day, every month, every year. Their objectives range all the way from lifetime goals to daily priorities.

Positive self-discipline. Positive self-discipline is the ability to *practice within*. Winners are masters of the art of simulation. Like astronauts, championship athletes, great stage performers, skilled surgeons, and truly professional executives and salesmen, they practice flawless technique in their minds over and over, again and again.

Positive self-dimension. Winners see their total person in such a full-formed perspective that they literally become part of the "big picture" of life—and it of them. They have learned to know themselves intimately. They have learned to see themselves through the eyes of others.

Positive self-projection. Winners practice positive self-projection. They project their best selves every day in the way they look, walk, talk, listen, and react. They specialize in truly effective communication, taking one hundred percent of the responsibility not only for communicating information to, but also for receiving information from every person they contact.

Source: Denis Waitley. *The Psychology of Winning.* Chicago: Nightingale–Conant Corporation.

from a particular report and will ignore anything not so related, judging it to be extraneous.

After receiving the stimuli, the manager processes the data, using three types of processes: cognitive, emotional, and physiological. *Cognitive processes* include the storage, retrieval, sorting, and assimilating of information. This logical thinking stage process makes heavy use of memory, recognition, recall, and analysis. *Emotional processes* are nonlogical responses to stimuli. Some of the variables that play a key role in these processes include beliefs, values, opinions, attitudes, and prejudices. *Physiological processes* are physical in nature. Some of the major variables include brain activity, blood pressure, heart rate, and body temperature. These variables affect the way the individual feels and acts, thus helping dictate both the interpretation of stimuli and the response to them.

In intrapersonal communication, the transmission process takes place through nerve impulses in the brain as the individual sends messages to himself or herself. When the brain reacts to these nerve impulses, the transmission is complete.

The messages or stimuli are then sent back to the person in the form of self-feedback. This feedback can be both external and internal. External self-feedback is the part of the message in which one hears oneself and corrects any mistakes. For example, a manager may talk to himself in trying to straighten out a problem. As he does so, he corrects or adjusts recommended solutions until, in his mind, he says, "That's it. That's how we'll solve the problem." Internal self-feedback is picked up through nerve endings or muscular movement. When a manager is reading a memo and suddenly flinches because of something in the directive, she can feel the muscle tension in her face. She is getting internal self-feedback regarding how she feels about what she is reading.

Intrapersonal Variables

How a manager interprets communications is a function of intrapersonal variables. These variables fall into three general categories: personal orientation, personality traits, and defense mechanisms.

Personal Orientation

A manager's personal orientation is a reflection of his or her values, attitudes, beliefs, opinions, and prejudices. These characteristics affect the way the person sees the world and responds to it. If a manager believes that more women should be promoted to higher-level positions, this belief will influence his or her evaluation of female workers. If a manager places a high value on hard work, this will affect his or her perception of other employees. A personal orientation dictates "where the manager is coming from" and influences the manager's approach to communication.[3]

Where the manager is coming from

Personality Traits

What kind of person the manager is

Personality traits also help determine how a manager communicates. Although there are many such traits, five of the most important are manipulation, dogmatism, tolerance for ambiguity, self-esteem, and maturity. Manipulative managers try to dominate or control others through the skillful use of verbal and nonverbal communications. Dogmatic managers are closed-minded and are typically unwilling to accept new ideas or opinions regardless of fact or logic. Managers who have a low degree of tolerance for ambiguity find it difficult to

---

[3] Benson Rosen and Thomas H. Jerdee, "Helping Your Managers Bridge the Generation Gap," *Training* (March 1985):42; and George E. L. Barbee, "Communicating with a Personal Touch," *Personnel Journal* (October 1989):38–45.

communicate in general, abstract, or nebulous terms; everything has to be spelled out clearly. Self-esteem helps determine personal confidence and often influences the way in which a person communicates with others. Maturity affects the manager's desire for such things as independence, approval, and affection; it therefore influences the way the person both transmits and interprets communiqués.[4]

Defense Mechanisms

How the manager deals with anxiety

When there is a conflict between one's inner psychological needs and the realities of the external world, anxiety results. If this anxiety is severe enough it can distort one's personal perception as well as one's view of the environment, bringing about a communication problem. To deal with this anxiety, people turn to the use of defense mechanisms. One of these is **rationalization**, which is an attempt to justify failures or inadequacies. Thus the person might say, "I would have gotten that promotion if they had judged the applicants on the basis of ability rather than past friendships." A second defense mechanism, **projection**, occurs when people ignore certain traits, motives, or behavior patterns in themselves and attribute them to others. The person says, "I can tell that Bob is still upset that I didn't get that promotion." A third is **reaction formation**, which involves dealing with "undesirable" behavior by taking just the opposite point of view. The manager who does not believe a college degree in business is very important but knows the company does, for example, may continually tell people, "We should never hire anyone who does not have a degree in business." Finally, **repression** is a defense mechanism that involves keeping down unpleasant or unacceptable feelings. The manager who really wants to tell off his or her boss but keeps these feelings well hidden is suffering from repression.

INTERPERSONAL COMMUNICATION

Interpersonal communication, the direct transmission of meanings between two or more persons, can be quite time consuming, especially if the manager eventually has to communicate the same message to a half dozen people. It is an extremely effective means of conveying information, however.

The interpersonal process can be diagrammed in the same basic way as the communication process was in Figure 11-1. Additionally we need to realize that

---

[4] J. Kevin Barge, Cal W. Downs, and Kenneth M. Johnson, "An Analysis of Effective and Ineffective Leader Conversation," *Management Communication Quarterly* (February 1989):357–86.

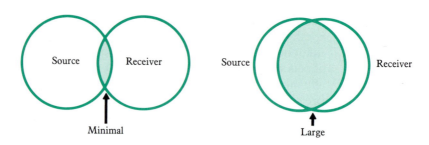

FIGURE 11-5
Degree of Message
Understanding

the source and the receiver must mutually understand one another. We can illustrate the idea by comparing two situations: one where the degree of understanding is minimal and the other where it is great. This comparison is made in Figure 11-5. Notice that the situation in the righthand diagram is more likely to produce effective results than is the situation in the lefthand diagram. Without considering the specifics of each situation, however, we cannot say how much message understanding is needed to produce the best results. We can only say a minimum amount is necessary in each situation. If it does not exist, communication breakdown will occur because of communication barriers.

Barriers to Interpersonal Communication

Barriers to interpersonal communication prevent the message from being understood in the way the sender intends. These barriers may be brought about by either the sender or the receiver, or they may be caused by environmental factors. Five of the major interpersonal communication barriers are perception, words, the source of the words, inconsistent behavior, and the environment.

Perception

People see things
differently

Perception is a person's view of reality. Personal values, education, and experience all influence individual perception. As a result, people often have different interpretations of the same situation. Consider the differences between the manager's perceptions and the subordinates in the following situation:

Situation 1
Manager said: "I need that report as soon as possible."

Manager meant: "I need that report as soon as you are done gathering those monthly sales figures."

Subordinate understood: "I'd better drop these monthly sales figures and get on that report right away."

Situation 2
Subordinate said: "If you need any help with that control plan, let me know."

Subordinate meant: "I'll be happy to look over a couple of sections of the plan and give you my input."

Manager understood: "If you need someone to rewrite or rework the plan, I'm available at any time."

Often, people see and hear what they want to. They interpret the communiqué based on what is in their own best interests, regardless of what was "actually" said.[5]

Words

Not everyone has the same meaning for the same word. Sometimes a word has a technical meaning.[6] For example, in the engineering world the word "burn" means to photocopy. Imagine an engineering manager's surprise if he tells a new secretary to burn the blueprints and finds out that the individual has literally done so.

Words can have different meanings

Words also take on meanings based on how they are used locally. For example, if today is Tuesday, the statement "We have a meeting next Thursday" would be interpreted differently by Californians and New Yorkers. To most Californians, the statement would mean there is a meeting in two days. For many New Yorkers the word "next" means next week, so they would think the meeting was going to be held in nine days. To get New Yorkers to come to a meeting in two days, the communication would have to say "this" Thursday.

Then, too, words sometimes cause confusion because people do not know their meaning. For example, what is meant by the phrase "biweekly meetings"? How often is "biweekly"? Most people know it means either twice a week or every other week, but which is it?

Finally, consider interpretive statements such as, "Do you have a minute?"; "I'll be with you shortly"; and "We need to impress this new candidate." In each case, the speaker probably has a very good idea of what he or she is talking about. The listener may not, however, because meanings are not in words, they are in the individuals who use them.

The Source

Who says something can be important

Sometimes what is said is not as important as who said it. This is particularly true when the receiver of the message has reason to believe that the sender is extremely knowledgeable, insightful, or trustworthy (or has the opposite characteristics). A typical example is provided by top managers who, when they are talking to other members of the management hierarchy, tend to be regarded as

---

[5] Sherron B. Ketton, "The Role of Communication in Managing Perceived Inequity," *Management Communication Quarterly,* (May 1989):536–43.

[6] Robert R. Max, "Wording It Correctly," *Training and Development Journal* (March 1985):50–51.

highly reliable. After all, they are part of the same team. On the other hand, when these top managers are discussing contract negotiations with the union, their statements may be regarded as inaccurate or misleading, especially if the negotiations are tough and the company feels it must hold the line on salary and benefits.

Analogous situations can be found throughout the organization. Individuals in departments or units where morale is high are more likely to believe communiqués from fellow workers merely because of their relationship to these employees. Conversely, when groups are fighting with each other it is common to hear each regarding the other's communiqués as self-serving, misleading, or just plain wrong.

Inconsistent Behavior

Inconsistency damages believability

How a person says something often influences the way in which the message is received. When the speaker acts disinterested or unconcerned, the listener often attributes little importance to the message. If the speaker communicates something while going out the door and ends with the statement, "This is really important," the listener is not likely to believe it. Really important information is conveyed in a more quiet, calm, serious setting. When the message content is inconsistent with the message environment, the subordinate discounts its importance accordingly. Finally, when people say one thing but do another, their communiqués are eventually treated as noncredible. For example, the manager who tells his people that work begins at 8:30 A.M. sharp while he continues to show up at 9:10 A.M. is unlikely to reduce employee tardiness with his communiqué. The manager who tells her people that they all have to help hold down expenses while she gets approval to attend a meeting in Hawaii in December is unlikely to get much support for her cost-cutting efforts. There is simply too much inconsistency between what these managers are saying and what they are doing.

The Environment

The physical setting is also important

Sometimes interpersonal communication fails because of noise or other environmental factors. If the listener cannot hear the speaker because too much activity is going on around them, communication breakdown is likely.

Environmental factors can also be more subtle, as when the setting is wrong. A manager who is talking to someone in the company cafeteria has to fight the never-ending interruptions by people who are dropping by to say hello or are waving from across the room. The same kinds of mental interruptions are also being encountered by the listener.

Finally, there is the environmental setting itself. The chairs in which the individuals are sitting, the colors in the room, and the location of the people (are they near each other or far apart?) all help convey nonverbal messages. These characteristics become part of the communication environment and can promote or hinder the reception of meanings.

Overcoming Interpersonal Communication Barriers

There are a number of ways to overcome interpersonal communication barriers. In large part, these methods are interdependent in that the use of one often involves the use of others. Nevertheless, for purposes of clarity we shall describe each individually. The following presents five of the most helpful approaches.[7]

Accuracy and Empathy

Accuracy is vital . . . Some communiqués fail because they are not conveyed accurately. Many examples of inaccuracy can be cited, some of which relate to written communication. When a manager is not confronting a subordinate on an interpersonal basis, the manager has to rely on message content to convey the desired meanings. To a large degree inaccuracy in written communications is related to perception. It can also be caused by other common written communication barriers, however, including poor sentence construction, improper grammar, lack of tact, and failure to plan the communiqué with the needs of the receiver in mind.[8]

One way to deal with problems like these is to use a written performance inventory like the one shown in Table 11-1. Notice that the problems involve qualities ranging from readability and correctness to appropriateness and thought. The inventory also emphasizes such behavioral factors as tact, diplomacy, motivational aspects, and persuasiveness.

as is empathy **Empathy** is the ability to see things from another person's point of view. When applied to communication, it means being able to look at a message from the receiver's standpoint and determine how this person will interpret the communiqué. To understand the receiver's standpoint, the manager must develop sensitivity. Perhaps the best way to develop empathy is by promoting two-way communication. As managers become more adept at this, their ability, figuratively speaking, to get into another person's shoes increases. Managers can also improve their ability to empathize by being able to read nonverbal communications.

Nonverbal Communication

Nonverbal communication incorporates a large range of factors, from body language to spatial relationships.[9] Body language relates to the way people sit, stand, and act in relation to others.[10] Spatial relationships relate to the

---

[7] See also Edward L. Levine, "Let's Talk: Tools for Spotting and Correcting Communication Problems," *Supervisory Management* (July 1980):25–37.

[8] John S. Fielden, "What Do You Mean You Don't Like My Style?" *Harvard Business Review* (May–June 1982):128–39.

[9] Lynn Renee Cohen, "Nonverbal (Mis)Communication," *Business Horizons* (January–February 1983):13–17.

[10] Ronald Zemke, ed., "Orchestrating Your Body Language," *Training* (January 1985):82.

TABLE 11-1   Written Performance Inventory

1. Readability

READER'S LEVEL
- ☐ Too specialized in approach
- ☐ Assumes too great a knowledge of subject
- ☐ So underestimates the reader that it belabors the obvious

SENTENCE CONSTRUCTION
- ☐ Unnecessarily long in difficult material
- ☐ Subject-verb-object word order too rarely used
- ☐ Choppy, overly simple style (in simple material)

PARAGRAPH CONSTRUCTION
- ☐ Lack of topic sentences
- ☐ Too many ideas in single paragraph
- ☐ Too long

FAMILIARITY OF WORDS
- ☐ Inappropriate jargon
- ☐ Pretentious language
- ☐ Unnecessarily abstract

READER DIRECTION
- ☐ Lacking of "framing" (i.e., failure to tell the reader about purpose and direction of forthcoming discussion)
- ☐ Inadequate transitions between paragraphs
- ☐ Absence of subconclusions to summarize reader's progress at end of divisions in the discussion

FOCUS
- ☐ Unclear as to subject of communication
- ☐ Unclear as to purpose of message

2. Correctness

MECHANICS
- ☐ Shaky grammar
- ☐ Faulty punctuation

FORMAT
- ☐ Careless appearance of documents
- ☐ Failure to use accepted company form

COHERENCE
- ☐ Sentences seem awkward owing to illogical and ungrammatical yoking of unrelated ideas.
- ☐ Failure to develop a logical progression of ideas through coherent, logically juxtaposed paragraphs

3. Appropriateness

A. UPWARD COMMUNICATIONS
TACT
- ☐ Failure to recognize differences in position between writer and receiver
- ☐ Impolitic tone—too brusk, argumentative, or insulting

SUPPORTING DETAIL
- ☐ Inadequate support for statements
- ☐ Too much undigested details for busy superior

OPINION
- ☐ Adequate research but too great an intrusion of opinions

- ☐ Too few facts (and too little research) to entitle drawing of conclusions
- ☐ Presence of unasked for but clearly implied recommendations

ATTITUDE
- ☐ Too obvious a desire to please superior
- ☐ Too defensive in face of authority
- ☐ Too fearful of superior to be able to do best work

B. DOWNWARD COMMUNICATIONS
DIPLOMACY
- ☐ Overbearing attitude toward subordinates
- ☐ Insulting and/or personal references
- ☐ Unmindfulness that messages are representative of management group or even of company

CLARIFICATION OF DESIRES
- ☐ Confused, vague instructions
- ☐ Superior is not sure of what is wanted
- ☐ Withholding of information necessary to job at hand

MOTIVATIONAL ASPECTS
- ☐ Orders of superior seem arbitrary
- ☐ Superior's communications are manipulative and seemingly insincere

4. Thought

PREPARATION
- ☐ Inadequate thought given to purpose of communication prior to its final completion
- ☐ Inadequate preparation or use of data known to be available

COMPETENCE
- ☐ Subject beyond intellectual capabilities of writer
- ☐ Subject beyond experience of writer

FIDELITY TO ASSIGNMENT
- ☐ Failure to stick to job assigned
- ☐ Too much made of routine assignment
- ☐ Too little made of assignment

ANALYSIS
- ☐ Superficial examination of data leading to unconscious overlooking of important pieces of evidence
- ☐ Failure to draw obvious conclusions from data presented
- ☐ Presentation of conclusions unjustified by evidence
- ☐ Failure to qualify tenuous assertions
- ☐ Failure to identify and justify assumptions used
- ☐ Bias, conscious or unconscious, which leads to distorted interpretation of data

PERSUASIVENESS
- ☐ Seems more convincing than facts warrant
- ☐ Seems less convincing than facts warrant
- ☐ Too obvious an attempt to sell ideas
- ☐ Lacks action-orientation and managerial viewpoint
- ☐ Too blunt an approach where subtlety and finesse called for

Source: John Fielden, an exhibit from "What Do You Mean I Can't Write?" *Harvard Business Review* (May–June 1964):147. Reprinted with permission of the Harvard Business Review. Copyright © 1964 by the President and Fellows of Harvard College; all rights reserved.

surroundings in which the communiqué takes place. If managers understand the impact of this type of communication, they can use it effectively.

BODY LANGUAGE   In **body language**, body movements are used to communicate ideas, interests, opinions, and objectives on a nonverbal basis. When two people meet for the first time, the way they shake hands says something. A soft handshake may be interpreted by the other person as a sign of weakness or an inability to take command. The same is true for the way people walk or stand. A fast, determined walk or an erect posture is often interpreted as a sign of a successful manager. Why? Because the individual seems to be saying, "I know where I'm going and I can see my way clear." He or she is coming across as believable and successful. Communiqués from such a manager are more likely to get the desired results.

A handshake is important (margin note)

Another important facet of body language is the eyes. Body language experts report that "our eyes (and face area around the eyes) are the most expressive and powerful parts of the body in terms of sending nonverbal messages."[11] Do not be fooled by the old adage that liars never look people in the eye. Actually, skilled liars have learned how to look right at their listener while telling their lies. On the other hand, changes in the eyes' pupil size may indicate whether a person is lying. Quite often when people lie they get emotional and this causes the size of their pupils to increase. Shifting of the eyes or blinking at a faster than normal rate also can indicate that a person is not being totally truthful. As the individual's stress level changes, the surface of the eyeball dries, causing increased eye movement. Still another thing to look for is "eye locks" between people during management meetings. Knowing who is looking at whom can help one understand the informal organization or the clique present in the meeting and figure out what different people are trying to do.

So are the eyes . . . (margin note)

Touching is another form of nonverbal communication. In addition to its use in shaking hands, touching is popularly used to convey orders and establish power relationships. Managers use it to let subordinates know who is in charge and to motivate them. For example, many managers put their hand on a subordinate's arm or shoulder when giving the person a directive. This touch creates a bond between them by which the manager says, "I'm counting on you to get this done right and I know you can do it. Now show me your stuff."

and touching . . . (margin note)

A physical attitude is another example of body language. It is a combination of gestures, postures, and face and hand signals. It is a composite of the way the individual acts when carrying out a task or completing an assignment. By studying this attitude, we get insights into the way the person goes about "selling" his or her ideas, objectives, and credibility. The manager uses body language as part of the strategy employed in swaying others to a given point of view. We need not confine our focus to managers exclusively, however. All organizational personnel use body language in communicating. Salespeople are an excellent example.

and physical attitude (margin note)

---

[11] Paul Preston, *Communication for Managers* (Englewood Cliffs, NJ: Prentice-Hall, 1979), 159.

FIGURE 11-6
Personal Space
Categories

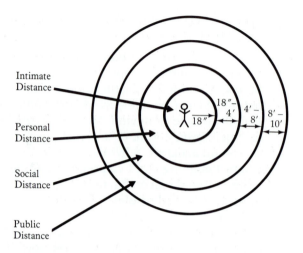

Intimate
Distance

Personal
Distance

Social
Distance

Public
Distance

. . . a good salesperson leans forward in an aggressive way when making a sales pitch; the prospect usually leans back. Also, a salesperson may use body language to spot certain facts about the prospective buyer. For example, sitting with arms folded is a traditional sign of resistance. When the prospect unlocks his arms and legs, he may be coming to the salesperson's side. Other traditional cues may be the prospect's uneasiness, displayed by juggling his foot or drumming his fingers, or doubt, displayed by holding his hands under his face.[12]

Space, Territory, and Status

Another nonverbal communication form is provided by space and territory. Where people stand in relation to others helps communicate a message. As seen in Figure 11-6, there are four principal zones of interaction in which interpersonal activities are conducted. The **intimate zone**, which extends to approximately an arm's length from a person, is the area in which sensitive communications are carried out. This zone is typically reserved for close relationships. If strangers enter the area, they usually feel uncomfortable and start to move away. The **personal zone** extends from arm's length to approximately four feet from the body. This zone is for relatives and good friends. The **social zone** extends approximately four to twelve feet from the body. This zone is the one in which we conduct most ordinary business and social activities. In offices, for example, most desks are wide enough to force people sitting on the opposite side to maintain this distance. The **public zone** extends approximately 12 to 25 feet from the body and is the area over which individuals exert little personal

The four principal zones of interaction

---

[12] Richard K. Allen, *Organizational Management Through Communication* (New York: Harper & Row, 1977), 164.

control. Activity in this area can often be ignored. When individuals are engaged in conversation groups eight to 10 feet apart, they often can block out activities going on around them and concentrate on the affairs within the more comfortable social and personal zones.

How managers fill their own territory, such as their office, also helps them communicate with people. For example, an office's size and furnishings tell us something about the person. When a subordinate enters a manager's office and sits in front of the desk, he or she is typically in the manager's social zone. The subordinate and the manager are functioning in a typical superior-subordinate relationship. If the manager comes out from behind the desk and sits opposite the subordinate, this action is designed to put the subordinate at ease. The manager and the subordinate are communicating within the manager's personal zone.[13]

Office size and furnishings convey status

A related factor is such things as wall-to-wall carpeting, a wooden desk, plush furniture, and windows. All indicate executive status, which helps influence communication.

Positive Persuasion and Negotiation

Sometimes an interpersonal communiqué fails because the manager fails to use positive persuasion or negotiation or both. This is unfortunate because every time a manager communicates, he or she is actually attempting to persuade the receiver to accept a given point of view. Of course, sometimes the persuasive attempt is more obvious than other times. For example, consider the following dialogue:

Manager: Bob, I've been waiting for the right time to send you into the field. I think this is that time and I'd like you to take that new position we have open in Buffalo.

Subordinate: Why do I have to take a sales position in the field? Why can't I stay here at headquarters and continue working in marketing research?

Manager: The answer is simple. Every single person in this company who has succeeded in the marketing area has had field experience. It is a prerequisite for moving up.

Subordinate: You know, you're right. I never thought about that. Management does view this experience as important for promotion, doesn't it?

Positive persuasion is useful . . .

As you can see, the manager did more than just provide the subordinate with information. The manager presented it from the subordinate's point of view, showing this person why it was important to have field experience and using persuasion to get the message across. As we can see from the dialogue, the subordinate was positively influenced.

---

[13] For more on this topic, see Jane W. Gibson and Richard M. Hodgetts, *Organizational Communication,* Chap. 5 (Orlando: Academic Press, 1991).

as is negotiation

Sometimes the manager will find that negotiation is required, particularly when he or she is dealing with other managers or with subordinates who are key employees and work best when there is some give and take on both sides. When these conditions exist the manager has to be willing to concede some ground in order to gain an advantage. One of the simplest techniques is to concede something to the other party immediately. For example, the manager might say, "If you will give me some assistance on project A, I will reciprocate by helping you with project B." Or consider the case of the subordinate who wants to move to a new sales territory because he feels that his current one is too crowded (there are three other salespeople in the same area). In this case, the manager might negotiate by saying, "Okay, I'll give you the new territory you want, but you'll have to increase your sales there by 10 percent before you qualify for a bonus."

Sometimes the manager's freedom to give ground is limited and little equivocation on the part of the subordinates can be allowed. When this situation occurs, the manager must resort to more direct and assertive communication approaches. The manager has to say: "This is what I need you to do by next Thursday." "I've just talked to J. J. and we have to cut costs across the board by 10 percent. Let me have your plan for accomplishing this by the day after tomorrow." "I've asked you to drop by because I want you to look at these figures and provide me with a report by Friday regarding how we can cut fixed expenses by 7 percent." Notice in all of these examples that the manager is giving the subordinate a deadline. Instead of requesting assistance, he or she is demanding it. In each case, however, the manager is exercising tact and diplomacy. The subordinate is not being threatened; he or she is simply being informed of a business situation and told what is expected. If there is some reason why the subordinate cannot fulfill the manager's expectations, the subordinate has the opportunity to explain why. Some of the ways in which this feedback can be elicited are explained later in the chapter. For the moment, however, let us conclude our discussion of positive persuasion and negotiation by noting that the manager can adhere to a number of useful rules, including the following:

Some basic rules of persuasion and negotiation

1. Let the other person make the opening statement; you may learn the company's needs and be able to satisfy them on your terms.
2. Phrase questions for a positive answer. That gets the other side used to saying "yes," which is what you want said.
3. Make an early concession on a minor point; the other side may feel called upon to reciprocate.
4. Never promise unless you can deliver.
5. Never suggest a range of values; the other side will choose the end that suits it.
6. Defer key issues until the end, when you know most about the other side's stance.

7. Take a position of prominence. Stand up when talking, if necessary; don't let them stare down on you.
8. Pick the right time of day. Don't hit the boss when he or she is thinking of the next appointment.
9. Have the strong points of your case on the tip of your tongue, ready to be unleashed strategically.
10. Guard emotions. Never show anger unless you know it will carry your point. Avoid gleeful expressions that could alienate.
11. Avoid snap decisions that you may regret. Better to insist on a delay to think the matter through.
12. Never underestimate the other side. It is already in a position of strength or you wouldn't be negotiating.
13. Remember that the boss is under pressure and faced with a decision that will reflect on him or her. Don't crowd.
14. Take along your sense of humor and be open and friendly.
15. Tell the truth. Exaggeration reduces your credibility.
16. Be yourself. Posturing is transparent.
17. End on a positive note regardless of the outcome, if only to express thanks and say that both sides have learned from the bargaining.
18. Adapt your messages to the receiver. Talk his or her language, and use examples and values that the receiver can appreciate.
19. Apply the "body messages" that strengthen your persuasive message.
20. Listen for the "relationship" messages when you negotiate or persuade. Don't simply rely on good content to bring about the persuasive goal you have in mind.[14]

Listening

Listening involves four phases

Hearing

Attention

Another way to overcome interpersonal communication barriers is through effective listening. Research reveals that managers spend more of their time listening than they do reading, writing, or speaking.[15] Listening involves four distinct phases: hearing, attention, understanding, and remembering.

Hearing takes place when the speaker's words are received by the listener. If the listener has poor hearing or there is noise in the local area, he or she may not hear what is being said.

Attention involves the selective perception of verbal messages. Usually a listener does not concentrate on each word but listens for the key ideas or phrases that he or she considers most important. The remainder of the message is either ignored or given minor consideration. The problem, of course, occurs

---

[14] Preston, *Communication,* 190–91.
[15] Beverly Davenport Sypher, Robert N. Bostrom, and Joy Hart Siebart, "Listening, Communication Abilities, and Success at Work," *Journal of Business Communication* (Fall 1989):293–301.

when the listener daydreams or ignores some key facts or opinions. The best way to avoid this problem is by forcing oneself to focus on what is being said and fight attempts to daydream, interrupt, or throw off the speaker by acting bored, irritated, or disinterested.

Understanding

Understanding requires an accurate interpretation and evaluation of the message. What is the speaker *really* saying? One of the most effective ways to ensure understanding is to have the listener recap the major points. If the manager is listening, when the subordinate is done the manager should say, "Okay, let me recap what I hear you saying." If the manager is speaking, a good recap question is, "Now before we close our discussion, I'd like you to give me your interpretation of what I want you to do." Remember that when trying to determine if understanding has occurred the manager must never ask *if* the other party understood the message but rather *what* the other party understood. The burden of understanding must be shifted to the listener. Then, if there is a problem the speaker can attempt to resolve it through additional clarification.

Remembering

The last stage of the listening process is remembering. The manager has to retain the essence of the message. Many managers retain information by taking notes and maintaining a file. In this way, they can consult their records when trying to recall what was said or agreed to. The human mind can remember and quickly recall only so much information. Note taking is an excellent supplement to the remembering stages of listening.

How can one improve one's listening ability? Some of the most useful guidelines include the following:

Listening guidelines

1. Ensure that the physical environment is conducive to listening by closing the door, shutting out noise, and sitting or standing close to the other person so as to create an atmosphere of trust and confidence.
2. Concentrate all of your physical and mental energies on listening to the other person.
3. Control your emotions by not getting upset at what the speaker says; otherwise, you will begin losing your concentration and the listening process will break down.
4. Try to be objective by listening to the logic and consistency of the message rather than to who is saying it.
5. Throughout the discussion demonstrate an interest and an alertness in what is being said; let the other person know you are listening.
6. Do not interrupt unless the speaker is confusing you by the order and logic of the presentation; and then do so only to get him or her back on track.
7. Encourage the speaker by nodding when you agree or understand a major point, and refrain from shaking your head "no" because this often throws the speaker off.
8. Listen closely for meanings and content but do not get hung up on

specific words that are either used incorrectly or erroneously by the speaker.

9. As you listen, be sure you are fulfilling your basic responsibilities to the speaker by remembering (a) to concentrate on being appreciative, courteous, and kind (if this is an informal discussion); (b) to concentrate on fact, logic, and objectivity (if this is a formal discussion); and (c) to pinpoint important details, follow the logic as closely as possible, and be prepared to ask for additional clarity and explanation where needed (if this is a critical discussion).

10. Demonstrate patience with the speaker by acting calm and collected; give the speaker a chance to fully and completely explain what he or she has to say.[16]

Giving and Getting Effective Feedback

Both during and after listening, the manager must be able to give and get feedback. Feedback keeps the communication process going and ensures a continual flow of ideas back and forth.[17] (See "Management in Practice: Learning to Inspire: Guidelines From the Top.")

Feedback is a circular process. After a message is transmitted to a receiver, a message is sent back to the sender. In the case of intrapersonal communication, the sender provides personal feedback. In the case of interpersonal communication, feedback comes from the receiver.[18]

Feedback serves a number of important functions. First, it provides data from which to evaluate what is right or wrong about a particular communiqué. Second, it can serve to stimulate change by showing the receiver what needs to be communicated differently. Third, it reinforces the sender through rewards ("Keep it up, George, you're doing a fine job") or punishments ("Alex, you'll have to improve your performance or I'll have to let you go").

Getting feedback

The manager can employ a number of useful techniques to achieve effective feedback. Some of these relate to *getting* feedback. For example, the manager can make an opening statement like the following:

- "Tell me more about this idea."
- "What makes you say that?"
- "How are you going to accomplish this?"

---

[16] See also John L. DiGaetani, "The Business of Listening," *Business Horizons* (October 1980):40–46.

[17] Charles E. Beck and Elizabeth A. Beck, "The Manager's Open Door and the Communication Climate," *Business Horizons* (January–February 1986):15–19.

[18] Kathleen Watson Dugan, "Ability and Effort Attributions: Do They Affect How Managers Communicate Performance Feedback Information?" *Academy of Management Journal* (January 1989)87–114.

MANAGEMENT IN PRACTICE

Learning to Inspire: Guidelines From the Top

In an effort to assess the skills needed to lead employees in today's corporations, *Fortune* magazine recently interviewed a number of top executives, including Beth Pritchard of Johnson Wax, Donald E. Paterson of Ford Motor Company, Michael R. Quinlin of McDonald's, James E. Burke of Johnson & Johnson, Frederick W. Smith of Federal Express, John Sculley of Apple Computer, and Barry Rand of Xerox. While each CEO had specific ideas on the skills needed to inspire their employees, the following seven guidelines were representative of the most often agreed-upon characteristics.

1. **Trust your subordinates.** You can't expect them to go all out for you if they think you don't believe in them.
2. **Develop a vision.** Some executive suspicions to the contrary, planning for the long term pays off. And people want to follow someone who knows where he or she is going.
3. **Keep your cool.** The best leaders show their mettle under fire.
4. **Encourage risk.** Nothing demoralizes the troops like knowing that the slightest failure could jeopardize their entire career.
5. **Be an expert.** From boardroom to mailroom, everyone had better understand that you know what you're talking about.
6. **Invite dissent.** Your people aren't giving you their best or learning how to lead if they are afraid to speak up.
7. **Simplify.** You need to see the big picture in order to set a course, communicate it, and maintain it. Keep the details at bay.

Source: Kenneth Labich, "The Seven Keys to Business Leadership," *Fortune* (October 24, 1988):58–66.

Notice that in each case the manager is encouraging the other party to offer feedback.

Giving feedback

Analogous statements can be used in *giving* feedback. For example, the manager might say:

- "Your ideas have merit, but before you continue let me share with you the latest thinking on this matter from top management."
- "I like your recommendations, but I think you should temper them in light of the latest financial report which I have just received."
- "Your progress has been much faster than I anticipated, so maybe now is the time for me to fill you in on the way in which your work is to dovetail with that of the people in advertising."

Again, feedback is promoted. The important thing to realize is that unless the manager can obtain and give feedback, communication remains basically a one-way process, and this is one of the major causes of communication breakdown.

FIGURE 11-7   Communication Flows

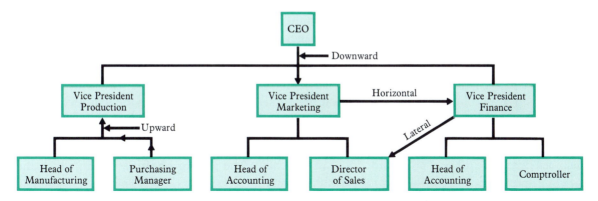

ORGANIZATIONAL COMMUNICATION

Organizational communication involves the formal transfer of information throughout the hierarchy. In many cases, organizational communication is a series of interpersonal communiqués in which one person verbally conveys information to another and so on, until the last person in the chain or network is informed. At other times this communication pattern is of a written nature. Yet when the process is examined in an organizational context, as opposed to an interpersonal one, its dynamics are much greater because both formal and informal communication networks are involved.

Formal Communication Flows

There are four basic communication flows

In an organizational setting, there are four basic communication flows: downward, upward, horizontal, and lateral. (See Figure 11-7.) **Downward communiqués** extend from superior to subordinate and are designed to convey such things as orders, directives, and guidelines for getting things done. **Upward communiqués** provide feedback on work assignments and are designed to keep the manager apprised of employee progress and problems. **Horizontal communiqués** occur between people on the same level of the hierarchy and are designed to ensure or improve coordination of work effort. **Lateral communiqués** take place between people on different levels of the hierarchy and are usually designed to provide information, coordination, or assistance to either or both parties.[19]

---

[19] Alan Zaremba, ''Communication: The Upward Network,'' *Personnel Journal* (March 1989):21–24.

These communiqués often are formal in nature, following the hierarchical chain of command, or they may be informal in nature and designed to cut through red tape and get things done as expediently as possible. When this approach is taken, the manager makes use of the informal organization.

Informal Communication Networks

Informal communication networks, often referred to as the **grapevine**, may take one of four forms: single strand, gossip, probability, or cluster chains. (See Figure 11-8.)

There are four informal networks

The **single-strand chain** is one in which each person passes the message to one other individual in the chain. The **gossip chain** is one in which the person with the information passes it to every other individual in the chain. The **probability chain** is one in which each person passes on information at random, without particular regard for who the receiver is, and the receivers use the same approach in their communication efforts. The **cluster chain** is one in which information is passed on selectively: the individual deliberately tells some people and does not tell others. Some of those getting the information pass it onto others while the remainder do not. The result is that a handful of people often account for all of the information that is passed along this informal chain.

FIGURE 11-8   Informal Communication Networks

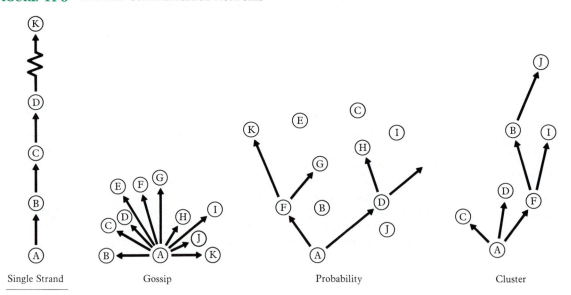

Single Strand   Gossip   Probability   Cluster

Barriers to Organizational Communication

Whether messages are being transmitted along formal or informal lines, communication barriers can prevent understanding. Five of the major barriers to organizational communication are status, the number of links in the chain, expansion and contraction of messages, organizational politics, and economic threats.

Status

As noted earlier, in an organizational setting, who says something is often more important than what is said. This statement is particularly true when we examine communication in terms of hierarchical position. The president tends to have more status or credibility than the vice president, who has more believability than the general manager, and so on down the line.

Status is not confined to hierarchical level

Status need not be confined to hierarchical position or title, however. Individuals with a reputation for getting things done, looking after their people, and knowing their job also have status in the organization. If a highly successful vice president of sales says the new product line will produce revenues in excess of $5 million this year, the person's status may be enough to sway the president into agreeing to add $500,000 to the advertising budget despite arguments to the contrary by the vice president of finance.

The problem with status, of course, is that the message itself is given secondary consideration. The source tends to be the most important factor.

Number of Links

When verbal communication is used, each person in the chain receives a message and then passes it on.[20] Like the old parlor game, however, the message that goes in at the beginning is seldom the one that emerges at the end. Each person modifies it, adding or deleting some things in the process. Table 11-2 illustrates this phenomenon. Notice that each person not only changes the message slightly but also tends to drop out some negative information and embellish the positive picture.

People modify verbal communiqués

Expansion and Contraction

Messages are often altered

Closely related to the barrier caused by the number of links is that of expansion and contraction of messages. As verbal messages come down the line, they tend to be expanded. Each person adds a little something. (See Table 11-3.) The

[20] For an interesting study see: Richard C. Huseman and Edward W. Miles, "Organizational Communication in the Information Age: Implications of Computer-Based Systems," *Journal of Management* (June 1988):181–202.

TABLE 11-2	The Number of Links Can Be a Communication Barrier
Unit Workers to Foreman	The new incentive payment plan doesn't look too bad. A couple of the guys are going to try it out. However, the salary offer is a good 2 percent too low and the fringe benefit package and new work rule proposals are lousy. We're telling the shop steward that if the company can't improve these, we should walk out.
Foreman to Supervisor	Some of the workers are going to support the new incentive payment plan, but the fringe benefit package and new work rules are going to be fought by the union. The proposed across-the-board salary increases are also a little low and we're going to get static on them, too.
Supervisor to Plant Manager	The workers seem fairly positive about our proposed incentive plan, but they don't like the fringe benefit package and they are somewhat opposed to the new work rules.
Plant Manager to Senior Vice President	The workers really like the new incentive plan, but I don't think the union will agree to our fringe benefit package.
Senior Vice President to Chief Executive Officer	The new incentive plan is being well received. We're getting a lot of positive feedback on it. I wouldn't be surprised if we had a new union contract signed by the end of next week.

reverse occurs with messages going up the line. In this case, they are contracted. One of the main reasons is that the higher one goes, the less time there is for long messages because time is money. A second reason for contraction is that managers typically hate to hear bad news. So the subordinate shortens the communiqué by reducing or omitting the negative parts. While this practice may be dangerous, no one wants to be penalized for being truthful, and some

TABLE 11-3	Message Expansion
Chairman	Bill, how many people would you estimate we have working in our claims division?
President	Fred, how many people do we have employed in our claims division? Find out for me, would you?
Vice President	George, get me a list of everyone who works in our claims division. Include both part-time and full-time people at all levels as well as any new hires through last Friday. I think they want it because they are planning a cutback in personnel.
General Manager	Kathy, I need a complete typewritten list of all employees in your division. Also, have their names, addresses, and telephone numbers included, as well as a copy of their latest performance evaluations. We're in the process of trimming back dramatically the number of personnel. We're going to get rid of a lot of deadwood.
Division Head	Tim, I want a complete list of everyone working in this division as well as their addresses, phone numbers, latest performance evaluations, and job descriptions. Send a copy of all of this to the general manager. There's a cut-back coming and we'll have to decide who goes. Then block out all day tomorrow on my calendar so you and I can decide how we can cut 25 percent of the staff without losing too much efficiency.

managers get the news and messenger confused. When it is time to evaluate the individual, all the manager remembers is the bad news the person always brings. This results in a less than accurate rating for the subordinate.

Organizational Politics

Throughout every organization there are managers who have built up little empires that they want to protect. There are also individuals with whom these managers work well and others with whom they do not. The result of all this is organizational politics, through which managers form alliances in an effort to achieve their objectives. Some people want to increase their power; others want money or autonomy over a given area of operations. Whatever the reason for the alliances, communication plays a key role in this process. People who know what is going on around the organization have the best chance to further their own aims. They are able to sift through the rumors and separate fact from fiction.[21]

Power plays may occur

Organizational politics is a barrier to communication in three ways. First, in pursuing personal aims some managers keep people in the dark about what is really going on. Second, misinformation or rumor is typically started in an effort to camouflage what is happening. Third, some managers or groups of managers make deals with each other in an effort to attain their objectives. When this occurs, communication is subverted for the sake of personal ambition, and the organization at large suffers.

Economic Threats

People are threatened economically

Whenever people's jobs and financial stability are threatened, they begin to communicate differently. An organization that introduces a new computer designed to help people with their paperwork must realize that these people may fear replacement by the machine. "If we cooperate," they reason, "we could end up out of work." As a result, they are not very open when explaining to the systems designer how the computer can be closely tied to their job. An analogous situation is found in the case of salespeople, who often do not tell the company about all of their sales leads for fear their sales quotas will be adjusted upward. "If you have that many potential customers," the sales manager will tell them, "you'll have no trouble increasing your sales 30 percent above our previously agreed-upon quota."

Economic threats are often psychological. The organization may have no intention of allowing anything negative to happen to the personnel, but the personnel are frightened and respond in a defensive manner. They reason that the less they communicate, the smaller the economic threat to them.

---

[21] Eric M. Eisenberg and Marsha G. Witten, "Reconsidering Openness in Organizational Communication," *Academy of Management Review* (July 1987):418–426.

Overcoming Barriers to Organizational Communication

How can these barriers to organizational communication be overcome? Some of the most effective ways were discussed earlier when barriers to interpersonal effectiveness were examined. Five additional guides are extremely useful.

Know the Audience

Know who is getting the message

Regardless of whether the manager is using written or verbal communication, and whether the formal or informal organization is involved, a knowledge of the audience is paramount. Who will receive this message? How are they likely to interpret it? What will the effect of this interpretation be? By answering questions like these, the manager follows the first rule of message communication: plan the communiqué.

Emphasize Value

Appeal to them

One of the surest ways to get a person's attention and win him or her over is to communicate something of value or importance. Rather than saying, "We are putting in a new computer because it is faster and more efficient than doing this work by hand," the manager should say, "This new computer we are going to be installing is designed to help you get your work done more efficiently and remove some of the time-consuming problems you are currently facing, allowing you more time for the rest of your job." Notice that the first statement presented the computer in terms of organizational value and could well be interpreted as an economic threat. The second presented the computer in terms of its value to the employee and was designed to win the latter's support of the work change. An emphasis on value can help overcome organizational communication barriers.[22]

Small Bites

Communicate simply

Messages that are simple and to the point are more effective than those that are complex and indirect. Unfortunately, sometimes a message must be long and must contain a number of important ideas. It is important to break these messages into a number of small pieces. Then, presenting each piece, one at a time, the manager can gradually convey the entire message. The manager should begin with a simple point and then move on to the more complex parts. Unless the message is conveyed this way, the receiver will begin to lose attention or will become overwhelmed by its complexity.

---

[22] Edward L. Levins, "Let's Talk: Effectively Communicating Praise," *Supervisory Management* (September 1980):17–25.

Consult With Others

Ask for advice
If the message is important, the manager should talk to someone about it or show it to someone. In this way if the message has a dual meaning or is likely to be misinterpreted by the receiver(s), the other person can notice the problems immediately. Remember that many of the messages we convey to others are crystal clear to us even though the receiver may have a great deal of difficulty with them. By allowing someone else to examine the communiqué, we reduce the chance of misinterpretation. Quite often others are able to pick up errors or interpretation problems that we ourselves (regardless of how many times we reviewed the message or read the memo), cannot see.

Encourage Trust and Openness

Encourage teamwork
Another valuable guideline for improving organizational communication is that trust and openness among the personnel should be encouraged. This certainly is the best way to overcome the problems associated with organizational politics. As long as people succeed in their political maneuvers they will probably continue to engage in power plays. These kinds of activities must be discouraged through both words and deeds. Through words, the manager should make it clear that teamwork is a prerequisite for organizational success. Through deeds, the manager can give merit increases and promotions to members of the team who do not engage in dysfunctional organizational politics. Naturally, it is impossible to completely eliminate all efforts to use organizational communication channels to further one's own ends. These problems can be minimized, however, if the management sets its mind to this task.[23]

In the final analysis, organizational communication effectiveness is determined by the willingness of the personnel to communicate with, trust, and work with others. If this organizational climate cannot be created, there is little chance that the enterprise can be either efficient or effective in the pursuit of its basic objectives.

SUMMARY

1. Communication is the process of transferring meanings from sender to receiver. This process involves a source, encoding, a message, decoding, a receiver, and feedback. There are three basic forms of communication: intrapersonal, interpersonal, and organizational.
2. Intrapersonal communication involves the reception, processing, and

---

[23] See: Fernando Bartolomé, "Nobody Trusts the Boss Completely—Now What?" *Harvard Business Reviews* (March–April 1989):135–42.

transmission of information to oneself. This process was illustrated in Figure 11-4. A number of variables affect this process. Some of these include the self, the self-concept, personal orientation, personality traits, and defense mechanisms. Defense mechanisms include rationalization, projection, reaction formation, and repression.

3. Interpersonal communication involves the direct transmission of meanings between two or more persons. This process typically occurs on a face-to-face basis.

4. There are a number of barriers to interpersonal communication. Five of the major ones are perception, words, the source, inconsistent behavior, and the environment. Some of the best ways to overcome these barriers include accuracy, empathy, the effective use of nonverbal communication, positive persuasion and negotiation, listening, and giving and getting feedback.

5. Organizational communication involves the transfer of meanings up and down the hierarchy. Sometimes this occurs in the form of formal communication flows: downward, upward, horizontal, and lateral. At other times it takes place in the form of informal network communiqués as represented by the single strand, gossip, probability, or cluster chains.

6. Some of the most common barriers to organizational communication include status, the number of links, expansion and contraction, organizational politics, and economic threats. These barriers may be overcome by knowing the audience, emphasizing value, communicating in small bites, consulting with others, and encouraging trust and openness.

KEY TERMS

Achieved roles   Roles that are earned through accomplishment.

Ascribed roles   Roles based heavily on sex, age, kinship, and general place in society.

Body language   The use of body movements to communicate ideas, interests, opinions, and objectives on a nonverbal basis.

Cluster chain   An informal communication network in which individuals pass information on a selective basis.

Decoding process   The way in which a receiver interprets a message from a source.

Downward communication   Organizational communiqués that travel from superior to subordinate and are used to convey orders and directive.

Empathy   The ability to see things from another person's point of view.

Encoding process   The way in which a source conveys meaning to a receiver.

Gossip chain   An informal communication network in which the person with the information passes it to every other individual in the chain.

Grapevine   Informal communication networks used to convey information throughout the hierarchy.

Horizontal communication   Organizational communiqués that occur between people on the same level of the hierarchy and are designed to ensure coordination.

Interpersonal communication   The direct transmission of meanings between two or more persons.

Intimate zone   The zone of interaction that extends to approximately an arm's length from one's body.

Intrapersonal communication   The way in which individuals receive, process, and transmit information to themselves.

Lateral communication   Organizational communiqués that take place between people on different levels of the hierarchy and are usually designed to provide information, coordination, or assistance to either or both parties.

Organizational communication   The formal transfer of information throughout the hierarchy.

Personal zone   A zone of interaction that extends from an arm's length to approximately four feet from the body.

Probability chain   An informal communication network in which individuals pass information on a random basis.

Projection   The ignoring of certain traits, motives, or behavior in oneself and the attributing of them to others.

Public zone   A zone of interaction that extends approximately 12 to 25 feet from the body.

Rationalization   An attempt to justify one's failures or inadequacies.

Reaction formation   Dealing with undesirable behavior by taking the opposite point of view.

Repression   Keeping down unpleasant or unaccepted feelings.

Selective perception   The acceptance from the external environment of only those stimuli that are of most importance or value to the receiver.

Self-concept   How people feel about themselves.

Single-strand chain   An informal communication network in which each person passes the message to one other individual in the chain.

Social zone   A zone of interaction that extends approximately four to twelve feet from an individual.

Upward communication   Organizational communiqués that travel from subordinate to superior and are designed to provide feedback on progress and problems.

QUESTIONS FOR ANALYSIS AND DISCUSSION

1. In your own words, what is meant by the term communication?
2. How does the communication process work? Be sure to include in your

answer a discussion of the source, encoding process, message, decoding process, receiver, and feedback.

3. How does the self affect intrapersonal communication? How does the self-concept influence intrapersonal communication?

4. How does the intrapersonal communication process work? What role is played by intrapersonal variables such as personal orientation, personality traits, and defense mechanisms?

5. In what way are the following barriers to interpersonal communication: perception, words, the source, inconsistent behavior, and the environment? Be complete in your answer.

6. How can a manager improve the accuracy of his or her written communiqués? Include a discussion of Table 11-1 in your answer.

7. What is meant by the term empathy? What role does it play in effective communication?

8. What does a manager need to know about nonverbal communication? Offer four useful guidelines.

9. What rules should managers follow in using persuasion and negotiation? Offer six of the most beneficial guides.

10. How can a manager improve his or her listening skills? Be sure to include in your answer the four phases of listening as well as at least five useful guidelines.

11. How should a manager go about giving feedback? Getting feedback? Provide at least two opening statements for achieving each of these forms of feedback.

12. There are four basic communication flows. What does this statement mean? Be complete in your answer.

13. Informal communication networks take one of four forms. What are these four? Identify and describe each.

14. In what way are the following barriers to organizational communication: status, number of links, expansion and contraction, organizational politics, and economic threats?

15. How can managers overcome barriers to organizational communication? Identify and describe four ways.

CASE

Getting the Business

It seems that every Monday morning is a busy one for Karl Proctor, vice president of the Commercial Loan Department. Monday of this week was particularly hectic because Karl had a very important meeting with a potential customer.

This individual had submitted his company's financial report to Karl a week ago. He told Karl, "I'd like to get a line of credit for $500,000. My construction business is expanding rapidly and my current bank is unable to provide me with the degree of financing I require. I need a bank I can grow with. I've looked around and gotten some excellent comments about your institution from other people in my line of work. I'd like to switch my business over to your bank if you can accommodate my credit needs. I want to make a decision within 10 days, however. If your bank turns me down, I'll need time to find someone else before my next fiscal year begins in 30 days."

Karl reviewed this applicant's financial records and did some in-depth checking. The man's business is doing quite well, but as a contractor, he is subject to economic ups and downs. A loan of $500,000 could be disastrous to the bank if the business went under. As a result, during his meeting with the businessman this Monday Karl tried to get him to agree to provide full collateral for all loans. Here is how part of the conversation went:

Karl: I've looked over your application and noticed that at your previous bank you had a credit line of $200,000. Your business seems to get on fine with this line; you never have a real cash shortage. Why do you need a larger line now?

Applicant: I want to expand and bid on some new jobs across town. I know the economy is not in great shape, but these remodeling contracts I'm looking at promise to provide a return of 21 percent net.

Karl: I see. That sounds promising. However, I should point out that the assets on your business are only worth $210,000. If we were to give you a $500,000 line of credit you'd have to cosign as an individual and be willing to put up your personal assets as collateral.

Applicant: Oh wow! I don't have to do that at my current bank. Why would I have to do it now?

Karl: Because your business assets have always had a greater value than your current line of credit. However, if you increase your loan line to $500,000 you'll have to increase your collateral coverage.

Applicant: Gee, I don't know. Maybe I should stay with my current bank.

Karl: You certainly can do that, but I can assure you that you'll also have to provide additional loan collateral coverage. Besides, for you $500,000 is probably only a temporary level. In two to three years you'll undoubtedly want to go higher. And since you are a fairly conservative risk taker, the chances of your having to sell personal assets to cover business loans is not very great. Additionally, our bank offers more business services than your current one. We're more equipped to help businesspeople meet their needs. Your bank gears itself toward individual accounts, not company business. Think about what I've said and call me later in the week. If you are interested in doing business with us, I'll bring your reports to our Wednesday weekly meeting and see what I can do.

The businessman thanked Karl, told him he would think about it, and left. The next day he called and told Karl he wanted the $500,000 line of credit and would agree to pledge his personal assets. This was approved at the Wednesday meeting. Early this morning the businessman's accountant was over at the bank opening up the necessary accounts and taking care of the requisite paperwork.

1. How did Karl manage to overcome the businessman's opposition to pledging his personal assets? What communication tools and techniques did he use?
2. In terms of effective negotiation, what principles or rules did Karl employ? Be complete in your answer.
3. How did Karl use the communication principle of "talk in terms of value to the other party?" How important was this in getting the businessman's account? Explain.

YOU BE THE CONSULTANT

A Centralized Move

The Shipley Company was having some financial difficulties when Mr. Brown accepted the presidency three months ago. Mr. Brown had 20 years of experience in a competitive firm.

After analyzing the situation, Mr. Brown decided that the company needed to centralize operations and to decrease costs. He thought it would be most efficient to centralize purchasing and warehousing and to have the field sales reps work out of their homes. This would enable the firm to close field offices, reduce inventory, and cut costs such as rent and utilities.

Mr. Brown knew that the company had decentralized seven years ago. Now he was making a reversal of this process. Yet he felt it was necessary if the company was to be profitable again.

When some employees heard rumors of the proposed centralization, they began to ask questions. Their managers denied these rumors and reaffirmed their support for a decentralized approach.

Last month Mr. Brown announced that all nonprofitable branches would be closed. Additionally, all stores with less than $1 million of annual sales would be closed, regardless of profitability, and sales reps would work out of their homes.

As a result of these decisions, Mr. Brown faces a number of problems. In particular, the personnel claims that he has not kept them informed about what was going on, that he simply sprung the decision on them. Mr. Brown has tried to explain that this had been a strategic decision that he did not want competitors to know about, that this was the reason for his secretiveness.

Your Consultation

Was Mr. Brown's decision to keep the centralization plan a secret a good one? How would you have had him handle it? What do you recommend be done now? Why? Explain.

12

The Motivation Process at Work

This chapter studies motivation at work. What drives people to work hard and do a good job? What role is played by money? Opportunity? Power? Prestige? The answers to these questions vary, depending on the individual. A large amount of research has been conducted on the subject of motivation, however, and in this chapter we will examine what is currently known about it.

Besides examining the nature of motivation, this chapter reviews some of the most important content and process theories of motivation, looks at the role played by money in the motivation process, and explores the impact of values. By the time you have finished reading the material in this chapter, you will be able to:

1. Define the term motivation and the three primary ingredients in the process.
2. Describe how motivation works.
3. Discuss in detail the four most important content theories of motivation: Maslow's need theory, Herzberg's two-factor theory, Alderfer's ERG theory, and McClelland's achievement motivation theory.
4. Describe three of the most important process theories of motivation: Vroom's expectancy theory, Porter and Lawler's model, and Adams's equity theory.
5. Explain the role of money in motivation.
6. Tell how values affect motivation in the modern organization.

THE NATURE OF MOTIVATION

Motivation defined

The word **motivation** comes from the Latin *movere,* which means to move. Today the term means stimulating people to action by means of incentives or inducements. This process is often generated through an *external* action such as offering someone more money to do more work. Whether or not this effort is successful is determined *internally,* however, because motivation is a psychological process. Furthermore, people are moved or motivated toward an objective only if they feel it is in their own best personal interest.[1] This fact was noted in Chapter 2 when Chester Barnard's acceptance theory of authority was discussed.

Primary Ingredients

There are three primary ingredients in motivation. These are best described in what can be called the *motivation formula:* motivation is a function of ability, effort, and desire.

Ability is the individual's capacity to do something. If a person has the ability to sell, he or she may be a terrific salesperson. But if the individual has little selling ability, her or she will never attain the same degree of success.

Effort is the time, drive, and energy the individual expends in the pursuit of an objective. Some goals cannot be attained by mere ability; they require the person to spend a considerable amount of effort as well. Many salespeople find, for example, that in order to close large sales, they have to make many calls on the customer before the latter is "sold" both on them and their product or service.

Desire is the wish, want, or urge for a particular objective. Unless someone truly desires to attain an objective, the chance of success is diminished and, even if the goal is attained, the degree of success is reduced. A salesperson who desires to make $1 million in sales during a given year has a much better chance of attaining this objective than does a colleague who hopes to sell $700,000 worth of merchandise.

Motion and Motivation

Motivation is more than movement

Motion is often confused with motivation. Often people see someone working very hard and assume that the person is motivated. Motion or effort (in the form of energy) is only part of good work, however. People who are not in motion

---

[1] Chester I. Barnard, *The Functions of the Executive* (Cambridge, MA: Harvard University Press, 1938): 165. Also see Michael E. Cavanaugh, "In Search of Motivation," *Personnel Journal* (March 1984):76–82.

FIGURE 12-1
One Model of
Motivation

may also be motivated. Many times employees may sit down to read something or ponder the answer to a particular problem, and they are indeed motivated toward a particular objective. Motivation can exist without motion and vice versa. For this reason, an initial investigation of motivation is best approached from a needs standpoint. When this approach is taken, behavior can be reduced to three common aspects.

Common Aspects of Motivation

The three common aspects of motivation deal with (1) what energizes human behavior, (2) how this behavior is directed or channeled, and (3) how the behavior can be maintained using a "needs" approach. Figure 12-1 expresses this idea.

People engage in
goal-directed
behavior

Referring to the figure, consider the case of a person who needs a new car (whether it be for transportation, status, ego, or whatever). This person is likely to engage in goal-directed behavior such as working overtime and saving money. The result is the purchase of the new car and the satisfaction of the need.[2]

Obviously this example is quite simple. People have many needs and sometimes their needs conflict. A person may want to be at home with his or her family (affiliation need) and at the same time may want to earn the next promotion at the office (power, ego, status needs). The fact that we cannot see into someone's mind limits our ability to determine which need will win out and become the focus of goal-directed behavior.

Moreover, people do not always attain their needs. Sometimes they are unsuccessful in their efforts and may end up engaging in what appears to be irrational behavior (yelling, screaming, blaming others for their failure to succeed). Motivation is a very complex subject. Many researchers have studied this process, and one of the most popular approaches to explaining it is through the use of a "needs" approach. This is only one way of looking at the subject, of course, but it is an excellent starting point because a wealth of research has been collected about needs and their role in human motivation.[3] These approaches generally can be clustered under the heading of content theories.

---

[2] Edwin A. Locke, Gary P. Latham, and Miriam E. Erez, "The Determinants of Goal Commitment," *Academy of Management Review* (January 1988):23–39.
[3] Terence R. Mitchell, "Motivation: New Directions for Theory, Research and Practice," *Academy of Management Review* (January 1982):80–88.

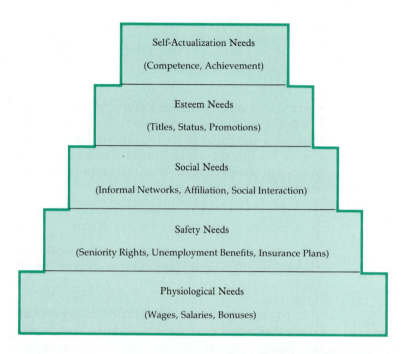

Self-Actualization Needs (Competence, Achievement)
Esteem Needs (Titles, Status, Promotions)
Social Needs (Informal Networks, Affiliation, Social Interaction)
Safety Needs (Seniority Rights, Unemployment Benefits, Insurance Plans)
Physiological Needs (Wages, Salaries, Bonuses)

CONTENT THEORIES OF MOTIVATION

Content theories of motivation attempt to explain what motivates people. Whenever managers are asked what motivates their personnel and they begin making a list of factors, they are taking a content theory approach. The four major content theories of motivation, all of which use a needs approach, are those by Abraham Maslow, Frederick Herzberg, Clayton Alderfer, and David McClelland.

Maslow's Need Hierarchy

Perhaps the best-known "needs approach" to the study of motivation is that of Abraham Maslow.[4] Based principally on his clinical experience, Maslow, a psychologist, presented his theory in terms of a need hierarchy. This hierarchy is illustrated in Figure 12-2.

Unsatisfied needs are motivators

Maslow's need theory holds that an individual strives for need satisfaction at a particular level. When needs at one level are basically satisfied, they no longer serve as motivators, and the individual moves on to the next level in the hierarchy. The upward movement continues until a lower-level need begins to

---

[4] Abraham H. Maslow, "A Theory of Human Motivation," *Psychological Review* (July 1943):370–396.

manifest itself again. At this point the individual drops back to the lower level and attempts to satisfy this need.

The Five Levels

The five levels in the hierarchy represent basic need categories that can be described as follows:

1. **Physiological needs** These are the most basic needs, often referred to as unlearned, primary needs. Typical examples include food, clothing, and shelter. Once these needs are basically satisfied, the next higher level of needs comes into play.
2. **Safety needs** This level represents the individual's need for security or protection. It extends not only to physical safety but to emotional safety as well.
3. **Social needs** This level represents the individual's need for affiliation, social interaction, and a sense of belonging. The person needs to give and receive friendship.
4. **Esteem needs** This level represents the individual's need to "feel good" about himself or herself. Often referred to as ego needs, the needs at this level are satisfied through the acquisition of power and status. The individual needs to feel important or worthwhile, and power and status provide a basis for these feelings.
5. **Self-Actualization needs** This level represents the apex of human needs. While it is the most difficult to describe, it is that level at which a person tries to become all he or she is capable of becoming. Many people pursue this need when they strive for competence or achievement in some area. They are trying to realize all of their potential.

Maslow never contended that everyone would be fully satisfied at a particular level before moving on to the next. He believed that people would seek the next level if they were "basically" satisfied at the current one. The higher they went, the lower the amount of basic satisfaction that would be realized, for example, 85 percent at the physiological level, 50 percent at the social level, 10 percent at the self-actualization level.[5]

Application of the Theory

In Figure 12-2, Maslow's basic hierarchy has been converted into a content model of work motivation. When Maslow first presented his hierarchy, however, he did not intend it to be used for describing the motivation of organizational personnel. This use did not come about until more than 20 years later.[6]

---

[5] Maslow, "Motivation," 388–89.
[6] Abraham H. Maslow, *Eupsychian Management* (Homewood, IL: Dorsey Press, 1965).

Much of what Maslow proposed has not been substantiated through research efforts. For example, one study of female clerks found his model fairly reliable as a way of measuring priority needs but open to question as an overall theory of work motivation.[7]

Another study, conducted among young managers at American Telephone & Telegraph over a five-year period, found that changes in managers' needs were attributable to their developing career concerns and not to the desire for the need gratification that Maslow described.[8] Mahmond Wahba and Lawrence Birdwell made a comprehensive review of the literature and found no support for Maslow's contention that satisfaction at one level led to activation of the next highest level. In addition, they discovered two primary clusters of needs, not five.[9]

The theory's value is limited

Research of this nature shows that while Maslow's theory may provide some insights into motivation, its value is limited. For example, the link between needs and motivation at work is not very well established. Nor is it clear exactly how many levels of needs each person has or whether everyone is actually motivated by all of these need levels. Maslow's ideas have been extended through the work of Frederick Herzberg.

Herzberg's Two-Factor Theory

Frederick Herzberg and his associates conducted motivation research among 200 accountants and engineers in the Pittsburgh area.[10] The researchers used the critical incident method to obtain their data, asking each person in the study to think of a time when he or she felt exceptionally good or bad about his or her job. Herzberg found the responses to be fairly consistent.

Satisfiers and dissatisfiers were identified

When reporting good feelings the participants in the study made comments related to their job experiences and to *job content.* When reporting bad feelings, they made comments associated with the environment or the *job context.* These two groups of factors—those related to the job content and those related to job context—became the basis of Herzberg's **two-factor theory of motivation.** The job content factors (the satisfiers) were labeled motivators. The job context factors (the dissatisfiers) were called hygiene factors. Herzberg's theory is shown in Table 12-1.

---

[7] Michael Beer, *Leadership, Employee Needs, and Motivation* (Ohio State University, College of Commerce and Administration, Bureau of Business Research, Monograph No. 129, Columbus, 1966), 68.

[8] Douglas T. Hall and Khahl E. Nougaim, "An Examination of Maslow's Need Hierarchy in an Organizational Setting," *Organizational Behavior and Human Performance* (February 1968):12–35.

[9] Mahmond A. Wahba and Lawrence G. Birdwell, "Maslow Reconsidered: A Review of Research on the Need Hierarchy Theory," *Proceedings of the Academy of Management* (1973):514–20.

[10] Frederick Herzberg, Bernard Mausner, and Barbara Bloch Snyderman, *The Motivation to Work* (New York: John Wiley, 1959).

TABLE 12-1 Herzberg's Two-Factor Theory	
Hygiene Factors	**Motivators**
Salary	Achievement
Supervision, technical	Recognition
Working conditions	Responsibility
Interpersonal relations	Advancement
Company policies and administration	The work itself

Motivators and Hygiene Factors

Herzberg called the job content factors **motivators** because they brought about satisfaction and resulted in motivation. The job context factors were labeled **hygiene factors** because, in Herzberg's view, they were like physical hygiene—they did not make things better but prevented them from getting worse.

Placing these two sets of factors, motivators and hygiene factors, in perspective, Herzberg concluded that hygiene prevented dissatisfaction, while motivators brought about satisfaction. Hygiene established a "zero level" of motivation; if management did not provide hygiene factors, dissatisfaction resulted. If hygiene factors were provided, then there was no dissatisfaction but there was no satisfaction either. Satisfaction resulted only from the presence of motivators.

One of the most important aspects of Herzberg's theory is the attention it focuses on the need to provide hygiene at least. In the past many organizations have emphasized such factors as salary, working conditions, and interpersonal relations. Herzberg recommended providing these hygiene factors and "shutting up about them." The real emphasis, he said, should be placed on motivators like achievement, recognition, and the chance for advancement.

Herzberg's theory is similar to Maslow's. Herzberg's hygiene factors coincide with Maslow's lower-level (physiological, safety, and social) needs. His motivators coincide with Maslow's upper-level (esteem and self-actualization) needs.

The basic two-factor theory is appealing if only because it seems to be intuitively correct. Many scholars and researchers have attacked the theory vigorously, however.

Criticisms of the Two-Factor Theory

One of the biggest arguments against the two-factor theory is that the conclusions drawn as a result of the research findings were not the only ones that could have been reached. Victor Vroom, a leading researcher in the area of motivation, put the argument this way:

It is . . . possible that obtained differences between stated sources of satisfaction and dissatisfaction stem from defensive processes within the individual respondent. Persons may be more likely to attribute the causes of satisfaction to their own achievements and accomplishments on the job. On the other hand, they may be more likely to attribute dissatisfaction not to personal inadequacies or deficiencies, but to factors in the work environment, i.e., obstacles presented by company policies or supervision.[11]

The theory appears to be methodologically bound

A second argument revolves around the fact that the theory appears to be "methodologically bound." This term means that the results are determined by the approach used in collecting the data. Other researchers have attempted to replicate Herzberg's theory using a data collection method other than the critical incident method and have not been able to get the same results.

Were the interviewers biased?

A third argument centers around the interpretations of the results by the interviewers. Since the respondents gave verbal answers, the interviewers may have misinterpreted some of the results and developed a theory that was at least partially fashioned by erroneous interpretations.

Finally, critics of the theory argue that Herzberg set up an "either/or" approach. According to his theory, something is either a hygiene factor or it is a motivator. Herzberg never proved, however, that something that is a hygiene factor for one person cannot also be a motivator for another. In fact, the two dimensions (motivators and hygiene factors) may not be nondimensional or independent. Robert House and Lawrence Wigdor, after making a review of the literature on the subject, have concluded that:

The dimensions are not independent . . .

Since the data do not support the satisfier-dissatisfier dichotomy, the . . . proposition of the Two-Factor theory, that satisfiers have more motivational force than dissatisfiers, appears highly suspect. This is true for two reasons. First, any attempt to separate the two requires an arbitrary definition of the classifications satisfier and dissatisfier. Second, unless such an arbitrary separation is employed, the proposition is untenable.[12]

but the theory does have value

On the positive side, it is important to realize that Herzberg made some important contributions to modern motivation theory. He provided a much better picture of job content factors and their relationship to motivation than anyone had before. Moreover, while his research findings may not hold true for every individual in every job, his basic theme — that more attention be paid to job content factors and less to job context factors — is an important one. For too long management has worried itself about the environment in which the work

---

[11] Victor Vroom, *Work and Motivation* (New York: John Wiley, 1964), 129.

[12] Robert J. House and Lawrence A. Wigdor, "Herzberg's Dual-Factor Theory of Job Satisfaction and Motivation: A Review of the Evidence and a Criticism," *Personnel Psychology* (Winter 1967):385–86.

is carried out and given insufficient attention to the psychological side of motivation.

Alderfer's ERG Theory

More recently, Clayton Alderfer has provided an extension of the Maslow and Herzberg models.[13] Alderfer's model is more in line with existing research findings in that he uses only three basic need categories: existence, relatedness, and growth (**ERG** for short).

Existence needs are related to survival and safety. They correspond to Maslow's physiological needs and safety needs of a material type. They also coincide with some of Herzberg's hygiene factors, such as working conditions and salary.

Relatedness needs stress interpersonal and social relationships. They correspond to Maslow's safety needs of an interpersonal type, social needs, and esteem needs of an interpersonal type. They also coincide with Herzberg's hygiene factors, such as interpersonal relations and supervision, and motivators such as recognition and responsibility.

Growth needs are related to the individual's desire for personal development. In Maslow's need hierarchy they can be found at the top of the esteem level and at the self-actualization level. In Herzberg's theory they include advancement, achievement, and the work itself.

Movement along a continuum

Alderfer goes further than simply expanding the Maslow and Herzberg models, however. He suggests that needs be thought of as a continuum. Instead of moving from one hierarchical level to the next, as Maslow's theory suggests, or from one factor group to another, as Herzberg argues, people can skip along the continuum. Some may spend a great deal of time trying to fulfill one particular need and very little trying to satisfy another. For example, individuals from a middle-class background are highly likely to spend most of their time trying to fulfill relatedness and growth needs. In contrast people of low economic status may spend a great deal of time trying to satisfy existence needs.

The theory is somewhat simplistic

While there has been no direct research on ERG theory, except for Alderfer's own work,[14] current motivation theorists have a great deal of respect for it. They feel it incorporates many of the strong parts of Maslow's and Herzberg's work while offering a less restrictive and limiting view of motivation. On the negative side, however, like Maslow and Herzberg, Alderfer does not really address the overall complexities of work motivation. This problem does not occur in all content theory research.[15] The work of David McClelland is an example.

---

[13] Clayton P. Alderfer, *Existence, Relatedness and Growth: Human Needs in Organization Settings* (New York: Free Press, 1972).

[14] Clayton P. Alderfer, "An Empirical Text of a New Theory of Human Needs," *Organizational Behavior and Human Performance* (May 1969):142–75.

[15] Bronston T. Mayes, "Some Boundary Considerations in the Application of Motivation Models," *Academy of Management Review* (January 1978):51–52.

Achievement Motivation Theory

David McClelland is most closely associated with **achievement motivation theory.** Over the last 35 years this theory has undergone considerable research and revision. The theory focuses on three specific needs: achievement, power, and affiliation. In contrast to the theories of Maslow and Herzberg, it is more limited in scope, tending to address only higher-level needs.

Those most interested in achievement motivation theory are concerned with the success and failure of organizational personnel. What do successful salespeople have in common? What characteristics do successful managers share? While achievement motivation parallels other content theories to some extent, it tends to go beyond the superficial treatment they afford. John Miner, a leading researcher, states the difference this way:

> The two major motives of the theory, achievement and power, would seem to fall within Maslow's esteem category, although achievement motivation has some aspects in common with self-actualization. Affiliation motivation would clearly fall in the social category. However, despite these overlaps and the origins of both theories in clinical psychology and personality theory, need hierarchy theory and achievement motivation theory represent distinctly different concepts of the motivational process.[16]

Need for Achievement

Achievement need is the drive to attain objectives or accomplish things. Through research, McClelland identified the specific characteristics of individuals with a high need to achieve.[17] They are the following:

1. *Moderate risk taking* A high achiever is neither a high nor a low risk taker. High risks involve too much luck; low risks are not sufficiently challenging. High achievers like moderate risks where they have a chance of winning, with the results dependent on their abilities.
2. *Personal responsibility* A high achiever wants to win or lose through personal effort. He or she wants to play a role in the successful attainment of an objective.

Characteristics of high achievers

3. *Feedback on results* A high achiever likes to know the score in terms of how well he or she is doing. In this way, if the individual is doing well, he or she can continue; if he or she is doing poorly, appropriate corrective steps can be taken.
4. *Accomplishment* A high achiever needs to accomplish things. The

---

[16] John B. Miner, *Theories of Organizational Behavior* (Hinsdale, IL: Dryden Press, 1980), 47.
[17] David C. McClelland, *The Achieving Society* (Princeton, NJ: Van Nostrand, 1961); David C. McClelland, "Business Drive and National Achievement," *Harvard Business Review* (July–August 1962):99–112.

rewards themselves are not unimportant, but they are usually not the most important thing. For example, a successful salesperson may be happy making $125,000 annually, but the money is often nothing more than a counting device to let the individual know how well he or she is succeeding. Rewards are often secondary to the internal satisfaction that accompanies the goal attainment.

5. *Task preoccupation* A high achiever tends to be preoccupied with a task until it is accomplished. The individual seldom leaves a job unfinished. For this reason, these people tend to be highly realistic and do not pursue objectives they cannot attain.

High achievers can be found in many occupations. One of the most typical is the area of sales, where it is possible to develop and nurture these five characteristics. It is also important to remember that high achievement, in and of itself, is not necessarily good, however. Many organizations have found that high achievers make excellent salespeople but extremely poor sales managers. These people are too interested in their own particular objectives to worry about others. If one is to become an effective manager, it is necessary to balance a concern for personal achievement with a desire to be helpful to subordinates.

Need for Power

During the mid-1970s McClelland expanded his initial interests and began studying the **need for power.** This need is manifested by a drive for control and influence. McClelland concluded that while achievement motivation is important in studying entrepreneurship, power is more important in an organizational setting. In fact, he determined that a good manager in a large company does not have a high need for achievement.[18]

According to McClelland, power motivation can be expressed in a number of different ways. The mode of expression, at least in part, is a function of the stage to which the power motive has developed in the individual. McClelland believes that there is a hierarchy of development and that people must experience one stage in order to reach the next. Some never rise above the first level, while others may be at any one of the four stages at a certain point in time. Table 12-2 illustrates these four stages.

McClelland also distinguished between personalized power and socialized power. *Personalized power* is characterized by win-lose situations and dominance-submission. A person exercising this type of power derives satisfaction from getting the better of others.[19] In contrast *socialized power* involves a

Personalized versus socialized power

---

[18] David C. McClelland and David H. Burnham, "Power is the Great Motivator," *Harvard Business Review* (January–February 1976):100–110.

[19] David C. McClelland et al., *The Drinking Man: Alcohol and Human Motivation* (New York: Free Press, 1972).

TABLE 12-2	**Power and Managerial Performance**	
Maturity Stage	**Power Motivational Pattern**	**Effect on Managerial Performance**
I	The desire to influence others is low.	Usually this pattern does not provide sufficiently assertive behavior for effective managerial performance.
II	The power motivation drive has little to do with other people; it is basically concerned with doing things for oneself.	Unrelated to the management of people.
III (early)	High power motivation coupled with low affiliation and low self-control.	Not very effective. The manager tends to push his or her weight around too much and be rude to the personnel.
III (late)	High power motivation coupled with low affiliation and low self-control.	More effective. The manager uses power to help out subordinates while maintaining a visible presence. Subordinates identify more with the manager than with the organization itself.
IV	High power motivation of an altruistic type coupled with low affiliation and high self-control.	Very effective. Selfless leadership. The manager helps out subordinates and encourages identification with the organization. The individual takes a back seat to the organization itself.

mix of power motivation and pragmatism so that there is a "concern for group goals, for finding those goals that will move men, for helping the group to formulate them, for taking initiative in providing means of achieving them, and for giving group members the feeling of competence they need to work hard for them." [20] When used in this way, power is employed as a means of getting things done, as opposed to a basis for simply making a person feel good because he or she is able to boss others around.

Table 12-2 shows the relationships between the various types of power motivation and managerial performance. Individuals at lower developmental stages may function effectively in some managerial roles. The effective manager usually does not begin to emerge until late stage III, however.

Power motivation is important for managers

This discussion illustrates that power motivation is extremely important to managerial performance. Power can manifest itself in many different ways, however. Some managers need power because it helps them dominate others (early stage III in Table 12-2); others need power because it helps them guide subordinates and develop a personal allegiance from them (late stage III); still others need power that allows them to be altruistic and develop subordinate talent that is well motivated and loyal to the organization (stage IV).

---

[20] David C. McClelland, *Power: The Inner Experience* (New York: Irvington Press, 1975), 265.

MANAGEMENT IN PRACTICE

Sam Walton = Motivation the Wal-Mart Way

Wal-Mart was listed number five in a recent *Fortune* survey of America's most admired corporations. This success is largely attributed to founder Sam Walton and his unique leadership style.

The legacy of Wal-Mart is colorful and much like the personality of Walton. Although the richest man in the United States, he promotes an image of simplicity. At age 71 Walton appears to be penny-pinching, since at home he drives an old 1978 pick-up truck. He attributes his success to the employees (who are called associates) and the willingness to listen to associates' ideas for change.

At Wal-Mart cost cutting is almost a religion, which is ingrained in the company's culture. The willingness to try anything once to reduce costs, coupled with a strict buyer-vendor relationship, is the key to implementation of their concept of "Every Day Low Prices," a concept which is now being emulated by Sears. Walton also believes in emulating the ideas of other companies, a practice he has held since his earliest days when he would visit other stores to get ideas that could be incorporated into Wal-Mart's operations.

Walton, in a down-home style, laughs, jokes, and motivates the employees by telling them how appreciative he is of the wonderful job they are doing, while at the same time challenging them to do better in a manner which inspires them to want to do better. He has been described as a "What you see is what you get" kind of individual, and his thrifty ways are emulated by the more than 200,000 employees. It is this style as a leader and motivator that are the wellsprings of his and Wal-Mart's phenomenal success, and as measured by profit, in most categories Wal-Mart leaves the competitors behind. During the last half of the 1980s, Wal-Mart's earnings growth has been an incredible 33 percent, more than triple that of most competitors.

Yet while Walton is a tough businessman, he has worked hard to take care of the people who work for him. Much is expected from each associate, but much is returned in the form of praise, recognition, and money. Employees are encouraged to offer their ideas and concerns. This has lead to an increased team concept among workers; and many of those who have been with him from the beginning are now millionaires.

Source: Sharon Reier, "CEO of the Decade: Sam Walton," *Financial World* (April 4, 1989):56–62, and John Huey, "Wal-Mart: Will It Take Over the World?" *Fortune* (January 30, 1989):52–59.

Need for Affiliation

The **need for affiliation** also plays a part in achievement motivation theory. Individuals with a high need for affiliation want to interact, socialize with others, and "belong." This need is best represented by the third level, social, on Maslow's hierarchy.

While achievement and power have been studied extensively, not much research has been done directly on affiliation.[21] However, in terms of

---

[21] Fred Luthans, *Organizational Behavior,* 3rd ed. (New York: McGraw-Hill, 1989), 236.

managerial performance, there have been some interesting findings. One of them, reported by McClelland and Burnham, was the following:

> The general conclusion of these studies is that the top manager of a company must possess a high need for power, that is, a concern for influencing people. However, this need must be disciplined and controlled so that it is directed toward the benefit of the institution as a whole and not toward the manager's personal aggrandizement. Moreover, the top manager's need for power ought to be greater than his need for being liked by people.[22]

Affiliation need
may subvert
managerial
performance

If managers are too concerned about wanting to get along well with their people, their effectiveness will suffer. For this reason, affiliation plays a significant role in achievement motivation. Strong affiliation motivation interferes with and possibly even subverts, effective managerial performance. Of course, this is not to say that the effective manager has no need to affiliate with others. He or she must keep this need in perspective, however, and exercise self-control by maintaining proper social distance. Commenting on an example of managerial behavior in which the affiliation need was allowed to override all others, McClelland and Burnham offer the following case:

> When President Ford remarked in pardoning ex-President Nixon that he had "suffered enough," he was responding as an affiliative manager would, because he was empathizing primarily with Nixon's needs and feelings. Sociological theory and our data both argue, however, that the person whose need for affiliation is high does not make a good manager. This kind of person creates poor morale because he or she does not understand that other people in the office will tend to regard exceptions to the rules as unfair to themselves. . . . [23]

Conclusions
regarding
achievement
motivation

When all three needs—achievement, power, and affiliation—are examined in terms of achievement motivation theory, three conclusions can be drawn. First, achievement drive is extremely important for entrepreneurs, salespeople, and others who depend exclusively upon their own abilities and drive for success. Power is most important for organizational managers, who must develop and nurture the talents of their personnel. Affiliation is most important for many of the nonmanagerial people but tends to have limited value for managers. These conclusions provide a general theory of motivation and help explain why some managers enjoy their roles while others do not seek managerial positions. Figure 12-3 provides a graphic summary of the four content theories described in this section.

---

[22] McClelland and Burnham, "Power," 101.
[23] McClelland and Burnham, "Power," 103.

FIGURE 12-3   A Summary of the Four Leading Content Theories

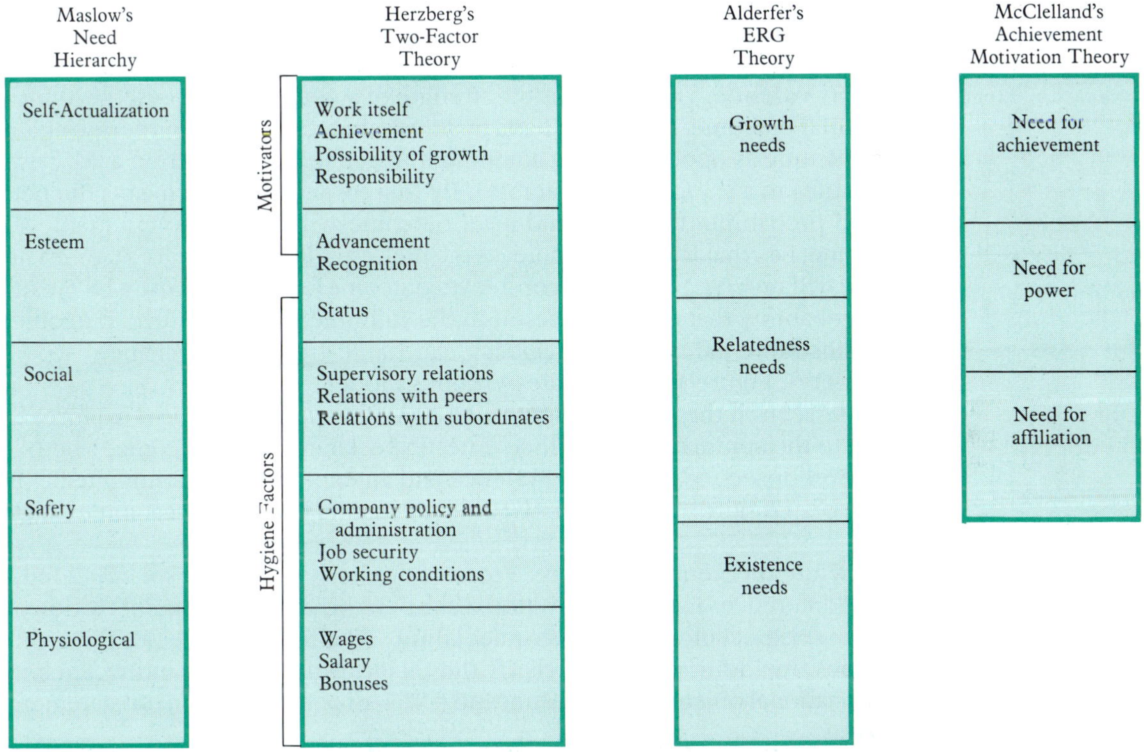

Maslow's Need Hierarchy	Herzberg's Two-Factor Theory	Alderfer's ERG Theory	McClelland's Achievement Motivation Theory
Self-Actualization	*Motivators:* Work itself / Achievement / Possibility of growth / Responsibility	Growth needs	Need for achievement
Esteem	Advancement / Recognition		Need for power
Social	*Hygiene Factors:* Status / Supervisory relations / Relations with peers / Relations with subordinates	Relatedness needs	Need for affiliation
Safety	Company policy and administration / Job security / Working conditions	Existence needs	
Physiological	Wages / Salary / Bonuses		

PROCESS THEORIES OF MOTIVATION

In contrast to content theories, **process theories** attempt to identify and explain how behavior is started, initiated, sustained, redirected, and terminated. The most important contributions to process theory have been made by Victor Vroom, Lyman Porter, Edward Lawler, and J. Stacy Adams.

Vroom's Expectancy Theory

In 1964 Victor Vroom proposed his **expectancy theory** of motivation[24]—a theory that derived from his belief that content models are inadequate in explaining the complex process of work motivation. Often referred to as "VIE" theory, the theory is built around three concepts: valence, instrumentality, and

---

[24] Victor H. Vroom, *Work and Motivation* (New York: John Wiley, 1964).

expectancy. Its basic assumption is that individuals are motivated to make choices among various alternative courses of action based on the results of these actions and how positively (or negatively) the individual views the payoffs.

Valence, instrumentality, and expectancy defined

By **valence,** Vroom means the strength of an individual's preference for a particular outcome. If a person has a positive valence, he or she prefers to attain the outcome as opposed to not attaining it. Valence can range from a +1 (very desirable) to a −1 (very undesirable). By **instrumentality** he means the perceived probability that a second-level outcome will follow from a first-level outcome, i.e., that if a person achieves the highest sales (first-level outcome) he or she will receive a bonus (second-level outcome). By **expectancy** he means the probability that effort will result in the attainment of a first-level outcome. Both instrumentality and expectancy can range from 0 (no chance) to +1 (certainty). Figure 12-4 illustrates Vroom's model.

Motivation is seen as a force

As seen in the figure, Vroom refers to motivation as a *force*. This force is equal to the summation of valence times expectancy. Each outcome, whether first-level or second-level, has a valence and an expectancy (instrumentality is incorporated here). Overall motivation is a result of this valence and expectancy.

The theory addresses individual differences . . .

While theoretical in nature, Vroom's model is useful in explaining individual differences in work motivation. Each person has a unique combination of valences, expectancies, and instrumentalities. The model addresses these differences. In addition, it helps clarify the relationship between individual and organizational objectives. J. G. Hunt and J. W. Hill commented on the statement this way:

> . . . instead of assuming (that) the satisfaction of a specific need is likely to influence organizational objectives in a certain way, we can find out how important to the employees are the various second-level work outcomes (worker goals), the instrumentality of various first-level outcomes (organizational objectives) for their attainment, and the expectancies that are held with respect to the employees' ability to influence the first-level outcome.[25]

but precludes direct application

On the negative side, Vroom's proposition is not only theoretical but precludes direct application. After all, what manager is really going to try to determine worker motivation via a computation of expectancy and valence? On the positive side, research in the field supports Vroom's basic model, and the model has served as a springboard for additional investigation into the subject of motivation.[26] The Porter-Lawler model is an excellent example of such research.

---

[25] J. G. Hunt and J. W. Hill, "The New Look in Motivation Theory for Organizational Research," *Human Organization* (Summer 1968):105.

[26] See, for example, Alan C. Filley, Robert J. House, and Steven Kerr, *Managerial Process and Organizational Behavior,* 2nd ed. (Glenview, IL: Scott, Foresman and Co., 1976), 200–201.

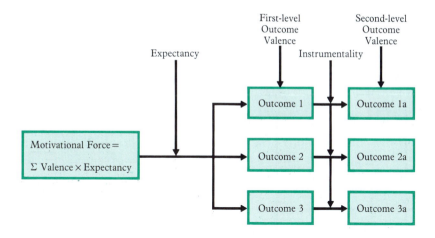

FIGURE 12-4
Vroom's
Expectancy Theory
Model

The Porter-Lawler Model

Vroom's model is extended

Lyman Porter and Edward Lawler have extended Vroom's model. In the process they have not only added more variables (expressed diagrammatically rather than mathematically, as in Vroom's case) but have also addressed the relationship between satisfaction and performance. Figure 12-5 is a diagram of their model.[27]

As the figure indicates, Porter and Lawler regard motivation as a force. This force is influenced by the value of the reward the individual is getting and the relationship the person sees between effort and the probability of attaining this reward. When effort is combined with abilities and traits (what the individual is capable of doing) and role perception (what the individual believes he or she should be doing), the outcome is performance (accomplishment). The result of performance is rewards. These rewards can be intrinsic (a feeling of having done a good job, self-satisfaction, personal enjoyment) or extrinsic (an increase in salary, a better office, a new title). The rewards, if perceived as equitable, result in satisfaction.

The performance-satisfaction link

Perhaps the most important part of the model is the righthand side, which addresses performance and satisfaction. The model presents satisfaction as the result of performance, that is, if an individual performs well and receives an equitable reward, he or she will be satisfied. This "performance causes satisfaction" approach is in marked contrast to that of many behaviorists who, prior to this time, held that "satisfaction causes performance" or "a happy worker is a productive worker." Are Porter and Lawler right in their contention that

[27] Lyman W. Porter and Edward E. Lawler, III, *Managerial Attitudes and Performance* (Homewood, IL: Richard D. Irwin, Inc., 1968).

FIGURE 12-5   The Porter-Lawler Motivation Model

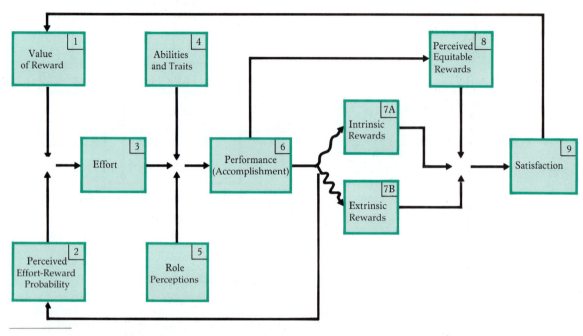

Source: Lyman W. Porter and Edward L. Lawler, III, *Managerial Attitudes and Performance* (Homewood, IL: Richard D. Irwin, Inc., 1968), 165. ©1968. Reprinted with permission.

performance brings about satisfaction? Research studies do basically substantiate their conclusion.[28]

The theory has been refined . . .   In more recent years, Lawler has proposed a number of refinements of the theory, suggesting that there are actually two types of expectancies. The first is the E→P, which is the probability that effort will lead to performance. The second is the P→O, which is the probability that performance will result in the desired outcome. In examining the E→P expectancy, he believes that the most important factors are the person's self-esteem, past experiences in similar situations, and communications from others. The P→O expectancy is influenced by many of the same basic factors, along with the attractiveness of the outcomes to the individual.

[28] For example, see David G. Kuhn, John W. Slocum, Jr., and Richard B. Chase, "Does Job Performance Affect Employee Satisfaction?" *Personnel Journal* (June 1971):455–59, 485; Jay R. Schuster, Barbara Clark, and Miles Rogers, "Testing Portions of the Porter and Lawler Model Regarding the Motivational Role of Pay," *Journal of Applied Psychology* (June 1971):187–95; and Rabi S. Bhagat, "Conditions Under Which Stronger Job Performance-Job Satisfaction Relationships May Be Observed: A Closer Look at Two Situational Contingencies," *Academy of Management Journal* (December 1982):772–89.

Overall, the Porter-Lawler model is an important contribution to the study of modern motivation. It identifies some of the most important variables in motivation and proposes a relationship between them. Commenting on the value of expectancy theory, in which the Porter-Lawler model plays a large role, Miner has noted that:

> . . . expectancy theory has obtained considerable acceptance among students of organizational behavior. It is, however, primarily a theory for the scholar and the scientists rather than the practitioner. The fact is manifested in the continued outpouring of expectancy theory research and the almost total lack of applications that can be clearly traced to the theory. It is becoming increasingly evident, though, that applications are possible and that they might well prove fruitful.[29]

but it has its limitations

A more negative assessment of the theory is that it is based on a hedonistic view of mankind. To the extent that a person is not hedonistic, the theory does not work. The model also suggests that human motivation is highly rational and conscious. Whenever unconscious motives cause people to behave unpredictably, expectancy theory misses its mark. Nevertheless, the expectancy theory approach is important in that it provides insights into human motivation at work.[30]

Equity Theory

Exchange relationships

Equity theory, another process theory of motivation, is most closely associated with the work of J. Stacy Adams.[31] In essence, **equity theory** deals with exchange relationships among individuals and groups. The theory holds that, in deciding whether or not they are being treated equitably or fairly, people compare what they are giving to an organization to what they and others are getting from the organization. Table 12-3 lists some of the inputs and outcomes that are involved in this comparison process.

When a person concludes that, in comparison to others, what he or she is giving to the organization is equal to what is being received, equity exists. When one side of the equation (either the input or the outcome) is larger, an imbalance exists.[32] The person feels either anger (because of being underrewarded) or guilt (because of being overrewarded). This tension typically results in one or more of the following steps being taken:

---

[29] Miner, *Organizational Behavior,* 160–61.

[30] Thomas L. Quick, "The Best Kept Secret for Increasing Productivity . . . Expectancy Theory," *Sales and Marketing Management* (July 1989):34–38.

[31] J. Stacy Adams, "Inequity in Social Exchange," in Leonard Berkowitz, ed., *Advances in Experimental Social Psychology* (New York: Academic Press, 1965):267–99.

[32] Robert P. Vecchio, "Predicting Worker Performance in Inequitable Settings," *Academy of Management Review* (January 1982):103–10.

TABLE 12-3   Some of the Typical Inputs and Outcomes Used by Individuals in Measuring Perceived Equity

Inputs	Outcomes
Education	Pay
Experience	Fringe benefits
Training	Job status
Skill	Seniority benefits
Job effort	Working conditions
Seniority	Job perquisites

Ways of dealing with inequity tension

1. The person alters the input by putting in more or less time (depending on whether there is an overreward or underreward).
2. The person attempts to alter the output by turning out more or less work (again depending on whether an overreward or underreward is perceived).
3. The person changes his or her perception of how much is being given or received, as in the case of the person who says, ''Sure I make $500 a year less than anyone else in this department, but my job has a lot less tension and anxiety so I don't mind the difference.''
4. The person simply stops comparing himself or herself with certain other people because there will always be a perceived inequity; instead the person chooses someone with whom a favorable comparison can be made.
5. The person acts against the individual or group with whom the comparison is being made by harassing them or inducing them to do something (such as more work) and thereby improves the perceived input/output ratio.

If the inequity tension is sufficiently strong, the person usually employs more than one of these five approaches. The important thing to remember, however, is that until there is a perceived balance between inputs and outputs, tension will result and individuals will seek to adjust these inputs and outcomes appropriately. If people feel they are being treated inequitably, even if they are not, motivation is affected.[33]

MONEY AS A MOTIVATOR

Before we conclude our discussion of modern motivation theory, some additional discussion of money as a motivator is in order. Earlier in the chapter it was noted that Herzberg felt that money was a hygiene factor — it does not bring

---

[33] Richard A. Cosier and Dan R. Dalton, ''Equity Theory and Time: A Reformation,'' *Academy of Management Review* (April 1983):311–19.

about satisfaction but it does prevent dissatisfaction. Many people find this idea hard to accept. For them, money is indeed a motivator. This seems to be as true for top executives as it is for members of the general workforce.[34] On the other hand, it is also true that money does not always motivate. For example, for someone in a very high income tax bracket, a raise of $500 has far less motivational potential than it would have for someone in a low income tax bracket. Moreover, the person's socioeconomic status must be taken into account. Was the person raised to believe that having a lot of money was a good thing? Do the person's current friends and relatives place a high value on money? If the answer to these two questions is yes, money is far more likely to be a motivator than if the answer is no. (See "Management in Practice: How "Rational" Is CEO Compensation?")

The Manager and the Managed

Many managers believe that their employees are lazy because they will not work an extra hour for time-and-a-half, or because they will not produce an extra 10 percent despite the fact that the organization has an incentive plan that is tied directly to output. These managers fail to distinguish between their own personal values and those of their employees.[35]

Managers assign significance to money . . .

Many managers are high achievers. They assign special significance to money rewards because doing so allows them to measure how well they are doing. Just because they use money as a counting device, however, does not mean their subordinates do also.

and often use it to manipulate

Furthermore, many managers regard money as a motivator because it is in their own best interest to do so. Why? Because money is a variable that is easy to manipulate. It can be given to those who obey the rules and denied to those who do not. It is a control device. If a manager can convince subordinates to accept money as a motivator, he or she can use money on a reward-penalty basis.

Money and Need Satisfaction

Money can satisfy virtually all needs

Money as a motivator is also difficult to understand because it means different things to different people. For the poor family that needs money for food, clothing, and shelter, it is a means for satisfying the most basic needs. Without it the family would be in dire straits.

Money also helps attain safety needs. A person with a lot of money can purchase protection in the form of health and disability insurance and can also store up a sufficient amount of savings to handle other crises that may arise. In short, money can help protect a person from environmental dangers (unemployment, sickness, disability).

---

[34] Susan Chin, "The Power and the Pay—The 800 Best Paid Executives in America," *Forbes* (May 29, 1989):159–88.

[35] Dennis T. Jaffe and Cynthia D. Scott, "Bridging Your Workers' Motivation Gap," *Nations Business* (March 1989):30–32.

How "Rational" is CEO Compensation?

In an effort to determine what factors actually influence the level of compensation received by CEOs of different companies, *Fortune* magazine recently commissioned a study of CEO pay in the top 100 companies in the *Fortune 500* and the top 100 companies in the *Service 500*. The following were found to be "rational" factors affecting the level of pay.

Company Size: For every 10 percent increase in the size of a company there was a 2 percent increase in CEO pay.

Company Performance: Increasing a company's Performance IQ (constructed using 5-year returns on equity, ratio of market value to book value, and total return to investors over the last 5 years) from 100 to 110 brings about a 31 percent increase in CEO pay.

Tenure: The longer a CEO works for a company the *less* he or she makes. A CEO with 30 years of service earned 6 percent less than one with 20 years of service.

Location: Companies headquartered in major cities pay more. For example, in New York City the pay is 7 percent higher than average and in Los Angeles the pay is 10 percent higher.

Ownership of stock in the company, age of the CEO, and the number of years serving as a CEO are all factors that did *not* have any effect on CEO pay.

Based upon the rational factors, the CEO of each company was given a "rational" pay to compare with their actual pay. Listed below are the top five, who exceeded their calculated rational pay and the top five who lagged behind their calculated rational pay.

CEOs Exceeding Their Rational Pay

		Pay			
Company	CEO	Actual $000	Rank	Rational $000	Percent Higher
Bear Stearns Cos.	Alan C. Greenberg	$5,712	2	$1,206	373%
Bally Manufacturing	Robert E. Mullane	2,549	11	697	266%
Warner Communications	Steven J. Ross	4,066	5	1,187	243%
Walt Disney	Michael D. Eisner	6,732	1	2,489	170%
Georgia-Pacific	T. Marshall Hahn, Jr.	2,623	10	1,119	134%

CEOs Lagging Below Their Rational Pay

		Pay			
Company	CEO	Actual $000	Rank	Rational $000	Percent Higher
Digital Equipment	Kenneth H. Olsen	$ 906	124	$1,566	−42%
Merck	P. Roy Vagelos	1,372	55	2,455	−45%
Caterpillar	George A. Schaefer	532	159	998	−47%
Texas Air	Francisco A. Lorenzo	505	163	964	−48%
Super Valu Stores	Michael W. Wright	551	157	1,053	−48%

Source: Graef S. Crystal, "The Wacky, Wacky World of CEO Pay," *Fortune* (June 6, 1988):68–78.

Money helps people meet their social needs. A person with a lot of money can afford to throw parties, join a country club, and socialize with others. In fact, money often serves as a magnet that attracts others to the person who has it.

Money also provides an excellent basis for meeting ego needs. After all, someone who is making $250,000 a year can reason: "I must be good. Look at how much money I'm making." Money cannot guarantee that a person will feel good about himself or herself, of course, but it certainly can help.

Finally, money is important in meeting self-actualization needs in that the individual with money can focus on becoming a better person. Dozens of examples can be cited, from John Kennedy and Nelson Rockefeller, whose personal wealth allowed them to enter and excel in politics, to Ray Kroc, the founder of McDonald's, whose wealth allowed him to do such things as build the swimming pool for the 1984 U.S. Olympics and construct Ronald McDonald houses coast-to-coast.

Naturally, money is not a prerequisite for all need satisfaction. The important thing to remember, however, is that some variables, such as money, allow an individual to fulfill more than one need. For this reason, money remains a rather elusive motivator. People use it in so many different ways, to fulfill so many varying desires, that it is impossible to say exactly what role it plays for people—except, of course, on an individual basis.

Of more importance to many of today's younger employees, however, is the chance to do things that are interesting, enjoyable, and meaningful. They believe that they will always be able to earn enough money to purchase what they need. The important thing is to earn this money in the most enjoyable and challenging way possible. In this way values enter the motivation process.

It is an elusive motivator

VALUES AND MOTIVATION

What do people want from their jobs? What are they willing to give to the organization in return for these rewards?

Not very long ago it would have been possible to answer these questions with the following list of values that most employees considered important:

Traditional employee values

- strong loyalty to the company
- strong desire for money and status
- strong desire for promotion up the management hierarchy
- critical concern about job security and stability
- strong employee identification with work roles rather than with personal roles[36]

---

[36] Lauren Hite Jackson and Mark G. Mindell, "Motivating the New Breed," *Personnel* (March–April 1980):54. See also Leonard Ackerman and Joseph P. Grunenwald, "Help Employees Motivate Themselves," *Personnel Journal* (July 1984):55–57.

FIGURE 12-6   Value Profile of a "Contemporary" Employee

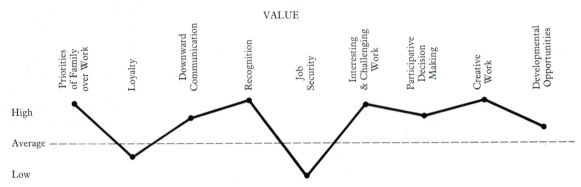

This employee places a much higher priority on his family role than on his work role, has high recognition needs, desires job duties that are varied and nonrepetitive, and likes to identify job-related problems and develop solutions to those problems independently. This individual does not value job security or place a high priority on company loyalty.

Source: Adapted, by permission of the publisher, from "Motivating the New Breed," Lauren Hite Jackson and Mark G. Mindell, *Personnel* (March–April, 1980):57. ©1980 by American Management Associations, New York. All rights reserved.

Many of these values were shaped by environmental factors. People learned their skills at the organization's expense and planned their careers around that enterprise. Today a majority of employees acquire their skills and knowledge independently of the enterprise and are not as loyal as before. Additionally, it is no longer the norm for a person to enter an organization and work his or her way to the top. Employees today often find that the fastest route to the top is to change jobs and move to another organization at a higher level.[37] Some of the values that characterize this contemporary employee have been identified as follows:

Contemporary employee values

- low loyalty or commitment to the organization
- a need for rewards geared to accomplishments
- a need for organizational recognition of his or her contributions
- decreased concern for job security and stability
- a view of leisure as being more important than work
- a need to perform work that is challenging and worthwhile
- a need to participate in decisions that ultimately affect him or her
- a stronger employee identification with his or her personal role rather than with his or her work role

---

[37] J. Daniel Sherman and Howard L. Smith, "The Influence of Organizational Structure on Intrinsic vs. Extrinsic Motivation," *Academy of Management Journal* (December 1984):877–85. Also see Martin G. Evans, "Organizational Behavior: The Central Role of Motivation," *Journal of Management* (Fall–Winter 1986):203–22.

FIGURE 12-7 Value Profile of a "Traditional" Employee

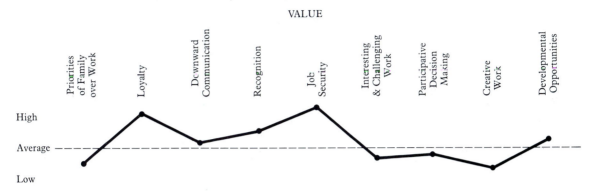

This employee places a much higher priority on his work role than on his family role and has high needs for job security. Further, this employee is extremely loyal to his or her organization. Of less importance are identifying problems and developing solutions to work-related problems himself, having different kinds of things to do on his job, and taking part in decisions affecting him or his work.

Source: Adapted, by permission of the publisher, from "Motivating the New Breed," Lauren Hite Jackson and Mark G. Mindell, *Personnel* (March–April, 1980):57. ©1980 by American Management Associations, New York. All rights reserved.

- a need for communication from management regarding what is going on in the company
- a need to rise above the routine and approach tasks creatively
- a need for personal growth opportunities on the job[38]

Traditional and Contemporary Employees and Managers

In a recent study, Lauren Hite Jackson and Mark Mindell used two research instruments, the Employee Value Inventory and the Management Style Inventory, to measure employee and management values. Their results are reported in Figures 12-6, 12-7, and 12-8.

Figures 12-6 and 12-7 show that contemporary employees have profiles that are quite different from those of traditional workers. In fact, as explained in the figures, the values of today's employee are almost the reverse of the values of his or her counterpart in the past.

Figure 12-8 provides the profiles of contemporary and traditional managers. The five values reported in this figure are

Contemporary managerial values

- locus of control—a manager with a high locus of control believes that there is a strong relationship between managerial effort and organizational success. This manager also feels that advancement

---

[38] Jackson and Mindell, "Motivating," 55.

FIGURE 12-8
Profiles of
"Contemporary"
and "Traditional"
Managers

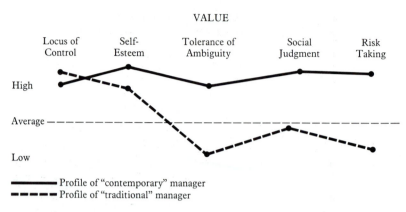

FIGURE 12-8
Profiles of
"Contemporary"
and "Traditional"
Managers

depends on achievement and that he or she has a great deal of control over subordinates' behavior.

- self-esteem — a high score here indicates that the manager considers his or her ideas to be creative, understood, and accepted. Managers with high self-esteem place high priority on employee feedback.
- tolerance of ambiguity — this value measures the degree to which managers are capable of functioning in an ambiguous or unstructured setting.
- social judgment — a high score on this scale characterizes managers with social perceptiveness, sensitivity, and a belief in the importance of good interpersonal relationships.
- risk taking — a person who scores high here tends to seek excitement rather than change and change rather than the status quo.

Taken together, the profiles of contemporary employees and managers, as reported by Jackson and Mindell, provide a clear, consistent picture. Today's employees do not intend to allow the organization to come before their family priorities. Meanwhile, on the job they are interested in what Herzberg referred to as motivators. These comments should not be taken as an endorsement of the two-factor theory, however. Rather they point to the fact that many employees simply want more control over their work and the chance to feel that what they are doing is meaningful and useful. Instead of supporting the two-factor theory, the results seem to point more to the desire for enriched jobs.

Managers have similar desires. They are less interested in being in direct control of subordinates and more interested in helping them get things done. They are also willing to operate in an unstructured environment, take risks, and work to develop good interpersonal relationships with their subordinates.

When motivation is placed in proper perspective, it becomes obvious that the manager and the employee must blend their interests. The values of the two groups cannot be at loggerheads.[39] If we think in terms of content theories, modern employees and managers both express a strong interest in higher-level need satisfaction. To the extent that an organization allows for the fulfillment of these desires, motivation can exist.[40]

SUMMARY

1. Motivation means stimulating people to action through incentives or inducements. This process is often generated through external action but is determined internally since motivation is a psychological process.
2. There are three primary ingredients in motivation: ability, effort, and desire. There are also three common aspects of motivation. They deal with: (a) what energizes human behavior, (b) how this behavior is directed or channeled, and (c) how the behavior can be maintained.
3. Perhaps the best-known "needs approach" to the study of motivation is that presented by Maslow. Basically, his theory is that only unsatisfied needs serve as motivators, and that as lower-level needs are satisfied, upper-level needs manifest themselves. In his hierarchy, there are five levels: physiological, safety, social, esteem, and self-actualization.
4. Herzberg has extended Maslow's model and applied it to the workplace with his two-factor theory of motivation. According to this theory, something is either a hygiene factor, like money or working conditions, or it is a motivator, like increased responsibility and the opportunity for advancement.
5. Alderfer's ERG theory is built around three needs: existence needs such as survival and safety, relatedness needs such as social relationships and recognition, and growth needs such as advancement, achievement, and the chance for self-actualization.
6. McClelland's achievement motivation theory addresses three needs: the need for achievement, the need for power, and the need for affiliation. McClelland holds that, of these three, the need for power is most important among managers.
7. Process theories attempt to identify and explain how behavior is started, initiated, sustained, redirected, and terminated. One of the most famous process theories is that of Vroom, who contends that motivation is the

---

[39] Jeffrey H. Greenhaus and Claudene Seidel, "The Impact of Expectations and Values on Job Attitudes," *Organizational Behavior and Human Performance* (June 1983):394–417.
[40] See: Jerry J. Sullivan, "Self Theories and Employee Motivation," *Journal of Management* (June 1989):345–63.

summation of valence times expectancy. While theoretical in nature, the model is useful in explaining individual differences in work motivation.

8. Porter and Lawler have extended Vroom's model by adding more variables and addressing the relationship between performance and satisfaction. In more recent years Lawler has proposed a number of refinements of the theory, especially by discussing the relationship of effort to performance and the relationship of performance to the desired outcome.

9. Equity theory deals with exchange relationships among individuals and groups. The theory holds that people compare what they are giving to an organization with what they are getting from it in deciding whether or not they are being treated equitably or fairly.

10. Money as a motivator is often misunderstood by managers because they assume that their subordinates attach the same importance to it as they themselves do. Money is also an elusive motivator because it can satisfy needs at any level of the need hierarchy and allow a person to fulfill more than one need at a time.

11. Values also influence motivation. The things that were important to employees 20 years ago are not necessarily those that are important to employees today. This means that if managers are going to be truly effective in motivating their people, they must understand what their employees regard as important and then help them attain these objectives.

KEY TERMS

Ability An individual's capacity to do something.

Achievement motivation theory A motivation theory that seeks to explain high achievement drive in people.

Achievement need The need to attain objectives or accomplish things.

Affiliation need The need to interact, socialize with others, and belong.

Content theories of motivation Theories of motivation that attempt to explain what motivates people.

Desire The wish, want, or urge for a particular objective.

Effort Time, drive, and energy expended in the pursuit of an objective.

Equity theory A process theory dealing with exchange relationships among individuals and groups in which employees compare what they are giving to an organization with what they are getting.

ERG theory An extension of the Maslow and Herzberg models, this theory examines three basic needs: existence, relatedness, and growth.

Esteem needs Needs related to feeling good about oneself.

Existence needs Needs related to survival and safety. They coincide with Maslow's physiological needs, safety of a material nature, and Herzberg's hygiene factors such as working conditions and salary.

Expectancy The probability that a specific action will yield a particular first-level outcome.

Expectancy theory A theory of motivation that states that motivation is equal to the summation of valence times expectancy.

Growth needs Needs related to an individual's desire for personal development.

Hygiene factors Factors identified by Frederick Herzberg (in his two-factor theory of motivation) that will not motivate people by their presence but will lead to dissatisfaction by their absence. Examples include money, good working conditions, and technical supervision.

Instrumentality The probability that a second-level outcome will follow from a first-level outcome.

Maslow's need theory A theory of human needs postulated by the psychologist Abraham Maslow which holds that unsatisfied needs are motivators and that as lower-level needs are satisfied one moves further up the hierarchy from physiological to, ultimately, self-actualization needs.

Motivation Stimulating people to action by means of incentives or inducements.

Motivators Factors identified by Frederick Herzberg (in his two-factor theory of motivation) that bring about satisfaction and result in motivation. Examples include recognition, advancement, and the work itself.

Physiological needs Basic human needs such as food, clothing, and shelter.

Power need The need for control or influence over a situation.

Process theories Theories of motivation that attempt to identify and explain how behavior is started, initiated, sustained, redirected, and terminated.

Relatedness needs Needs that stress interpersonal and social relationships as well as safety needs and ego needs of an interpersonal type.

Safety needs Needs for physical and emotional security or protection.

Self-actualization needs The need to become all one is capable of becoming by realizing one's total potential.

Social needs Needs for affiliation, interaction with others, and belongingness.

Two-factor theory A theory of motivation formulated by Frederick Herzberg in which all job-related factors are divided into two groups: hygiene factors and motivators.

Valence The strength of an individual's preference for a particular outcome.

QUESTIONS FOR ANALYSIS AND DISCUSSION

1. In your own words, what is meant by the term motivation? How does Chester Barnard's acceptance theory of authority help explain how motivation works?

2. What are the three primary ingredients in motivation? Identify and explain each.

3. There are three common aspects of motivation. What does this statement mean? Explain your answer.

4. How do content theories of motivation differ from process theories of motivation? Compare and contrast the two.

5. In your own words, what is Maslow's need hierarchy all about? Be sure to discuss all five levels in the hierarchy.

6. In what way is Maslow's need theory helpful in understanding motivation?

7. What is Herzberg's two-factor theory all about? In your answer be sure to identify and define the two types of factors.

8. How useful is Herzberg's theory in explaining motivation in the workplace? In your answer be sure to discuss both the strengths and the weaknesses of the theory.

9. In what way does Alderfer's theory extend the Maslow and Herzberg models? How useful is Alderfer's theory?

10. What is achievement drive? What are the basic characteristics of high achievers?

11. How important is a need for power among successful managers? In your answer be sure to incorporate a discussion of the material in Table 12-2.

12. What is affiliation need? How important is it for success in a management position? Explain.

13. In what way are the Maslow, Herzberg, Alderfer, and McClelland motivation theories alike? Compare and contrast them.

14. What is Vroom's expectancy theory? In your answer be sure to discuss the terms valence, instrumentality, and expectancy.

15. How does the Porter-Lawler model expand Vroom's findings? What else does their model do to help us better understand motivation?

16. Of what value is equity theory to the study of motivation at work? Defend your answer.

17. What role does money play in motivation? Be as complete as possible in your answer.

18. How do personal values affect individual motivation? In your answer be sure to incorporate a discussion of Figures 12-6, 12-7, and 12-8.

CASE

Who Will It Be?

Every three months one of the country's largest drug manufacturers holds a sales contest. The individual who produces the most sales during this time is given a two-week, all-expense-paid vacation for two. If the person is not married, the difference is given in the form of a bonus payment.

The latest contest will end in four weeks. At present it appears that the winner will be one of three people: Helen Radwin, Karl Melcher, or Roger O'Flaherty. The winner will be sent to London. The national marketing manager, Albert Chesser, is on the road quite a bit so he has had the opportunity to talk to all three of these salespeople. Here is his summary of how each feels about winning the contest.

Helen: Boy, am I excited! I have never won the sales contest before. Probably that's because it has taken me this long to hone my sales skills. Now I really feel as if I know both my product line and how to sell and it's all beginning to pay off. As far as London is concerned, I've never been there. It will be great to go. Every morning when I get up, I think about the trip. This starts me going and I can't wait to get out on the road and make my first call.

Karl: London must be beautiful this time of year. I sure would like to see it. My wife and I have never been to Europe. It would be a chance for both of us to take a vacation and relax. I'm not holding my breath about winning this contest, however. I've come close a couple of times before but I always get beaten out by someone. So if it happens this time, it happens. I'm just going to keep plugging along and do my best. I know that sooner or later I'm going to win one of these contests; so if I miss this one it's not going to be the end of the world for me.

Roger: I like sales contests, although I don't know if I particularly want to go to London. I won twice last year and three times the year before. In each case I was sent somewhere—Paris, Tokyo, Rio, Montreal. It's very nice. However, I didn't join the company to see the world. If I win this time, I think I'll ask the company to send me someplace locally for a week and then let me come home and put my feet up for the other week. Now don't get me wrong. I love to win. However, I don't necessarily care for the rewards the company gives out. I suppose it's just getting to be "old hat" for me.

1. Which of the three individuals has the greatest valence for winning the contest? Which one has the strongest belief that he or she will win?
2. Which of the three salespeople is most motivated to win the contest? Defend your answer.
3. In addition to getting the free vacation, what other needs might be satisfied by winning the contest? Explain.

YOU BE THE CONSULTANT

The Survey Results

Sergio Campanella, administrator of a large hospital, just had a survey conducted among his managerial personnel. The focus of the survey was on what these individuals want from their jobs. In addition to a list of factors that were provided in the survey, the respondents were each given the opportunity to add additional factors. The top 15, based on the number of times they were ranked and where on the list they appeared (first, second, third), were the following:

1. A chance to do something that I feel is important.
2. The opportunity to use my skills and abilities.
3. The opportunity to help others.
4. The chance to learn new things.
5. The opportunity to excel at something I am good at.
6. The opportunities that are available for promotion.
7. The amount of freedom I have to do the job my way.
8. The amount of money I receive.
9. The respect I receive from those with whom I work.
10. The job security that is afforded to me.
11. The support I get from my boss.
12. The fringe benefits that are provided to me.
13. The praise I am given for doing a job well.
14. The information I receive regarding my specific job performance.
15. The chance to participate in decision making.

Sergio has had the responses classified both by department and by level in the organization. The classification reveals very little difference in the responses. The list basically represents the way all managerial personnel feel regarding motivational factors.

Sergio is a little unsure of what the results mean. He had believed that the first items on everyone's list would be money, job security, and fringe benefits.

Nevertheless, he is not discouraged. He still feels that he can use the results to develop a plan for motivating personnel over the next 12 months. It is all a matter of deciding how to take advantage of the survey information. At the same time, he will be conducting a similar survey at the workers' level. An initial effort along these lines was made last week when 35 people in one of the departments were surveyed. Although Sergio has not yet seen the results, the department head had them compiled and gave Sergio a brief verbal summary. From what Sergio can glean from the conversation, the results are very similar to those of the managerial survey.

On the negative side, Sergio is concerned that in both cases he was apparently unable to anticipate the responses of the personnel. On the positive side, if the results from both hierarchical groups are similar, it means that one overall motivational plan can be used for the entire organization. Right now Sergio feels his first priority should be to decide what action to take in light of the results.

Your Consultation

Assume you are Sergio's consultant. He has just called you in and shown you the results reported in the case. What is your conclusion regarding what the data show? Drawing upon the information in the chapter, can you cite any research findings that would support your conclusions? Finally, based on your findings, what specific actions would you recommend Sergio take? Be as complete as possible in your report to him.

13

Group Behavior and Dynamics

OBJECTIVES

Every organization is made up of groups, formal and informal. Motivating and leading the members of these units requires a basic understanding of group behavior. This chapter studies the nature and characteristics of groups, the ways in which individuals within groups use power, and the way human interaction occurs both within and between groups. When you have finished studying all of the material in this chapter, you will be able to:

1. Define the term groups.
2. Describe formal, informal, and combination groups.
3. Explain why people join groups.
4. Identify and describe the five most meaningful characteristics of groups.
5. Describe the five most common types of power.
6. Discuss group dynamics in action.

THE NATURE OF GROUPS

There is no universal definition of the word "group." Some researchers argue that two or more people constitute a group if they perceive themselves as a group. Others define the word in motivational terms, arguing that a group is a collection of individuals whose existence is beneficial to the members. Still others argue that if individuals *communicate and interact* with each other over time, they are a group.[1]

Perhaps the best way to define the word is on the basis of common characteristics. Every **group** has three characteristics: (1) it is a social unit of two or more people, each of whom interacts with one or more of the others; (2) its members are dependent on each other in some way, if only to get their work done; and (3) its members receive satisfaction from their mutual association. These three characteristics—interaction, dependence, and satisfaction—are quite easy to understand. Unless individuals come in contact with each other, directly or indirectly, they cannot truly be members of a group. Nor would they come in contact if they were not dependent on one another for some reason. Finally, if any one of them did not derive satisfaction from this association he or she would attempt to leave the group. So in general terms, we can draw together

A group defined   these three characteristics and define a group as a social unit consisting of two or more interdependent, interactive individuals who are striving to attain common goals.

Types of Groups

Every organization contains formal and informal groups as well as combination groups which combine the characteristics of the two.

Formal Groups

Groups can be formed by organizations or by the individuals themselves   **Formal groups** are established by the organization and typically can be described as either functional or project groups. A **functional group** is made up of individuals performing the same basic tasks. For example, in a large organization one can expect to find all accountants in the accounting department, lathe operators in the production department, and salespeople in the marketing department. **Project groups**, as seen in Chapter 9, are multifunctional in composition and are formed to carry out a particular assignment. As soon as this objective is attained, the project group is disbanded.

---

[1] Richard M. Steers, *Introduction to Organizational Behavior,* 2nd ed. (Glenview, IL: Scott Foresman and Co., 1984), 222.

Informal Groups

Informal groups are set up by the members themselves and often cross departmental lines and span hierarchical levels. There are various bases for their formation. Two of the most common are interests and friendship. People in an organization who have similar interests (both are in the R&D department working on the same invention) or personalities (they hit it off well together) are likely to be members of the same informal group.

Combination Groups

Many people are members of more than one group

An individual can be a full-fledged member of more than one group. For example, someone can be in the accounting department (functional group), or a task force chosen to audit the operations of a subsidiary (project group), and in continual contact with two friends who work in the marketing department (informal group). Moreover, people do not always separate business from pleasure when interacting with other group members. For example, in most formal groups members spend time socializing as well as "getting down to business." Conversely, while the informal group often serves as an outlet for social interaction, it is also commonly used for getting things done. For example, in auditing the operations of the subsidiary, the accountant may call and talk to one of his or her friends in marketing in order to get some inside information on the way salespeople write up their orders and the type of sales pattern that is typical for this subsidiary. The accountant uses the informal organization to supplement formal sources of information.

When the interactions of groups in a modern enterprise are depicted on an organization chart, there can be lines running all over the page. This point is illustrated in Figure 13-1, where special attention has been given to illustrating *only* the flow of informal communiqués. Four informal relationships are shown. Here is what has happened:

1. A worker has contacted the manager of Plant A to remind her that they are bowling for the league championship that evening.
2. One supervisor has contacted a fellow supervisor to ask some questions regarding how to properly fill out the new monthly control report.
3. Another supervisor has contacted the manager of Plant B, a fellow college chum, and urged him to read an article in the business section of the local paper.
4. The manager of Plant A has contacted a foreman who lives down the block from him to ask if he can hitch a ride home this evening.

Notice from these explanations that some of the informal communiqués are business related and others are of a more personal nature. The manager is faced with the challenge of dealing with both formal and informal groups.

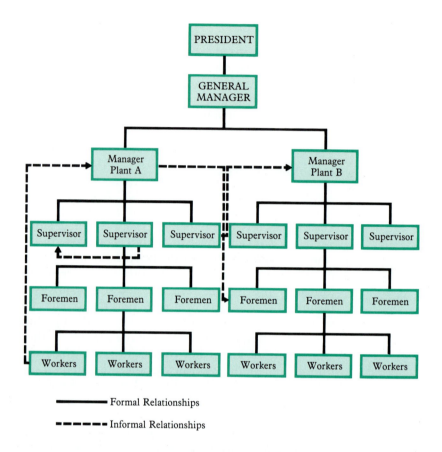

FIGURE 13-1
Formal and
Informal
Relationships

WHY PEOPLE JOIN GROUPS

Why do people join groups? A number of theories have been formulated to answer this question.

Theories of Group Formation

Closeness counts

The most basic theory of group formation explains it in terms of "propinquity," which means nearness or close proximity. In other words, people affiliate with others because they are located near them. As applied to modern organizations, this theory holds that people who work in the same area are more likely to join the same group than are people who work a great distance apart.[2] Unfortunately,

[2] Leon Festinger, Stanley Schachter, and Kurt Back, *Social Pressures in Informal Groups: A Study of Human Factors in Housing* (Stanford, CA: Stanford University Press, 1963).

the theory is superficial, failing to address the real complexities of group formation.

A more comprehensive approach has been provided by George Homans.[3] His theory is based on three elements: activities, interactions, and sentiments. An *activity* is something that an individual or group does. An *interaction* is a communication, whether verbal or nonverbal, between people. A *sentiment* is an idea, a belief, or a feeling that an individual has about someone or something.

So do activities, interactions, and sentiments

> The more activities persons share, the more numerous will be their interactions and the stronger will be their sentiments . . . the more interactions among persons, the more will be their shared activities and sentiments; and the more sentiments persons have for one another, the more will be their shared activities and interactions. This theory lends a great deal to the understanding of group formation and process. The major element is *interaction*. Persons in a group interact with one another, not in just the physical propinquity sense, but also to accomplish many group goals such as cooperation and problem solving.[4]

Another theory explaining group formation is often referred to as **balance theory**. This theory contends that people are attracted to one another because of similar attitudes toward the same goals or objects. For example, they feel the same way about religion, politics, work, lifestyle, sports, or marriage. Perhaps the cliche "similarities attract" best describes the essence of balance theory, although it does tend to integrate two of the ideas that the other two theories focus on: propinquity and interaction.

Similar attitudes are important

The theory that has received the greatest attention in recent years, however, is **exchange theory**. This theory is similar to equity theory, which was discussed in the previous chapter, in that it holds that a person's decision to join and remain with a group is based on the reward cost outcome of the interaction. As long as what the person is getting from being a member of the group (friendship, support, satisfaction) exceeds the cost of being a member (time expended, favors given), he or she will remain a member. Propinquity, interaction, and common attitudes all play a role in this theory.

So are reward cost outcomes

Economics of Group Formation

While these four theories certainly sum up many of the reasons why people join groups, it is not necessary to couch an answer in strictly theoretical terms. We can examine the question from the standpoint of economics or payoffs. And while balance theory and exchange theory certainly do pay some attention to

---

[3] George Homans, *The Human Group* (New York: Harcourt Brace Jovanovich, 1950), 43–44.
[4] Fred Luthans, *Organizational Behavior,* 5th ed. (New York: McGraw-Hill, 1989), 371.

this approach, we can go further. Many people join groups because it helps them satisfy one or more of their needs. This statement is particularly true when examined in terms of Maslow's need hierarchy. For example, in addition to feeling the obvious satisfaction of social needs

Groups help people satisfy needs . . .

. . . people in groups feel secure (safety), and such social interaction also helps them feel important (esteem). Additionally, members of a group may be of use to each other by demonstrating shortcuts for doing their jobs, thereby enabling the individuals to increase their pay and satisfy physiological needs in the process. Finally, group members often help each other in self-actualizing by encouraging the development of competence.[5]

and meet people with similar interests

When presented in terms of balance theory, similar interests are also a very practical reason for joining a group. And we need not confine this similarity to one of viewpoint, as when two people see things the same way. It can be extended to include the need to cluster together to deal with problems or ward off danger. Workers and managers who are confronted with a situation that threatens the profitability of the firm or their continued employment are much more likely to band together and work as a team than are those who do not face such potential calamities.

CHARACTERISTICS OF GROUPS

Another way to examine groups is on the basis of their characteristics or distinguishing features. Five of the most meaningful are group size, norms, roles, status, and cohesiveness.

Group Size

Group size influences interaction . . .

Work groups can be found in various sizes; some are quite small (three to four people) while others are quite large (20 people or more). Research indicates that size may affect a number of behavioral variables. For example, as the size of the group increases, the way in which members interact with each other changes. Robert Bales and Edgar Borgatta found that as the group size went up, the time and attention given to group harmony went down.[6] In small groups the members typically exhibited greater agreement and sought each other's opin-

[5] Richard M. Hodgetts, *Modern Human Relations at Work,* 2nd ed. (Hinsdale, IL: Dryden Press, 1984), 102.
[6] Robert F. Bales and Edgar F. Borgatta, "Size of Group as a Factor in the Interaction Profile," in A. P. Hare, Edgar F. Borgatta, and Robert F. Bales, eds., *Small Groups* (New York: Knopf, 1955), 396–413.

ions more frequently. In large groups data were communicated directly in the form of either suggestions or information. The need for group approval diminished, and, realizing that there was increased competition for attention, members were more direct and to the point with their communiqués.

On the other hand, research also shows that satisfaction tends to decline as group size increases. Porter and Lawler found that people working in smaller groups or work units reported higher levels of satisfaction than did those in larger units.[7]

Researchers have also found that as group size increases, so does turnover.[8] One of the primary reasons appears to be the difficulty of attaining upper-level need satisfaction. The work becomes highly specialized, group cohesion declines, and the average worker begins to find the job less appealing. The result is that the person quits.

A similar pattern exists in the case of absenteeism. In particular, absenteeism tends to be higher among blue-collar workers than among white-collar workers.[9] One explanation is that as group size increases, blue-collar workers are less able than white-collar workers to satisfy their upper-level needs because fewer avenues are available to them. For example, white-collar jobs tend to have more job autonomy and control than blue-collar jobs. The inability to satisfy upper-level needs may cause blue-collar workers to begin to stay away from work.

Richard Steers and Susan Rhodes made an investigation of both turnover and absenteeism in industry and found that two primary factors influence attendance: the individual's satisfaction with the job situation and pressures to attend. If a person is satisfied with a job, he or she wants to come to work. If there are pressures to attend, he or she is reluctant to stay away. Figure 13-2 shows Steers and Rhodes's model outlining the major influences affecting employee attendance.

Notice in the figure that one of the primary factors influencing job attendance is the situation itself. If a person has a great deal of job scope (autonomy, responsibility, variety, feedback), a high job level, an acceptable amount of stress, opportunity for advancement, and so forth, he or she is favorably influenced to attend work. Another important set of criteria are the pressures to attend. If the person needs the job, is motivated by the reward system, is pressured by fellow workers to attend, or has a high organizational commitment, he or she is more likely to come to work. Some of the factors in Figure 13-2 are a result of group size. Others are a result of group norms, another important group characteristic.

(margin notes) as well as satisfaction · Size also affects turnover . . . · and absenteeism

---

[7] Lyman Porter and Edward Lawler III, "Properties of Organization Structure in Relation to Job Attitudes and Job Behavior," *Psychological Bulletin* (July 1965):23–51.

[8] Lyman W. Porter and Richard M. Steers, "Organizational, Work, and Personal Factors in Employee Turnover and Absenteeism," *Psychological Bulletin* (August 1973):151–76.

[9] Richard M. Steers and Susan R. Rhodes, "Major Influences on Employee Attendance: A Process Model," *Journal of Applied Psychology* (August 1978):391–407.

FIGURE 13-2   Major Influences on Employee Attendance

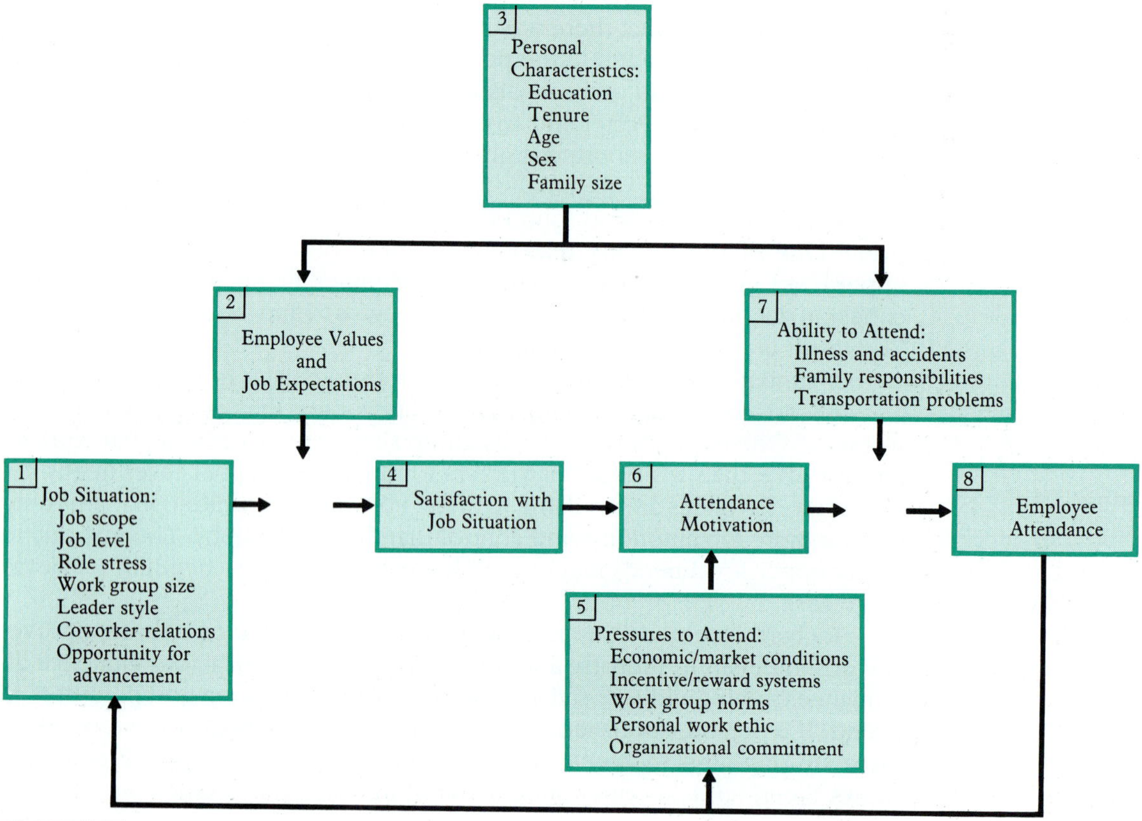

Source: Richard M. Steers and Susan R. Rhodes, "Major Influences on Employee Attendance: A Process Model," *Journal of Applied Psychology*, 63, no. 4 (August 1978):393. Copyright 1978 by the American Psychological Association. Reprinted by permission of the publisher and author.

Group Norms

Norms are behavioral rules of conduct

Norms are behavioral rules of conduct that are adopted by group members. Norms tell how an individual ought to act. In essence, they serve five purposes: (1) to provide a frame of reference for viewing the environment, (2) to establish the attitudes and behaviors to be employed in this environment, (3) to help prescribe feelings about right and wrong attitudes and behavior, (4) to help determine tolerance (or lack of it) toward those who violate the norms, and (5) to help establish the positive and negative sanctions by which acceptable behavior is rewarded by group members and unacceptable behavior is punished.

Norms are important to group development for two reasons. First, they provide the members with an understanding of the way to act by telling them what is right behavior and what is wrong behavior. Second, they ensure that all of the members of the group act in unison. Without uniformity of action, the members might all be going in different directions. Thanks to these behavioral rules of conduct, however, all of the members act as one.

On the other hand, there are limits beyond which norms do not extend. The following list summarizes some of these limits:

Limits beyond which norms do not extend

1. Norms apply only to behavior; they do not carry over to private feelings or thoughts. Nor is it necessary to accept group norms privately, only publicly.
2. Norms are developed only for behavior that is viewed as important by most of the group members. They are commonly restricted to such areas as the amount of work people should be doing, the way in which they should interact with the manager, and the way they should behave with other members of the group. It is uncommon to find norms relating to one's personal life away from the group.
3. Norms usually develop over time. As the group increases its interaction and informal goals are developed, norms of conduct are formulated. This development of norms can be hastened, however, if some emergency arises. If new work rules are introduced, for example, the members need to know how to react.
4. Not all of the norms apply to all of the members. For example, younger members of the group may be required to show respect to the older members but the latter may be allowed to openly correct or criticize young people who have done things wrong. Such factors as seniority, age, and experience often dictate which norms apply and to what extent.
5. There are degrees of conformity. Not everyone has to toe the mark perfectly. For example, while a particular work group may have an informal output norm of 50 pieces an hour, a deviation of five pieces either way may be tolerated. Also, if someone in the group has a sick child and needs to earn additional income to meet the hospital bills, the output norm may not be applied to this person at all.

Individuals who want to be members of the group must adhere to these norms or be willing to suffer the consequences, which can take numerous forms. The most common is exclusion from social interaction with the other members. A second and somewhat related consequence is lack of assistance in job-related matters. A third is to be made the object of outright hostility or tension-building behavior such as name calling. The person may also be made to look foolish or ridiculous in front of the other members of the group or the supervisor, or, if things really get out of hand, he or she may be subjected to physical abuse of some sort such as being "accidentally" bumped by others or having work knocked on to the floor. The degree to which these negative consequences are carried is determined by the situation. If the group cannot afford to allow deviation from its ranks because the existence of the group is being threatened, the penalties are much more severe than if the person has a poor personality and is not popular with the group.[10]

Role

A **role** is an expected behavior. In many organizations job descriptions provide the basis for one's role. By carefully reading the description an individual can understand what he or she is supposed to be doing. The job description provides an initial basis for determining one's role. There is more to the topic of role, however, than a job description can explain.

A role is an expected behavior

Sometimes a person does not fully understand what is expected of him or her because the description is either too general or too vague. When this occurs, **role ambiguity** can result. Most people deal with this problem by learning their responsibilities as they go along. Additionally, the further up the hierarchy people go, the more likely it is that they will face role ambiguity.

Role-related problems

A second major role-related problem is **role conflict**. It occurs when an individual is forced to assume two roles but the performance of one precludes the performance of the other. For example, in order to be most effective, a supervisor believes that she needs to exercise a lenient leadership style. On the other hand, her boss has just told her that top management wants supervisors to crack down hard on output and that she will be evaluated heavily on her ability to make the workers toe the mark.

Finally, there are manager and employee **role perceptions**. The manager not only has a perception of his or her own role but also of each employee's role and of his or her own role as seen by the employees. The employees have the same set of three perceptions: their own role, the manager's role, and the manager's perception of their role. See Figure 13-3. These role perceptions influence both how people act and how they expect others to act. Knowing one's role and carrying it out is not enough for intragroup harmony. The other members of the group must feel that the individual is carrying out the "proper" role.[11] For example, in many organizations managers are expected to maintain their distance from other employees. Those who do not are regarded as acting improperly—not only by fellow managers but by employees as well!

Status

Status is the relative ranking of individuals in organizations or groups. This ranking is typically based on criteria such as job position, job function, personality, and competence.

Status is the relative ranking of individuals

---

[10] Robert Albanese and David D. Van Fleet, "Rational Behavior in Groups: The Free Riding Tendency," *Academy of Management Review* (April 1985):244–55.

[11] Randy Y. Hirokawa and Dennis S. Gouran, "Facilitation of Group Communication," *Management Communication Quarterly* (August 1989):71–92.

FIGURE 13-3
Manager-Employee
Role Perceptions

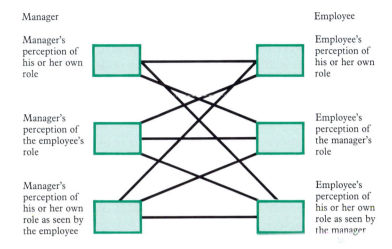

Manager

Manager's
perception of
his or her own
role

Manager's
perception of
the employee's
role

Manager's
perception of
his or her own
role as seen by
the employee

Employee

Employee's
perception of
his or her own
role

Employee's
perception of
the manager's
role

Employee's
perception of
his or her own
role as seen by
the manager

Determinants of Status

Hierarchical level
helps determine
status . . .

The employee's place in the organizational hierarchy helps dictate status. For example, a vice president has more status than a general manager; a supervisor has more status than a laborer.

as does one's job

Another status determinant is the job the individual performs. For example, in manufacturing firms tool and die makers have more status than machinists; in sales organizations, the high-achieving salesperson has greater status than the office manager and the advertising manager has greater status than the purchasing manager.

Personality makes a
difference . . .

Personality also affects status. An individual who gets along with others, is easy to work with, and is always ready to say a kind word is more likely to be given status by other members of the organization than an individual with whom no one can work easily because he or she is unpleasant.

as well as work
competence

Job competence also plays a role, because the better a person knows his or her job, the more likely it is that he or she will be accorded status by members of the peer group. Among workers with a high productivity objective, the greatest producer is likely to have high (if not the highest) status.

Status can be
situationally
determined

Who will have the most status in the group, or in the enterprise at large, at any given moment? This question can be answered only by analyzing the specific situation. For example, if the group is confronted with a particular advertising problem, the person with the greatest expertise in this area undoubtedly will have the highest status. On the other hand, if the group is in the process of entertaining a potential client, the person with the most pleasing personality will move to the fore. If the group is having a weekly meeting, the chairperson will have the most status. If the group is meeting away from the job, the specifics of the situation must be analyzed again. Is it a business meeting? If so, the person with the highest rank (president, vice president) may well have the greatest status. If it is a golf match, the person who is the best golfer has the greatest status.

Figure 13-4 illustrates this idea. The figure shows four people: an insurance company president, a company client, a professor of insurance, and an MBA student who is specializing in insurance. On the golf course, the insurance company client (who is the best golfer of all four) has the greatest status. In the company itself, the president has the most status. If the four go over to the university, they are in the bailiwick of the professor and he or she has the highest status.

Informal Organizational Status

Three basic groups

Status can also be examined from the standpoint of the informal organization. Within this kind of organization, there are three basic groups. First, people who are full-fledged members of the organization constitute what is called the **nucleus group**. Next, people who are seeking admission to the informal organization and from whose numbers new members will be chosen constitute the **fringe group**. Finally, people who have been rejected for membership for reasons that include doing too little work, doing too much work, or having an unpleasant personality constitute the **outer group**.

Figure 13-5 shows arrows between the people who are members of the nucleus group, indicating that they interact and socialize with each other. The people in the fringe group have been placed in the inner portion of their circle, close to the nucleus group because this is the direction in which they want to move. Meanwhile, those in the outer group are placed toward the outer edge of their respective circle as far away from the nucleus group as possible, because they are not permitted admission.

Status Problems

Although most members of groups, formal and informal, seek status, status-related problems must sometimes be addressed. The two most common are status incongruency and status discrepancy.

FIGURE 13-4
Status Varies with the Environment

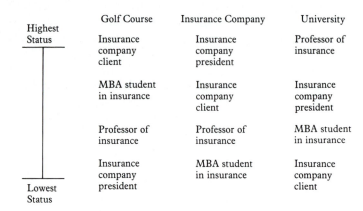

	Golf Course	Insurance Company	University
Highest Status	Insurance company client	Insurance company president	Professor of insurance
	MBA student in insurance	Insurance company client	Insurance company president
	Professor of insurance	Professor of insurance	MBA student in insurance
Lowest Status	Insurance company president	MBA student in insurance	Insurance company client

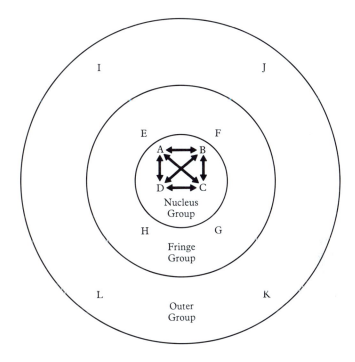

FIGURE 13-5
Status Positions
in Informal
Organizations

Nucleus
Group

Fringe
Group

Outer
Group

Sometimes an
individual's status
is in doubt

Status incongruency occurs when group members disagree regarding an individual's status. For example, if a vice president has just been reassigned a parking spot in the supervisory area, the assignment is incongruent with his position. People immediately begin to ask: Is he about to be demoted? Or if a lower-level manager is suddenly given new carpeting in her office and a new desk, what does it mean? Is she about to be promoted? When status symbols are out of place, people have difficulty knowing how much respect or deference to accord to an individual. Things are not as they should be, and people begin trying to interpret the reasons. In the case of the vice president, the truth may be that the company is putting in a storm drain on his usual spot so he has to park elsewhere for a few days until the job is done. In the case of the lower-level manager, the company may be giving new carpeting and desks to all lower-level managers and she has been chosen as the first one; no hidden meaning or intention is involved.

Status imbalance
may occur

Status discrepancy occurs when people do things that simply do not fit with their status in the group. There is an imbalance or discrepancy between who they are and how they act. Top-level managers can create such a discrepancy just as low-level managers can. For example, if a senior vice president begins to socialize with supervisors during lunch hour, his actions may be regarded as "inappropriate" both by other top managers and by lower-level managers. Analogously, a supervisor may attempt to improve his or her status by trying to associate with upper-level managers, only to be rebuffed by them and

What Happened to Gung Ho?

Drastic cost-cutting programs and massive layoffs in the U.S. corporations have left many employees fearful that each year may be their last. According to the Department of Commerce, since 1983, 4.7 million workers have been dismissed after holding their jobs for at least three years. Of that total, one-third took at least a 20 percent pay cut in their next position and one-fourth have not found new positions.

The term "downsizing" has been replaced by the term "rightsizing," referring to the corporations that hire to meet increased demand and then quickly layoff to reduce costs if the demand diminishes. For example, during the past year Chrysler, Kodak, Campbell Soup, Sears, and RJR Nabisco have all announced layoffs that total 13,000 jobs. In addition, General Motors has eliminated 150,000 jobs since 1980. With these figures in mind, Time/CNN conducted a poll of 520 employed adults to find out the general feeling of workers about their current jobs. The question and response percentage is listed below.

Compared with ten years ago, are companies today more loyal or less loyal to their employees?

More 25%
Less 57%

Compared with ten years ago, are employees today more loyal or less loyal to their companies?

More 22%
Less 63%

Do you think it is likely or unlikely you will change jobs within the next five years?

Likely 50%
Unlikely 45%

What do you like most about your job? (choose one)

What you do at work 38%
The people you work with . . 30%
Your salary 9%
Your chances of being
promoted 5%
Your boss or supervisor 4%

The perception of sagging loyalty of employers and employees is obvious from the first two responses. For managers, the last question/response may pose the greatest challenge. The percentages that like their salary, promotional opportunities, or boss, are quite low. Thus, management has the challenge to readjust their strategies in order to reinvigorate morale in the workforce.

Source: Janice Castro, "Where Did the Gung-Ho Go?" *Time* (September 11, 1989):52–56.

chastised by his or her peers. Status discrepancy can occur any time people go outside of their own status level.

Cohesiveness

Cohesiveness is important to group membership

Cohesiveness is the extent to which individual members of a group are motivated to remain in the group.[12] (See "Management in Practice: What Happened

---

[12] Jeffrey P. Davidson, "A Task-Focused Approach to Team Building," *Personnel* (March 1985):16–18. See also: Wolfe J. Rinke, "Empowering your Team Members," *Supervisory Management* (April 1989):21–24.

to Gung Ho?'') The numerous determinants of group cohesiveness have been covered in our earlier discussion of group formation theories: (a) similarity of goals, (b) need for affiliation, (c) security, (d) recognition, and (e) the belief that such an association will be useful in achieving personal goals.

Of more importance are the consequences of group cohesiveness. What happens when a group is highly cohesive? The most probable result is that the group has considerable power over its members. Realizing that they have more to gain by remaining members of the group than by leaving, the group members agree to adhere to established norms and work for the continued survival of the group. Furthermore, with high cohesion there is more likely to be frequent communication among the members and more participation in group activities. Other results include less absenteeism and turnover along with high levels of satisfaction.

High cohesion does not always lead to high output

On the other hand, high cohesion does not automatically result in high productivity or performance. Numerous studies can be cited to illustrate that unless the group accepts management's goals as its own, productivity may be quite low. The group members may simply agree among themselves not to do a great deal of work. One of the most famous studies supporting this conclusion is that by Stanley Schachter in which he created four groups of participants and studied them under controlled conditions.[13]

All of the groups were to make checkerboard squares and then pass them through a window to other team members, whom they did not see, on the other side. Two of the groups were told that they would like their counterparts on the other side of the window; the other two groups were not told this. The effect was to create high cohesion among the first two groups and their ''unseen'' associates. Then, during the experiment one of the highly cohesive groups was encouraged by its unseen associates (actually the researchers themselves) to turn out more work and the other group was encouraged to turn out less work. The result was that the first of these two groups had the greatest output and the second had the smallest. Schachter showed that high cohesion alone does not guarantee high output. The goals of the group must be considered. If high cohesion is coupled with high output goals, productivity will be high. If high cohesion is coupled with low output goals, productivity will be low.

Other researchers have reported similar results. For example, a classic study of productivity among British coal miners was conducted by E. Trist and K. Bamforth.[14] They found that before the introduction of mechanization in the coal mines, coal was gathered by teams of six men who worked together as a cohesive unit. With mechanization, these small groups were broken up and each worker was given a specific task to perform. The old cohesive units ceased to exist. In many locales, however, the miners adapted the new procedures to

---

[13] Stanley Schachter et al., ''An Experimental Study of Cohesiveness and Productivity,'' *Human Relations* (August 1951):229–39.

[14] E. Trist and K. W. Bamforth, ''Some Social and Psychological Consequences of the Longwell Method of Coal-Getting,'' *Human Relations* (February 1951):3–38.

suit themselves. The miners made the new technology work for them instead of working for the technology because they refused to work in noncohesive groups.

The adaptation of technology to social needs has also been incorporated at organizations like Saab-Scania, the Swedish auto manufacturer. In this case, however, the organization addressed itself to building highly cohesive work teams before making changes in the assembly line. Employees were brought into the decision-making process to help the organization deal with productivity and morale problems. The result of this step was impressive: unplanned work stoppages dropped from 6 percent to 2 percent of the total work time, extra work and adjustment needed to correct omissions and errors in the finished product declined by 33 percent, and turnover dropped from an average of 55 percent to 20 percent per year. Allowing the workers greater involvement in problem solving brought about increased cohesiveness among group members and greater commitment to group goals. In short, cohesiveness is vital to group survival and performance.

POWER AND GROUP BEHAVIOR

No discussion of group behavior in organizations would be complete without a consideration of power. As we saw in an earlier chapter, *power* is the ability to influence, persuade, or move another person to accept one's own point of view.[15] In modern organizations, power is used both by formal and by informal leaders.

Types of Power

There are five commonly cited types of power: reward, coercive, legitimate, referent, and expert.[16]

Reward Power

Positive payoffs

Reward power is held by individuals who have the ability and resources to reward people who do their jobs well. These rewards may take numerous forms, including pay increases, bonuses, promotions, praise, and increased responsibility. Both formal and informal leaders have reward power, and to ensure continued commitment to their organization's goals, they give or withhold rewards to their members. While the formal leader can make use of both intrin-

[15] Richard M. Hodgetts, *Human Relations At Work,* 4th edition (Hinsdale, IL: Drydren Press, 1990), 156.
[16] John R. P. French, Jr. and Bertram Raven, "The Bases of Social Power," *Studies in Social Power,* Dorwin Cartwright, ed. (Ann Arbor, MI: Institute for Social Research, 1959), 155–64.

sic and extrinsic rewards, however, the informal leader must rely exclusively on intrinsic payoffs since the individual has no control over salaries, bonuses, or promotions.

Coercive Power

Coercive power is held by people who have the ability to inflict punishment or other negative consequences on others, for example, by demoting them, docking their salary, or terminating their employment. This power also extends into the psychological arena, as when individuals are denied social need satisfaction by the person wielding coercive power. David Kipnis has summed up the range of this influence by noting that "individuals exercise coercive power through a reliance upon physical strength, verbal facility, or the ability to grant or withhold emotional support from others. These bases provide the individual with the means to physically harm, bully, humiliate, or deny love to others." [17]

Note that it is not necessary actually to use such sanctions; as long as the other party conforms because he or she wishes to avoid a negative outcome, the individual possesses coercive power. Because this power involves psychological as well as physical reward denial, it can be employed by both formal and informal leaders. Many behavioral scientists believe that "much of organizational behavior may be explained in terms of coercive power rather than reward power." [18]

Coercive power involves negative consequences

Legitimate Power

Legitimate power arises from the values of the people who are being influenced. These people feel that the person influencing them has a legitimate right to do so, so they obey. Legitimate power is similar to authority because the person who has it also is in a position to reward and punish people who do not obey. Managers have legitimate power by virtue of their position in the firm. Additionally, a vice president has greater legitimate power than a district manager, who has greater legitimate power than a supervisor. Legitimate power is often referred to as "delegated authority" since managers get it from their bosses and give some of it to their subordinates. This process helps fashion the scalar chain of authority, linking the top and bottom of the organization.

Legitimate power is similar to authority

Referent Power

Referent power is based on the follower's identification with the leader. This type of power is emotional in nature and can lead to enthusiastic and unquestioning trust and loyalty. The followers obey because of *who* the leader is rather than *what* he or she asks them to do. A person can obtain referent power in

Referent power is based on identification with the leader

---

[17] David Kipnis, *The Powerholders* (Chicago: University of Chicago Press, 1976), 77–78.
[18] Luthans, *Organizational Behavior,* 431.

various ways, such as by having a reputation for fairness, by possessing a "winning" personality, or by being able to empathize with others and bring them around to his or her own personal point of view.

Expert Power

Expert power depends on knowledge and ability

Expert power derives from an individual's knowledge and expertise. Others listen to and follow the person with expert power because he or she is regarded as capable and knows how to do things right. Leaders who have demonstrated competence to implement, analyze, evaluate, and control group tasks are often seen as knowledgeable in their jobs. As a result, they acquire expert power and people rely on them for guidance and direction. Another characteristic of expert power is trust. Because this form of power is fairly impersonal and more concerned with task performance than with subordinates as people, it is important for the individual with expert power to wield it carefully. If the followers begin to learn that someone is using expert power for personal gain or to their detriment, they will turn away from this person. The following excerpt about Henry Kissinger, former secretary of state, tells how someone can lose expert power:

> . . . expert power is highly selective and besides credibility, the agent must also have trustworthiness and relevance. By trustworthiness is meant that the person seeking expert power must have the reputation of being honest and straightforward. In the case of Kissinger, events such as the scandal of Nixon's corrupt administration and Kissinger's role in getting the Shah of Iran into this country undoubtedly eroded his expert power in the eyes of the American public. He still has unquestionable knowledge about foreign affairs, but he has lost expert power because he may no longer be trustworthy.[19]

Of all the types of power, expert power is the one most difficult to retain because one's expertise may be surpassed by someone else's or the knowledge may become irrelevant. Nevertheless, because so many people in modern organizations rely upon knowledge as a source of power, including engineers, accountants, and other staff specialists, expert power continues to be nurtured and cultivated.

The Use of Power

Which of the five types of power is the "best" one to employ? Which should be one's last choice? While specific answers depend on the situation, research has

---

[19] Luthans, *Organizational Behavior,* 4th ed., 394.

been devoted to examining the use of each of the power categories.[20] On the basis of organization studies conducted in a branch office, a college, an insurance agency, production work units, and a utility company work group, Jerald Bachman and his associates drew the following conclusions regarding each of the five bases of power:

Conclusions regarding power bases

1. Expert power is most strongly and consistently correlated with satisfaction and performance.
2. Legitimate power, along with expert power, is rated as the most important basis for complying with a supervisor's wishes but is an inconsistent factor in organizational effectiveness.
3. Referent power is of intermediate importance as a reason for complying and in most cases is positively correlated with organizational effectiveness.
4. Reward power is also given intermediate importance for complying but has inconsistent correlations with performance.
5. Coercive power is by far the least prominent reason for complying and is actually negatively related to organizational effectiveness.[21]

These findings illustrate that informal bases of power can have a more favorable impact on organizational effectiveness than formal bases. Expert power, an informal basis, was more important than the other kinds of power in producing satisfaction and performance. Legitimate power (a formal basis) had an inconsistent effect on organizational effectiveness. And while referent power (an informal basis) was of intermediate importance, it ranked ahead of reward and coercive power (both formal in nature).

More recent work, such as that by Y. K. Shetty, supports these earlier findings. For example, in his review of both the empirical and theoretical literature related to the management of people at work, Shetty reported the following:

Additional conclusions

1. Expert power is closely related to a climate of trust and can result in internalized motivation on the part of the subordinates. This type of power can at least diminish, if not eliminate, the need for employee surveillance.
2. At least initially, legitimate power can be relied on. Continued dependence on it can create problems, however, such as the feeling of powerlessness and dissatisfaction, resistance, and frustration among the employees. If legitimate power does not coincide with expert power, an

---

[20] Gary Yukl and Tom Taber, "The Effective Use of Managerial Power," *Personnel* (March–April 1983):37–44.

[21] Jerald G. Bachman, David G. Bower, and Philip M. Marcus, "Bases of Supervisory Power: A Comparative Study in Five Organizational Settings," *Control in Organizations,* Arnold S. Tannenbaum, ed. (New York: McGraw-Hill, 1968), 236.

ineffective use of human resources can occur, resulting in lower productivity. Finally, the use of legitimate power may be inconsistent with some modern employees' work life values and may lead to minimum compliance and increased resistance.

3. Referent power can bring about internally motivated employees. The use of this type of power can also lead, however, to highly personal, selfish gains and manipulation of subordinates.

4. Reward power can directly influence employee behavior. Dependence on this type of power can produce problems, however, because in some organizations (a) there is very little money or few promotions that can be given out to those who comply with the manager's directives; (b) these rewards may have only a short-run impact; and (c) the use of such rewards may result in the subordinates' feeling manipulated and used.

5. Coercive power may bring about temporary compliance of subordinates or group members. It also produces numerous undesirable side effects, however, including fear, frustration, and alienation. The ultimate result is often poor performance, dissatisfaction, and turnover. When employing this type of power the manager must continually use surveillance of the employees to ensure that they are doing their work. Once out from under the watchful eye of the manager, many of them begin to slow up or stop working altogether.[22]

These conclusions echo those of Bachman and his associates. The informal bases of power—expert and referent—have a more favorable impact on organizational effectiveness than do the more formal power bases.

Power and People

Some people are more easily influenced than others

Some individuals are quite easily influenced. It does not take much effort to attain power over them. Conversely, some seem to be above all attempts at influence or domination. What accounts for these differences?[23] Why are some people easy targets of power while others are not? As researchers attempt to answer this question, it is becoming increasingly clear that the subject of power and people involves a *reciprocal* relationship. On the one hand is the individual who is wielding the power; on the other is the person or group toward whom it is being wielded—the power target. Six characteristics have been found to be especially important in determining how easily these targets can be influenced.[24]

[22] Y. K. Shetty, "Managerial Power and Organizational Effectiveness: A Contingency Analysis," *Journal of Management Studies* (May 1978):178–81.

[23] W. Graham Astley and Paramjit S. Sachdeva, "Structural Sources of Intraorganizational Power: A Theoretical Synthesis," *Academy of Management Review* (January 1984):104–13.

[24] Stephen B. Robbins, *Organizational Behavior* (Englewood Cliffs, NJ: Prentice-Hall, 1979), 276.

One characteristic is the *dependency* of the individual or group on the person who is attempting to do the influencing. A manager often has subordinates in a difficult position. If they do not comply, reward or coercive power can be used against them. Of course, this is not always the case. If the manager needs the subordinates because they have certain skills that the department or unit cannot afford to lose, the shoe is on the other foot. Now the subordinates can use expert power either to reduce or overcome the manager's reward/coercive power options.

A second characteristic is the *degree of uncertainty* that others have regarding how to behave or go about attaining their desired objectives. The greater their uncertainty, the easier it is for someone to influence their behavior. In this case, expert power is one of the most influential means of doing so.

What makes people power targets

A third factor is the *personality* of the individual who is attempting to do the influencing. There are many reasons why personality can be influential. If the other members of the group are highly susceptible to influence, a person with a strong personality can dominate. If the group members have a high need for affiliation (one of the primary reasons for group membership), a person with a winning personality can often influence them. If they do not know how to achieve their objectives, the personable individual can persuade them to carry out a particular line of action.

Intelligence is a fourth factor, but in this case the relationship is inverse. The higher the intelligence of the members of the group, the lower their susceptibility to influence. For example, while highly intelligent people may be more willing to listen than the average person, they are also more likely to pick out flaws in someone's argument or statements. Additionally, highly intelligent people are accustomed to being held in high esteem, so attempts to influence them are usually less successful than the same attempts are with other people. Intelligent people are more resistant to influence.

Age is another important factor. Younger people tend to be more easily influenced than older people. Workers who have been around for a long time are more likely to resist attempts by management to influence them. Younger workers are more flexible and willing to go along with things, if only to see how well they work. This is why the introduction of new work changes is often fought most strongly by older members of the work group.

Finally, *culture* influences the effectiveness of power. In western cultures such as the United States, individuality, dissent, and diversity are encouraged. People tend to fight attempts to be influenced; they try to protect their own identities. On the other hand, in many Asian cultures there is an emphasis on agreement, uniformity, and cohesiveness. These cultural norms influence the way people respond to power sources.

Some of these factors are more important for some people than for others. Additionally, while three or four of them may be present at the same time, one is usually more important than the others. For example, even if the members of a group are highly intelligent, if they are uncertain how to handle a particular project, their uncertainty may overshadow everything else and the individual who offers a solution to their dilemma may emerge as the most powerful member of the group. On the other hand, regardless of an individual's personality, if the members of the group have no need to depend on him or her for anything, this person may be unable to influence the group.[25]

GROUP DYNAMICS

A group is more than the sum of its individual members. In the study of group behavior in the workplace, it is necessary to look at the way groups function both internally and with other groups. This is what **group dynamics** is all about. (See "Management in Practice: Volvo's Experiment in Team Craftsmanship.")

Of course, there are many aspects of intra- and intergroup relations that can be examined. We will confine our attention, however, to two of the most important ones: how decisions are made within groups and how groups interact externally with other groups.[26]

Intragroup Behavior

Intragroup behavior consists of the interactions that occur between group members. The characteristics and dimensions of groups that were examined earlier in the chapter help explain some of this behavior. Group size, norms, roles, status, and cohesiveness all dictate acceptable behavior. Yet intragroup behavior depends on other conditions as well. These group factors are often supplemented by two others: the risky-shift phenomenon and groupthink. Both of these can seriously influence group decision making.

Risky-Shift Phenomenon

The **risky-shift phenomenon** has long intrigued students of group behavior. The phenomenon can be explained quite simply: people tend to make riskier

[25] For more on power, see David C. Calabria, "CEOs and the Paradox of Power," *Business Horizons* (January–February 1982):29–31. Also see A. J. Patrellis, "Producing Results: Using Power with Your Employees," *Supervisory Management* (March 1985):32–37.

[26] Frederick C. Miner, Jr., "Group Versus Individual Decision Making: An Investigation of Performance Measures, Decision Strategies, and Process Losses/Gains," *Organizational Behavior and Human Performance* (February 1984):112–24.

Volvo's Experiment in Team Craftsmanship

*I*n 1988 Volvo had sales of $16.1 billion and operating profits of $1.2 billion. This was a 50 percent increase since 1983. Yet even though performance appeared satisfactory, the firm faced the challenge confronting all manufacturing plants: How to motivate a workforce that is well-educated and well-trained in assembly line jobs?

The average Volvo plant in Sweden has an annual 20 percent absentee rate and 33 percent turnover. Money alone does not motivate the workers since taxes take up to 70 percent of overtime pay and the unemployment rate is a low 1.6 percent, which indicates jobs are plentiful.

Volvo's solution to this challenge was the creation of a $220 million plant in Uddevalla, Sweden. Within this manufacturing plant, Volvo divided workers into teams of 7 to 10 hourly workers that are assigned to one of six assembly areas. Each team manages itself by monitoring scheduling, quality control, hiring, purchasing, etc., in order to completely assemble four cars

per shift. There are no foremen, but each team has a spokesperson who reports to one of the six plant managers. Teams determine the requirements on each car body and then take responsibility for any defects. The main idea is to induce the concept of craftsmanship within each team.

Is the idea working? In 1989, absenteeism was only 8 percent and morale appeared to be high. Volvo's goal is to produce 40,000 cars a year in single shift production by the mid-1990s. This would be relatively less than the average 120,000 cars of other plants but two critical areas will be addressed: worker motivation through group efforts and autonomy, and quality control through a team craftsmanship idea.

Volvo's executive Leif Kalberg says, "This isn't just new production technology, it is the death of the assembly line. We've brought back craftsmanship to auto making."

Source: Jonathan Kapstein and John Hoerr, "Volvo's Radical New Plant: The Death of the Assembly Line?" *Business Week* (August 28, 1989):92–93.

decisions when in a group than when acting independently.[27] Why is this so? Earl Cecil and his associates have provided five of the most common explanations:

Explanations for the risky-shift phenomenon

1. Making a decision in a group allows for diffusion of responsibility in the event the decision is wrong.
2. Risky people are more influential in group discussions than conservative people and so are more likely to bring others to their point of view.

---

[27] Dorwin Cartwright, "Risk Taking by Individuals and Groups: An Assessment of Research Employing Choice Dilemmas," *Journal of Personality and Social Psychology* (December 1971):361–78; Russell D. Clark, III, "Group-Induced Shift Toward Risk: A Critical Appraisal," *Psychological Bulletin* (October 1971):251–70.

3. Group discussion leads to deeper consideration of, and greater familiarization with, the possible pros and cons of a particular decision. In turn, greater familiarization and consideration lead to higher levels of risk taking.
4. Risk taking is socially desirable in our culture, and socially desirable qualities are more likely to be expressed in a group than alone.
5. According to a modification of the fourth explanation, a moderate risk is valued in our culture on certain kinds of issues, while on other kinds of issues moderate caution is valued. When the value of risk is engaged, people will choose a risk level which they believe is equal to or slightly greater than the risk the average person will take. When a decision-making group is formed, members discovering that they are more conservative than the average will become riskier. . . . Likewise . . . those discovering that they are more risky than the average will shift in a conservative direction.[28]

These explanations help tell why a group's actions may be different from the actions of any particular member of that group. Additionally, it should be noted that if there is group pressure toward accepting riskier courses of action, this pressure will often influence the superior to follow a similar course. Decision making within a group context is a two-way street: the subordinates influence the formal or informal leader and the leader influences the group. Of course, the people recommending the greatest risk are not followed automatically. Remember from explanation number five that the group decision often involves only a slightly greater risk than the average risk taken by the group members individually. Nevertheless, to repeat our earlier statement: the decision of a group is more than the sum of the individual decisions. The interaction of the members greatly influences the final course of action.

Groupthink

A second major phenomenon of intragroup behavior is groupthink. **Groupthink** is conformity to group ideas by members of the group.[29] Groupthink may have an especially adverse effect on highly cohesive groups because there is pressure by group members on those who are unwilling to go along with the majority. Irving Janis, who popularized the concept of groupthink, has noted that a number of historic fiascos by government policy-making groups can be accounted for by this phenomenon. Examples include the unpreparedness of

---

[28] Earl A. Cecil, Larry L. Cummings, and Jerome M. Chertkoff, "Group Composition and Choice Shift: Implications for Administration," *Academy of Management Journal* (September 1973):413–14.
[29] Hodgetts, *Human Relations,* 133–134.

the U.S. forces at Pearl Harbor, the invasion of Cuba at the Bay of Pigs, the escalation of the Vietnam War, and the Watergate scandal.[30]

In essence, groupthink has a number of common symptoms. One of these is the illusion, on the part of the group, that what it is doing is right. Second, any warnings the group has that its actions are wrong are either ignored or rationalized away. Third, if any member disagrees, pressure is placed on the person to "go along" with the group. Fourth, there is at least the illusion of unanimity among the members, especially when it comes to major areas of concern. Fifth, members of the group work to protect each other from adverse information that might shake the complacency they share. As a result, the group ends up isolating itself from the outside world.

Groupthink might seem farfetched until one remembers how the group feels about what it is doing. Typically the members believe their actions are humanitarian and are based on high-minded principles. ("Honest people everywhere would applaud us for our actions.") Second, in order to remain a member of the group, a person has to avoid criticizing it. ("Let's get behind the boss on this one.") Third, the high *esprit de corps* among the members results in their believing that people who criticize them are irrational and totally wrong. ("Those other guys are totally nuts.") Not only is the group isolated from the world around it, but it believes its actions are justified. Fortunately, not all groups fall victim to groupthink, and there are ways of avoiding any tendency toward this happening.

> Groupthink illustrates the serious consequences of a work team's becoming victim of its own group norm. Fortunately, managers can combat this phenomenon by following a handful of simple rules. First, the manager must encourage the open airing of objections and doubts. Second, one or more outsiders should be invited into the group to challenge the views of the members. Third, one member of the original group should be appointed to function as a "lawyer" who is challenging the testimony of the other members. Finally, after reaching a preliminary decision, the group should hold a "second chance" meeting at which every member expresses, as vividly as possible, all his or her doubts and thinks through the entire issue again before making a final decision.[31]

Intergroup Behavior

Intergroup behavior consists of the interactions that occur between or among two or more groups. Sometimes these groups are in the same department; at other times they are not. In any event, they come into contact with each other.

---

[30] Irving L. Janis, *Victims of Groupthink* (Boston: Houghton Mifflin, 1972); Irving L. Janis, "Group Think," *Psychology Today* (November 1971):43–46, 74–76.
[31] Hodgetts, *Human Relations,* 134.

Two of the most common reasons are for coordination purposes or because a power struggle has arisen.

Coordination Purposes

Objectives, cooperation, and planning are needed

The most typical reason for group coordination is goal achievement. When this is the purpose, the groups work to synchronize their efforts. Coordination requires an emphasis on three factors. First, each group must clearly establish what it is supposed to be doing. Second, there must be joint cooperation. Third, interfaces between the groups must be carefully planned, so that if one fails to meet certain targets or goals, the others can work to straighten out the situation. When groups are cooperating for the purpose of achieving high performance, planning and liaison work are vital. Unfortunately, not all intergroup behavior consists of harmonious cooperation. Sometimes power struggles develop in which one group attempts to dominate or influence the others.[32]

Power Struggles

Groups secure power in many different ways

Modern complex organizations tend to create a climate that promotes power seeking and political maneuvering. Groups carry out these power struggles in many ways. One of the simplest ways is by providing other groups with services they either cannot, or will not, provide for themselves. For example, the Industrial Relations Department in large organizations is responsible for negotiating union contracts and working out the finer points of management-union prerogatives. Whenever union-management problems arise, the people in Industrial Relations take on a great deal of power. They interpret how management is to act and how much leeway will be given to the union. Since most departments or units in the company are ill-equipped to interpret the terms of the contract, Industrial Relations holds sway over the others. The services it provides give it the necessary basis for this power.

A second basis of power is the degree of *integrative importance* the group holds. Figure 13-6 illustrates this concept. Since there is only one Quality Inspection Department, it constitutes a bottleneck. If this department approves of the manufactured, assembled, and painted units, they can be passed on to the Packing Department. If the quality inspection people do not approve, the units are sent back for the necessary reworking. If some people are absent from the manufacturing, assembling, painting, or packing groups, the flow of work is not necessarily slowed up. If one or two people are missing from the quality inspection group, however, the smallest one of all, overall output can be affected.

---

[32] Toby D. Wall, Nigel J. Jackson, Paul R. Clegg, and Chris W. Clegg, "Outcomes of Autonomous Work Groups: A Long-Term Field Experiment," *Academy of Management Journal* (June 1986):280–304.

FIGURE 13-6   The Integrative Importance of Groups

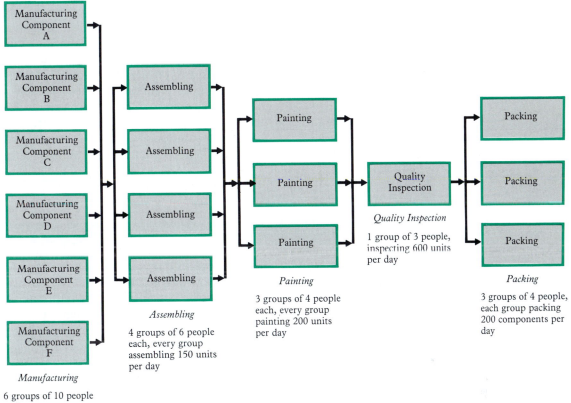

Manufacturing

6 groups of 10 people each, every group producing 100 units per day

Assembling

4 groups of 6 people each, every group assembling 150 units per day

Painting

3 groups of 4 people each, every group painting 200 units per day

Quality Inspection

1 group of 3 people, inspecting 600 units per day

Packing

3 groups of 4 people, each group packing 200 components per day

A third common intergroup power struggle is related to *budget allocation.* In virtually every organization there is a limited amount of money in the budget. Every dollar obtained by one department is lost to the others, so each department or unit tries hard to justify the need for more money. Quite obviously this is a win-lose situation. Not every department gets all of its budget requests.

Effective managers realize the power struggles are inevitable. They do not try to prevent these struggles, only to manage them properly. Proper management involves techniques of *conflict resolution.* The four most common forms of conflict resolution for dealing with intergroup power struggles are these: (1) confrontation, in which, because the groups have been unable to get along in the past, they are forced to face each other, discuss their common problems, and work to overcome them to the good of all; (2) collaboration, in which groups are shown how they can all achieve their aims if they simply cooperate; (3) compromise, in which each group gives up some of its demands, no group emerges as the clear winner, but the conflict is resolved; and (4) altering of the organizational structure, in which people are transferred to other departments or work assignments are changed in an effort to resolve the dispute.

Modern organizations generally use one or more of these approaches, depending on how serious the problems prove to be. Unfortunately, it is often easier to talk about how to deal with intergroup differences than it is to resolve them. A great deal of the success of such resolution is a result of the effectiveness of the group leadership, a topic that will be the focus of our attention in the next chapter.

SUMMARY

1. A group is a social unit consisting of two or more interdependent, interactive individuals who are striving to attain common goals. In every organization there are two basic types of groups: formal and informal. Formal groups are established by the organization; informal groups are set up by the members themselves and often cross departmental lines and span hierarchical levels.

2. Formal groups fall into one of two categories: functional or project. A functional group is made up of individuals performing the same basic tasks. Project groups are multifunctional in composition and are formed for the purpose of carrying out a particular assignment. They are disbanded when the project is completed. In many cases individuals are members of more than one group.

3. People join groups for many different reasons. Some of the most common theories explaining group formation include: (a) propinquity theory, which holds that people affiliate with others because they are located near them; (b) Homans's theory, which holds that group formation is explained in terms of activity, interaction, and sentiment; (c) balance theory, which holds that people are attracted to one another because of similar attitudes toward the same goals or objects; and (d) exchange theory, which holds that a person's decision to join and remain with a group is based on the reward-cost outcome of the interaction.

4. Another way to examine groups is on the basis of their characteristics or distinguishing features. One of these is group size. Research shows that as size increases, satisfaction tends to decline, communication with other members of the group is more direct, the need for group approval diminishes, and absenteeism and turnover increase.

5. Norms are behavioral rules of conduct that are adopted by group members. They tell how an individual ought to act. While norms regulate group behavior, however, they do not apply off the job and they are limited in terms of who has to follow them and to what degree.

6. A role is an expected behavior. A role helps an individual understand how to behave in a group. Sometimes this understanding is hampered by such problems as role ambiguity, role conflict, and role perception.

7. Status is the relative ranking of individuals in organizations or groups. This ranking is determined by such things as a person's place in the hierarchy, the job he or she performs, personality, and job competence. The specific status of the person is often situationally determined, however. Status exists in both formal and informal organizations. In the latter, there are three basic groups: the nucleus group, which consists of full-fledged members of the informal organization; the fringe group, whose members are seeking admission to the informal organization; and the outer group, whose members, for some particular reason, have been denied admission to the informal organization. Some common status-related problems that must sometimes be addressed are status incongruency and status discrepancy.

8. Cohesiveness is the extent to which individual members of a group are motivated to remain in the group. There are numerous determinations of group cohesiveness, including similarity of goals, need for affiliation, security, recognition, and the belief that such an association will be useful in achieving personal goals. It should be noted, however, that high cohesiveness does not guarantee high output. The group must also have a desire for high output.

9. Power is the ability to influence, persuade, or move another person to accept one's own point of view. There are five basic types of power: reward, coercive, legitimate, referent, and expert. Of these five, expert power is most strongly and consistently correlated with satisfaction and performance, while coercive power is the least prominent in attaining organizational effectiveness.

10. Power involves a reciprocal relationship. One person attempts to wield power and the other, known as the power target, is the individual toward whom it is wielded. Six characteristics have been found to be especially important in determining the influenceability of these targets: dependency, degree of uncertainty, personality, intelligence, age, and culture.

11. Researchers interested in group behavior in the workplace study group dynamics. Group dynamics involve both intragroup and intergroup behavior. In the case of intragroup behavior, two important factors merit attention. The first is the risky-shift phenomenon, or the likelihood that when in a group people will make riskier decisions than when they are acting alone. The second is groupthink, or the likelihood that an

individual will conform with the ideas of other members of the group because of an unwillingness to break with them.

12. Intergroup behavior consists of the interactions that occur between or among two or more groups. The most typical reason for such behavior is to promote coordination, which depends on three things: clearly established objectives, joint cooperation, and careful planning. Sometimes, however, power struggles develop between groups or one manages to obtain some degree of control over the others. When this happens, effective managers work to prevent things from getting out of control. Four of the most common forms of conflict resolution for intergroup power struggles are confrontation, collaboration, compromise, and an altering of the organizational structure.

KEY TERMS

Balance theory   A theory of group formation that holds that people are attracted to one another because of similar attitudes.

Coercive power   Power held by people who have the ability to inflict punishment or other negative consequences on others.

Cohesiveness   The extent to which individual members of a group are motivated to remain in the group.

Exchange theory   A theory that holds that a person's decision to join groups and remain with them is based on the reward-cost outcome of the interaction.

Expert power   Power that derives from an individual's knowledge and expertise.

Formal group   A group established by the organization, as in the case of a functional or project group.

Fringe group   Individuals seeking admission to an informal organization.

Functional group   A group made up of individuals all performing the same basic tasks.

Group   A social unit consisting of two or more interdependent, interactive individuals who are striving to attain common goals.

Group dynamics   Intra- and intergroup behavior and functioning.

Groupthink   Conformity to group ideas by members of the group.

Informal group   A group set up by the organizational personnel themselves on the basis of such things as friendship or personal interest.

Legitimate power   Power that arises from the values of the people being influenced, who feel that the person influencing them has a legitimate right to do so.

Norms   Behavioral rules of conduct that are adopted by group members.

Nucleus group   Full-fledged members of an informal organization.

Outer group   Individuals who have been rejected for membership in an informal organization.

Project groups   A group formed for the purpose of carrying out a particular objective and then disbanded.

Referent power   Power based on the follower's identification with the leader.

Reward power   Power held by people who have the ability and resources to provide rewards to those who do their jobs well.

Risky-shift phenomenon   A development that occurs in groups when people make riskier decisions than they would when acting independently.

Role   An expected behavior.

Role ambiguity   A role-related problem that exists when a person is unsure of what he or she is expected to do.

Role conflict   A role-related problem that occurs when an individual is forced to assume two roles but the performance of one precludes the performance of the other.

Role perceptions   The way managers and subordinates perceive their own role, the others' role, and their perception of their own role as seen by the others.

Status   The relative ranking of individuals in organizations or groups.

Status discrepancy   A status-related problem that occurs when people do things that do not fit with their status ranking in the group.

Status incongruency   A status-related problem that occurs when there is disagreement among group members regarding an individual's status.

QUESTIONS FOR ANALYSIS AND DISCUSSION

1. In your own words, what is meant by the term group?
2. How do the following kinds of groups differ from each other: formal, informal, and combination? Compare and contrast them.
3. Why do people join groups? In your answer include a discussion of such theories as propinquity, balance, exchange, and Homans's.
4. In what way does group size affect group behavior? Cite research findings to support your answers.
5. What are group norms? How do they affect group behavior? When do they not apply to group members?
6. What is a role? How do the following create role-related problems: role ambiguity, role conflict, role perception?
7. Of what significance is cohesiveness to group behavior? Does group cohesion have any effect on group output? Explain.
8. How is an individual's status within a group determined? What are some of the key variables that determine the person's status ranking?

9. In the informal group, who is a member of each of these subgroups: the nucleus group, the fringe group, the outer group?
10. How do status incongruency and status discrepancy affect one's group status? Use examples in your answer.
11. How would a manager use each of the following types of power: reward, coercive, legitimate, referent, and expert? Which would result in the highest satisfaction and performance among the group members? Which would bring about the lowest satisfaction and performance? Explain.
12. In what way is power a reciprocal relationship? What are some of the characteristics that have been found to be especially important in determining the influenceability of people as targets of power? Identify and describe four.
13. How does the risky-shift phenomenon work? What impact does it have on group dynamics?
14. How does groupthink work? What impact can it have on group behavior?
15. What are three of the most common ways in which groups attempt to gain power over other groups? How can effective managers work to resolve intergroup conflict resulting from these power struggles? Be complete in your answer.

CASE

The Group Paper

Dick Biltmore is a junior at State University. For the term paper in his management class this semester, Dick decided to write on "Group Norms and Work Group Behavior." His father owns a locally based, medium-sized manufacturing firm, and Dick arranged with one of the supervisors to have himself assigned to a work group for five days. He took the second shift so it would not interfere with his class schedule. Initially, both his professor and his father believed he could obtain all the information he would need within this time period. Dick is not so sure he has been successful, however. Yesterday, he sat down with all of his notes and sketched out his findings. Here is a summary of his observations.

1. There were 10 people in the group to which he was assigned.
2. Seven of these people seemed to get along quite well. Two of them were loners, however, and did not interact at all with the others and the last one was continually arguing with the other seven.
3. The amount of work that each did varied significantly. The two loners produced 115 widgets an hour, 15 more than the norm established by the

company. The person who argued a great deal did 125 widgets an hour, but some (usually 10) of these were stolen by one or more of the seven people who got on well. Three of the seven people who get on well produced exactly 100 widgets an hour for their own account. This took about 50 minutes an hour. The other 10 minutes were spent helping out the other four people in their clique.

4. Of the four people being helped out, one was the group's main interface with the foreman. Whenever problems arose, this individual would work to straighten things out. He was identified by Dick as the informal group leader. A second person was 64 years old, had rheumatism, and was unable to keep up to company production standards. A third person produced 110 widgets for himself and was "given" 20 more by others. This individual's baby daughter was in intensive care, and he was working extra hard to meet the large medical bills that were accumulating. The fourth person was a part-time college student paying his own tuition. The group admired his drive.

Answer the following questions:

1. Was there an informal group in the room? Explain your answer.
2. What were the norms of this group? How were they enforced?
3. What would you advise Dick to include in his paper? Sketch out an outline for him.

The Low Output Problem

Hand-held computer games have had exceptionally good reception by the consumer market. Hatwick Industries has a large contract with one of the nation's leading retail stores to provide such games. The firm is given the technical blueprints and 11 of the machines needed to produce the 10 computer games called for by its contract. The company's job is to manufacture the games according to specifications and then assemble, test, package, and send them to the respective retail outlets (see Figure 13-7). Output is a major consideration in that the firm must produce 1,000 of these games a day in order to stay on schedule.

Unfortunately, Hatwick's daily output has been slipping gradually. Six months ago, it was 1,037. Three months ago it was down to 988. Last month it was 949. The most recent count shows that while output is higher on some days

FIGURE 13-7
Hand-Held
Computer
Production Process

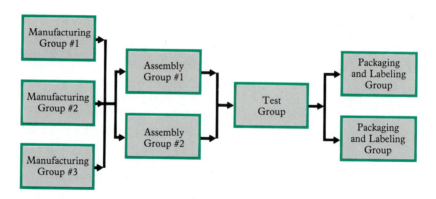

than others, current output is now averaging 934 units daily. In an effort to find out what is causing the problem, management has sent in a fact-finding group to analyze the situation. Here is what the team has discovered:

1. Among the three manufacturing groups, output varies significantly. Group 1 meets its output objectives each day. Group 2, which has extremely high morale, is producing 109 percent of its output objectives. Group 3, which also has extremely high morale, is producing only 35 percent of its output objectives.

2. Assembly Group #1 is doing fine. Group #2, however, continually falls behind, and the only way it has been able to keep up is by having the group manager pitch in and help out. This action has not gone unnoticed by the other groups, most of which feel the manager has no business doing this. They feel the manager should manage and leave the assembly work to the assemblers.

3. Both packaging and labeling groups are turning out only 94 percent of expected daily output. There is a great deal of concern in the two groups that the new packaging and labeling machines scheduled to be introduced next month will result in layoffs of some personnel.

4. The test group personnel are fighting with each other. The situation is so bad that the only solution appears to be to transfer some people out of the group to other jobs in the company.

5. In an effort to get the overall hand-held computer production process group back on target, the general manager has announced an incentive plan. All salary raises will be tied directly to group output. Those groups turning out less than they should can expect to receive salary raises in the 3 to 5 percentage range; those doing more than their output quota can expect raises in the 10 to 14 percent range.

Your Consultation

Assume that you have just been called in by the president of this firm to act as a consultant regarding how to handle the situation. First, drawing upon your knowledge of norms, cohesion, status, group size, and other group-related characteristics, tell the president why some groups are not producing up to par. Then describe any other problems you have uncovered in the case and explain the reasons for these problems. Finally, offer the president your recommendations for straightening out the entire situation.

14

Managerial Leadership

OBJECTIVES

One of the most important functions of a manager is to be able to lead. In fact, effective leadership is often the key both to individual and to organizational success. This chapter explores the nature of leadership by examining leader traits, abilities, and behavior. It also describes two of the most popular contingency theories of leadership and reviews selective leadership theories on an applied level. When you have finished studying all of the material in this chapter, you will be able to:

1. Define the term leadership.
2. Discuss some of the traits or characteristics commonly found in effective leaders.
3. Compare and contrast autocratic, paternalistic, democratic/participative, and laissez-faire leadership styles.
4. Compare and contrast the assumptions and managerial implications of Theory X and Theory Y.
5. Discuss the three alternative models of management: traditional, human relations, and human resources.
6. Describe the managerial grid.
7. Explain the contingency and path-goal theories of leadership and discuss the value of each for practicing managers.
8. Discuss the leader follower continuum and the situational theory of leadership and describe the practical value of each for modern managers.

THE NATURE OF LEADERSHIP

The term leadership has been defined in many different ways. Bernard Bass, after making a systematic review of research on the topic, reports that "There are almost as many different definitions of leadership as there are persons who have attempted to define the concept."[1] It is generally accepted, however, that effective leadership consists of successful influence by the leader, resulting in goal attainment by the followers.[2] For our purposes, therefore, we shall define leadership as the process of influencing people to direct their efforts toward the attainment of some particular goal or goals.

Leadership defined

The way in which this process of influencing is carried out varies from manager to manager.[3] Some spend a great deal of their time formulating objectives for subordinates, setting out detailed lists of what is to be done, and closely following up to ensure that everything goes according to schedule. Others prefer to set general objectives, allowing the subordinates to determine their own approach while maintaining an open-door policy for those who feel they require additional assistance. Still others provide the least amount of direction possible; if the subordinates run into any problems, they must work things out for themselves. The first of these kinds of managers delegates very little authority to subordinates; the second delegates a fair amount of work; the third delegates virtually everything. Which of these three styles is most effective? The answer is: all three may be equally effective. There is simply no such thing as one best leadership style. Perhaps this is why leadership is such an interesting topic and why it has led one well-known author to write, "Leadership has probably been written about, formally researched, and informally discussed more than any other single topic."[4] The result of all this research and interest has been the accumulation of a wealth of information about leadership behavior and leadership style.[5] One of the primary areas of interest has been the traits and abilities that leaders have in common.

Traits and Abilities

A common approach to the subject of leadership is to try to isolate the traits and abilities that leaders possess and nonleaders do not. This approach has come to be known as the **trait theory.** From 1920–1950 a great deal of trait theory

---

[1] Bernard M. Bass, *Stogdill's Handbook of Leadership* (New York: Free Press, 1982), 9.

[2] Bass, *Leadership,* 10.

[3] Craig M. Watson, "Leadership, Management, and the Seven Keys," *Business Horizons* (March–April 1983):8–13. Also see Andre Van der Merwe and Sandra Van der Merwe, "Strategic Leadership and the Chief Executive," *Long Range Planning* (February 1985):100–111.

[4] Fred Luthans, *Organizational Behavior,* 4th ed. (New York: McGraw-Hill, 1985), 475.

[5] See: Gary Yukl, "Managerial Leadership: A Review of Theory and Research" *Journal of Management* (March 1989):251–89.

research was conducted in an effort to isolate the factors that contribute to leadership effectiveness. The biggest problem, unfortunately, was that investigators were unable to develop one universal list. Nevertheless, there are some general findings that many of them have reported. For example, after reviewing the literature of this period, Bass found uniformly positive evidence from 15 or more studies to support the following conclusions:

Some leadership traits

The average person who occupies a position of leadership exceeds the average member of his group in the following respects: (1) intelligence; (2) scholarship; (3) dependability in exercising responsibilities; (4) activity and social participation; and (5) socioeconomic status.[6]

Additionally, he found 10 or more studies supporting the following findings:

a. The qualities, characteristics, and skills required in a leader are determined to a large extent by the demands of the situation in which he is to function as a leader.

b. The average person who occupies a position of leadership exceeds the average member of the group to some degree in each of the following aspects: (1) sociability, (2) initiative, (3) persistence, (4) knowing how to get things done, (5) self-confidence, (6) alertness to, and insight into, situations, (7) cooperativeness, (8) popularity, (9) adaptability, and (10) verbal facility.[7]

Because there is such intuitive appeal in discovering common leadership traits, this approach still remains popular in the literature today. For example, Harry Levinson, a well-known psychologist and frequent contributor to the *Harvard Business Review,* has offered the following 20 dimensions of leader

Dimensions of leader personality

personality as those that should be considered when choosing a top executive:

1. The capacity to abstract, to conceptualize, to organize, and to integrate different data into a coherent frame of reference.
2. A tolerance for ambiguity.
3. Intelligence.
4. Good judgment.
5. The ability to take charge.
6. A capacity for attacking problems both vigorously and strategically.
7. An achievement orientedness.
8. A sensitivity to the feelings of others.
9. Participation as a member of the organization.

---

[6] Bass, *Leadership,* 65.
[7] Ibid.

10. Maturity.
11. An ability to stand on his or her own while accepting information, criticism, and cooperation from others.
12. An ability to articulate.
13. High physical and mental stamina.
14. The ability to adapt and to manage stress.
15. A sense of humor.
16. Well-defined personal goals that are consistent with organizational needs.
17. High perseverance.
18. The ability to organize time well.
19. High integrity.
20. An appreciation for the need to assume social responsibility and leadership.[8]

Even in this discussion, however, Levinson admits that there is no statistical validation of these dimensions. Rather, he offers them merely as a way of calling attention to characteristics related to executive success. Nevertheless, such traits are important in understanding the nature of leadership. The specific relationship of each to leader effectiveness may not be clear, but when the traits are examined as a composite, they certainly provide a general picture of what is needed in a good leader.[9] (See, for example, "Management in Practice: Leadership Practices for the Year 2000.")

Behavior

Another important way to study leadership is to examine what leaders do. Many individuals believe that one can become a better leader by emulating successful leadership behavior. While this idea is debatable, there is currently a great deal of interest in leadership behavior.[10] Many approaches have been used to describe how leaders conduct themselves. One describes leader-subordinate interactions.

Leader-Subordinate Interactions

As illustrated in Figure 14-1, leaders and subordinates can interact in four basic ways, depending on whether the manager's leadership style is autocratic, paternalistic, democratic/participative, or laissez-faire.

---

[8] Harry Levinson, "Criteria for Choosing Chief Executives," *Harvard Business Review* (July–August 1981):114–18. Also see "Should Companies Groom New Leaders or Buy Them?" *Business Week* (September 22, 1986):94–96.

[9] Morgan W. McCall, Jr. and Michael M. Lombardo, "What Makes a Top Executive," *Psychology Today* (February 1983):26–31. See also: R. H. G. Field, "The Self-Fulfilling Prophecy Leader: Achieving the Metharme Effect," *Journal of Management Studies* (March 1989):151–68.

[10] Stanley F. Slater, "The Influence of Managerial Style on Business Unit Performance," *Journal of Management* (September 1989):441–53.

Leadership Factors for the Year 2000

*I*n a study conducted by Columbia University, 1,500 senior executives (870 were CEOs from 20 nations) were surveyed to determine the current CEO characteristics. In addition, the executives were asked to assess the characteristics that CEOs will need in the year 2000. The results listed below show the percentage of the executives that selected each trait or skill now and in the year 2000.

Personal Behavior	Now	Year 2000	Knowledge & Skills	Now	Year 2000
Conveys a strong sense of vision	75%	98%	Strategy formulation	68%	78%
Links compensation to performance	66%	91%	Human resource management	41%	53%
Communicates frequently with employees	59%	89%	International economics and politics	10%	19%
			Science and technology	11%	15%
Emphasizes ethics	74%	85%	Computer literacy	3%	7%
Plans for management succession	56%	85%	Marketing and sales	50%	48%
Communicates frequently with customers	41%	78%	Negotiation	34%	24%
			Accounting and finance	33%	24%
Reassigns or terminates unsatisfactory employees	34%	71%	Handling media and communications	16%	13%
Rewards loyalty	48%	44%	Production	21%	9%
Makes all major decisions	39%	21%			
Behaves conservatively	32%	13%			

Source: Lester B. Korn, "How the Next CEO Will Be Different," *Fortune* (May 22, 1989):157–59.

Some leaders place little emphasis on people

AUTOCRATIC LEADERSHIP   **Autocratic leadership** is practiced by managers who tend to be heavily work-centered, placing most of their emphasis on task accomplishment and little on the human element. These leaders fit the classical model of management, in which the workers are viewed as factors of production. It should not be assumed, however, that these leaders are ineffective: sometimes they are extremely successful. In crisis situations, for example, get-tough managers are often needed. Organizations having productivity, cost control, or high inefficiency problems often turn to autocratic leaders to straighten out the situation.

Autocratic leaders are characterized by an emphasis on close control and a willingness to delegate very little authority. They retain decision-making authority on all important matters, ensuring that they will have the final say. As represented in Figure 14-1, leader-subordinate interaction is characterized by order giving on the leader's part. There is virtually no flow of information from

FIGURE 14-1   Leader-Subordinate Interactions

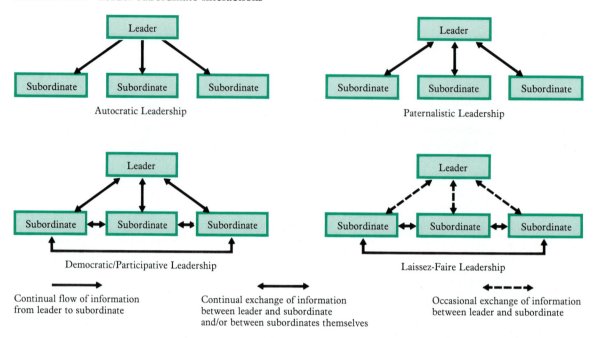

Continual flow of information
from leader to subordinate

Continual exchange of information
between leader and subordinate
and/or between subordinates themselves

Occasional exchange of information
between leader and subordinate

the subordinates back to the leader. Communication is primarily downward and is used for conveying directives and orders related to the work itself. If there is any upward flow of information, it is commonly restricted to reports related to work progress and is used by the leader to monitor operations further.

PATERNALISTIC LEADERSHIP   **Paternalistic leadership** is heavily work-centered but managers who adopt this leadership style also have some consideration for the personnel. In fact, they are sometimes confused with democratic/participative leaders because they seem to be as interested in the people as the work. One distinguishing characteristic, however, prevents them from being truly democratic: they believe in the philosophy "Do as I say and the organization will take care of you." These leaders tend to be very much like parents. They will look after their subordinates, but the subordinates have to behave themselves and stay in line. If there is any deviation, some form of punishment (demotion, poor performance evaluation, low salary increase) is likely to follow. When paternalistic leaders are described in terms of Theory X and Theory Y, they typically are identified as "soft" Theory X. Notice in Figure 14-1 that these managers have a continual exchange of information with their employees but that the employees do *not* interact with each other. In this way the leader still maintains final control. Everyone is managed directly by him or her, and intergroup teamwork never develops.

Others are parental in their approach

Many managers are paternalistic leaders because they believe their subordinates really want someone to look after them. Additionally, although they do not believe that the workers are truly lazy (hard Theory X), they do feel that the workers have a tendency toward acting this way (soft Theory X philosophy). Paternalistic leaders tend to be most effective when dealing with subordinates who are insecure or who are just learning their jobs and welcome advice, assistance, and protection.[11]

DEMOCRATIC/PARTICIPATIVE LEADERSHIP   **Democratic/participative leadership** is characterized by a high concern for both people and work. As seen in Figure 14-1, democratic/participative leaders encourage a continual flow of information between themselves and their subordinates. They also support a continual exchange of information between the subordinates themselves. In bringing about this open flow of information in their unit or department, democratic leaders delegate a great deal of authority to their people and encourage them to play an active role in the operation of the enterprise.

Others have a high concern for people and work

A number of advantages commonly result from this form of leadership behavior. Some of the most typical are that (1) decision making is improved because the leader is able to rely upon others for information and assistance before rendering a final judgment; (2) morale goes up because the followers like the openness and freedom of their work environment; (3) high achievement drive is nurtured and developed because the subordinates know what is expected of them and are given the necessary freedom to pursue these objectives; and (4) when changes have to be made, the personnel are less likely to oppose them because they will be playing a role in fashioning and implementing these new rules or regulations.

In the main, participative leadership is well thought of in the United States, perhaps because most Americans prefer to work in this type of environment.[12] This approach does not work for every organization, however. Dale D. McConkey, a management researcher and writer, put the issue in perspective when he wrote: "Participative management . . . starts off by making clear to each manager that the primary reason he or she is employed is to help carry out the requirements of the organization. Then . . . each manager is asked how he or she can help carry out the organization's objectives and priorities. In responding to this question each manager is given the greatest possible (practical) latitude or participation in determining his or her own future within the organization which is *consistent with the requirements of the organization.*[13]

Participative management is not for everyone

---

[11] Dean Tjosvold, "Interdependence and Power Between Managers and Employees: A Study of the Leader Relationship," *Journal of Management* (January 1989):49–62.

[12] Peter R. Richardson, "Courting Greater Employee Involvement through Participative Management, *Sloan Management Review* (Winter 1985):33–44. See also: Edward E. Lawler III and Susan A. Mohrman, "High-Involvement Management," *Personnel* (April 1989):26–31.

[13] Dale D. McConkey, "Participative Management: What It Really Means in Practice," *Business Horizons* (October 1980):67.

Some organizations do not function well in a highly participative environment; some subordinates do not respond well to this form of leadership behavior.

Three conditions are necessary for the effective use of participative leadership. First, this approach works best only when a manager is able to anticipate problems and plan ahead; if the problems turn into crises, the authoritarian style may be required. Second, both the subordinates and the manager must believe that this approach will be beneficial to them; if either feels it is inappropriate, it will not work. Third, the leader must remember that he or she has a responsibility to two groups: the subordinates and the enterprise. Democratic leadership does not mean turning over the management of the unit to the subordinates. It means developing group teamwork in the pursuit of the organization's goals.

Many organizations today express an interest in moving from their semiauthoritarian leadership approach to a more participative one. Such a change takes time to implement. Moreover, the organization has to be sure that it is ready to make such a transition. The readiness checklist in Table 14-1 is one of many that can be used for this purpose. The checklist can help an organization determine its overall readiness or current posture in regard to the major aspects of participative management. Many researchers recommend that at least three levels of management take part in completing these types of checklists so as to uncover any major problems that can accompany the decision to become a more participative enterprise.

LAISSEZ-FAIRE LEADERSHIP   **Laissez-faire leadership** is employed by managers who are basically uninvolved in the operations of the unit. These managers tend to turn things over to the subordinates. If a leader does make an appearance, it is to check and see how things are going. There is no active involvement on the leader's part. As seen in Figure 14-1, there are only occasional exchanges of information between the leader and the subordinates.

Some leaders are basically uninvolved in operations

Does laissez-faire leadership ever work well? The answer is that it can, but such situations are rare. The most commonly cited example of successful laissez-faire leadership is that of a manager in a research and development laboratory. The subordinates are usually all highly skilled, well-trained professionals. The manager's job is to provide them with the assistance and equipment they require to get their work done. The subordinates are typically highly motivated and do not need to be told what has to be done. By simply ensuring that they have what they need and staying out of their hair, the manager can achieve excellent results.[14] This example is the exception to the rule, however. In most cases laissez-faire leaders are not effective because they fail to carry out the

---

[14] Charles C. Manz, "Self-Leadership: Toward an Expanded Theory of Self-Influence Processes in Organizations," *Academy of Management Review* (July 1986):585–600. See also: Colette A. Frayne, "Improving Employee Performance Through Self-Management Training," *Business Quarterly* (Summer 1989):46–50.

TABLE 14-1   A Readiness Checklist for Participative Management

Factor	Major Thrust	Little if any 1 2 3	Exception rather than rule 1 2 3	Rule rather than exception 1 2 3	Extensive 1 2 3
Support and participation by top management	Active involvement vs. lip service	☐☐☐	☐☐☐	☐☐☐	☐☐☐
Favorable environment for change	Willingness to change vs. protecting landed interests	☐☐☐	☐☐☐	☐☐☐	☐☐☐
Open, nonthreatening environment	Trust and respect vs. fear	☐☐☐	☐☐☐	☐☐☐	☐☐☐
Willingness of senior managers to share authority	Secure vs. insecure manager	☐☐☐	☐☐☐	☐☐☐	☐☐☐
Quality of subordinate managers	Ability and willingness to accept responsibility	☐☐☐	☐☐☐	☐☐☐	☐☐☐
Willingness of subordinates to accept objective measurement on the job	Results vs. effort or busyness	☐☐☐	☐☐☐	☐☐☐	☐☐☐
Willingness to comply with disciplined approaches	Planning vs. seat-of-the-pants	☐☐☐	☐☐☐	☐☐☐	☐☐☐
Environment predictable enough for planning	Stability vs. instability	☐☐☐	☐☐☐	☐☐☐	☐☐☐
Participation in objective setting	Self-management vs. dictation from above	☐☐☐	☐☐☐	☐☐☐	☐☐☐
Relationship between objectives of the organization and lower level objectives	Supportive vs. fragmented	☐☐☐	☐☐☐	☐☐☐	☐☐☐
Verifiable objectives	Measurable vs. vague/nebulous	☐☐☐	☐☐☐	☐☐☐	☐☐☐
Relationship between achievement of objectives and reward system	Results-oriented rewards vs. subjective ones	☐☐☐	☐☐☐	☐☐☐	☐☐☐
Willingness to take risks	Innovative vs. playing it safe	☐☐☐	☐☐☐	☐☐☐	☐☐☐
Free and open interdepartmental communications	Team building vs. empire building	☐☐☐	☐☐☐	☐☐☐	☐☐☐
Degree of interdepartmental coordination among managers on matters of common concern	Freedom and willingness to consult with other involved managers	☐☐☐	☐☐☐	☐☐☐	☐☐☐
Data/information in focus for decision making	Decentralization vs. centralized	☐☐☐	☐☐☐	☐☐☐	☐☐☐
Job responsibilities clearly delineated	Agreement between superior and subordinate on job scope and content	☐☐☐	☐☐☐	☐☐☐	☐☐☐
Priorities can be determined	Most important vs. less important	☐☐☐	☐☐☐	☐☐☐	☐☐☐

Source: Dale D. McConkey, ''Participative Management: What It Really Means in Practice,'' *Business Horizons* (October 1980):72. Reprinted by permission of the publisher.

most important function of a leader—they do not attempt to influence their people to direct their efforts toward goal attainment.

Theory X and Theory Y

A basic approach to examining leadership behavior was presented by Douglas McGregor in his now-famous Theory X and Theory Y.[15] **Theory X** is a set of assumptions that many managers use in supervising and leading their personnel. In McGregor's view, managers who subscribe to Theory X employ the following assumptions:

Theory X assumptions

1. The average person has an inherent dislike of work and, whenever possible, will avoid it.
2. People have little ambition, tend to shun responsibility, and prefer to be directed.
3. Above all else, people want security.
4. In order to get people to attain organizational objectives it is necessary to use coercion, control, and threats of punishment.[16]

These assumptions, if accepted by the manager, lead to the use of a "carrot and stick" approach. In front of the worker are placed job security and other financial rewards—the carrot. If the worker does not move forward, the stick (loss of pay raises, demotions, outright firing) is used.

The assumptions of **Theory Y** are quite different from those of Theory X. Theory Y employs a more optimistic, dynamic, and flexible philosophy. The assumptions of Theory Y are:

Theory Y assumptions

1. Work is a natural phenomenon and, under the right conditions, people not only will accept responsibility but also will seek it.
2. If people are committed to organizational objectives, they will exercise self-direction and self-control in pursuing these aims.
3. Commitment to organizational objectives is a function of the rewards associated with goal attainment; the more the organization is willing to give to its people, the harder the latter will work in pursuing enterprise goals.
4. The capacity for ingenuity and creativity is widespread throughout the population but under conditions of modern industrial life, this potential is only partially tapped.[17]

---

[15] Douglas McGregor, *The Human Side of Enterprise* (New York: McGraw-Hill, 1960).
[16] McGregor, *Enterprise,* 33–34.
[17] McGregor, *Enterprise,* 47–48.

TABLE 14-2	A Comparison of Theory X and Theory Y	
Selected Management Functions	Theory X Managerial Behavior	Theory Y Managerial Behavior
Planning	Superior sets objectives for subordinates.	Superior and subordinates jointly set objectives.
Decision making	Superior makes decisions and announces them to subordinates.	Superior establishes broad guidelines and lets subordinates make decisions within these parameters.
Organizing	Superior determines what everyone will do and all authority is based on job position and title.	Superior and subordinates jointly determine job design. Authority is based on job knowledge and initiative as well as hierarchical position.
Communicating	All communication flows from superior to subordinates.	Communication flows in all directions: vertical, horizontal, lateral, and diagonal.
Motivating	Motivation is based on threats, fear, and the potential loss of job security.	Motivation is based on helping subordinates achieve a feeling of self-fulfillment for a job well done.
Leading	Leadership is autocratic; people do as they are told—or else.	Leadership is participative and teamwork is both encouraged and nurtured.
Controlling	Subordinates are evaluated based on past mistakes. Those who have erred are punished.	Subordinates are evaluated based on accomplishments. Mistakes are used as learning examples for preventing further occurrences.

Table 14-2 shows how a Theory X manager differs from a Theory Y manager in carrying out selected management functions.

Miles' Theories of Management

Raymond E. Miles points out that the managerial task is to integrate organizational variables (goals, structure, technology) with human variables (abilities, values, attitudes, personal needs). The result is an efficient sociotechnical system in which the needs of both the organization and the personnel are met.

Into this environment the manager brings his or her own personal concepts about how to deal with people. Miles' model goes past Theory X and Theory Y and incorporates both the policies of the manager and the expectations of management. Table 14-3 illustrates his three-theory model.

This table shows that there are three theories of management: traditional, human relations, and human resources. In practice managers subscribe not to one of these theories but to two. The first is the one they use to manage their own subordinates. The second is the way they believe they should be managed by their own superior.

TABLE 14-3   Alternative Models of Management

Traditional Model	Human Relations Model	Human Resources Model
Assumptions		
1. Work is inherently distasteful to most people 2. What workers do is less important than what they earn for doing it 3. Few want or can handle work which requires creativity, self-direction, or self-control	1. People want to feel useful and important 2. People desire to belong and be recognized as individuals 3. These needs are more important than money in motivating people to work	1. Work is not inherently distasteful. People want to contribute to meaningful goals which they have helped establish 2. Most people can exercise far more creative, responsible self-direction and self-control than their present jobs demand
Policies		
1. The manager's basic task is to closely supervise and control subordinates 2. The manager must break tasks down into simple, repetitive, easily learned operations 3. The manager must establish detailed work routines and procedures and enforce these firmly but fairly	1. The manager's basic task is to make each worker feel useful and important 2. The manager should keep subordinates informed and listen to their objections to his plans 3. The manager should allow subordinates to exercise some self-direction and self-control on routine matters	1. The manager's basic task is to make use of "untapped" human resources 2. The manager must create an environment in which all members may contribute to the limits of their ability 3. The manager must encourage full participation on important matters, continually broadening subordinate self-direction and control
Expectations		
1. People can tolerate work if the pay is decent and the boss is fair 2. If tasks are simple enough and people are closely controlled, they will produce up to standard	1. Sharing information with subordinates and involving them in routine decisions will satisfy their basic needs to belong and to feel important 2. Satisfying these needs will improve morale and reduce resistance to formal authority— subordinates will "willingly cooperate"	1. Expanding subordinate influence, self-direction, and self-control will lead to direct improvements in operating efficiency 2. Work satisfaction may improve as a "by-product" of subordinates making full use of their resources

Source: From *Theories of Management: Implications for Organizational Behavior and Development* by R. E. Miles. Copyright 1975 by McGraw-Hill Book Company. Used with permission of McGraw-Hill Book Company.

The emphasis is on
controlling and
direction

The **traditional model** emphasizes controlling and directing. The underlying assumption in this model is that the members of the organization will comply if they are given specific tasks and procedures and if they are properly selected, trained, and paid for their efforts.

The **human relations model** is a modified version of the traditional

Attention is paid to social and egoistic needs

model. The major difference is that the human relations model pays attention to personal needs such as social and egoistic needs. Social needs are addressed by allowing personnel to interact with other members of the workforce and feel part of a team. Egoistic needs are met by allowing people to feel that they are doing something important and meaningful.

The manager serves as a developer

The **human resources model** presents the manager as a developer and facilitator who assists the subordinates in achieving goals. Under this model there is a great deal of participation in goal setting. Self-direction and self-control are not only encouraged but are rewarded. The employee is given the opportunity to become all he or she is capable of becoming.

These three theories are somewhat similar to McGregor's, with Theory X most represented by the traditional and (to some extent) the human relations model, and Theory Y most represented by the human resources model.

The Managerial Grid

Another popular way of describing leadership behavior is through the use of the **managerial grid** developed by Robert Blake and Jane Mouton.[18] The managerial grid provides a detailed description of leadership behavior, in addition to serving as a training and development tool. At this point in the book, we will examine the grid only in terms of its descriptive value.

BASIC STYLES   The managerial grid, illustrated in Figure 14-2, is a two-dimensional leadership model. One axis is labeled "concern for production" and the other is labeled "concern for people." Each axis has nine degrees, ranging from low concern (1) to high concern (9). As a result, 81 leadership combinations are possible. Only five are considered to be major leadership styles, however. These are shown in the figure.

Basic management styles

The 9,1 manager is most interested in production or work output and has a low concern for people. In direct contrast, the 1,9 manager is very interested in people but has a low concern for production. The 1,1 manager has a minimum concern for both work and people, exerting a minimum of effort in getting things done. The 5,5 manager is a middle-of-the-road type who balances an intermediate concern for production with a similar concern for people. Finally, the 9,9 manager has a high concern for both people and work.

In contrast to a leader-subordinate interaction approach which describes how a leader *can* act, the grid is designed to teach managers how they *ought* to act. Blake and Mouton, drawing on their research and experience, claim that the 9,9 style is the best one for all situations. In so doing they directly reject the contingency approach to leadership, which holds that the most effective style

---

[18] Robert R. Blake and Jane Syrgley Mouton, *The Managerial Grid* (Houston, TX: Gulf Publishing Co., 1964).

FIGURE 14-2
The Managerial
Grid

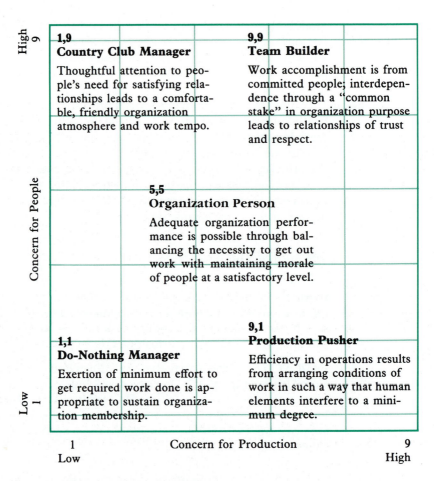

High 9

1,9
Country Club Manager
Thoughtful attention to people's need for satisfying relationships leads to a comfortable, friendly organization atmosphere and work tempo.

9,9
Team Builder
Work accomplishment is from committed people; interdependence through a "common stake" in organization purpose leads to relationships of trust and respect.

Concern for People

5,5
Organization Person
Adequate organization performance is possible through balancing the necessity to get out work with maintaining morale of people at a satisfactory level.

9,1
Production Pusher
Efficiency in operations results from arranging conditions of work in such a way that human elements interfere to a minimum degree.

1,1
Do-Nothing Manager
Exertion of minimum effort to get required work done is appropriate to sustain organization membership.

Low 1

1   Concern for Production   9
Low   High

depends on the situation the leader faces at that particular time. Defending their position, Blake and Mouton argue that:

> Rejection of the "one best way" is equivalent to repudiating the proposition that effective behavior is based on scientific principles or laws. Yet the view that principles of behavior undergird specific events is consistent with all other areas of scientific inquiry. We know that principles of physics underlie a vast range of phenomena in inanimate nature. Principles of biology account for phenomena of life and make them predictable. By analogy, behavioral science principles underlie human conduct, provide guidelines for soundness, and also make it predictable . . . Shifting from an "it all depends" to a "one best way" concept of leadership is what managerial effectiveness training is—or should be—all about.[19]

---

[19] Robert Blake and Jane Syrgley Mouton, "Should You Teach There's Only *One* Best Way To Manage?" *Training HRD* (April 1978):25–29.

CONTINGENCY THEORIES OF LEADERSHIP

At the present time the contingency approach to leadership is the most highly regarded. There are a number of contingency theories but they all have one thing in common: they tell how a leader should act in a particular situation.[20] These theories make wide use of "if-then" propositions such as: if the leader is in a moderately favorable situation, he or she should use a people-oriented style; if the leader faces a crisis situation, he or she should be task oriented. These theories are also heavily research-based, in contrast to most other leadership theories, which are simply descriptive or are based on intuition or personal experience or both. The two that will be examined here are Fred Fiedler's contingency theory of leadership and Robert Houses's path-goal theory. These are currently the two most prominent contingency theories of leadership.

Fiedler's Contingency Theory

Fiedler's contingency theory has been well accepted because of its empirical nature. The development of this theory can be divided into two major stages. The first extended from the early 1950s to the early 1960s and was basically explorative. The second began with a statement of the theory, has been characterized by testing and modification to fit research findings, and continues to the present day.

Fiedler published his findings in 1964.[21] A few years later he published a comprehensive and detailed explanation of the theory.[22] In so doing he sought to explain the reasons why leaders are effective. At the heart of his contingency theory are a research instrument called the **least preferred coworker scale** (LPC) and a classification of three situational dimensions in which a leader functions.

The LPC and Situational Variables

The LPC (see Table 14-4) is a scale containing paired adjectives. The person filling out the instrument is asked to describe the coworker with whom he or she can work least well. This coworker does not have to be someone with whom

---

[20] Noel M. Tichy and David O. Ulrich, "The Leadership Challenge—A Call for the Transformational Leader," *Sloan Management Review* (Fall 1984):59–68. See also: David V. Day and Robert G. Lord, "Executive Leadership and Organizational Performance: Suggestions for a New Theory and Methodology," *Journal of Management* (September 1988):453–64.

[21] Fred E. Fiedler, "A Contingency Model of Leadership Effectiveness," *Advances in Experimental Social Psychology,* Leonard Berkowitz, ed. (New York: Academic Press, 1964):149–60.

[22] Fred E. Fiedler, *A Theory of Leadership Effectiveness* (New York: McGraw-Hill, 1967).

TABLE 14-4   The Least Preferred Coworker (LPC) Scale

Pleasant	__:__:__:__:__:__:__:__ 8 7 6 5 4 3 2 1	Unpleasant
Friendly	__:__:__:__:__:__:__:__ 8 7 6 5 4 3 2 1	Unfriendly
Rejecting	__:__:__:__:__:__:__:__ 1 2 3 4 5 6 7 8	Accepting
Helpful	__:__:__:__:__:__:__:__ 8 7 6 5 4 3 2 1	Frustrating
Unenthusiastic	__:__:__:__:__:__:__:__ 1 2 3 4 5 6 7 8	Enthusiastic
Tense	__:__:__:__:__:__:__:__ 1 2 3 4 5 6 7 8	Relaxed
Distant	__:__:__:__:__:__:__:__ 1 2 3 4 5 6 7 8	Close
Cold	__:__:__:__:__:__:__:__ 1 2 3 4 5 6 7 8	Warm
Cooperative	__:__:__:__:__:__:__:__ 8 7 6 5 4 3 2 1	Uncooperative
Supportive	__:__:__:__:__:__:__:__ 8 7 6 5 4 3 2 1	Hostile
Boring	__:__:__:__:__:__:__:__ 1 2 3 4 5 6 7 8	Interesting
Quarrelsome	__:__:__:__:__:__:__:__ 1 2 3 4 5 6 7 8	Harmonious
Self-assured	__:__:__:__:__:__:__:__ 8 7 6 5 4 3 2 1	Hesitant
Efficient	__:__:__:__:__:__:__:__ 8 7 6 5 4 3 2 1	Inefficient
Gloomy	__:__:__:__:__:__:__:__ 1 2 3 4 5 6 7 8	Cheerful
Open	__:__:__:__:__:__:__:__ 8 7 6 5 4 3 2 1	Guarded

Source: Fred E. Fiedler, *A Theory of Leadership Effectiveness.* Copyright © 1967, McGraw-Hill Book Company. Used by the permission of the author.

the person is working currently; he or she can be a past colleague or subordinate. The interpretation of the LPC score was explained by Fiedler in this way:

The LPC score explained

. . . we visualize the high-LPC individual (who perceives his least-preferred coworker in a relatively favorable manner) as a person who derives his major satisfaction from successful interpersonal relationships, while the low-LPC person (who describes his LPC in very unfavorable terms) derives his major satisfaction from task performance.[23]

---

[23] Fiedler, *Leadership Effectiveness,* 45.

TABLE 14-5 Fiedler's Findings on Leadership Style and Performance

Major Situational Variables

Condition	Leader-Member Relations	Task Structure	Position Power	Effective Leadership Style
I	Good	Structured	Strong	Task-Oriented
II	Good	Structured	Weak	Task-Oriented
III	Good	Unstructured	Strong	Task-Oriented
IV	Good	Unstructured	Weak	Human Relations
V	Moderately Poor	Structured	Strong	Human Relations
VI	Moderately Poor	Structured	Weak	No Data
VII	Moderately Poor	Unstructured	Strong	No Relationship
VIII	Moderately Poor	Unstructured	Weak	Task-Oriented

Situational variables

Initially Fiedler hoped to find a relationship between the LPC score and the leader's performance. He eventually concluded, however, that more attention had to be given to situational variables. The three he found to be most important were (1) **leader-member relations**—the degree to which the group leader is accepted by the group members and is able to maintain their loyalty; (2) **task structure**—the degree to which rules, regulations, job descriptions, and policies are clearly specified; and (3) **position power**—the degree to which the leader is able to apply both positive (reward) and negative (punishment) sanctions. If the leader has good relations with the group members, high task structure, and strong position power, the situation is favorable. If just the opposite is true, the situation is unfavorable.

Choosing the most effective leader

Fiedler then brought together the LPC scale, the situational variables, and his findings. The results are presented in Table 14-5 and Figure 14-3.[24] Notice that the "V" shaped curve can be used to determine what type of leader is most effective in a particular situation. In a very favorable situation ("A" in the figure), a task-oriented leader is best; in a moderately favorable situation ("B" in the figure), a human-relations-oriented leader is best; in a moderately unfavorable situation ("C" in the figure), a human-relations-oriented leader is best; in a very unfavorable situation ("D" in the figure), a task-oriented leader is best.

---

[24] For more on the LPC, see John K. Kennedy, Jr., "Middle LPC Leaders and the Contingency Model of Leadership Effectiveness," *Organizational Behavior and Human Performance* (August 1982):1–14.

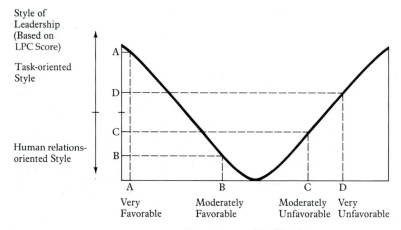

FIGURE 14-3
Fiedler's Findings
Regarding
Leadership
Effectiveness

Favorableness of the Situation

LEADER MATCH   As well as identifying these relationships between leader-ship style and situation, Fiedler has also encouraged the use of a leader match concept. Since effective leadership is a function of *both* the individual leader and the situation, two alternatives are available to the leader who wants a better match between the two. The leader can either attempt to change his or her personality or work to change the situational variables and make them more favorable. Fiedler argues that it is too difficult to get leaders to change their personalities; it is more effective to change the situation. As a result, Fiedler and his associates have developed a self-paced program instruction workbook for this purpose.[25] The booklet teaches leaders how to (1) assess their leadership style based on their LPC score, (2) assess the amount of situational favorable-ness that currently exists in their environment, and (3) change the situation so that it matches their style. The theory has been applied quite successfully.

Matching the leader with the situation

BASIC VALUE   How well has Fiedler's theory been accepted? At present it is well regarded. Much of what Fiedler has to say is grounded in empirical re-search, and he continues to address criticisms and conduct further testing. He himself described the situation best when he wrote:

> A number of the Contingency Model's critics have charged that ". . . the theory keeps changing to fit the data" and that is becoming increasingly complex. Both of these observations are accurate . . . . The theory will, of course, continue to change as new data become available . . . We simply

[25] Fred E. Fiedler, Martin M. Chemers, and Linda Mahar, *Improving Leadership Effectiveness: The Leadership Match Concept* (New York: John Wiley, 1976).

have to live with the fact that any attempt to predict pretzel-shaped relationships will require the development of pretzel-shaped hypotheses.[26]

The Path-Goal Theory of Leadership

The nature of the job affects the approach

The **path-goal theory,** another contingency leadership theory, seeks to explain how the nature of the group's job affects whether a task orientation, human relations orientation, or some combination of the two will result in the greatest degree of group satisfaction and effectiveness. This theory has been popularized through the work of Martin Evans and Robert House.[27] It is actually derived from the expectancy theory of motivation in that it draws heavily on such concepts as valence and expectancy in explaining how a leader should act. Hence, the path-goal theory blends the subjects of motivation and leadership.

In essence, the path-goal theory holds that the leader's job is to (1) clarify the tasks to be performed by subordinates (2) clear away any roadblocks that prevent goal attainment, and (3) increase the opportunity for subordinates to attain personal satisfaction. The major question, of course, is: What degree of task or human relations orientation will be best? As initially postulated, the theory suggested that in situations in which subordinates did not know what they were supposed to do or were unclear about the way to get the job done, a high task orientation was warranted. Conversely, when the subordinates knew what they were supposed to do and were capable of performing adequately, a human relations orientation was best.

> What does this mean in practice? For one thing, it means that if subordinates are confused as to what to do next, then a lot of "initiating structure" might be called for — you tell them what to do and how to do it. That way the leader gives them a clear path to follow. It also means that if subordinates' tasks are already very clear — as they might be on an assembly line — then the leader wants to "stay out of their hair." In this case, their "paths" are already clear enough. The path-goal theory also assumes that setting clear goals for subordinates and explaining to them why these goals are important are basic functions all leaders should perform.[28]

The theory can also be turned around to examine what will happen if the leader does not act properly. For example, if the leader fails to give adequate

---

[26] Fred E. Fiedler, "Predicting the Effects of Leadership Training and Experience from the Contingency Model: A Clarification," *Journal of Applied Psychology* (April 1973):113.
[27] Martin G. Evans, "The Effect of Supervisory Behavior on the Path-Goal Relationship," *Organizational Behavior and Human Performance* (May 1970):277–98; Robert J. House, "Path-Goal Theory of Leadership Effectiveness," *Administrative Science Quarterly* (September 1971):321–38.
[28] Gary Dessler, *Management Fundamentals,* 3rd ed. (Reston, VA: Reston Publishing, 1982), 393.

support to the subordinates performing the tasks, they will be dissatisfied and ineffective. Likewise, if the leader gives too much attention or direction to individuals who already know how to carry out their tasks, they will not like it and will be dissatisfied and not fully effective.

Research results are mixed . . .

How accurate has the path-goal theory proven to be? To date the results are mixed.[29] For example, some researchers have found that while increased task orientation on ambiguous jobs can lead to increased subordinate satisfaction, it does not necessarily lead to increased subordinate performance. Others have found that in an unstructured situation the subordinates welcomed attempts by the leader to be friendly and personable but did not want as much structure as had been predicted by the theory.

but the value of the path-goal theory cannot be disputed

At the present time research on the theory is continuing. On an overall basis, the path-goal theory has value, especially as a supervisory theory of leadership. It not only suggests the type of leadership style that may be most effective in a given situation but also attempts to explain why that style is most effective, thereby serving as a basis for further research and refinement. Also, the linkage between the path-goal theory and the expectancy theory in work motivation may yet provide a basis for more effectively integrating the study of motivation and leadership.

LEADERSHIP EFFECTIVENESS

In recent years increased attention has been given to answering the question: How can leadership research be brought down to an *applied* level? Blake and Mouton attempt to answer this question with their grid training. Their critics decry the lack of flexibility provided by the approach, however — for example, its contention that the 9,9 style is *always* superior. Students and practitioners alike express an interest in a more contingency-based approach. The result has been the emergence of two different types of leadership effectiveness models. One is based heavily on management theory and attempts to integrate current knowledge into a logical framework for management action. The other is based more heavily on training and development in organizations and represents the experience and judgment of the particular researchers. Both approaches, however, are likely to rely heavily on Fiedler's leader match concept. The following discussion examines each of these two approaches. (See also, "Management in Practice: The CEO Test.")

---

[29] For an excellent summary of research studies that have provided both supportive and mixed results on the theory, see Bass, *Leadership,* 445–47; Janet Fulk and Eric R. Wendler, "Dimensionality of Leader-Subordinate Interactions: A Path-Goal Investigation," *Organizational Behavior and Human Performance* (October 1982):241–64.

FIGURE 14-4
A Leadership
Continuum

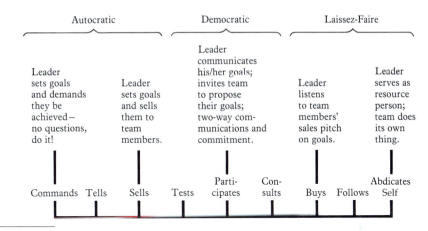

A Leadership Continuum

Leader-Follower Continua

The approach that is perhaps the most popular for explaining how to achieve leadership effectiveness uses a synthesis of current information. One such comprehensive view has been offered by Robert W. Johnston, a management and organizational development specialist. He seeks "to develop a practical, conceptual model of leader-follower behavior designed for use as a tool for diagnosing, planning, and working through leader-follower issues for more productive relationships.[30]

A matching of the styles of the leader and the followers

Every leader can adopt a number of different styles. The three most commonly accepted are autocratic, democratic, and laissez-faire. These three are arrayed along a continuum and described in Figure 14-4.

In the same way, every follower also can adopt a number of different behavior patterns. In Johnston's terminology, these behavior patterns are dependent, interdependent, and independent; each of these is described in Figure 14-5.

When the leadership continuum in Figure 14-4 and the followership continuum in Figure 14-5 are brought together, the result is the leader-follower continuum depicted in Figure 14-6. Notice in this figure how the styles of the leader and the followers are matched. When the leader is autocratic and the follower is dependent, everything moves smoothly. The same is true when

[30] Robert W. Johnston, "Leader-Follower Behavior in 3-D, Part 1," *Personnel* (July–August 1981):32.

MANAGEMENT IN PRACTICE

The CEO Test

HOW TO MAKE YOUR MARK

Circle the letter, as illustrated to the right, that best represents your acceptance or rejection of the statements that follow.

Strongly disagree:	(D)	d	?	a	A
Moderately disagree:	D	(d)	?	a	A
Neutral or uncertain:	D	d	(?)	a	A
Moderately agree:	D	d	?	(a)	A
Strongly agree:	D	d	?	a	(A)

FORTY QUICK DECISIONS

1. You would deliberately modify your style or opinions in order to achieve your ends.   D d ? a A
2. You have a highly developed sense of intuitive judgment, common sense and problem-solving ability.   D d ? a A
3. You seldom try to do more than one thing at a time (talk on the phone while watching the news or reading the mail, etc.).   D d ? a A
4. You consider many jobs/tasks to be beneath you.   D d ? a A
5. You try to influence strongly the outcome of events.   D d ? a A
6. Even though you really enjoy what you are doing, you find that your mind is easily distracted.   D d ? a A
7. You are more sensitive to rejection than most people.   D d ? a A
8. It irritates you when others treat life as nothing more than a game.   D d ? a A
9. You read a minimum of 20 books a year (fiction and nonfiction) and at least 10 different magazines and articles per month.   D d ? a A
10. You rarely remember your dreams.   D d ? a A
11. You have a deep dislike of regularity or systemization.   D d ? a A
12. Although you know you have a lot of potential, you have seldom taxed your capacity to the maximum.   D d ? a A
13. You are more competent and better able to motivate others than most people.   D d ? a A
14. You find it hard to keep your motivation on one task or one job at a time.   D d ? a A
15. You have contempt for what may be called a conformist society.   D d ? a A
16. It is very easy to ruffle your feathers or to get your back up.   D d ? a A
17. You consider yourself more of a practical person than a creative person.   D d ? a A
18. You are always ready and willing to make changes.   D d ? a A
19. You prefer to stay unstructured and seldom like to plan things out in advance.   D d ? a A
20. You exert so much energy at work that there is little left for play.   D d ? a A
21. Being successful at work is the most important priority in your life.   D d ? a A
22. You try your hardest when your work is being evaluated by others.   D d ? a A
23. You believe the present is all that really counts and have little interest in postponing your pleasures.   D d ? a A

24. It really gets on your nerves when you make small mistakes or experience even trivial setbacks.   D d ? a A

25. The logical and factual part of your mind appears stronger than the intuitive (feelings) part of your mind.   D d ? a A

26. In school, math was one of your best subjects.   D d ? a A

27. It is better to do something 70% correct than waste your time trying to get it perfect.   D d ? a A

28. When things go wrong, you do not feel most responsible or blame yourself more than others.   D d ? a A

29. Without a full-time career/job, you doubt if you could be happy.   D d ? a A

30. You need to be psyched up or encouraged by others in order to do your best.   D d ? a A

31. When making speeches, you usually like to wing it rather than carefully planning what to say.   D d ? a A

32. You would dislike a job that caused you to suffer headaches, acid indigestion and ulcers due to the competitive stress level.   D d ? a A

33. When all the facts say, "Go for it!" but a nagging inner feeling says no, you follow the inner feeling.   D d ? a A

34. You would rather be known as a person who makes an occasional wrong decision than one who makes few but always accurate decisions.   D d ? a A

35. You have a difficult time doing a job well when you personally dislike the task.   D d ? a A

36. Resigning your position or job as a matter of principle to support a cause that you believe in seems immature to you.   D d ? a A

37. You are a fast-moving person on the go from morning to night.   D d ? a A

38. You insist on having total advance knowledge of any new venture before you enter into it.   D d ? a A

39. You usually have difficulty stating your ideas when around well-educated or intelligent people.   D d ? a A

40. You are quick to criticize or discount the foolish opinions and actions of people you do not respect.   D d ? a A

EXECUTIVE SCORECARD

Thinking

For questions 1, 2, 9, 10, 17, 18, 25, 26, 33 and 34, give yourself:

5 points for each "A" circled   4 points for each "a" circled   2 points for each "?" circled

Total raw score: _____   Percentile: _____

Work habits

For questions 3, 4, 11, 12, 19, 20, 27, 28, 35 and 36, give yourself:

5 points for each "D" circled   4 points for each "d" circled   2 points for each "?" circled

Total raw score: _____   Percentile: _____

(continued)

MANAGEMENT IN PRACTICE *(Continued)*

Motivation

For questions 5, 13, 21, 29 and 37, give yourself:

  5 points for each "A" circled   4 points for each "a" circled   2 points for each "?" circled

For questions 6, 14, 22, 30 and 38, give yourself:

  5 points for each "D" circled   4 points for each "d" circled   2 points for each "?" circled

  Total raw score: _____   Percentile: _____

Self and others

For questions 7, 8, 15, 16, 23, 24, 31, 32, 39 and 40, give yourself:

  5 points for each "D" circled   4 points for each "d" circled   2 points for each "?" circled

  Total raw score: _____   Percentile: _____

Find out your percentiles by using the conversion chart.

HOW YOU STACK UP WITH THE BEST

CONVERSION CHART

Use the table to the right to convert your raw score on each trait into a percentile score (the average business person scores at the 50th percentile). Then use the chart below to compare your results with those of other executives. For example, if your raw score in the Thinking category is 23 points, your percentile score is 55. This means you are more competent in this area than 55% of business people. But, as illustrated, it also means you are 20% below the average percentile for Cash Newton and Associates' sample of successful top executives.

Raw score	Percentile score	Raw score	Percentile score
47–50	99	21–22	50
44–46	97	19–20	45
41–43	95	18	40
38–40	90	16–17	35
36–37	85	14–15	30
34–35	80	12–13	25
31–33	75	11	20
29–30	70	10	15
27–28	65	9	10
25–26	60	0–8	5
23–24	55		

EXECUTIVE TRAITS	*Your percentile score*	*Average percentile for sample of successful top executives*
Thinking: tendency to think logically, pragmatically, inventively; to act decisively; and to stay open to progressive ideas	_____.	75
Work habits: degree to which you act in an expedient, well-organized, dedicated and responsible manner with attention to quality	_____.	65
Motivation: ambition and energy level, desire to lead, initiate and act with courage in the face of failure	_____.	75
Self and others: degree to which you appear good-natured, mature, open to constructive criticism and possess good human-relations skills	_____.	70
Average score: add up total scores from all four areas and divide by four	_____.	70

WHAT IT ALL MEANS

76%ile – 100%ile: Exceptional performer

You are destined to do very, very well. You consistently display an exceptional level of performance. Expressions used to describe you include a "superachiever" and "can't say enough good about him/her." You do just about everything with an eye to excellence. You have an exceptional business sense, and people are amazed by your proficiency. You have the ability to detect a potentially successful endeavor—to know a good thing when you see it. Your desire to influence results is very high, and you do so with ease. Only jobs that have the highest levels of responsibility and challenge and that have an overriding effect on company results will, in the long run, interest you. Frustration, boredom and poor performance will occur early if challenge or promotion is not provided quickly.

70%ile – 75%ile: Superior performer

You will almost certainly do very well. Terms used to describe you include "excellent performer" and "organized." Highly proficient, you have the ability to grasp essential concepts quickly and easily even when lacking formal education or training. You are predictably consistent in your performance and prove to be a superior producer due to the standards and demands you set for yourself. You combine good people skills and a desire to be liked with resultant good rapport with peers and staff. You perform best under pressure to achieve, but when the crisis is over or a project has succeeded, you have a tendency to relax your performance. You are good at initiating, planning and implementing new projects but may become too easily bored once you have grasped the complexity of the job. A strong manager, as well as positive feedback expressed both in salary and in encouragement, can provide the structure and supervision needed to get the best from you. Your skills can be best used in a variety of functions such as a consultative or staff-management job or a line-delivery position. Your performance in a senior role would be expected to be outstanding.

(continued)

MANAGEMENT IN PRACTICE *(Continued)*

65%ile – 69%ile: Above-average performer

You are an above-average achiever, expected to give solid, dependable performance. You follow a well-thought-out direction in a realistic, progressive and disciplined manner. Generally, you would do an above-average job in senior- to middle-line positions. Initially, you appear to be intelligent, aggressive, bright, results oriented, positive and quick with answers. However, terms used after being on the job for a while are "not always working to his/her potential" and "needs too much direction to get his/her best." Often, you lack the necessary ego drive found in most successful executives. You have excellent potential but may never get around to fulfilling your talent. You need a lot of encouragement and feedback to put in a full, consistently high effort on the job. If you were a little more aggressive and stretched yourself, your performance would improve faster, encouraging others to trust you with more responsibility. You may tend to change jobs frequently when you feel your talents are not appreciated. This may not be in your best interest in the long term.

50%ile – 64%ile: Average performer

You appear to have some key traits, attitudes and behavioral habits working against your best interests. Terms often used to describe you by supervisors are "weak industry knowledge," "gives up too quickly" and "lacks aggression." You are capable of handling a job, subject to practices and

the leader is democratic and the follower is interdependent, or when the leader is laissez-faire and the follower is independent.

Why the theory has value

On a more specific level, Table 14-6 shows how the leader should act, given the followers' needs and the specifics of the situation. The Johnston model, of course, is much more complex than what is presented here. In

FIGURE 14-5

A Followership Continuum

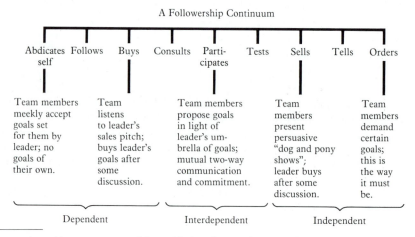

A Followership Continuum

procedures covered by precedents or well-defined policy, under constant supervisory review. You have the knowledge to be above average in competency but may not find your job or career path appealing. You seem to work mostly to earn a living. Your performance will not improve without a change in attitude or career shift. If criticized, you may respond negatively toward both the critic and the company rather than face the fact that your own attitudes and behavior require improvement.

0%ile – 49%ile: Below-average performer

As an employee, you project many difficulties that simply interfere with efficient performance on the job. You are either ambivalent about being successful or lack many of the attributes required in a work setting. When asked to comment on this type of individual, managers often say, "Weak career potential . . . needs more motivation than I can give." You would perform best in maintenance or administrative duties governed by rules, instructions, established routines and firm deadlines that offer few surprises. If you will not or cannot change the difficulties that interfere with your ability to perform at an average level, consider changing to another career to which you'll be better suited. Management of others does not appear to be your strength at this time.

Source: Michael Clugston and Janice Zemdegs, "Are You CEO Material?" *Canadian Business* (June 1986):67–73.

essence, however, these figures and tables provide an accurate summary of Johnston's leader-follower behavior theory.

The theory is useful for four reasons: it encourages the leader to conduct self-analysis regarding his or her style; it focuses on the followers' styles, a topic that has not been given sufficient attention in the leadership literature; it helps explain how to achieve an effective leader-follower match; and it offers specific suggestions regarding the style to use given the needs of the followers and the specifics under which all are operating.[31]

The Situational Leadership Model

One of the most popular "applied" leadership theories to emerge in the last two decades is the **situational leadership model** developed by Paul Hersey and Kenneth Blanchard.[32] Originally known as the life cycle theory of leadership, the model has been gradually modified, retitled, and made more applicable. Figure 14-7 illustrates the latest model.

The four quadrants in Figure 14-7 are very similar to those of the managerial grid of Blake and Mouton. The general thrust is quite different, however. For example, unlike Blake and Mouton, Hersey and Blanchard argue that there

[31] For more on this topic, see William Litzinger and Thomas Schaefer, "Leadership Through Followership," *Business Horizons* (September–October 1982):78–81.
[32] Paul Hersey and Kenneth Blanchard, *Management of Organizational Behavior: Utilizing Human Resources,* 4th ed. (Englewood Cliffs, NJ: Prentice-Hall, 1982).

FIGURE 14-6
The Leader-Follower Continua

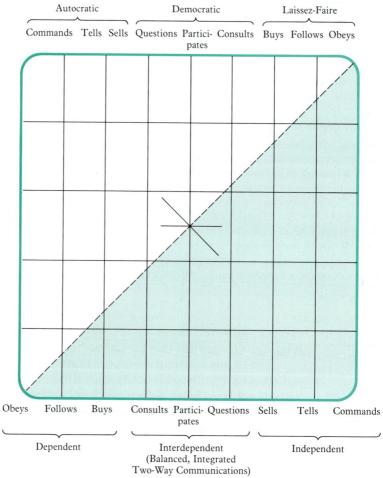

The Leader-Follower Continuums

Leader's range of power, authority, and responsibility
Follower's range of power, freedom, and responsibility

Source: Adapted by permission of the publisher, from Robert W. Johnston, "Leader-Follower Behavior in 3-D, Part 1," *Personnel* (September–October 1981), 54. © 1981 American Management Association, New York. All rights reserved.

Matching
leadership styles
with maturity levels

is no one best leadership style. Instead, the most effective leadership style is determined by the task-relevant maturity level of the individual or group. As seen in Figure 14-7, there are four degrees of maturity, and each is related to a different leadership style. These styles are referred to as telling, selling, participating, and delegating, and they represent different combinations of task and relationship behavior.

TABLE 14-6   A Synopsis of Three Choices of Leadership Behavior Considering Followers' Needs and Situations

Consider Being Autocratic When . . .	Consider Being Democratic When . . .	Consider Being Laissez-Faire When . . .
Leader/Manager:	*Leader/Manager:*	*Leader/Manager:*
Has complete power and no restraints on its use.	Has limited power and authority.	Has no power to compel action.
Has a way of saving matters in an emergency.	Has restraints on use.	Has no time pressures.
Has some unique knowledge.	Group might reject his/her authority and succeed at it.	Possesses tenure based on pleasure of the group.
Is firmly entrenched in his/her position.	Has *some* existing time pressures.	Has no sanctions to exert.
	Has *limited* sanctions he/she can exert.	Has no special knowledge.
Followers:	*Followers:*	*Followers:*
Are leader-dependent persons.	Expect to have some control over methods used.	Have more power than the leader.
Are rarely asked for an opinion.		Dislike orders.
Have low educational background (not always).	Have predominantly middle-class values.	Will rebel successfully if they so choose.
Recognize emergencies.	Are physicians, scientists, engineers, managers, staff persons.	Choose own goals and methods.
Are members of a "labor surplus" group.	Possess relatively scarce skills.	Are volunteers, loosely organized, or in short supply.
Are autocrats themselves.	Like system, but not authority.	Are physicians, scientists, or others with rare skills.
Have low independence drives.	Have high social needs.	
Work Situation:	*Work Situation:*	*Work Situation:*
Features tight discipline.	"Umbrella" organization objectives understood.	Has no clear purpose apparent except as the individual chooses.
Is characterized by strong controls.	Involves shared responsibility for controls.	Is unstructured.
Is marked by low profit margins or tight cost controls.	Has some time pressures.	Is one in which only self-imposed controls exist.
Includes physical dangers.	Consists of gradual changes or regularly spaced changes.	Has no time pressures.
Requires low skills from workers.	Involves actual or potential hazards occasionally.	Features few or only gradual changes.
Requires that frequent changes be made quickly.	Is one in which teamwork skills are called for.	Takes place in a safe, placid environment.
		Requires high individual skill or conceptual ability.
Effect of Autocratic Leadership Carried to Extreme or Overused:	**Effect of Democratic Leadership if Carried to Extreme or Overused:**	**Effect of Laissez-Faire Leadership if Carried to Extreme or Overused:**
May result in poor communication, rigidity of operation, slow adaptation to changing conditions, and stunting of the growth of people.	May result in loss of ability to take individual initiative when necessary (in favor of group decisions); also may result in slow decision making in emergencies.	May result in organization fragmentation, member isolation, chaos, and anarchy.

Source: Reprinted by permission of the publisher, from Robert W. Johnston, "Leader-Follower Behavior in 3-D, Part 1," *Personnel* (July–August 1981):41. © 1981 by American Management Association, New York. All rights reserved.

FIGURE 14-7
Situational Leadership

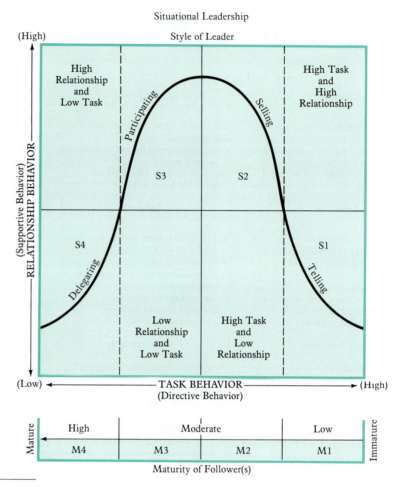

Source: Paul Hersey and Kenneth H. Blanchard, *Management of Organizational Behavior: Utilizing Human Resources,* 4th ed., 248. © 1982. Reprinted by permission of Prentice-Hall, Inc., Englewood Cliffs, NJ.

Task behavior relates to the extent to which a leader provides direction for subordinates, such as by telling them what to do, when, where, and how. *Relationship behavior* relates to the extent to which a leader engages in two-way or multi-way communication by providing assistance, advice, and socio-emotional support. These two types of behavior, task and relationship, combine to provide four basic leadership styles: (1) high task and low relationship, (2) high task and high relationship, (3) high relationship and low task, (4) low relationship and low task. As seen in Figure 14-7, these four task-relationship combinations are labeled S1, S2, S3, and S4, respectively. Also, at the bottom of Figure 14-7 there are four degrees of follower maturity which match up with the four leadership styles. By determining the maturity level of the individual or group, a leader can identify the appropriate style (S1 through S4) along the prescriptive curve.

Choosing a Style

The style in the lower righthand corner of Figure 14-7 (S1) is considered most effective for individuals with low maturity. These people are both unable and unwilling to perform specific tasks. They need clear direction and close supervision. The leader should deal with these people by telling them what to do and by providing minimal supportive behavior to avoid being seen as tolerant of poor performance.

Sometimes the leader must tell the subordinates what to do

Individuals of low to moderate maturity should have a leader who can sell them on what needs to be done. These people are willing to do the work but are unable to take responsibility for a specific task or function. The leader needs to display directive behavior but must also be very supportive of the followers' willingness and enthusiasm. Through the use of two-way communication to explain decisions and gain subordinate support, the leader sells the followers on a course of action.

At other times a selling approach works best

Subordinates with a moderate to high level of maturity are handled most effectively through the use of a participating leadership style. The followers at this level have the ability to perform specific tasks but they lack confidence or enthusiasm or both. By providing low task direction the leader allows them to use their own judgment and ability. At the same time the leader offers strong support and is continually available to listen and to praise. The leader's primary emphasis is to build up the personal confidence of the followers.

Leaders may participate . . .

Individuals with a high level of maturity work best under a leader exercising both low task and low relationship behavior. The followers are self-directed and self-motivated. They can perform their jobs with a minimum amount of assistance from the leader, who therefore employs a delegating style.

or they may delegate

How does the leader determine the maturity of the followers? Hersey and Blanchard recommend two simple steps:

1. Determine the goal or task to be accomplished by the followers.
2. Determine the maturity level of the follower or group that is relevant to the task by assessing:
   a) achievement motivation — the ability of the followers to set high but realistic goals.
   b) responsibility — the willingness and ability of the followers to assume responsibility.
   c) education/experience — the education and experience of the group related to the accomplishment of the task.

Assessing the maturity of the followers

After determining the maturity level of the followers (M1, M2, M3, or M4) the leader simply draws a line from this level up to the leadership style curve in Figure 14-7. The point at which the line intersects with the leadership style (S1, S2, S3, or S4) indicates the most effective approach to employ.

This model can also be used to help followers develop in maturity by showing leaders how to move through the four styles on the prescriptive curve. The leader can adjust his or her style to move forward along the curve or to move backward, depending on the situation.

> The developmental cycle is accomplished through a series of two-step processes: first, the leader reduces directive behavior to encourage the follower to assume greater task-relevant responsibility; second, as soon as performance improvement is noted, the leader rewards the follower by increasing supportive behavior as positive reinforcement; and finally, as the follower reaches higher levels of maturity (M3 and M4), the leader responds by decreasing both task and relationship behavior, because very mature people tend to need autonomy more than socioemotional support.

The leader can help followers develop maturity

> Conversely, the leader can arrest and reverse tendencies toward declining performance in followers by reassessing their maturity level and moving backwards through the prescriptive curve (the regressive cycle) to provide the necessary amounts of task and relationship behavior.[33]

Leadership Match and Effectiveness

At the heart of the situational leadership model is the issue of identifying the most effective style. Hersey and Blanchard have developed a diagnostic instrument that aids in this process. This instrument measures both job maturity and willingness to do the job. Of perhaps even greater value is a process they call "contracting for leadership style." After the leader and the follower agree on the goals the latter will pursue, they discuss the most appropriate leadership style to be used. In a manner of speaking, the two negotiate the style to be employed by the leader.

Negotiating a "contract" for leadership style

If the subordinate finds the choice to be unrealistic, he or she can then contact the leader and set up a meeting to negotiate a different style. For example, the subordinate may feel that the leader is not being sufficiently helpful and that a change from S3 back to S2 will improve work performance. Analogously, the leader may request a change in style because the subordinate is not producing the expected results. For example, the worker may have negotiated an S1 style but the leader may feel this choice is too time consuming because of the amount of attention that must be given to providing specific instructions and close supervision. An S3 style will give the subordinate more freedom, increased supportive behavior, and a chance to increase the amount of work output. This form of contracting results in a leadership match and tends to be superior to the typical situation in which the leader simply assumes the role that he or she believes will produce the best results without discussing this choice with the subordinates.

Of course, even with leader-subordinate discussion, the leader match may

---

[33] Paul Hersey and Marshall Goldsmith, "A Situational Approach to Performance Planning," *Training and Development Journal* (November 1980):39.

TABLE 14-7	Matching Maturity Level and Leadership Style			
Maturity Level	Most Effective Style	Second Most Effective Style	Third Most Effective Style	Least Effective Style
M1 Low	S1 Telling	S2 Selling	S3 Participating	S4 Delegating
M2 Low-Moderate	S2 Selling	S1 Telling or S3 Participating	—	S4 Delegating
M3 Moderate-High	S3 Participating	S2 Selling or S4 Delegating	—	S1 Telling
M4 High	S4 Delegating	S3 Participating	S2 Selling	S1 Telling

Degrees of leadership effectiveness

not be the best one. On the other hand, it may not be that far off. Given the fact that effectiveness is a dimension that ranges from most effective to least effective, if the leader match does not result in a choice of the best style it may produce a choice of the second best style. To assess the probability that the other styles will be successful, if the leader is unwilling or unable to use the ideal style, Hersey and Blanchard offer the leader match success probabilities presented in Table 14-7. Commenting on the table data, they note that:

> . . . the "desired" style always has a second "best" style choice, that is, a style that would probably be effective if the highest probability style could not be used. In attempting to influence people at the low to moderate (M2) and moderate to high (M3) maturity levels, you will notice that there are two second "best" style choices: which one should be used depends on whether the maturity of the individual is getting better, indicating that the leaders should be involved in a developmental cycle, or getting worse, revealing that a regressive cycle is occurring. If the situation is improving, "participating" and "delegating" would be the "best" second choices, but if things are deteriorating "telling" and "selling" would be the most appropriate backup choices.[34]

Why the model is useful

The situational leadership model approach is useful for four reasons. First, it encourages leader-subordinate matching, applying Fiedler's idea on a much more practical level. Second, it helps develop communication flows between leaders and subordinates through the "contracting for leadership style" process. Third, the model encourages managers to view leadership effectiveness as

---

[34] Hersey and Blanchard, *Management of Organizational Behavior,* 236.

a continuum that ranges from most effective to least effective rather than as an "all or nothing" concept. Fourth, the developers of the theory set forth an easy-to-understand approach for matching maturity level and leadership style and offer success probabilities at each level (from M1 through M4) for each style (S1 through S4).[35]

SUMMARY

1. Leadership is the process of influencing people to direct their efforts toward the achievement of some particular goal or goals. Some of the common traits or characteristics found among successful leaders include intelligence, scholarship, dependability, social participation, and socioeconomic status.
2. Leader behavior can be described in many ways. One is through the use of leader-subordinate interactions as typified by autocratic, paternalistic, democratic/participative, and laissez-faire leadership styles.
3. Some managers accept Theory X assumptions, which, in the main, hold that the employee is lazy, works best when threatened or coerced and, above all, wants security. Other managers subscribe to Theory Y, which holds that people do not dislike work, do their best when under self-direction, and are willing to assume responsibility.
4. Another way to view leadership in organizations is to examine the three models of management: traditional, human relations, and human resources. Depending on the assumptions, policies, and expectations of the manager, any one of these three may be used. While many managers believe that their own people work best under the human relations model they believe they themselves should be managed via the human resources model.
5. Another popular way to describe leader behavior is through the use of the managerial grid. By examining the five basic styles on the grid—9,1 management, 1,9 management, 1,1 management, 5,5 management and 9,9 management—one can obtain an excellent understanding of the way leaders combine a concern for work with a concern for people in getting things done.
6. At the present time the contingency approach to leadership is the most highly regarded. One contingency theory has been proposed by Fred Fiedler. Combining the LPC score with situational variables. Fiedler reports that task-oriented managers do best in highly favorable or highly unfavorable situations while human-relations-oriented managers do best in moderately favorable or moderately unfavorable situations. Fiedler recommends matching the leader to the situation.

---

[35] For more on this theory, see Claude L. Graeff, "The Situation Leadership Theory: A Critical View," *Academy of Management Review* (April 1983):285–91.

7. Another contingency leadership theory, path-goal, seeks to explain how the nature of the group's job affects whether a task orientation, human relations orientation, or some combination of the two will result in the greatest degree of group satisfaction and effectiveness. The theory holds that the leader's job is to clarify subordinate tasks, clear away roadblocks preventing goal attainment, and increase the opportunity for subordinates to attain personal satisfaction. While research continues, path-goal offers great promise as a supervisory theory of leadership.

8. Increased attention has been given in recent years to answering the question: How can leadership research be brought down to an applied level? Two different types of leadership models have emerged. One is based heavily on management theory; the other is grounded in training and development research.

9. Robert Johnston has offered one type of "applied" theory in developing his leader-follower continua. This approach is based on the idea that the leader must match his or her style with that of the followers. An autocratic leader will do best with dependent subordinates; a democratic leader will succeed with interdependent subordinates; a laissez faire leader will excel with independent subordinates.

10. One of the most popular "applied" leadership theories is the situational leadership model developed by Hersey and Blanchard. This model is designed to help managers identify the maturity level of their subordinates and from this determine the leadership style that will be most effective. Along a continuum ranging from low to high maturity, the leader uses varying degrees of task and relationship behavior. Figure 14-7 illustrated this idea in detail. The model also recommends leader match preferences as explained in Table 14-7.

KEY TERMS

Autocratic leadership   A leadership style characterized by a heavy emphasis on task accomplishment and very little on the human element.

Democratic/participative leadership   A leadership style characterized by a high concern for both people and work.

Fiedler's contingency theory   A leadership theory that seeks to explain managerial effectiveness in terms of LPC score and situational variables.

Human relations model   A model of management that describes the manager's job as one in which personal attention must be paid to both the job and the personal needs of the people.

Human resources model   A model of management that presents the manager as a developer and facilitator who encourages self-direction and self-control on the part of subordinates, allowing them to become all they are capable of becoming.

Laissez-faire leadership   A leadership style characterized by the manager's general uninvolvement in the operations of the unit or department.

Leader-member relations   The degree to which a group leader is accepted by the group and is able to maintain the loyalty of the members.

Least preferred coworker scale   A scale containing paired adjectives that are used to describe the person with whom the respondent can work least well. It is used to classify the respondent as a task-oriented or human-relations-oriented manager.

Managerial grid   A two-dimensional leadership model used to measure a manager's concern for work and concern for people.

Paternalistic leadership   A leadership style characterized by the philosophy "Do as I say and the organization will take care of you."

Path-goal theory   A theory of leadership that seeks to explain how the nature of a group's job affects whether a task orientation, a human relations orientation, or some combination of the two will result in the greatest degree of group satisfaction and effectiveness.

Position power   The degree to which a leader is able to apply positive (reward) and negative (punishment) sanctions.

Situational leadership model   A leadership model that brings together task behavior, relationship behavior, and the maturity of the followers in identifying the most effective leadership style to employ.

Task structure   The degree to which rules, regulations, job descriptions, and policies are clearly specified.

Theory X   A set of assumptions that hold that people (1) dislike work, (2) have little ambition, (3) want security above all, and (4) must be coerced, controlled, and threatened in order to attain organizational objectives.

Theory Y   A set of assumptions that hold that (1) if conditions are favorable, people will not only accept responsibility but will seek it; (2) if people are committed to organizational objectives, they will exercise self-direction and self-control; and (3) commitment is a function of the rewards associated with goal attainment.

Traditional model   A model of management that describes the manager's job as one of controlling and directing people. It is based on the belief that people will comply only if their tasks are specified and they are properly trained and paid for their efforts.

Trait theory   An approach to the study of leadership characterized by attempts to identify the traits or abilities that are unique to effective leaders.

QUESTIONS FOR ANALYSIS AND DISCUSSION

1. In your own words, what is meant by the term leadership?
2. Are there any traits or characteristics that seem to be of importance for effective leadership? Identify and describe five.
3. How do each of the following types of leaders act: autocratic,

paternalistic, democratic/participative, and laissez-faire? Describe each in terms of concern for work and concern for people.

4. What are the Theory X assumptions? Theory Y assumptions? Compare and contrast both sets of assumptions and discuss their managerial implications.

5. How does each of these models of management differ from the others: traditional, human relations, and human resources?

6. One way of describing leadership behavior is through the use of the managerial grid. How can this be done? In your answer be sure to incorporate the five major styles described by Blake and Mouton.

7. Drawing upon your knowledge of Fiedler's contingency theory of leadership, explain what the LPC is all about. What were the three situational variables Fiedler found to be most important to effective leadership? How did he bring together the LPC and the situational variables in constructing his leadership model? In your answer be sure to incorporate a discussion of Table 14-3.

8. What did Fiedler conclude regarding leadership style and effectiveness? Who does best under what conditions? Be sure to include reference to Figure 14-3 in your answer.

9. According to the path-goal theory of leadership, what is the leader's job? How will the clarity or ambiguity of the subordinate's task affect the style of an effective leader?

10. Of what practical value to managers is the path-goal theory of leadership? Put the answer in your own words.

11. Drawing upon Johnston's leader-follower continuum, presented in Figure 14-6, describe the relationship between leadership style and follower behavior. Explain, incorporating a discussion of autocratic, democratic, and laissez-faire styles into your answer.

12. Drawing upon Johnston's findings, as presented in Table 14-4, when should a leader consider being autocratic? Democratic? Laissez-faire?

13. According to Hersey and Blanchard, how can one determine the maturity of subordinates? What type of leadership style is most effective when dealing with subordinates of low maturity? Low to moderate maturity? Moderate to high maturity? High maturity?

14. How does the Hersey and Blanchard model help explain leadership match? Use Table 14-5 in your answer.

CASE

Ralph's Way

Salespeople in the pharmaceutical firm where Ralph Holloway works have always made good money. In fact, those who do not are terminated. If they cannot sell, they are not kept around.

Over the last 15 years Ralph has become one of the company's outstanding salespeople. Two years ago he was number seven companywide; last year he was number six. Three months ago, however, he decided to make a career change, applying for a district sales manager's job and getting it. For the last 90 days Ralph has been supervising 12 salespeople.

Two of Ralph's people are new, having just finished their training at company headquarters. There they learned about the product lines, how the drugs work, what the competitive products are, and how to sell in the face of both doctor/hospital resistance and competition. Since the two new people are totally unfamiliar with their territory or how to call on doctors and hospitals, Ralph is spending a great deal of time working with them.

He is not confining himself to these two people, however. He is also spending time with the other 10 salespeople. During this time Ralph calls on medical personnel with the salesperson, helps with the presentation, and even pitches in to close the sale.

The new salespeople seem to like having Ralph along. They believe his advice and assistance are helping them improve their sales skills and overall performance. The other salespeople do not feel this way. They believe Ralph is too close-control in his approach. One of them put their feelings this way, "I know how to sell. Oh sure, it's nice to have Ralph along in terms of advice. He sure knows how to sell and can pick out little things I'm doing wrong or could do better. However, I don't need him to sell for me. He's supposed to be a manager now, not a salesperson. If anything, he tends to be too autocratic in his approach. He wants me to do things his way. I wish he'd just stay out of my hair and let me sell my way." Most of the other experienced salespeople feel the same way, although Ralph certainly does not. When talking to his boss last week, Ralph commented:

> Sales are up 21 percent over this time last year and I think they are going to go even higher. One of the reasons is the two new people we have in the district. They are a lot better than the two they replaced. Also, my approach of working closely with the salespeople is helping a lot. It keeps them on their toes and assists them in developing their selling techniques. If more district sales managers would follow my leadership style, their sales forces would also improve.

1. Using the managerial grid as your guide, describe Ralph's leadership style. What style would the experienced salespeople like Ralph to use? Explain.
2. In terms of the path-goal theory of leadership, how should Ralph go about managing his people? Be complete in your answer.
3. What contingency-based recommendations would you offer to Ralph regarding how to lead his people? Draw upon Fiedler's and Hersey and Blanchard's ideas in constructing your recommendations. Provide Ralph with at least three useful leadership guidelines.

The Foreman — "X" Style

Bruce Leesguard is the factory foreman for the Chicago division of the Kendon Corporation. Plant productivity in this factory has continually surpassed the six other company plants throughout the U.S. Kendon operates its facilities on long hours, hard work, and assembly line deadlines.

Bruce leads his workers with an "iron fist." He lives directly above the plant in a large, 5-room apartment which allows for security of the building in the off-hours. Every morning, Bruce enters the plant and bellows, "Let's get this operation moving!" There are 30 employees, all of whom must be clocked in by 7 A.M. The typical workday is from 7 A.M. to 5 P.M. with ½ hour for lunch. It is a 5-day workweek that encompasses 50 hours of strict deadlines, difficult welding, the cutting of iron channel, and the loading and unloading of delivery trucks. Amidst this bursting activity, Bruce, who stands 6'8" and weighs 290 lbs., calls out orders in his deep, bellowing voice. And his orders are simple — work and work hard! Bruce is a no-nonsense boss who expects his employees to work continuously at peak performance. He paces the factory calling out his orders, with his physical presence adding a dimension of fear.

Every Friday after work, Bruce has a weekly gathering of the workers at his favorite tavern, The Village Pub. Bruce buys the first two rounds of refreshments and toasts "his boys" proudly as he exclaims to one and all in the tavern, "This is the greatest group of workers in the U.S.A. They're my boys and I'm proud of 'em!" And so the Friday gathering goes, with Bruce bragging about the workers, discussing various topics with them, and, in a sense, being "with them" instead of "above them."

When Monday morning comes along, Bruce is back on the factory floor demanding the most from his workers again.

Your Consultation

The president of Kendon has called you to witness the above scenario. Worried about the harsh style that Bruce employs as a manager, the president has asked you for your consultation. What is your evaluation of Bruce's managerial style? Explain.

Integrative Case Study
PLASTIC SUPPLIERS, INC.

Company History

Plastic Suppliers, Inc. (PSI), commenced operations in April, two years ago. The company was an offshoot of its founder's lifelong dream of owning his own business by providing services which he enjoyed and was considered to have been highly qualified to do. At the onset he was named as the chief executive officer (CEO) and the two other people who joined him were part owners and heads of the various functions within the organization. All three were friends who had worked in the plastics business as technicians for many years and shared the founder's personal objective of being their own bosses.

Mr. Edmunds, the founder, worked sixteen years at IBM, where he started from the bottom and worked his way up until he became Head, New Products Division. Despite his position with IBM, Mr. Edmunds's enterpreneuring spirit could not hold him down to a job at a prestigious internationally acclaimed company like IBM. Therefore, he and two of his friends with the same technical background invested their lifetime savings in a small company, Plastic Suppliers, Inc. (PSI), and started operations in McAllen, Texas.

Several advantages accrued from the choice of location in south Texas. First, Mr. Edmunds was a native of south Texas. Second, most of the existing plastics injection molding outfits were located in the northeast or midwest states and the nearest (a very small facility) was in Dallas, some 550 miles to the north of McAllen. Thirdly, the maquiladoras were located just across the border in Mexico, some 12 miles away. Maquiladora plants are usually one-half of twin plant operations: parts are manufactured and technical operations are performed on the U.S. side; and manual operations are performed on the Mexican side. Mr. Edmunds realized that the maquiladora was a rapidly growing industry, with a need for various manufactured parts for its many operations requiring parts made from plastic.

Having a supplier that was close to the maquiladoras could cut delivery time enormously. Inventory levels could be kept low (resulting in lower investments in inventory and all the pluses and minuses of JIT—Just-in-Time—inventory methods). The distance alone was an advantage for PSI as a supplier. If for any reason problems occurred about the supplied parts, customers (maquiladoras) could easily cross the border to correct the problem(s).

Maquiladoras choose suppliers from the U.S. rather than Mexico primarily

Source: This case was prepared by Dr. Walter E. Greene of Pan American University, Edinburg, Texas. Research assistance was provided by Mark E. George and Carminia D. Oris, graduate assistants, Pan American University. Presented to the Midwest Society for Case Research Workshop, 1988. All rights reserved to the author and to the Midwest Society for Case Research. Copyright © 1988 by Walter E. Greene. Reprinted by permission.

due to higher quality and service available. Finally, in the Rio Grande Valley region of Mexico alone, there had been a 43 percent increase in maquiladoras in the nine-year period 1978–1986, increasing from 49 to 70 plants. Mr. Edmunds had projected, barring any drastic changes, a 10 percent annual growth rate for PSI, with 95 percent derived from the Mexican maquiladoras.

During the first two years of operation, growth was tremendous. The first operation was equipped with four 150-ton plastic injection molding machines (similar to the plastic injection molding machines that make toy soldiers, etc., only much larger). Four additional machines had been installed, three additional 150-ton and one 500-ton machine. The plant had been expanded to accommodate the new equipment and the work force had grown from the original three to a work force of eighty-six.

Company Objectives

Aside from Mr. Edmunds's desire to run his own business, the company had one major objective. All three partners agreed that the company was to become a full-service supplier of plastic injection molding parts to local manufacturing firms on both sides of the border; i.e., in U.S. plants and in the Mexican maquiladora operations.

An organizational chart is shown in Exhibit 1. PSI was Mr. Edmunds's dream of a lifetime, he had worked hard, and put his lifetime savings into founding it. As a technician his major concerns were meeting client specifications and providing quality services and products. PSI found a niche in the market and grew at a tremendously fast pace during its first two years. As is common with entrepreneurs, they outgrew their original investments, and venture capitalists from both U.S. and Mexico stepped in and provided much needed capital.

Products and Services Provided

PSI had three profit-generating departments: engineering, tooling, and production. The engineering department crated mold designs, the tooling department made the actual molds and mold repairs, and the production department ran the mold to produce the various plastic parts.

Although each department's function could be considered a continuous flow from mold design to parts production, clients came in needing one or two or all of the services that PSI offered. Some clients had their own molds (which they brought down from northern U.S. locations, so that delivery would be faster) so all that PSI had to do was produce the plastic parts and maintain the molds. Other customers came with specifications for the part that they wanted to produce, so PSI had to design and make the mold, then produce the parts. Added to all these functions, PSI could provide local delivery services following the purchase of its own small delivery van.

EXHIBIT 1   Organization Chart* Plastic Suppliers, Inc.

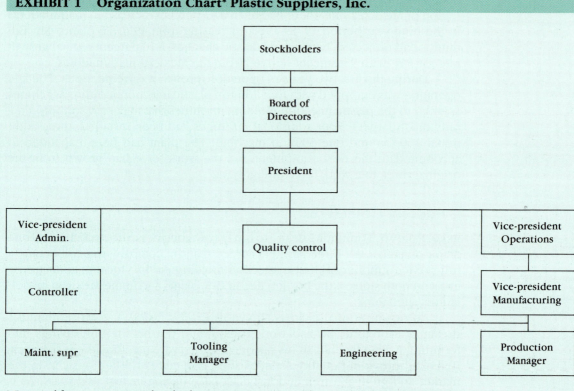

* Prepared from a report issued to third parties, customers, suppliers, and prospective investors.

The engineering department was responsible for designing the molds that would be used to make the parts. Its head was one of the original three that started the business. His two assistants prepared drawings showing all details of the mold. The drawings were generated by a computer (CAD/CAM-Computer Assisted Design/Manufacturing), making the task easier. Designing the molds required highly skilled people, unavailable in the local job market.

The tooling department, supervised by another of the founders, made the molds based on the drawing specifications from the engineering department. Making a mold took anywhere from a couple of weeks at the very least to three months or more. Skilled personnel were a must for this department because of the complexity of the tasks involved. However, as was the case with the engineering department, skilled personnel were unavailable in the local job market. After the molds were built, they were moved to the production floor for preliminary testing. If any flaws were discovered, the molds were sent back to tooling for adjustments.

Adjusted and tested molds were turned over to the production department, manned mostly with semi-skilled operators. The only skills required in this department were in setting up the machine specifications to turn out the right number of plastic parts. Knowledge of cycle times, water levels, etc., was an important factor. Apart from this the machines did most of the work. Each machine was manned by a worker who saw to it that the parts were produced according to the quantity on the specification sheet and that the machine did not run out of water. This task did not require any special skills. Normally the only way big production schedules could be met was by second-shift operations in the production department, and on rare occasions even a third shift (24-hour operations).

Quality Controls and Problems

Mr. Edmunds realized that quality control was of the highest priority with maquiladora operators. Since PSI produced plastic parts which form part of larger components, all parts had to fit perfectly (e.g., one of PSI's customers, which used a large portion of PSI capacity was a maquiladora plant which required the plastic parts for automobile seat belts. This maquiladora plant produced all seat belts required by one of the big three U.S. automobile manufacturers). This required strict measurement and material quality controls. Therefore, a quality control department was added.

Frequently, problems arose concerning a work order. Usually time schedules were set up to insure that the parts got to the customer on time and to maximize the utilization of personnel and machines. However, delays could and did occur often, caused by any of the following factors:

1. Too much time spent on designing the molds (engineering), or in making the molds (tooling), or in producing the parts (production).
2. Sometimes parts did not conform to quality control standards, and then each of the departments blamed the other department for the failure.
3. Sometimes the molds broke or did not work correctly even if they passed quality control checks.
4. Finally, machine breakdowns were a much too frequent problem.

Economic Environment

PSI's economic environment was greatly influenced by the fact that it was situated in the Rio Grande Valley of south Texas. While the U.S. national unemployment rate was about 7 percent, as it was for the state of Texas, unemployment in the valley area was between 15 and 18 percent during this period. Starr County (one of the four counties in the valley) had the dubious honor of being one of the four poorest counties in the U.S.A., with an average annual income of $3,300. Poor health, low educational achievement, and limited job opportunities characterized this region. The local economy was highly influenced by what happened to the oil industry and the Mexican economy. Mexico's rate of inflation during the first years PSI was in operation was 160 percent and had averaged over 100 percent for each of the past three years.

Most Mexicans residing near the border brought business to the area by purchasing goods on the U.S. side of the border. With the Mexican peso devalued a few years earlier, the high rate of Mexican inflation, and the bottom dropping out of the oil market, followed by the killing freeze that had destroyed the valley's citrus crop three years before, business on the U.S. side of the border was basically at a standstill.

Unfortunately, in view of the area's past economy, local banks were geared to agriculture, oil, and small retail establishments. The failure rate of Texas banks during this period had been one of the highest of any state in the country. Bankers were scared, and in addition, none had any experience with manufacturing establishments like PSI.

Public officials in the region exhorted the development of a manufacturing sector. With high unemployment, firms of any kind were encouraged to relocate to the valley from the industrial north. Aware that the economy had to become multifaceted to lessen the impact of drastic changes in the local economy, a strong desire developed to encourage the manufacturing sector to grow in the valley region.

Fast Expansion

Rapid expansion was triggered by the increased demand from maquiladora operators. At the onset, PSI was doing small jobs and one big project (to manufacture bag handles). One machine was devoted entirely to the plastic handles. The other three machines were almost always idle because of small production runs. Then when the word spread that PSI was located in the valley, jobs came pouring in. Two maquiladora plants, Zenith Televisions and TRW (seat belts), together took practically all of the original capacity. Expansion was inevitable, and four additional machines were acquired.

The production department's capacity, in terms of machine hours, had more than doubled over its first two years. Raw materials were stacked in boxes alongside the machines due to lack of storage space. A small nearby warehouse had been leased for extra storage space. A small office for the engineering department had to be added due to overcrowding in the administrative office.

Financial Problems

During the first twenty months no accurate financial reports were maintained. The new stockholders were concerned about the lack of accounting information to support decision making. The original bookkeeper was just that, a bookkeeper. A CPA with consulting and work experience in one of the major accounting firms was hired.

The CPA, Mr. Earl, set up the accounting system from scratch (see Exhibit 2). As the controller, he performed functions like financial sourcing, financial information analysis, and general accounting. He did manage to secure several short- and long-term loans. Cash flow problems had beset PSI from the start. Collections were very late. To meet current expenses (such as payroll and regular monthly payments) short-term loans had been obtained. However, as loans matured, interest and principal payments became too high for PSI to handle. Eventually the debt grew so large that the debt-to-equity ratio and the debt-to-asset ratio precluded conventional debt financing. Long-term loans were hard to come by because of the banking system's reservations about lending to manufacturing organizations.

When job costs were derived and compared to the revenues, it was discovered that PSI was barely making a profit on most of its contracts. In the absence of cost standards and a cost accounting system, the price quotations given to clients were not enough to cover costs of manufacturing the parts. A consulting team was hired to determine the standard costs for labor, raw materials, and overhead, and to also set up a system to monitor expenses on a per job basis. However, the resulting cost accounting system was not implemented because Mr. Edmunds, the CEO, was too busy searching for more sales and financial sources.

With the existing plant already filled to capacity, management had plans for a bigger facility that could accommodate twenty plastic injection molding machines in the production department and officers for each of the departments. The number of jobs had increased, and the company was producing at maximum capacity; therefore, management believed that the proposed new facility was a must, and no financing was available.

Change of Management

Mr. Edmunds relinquished his position to the CPA. He felt that the administrative duties were too much for him to handle and paperwork was piling up in the office. Besides, Mr. Edmunds was a technician and not fond of paper work, and the CPA had done an outstanding job of compiling PSI's financial statements.

Almost immediately, conflicts between Mr. Earl and the partners arose about strategic policies.

At the board meeting, Mr. Earl tendered his thirty-day notice of resignation. Mr. Edmunds stated in the meeting that he would not resume duties as CEO, because he had more than he could handle generating sales (technical marketing).

Takeover Problems

Aware of the financial problems of PSI and of their prospects as a maquiladora supplier, one of PSI's newest clients had become interested in acquiring PSI. This client was one of the larger maquiladora operators and it was its intention

EXHIBIT 2   **Plastic Suppliers, Inc. Balance Sheet***

Assets
Current Assets:

Cash	($8,689)	
Accounts Receivable	146,547	
Inventory	266,449	
Prepaid Expenses	3,765	
Deposits	579	
TOTAL CURRENT ASSETS		$408,651
FIXED ASSETS:		
Autos & Trucks	$75,880	
Furniture & Fixtures	14,191	
Equipment	2,084,960	
Building	283,246	
Less accumulated depreciation	(98,470)	
Land	81,383	
Leasehold Improvements	49,525	
Less accumulated amortization	(3,186)	
TOTAL FIXED ASSETS		$2,487,529
TOTAL ASSETS		$2,896,180

Liabilities

CURRENT:		
Notes Payable	$152,049	
Accrued Payable	22,590	
Taxes Payable	91,519	
Other Payable	52,421	
Current Portion L/T Debt	343,487	
Deferred Income	67,771	
TOTAL CURRENT LIABILITIES		$ 729,837
LONG-TERM:		
Mortgage Payable	$361,154	
Notes Payable	1,694,265	
TOTAL LONG-TERM LIABILITIES		$2,055,419
TOTAL LIABILITIES		$2,785,256
STOCKHOLDER'S EQUITY		
Common Stock	$466,575	
Paid-in Capital	579,236	
Treasury Stock	(180,432)	
Retained Earnings	(754,455)	
TOTAL STOCKHOLDER'S EQUITY		$110,924
TOTAL LIABILITIES & EQUITIES		$2,896,180

*Taken from a report issued to third parties, i.e., suppliers, bankers and prospective investors.

	Department			
	Production	*Mold Build*	*Repairs*	*Total*
Sales	$120,000	$140,000	$34,000	$294,000
Cost of Sales				
Materials Used	68,345	20,496		88,841
Direct Labor	32,492	123,932	566	156,990
Overhead	31,433	26,058	3,515	61,007
TOTAL COST OF SALES	132,271	170,486	4,081	306,838
GROSS PROFIT	(12,271)	(30,486)	29,919	(12,838)
General & Administrative Expenses				
Payroll				108,232
Maintenance				24,289
Depreciation				36,114
Amortization				1,213
Rents and Leases				311
Insurance — assets				7,887
Travel and Entertainment				11,546
Shipping				507
Taxes				741
Consulting Fees				30,428
Office Supplies				7,324
Telephone & Telegraph				5,622
Mail/Postage/Courier				2,596
Electricity and Water				19,835
Fuel and Oil				122
Contributions and Donations				51
Licenses and Permits				491
Memberships, Dues & Subscriptions				1,418
TOTAL GENERAL AND ADMINISTRATIVE EXPENSES				258,728
Operating Income				(271,565)
Less Other Expenses (Revenues)				
Financial Expenses				42,083
Other Expenses				3,824
Net Income				($317,471)

to integrate vertically and thus ensure an adequate supply of plastic parts at cheaper prices. This potential acquirer saw a definite advantage of a supplier located as close as PSI. In an attempt to prevent the takeover, the existing stockholders had infused additional equity of approximately twice their original investments. Despite this, PSI still needed additional financing to start the-new facility.

Questions

1. What was the root cause of all the problems or symptoms besetting PSI?
2. Is expansion the right move for PSI?
3. What specific strategies would you propose to solve their financial problems? Are there alternatives to financing outside of the local region? If so, what type (equity or loans)?
4. How can interdepartmental problems be resolved?
5. What did PSI top management do wrong? How should they have handled those problems?
6. Identify the strengths and weaknesses of the company. How should the company use these?
7. What was the bank failure rate in the U.S.A.? In Texas?
8. What are the basic problems you foresee for the company as far as having a customer base composed of 95 percent maquiladoras?
9. What can you suggest to solve the personnel problems? Do the maquiladora operations really take jobs away from U.S. workers as some claim, or do they merely relocate jobs away from the northeast to the southwest as others claim?
10. What strategies would you suggest to combat competition?
11. What strategies would you suggest for the PSI to protect itself from any drastic changes in the maquiladora industry? From changes in the Mexican (or U.S.) political situation?

FIVE

CONTROLLING THE ENTERPRISE'S OPERATIONS

This part of the book studies the ways in which modern organizations control their operations and their human resources. The control process has two important elements: physical resources and human beings. The tools and techniques used in controlling one are quite different from those used in controlling the other.

Chapter 15 focuses on the basics of operational control. It examines the control process in action; the way in which budgets work and the types of budgets commonly used by modern organizations; the nature of comprehensive budgeting and its value to overall control; financial statement analysis, break-even analysis, and program evaluation and review technique; the way overall performance control works; the ways in which management audits help an enterprise monitor its operations; and the role played by computerized information systems in helping managers control operations.

Chapter 16 examines the nature of operations management and its role in the controlling process. Particular attention is given to the major dimensions of operations

management: product design, production planning, purchasing, inventory control, work flow layout, and quality control and to the way in which these dimensions are helping management improve productivity and meet the challenge from Japanese competition.

Chapter 17 examines the ways in which today's enterprises control personnel performance. In this chapter, attention is first focused on the performance appraisal process. The chapter then considers how conflict and change can be controlled. The last part of the chapter is devoted to an examination of some of the properties of organizational climate, the ways in which this climate can be measured, and the role that organizational development techniques can play in improving it.

When you have finished studying all of the material in this part of the book, you will have a working knowledge of the ways in which management controls its operations. You will also know some of the tools and techniques used specifically in controlling organizational operations and personnel performance.

15

Controlling Organizational Performance

OBJECTIVES

At some point in time, every organization has to measure its progress and determine the adequacy of its performance. This control process can be applied at each level of the organization and can incorporate all enterprise activities. In carrying out the process, organizations employ many different control tools and techniques, from budgeting and financial statement analysis to break-even analysis, overall performance analysis, and management audits. Sometimes these tools are tied directly to the computer, which provides managers with the kind of information they need for carrying out timely and economical control.

This chapter examines the ways in which modern organizations control organizational performance. It analyzes the nature of the controlling process and reviews some of the primary ways to monitor organizational performance through the use of financial control. It also explores some of the major forms of operational control, as well as the overall performance control measures used by modern organizations. Attention is also focused on the role, scope, and purpose of management audits, and the role that computers and management information systems play in the control process. When you have finished studying the material in this chapter you will be able to:

1. Define the term controlling and describe the control process in action.
2. Explain how budgets work and the types of budgets most commonly used by modern organizations.

3. Describe how zero-base budgeting and comprehensive budgeting can improve budgeting effectiveness.
4. Discuss financial statement analysis, break-even analysis, and program evaluation and review techniques and explain their value to the controlling function.
5. Explain how overall performance control works and how management audits help an organization monitor its operations.
6. Describe the role played by computerized information systems in assisting managers to control organizational operations.

THE NATURE OF CONTROLLING

The controlling process defined

As we learned in a previous chapter, controlling is the process in which management evaluates performance using predetermined standards and, in light of the results, makes a decision regarding corrective action. Figure 15-1 illustrates the basic steps in this process.

The Control Process in Action

In studying how the control process works, we have to refer back to planning, for the two are closely linked. In fact, it is sometimes difficult to determine where one ends and the other begins.[1]

Controlling and planning are closely linked

Consider, for example, an organization that wants to capture 15 percent of its market. It currently holds 11 percent and has determined that strong advertising will help it close the gap. In January the firm begins a vigorous ad campaign, and when progress is measured in June, market share is up to 13 percent. What will the firm do now? Most likely it will keep up the ad campaign and may pump in even more money. The control process, which identified market share as 13 percent, has provided feedback for the next six-month plan. As this example indicates, the planning and control processes are irrevocably intertwined.

More specifically, the control process forces management to review the standards or objectives that were set in the planning process and make decisions about the adequacy of progress toward them. Two areas of this process merit consideration.

---

[1]See T. K. Das, "Organizational Control: An Evolutionary Perspective," *Journal of Management Studies* (September 1989):459–73.

FIGURE 15-1
The Control
Process in Action

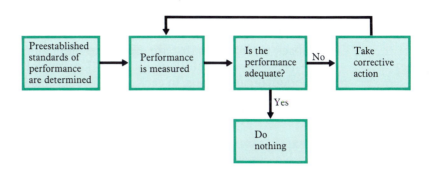

FIGURE 15-1
The Control
Process in Action

Predetermined
standards must
exist

First, there must be a predetermined basis for comparing performance and standards. Sometimes this basis will be heavily quantitative, as when the return on investment in one year is compared with that of the previous year. At other times the basis will be more qualitative, as when the public's view of the enterprise is examined and management attempts to answer the question: Is our image getting better or becoming worse?

Not every deviation
requires action

Second, not every deviation from the plan requires corrective action. Sometimes the results can be considered good enough, as when there is a desired profit of $1 million and an actual profit of $988,000. Medium-sized and large firms often sidestep this problem by establishing a range of acceptable performance, such as a return on investment of between 14.8 and 15.2 percent. In this case action need be taken only if the return is outside this range. If it is less than 14.8 percent, such things as production efficiency, product quality, advertising, and sales programs might be analyzed to determine what is wrong. If the return on investment is higher than 15.2, the enterprise may simply want to set higher goals for itself in the future.

Characteristics of Effective Control Systems

Every control system should be accurate, timely, economical, and understandable. Accuracy is essential because if the information that is received is not correct, the resulting decisions are likely to make things worse rather than better. The information being fed back must be timely to allow management to obtain full benefit from the data, and it must be economical because it would be pointless, for example, for management to spend $1,000 on a reporting system that saved the company only $10 a month. The information also must be understandable, because unless the manager knows what it is all about, he or she may make unnecessary mistakes in interpreting and using it.

Effective control
characteristics

In addition to having these four characteristics, a control system must help the manager focus on key control points, and it must be acceptable to managers. A manager does not have time to control every aspect of operations. As a result, the control system should single out specific areas that provide overall comprehensive control. Acceptability also is essential because if the data is impractical, calls for a great deal of extra analysis, or takes too long to implement, managers will find ways to work around the control system by developing their own feedback mechanisms that are easier and more efficient.

The material that follows illustrates key control tools and techniques used in modern organizations. In each case these six characteristics are incorporated into the specific control procedure or process.

FINANCIAL CONTROL

One of the primary ways to monitor organizational performance is through the use of financial control. (See "Management in Practice: Controlling Costs at The Enquirer.") Some of the control techniques used in this process are quite simple while others are extremely sophisticated. Two major approaches to financial control used by both large and small organizations are budgets, the most popular method, and financial statement analysis, which is important in analyzing past performance, identifying problem areas, and determining a future course of action.

Budgets

Budgets defined | Budgets are plans that specify results in quantitative terms and serve as a control device for feedback evaluation and follow-up. There are many different types of budgets but all have three common characteristics: (1) they help establish goals and provide general direction to management by showing, in quantitative terms, what is to be done and how much it will cost; (2) they establish control points against which progress can be measured and performance can be evaluated; and (3) they provide a means for coordinating organizational activity on both an intra- and interdepartmental basis.

The way in which budgets are drawn up and approved varies by organization. Typically, the process begins at both the upper and lower levels of the hierarchy. At the upper levels top management examines overall forecasts related to expected annual revenue and determines how much it can afford to spend on operations. This number serves as the overall limit for all budget requests and is broken down by division or department for the organization at large. At the lower levels, each unit or department draws up its own budget and forwards the request to the respective superior. As these proposals make their way up the line, superiors compare the requests with the initial allocations they have received from higher-level management. In this way a paring of budgets takes place at all levels as management attempts to reconcile requests with available funds.

Few divisions or departments ask for less than what they think they can get. Most request more and hope to secure at least part of this additional

Controlling Costs at The Enquirer

When MacFadden Holdings purchased the sensational tabloid *The Enquirer* for $412.5 million, financial experts questioned the logic of the deal. Why? Because MacFadden borrowed $300 million for the purchase which required the company to have debt payments of $23 million a year. The problem was that *The Enquirer* was churning out only $17.4 million in cash flow. However, MacFadden's strategy was to *cut* and *control* and thus triple the amount of cash flow to $50 million per year.

First, MacFadden closed one of *The Enquirer* printing plants and cut the firm's payroll by 15 percent for a savings of $5 million. Next, they slashed the television advertising budget from $13 million to $3 million. Then they raised the newsstand price of the paper from 75 cents to 85 cents, producing an additional $13 million.

Are the reductions costing the company in sales? Apparently not, since *The Enquirer* is selling steadily 4.3 million copies a week and producing $146 million in revenues each year.

However, MacFadden still plans further controls. For example, every Christmas the company used to decorate its 7.5 acres of trees with Christmas lights at a cost of $1 million. That tradition is now gone.

Other strategies that MacFadden plans for *The Enquirer* include a hotline for telephone information on the latest "gossip stories," a television show entitled "The Enquirer," a soap opera guide in each issue, and a Spanish edition of the paper. Finally, the most aggressive strategy will be to increase the sale of advertising space in *The Enquirer*. Previously, only 20 percent of the company's revenues were generated through major advertisers.

The new cost-cutting and control measures appear to be paying off. Financial analysts now predict a healthy future for the firm.

Source: Antonio N. Fins, "Alien Beancounters Invade *The Enquirer*," *Business Week* (September 11, 1989):35.

amount. Still others have special problems or projects that do indeed require a greater amount of money than that initially allocated. Realizing this, management usually holds back part of the budgetary funds to cover emergencies or special cases.

Types of Budgets

A wide array of budgets are used in modern organizations. Most organizations make use of operating budgets and financial budgets. Some also employ various tools and techniques designed to tie these budgets as closely as possible to variations in the level of operational activity.[2]

---

[2] Neil C. Churchill, "Budget Choice: Planning vs. Control," *Harvard Business Review* (July–August 1984):150–64.

Operating budgets
monitor expenses
and revenues

Operating budgets are used for monitoring expenses, revenues, and, in the case of business firms, profit. The *expense budget* is designed to control things like production, marketing, personnel, research, administration, and other expenses vital to the operations of the organization. The *revenue budget* is used to measure marketing and sales effectiveness or, in the case of public agencies, to keep track of fund allocations. In this way, both outflows and inflows are tied to a budget. A business firm may also use a supplemental budget known as the *profit budget.* It is particularly important to a division head or product manager who is charged with achieving a particular return on investment or profit.

Financial budgets
integrate the
financial and
operational plans

Financial budgets integrate the organization's financial plan with its operational plan. Will the firm have the money it needs to carry out its operations? To answer this question organizations commonly use four financial budgets: the *capital expenditure budget,* used for constructing or expanding buildings, property, equipment, and other physical assets; the *cash budget,* used to monitor the flow of funds and the pattern of receipts and cash disbursements; the *financial budget,* used to balance any shortages of capital whether they be short-, intermediate-, or long-range in nature; and the *balance sheet budget,* used for bringing together all of the other budgets and projecting how the balance sheet will look at the end of the period if actual results conform to budgets.

Budget Flexibility

One of the biggest problems with budgets is inflexibility. Managers often reveal this inflexibility when they say, "I'm sorry, but we can't buy that piece of equipment. It's not in the budget." In cases like this, the budget is being treated as a fixed entity instead of as a control tool that can be altered or changed to meet the needs of the organization. Perhaps the enterprise really should increase the budget to buy the piece of equipment.

Variable budgets
are tied to volume
of activity

In an effort to avoid inflexibility, many organizations have turned to the use of **variable budgets**. These budgets are tied to volume of activity in that the more output the enterprise produces or the more sales it generates, the greater its expenditure budget. Conversely, if the organization finds it must contract operations, the budget is decreased. The costs affected by changes in activity are those directly related to production and sales. Examples include materials, parts, maintenance, utilities, personnel salaries, advertising, and entertainment costs.

One of the major advantages of variable budgets is that they encourage the organization to examine its costs. In all, there are three types of costs: fixed, variable, and semivariable. A **fixed cost** is one that does not change, regardless of the amount of work being done. Property taxes, rent, and flood insurance are examples. **Variable costs** are expenses that vary directly with the quantity of work being performed. Raw materials, supplies, and scrap are all examples.

Semivariable costs are those that vary with the quantity of work being performed but not in a directly proportional way. Examples include labor salaries, utilities, and machine maintenance. By systematically identifying and analyzing its costs, the organization is better able to control these expenses.

Advantages and Disadvantages

A number of important advantages are associated with budgeting, but managers also should be aware of some distinct drawbacks.

On the positive side, budgets help coordinate the work of units, departments and, if used on an overall organizational basis, the entire enterprise. They also provide feedback for correcting errors and, if properly installed, are able to generate this information on a timely and economical basis. Budgets help managers learn from their past mistakes and serve as a basis for the future allocation of resources. They help clarify planning efforts by communicating how progress will be evaluated and when this evaluation will take place. Finally, they help reduce anxiety and tension because they tell people what is expected of them.

On the negative side, however, budgets can create problems. One of the most common occurs when managers begin fighting with each other over budgetary allocations in an effort to maintain the size of their previous allocation or build onto it. A second problem is the failure of management to tell employees when they have deviated from their budget and give them an opportunity to correct the situation. Other problems arise when budgets are allowed to dictate what happens in the organization instead of being used as tools and techniques for controlling and monitoring operations. Problems also arise when budgetary allocations are not tied directly to the job and cut backs must be made to critical operations while others have plenty of fat.

Effective Budgeting

Many organizations seek ways to maintain the advantages of budgeting while sidestepping the disadvantages. One of the most effective approaches is to look at each department's or unit's budget solely in terms of objectives and resource requirements. If this approach is used, a department that received a large budget last year will not necessarily receive a large one this year. During the late 1970s this approach gained in popularity as **zero-base budgeting** (ZBB) was adopted by organizations throughout the private and public sector. In its essence, ZBB calls for the allocation of organizational funds on the basis of a cost-benefit analysis of major activities. This process is carried out via three major steps:

The ZBB process
1. Each department justifies what it is going to be doing and how much it will cost. This constitutes the unit's "decision package."

2. The unit then does a comparison of the costs and benefits of the activities in the decision package. Attention is also focused on alternative ways to perform these activities, such as hiring temporary help, and what the unit would do if it received additional money and could expand its activities.

3. Activities are then ranked in order of benefit to the organization. The budget proposal and the ranking are then passed up the line and the next manager in the hierarchy performs the same ZBB procedures.[3]

In recent years, the overall use of ZBB has declined. The amount of paperwork generated by the approach and the time and effort that were required for its implementation convinced many that there had to be a better way.[4] As a result, many organizations have developed their own simplified version of ZBB.

Comprehensive budgeting covers all phases of operations

A second effective technique is **comprehensive budgeting**, in which all phases of operations are covered by budgets. Beginning at the bottom of the hierarchy and working up to the top, each unit develops a budget that fits in with that of the next highest level. In this way, management is able to integrate comprehensive planning (what each department will be doing) with comprehensive budgeting (how much money each department will need to accomplish these objectives).

Budgets should have some flexibility

A third useful technique is that of not budgeting too strictly. If every penny is designated for particular activities and projects, the manager will have no flexibility in moving funds from one departmental program to another. This philosophy encourages waste. Since funds cannot be transferred to other projects, the department will simply spend them on the designated programs regardless of the cost/benefit ratio.

Communication is vital

Finally, effective budgeting requires that everyone know what is going on. When personnel understand how much money they have to work with, the objectives that are to be accomplished, the time frame within which everything is to be done, and how performance will be evaluated, there is an excellent chance of developing high morale and teamwork. Budgets are more than just control tools. They are also important in effective planning, organizing, influencing, and leading. They are crucial to the overall management process.

Financial Statement Analysis

There are two major financial statements: the balance sheet (see Table 15-1) and the income statement (see Table 15-2).

---

[3] Peter A. Pyhrr, "Zero-Base Budgeting," *Harvard Business Review* (November–December 1970):111–21.

[4] Stanton C. Lindquist and K. Bryant Mills, "Whatever Happened to Zero-Base Budgeting?" *Managerial Planning* (January–February 1981):31–35.

TABLE 15-1   Jones Manufacturing, Inc., Consolidated Balance Sheet as of December 31, 1988

Assets				Liabilities and Owners' Equity			
Current assets				*Current liabilities:*			
Cash	$180,000			Accounts payable	$ 10,000		
Accounts receivable	160,000			Notes payable	30,000		
Notes receivable	55,000			Income taxes payable	250,000		
Inventory	330,000			Total current			
Total current assets			$ 725,000	liabilities		$290,000	
Fixed Assets				*Long-term liabilities*			
Plant and equipment	$800,000			Mortgage payable	$180,000		
Less: Accumulated				Notes payable	100,000		
depreciation	225,000	$575,000		Long-term bonds			
Building	$600,000			outstanding	200,000		
Less: Accumulated				Total long-term			
depreciation	150,000	$450,000		liabilities		$480,000	
Land		250,000		Total liabilities			$770,000
Total fixed assets			$1,275,000	*Owners' equity*			
Total assets			$2,000,000	Common stock	$500,000		
				Preferred stock	200,000		
				Retained earnings	500,000		
				Total owners' equity			$1,230,000
				Total liabilities and			
				owners' equity			$2,000,000

TABLE 15-2   Jones Manufacturing Statement of Income for the Year Ended December 31, 1988

Revenue from Sales

Gross sales	$4,000,000	
Less: Sales returns and allowances	250,000	
Net Sales		$3,750,000

Cost of Goods Sold

Beginning inventory	$ 330,000	
Purchases	1,870,000	
Total goods available for sale	2,200,000	
Less: Ending inventory	200,000	
Total cost of goods sold		$2,000,000
Gross profit		$1,750,000

Expenses

Selling expenses	$ 700,000	
Administrative expenses	300,000	
General expenses	200,000	
Total expenses		$1,200,000
Net income before taxes		$ 550,000
Federal and state income taxes		250,000
Net income		$ 300,000

Tools for measuring performance

The **balance sheet** is a financial statement that shows a firm's financial position at a specified point in time. It consists of three major parts: assets, liabilities, and owners' equity. Assets are the things the company owns. Liabilities are the firm's debts. Owners' equity is the difference between assets and liabilities and represents the net worth the owners have in the business.

The **income statement** summarizes a firm's financial performance over a given period of time, typically one year. The four major parts of an income statement are revenues, cost of goods sold, expenses, and net income.

Using these two financial statements, an organization can conduct analysis and determine where it is doing well and where it is doing poorly. The most common way in which this is done is through ratio analysis.

Ratio Analysis

A ratio is a relationship between two numbers

A **ratio** is a relationship between two numbers. In regard to financial statements, it is possible to conduct balance sheet ratio analysis, income statement ratio analysis, and combination ratio analysis. The latter draws upon data from both the balance sheet and the income statement. The four most common types of ratio analyses relate to liquidity, debt, operations, and profit.

Liquidity ratios measure the ability to meet current debts

Liquidity ratios are designed to measure how well the organization can meet its current debt obligations. Can it pay the monthly mortgage? Are there funds for meeting the payroll? Will the utility bill be paid on time? If an organization has the necessary cash, or can raise it quickly, it is said to be liquid. One of the most common ratios for measuring liquidity is the **current ratio**, which is computed by dividing current assets by current liabilities. For Jones Manufacturing in Table 15-1, this computation is $725,000/$290,000 = 2.5. The firm's current assets are two-and-a-half times its current liabilities. A standard rule of the road in manufacturing is 2.0 for the current ratio. So Jones Manufacturing, with a current ratio of 2.5, should have no trouble meeting its current debts. Liquidity is more than adequate.

Debt ratios measure the amount of financing by creditors

Debt ratios measure the amount of financing being provided by creditors. One kind is the **debt/asset ratio**, which expresses the relationship between the firm's total debt and total assets. In the case of Jones Manufacturing $770,000/2,000,000 = 38.5 percent. This means that 38.5 percent of all assets were purchased with debt. For a manufacturing firm, this ratio is acceptable. A second debt ratio is **debt/equity** which measures the amount of assets financed by debt compared to the amount financed by stock and profits that are retained in the firm. In the case of Jones Manufacturing this ratio is $770,000/1,230,000 × 0.642 to 1. For every 64.2¢ of debt there is $1 of equity. Many banks prefer to keep this ratio below 1 : 1. In Jones Manufacturing's case, there is still some room for additional borrowing.

Operations ratios measure internal performance

Operations ratios measure internal performance such as how fast inventory is turning over or how fast accounts receivable are being collected. Let us address just the first of these, the **inventory turnover ratio**. If a firm can turn its inventory over 12 times a year, it can get by with a much smaller inventory investment than a competitor with equal sales but an inventory turnover of only three. Inventory turnover is determined by taking the average inventory for the year (beginning inventory plus ending inventory divided by two) and dividing it into the cost of goods sold. Drawing upon data from both the balance sheet and the income statement, the calculations for Jones manufacturing are

$$\text{Average inventory} = \frac{\$330,000 + 200,000}{2} = \$265,000$$

$$\text{Inventory turnover} = \frac{\$2,000,000}{265,000} = 7.55 \text{ turns}$$

The company is turning over its inventory 7.55 times per year. Although the manager would have to compare this turnover to that of the competition in determining its adequacy, for most manufacturing firms this is a very good turnover rate.

FIGURE 15-2   Return on Investment Computation

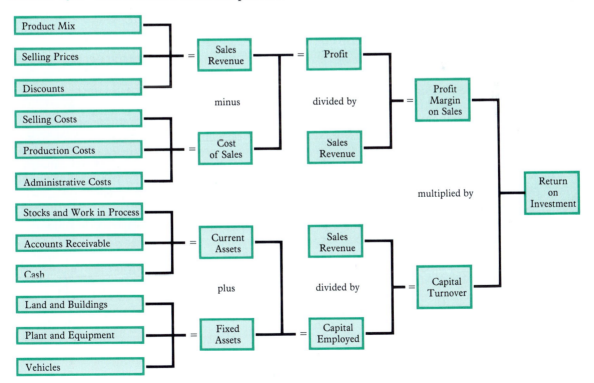

Profitability ratios measure performance vis-à-vis the competition

Profitability ratios measure a company's effectiveness vis-à-vis its own performance and that of the competition. One of the most popular profitability ratios is **return on investment** (ROI), which is measured by comparing net income with total assets. In the case of Jones Manufacturing, this ratio is $300,000/2,000,000 = 15$ percent. This is quite good in light of the fact that we used net income after taxes in our calculations. If we opted for net income before taxes, the percentage would have risen to 27.5 percent. In its comprehensive form, ROI includes a large number of key factors. Figure 15-2 presents these and illustrates the relationship between them. By examining performance in each of these factors, an organization can identify problem areas and work to resolve them, increasing ROI in the process. (See "Management in Practice: From 'Low Cost Operator' to 'Total Quality Management.'")

MANAGEMENT IN PRACTICE

From 'Low Cost Operator' To 'Total Quality Management'

*I*n 1979 Anthony J. F. O'Reilly became the CEO of the H. J. Heinz Co. and instituted an austerity program for a slumping company. The cost-cutting measures were termed "low cost operator" and they immediately turned Heinz's efforts into successes. For example, Heinz's ketchup increased its market share from 25 percent to 54 percent through aggressive marketing, innovative packaging, and extensions of the product line.

In order to meet the new corporate goals, Heinz manufacturing facilities began to cut workers, reduce training, speed up production lines, and change the storage as well as cooking procedures. While the austerity program worked for a while, it began to erode the quality of the company's products. By 1987, the sales of Ore-Ida Tater Tots (frozen fried potatoes) were falling drastically. When management investigated the reasons, it found that the cost-cutting measures had destroyed the taste and quality. It was apparent that what worked in the short run for the 1980s was not going to carry over in the long run for the 1990s.

O'Reilly then implemented a new approach called "total quality management." Training budgets tripled and quality teams were created to formulate solutions to the production process problems.

The results have been dramatic. By concentrating on a quality manufacturing process instead of merely a low cost process, Heinz's rejection rates are down, sales are up 18 percent, and profit margins are up 15 percent. The company now expects to save $125 million each year by 1994. Not bad for Heinz, which already earns $500 million in profit on sales of $6.5 billion.

In addition, Heinz has spent $500 million to acquire 44 subsidiaries ranging from pastries to dog food. With a coordinated advertising and marketing effort, the company is seeking to increase profits at least 10 percent a year for the next five years.

Source: Gregory L. Miles, "Heinz Ain't Broke, But It's Doing a Lot of Fixing," *Business Week* (December 11, 1989):84–88.

A second major form of control is operational control. The tools and techniques used in operational control are designed to help the organization monitor its operations or activities. One of the most popular tools, particularly among manufacturing firms, is break-even analysis. Another, used for controlling sophisticated or one-of-a-kind projects, is program evaluation and review technique.

Break-even Analysis

The purpose of break-even analysis is to determine the point at which the firm covers all of the costs associated with producing a particular product. If the company cannot sell enough units to reach this point, it will lose money on the product. If the firm can sell more than this number of units, it will earn a profit. Before we explain how the break-even point is calculated, however, we should stress one point. A firm will not necessarily produce a product just because it can break even on it. In most cases, a return on investment objective is set, and if the firm cannot reach this target, which may mean selling 10,000 units above break-even, it will refuse to produce the good or will terminate the current production plan.

Calculation and Advantages of Break-Even

Break-even analysis requires an analysis of two types of costs: fixed and variable. Fixed costs, as noted earlier in the chapter, do not change in relation to output. Variable costs do change in relation to output, that is, the greater the output, the higher the variable costs and vice versa. Breakeven occurs when the organization can cover all of the fixed and variable costs associated with production of the product.

Break-even occurs when costs are covered

For example, suppose that Firm G is thinking about producing Product H. In order to set up all of the machinery and buy the necessary equipment to produce the product, a $50,000 investment is needed. Also assume that each unit will require $6 of labor, materials and parts and will sell for $10. How many units will the firm have to produce in order to break even? The formula for the break-even point (BEP) is fixed cost/selling price minus variable cost. In our example, the break-even point will occur at 12,500 units ($50,000/$10 − 6). This solution is graphed in Figure 15-3. Because of its simplicity, however, we can explain the logic in writing. On every unit sold, the company will clear $4 over and above the costs associated with building the unit. This $4 must be used to reduce the fixed cost associated with setting up the machinery and getting the production process in order. Since there was a $50,000 fixed cost, it will take 12,500 units, each contributing $4, to cover all fixed costs.

FIGURE 15-3   **Illustration of a Break-Even Point**

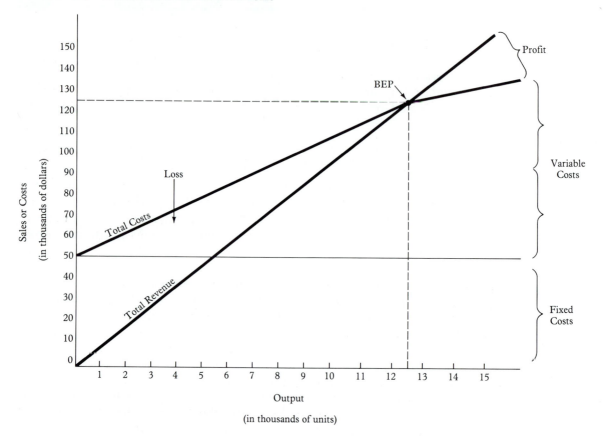

Once the firm has achieved break-even, assuming there is no change in selling price, fixed cost, or variable cost, it will make $4 on every unit produced and sold. The thing to keep in mind about break-even analysis is that it is usually not this simple. Quite often, the selling price, fixed cost, or variable cost will change, and this change will alter the BEP. For example, because of competition, the firm may find it necessary to lower the selling price from $10 to $9. When this happens, the BEP is raised. Conversely, if the variable cost per unit declines from $6 to $5.50, the BEP goes down. So the break-even point cannot be computed just once. The firm has to make these calculations on a periodic basis, and if costs are rising it can either raise prices in order to maintain profitability or begin to phase out production of the line.

Benefits of BEP analysis   One of the biggest benefits of break-even point analysis is that it forces the organization to analyze costs. It also helps the firm tie production to marketing demand, and it helps the manager integrate production with ROI objectives.

Program Evaluation and Review Technique

In some cases an organization needs to go beyond break-even point analysis in controlling operations. This is particularly true when the enterprise is engaged in a one-time, nonrepetitive project that is complex and requires the monitoring of many different activities. Typical examples include building sophisticated aerospace hardware, constructing high-technology telecommunication systems, and using state-of-the-art R&D to oxygenate polluted bodies of water. Given the fact that these projects typically are performed under a contract arrangement that penalizes late completion, management needs to monitor progress very closely. In so doing, management often uses a tool known as **Program Evaluation and Review Technique (PERT)**, which is designed for one-time and complex projects. PERT was developed by the U.S. Navy and the consulting firm of Booz, Allen and Hamilton in connection with the Polaris missile. Since then, its use has been expanded to many types of undertakings.

Stages of PERT

First comes the formulation stage . . .

PERT has three stages: formulation, planning, and monitoring and control. In the formulation stage, the project is broken down into events and activities. An **event** in this context is defined as a milestone or specific accomplishment, such as completing the hiring of all necessary personnel for the project. An **activity** is defined as the effort, resources, and time associated with an event. Placing employment ads, interviewing candidates, and hiring qualified personnel may all be considered activities. These events and activities are then laid out in sequential order so that management knows what has to be done first, second, third, and so on. Then every event-activity is brought together in the form of a diagram or PERT network, and the time for each activity is indicated. An example of such a network, related to a lake restoration project, is presented in Figure 15-4. In this network, the activity associated with each event is indicated by an arrow, and the time for this activity is placed along the top of the arrow. For example, to complete event 2 will require six weeks; to finish event 5 will take eight weeks; to complete event 8 will take three weeks.

followed by the planning stage . . .

In the planning stage, the **critical path** (the longest path) through the PERT network is computed. In Figure 15-4 there are three paths through the network. These paths, along with their respective times, are as follows:

Path	Time	Total
$1-2-3-6-7-8$	$6+10+4+9+3$	32
$1-2-4-6-7-8$	$6+10+6+9+3$	34
$1-2-5-6-7-8$	$6+8+2+9+3$	28

As can be seen, the second path is the critical one.

FIGURE 15-4

A PERT Network

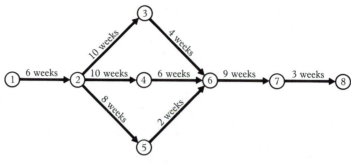

Event	Activity Associated with the Event
1	Lake restoration project begun
2	All necessary personnel hired
3	All materials purchased
4	All equipment assembled
5	Oxygenation plan finalized
6	All resources moved to lake project site
7	Oxygenation process carried out
8	Progress measured and evaluated

After this evaluation is made, the total of the critical path time is compared with the allotted time for the project. Assuming that this project has a completion date of 39 weeks, management will complete it in time if none of the activities take any longer than the estimates indicate. In fact, the critical path $(1 - 2 - 4 - 6 - 7 - 8)$ can slip by as much as five weeks and the project still will be completed on time. If the contact time is 32 weeks, however, the critical path must be reduced by two weeks.

and, finally, the monitoring and controlling stage

In the monitoring and controlling stage, steps are taken to ensure that the project does not run late. If the critical path must be reduced, management must decide how this should be done. For example the activities associated with events 4 or 6 might be cut by a total of two weeks. The firm could take personnel off other activities where there was extra time and allocate them to activities on the critical path.

Advantages of PERT

Why use PERT?

PERT offers some very important advantages, including the following:

1. It helps management plan in detail, defining exactly what must be done in order to accomplish the project's objectives on time.

2. It forces management to make commitments regarding execution times and completion dates.
3. By identifying critical activities, it helps management monitor work progress more efficiently.
4. It assists management in identifying potential problem areas and formulating contingency plans.
5. The overall concept is easily understood because it provides a method for visualizing the entire project and explaining it to all who will be involved.[5]

OVERALL PERFORMANCE CONTROL

Financial and operational control are important at the lower and middle levels of the hierarchy. At the upper levels, however, managers are more interested in overall performance control. Typically, their attention is focused on five to seven key performance factors that provide the necessary control information for the organization at large. Identifying these key factors is the most important phase of overall performance control.

Identification of Key Factors

Some performance control factors are a result of strategic objectives

The most common overall performance control factor is ROI. Other popular ones include market share, growth, profit, and customer relations. In deciding which factors are most important, the organization typically begins by reviewing its strategic objectives. Quite often, these objectives serve as both planning goals and key control points.

Others are tied to key success factors

Additional key control factors are identified by answering the questions: Where do we need to do well in order to succeed? What are our key success factors? In every industry there are, at most, a handful of such factors. For example, in the computer industry, technology and customer service are two of the primary success factors. In laboratory animal breeding, research and development (R&D) is the most significant factor. In the automobile industry, production quality and customer service are of great importance. In the watchmaking business, production efficiency and marketing effectiveness are two key success variables.

Some are highly quantifiable

In some cases, these key factors are quantifiable. Every week, Detroit auto sales are reported. If General Motors wants to hold 60 percent of the market of autos produced domestically, the company can measure its progress on a weekly basis.

---

[5] Efraim Turban and Jack R. Meredith, *Fundamentals of Management Science,* 3rd ed. (Dallas, TX: Business Publications, Inc., 1985), 323.

Others are partially quantifiable

In other cases, the key factor is only partially quantifiable. An organization that wants to be a leader in R&D innovation cannot know its position on a weekly basis, so it must remain alert to environmental changes. Particular attention must be directed toward the competition's current product offerings and any news regarding new R&D developments in the industry. The organization does not know exactly what is happening in the environment, but it tries to assess these developments as objectively as possible.

Still others are qualitative

In still other cases key factors are heavily qualitative in nature. Consider a company that wants to mesh long-, intermediate-, and short-range planning in an overall, comprehensive way. The state of progress is usually judged by an in-house management team, and the final decision regarding the company's progress is often based heavily on qualitative factors.

Tying Control to Performance

While key factor control allows the enterprise to focus on a limited number of performance variables, these variables often are tied closely to performance. For example, an organization may desire a 20 percent ROI, which can be attained only with a production of 500 units or more a day. In this case, the primary focus must be on production; ROI will be taken care of in the process. This is particularly true for businesses that can sell everything they can produce. During the early 1980s, many video game manufacturers fell into this category. The Rolls Royce auto division, of course, has been in it for years.

A second important fact in tying control to performance is that the required emphasis on specific key control variables may change. For example, in the early 1970s, a few firms introduced the digital wristwatch. In the initial version of this watch, the user pressed a button on the side of the watch and the time was displayed in red digital numbers. Depending on whether the casing was silver or gold, the watches retailed in the $250 to $400 range. The product was a novel one and in controlling overall performance, the manufacturers initially concentrated their attention on R&D. As sales began to increase and the market matured, however, attention shifted away from R&D to production and then to marketing. Figure 15-5 illustrates this pattern for a manufacturing industry similar to the one we are discussing.

Control is often tied to product/ market evolution

Notice in the figure that control emphasis must be tied directly to the product/market evolution. In product manufacturing, technology and R&D initially are more important than anything else. As the market matures, however, the emphasis moves to production and then on to marketing and finance. Unless R&D is used to develop a better product, its function is complete. At this stage the company's task is to produce the good as efficiently as possible and market it to the consumer. Since many firms are engaged in the production of goods or services, Figure 15-5 is an excellent one with which to illustrate how key control factors are tied to specific operations. It is also useful in explaining why many firms do not achieve their desired strategic objectives: they fail to adjust their control variables.

FIGURE 15-5   Product/Market Evolution and Key Area Control

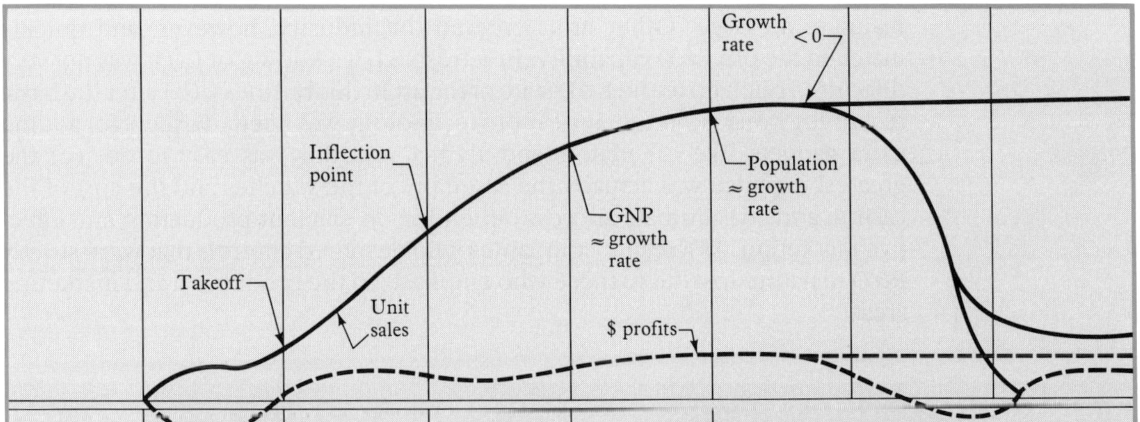

Stage	Development	Growth	Shakeout	Maturity	Saturation		
					Saturation	Decline	Petrification
Market growth rate	Slight	Very large	Large	GNP growth	Population growth	Negative	Slight to none
Change in growth rate	Little	Increases rapidly	Decreases rapidly	Decreases slowly	Little	Decreases rapidly, then slow. May increase, then slow	Little
Number of segments	Very few	Some	Some	Some - to - many		Few	Few
Technological change in product design	Very great	Great	Moderate	Slight	Slight	Slight	Slight
Technological change in process design	Slight	Slight/ moderate	Very great	Great moderate	Slight	Slight	Slight
Major functional concern	Research and development	Engineering	Production	Marketing-distribution-finance		Finance	Marketing and finance

Source: C. W. Hofer, "Conceptual Constructs for Formulating Corporate and Business Strategy," (Dover, MA: Lord Publishing Company, BP-0039, 1977), p. 7. Copyright © 1977 by Charles W. Hofer. Reprinted by permission.

In the case of the early digital watch manufacturers, this is precisely what happened. They believed that the most important factor was R&D and strove to maintain an edge. Other firms entered the industry, however, and quickly matched the old R&D capability. In retrospect, we know that (a) it was not very difficult to catch up to the R&D state of the art in this business; (b) after the basic technology was mastered, little more technology was needed except for adding extra gadgets like calculators and alarms, and this was easy to do; (c) the greatest expense was actually the assembly of the watches and the cost of the casing; and (d) ultimate success depended on efficient production and effective marketing. As a result, companies who designed controls that were strictly R&D in nature lost out to those who emphasized the production and marketing areas.

MANAGEMENT AUDITS

Regardless of the control measures an organization employs, it is becoming common, especially among intermediate-sized and large enterprises, to find management audits being used to supplement these measures. The term "auditing" typically is employed to refer to an external financial evaluation of an enterprise's transactions and accounts that is carried out by a certified public accounting firm. In the last few decades, however, organizations have begun to realize that they also can benefit from management audits. A **management audit** is an evaluation of the abilities and successes of the executives who are operating the enterprise.

External Audits

External audits are conducted by outside personnel

An external management audit is conducted by outside personnel. These individuals examine industry trends, organizational resources, and strategic and operating performance to help management pinpoint problem areas. They also offer recommendations for action. In recent years a number of accounting firms have begun carrying out management audits for their clients. Since the company is already reviewing the enterprise's financial records, why not go on to evaluate overall operations? Many accounting firms feel that such consulting activities are a natural extension of their current task. Yet they are not the only group interested in management audits. Some firms specialize in this type of activity and, for a fee, will carry out an overall organizational evaluation of enterprise activities ranging from health of earnings, sales vigor, fiscal policies, and corporate structure to research and development policies, production efficiency, stockholder relations, and executive ability.[6]

---

[6] Jackson Martindell, *The Scientific Appraisal of Management* (New York: Harper & Brothers, 1950), and *The Appraisal of Management* (New York: Harper & Brothers, 1962).

TABLE 15-3   Partial Outline for Evaluation of a Firm

I. Product Lines and Basic Competitive Position

A. Past

What strengths and weakness in products (or services) have been dominant in this firm's history—design features, quality-reliability, prices, patents, proprietary position?

B. Present

What share of its market(s) does the firm now hold, and how firmly? Is this share diversified or concentrated as to number of customers? In what phases of their life cycles are the present chief products and what is happening to prices and margins? How do customers and potential customers regard this firm's products? Are the various product lines compatible marketing-wise, engineering-wise, manufacturing-wise? If not, is each product line substantial enough to stand on its own feet?

C. Future

Is the market(s) as a whole expanding or contracting, and at what rate? What is the trend in this firm's share of the market(s)? What competitive trends are developing in numbers of competitors, technology, marketing pricing? What is its vulnerability to business cycle (or defense spending) changes? Is management capable of effectively integrating market research, R&D, and market development programs for a new product or products?

II. Top Management

A. Identification of Top Management and Its Record

What person or group constitutes top management? Has present top management been responsible for profit-and-loss results of the past few years?

B. Top Management and the Future

What are top management's chief characteristics? How adequate or inadequate is this type of management for coping with the challenges of the future? Will the present type and quality of top management continue? Will it deteriorate, will it improve, or will it change its basic character?

C. Board of Directors

What influence and/or control does the Board of Directors exercise? What are the capabilities of its members? What are their motivations?

III. Summary and Evaluation Strategy

What other factors can assume major importance in this particular situation? (Use a checklist.) Of all the factors studied, which, if any, is overriding in this particular situation? Which factors are of major importance by virtue of the fact that they govern other factors? What are the basic facts of life about the economics and competition of this industry now and over the next decade? In view of this firm's particular strengths and weaknesses, what are levels of success in this industry? What are the prospects of its succeeding by diversifying out of its industry?

Source: Reprinted with permission from Robert B. Buchele, "How to Evaluate a Firm," *California Management Review* (Fall 1962):6–7. © 1962 by the Regents of the University of California. Condensed from *California Management Review,* vol. 5, no. 1. By permission of The Regents.

External audits offer some important advantages. One is that the consultants can be objective without fear of reprisal by management. Also, in many cases they have seen similar performance in other firms and know what to look for and what to overlook during the management audit. And since the reputations of these firms are based on how well they help out their clients, they have everything to gain from doing a good job and nothing to lose.

Internal Audits

Internal audits are performed by in-house people

An internal management audit is similar in nature to an external one. In making an evaluation, the audit team is generally directed by questions such as those presented in Table 15-3. Notice that these questions are directed toward analyzing key internal and external areas of management performance. Of course, depending on the firm, the questions also may address other areas, including research and development, production, personnel, financial performance, and customer relations.

Internal audits provide some important benefits to the enterprise. Because the inside people are more likely to know the inner workings of the organization, they should have less difficulty pinpointing both strengths and weaknesses than outside auditors would. In addition, the cost of using inside people is usually lower, and if there is a problem following through on some recommendations, the internal auditors can easily be called back for consultation.

In recent years, there has been a trend towards using internal auditors when possible. Of course, these people can be biased, and there is always the chance that they will be pressured to paint a rosier picture than actually exists. From a cost/benefit standpoint, however, many organizations are questioning whether external audits are worth the expense in terms of both company time and money. Some firms are compromising on the matter by using internal consultants whenever possible and bringing in outside consultants for special situations.

However management audits are done, they are an excellent way to supplement the overall control program. They provide a follow-up and appraisal of financial, operational, and key area control.

COMPUTERIZED INFORMATION SYSTEMS

Over the last 25 years, computers have begun to play an increasingly important role in the control process. In particular, these machines are now being used to compile, analyze, and report information needed for control purposes.

The Computer Evolution

Computer power has increased

Modern computer technology has evolved through a number of generations. The term "generation" is applied to different types of computers in order to better delineate the major technological developments in hardware and software. Currently five distinct generations are recognized by most computer experts.

The first generation (1944–1958) were the earliest general-purpose computers using punch cards and magnetic tape. The main memory was made up exclusively with vacuum tubes. These machines could do 1,000 five-digit decimal additions per second. The second generation (1959–1963) replaced the vacuum tube with transistors and some solid-state devices. Those machines tended to be smaller, more reliable, and increased decimal additions to 10,000 per second. The third generation (1964–1970) made use of small integrated circuits and decimal additions rose to 25,000 per second. More importantly, the use of magnetic discs became widespread, introducing new capabilities, such as multiprogramming and timesharing. The fourth generation (1971–present) introduced thousands of integrated circuits on a single chip (large scale integration circuits) and the microprocessor which combined all of the circuitry for the central processing unit on one chip. It is still debated as to what actually constitutes the fifth generation. However, it is widely recognized that the new microcomputers with faster operating speeds, greater processing capacity, and virtually unlimited memory should be included. Scientists have also tried to develop new superconductors that can conduct electricity with no resistance, thus generating no heat but great speed. Many fifth-generation computers will also incorporate hundreds or thousands of processors that operate in parallel —that is, simultaneously. Traditional computers act on only one problem at a time; parallel processing means that many processors will work on the problem at the same time.

Relative costs have declined

More important for modern enterprises is the relationship between performance and price. As the power of computers has risen, the cost has declined. By 1990, one dollar of hardware expenditure could have purchased 100,000 times the computing power it would have in 1955! (See Table 15-4.)

As the range and power of the computer have risen, organizations have increased the ways in which they are using these machines. In the 1950s and 1960s computers performed a great number of paperwork functions such as payroll, accounting, and billing. Now their scope of operations is broadening with the development of computerized management information systems.

Management Information Systems

MIS defined

A **management information system (MIS)** is a formally designed data network used to provide managers with timely and useful information for effective

TABLE 15-4	The Four Kinds of Computers and Their Approximated Costs*			
Component	Microcomputer	Minicomputer	Mainframe	Supercomputer
Main memory	64,000–7,000,000 characters	1,000,000–50,000,000 characters	32,000,000–200,000,000 characters	64,000,000–2,000,000,000 characters
Storage capacity	64,000–16,000,000 characters	4,000,000–64,000,000 characters	32,000,000+ characters	No limitation
Processing speed	60–1,000,000 instructions per second	1–5 mips	5 mips and up	10 mips and up
Cost	$200–$15,000	$10,000–$475,000	$250,000–$10,000,000	$10,000,000–$20,000,000

*The figures in this table are approximations. These numbers change rapidly as changing technology blurs the distinctions between categories.
Source: Sarah E. Hutchinson and Stacey C. Sawyer, *Computers: The User Perspective* (Homewood, Ill.: Irwin, 1989).

planning and control. The system is specially designed so that managers get only the information they need, in the most useful form possible.[7]

MIS Design

Every manager needs information. Specific demands vary, however, with the manager's function and hierarchical level. Using the latter as an example, we can compare the MIS needs of first-line managers and executives as in Table 15-5. If we added middle managers to the table, they would fall between the two, requiring less specific on-the-spot decision-making information than first-line managers but more than that needed by executives.

How can the organization ensure that its MIS design provides managers the data they need? There are four basic stages.[8]

Stages in MIS design

The first is a preliminary survey of what the MIS will entail. At this point, the informational, operational, and functional objectives of the organization are reviewed. The question the designers seek to answer at this stage is: What kinds of problems do the managers have to deal with and what kind of information can help them do so?

The second stage is that of conceptual design. What should the MIS look like? How can the purpose and nature of the system be communicated to the

[7] See: John Burch and Gary Grudnitski, *Information Systems: Theory and Practice,* 5th ed. (New York: John Wiley & Sons, 1989); and Robert K. Wysocki and James Young, *Information Systems: Management Principles In Action* (New York: John Wiley & Sons, 1990).
[8] Robert G. Murdick, "MIS Development Procedures," *Journal of Systems Management* (December 1970):22–26.

TABLE 15-5 Information Requirements Based on Hierarchical Level	First-Line Manager	Executive
This information will be gathered from:	internal environment	external environment
The nature of this information will be:	specific, narrow, well-defined	general, broad, ill-defined
The focus of the information will tend to be on:	technical issues	general issues
The accuracy of this information will be:	high	high-low, depending on its nature
The information will relate to:	the current situation	past, current and future situations
The information will be used for planning and controlling:	current operations	current and future operations
This information will be provided:	daily or weekly	monthly or quarterly

people who will be using it? At this point the designers work on bringing together the system and the personnel so that the latter will know the value of the MIS and support it.

The third stage involves a detailed design of the information system. All of the specifics are worked out and, if the MIS is tied to the computer, the necessary program and other parts of the software package are completed at this point. Any personnel training related to the use of the system is also carried out during this stage.

The fourth stage is that of final implementation. At this point, the system is put into practice. If the designers have done their job right, management should find itself receiving both accurate and timely information.

MIS and Decision Making

In the last decade there has been a dramatic change in the way managers use information systems. In particular, reliance on written reports and similar forms of information is beginning to be replaced by what are called **decision support systems (DSS)**. This is a collective term that refers to systems that are designed to provide the manager with information that is useful in making current decisions. Personal computer technology has gone a long way toward making these

Microcomputers allow for on-line decisions

systems possible. Now, managers who know how to operate microcomputers and whose companies have the necessary computer software can request the current status of a project, make decisions regarding what needs to be done, and be assured that these commands are communicated to the people working on the project. The microcomputer is also allowing managers to make "what if" decisions for dealing with problems that occur on the line. As these machines become less expensive and managers become accustomed to operating them, we will probably see managers staying at home part of the day and making decisions from there and making decisions over the weekend on matters that will be carried out on Monday.

By the early 1980s two impressive breakthroughs had made headlines in the computer field. IBM's personal computer, first introduced in 1981, soon began to dominate the industry. In 1983, when Apple introduced Lisa, it was touted as the most powerful and versatile personal computer available on the market.[9] The next year saw the introduction of IBM's PC jr. and Apple's Macintosh, offering still more computer power. Technological developments and the intense competition among computer manufacturers have created a climate in which new advances occur with regularity, making one day's technology obsolete the next.

Other important uses of computers in decision making are offered in the form of up-to-date printouts that provide managers with the current status of inventory, sales, receivables, and other similar information. Provided on a daily or weekly basis, these reports are useful when decisions do not have to be made on the spot. Managers unfamiliar with microcomputers (or computers in any form) usually encounter fewer problems with computerized printouts than they do with machines that allow them to ask for and receive information that they request. As managers become more familiar with computers, we are likely to see less resistance to linking information systems, computers, and managers on an interactive basis.[10]

In fact, the proliferation of microcomputers in managerial offices has now caused a greater use of computers by executives in the planning and controlling functions of their businesses.[11] As demonstrated in Table 15-6, 106 CEOs of the top 500 corporations utilize a computer—an indication that microcomputers are becoming a well-recognized tool for middle and upper management.

MIS and Human Behavior

Before completing our discussion of MIS implementation, we need to touch on the behavioral effects of this process.[12] As noted earlier in the chapter, MIS output must be acceptable to those who receive it.

---

[9] Peter Nulty, "Apple's Bid to Stay in the Big Time," *Fortune* (February 7, 1983):36–41.
[10] For more on the subject of computerized information systems, see Robert J. Mockler and D. G. Dologite, "Put Data Processing Where the Action Is," *Business Horizons* (May–June 1981):25–31; Raymond McLeod, Jr. and Jack W. Jones, "Making Executive Information Systems More Effective," *Business Horizons* (September–October 1986):29–37.
[11] See "Top Executives Increase Use of Computers in Decision-Making," *Journal of Accounting* (March 1985):29.
[12] In addition to the discussion here, see Archie B. Carroll, "Behavioral Aspects of Developing Computer-Based Information Systems," *Business Horizons* (January–February 1982):42–51.

TABLE 15-6   Top CEOs Who Compute

Name	Company/Title	Office/Home	Name	Company/Title	Office/Home
Jeff K. Coors	Adolph Coors/President	N/Y	William E. LaMothe	Kellog/Chairman & CEO	N/Y
Edward Donley	Air Products & Chemicals/CEO	Y/N	Joseph E. Luecke	Kemper/Chairman & CEO	N/Y
Robert J. Buckley	Allegheny International/CEO	Y/Y	Gerald C. McDonough	Leaseway Transportation/Chairman & CEO	N/Y
George J. Stella, Jr.	American Cyanamid/Chairman, President & CEO	N/Y	Darryl F. Allen	Libbey-Owens-Ford/President & CEO	N/Y
Willis S. White, Jr.	American Electric Power/Chairman of the Board & CEO	N/Y	Lawrence O. Kitchen	Lockheed/Chairman & CEO	N/Y
James D. Robinson III	American Express/Chairman of the Board	Y/U	Robert M. Long	Longs Drug Stores/President & CEO	Y/U
Harold S. Hook	American General/Chairman & CEO	Y/Y	John M. Lillie	Lucky Stores/Chairman & CEO	N/Y
Paul D. Meek	American Petrofina/Chairman	N/Y	Gene H. Bishop	M Corp./Chairman & CEO	Y/N
William B. Boyd	American Standard/Chairman of the Board & CEO	N/Y	Sanford McDonnell	McDonnell Douglas/Chairman & CEO	Y/N
John Sculley	Apple Computer/Chairman, President & CEO	Y/Y	John F. McGillicuddy	Manufacturers Hanover/Chairman & CEO	N/Y
John R. Hall	Ashland Oil/Chairman of the Board & CEO	Y/Y	William G. McGowan	MCI Communications/Chairman & CEO	Y/Y
Ernest H. Clark, Jr.	Baker International/Chairman & CEO	N/Y	Burnell R. Roberts	Mead/Chairman & CEO	Y/Y
Charles E. Rice	Barnett Banks of Florida/Chairman & CEO	Y/Y	P. Roy Vagelos	Merck/Chairman & CEO	Y/Y
Vernon R. Loucks, Jr.	Baxter Travenol Laboratories/President & CEO	Y/Y	Allen Jacobson	Minnesota Mining & Manufacturing/Chairman & CEO	Y/Y
Finn M.W. Casperson	Beneficial Corp./CEO	Y/Y	Charles S. Locke	Morton Thiokol/Chairman & CEO	Y/N
Andrew M. Lewis	Best Products/Chairman & CEO	N/Y	Donald D. Lennox	Navistar International/Chairman of the Board & CEO	Y/N
Eugene J. Sullivan	Borden/Chairman & CEO	N/Y	Charles E. Exley Jr.	NCR/Chairman & President	Y/Y
William A. Klopman	Burlington Industries/Chairman & CEO	Y/Y	Samuel Huntington	New England Electric System/President & CEO	N/Y
Robert A. Charpie	Cabot/President	Y/Y	Theodore C. Rogers	NL Industries/Chairman & CEO	Y/N
			William B. Ellis	Northeast Utilities/Chairman, President & CEO	N/Y

(Continued)

TABLE 15-6   Top CEOs Who Compute *(Continued)*

Name	Company/Title	Office/Home	Name	Company/Title	Office/Home
Thomas C. Simons	Capital Holding/ Chairman & CEO	N/Y	Donald W. McCarthy	Northern States Power/Chairman & CEO	N/Y
Philip M. Hawley	Carter Hawley Hale Stores/Chairman & CEO	Y/Y	C.J. Silas	Phillips Petroleum/ Chairman of the Board & CEO	N/Y
John D. Macomber	Celanese/Chairman & CEO	N/Y	William R. Howard	Piedmont Aviation/Presi- dent & CEO	N/Y
Robert P. Reuss	Centel/Chairman & CEO	Y/Y			
John S. Reed	Citicorp/Chairman & CEO	Y/Y	Frederick S. Hammer	PSFS/Chairman & CEO	Y/Y
Reuben Mark	Colgate-Palmolive/ Chairman, President & CEO	N/Y	Richard F. Walker	Public Service of Colorado/Chair- man of the Board	N/Y
Charles M. Harper	ConAgra/Chairman & CEO	Y/Y	William D. Smithburg	Quaker Oats/Chair- man & CEO	Y/Y
George J. Tankersley	Consolidated Natural Gas/Chairman & CEO	Y/N	Robert R. Frederick	RCA/President & CEO	Y/N
			J. Tylee Wilson	R.J. Reynolds Industries/Chair- man & CEO	Y/N
John P. Mascotte	Continental Corp./Chairman & CEO	Y/N	Robert Anderson	Rockwell International/ Chairman & CEO	Y/Y
John N. Lemasters	Continental Telecom/Presi- dent & CEO	Y/Y	M. Anthony Burns	Ryder Systems/ Chairman, President & CEO	Y/N
James R. Houghton	Corning Glass Works/Chairman & CEO	Y/N	Philip E. Lippincott	Scott Paper/Chair- man & CEO	N/Y
Hays T. Watkins	CSX/Chairman & CEO	N/Y	Raymond Zimmerman	Service Merchan- dise/President & CEO	Y/N
William H. Knoell	Cyclops/President & CEO	N/Y	Henry Wendt	Smithkline Beckman Corp./ President & CEO	N/Y
John J. Murphy	Dresser Industries/ Chairman, President & CEO	N/Y	Edward L. Addison	Southern Co./President & CEO	Y/N
William S. Lee	Duke Power/CEO	Y/Y			
Charles W. Moritz	Dun & Bradstreet/ Chairman & CEO	Y/N	Gerald G. Probst	Sperry/Chairman & CEO	Y/Y
Colby H. Chandler	Eastman Kodak/ Chairman & CEO	Y/Y	Dalton L. Knauss	Square D/Chair- man, President & CEO	N/Y
Frederick W. Smith	Federal Express/ Chairman & CEO	Y/Y	Richard M. Furlaud	Squibb/Chairman & CEO	N/Y
John J. Byrne	Fireman's Fund/Chairman	Y/Y	Evans W. Erikson	Sundstrand/Chair- man	N/Y
John J. Nevin	Firestone Tire & Rubber/Chair- man, President & CEO	Y/Y	John V. Roach	Tandy/Chairman, President & CEO	Y/Y
A. William Reynolds	GenCorp/President & CEO	Y/N	Dr. Henry E. Singleton	Teledyne/Chairman	Y/U
			I. David Bufkin	Texas Eastern/ Chairman & CEO	Y/N
Stanley C. Pace	General Dynamics/ Chairman & CEO	N/Y	Jerry R. Junkins	Texas Instruments/ President & CEO	Y/Y

Name	Company/Title	Office/Home	Name	Company/Title	Office/Home
Robert E. Mercer	Goodyear Tire & Rubber/Chairman & CEO	Y/N	Perry G. Brittain	Texas Utilities/ Chairman & CEO	N/Y
James S. McDonald	Gould/President & CEO	N/Y	Edward H. Budd	Travelers/Chairman & CEO	Y/N
James Wood	Great Atlantic & Pacific Tea/Chairman	N/Y	Nelson Peltz	Triangle Industries/ Chairman & CEO	Y/N
James F. Montgomery	Great Western Financial/Chairman & CEO	Y/U	Stanton R. Cook	Tribune Co./President & CEO	N/Y
Alexander F. Giacco	Hercules, Inc./Chairman, President & CEO	Y/N	William T. Esrey	United Telecommunications/ President & CEO	
John A. Young	Hewlett-Packard/ President & CEO	N/Y	Jack A. MacAllister	US West/Chairman & CEO	Y/Y
George Scharffenberger	Home Group/ Chairman	N/Y	Michael D. Eisner	Walt Disney/Chairman & CEO	N/Y
Donald C. Clark	Household International/ Chairman, President & CEO	N/Y	Ward Smith	White Consolidated Industries/Chairman	Y/Y
John F. Akers	IBM/Chairman	Y/Y	Sanford C. Sigoloff	Wickes Cos./Chairman, President & CEO	Y/Y
Frank W. Luerssen	Inland Steel/Chairman & CEO	N/Y	Charles S. McNeer	Wisconsin Electric Power/CEO	Y/Y
Rand V. Araskog	ITT/Chairman & CEO	Y/Y	David T. Kearns	Xerox/Chairman & CEO	Y/Y
			Jerry K. Pearlman	Zenith Electronics/ Chairman	Y/Y

N = No, Y = Yes, U = Unknown. Total number of respondents: 488.

Negative reactions may occur . . .   One of the biggest problems occurs when the users are not included in the design of the system. When this happens the information frequently is presented in the wrong form, requires too much time to decipher, or provides data of only marginal use. In any event, the managers make only minor use of the MIS output.[13]

A second major problem is that many managers fear the information system because they are afraid of being subjected to excessively close control by upper management. These managers also view the MIS as a means of reducing the power they hold over their units. Many of them run their departments like little empires and are reluctant to see this power base threatened.

MIS systems also may trigger a feeling of insecurity. Some managers feel that MIS will uncover many of their shortcomings and, perhaps, will bring about

[13] Albert L. Lederer and Aubrey L. Mendelow, "Information Systems Planning: Top Management Takes Control," *Business Horizons* (May–June 1988):73–78.

their replacement. They reason that it will now be easier to identify managers who are not getting their jobs done efficiently, and no room for error will be tolerated.

Finally, there is the fact that MIS brings about change, and many people are wary of what will happen. They do not know what the ultimate effect of the MIS will be, and they start becoming defensive and fighting the system before they give it a chance.

but these problems can be dealt with

How can management deal with these problems? The best way is to incorporate the user into the design of the system and show the individual how the MIS will assist in getting more work done. Doubts and worries should be seriously considered and action should be taken to show managers that they have nothing to fear from MIS. Then, after the system has been implemented, the organization should follow up and see that everything is going according to plan. If some managers are still concerned about the system, the superior should talk to them and help resolve their problems. There may, of course, be occasions when problems cannot be resolved completely, but if the organization approaches MIS implementation from the standpoint of both the user and the enterprise, behavioral problems can be minimized.[14]

Trends in Management Information Systems

Perhaps no management area has evolved as rapidly as that of information systems. In particular, over the past five years there has been a dramatic growth in the advent of "user friendly" software programs which allow people to quickly and easily interact with the computer. Now managers can ask for information they need for decision making and get it in understandable form. As a result, the computer is becoming a valuable management tool.[15]

A second important development is the use of distributed data processing which involves the decentralization of at least some computing facilities so that managers throughout the firm can directly use the computer. This has been made possible by the rapid development of microcomputers.

Associated with these two trends has been the emergence of "telecomputing." Thanks to this development, the manager does not need to go into the traditional office environment to function effectively. Instead, through the use of communications systems and microcomputers, this individual can use the information system at his or her home to make decisions. This trend allows for greater flexibility in the traditional office and working environment. Many people feel that management will be able to function as well (if not better) away from the office, since the personnel will be working in a more relaxed and comfortable setting. This trend could also do away with a great deal of lost time due to physical commuting from home to the office.

---

[14] Thomas H. Davenport, Michael Hammer, and Tauno J. Metsisto, "How Executives Can Shape Their Company's Information System," *Harvard Business Review* (March–April 1989):130–34.
[15] Bernard C. Reimann, "Decision Support Systems: Strategic Management Tools for the Eighties," *Business Horizons* (September–October 1985):71–77.

A fourth major development is the emergence of artificial intelligence in the form of "expert systems."[16] An expert system puts in the hands of its user a means to access the collected expertise of persons who are authorities in the area in which the system is designed. Thus, a manager, by using an expert system, could draw not only on his or her own collective knowledge and background, but could also use that of others when making decisions. The promise of expert systems is the ability to make better-informed decisions based on a wider base of knowledge.

In comparing Decision Support Systems to Expert Systems one author has noted the following benefits derived from each as decision aids:

DSS
- flexibility to conform to individual decision styles
- decision maker controls nature and type of information acquired
- decision maker controls model selection
- decision maker controls number and nature of alternatives examined

EXPERT SYSTEMS
- capture and disseminate expert knowledge
- improve consistency in decision reached
- ability to be used as a decision training aid
- allow experts to deal with more difficult problems
- reduced decision making time.[17]

As might be inferred from this description of trends in information systems, there are many different applications which may be made using automated information systems. It is quite clear that in order to remain in a competitive posture, management must be able to use the resources of information systems.

SUMMARY

1. Controlling is the process in which management evaluates performance using predetermined standards and, in light of the results, makes a decision regarding corrective action. Controlling is closely linked to planning in that results serve as a basis for future decisions.
2. One of the most common control techniques is the budget. A budget is a plan that specifies results in quantitative terms and serves as a control

---

[16] Beau Sheil, "Thinking About Artificial Intelligence," *Harvard Business Review* (July–August 1987):91–96.

[17] Paul E. Juras, "The Practitioner and the Computer," *The CPA Journal* (May 1989):72–74. See also: Dennis Yablonsky, "Solving Problems with AI," *Automation* (July 1989):47–48; and Beth Enslow, "The Payoff from Expert Systems," *Across the Board* (January–February 1989):54–58.

device for feedback, evaluation, and followup. Two of the most common types of budgets are operating budgets and financial budgets. Operating budgets are used for monitoring expenses, revenues, and, in the case of business firms, profit. Financial budgets integrate the financial plan of the enterprise with its operational plan.

3. Many organizations try to avoid budget inflexibility. One of the ways is by using variable budgets in which the volume of activity and the budget are tied together. Other useful approaches for increasing budget effectiveness include zero-base budgeting and comprehensive budgeting.

4. Financial statement analysis is an important financial control tool. Using data from the balance sheet or income statement, an organization can analyze financial performance. Four of the most common types of financial analysis are those related to liquidity, debt, operations, and profitability.

5. Another major form of control is that designed to monitor and evaluate operations. One of the most common tools used for this purpose, especially among manufacturing firms, is break-even analysis. Another, used for one-of-a-kind and computer projects, is PERT. By carefully spelling out all of the events and activities associated with the project and monitoring progress via the critical path, the organization can effect operational control.

6. In achieving overall performance control, an organization focuses attention on key control factors. Typical examples include ROI, market share, growth, and profit. Others are identified as the enterprise analyzes how to tie performance and control together in a harmonious fashion.

7. Over the last 25 years, many organizations have begun using computers to help them ensure that managers have both accurate and timely information for decision purposes. The design of an effective management information system entails four basic steps: a preliminary survey, a conceptual design, a detailed design, and final implementation. The introduction of MIS can bring about dysfunctional behavior, but there are ways of dealing with these problems. In addition, there were new trends developing in MIS including "user friendly" software, distributed data processing, telecomputing, and artificial intelligence.

KEY TERMS

Activity   The efforts, resources, and time associated with completing a PERT event.

Artificial intelligence   The use of an expert system that allows a computer user a means to access the expertise of persons who are authorities in a certain area of knowledge.

Balance sheet   A major financial statement that shows an enterprise's financial position at a specific point in time. It consists of three major parts: assets, liabilities, and owners' equity.

Comprehensive budgeting   A process by which all phases of operations are covered by budgets.

Critical path   The longest path in a PERT network.

Current ratio   A liquidity ratio computed by dividing current assets by current liabilities. Its purpose is to provide a measure of the enterprise's ability to meet current debt obligations.

Debt/asset ratio   A debt ratio used to express the relationship between a firm's total debt and total assets.

Debt/equity ratio   A debt ratio used to determine the amount of assets financed by debt and equity.

Debt ratios   Financial ratios used to measure the amount of financing provided by creditors.

Decision support systems (DSS)   Systems that are designed to provide the manager with information that is useful in making decisions.

Distributed data processing   A decentralized use of computer systems that allows managers easy access to the computer from a variety of locations.

Event   A milestone or specific accomplishment of a PERT network.

Expert system   A computer application that allows access to the expert knowledge of authoritative persons in a designated field.

Financial budgets   Budgets that integrate the organization's financial plan with its operational plan.

Fixed costs   Costs that do not change in relation to output.

Income statement   A major financial statement that summarizes a firm's financial performance over a given period of time. It consists of four parts: revenues, costs of goods sold, expenses, and net income.

Inventory turnover ratio   An operating ratio computed by dividing average inventory into cost of goods sold. Its purpose is to provide a measure of how quickly the enterprise is turning over its inventory.

Liquidity ratios   Financial ratios designed to measure how well an enterprise can meet its current debt obligations.

Management audit   An evaluation of the abilities and successes of the executives operating an enterprise. It may be conducted either by external consultants or in-house specialists.

Management information systems (MIS)   A formally designed data network used to provide managers with timely and useful information for effective planning and control.

Operating budgets   Budgets used for monitoring expenses, revenues and, in the case of business firms, profit.

Operations ratios   Financial ratios used to measure internal performance.

Profitability ratios   Financial ratios used to measure a company's effectiveness vis-à-vis its own performance and that of the competition.

Program evaluation and review technique (PERT)   A planning and control tool used for handling one-time, nonrepetitive and complex projects.

Ratio   A relationship between two numbers.

Return on investment   A profitability ratio used to compare a company's performance with that of the competition. The calculation is: profit/assets.

Semivariable costs   Costs that vary with the quantity of work being performed, but not in a directly proportional way.

Telecomputing   A contemporary development through the use of communication systems and microcomputers that allows individuals access to information and decision-making applications from a home office.

Variable budgets   Budgets that are tied to volume of activity so that the more output the enterprise produces, the greater the size of these budgets and vice versa.

Variable costs   Costs that change in relation to output.

Zero-base budgeting   A budgeting process in which funds are allocated on the basis of carefully developed decision packages and the use of cost/benefit analysis at each level of the hierarchy.

QUESTIONS FOR ANALYSIS AND DISCUSSION

1. What is meant by the term controlling? Put the definition in your own words and then describe the control process in action, being sure to incorporate Figure 15-1 into your answer.
2. Every control system should have certain characteristics if it is to be effective. What does this statement mean? Be sure to include a discussion of at least five characteristics in your answer.
3. How is the budgeting process conducted in most modern organizations? Describe the process.
4. How do operating budgets differ from financial budgets? Of what value is each to the controlling process?
5. How can variable budgets help overcome a tendency toward budget inflexibility?
6. What are some of the most important advantages of budgeting? What are some of the major drawbacks? Identify and describe three of each.
7. How can ZBB help ensure an effective budgeting process? What other techniques can be used to improve effectiveness? Explain.
8. In what way does financial statement analysis help management control operations? Include in your answer a discussion of liquidity, debt, operations, and profitability ratios.
9. How does break-even analysis work? Explain with an example. Then discuss the benefits of this kind of analysis to the control process.
10. How is a PERT network constructed? Include in your answer a discussion

of events, activities, and the critical path. What benefits does PERT offer? Discuss four of them.
11. What are some common key factors used in overall performance control? Identify and discuss three of them.
12. How do modern organizations tie control to performance? Include a discussion of Figure 15-5 in your answer.
13. How does a management audit work? What is the difference between external and internal management audits? Which is best? Explain.
14. Of what value is a management information system to a modern organization? What are the four basic stages in an MIS design? Describe each.
15. What behavioral problems are associated with the implementation of a new MIS? How can management try to resolve them? Explain.

CASE

Ferdie's Expansion Plans

Ferdie Fernandez owns an optical manufacturing firm that specializes in the grinding of lenses for ophthalmologists and optometrists. The doctors' offices call in the prescriptions and the company makes the lenses and delivers them the next day. The company also wholesales eyeglass frames to small retail firms. The company is now thinking about expanding its operations.

At present, Ferdie is considering a contract with a local retailer to open an optical center in each of the latter's 10 outlets. Ferdie's firm would sell lenses, frames, and other accessories directly to retail clients. The fixed costs associated with setting up each store—including annual salaries, administrative overhead, inventory, and equipment for grinding the lenses—are $100,000. On average, each pair of glasses costs $25 and retails for $65. The contract that Ferdie is considering calls for the retailer to provide free space and utilities. Then, after break-even is reached, the manufacturer and retailer split all profits per pair of eyeglasses ($40) on a 50-50 basis. An initial estimate by both parties is that 5,000 sets of eyeglasses can be sold annually at each location.

In order to raise the necessary capital for opening the 10 optical centers, Ferdie is going to have to seek bank financing. He will also have to develop a comprehensive budget so that expenses are closely controlled. In this regard, he is asking his accountant to help him devise an effective financial control system.

If all goes well, Ferdie has plans for the future. He currently pays $5 for each blank lens. If he could invest $700,000 in new machinery, he could make his own blanks. The annual variable cost associated with each blank is $3 for the first 200,000 blanks and $2 for every blank thereafter. Ferdie feels that if he can cut his own costs per lens and sell to other optical retailers, both local and national, he can increase his profits dramatically.

1. If Ferdie signs the contract with the retailer, how many pairs of eyeglasses will he have to sell per store in order to break even? If he sells 5,000 per store, how much profit will his firm make? What will be his ROI? If he sets a minimum ROI of 25 percent for his firm, how many pairs of glasses will he have to sell at each store?
2. What characteristics must Ferdie's control system have in order to be effective? Identify and describe five of these characteristics.
3. If Ferdie does get into the manufacture of blank lenses, what will be his annual break-even point? If he sets a minimum ROI of 20 percent, what is the minimum number he must sell? Could he sell this number by simply filling the demand he will have from his 10 retail outlets, or will he have to have outside customers as well? Show your calculations.

YOU BE THE CONSULTANT

John's Proposed Expansion

When John Harrison started in business he had only $38 in his pocket. He bought 76 boxes of Christmas cards wholesale and began selling them door-to-door. Before that Christmas season was over, he had sold 1,600 boxes of cards at a profit of 50 cents each. John was 15 years old at the time.

During the 25 years since then, John has been quite successful in the retail business. Most of his success is a result of the three general merchandise drugstores he owns. When he opened his first store, John offered a typical line of merchandise: drugs (prescription and nonprescription), greeting cards, magazines, and candy. There was also a luncheon counter. Over time, however, he began to expand into other offerings: ice cream, paperback books, office and school supplies, and most recently, appliances such as TVs, radios, heaters, and fans. John is also planning to put in a small store next to each of the current ones for the sale of beer, wine, liquor, mixers, and ice.

John believes that people will pay for convenience, and so far he has been right. His markup on paperback books and appliances, for example, is not extremely high. His return on investment on these lines, however, is in excess of 23 percent because of high inventory turnover. John believes he can also attain a high turnover on the new stores he is planning to open, ensuring him a continued high ROI.

Since location is so important to retail store success, John also has been looking into buying competitive stores. He has had his eye on one for more than six months and has made a tentative acquisition offer. The owner appears agreeable, and the two of them may be completing the deal shortly. In the interim, and before making a final determination on price, John has requested and obtained the right to look over the man's financial records. John is particularly interested in the store's ROI on its different lines. Also, this store is very conservative and has none of the latest offerings: paperback books, fast foods, appliances, or supplies. John believes that the addition of these lines could raise ROI by as much as 35 percent. If he can also put in a small store to handle beer, wine, and liquor, he believes he can boost ROI to 50 percent annually.

John foresees a few potential problems, however. One is that the initial offer to the owner calls for the latter to continue running the store for five years. This will allow the current owner to work to retirement, something he insists on doing. A second problem is the potential difficulty that might ensure when adding new lines, since the owner is not familiar with selling this type of merchandise. Third, John is not certain that the current clientele will welcome these changes. They are accustomed to a different product line. John may have to work on drawing in a new clientele. Finally, all of John's operations are controlled via computerized feedback. His store managers get computer printouts every Monday morning listing inventory on hand and on order. An ROI per product line is also provided, and once a month John meets with the store managers to evaluate progress and discuss changes in strategy.

Since he has never purchased a store before, John is concerned about whether he will be able to install his management system in an ongoing operation. He believes the best approach is to review the operations of the new business and determine its profitability. If things then look good, he will put in an assistant store manager to help ensure proper control of operations. From then on, it is going to be a matter of effective management.

Your Consultation

Assume that John has called you in as a consultant. After reviewing the facts in the case, outline the types of control procedures and techniques that should be used in controlling this new store. Be sure to discuss the roles of budgets, financial analysis, and key area control. Also, tell John how he can carry out a management audit of this new store. Be as complete as possible in your answer.

16

Production and Operations Management

Many organizations produce goods and services that they sell to others. Manufacturing firms are an excellent example. These types of companies must be particularly concerned with operations management in the form of effective product design, production planning, purchasing, inventory control, work flow layout, and quality control. Additionally, many American firms are finding that they must increase their productivity if they hope to compete effectively. Operations management tools and techniques are very helpful to them in doing these things.

This chapter examines what operations management is all about and tells how it can help organizations control productivity and remain competitive. It examines the nature of operations management, emphasising the production/operations process. Attention is focused on the current productivity challenge and the role that operations management can play in meeting this challenge. The importance of product design, production planning, purchasing, inventory control, and work flow layout is explored as a way of describing the range and scope of operations management. Quality control is addressed with particular attention given to the philosophical differences between American and Japanese firms. Finally, consideration is given to worker involvement and the role of monetary rewards in getting things done. When you have finished studying the material in this chapter, you will be able to:

1. Describe the current productivity challenge facing American firms and suggest how they can deal with it.
2. Describe the production/operations process.
3. Discuss the role of technology in operations management.
4. Explain product design and the role of value engineering and value analysis.
5. Describe how the production planning process is carried out and the importance of master production schedules and product life cycles in this process.
6. State the role of purchasing and inventory control in operations management.
7. Discuss the three major types of work flow layout and when each is used.
8. Discuss the importance of quality control in operations management and tell how American firms can meet the Japanese challenge in this area.
9. Explain the importance of rewards when operations management is used for control purposes.

THE PRODUCTIVITY CHALLENGE

Productivity is measured by output/input

Productivity is measured by using the equation: output/input. If a company produces 10 widgets with an input of $10, the cost per widget is $1. If through labor saving tools and techniques the firm can reduce its input to $9 and still turn out the 10 widgets, productivity has increased. Another way of improving productivity is to use the same input while increasing the output, for example by turning out 11 widgets with $10 of input. A third way is to increase output faster than input. For example, the firm might replace an old machine with a new, expensive one and find that the increase in output more than justifies the expense of the new machine because of the boost it gives to productivity. In the area of operations management and control, productivity is a key consideration.

By the mid-1970s it had become obvious that productivity was a major problem for many American firms. Statistics showed that the productivity levels of most industrialized countries were outrunning those of the United States. Of greatest concern, perhaps, was the fact that U.S. productivity was slowing up dramatically.

However, during the 1980s things turned around. Productivity in the private nonfarm sector increased at a rate of 1.7 percent annually between 1982 and 1990 and is expected to increase by 1.4 percent each year during the 1990–1995 period; and increases in manufacturing labor productivity are expected to average 2.2 percent annually over the entire period.[1] As a result, the projections for productivity are quite optimistic when compared to more recent experience. Yet there is still a long way to go as management seeks additional ways to improve productivity.[2]

Productivity Truths

As management has searched for answers to the productivity problem, three basic truths have come to the fore. Arnold Judson, a management consultant, has explained them this way:

Basic truths about productivity

1. Management effectiveness is by far the single greatest cause of declining productivity in the United States.
2. Most companies' efforts to improve productivity are misdirected and uncoordinated.
3. Tax disincentives, the decline of the work ethic, problems with government regulation, obsolete plant and equipment, insufficient R&D, and poor labor relations all have little to do with industry's faltering productivity.[3]

After conducting research among 236 top-level executives representing a cross section of 195 U.S. industrial firms, Judson found that there were a number of things American firms were doing wrong in their efforts to increase productivity. The major one was that their scope of productivity improvement was too narrow. They were focusing almost exclusively on cost savings in one or another part of the company. This piecemeal approach was providing short-run benefits only.

A second major problem was that many firms were focusing their efforts on the symptoms rather than on their causes. They addressed productivity problems as they appeared rather than trying to find out what was behind the problems in the first place.

Third, few companies had top management involved in their productivity efforts. In the main, the top staff were lukewarm in their support.

How must the productivity problem be addressed? Judson has recommended two important steps. First, management must view productivity as an overall organizational problem and not one that is confined to specific

---

[1] U.S. Department of Labor, Bureau of Labor Statistics, "Economic Projections for 1995," 1988, pp. 13–15.

[2] Steven C. Wheelright, "Restoring our Competitive Edge in U.S. Manufacturing," *California Management Review* (Spring 1985):26–42, and Kim B. Clark and Robert H. Hayes, "Recapturing America's Manufacturing Heritage," *California Management Review* (Summer 1988):9–33.

[3] Arnold S. Judson, "The Awkward Truth About Productivity," *Harvard Business Review* (September–October 1982):93.

departments or units. Second, management must attack the problem on a long-term basis, developing and executing productivity plans that will solve today's problems and also address those that may arise in the future.[4]

Achieving Increased Productivity

Recent research reveals that firms seeking to increase their productivity have certain key elements in their programs. After talking to firms such as Beatrice Foods, Burger King, General Foods, Honeywell, Hughes Aircraft, and Kaiser Aluminum, Y. K. Shetty, a well-known researcher, reports that successful productivity improvement programs have six key elements.[5]

Top management support is needed

First, as Judson also found, top management support is required. Unless an organization's managers and employees are convinced that a productivity improvement program has top management's support, they are unlikely to take the program seriously. This support can come in various ways. For example, at Beatrice Foods, the firm uses speeches, meetings, and a productivity philosophy booklet to illustrate its support for the program. At Honeywell a memo is used to announce the program, and then a meeting between top management and the general managers of the operating divisions lets the latter know that the program has executive support.

A support structure is required

Second, an organizational structure has to be established to support the productivity improvement objective. Quite often there is one person charged with this function, but he or she is given additional support in the form of a committee. For example, at Honeywell a corporate productivity administrator is responsible for assisting in the day-to-day implementation of productivity programs. A productivity steering committee, consisting of five top officials and the administrator, shares the responsibility for developing a program both to educate and to assist divisions and functional groups in measuring and improving productivity. Additionally, the firm uses productivity coordinators in its divisions, plants, and departments to chair group meetings with the workers in these units. At Beatrice Foods an operating service department is responsible for productivity efforts. It provides productivity improvement orientation and assistance to operating units and conducts productivity improvement projects. At Detroit Edison the top-level Productivity Committee is charged with surveying the firm's 65 departments, establishing productivity training programs for the managers and supervisors, and assisting the departments in establishing measurement systems and action programs.

---

[4] For more on productivity and management, see Carlton P. McNamara, "Productivity Is Management's Problem," *Business Horizons* (March–April 1983):55–61, "The Revival of Productivity," *Business Week* (Feb. 13, 1984):92–100, and Wickham Skinner, "The Productivity Paradox," *Harvard Business Review* (July–August 1986):55–59.
[5] Y. K. Shetty, "Key Elements of Productivity Improvement Programs," *Business Horizons* (March–April 1982):15–22.

Third, the company climate must be conducive to a productivity effort. Shetty reports that there are four major things that can be done to create the "right" company climate. The first is to make the employees aware that management is pushing for increased productivity. During this phase a company should announce its productivity objectives and describe the tools and techniques that are available to attain its goal. The second thing management must do is communicate with the employees to be sure that they understand these objectives. In the third phase the company must encourage employee involvement. This is typically done by putting the personnel on committees and involving them in discussions about ways to improve productivity. Finally, the company must recognize the contributions of the personnel through appropriate reward systems. Many companies give bonuses to individuals or groups that develop cost-saving techniques. Citations and employee- or manager-of-the month awards are other common rewards used to recognize contributions.

A conducive corporate climate is important

Fourth, the firm must design methods of measuring productivity progress and set realistic goals. Some of the most common measurements of progress include units per man hour, sales per payroll dollar, sales per employee, sales per asset dollar, and costs per unit. Given the wide range of possible measurements, each firm chooses those that are most useful for its own operations. In setting realistic goals, most firms seek attainable and quantifiable objectives on which they can secure data for measurement purposes. Then based on this information, the company can determine how well it is doing, where problems still exist, and how to correct them.[6]

Productivity progress must be measured

Fifth, the firm must be continually on the lookout for new techniques for productivity improvement. Some of the most common approaches include work simplification, value analysis, value engineering, automation, suggestions systems, time and motion studies, simulation models, and job enrichment. (See also "Management in Practice: Robots Increase in Functional Positions.") On an overall company basis, many companies are turning to produce specialization, cutting away their excess plant and equipment, and turning out low cost, high quality, consumer-demanded items.[7]

New productivity techniques must be sought

Sixth, there must be a schedule for implementing the productivity program and committing resources. As Shetty puts it, "productivity improvement . . . has to be planned and systematically pursued."[8] Recent research shows that many firms are indeed implementing productivity improvement programs. Since the early 1980s, business has been increasing the amount of money it has been pumping into R&D. The American work force is becoming more experienced at its jobs; more capital per worker is being invested; and productivity is beginning to rise.

Implementation schedules must be formulated

---

[6] See also: W. Bruce Chew, "No-Nonsense Guide to Measuring Productivity," *Harvard Business Review* (January–February 1988):110–118.

[7] See, for example, Agis Salpukas, "Plants to Be Smaller, More Effective," *New York Times* (February 2, 1984):D 1.

[8] Shetty, *Key Elements,* 22.

Robots Increase in Functional Positions

Three companies have recently introduced modern robotic advances for the 1990s. Ford Motor Company's assembly line in Lorain, Ohio, covers 61,000 square feet and produces 78 Ford Thunderbirds and Mercury Cougars per hour. The line, which was built to significantly increase productivity and to achieve consistent quality, is being used by Ford to introduce an entirely new concept of building cars. The system completes assembly of front suspensions and rear axles, assembles the under carriages and power trains, and joins the chassis module to the body (a process known as decking). Each of the two decking lines contains a declining station, a fully automatic bolt-fastening station, and a delatch station. The system also features 11 jointed arm robots and 3 gantry robots; 6 gantry pick-and-place devices; 15 automatic bolt-fastening stations; and 31 automatic assembly stations.

Battelle of Columbus, Ohio, has designed a concept for a robotic vehicle that NASA could build to help erect a radio observatory on the moon early in the next century. The vehicle has been designed to deploy itself based on radio signals from earth instructing it on specific direction, speed, and range of travel. As it has been designed to operate without humans aboard; the onboard computer allows the vehicle to avoid obstacles. Additionally, it can scale slopes up to 30°, climb over objects up to one foot high, and travel through crevasses up to one meter wide. Finally, the vehicle's navigation system will use laser triangulation calibration to determine precise locations.

Cybernation, Inc. of Roanoke, Virginia will fill an order for an environmentally hardened version of an autonomous, mobile robot for deployment in one of the Savannah River's operating nuclear reactors. The order includes one robot of Cybernation's advanced sonar imaging system, several optical docking and auto charging stations, and base station equipment. The robot navigates by a hierarchical system including dead reckoning, optical docking, and sonar imaging. Communications with the robot will be by redundant radio modems and an infrared optical transponder. The robot will also be equipped with a radiation hardened TV camera and video transmitter. The robot will be directed by a remote dispatcher computer which will compile optimized patrol programs and download them for execution. These three examples clearly illustrate that during the 1990s robots will be used increasingly in functional positions.

Source: Anne M. Hayner, Rita R. Schreiber, and Robert N. Stauffer, "Assembly Automation Builds Better Fords," *Manufacturing Engineering* (December 1989):38; and "Moon Bound Robot," *Manufacturing Engineering* (May 1989):36; and "Robot Roams Reactor," *Manufacturing Engineering* (July 1989):32.

THE NATURE OF OPERATIONS MANAGEMENT

Operations management is receiving renewed interest

Operations management is the process of designing, operating, and controlling a production system that transforms physical resources and human effort into goods and services. The field of operations management includes production management and is often referred to as "Ops Management" or "P/OM," which stands for production and operations management. In any event, over the last decade the field of operations management has received renewed interest. Not since the days of Frederick Taylor and his followers has management been as concerned with this subject. One reason is that, again and again, other countries, most notably Japan, are proving that they can produce lower-cost and higher-quality goods than the United States. In an effort to become competitive, management is again looking to the factory floor.

Given these latest developments, students of management need at least a basic understanding of operations management. Other important reasons for a knowledge of the field include the following: (1) production, in one form or another, is a major area of concern for all organizations; (2) this function has extensive command over the total resources and assets of most organizations; (3) industrial societies depend heavily on the outputs of production organizations; and (4) the production function is directly related to many of society's most urgent problems, including inflation, productivity, and resource scarcity.[9]

Production/Operations Process

The production/operations process has three basic phases: input, transformation process, and output. The **inputs** are the resources used in creating the goods and services. The transformation process uses machinery, tools, and techniques to convert the inputs into outputs. The outputs are the finished goods or services that will be sold to the customer or used to create still other goods or services.

Inputs

Inputs include materials and human talent

The most common inputs are materials and human talents. In the production of an automobile, for example, materials include such things as aluminum, steel, glass, plastic, and rubber. The human talents include semiskilled and skilled laborers as well as management and the administrative staff. In the case of hospital health care, the inputs include ambulances, hospital rooms, beds, medicines, and equipment, while the human talents consist of the medical skills of the doctors and the nursing staff and the support services of the other personnel. As seen in Figure 16-1, the production/operations process relates to any conversion process used in producing goods and services.

Transformation Process

The transformation process changes inputs into outputs

The **transformation process** consists of the production activities that take the inputs and combine them in some special way so as to produce the desired

---

[9] Charles G. Andrew and George A. Johnson, "The Crucial Importance of Production and Operations Management," *Academy of Management Review* (January 1982):145.

FIGURE 16-1
Production/
Operations Process
in Action: Four
Examples

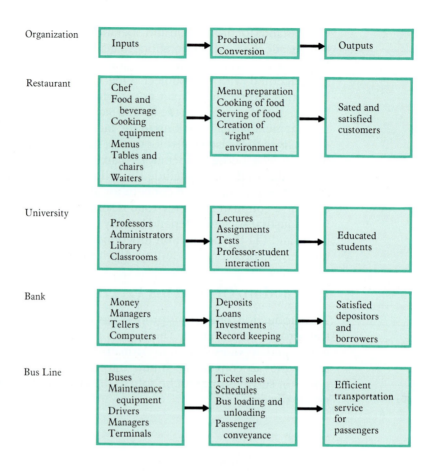

outputs. In the case of the automobile, transformation involves manufacturing the various parts of the car and then assembling them properly. The nature of the process becomes particularly clear when one watches an auto frame make its way down the assembly line. In the case of a hospital, the transformation process consists of such activities as assigning patients to rooms, evaluating their current state of health, providing medication, operating on those who require such procedure, providing food, taking X rays, charting recovery progress, and discharging patients on the doctor's approval.

Output

Outputs are the result of the transformation process

The **output** is the final result of the transformation process. In the case of the automobile, it is a completely assembled, ready-to-drive car. In the case of a patient, it is an individual who is well enough to leave the care of the hospital and complete the medical recovery at home.

Technology and Operations Management

Sweeping economic and technological changes are challenging manufacturing operations worldwide. Companies that are not aggressively seeking to transform their operations into cost-competitive systems are finding themselves losing market share quickly. A recent survey by SRI International revealed the following facts related to global manufactures:

- Nearly all are focusing on ways to improve quality and productivity while reducing costs on a continuing basis.
- Most now view manufacturing operations as strategic — which is as it should have been.
- Only 20 percent are satisfied with their manufacturing competitiveness and productivity.
- All are trying to increase the use of manufacturing technology.[10]

These facts have lead to a new awareness of the importance of technology and operations management. As one researcher states:

> The main goal is to reduce time and cost of delivery while maintaining the highest quality product. Consequently, the mission statement of manufacturing must be: To manufacture and distribute diversified products through innovative, flexible processes that optimize resources to achieve the required standards of quality, consistency, cost, and delivery in order to enable marketing to profitably sell the products.[11]

The Automated Factory

The dollars invested in automation are growing worldwide. In 1988 America invested $19.4 billion in material-handling equipment, machine-vision systems, process controls, robotics, and manufacturing software. This was a 13 percent increase over the investment in 1987. Figure 16-2 illustrates the projected increases through 1992. Currently, the U.S. accounts for approximately 43 percent of the world's manufacturing-automation market of $45 billion. In Europe, West Germany accounts for approximately 26 percent, while in Asia Japan accounts for 28 percent.

More and more firms are realizing that they cannot compete in the marketplace unless they are able to reduce their costs and increase their outputs. Technology in the form of the automated factory is helping them to achieve these goals. For example, the Flexible Manufacturing Laboratory at the Robotics

---

[10] Otis Port, "A New Vision for the Factory," *Business Week* (June 16, 1989):146.
[11] Nick W. McGaughey, "The Manufacturing Connection: A Competitive Requirement," *Industrial Management* (January – February 1988):23.

FIGURE 16-2
America's Rising
Investment In
Automation

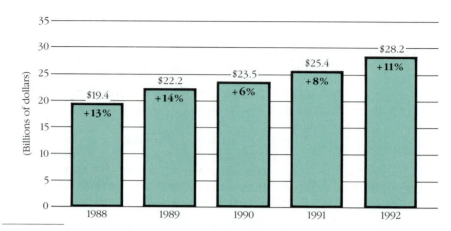

Source: Dataquest reported in John S. McClenahen, "Automation's Global Game," *Industry Week* (June 20, 1988):40.

Institute of Carnegie Mellon University is developing a physical environment to completely automate machining. The idea is to replace the eyes, ears, touch, and hands of a machinist by providing motive power from a collection of "expert" systems. During 1989 Volkswagen AG placed a $28 million dollar order for robotics, which represents one of the largest robot orders ever by a European company. By 1985 the industrial robot population of the USSR had increased to 14,300, and that number is projected to triple by 1990. In addition, socialist countries alone are expected to have 200,000 industrial robots installed by 1990.[12] In the United States a total of $249.3 million of robots were sold in 1987.[13] (Also see "Management in Practice: The New Robot with the Human Touch.")

Over the last two decades many technological advances have been made. First came numerically controlled machine tools that performed automatic operations according to coded instructions received from paper or tape. Then came computer-aided design and computer-aided manufacturing, CAD and CAM for short, which replaced the drafting board with a cathode ray tube screen. At the same time the numerical control tape was replaced with a computer. One of the most recent developments has been **flexible manufacturing systems**, FMS for short, which integrates all of these elements. Here is how *Fortune* described these systems:

> They consist of computer-controlled machining centers that sculpt complicated metal parts at high speed and with great reliability, robots that handle the parts, and remotely guide cars that deliver materials. The components

---

[12] Robert Eade, "Robots on the Comeback," *Manufacturing Engineering* (October 1989):51.
[13] John S. McClenahen, "Automation's Global Game," *Industry Week* (June 20, 1988):37–64.

The New Robot With the Human Touch

A new microelectric sensing device—an electronic fingertip—developed at the University of Michigan (UM) will now allow robots to closely mimic the human sense of touch, according to Kensall D. Wise, UM professor of electrical engineering and computer science. Robots equipped with this sensing device will now be able to select parts or objects from a bin of assorted parts with great reliability.

This tactile imager converts degrees of pressure to electronic signals that are then processed by a computer. The greater the pressure, the stronger the signal. Then, by analyzing the electronic pattern produced by the raised projections of an object pressing against the tactile sensor, the computer can tell the robot whether it has selected the correct object.

A feedback mechanism between the tactile imager and the computer allows the robot to handle delicate objects, while a control mechanism in the computer's software compares pressure on the tactile imager with programmed information about the optimum force for the type of object that the robot is handling. The computer then directs the robot to increase or decrease the pressure as necessary.

According to Wise, the UM sensor has the highest resolution and accuracy of any imager developed yet due to its capacitor-based design. These capacitors, which are made of silicon, do not lose their resiliency over time, as do most commercial tactile imagers using carbon-impregnated foam rubber or polymer pads. As a result, we now have a robot with a human touch.

Source: "Bin-Picking Robot Has Electronic Fingers," *Manufacturing Engineering* (August 1989):30–32.

are linked by electronic controls that dictate what will happen at each stage of the manufacturing sequence, even automatically replacing wornout or broken drill bits and other implements.[14]

FMS allows for flexible manufacturing

Best of all, FMS allows companies to produce small quantities of goods at a low price. In the past, large volume production was necessary in order to achieve low cost per unit or economy of scale. With flexible automation it is possible for firms to produce one, two, or a handful of items as efficiently as a production line designed to produce one million of them. FMS allows more frequent setups which allow product batch sizes to be reduced. As a result, defects are detected faster. With smaller quantities scrap and rework are reduced, manufacturing lead times are cut, and inventories are slashed dramatically. Additionally, by carefully designing the factory layout, an organization can reduce the number of people needed to run the operation. For example, the

---

[14] Gene Bylinsky, "The Race to the Factory Floor," *Fortune* (February 21, 1983):53. See also "FMS—Where the Action Is," *Production* (August 1986):74–94, and Ramchandran Jaikumar "Post Industrial Manufacturing," *Harvard Business Review* (November–December 1986):69–76.

Yanazaki plant near Nagoya, Japan has 65 computer-controlled machine tools and 34 robots linked by a fiber optic cable to the computerized design center back at plant headquarters. The facility is so automated that it needs less than 10 percent of the workforce found in the average factory. With many of these systems, the automation computer provides the plant's management with a real-time link to exactly what is occurring on the production lines.

This highly automated approach is now spreading to the United States. In 1987, the total FMS market was $870 million, and by 1992 it is projected to be $2.9 billion.[15] What managers seem to like best about it is that a firm can automate gradually. It does not have to stop production and convert everything to computers. The areas that would profit most from computerization can be converted while everything else is done as before. The "smart" factory of the 1990s will offer new possibilities just as FMSs gave new promise in the 1980s. Smart factories are ones in which electronic causeways between all of the separate automated islands are connected not only to each other but also to a managing database that governs all operation assembly functions in separate local area networks (LANs).

Developments such as these are leading businesses to realize that they have too long neglected the operations management side of things. New concepts and terminology such as statistical process control (SPC), just-in-time production (JIT), quality assurance (QA), team-oriented problem solving (TOPS), quality functional deployment (QFD), and total quality management (TQM) have become "buzzwords" of both business and manufacturing firms for the 1990s. The old manufacturing plant that thrived on large production runs is being replaced by more efficient, flexible systems. Most important, managers are beginning to realize that a focus on operations management and technology is perhaps the best way to make the U.S. competitive in the world market.

Time — The Competitive Edge

Automation is only part of the solution to the challenges confronting U.S. manufacturing. The other factor for success is the management of time — in production, new product development, sales, and distribution. Quickly developing, producing, and distributing products can bring about a new competitive advantage. Figure 16-3 illustrates the improvements in development time and production time for some companies. One author believes that as a strategic weapon, time can be as powerful as money, productivity, quality, and even innovation.[16]

---

[15] Yash P. Gupta, "Human Aspects of Flexible Manufacturing Systems," *Production and Inventory Management Journal* (Second Quarter 1989):30–35.

[16] George Stalk, Jr., "Time — The Next Source of Competitive Advantage," *Harvard Business Review* (July–August 1988):41–51.

FIGURE 16-3
Superfast
Innovators and
Producers

Innovators		Development time	
Company	Product	*Old*	*New*
Honda	cars	5 years	3 years
AT&T	phones	2 years	1 year
Navistar	trucks	5 years	2.5 years
Hewlett-Packard	computer printers	4.5 years	22 mos.

Producers		Order-to-finished-goods time	
Company	Product	*Old*	*New*
GE	circuit breaker boxes	3 weeks	3 days
Motorola	pagers	3 weeks	2 hours
Hewlett-Packard	electronic testing equipment	4 weeks	5 days
Brunswick	fishing reels	3 weeks	1 week

Source: Brian Dummaine, "How Managers Can Succeed Through SPEED," *Fortune,* (February 13, 1989):56.

In order to slash production times, U.S. manufacturers are implementing new approaches, such as DFM—design for manufacturability and concurrent engineering. With DFM, the product is engineered for easy assembly—by reducing the number of parts or shunning screws for snap-fit fasteners. NCR Corporation used DFM on its latest point-of-sale terminal and fashioned a system that can be put together in less than two minutes—blindfolded. Concurrent engineering, meanwhile, involves simultaneous development of both the product and the process to make it.[17]

Thus, ideas are getting into the production cycle faster, manufacturing systems are becoming more automated in the concept-to-production style, and ongoing refinements can be made more easily than ever before.

DESIGN OF A PRODUCTION SYSTEM

One of the major dimensions of operations management is the design of a production system.[18] This phase of operations comes early in the process. During this phase management decides the specific physical dimensions of the

---

[17] Port, *op cit.*, p. 146.
[18] James W. Dean and Gerald I. Susman, "Organizing For Manufacturing Design," *Harvard Business Review* (January–February 1989):28–36.

goods or services to be produced. Quite often the process begins with research designed to generate new product or service ideas. After the research is complete, the company selects the ideas that are feasible, marketable, and compatible with the organization's strategy. Finally, it designs the product or service. During this final step the company addresses issues such as quality, cost, and reliability. Figure 16-4 provides an overall view of the product design process.

In recent years management has come to realize that a well-formulated product or service can greatly increase profit. In fact, if the offering is well designed, the costs of making changes or correcting mistakes can be foregone and greater profit can be generated. Unfortunately, this seldom happens. Firms tend to be in too much of a hurry to get things produced. For example, a few years ago Ford Motor found that 2.7 million of its four- and six-cylinder engines had a design flaw. They were susceptible to wearing out in cold climates. In an effort to save money, two oil holes that would normally have been drilled into the piston connecting rods had been left out. The financial results were disastrous. The cost of correcting the flaw in the 56,000 recalls was $250 per car for a total of $14 million.[19] Such problems can often be minimized, if not avoided, if a firm uses effective value engineering and value analysis techniques.

Value Engineering/Value Analysis

Value engineering (VE) is the analysis of new products and the application of research and development concepts to these products for the purpose of designing the most efficient, lowest cost, highest quality output. **Value analysis** (VA) is the analysis of existing production products, specifications, and requirements demanded by production documents and purchase requests. Together VE/VA helps an organization attain its desired production objectives at the lowest cost and highest quality.[20]

If VE were properly applied in the design stage, VA could be eliminated. This usually does not happen, however. Typically, something goes wrong and the company has to turn to value analysis to straighten it out. In doing so, many firms use a team approach. The team often consists of personnel from engineering, design, purchasing, production, marketing, quality, and cost departments. The group uses its collective judgment to improve both the design and the follow-up value analysis. The results can be impressive as seen by the following reported examples:

Reported benefits of VA and VE

A machinery contractor using regular carbide inserts doubled output by switching to coated carbide cutting tools without adding machines or increasing the size of the workforce.

---

[19] "What Clouds Ford's Future?" *Business Week* (July 31, 1978):73.
[20] Vincent G. Reuter, "Value Engineering/Value Analysis: Valuable Management Techniques," *Industrial Management* (November–December 1983):2.

FIGURE 16-4
Design of a
Production System

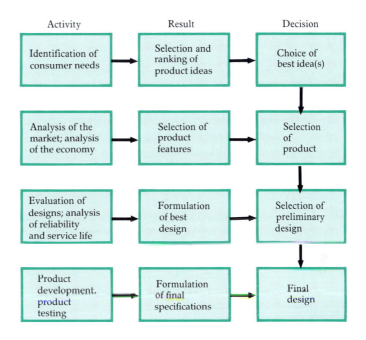

A firm packaging bottles of shampoo for distributors in plain chipboard cartons changed to a 6-pack holder similar to that used in the beverage industry and saved over $100,000 in the first year.

A large equipment manufacturer saved $18 for each dollar spent in VE/VA effort covering 2,000 projects and using a permanent four-person committee to head up the program.

Honeywell, on defense contracts and within the company, found that the costs of VE/VA implementation were never more than one-tenth of the savings therefrom and that in a recent year they saved 18.1 dollars for every VE/VA dollar spent.[21]

Computer-Aided Design

Applications of
CAM

Another product design development that is being used by many firms is CAD/CAM (computer-aided design/computer-aided manufacturing). In the case of CAD, for example, engineers can now produce blueprints without ever lifting a pencil. Using an input device, the engineer can draw directly on a cathode ray tube (CRT). The pen, which is connected to the CRT by a wire, feeds information to the computer system. Once the outline is placed on the CRT, the engineer can then rotate it, view the design from any angle, stretch it out, color or shade it, and change or add depth so as to produce a 3-D version of the drawing.

---

[21] Reuter, "Value Engineering/Value Analysis," 1–2.

The engineer can also call up reference drawings that have been programmed into the computer's memory and incorporate them into the engineering design. If the engineer wants to redesign just a section of the drawing, he or she merely fits the redesigned piece into the sketch. The entire design does not have to be redrawn. As a result of such computer-aided techniques, the engineer can correct mistakes and make changes as he or she goes along. Then, when the design is finished, a hard copy can be produced with just the touch of a button.[22]

CAM is also proving to be very useful. In particular, it allows manufacturers to produce different sizes of a particular part, as well as a number of different parts within a given size range, by simply changing the programmed instructions that guide the machine.

> Caterpillar, the large tractor company, for example, uses CAM to make components for an engine drive assembly. About a dozen machines stand on both sides of a railroad-like track . . . along which a transfer device shuttles parts among the work stations, where some 30 to 40 separate machining operations are carried out. Operators at entry and exit points clamp the part on and off the transfer mechanism; the rest of the process is computer driven.
>
> Another use of CAM is illustrated by a leading automobile manufacturer which uses the technology to weld gas tanks. In designing the tank, engineers chose a five-sided, irregular shape in which no two sides were parallel. Were the operation manual, someone would have to turn the tank at each stage; but with CAM, a complex welding system molds the individual sides precisely to the specifications—ensuring quality control even for such a nonstandard design.[23]

PRODUCTION PLANNING

Production planning is the process whereby management meshes demand forecasts for goods and services with scheduled resource outputs. At this phase the firm's strategic sales forecast and production plan are brought together. After determining annual demand for each good and service, the firm breaks down these forecasts into short-term production plans with detailed schedules. The schedules describe manpower, equipment, and inventory requirements. During this process, management answers questions such as:

---

[22] John McElroy, "CAD/CAM Comes of Age," *Automotive Industries* (July 1981):36.
[23] Bela Gold, "CAM Sets New Rules for Production," *Harvard Business Review* (November–December 1982):90. For still more on this subject, see Donald Gerwin, "Manufacturing Flexibility in the CAM Era," *Business Horizons* (January–February 1989):78–84.

1. What product lines will be produced?
2. How much of each line will be produced?
3. How much material and other inputs will be needed to turn out each of these lines?
4. How many personnel will be required to produce these goods?
5. What types of technology and machinery will be needed to get all of this work done?

Master Production Schedules

If there are many different items being produced at the same time, coordination of production activities becomes extremely important. In meeting the challenge to coordinate activities, many firms use a master production schedule. This schedule takes into account all of the raw materials, subcomponents, components, machines, fabrication, and assembly operations that have to be carried out to produce the desired goods. If properly drawn up, the master schedule incorporates all of the production activities; and if properly implemented, it serves to ensure that everything is done efficiently and on time.

Unfortunately, bottlenecks occur frequently in production operations. Some crucial component does not arrive from the supplier, or a machine breakdown results in the need to delay the final assembly of a unit. When a bottleneck occurs, the master schedule can be consulted in order to find ways of working around the problem and to keep other jobs on time. In determining how to reschedule jobs, the master schedule is a vital document. It helps management keep track of the current status of all work and decide how to deal with problems. The schedule also provides a sound basis for decisions about staffing.

Product Life Cycles

Production planning and scheduling have to be tied to the product life cycle of the goods. Some products have very long life cycles (5 years or more) while others have very short ones. Working closely with the marketing department, the operations management people schedule production so that it coincides with the various phases of the product's life cycle.

In recent years many firms have found that the life cycle for their products is growing shorter. Competitors are flocking into the marketplace at a rapid rate, making older products obsolete more quickly. As a result, firms are turning to shorter production runs for their goods. When these runs are complete, the firm then tools up and begins production of another product. Quite often it is a more up-to-date version of the earlier offering. In this way the company reduces the problems associated with manufacturing goods for which there is little, if any, demand. The Japanese have been particularly skillful at tying production planning and scheduling to product life cycles. Casio, famous for its manufacture of watches and pocket calculators, is a good example. An engineering, marketing, and assembly company, with only a small investment in production facilities and marketing channels, Casio relies heavily on its production-marketing flexibility. It produces goods with very short product life cycles. As soon as Casio comes out with a product such as a calculator, it begins reducing the price to discourage competition. Then, within a few months, it introduces an improved version of the product, for example a calculator that plays musical notes when the numerical keys are touched.

> In Casio's case, the . . . strategy is to integrate design and development into marketing so that consumers' desires are analyzed by those closest to the market and quickly converted into engineering blueprints. Because Casio has this function so well developed, it can afford to make its new products obsolete quickly. Its competitors, all organized vertically on the assumption of a one- or two-year life cycle for this type of product, are at a severe disadvantage.[24]

PURCHASING AND INVENTORY CONTROL

Two other major areas of operations management are purchasing and inventory control. The two are interrelated in that firms usually purchase materials and parts and store them until they are used. Not wanting to have too much on hand at any one time, however, they seek to balance the risk associated with stockouts against the costs of storing excess amounts.

Purchasing Practices and Organization

Almost every firm purchases some things from outside suppliers. Even large corporations rely on external vendors to provide them with some of the materials and parts needed in operations. As a result, it is important to have well-defined purchasing practices and an organizational structure that can efficiently handle purchase decisions.

Purchasing practices differ from firm to firm, but there are some general ones used by many. Some of the most common include the following:

Common purchasing practices

1. A centralized purchasing department buys all of the major items that are supplied by outside vendors.
2. Minor purchases or one-of-a-kind items are bought directly by the departments that need them.

---

[24] Kenichi Ohmae, *The Mind of the Strategist: The Art of Japanese Management* (New York: McGraw-Hill Book Company, 1982), 117–118. For more on this topic, see Robert H. Hayes and Steven C. Wheelwright, "Link Manufacturing Process and Product Life Cycles," *Harvard Business Review* (January–February 1979):133–40.

3. Buyers are required to have a solid understanding of the engineering specifications and requirements of all items being purchased from outside.
4. All purchases in excess of $10,000 are handled on the basis of low bid commensurate with the reputation of the supplier.
5. No special rebates or favors are accepted from any suppliers regardless of the conditions under which they are offered.

Guidelines of this nature are designed to ensure that the company is able to obtain the best quality merchandise at the fairest possible prices. In many cases these guidelines apply directly to the purchasing department since it is responsible for the purchase of expensive components and parts as well as for all large orders, regardless of the individual cost per item in the order. The centralization of large purchase orders is both logical and cost saving. From the standpoint of logic, as the purchasing people become increasingly familiar with how and where to buy, they begin to save the firm money. In shopping for vendors, they learn the questions to ask and the ways to size up the seller. Additionally, since they are doing this job on a full-time basis, they will eventually prove superior to the individual department personnel for whom purchasing is a side duty. By buying in large quantities, the purchasing department is also in a better position to negotiate the best possible price with the suppliers.

Inventory Control Practices

Earlier in the text the value of the economic order quantity formula was discussed. At that point it was noted that every firm attempts to balance product demand with the amount of product inventory on hand. Operations management is concerned with more than just computing an EOQ formula for each product line, however. Many firms are also using material requirements planning and just-in-time production methods.

Material Requirements Planning

MRP helps control materials and inventory

Material requirements planning (MRP) is a systematic, comprehensive manufacturing and controlling technique used to increase the efficiency both of material handling and of inventory control. The master production schedule is the basis of an MRP system, and most MRPs are computerized because of the large amount of data processing that must be done. The formulation of an MRP begins with an annual sales forecast, which is used to get an initial idea of the demand for the company's products. Each of these products is "exploded" to determine the materials and parts that will be needed to produce it. The amount of inventory on hand is then subtracted from the total that will be needed, to arrive at the amount that has to be ordered. Then the time between the placement of an order and the expected delivery date is calculated along with lead time necessary to ensure that materials and parts are received in time for production. The forecast and the materials requirement plan often have to be revised on the basis of actual sales so that demand and supply can be kept in balance. When the system works properly, the firm can avoid costly ripple effects from either a sharp, unexpected drop in sales or delivery problems created by suppliers.

MRP is becoming increasingly popular because of the benefits it offers in controlling inventory and adjusting for changes in the economic environment. One national study of MRP found that the benefits of the system can be extremely high.

> Installation costs ranged from less than $100,000 for small companies to more than $1 million for large ones. But the average increase in annual inventory turnover was an astounding 50.3%. For the typical company with $65 million in annual sales, that made possible an inventory reduction of about $8 million, and a saving of $1.8 million per year in carrying costs calculated at recent interest rates. Some companies reported that MRP had enabled them to cut in half the amount of money tied up in inventories for each dollar of sales. The new system also improved service to customers: the average lead time for deliveries declined 18%.[25]

JIT Production

JIT production is hand-to-mouth

Another development, related to inventory control, is just-in-time (JIT) inventory production. **JIT production** is the purchase, the production, or both the purchase and production of small quantities of products just in time for use. This hand-to-mouth approach leads to smaller inventories and reduces the need for storage space, inventory-related equipment such as forklifts and racks, and material support personnel. Most important, because of the absence of extra inventories, the organization is able to run an error-free operation.[26]

In some ways, JIT production is not new. Large organizations have always sought to minimize inventories while maintaining full-scale production. For example, at the Anheuser-Busch brewery in St. Louis there is only a two-hour supply of unfilled cans on hand at any time. The firm brings in empty cans on a continuous basis to replace depleted inventory allowing manufacturing to continue unimpeded. It is not necessary to produce a standard product, however, in order to use JIT production. It can also be employed in small operations and with multiple product lines.

The big problem with JIT production is that the company may run out of

---

[25] Lewis Beman, "A Big Payoff from Inventory," *Fortune* (July 27, 1981):78–79.
[26] G. H. Manoochehri, "Improving Productivity with Just-In-Time Inventory," *Journal of Systems Management* (January 1985), and Arjan T. Sadhwani, M. H. Sarhan, and Dayal Kiringoda, "Just-In-Time: An Inventory System Whose Time Has Come," *Management Accountant* (December 1985).

inventory from time to time, resulting in work stoppages. Yet this feature is not looked on negatively by operations management people. They see it as a way of pinpointing problem areas and working out solutions.

> . . . now the analysts and engineers pour out of their offices and mingle with foremen and workers trying to get production going again. Now the causes — bad raw materials, machine breakdown, poor training, tolerances that exceed process capabilities — get attention so that the problem may never recur.[27]

After these matters are resolved inventories are often cut again, creating still more problems. These, too, are addressed as the operations management people seek to improve efficiency still further. Is this really possible? Japanese firms have proven that it is, leading more American firms to follow suit.

Research shows that companies not using JIT production are now beginning to look seriously into adopting this technique. Richard Schonberger, an international expert on Japanese manufacturing techniques, has noted that the best way to adopt it is often "cold turkey." He recommends that firms get going and, "remove inventories from the shop floor, dismantle distance-spanning conveyors, move machines close together and permanently reallocate floor space that once held inventory." As a result, he predicts, "Spasms of work stoppage for lack of parts will soon get everyone involved in solving underlying problems.[28] For firms that want to employ a slower approach, incremental methods are available. One of the most common is to reduce machine setup costs. A second is to cut back inventory in an effort to implement JIT production. A third is to find local suppliers, thereby reducing delivery time.

> The only significant obstacles to JIT are those that stand in the way of any major change in management system: reorienting people's thinking. Much of that task has been done. Just-in-time programs have been established at General Electric, the big-three auto makers, Goodyear . . . and various other American industrial companies.
>
> Transforming our coughing, sputtering plants into streamlined just-in-time producers sounds like a 10- or 20-year project. It may not take that long because the innovating has been done for us. Taylor's innovation, scientific management, was readily exportable and implementable in Europe and Japan. . . . The Japanese innovation, just-in-time, is equally transportable.[29]

---

[27] Richard J. Schonberger, "A Revolutionary Way to Streamline the Factory," *Wall Street Journal* (November 15, 1982):24. See also: Uday Karmarkar, "Getting Control of Just-In-Time," *Harvard Business Review* (September – October, 1989):122 – 131.

[28] Schonberger, "Revolutionary Way," 24.

[29] Schonberger, "Revolutionary Way," 24.

WORK FLOW LAYOUT

Another critical area of operations management is **work flow layout**, the process of determining the physical arrangement of the production system. Work flow processes are important in converting inputs into outputs. If personnel and machines are scattered in a haphazard arrangement, productivity will suffer. If these machines can be arranged in an orderly, logical, cost-effective manner, productivity can be increased. In a well-designed work layout arrangement, some of the major benefits include (a) a minimization of investment, (b) more effective use of existing space, (c) a reduction in material handling costs and overall production time, (d) the maintenance of operational flexibility, and (e) the guarantee of employee safety and convenience.

Basic Layout Formats

Although there are many production layout configurations, there are three basic formats. These are the product layout, the process layout, and the fixed-position layout. All other layouts are simply variations of these three.

Product Layout

A product layout arranges resources in progressive steps

In a **product layout**, machines, equipment, and personnel are arranged according to the progressive steps used in building the product. A good example is found in auto assembly plants. As the basic frame of the car moves down the line, parts are put on it until a finished auto emerges at the end of the line. (See Figure 16-3). When large numbers of manufactured products are to be assembled, machines and personnel are often placed at fixed work-stations along the line with each making a contribution to the product as it moves past.

This type of layout has both advantages and disadvantages. On the positive side, the workers do not have to be very skilled. Most assembly lines are staffed with unskilled and semiskilled personnel. Additionally, one supervisor can usually oversee the work of many people. Some direct management costs tend to be low. On the negative side, the firm is locked into one type of layout. Changing to another major form is extremely costly. Second, the assembly line is no stronger than its weakest link. If a person cannot keep up or a machine goes down, it may be necessary to stop the line; if the firm runs out of an inventory item, such as headlights for the cars, it will be impossible to continue assembly. Finally, in recent years more and more workers have begun to rebel against the monotony, boredom, and specialization of the line. They want more authority and control of their work environment.

Process Layout

A process layout groups components on the basis of function

A **process layout** is one in which all components are grouped on the basis of the functions they perform. All lathe machines are placed in one area; all welding machines are placed together in another. In job shops where the product can be moved from one area to another, process layout works well. Yet the layout is not restricted to manufacturing. Hospitals (see Figure 16-5) also employ this layout. The patient is literally moved to some departments (X ray, surgery) while others come to him or her (dietetics, pharmacy). In any event, the functional arrangement of a process layout is infinitely superior for hospitals to that of a product layout.

The process layout has both advantages and disadvantages. On the positive side, process layouts are more flexible than product layouts. They are also more suitable for the custom processing of diverse outputs because they can address themselves to the specific needs of such processing. On the negative side, work must be scheduled carefully. Otherwise some departments will be overscheduled while others sit idle.

Fixed-Position Layout

With fixed-position layout, the workers come to the work

A **fixed-position layout** is one in which the workers come to the work. (See Figure 16-5). Aircraft, diesel locomotives, and oil tankers are produced using this kind of layout. The product is too large or heavy to be moved so the workers and the equipment come to the product.

FIGURE 16-5
Basic Layout Formats

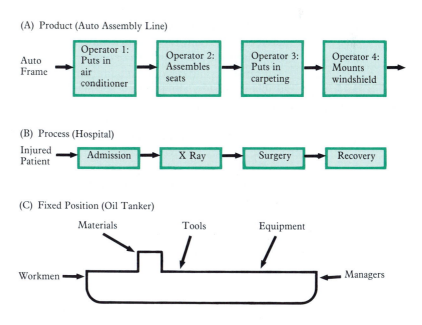

(A) Product (Auto Assembly Line)

Auto Frame → Operator 1: Puts in air conditioner → Operator 2: Assembles seats → Operator 3: Puts in carpeting → Operator 4: Mounts windshield →

(B) Process (Hospital)

Injured Patient → Admission → X Ray → Surgery → Recovery

(C) Fixed Position (Oil Tanker)

Materials   Tools   Equipment

Workmen →   ← Managers

Like the other kinds of layouts, this one has both advantages and disadvantages. On the positive side, the resources are efficiently used because it is too costly to build the product any other way. Additionally, workers like this form of layout because it allows them to move about during their work day. On the negative side, this work design is expensive because it requires the firm to duplicate resources. For example, if there are three ships being built simultaneously, the company has to have three times as many crews and three times as much equipment and materials.

QUALITY MANAGEMENT

The quest for product quality became a major strategy in the 1980s and this will continue in the current decade. For example, quality improvement and quality control programs have been gaining momentum in U.S. companies such as Westinghouse, Polaroid, Motorola, Ford, Hewlett-Packard, and Honeywell. However, the quality issue is a complex one because there are a number of attributes and aspects associated with quality.

> Quality attributes vary among industries. Perceived quality of an automobile, for example, may include performance, durability, styling, comfort, safety, finish, speed, competence of repair, and value. Airline quality may include ease of check-in, timely departure and arrival, safety, ease of check-out, seating comfort, cabin cleanliness, food, and flight attendants' courtesy.
>
> Quality attributes may also vary between firms. Perceived quality may be different at Lord and Taylor than K mart. The quality standards for Mercedes may differ from those for Volkswagen.
>
> Target markets and customer requirements are the basis for quality. Quality attributes include both products and service.[30]

In order to manage for quality one expert author in the area, J. M. Juran, established the Juran Trilogy. This trilogy consists of quality planning, quality control, and quality improvement.[31]

> Quality planning is the activity of developing the products and processes required to meet customers' needs. It involves a series of universal steps, essentially as follows:
>
> 1. Determine who the customers are.
> 2. Determine the needs of the customers.

---

[30] Y. K. Shetty, "Product Quality and Competitive Strategy," *Business Horizons* (May–June 1987):46–47.

[31] J. M. Juran, *Juran on Leadership for Quality* (New York: The Free Press, 1989), p. 21.

3. Develop product features that respond to customers' needs.
4. Develop processes that are able to produce those product features.
5. Transfer the resulting plans to the operating forces.[32]

Quality control is the process of ensuring that goods and services are produced according to predetermined specifications. Earlier in the text, quality circles were discussed. These circles are certainly one way of improving output quality, but they are not the only way. Many other approaches currently are being used, as American managers begin to emphasize quality.

Feedback and Feedforward

In Chapter 15, the control process was examined. Using feedback, the process seeks to correct mistakes after they are made. Quality control also makes use of **feedforward control** to help *avoid* problems in the first place. This kind of control focuses on the quality of the production inputs and the work process. By ensuring that inputs and conversion/transformation processes are being handled properly, the organization reduces the likelihood of product recalls, consumer complaints, and lost business.[33]

Feedforward control seeks to avoid problems

Operations management people work to balance the costs of feedback with the expenses associated with lack of quality. There is always a tradeoff between the two. For example, a company building an aircraft puts heavy emphasis on purchasing quality raw materials, subcomponents, components, and parts. As the work proceeds the firm also checks progress, ensuring that the craft is being built according to specifications. When the plane is completed, another series of quality checks is made. Finally, the machine is delivered to the customer. For the rest of its life, the plane's quality is judged on the basis of needed repairs and customer complaints.

Many of the control steps described in this example are feedforward in nature. Operations management people catch and correct quite a few errors. Some errors go undetected, however, and have to be picked up later. Still others are not sought because the cost of conducting the inspection is too high; it is more cost efficient to wait and get them later.

Philip B. Crosby, another noted quality expert, describes determination, education, and implementation as key elements in the installation of a quality program.[34] Obviously, the good in all of the aspects of quality management is to inject the quality element into the entire manufacturing system. The Japanese have paced the competition with their quality efforts and the U.S. must meet that challenge.

---

[32] Juran, *op. cit.,* p. 20.
[33] David M. Lascelles and Barrie G. Dale, "The Buyer-Supplier Relationship is Total Quality Management," *Journal of Purchasing and Materials Management* (Summer 1989):10–19.
[34] Philip B. Crosby, *Quality Without Tears* (New York: McGraw-Hill, 1984).

Meeting the Japanese Challenge

Beginning in the late 1960s, the Japanese started to provide strong competition in a number of different fields including household electronics, optics, shipbuilding, and steel. Since then they have expanded their offerings to include air conditioners, automobiles, calculators, computers, musical instruments, textiles, and watches, to name but six. In each case they have been successful in no small measure because of product quality. This quality emphasis is based on two points ingrained at all levels of Japanese industry:

- Do it right the first time. It is a waste of time, material, labor, and machines to separate good from bad production.
- Quality control is not a specialized production function. If there is a quality problem, it cannot be corrected by supervisors. Quality problems are due to problems in the production system and the system must be corrected.[35]

Japanese firms encourage quality consciousness

Japanese concepts of quality control are different from those followed by many western firms. (See Table 16-1.) Their ideas are put into practice by having the personnel assume a more involved role in responsibility for quality. Table 16-2 illustrates this contrast between American and Japanese firms. At Matsushita, for example, the philosophy of quality control includes such key elements as encouraging quality consciousness in the personnel, involving them in quality control circles, removing the potential for human error through automation, designing quality into the process, securing good quality components, and randomly inspecting the product.

> . . . design engineers meet twice a month with the component manager and quality reliability and related specifications. One to two product planning and cross-functional meetings take place each month for an exchange of ideas. Although the design engineer is responsible for design, he has frequent contact with customers. The first outline of the product plan includes careful calculation of quality, reliability, and cost. After this, drawings are made of the concept, and pilot production and testing begin. If the latter two processes are successful, a mass production sample is made, tested, and mass production begins. New or redesigned production systems are always considered in light of total quality control. Matsushita believes that each parameter of quality is new for each product, and design and production engineers determine the parameter jointly.[36]

In ensuring that the best quality components are received from the vendors, Japanese firms often have a personal financial investment in these sup-

---

[35] William A. Mahon and Richard E. Dyck, "Japanese Quality Systems From A Marketing Viewpoint," *Industrial Management* (September–October 1982):10.

[36] Mahon and Dyck, "Japanese Quality Systems," 12.

TABLE 16-1   Concepts of Quality

Western	Japanese
Higher quality will bring about higher cost and lower productivity.	Higher quality will bring about lower costs and high productivity.
Quality is the responsibility of the Quality Control Department people.	Everyone is responsible for quality control.
With large production runs, low costs per unit can be achieved.	With small production runs, low costs per unit can be achieved.
There is a tradeoff between cost, quality, and delivery.	There need never be a tradeoff between cost, quality, and delivery.
Poor quality should be kept at a minimum.	Poor quality should be totally eliminated.

pliers. They also work closely with them, helping the vendors improve their quality and delivery time. The firms believe in "co-prosperity" with the suppliers. At Toshiba, for example, the Quality Assurance Systems Department develops instructions for component suppliers and makes an annual review of all vendors to determine which should be given additional business and which should be terminated.

Japanese firms also make heavy use of computerized operations. They have come to realize that a highly mechanized, technologically advanced production system is not only efficient but eliminates human error. This approach is complemented by random inspections made by quality control people. In the case of many products, the inspection is quite rigorous. For example, Matsushita carefully inspects one out of ten TV sets, switching the machine on for six

TABLE 16-2   Role of Personnel in Quality Control

American	Japanese
Management has a short-term view of operations.	Management has a long-term view of operations.
Employees are judged on productivity and their individual contribution.	Employees are judged on work contribution, quality, cleanliness, and assistance to others.
Employees perform specific tasks within well-defined job descriptions.	Employees perform their own jobs and others for which they have the ability and time.
Employees have low organizational commitment and are responsible for their jobs only.	Employees have high organizational commitment and share responsibility for accomplishment.
Scrap rates vary between 1 and 5 percent and there is a large amount of work in progress.	Scrap rates are usually less than one half of 1 percent and there is a minimum amount of work in progress.
Quality checks are performed by inspectors.	Quality checks are performed by each worker.
Unions have an adversary relationship with management. Strikes are accepted as legitimate bargaining tools.	There are company unions and no adversarial relationships. Most grievances are quickly settled; strikes are vary rare.

hours and off for two, at a temperature of 40°C and 80 percent humidity to ensure that it will more than stand up to the demands of everyday use.

If there are quality problems, Japanese firms respond quickly. Quite often the design engineer who first drew the blueprints for the product becomes involved. If a redesign is needed, the engineer knows what has to be done.

The success of the Japanese is leading more and more American firms to study and emulate their methods. It has become obvious that this success is a result of both technology and more effective personnel practices. As the philosophy of American companies begins to change to accommodate the emphasis of production quality, we should see a closing of the quality gap between the two countries.

OPERATIONS MANAGEMENT AND REWARDS

Operations management is heavily concerned with product design, plant layout, and work quality. There is one area crucial to productivity and efficiency that warrants consideration, however, even though it is peripheral to the main concerns of operations management. That area is reward systems.

Reward Systems

Money is an important motivator

When an organization implements an effective plant layout, it should achieve productivity increases. The overall success of the effort, however, is often a result of the reward systems that accompany the implementation. When motivation was discussed in Chapter 12, the value of intrinsic rewards was noted. Attention was also given to money as a motivator. To a large degree, the implementation of successful operations management concepts depends more on monetary rewards than it does on the psychological satisfaction brought about by job enrichment. Mitchell Fein, a consultant and frequent contributor to the literature, reports that

> worker involvement programs which offer only job satisfaction as the prime reward for involvement will be supported by only a small proportion of the work force and tap a fraction of the potential for improvement in the organization.
>
> Worker involvement programs which offer financial rewards by sharing productivity improvement with employees through formal productivity sharing plans create high levels of involvement, produce results very quickly, and raise productivity to much higher levels than are attained by nonfinancial reward programs only.[37]

---

[37] Mitchell Fein, ''Improved Productivity Through Worker Involvement,'' *Industrial Management* (May–June 1983):4.

These findings point out the need to combine operations management decisions with personnel rewards. In this way greater control of productivity can be ensured.

Presently, there are a number of productivity plans designed to involve employees in productivity improvement and share the gains with the workers. According to the General Accounting Office, the most popular one is the **Scanlon plan**.[38] Under this plan the total payroll dollars are divided by the total dollar sales value of production in determining productivity gains. These are then shared with the workers. For example, consider a firm that has found from past performance that for $1 million in payroll it is able to produce goods worth $2 million in sales revenue. Under the Scanlon plan, if $2 million worth of goods can be produced for less than $1 million in payroll or more than $2 million worth of goods can be produced for $1 million in payroll, there is then a productivity gain. This gain is then shared between the workers and the management on a 75/25 basis.

Productivity plans tell how gains are to be shared with the workers

Another popular productivity sharing arrangement is the **Rucker plan**, which is similar to Scanlon but more sophisticated in design. Under the Rucker plan, using past performance, the company establishes the relationship between the total earnings of the hourly rated employees and the production value created by the company. Productivity gains are then shared with the workers. David Belcher, a compensation expert, has explained the specifics of the Rucker plan this way.

> Assume that the company puts $.55 worth of materials, supplies, and power into production to obtain a product worth $1.00. Value added or production value is thus $.45 for each $1.00 of sales value. Assume also that analysis shows that 40 percent of production value is attributable to labor. The productivity ratio becomes 2.5, and for a payroll (plus benefits) of $100,000 standard production value is $250,000. If actual production value for the month is $300,000 a gain of $50,000 is available for bonus and is distributed 40 percent to labor and 60 percent to the company. Labor's bonus share for the month is $20,000.[39]

There are many other group productivity plans from the Kaiser Plan to Improshare, but they all have one thing in common: using some predetermined formula they reward employees for productivity increases. In some cases, these gains have proven to be dramatic. For example, using Improshare, a plan he developed, Fein reports that he was able to increase productivity in a highly

---

[38] General Accounting Office, *Productivity Sharing Programs: Can They Contribute to Productivity Improvement?* U.S. GAO, Document Handling & Information Services Facility, PO Box 6015, Gaithersburg, MD 20760, AFMD-81 (March 3, 1981):22.
[39] David W. Belcher, *Compensation Administration* (Englewood Cliffs, NJ: Prentice-Hall, Inc., 1975), 332.

mechanized brick plant by 30 percent in 3 weeks and raise productivity in a plywood plant by 24 percent in 4 weeks and 34 percent for the overall year.[40]

In all of these productivity sharing plans there are two major considerations. First, financial rewards must be given to the employees. Second, management must secure worker support. Without these two elements, operations management efforts are less than ideal. Job redesign coupled with improved work layout and technology is incomplete. There must be monetary rewards as well. Money is still a major motivator. In fact, in the view of many researchers it remains the most important one. Edwin Locke, a well-known behavioral scientist, and his associates have noted that, "For the last several decades ideological bias has led many [social scientists] to deny the efficacy of money as a motivator and to emphasize the potency of participation. The results of research to date indicate that the opposite point of view would have been more accurate.[41] Management must realize that in controlling operations it must tie its efforts to a reward system that encourages work participation. Only in this way will it be able to obtain the greatest benefits from the ideas set forth in this chapter.

SUMMARY

1. Productivity is measured by using the equation: output/input. There are a number of reasons for the productivity lag in the United States. One is the failure of firms to develop an overall, long-range plan for dealing with the problem. A second is a focus on productivity symptoms rather than on its causes. A third is the failure of top management to become active in the process. Some of the most effective ways of increasing productivity include getting top management involved, organizing to support the productivity objective, developing a climate conducive to this objective, designing methods of measuring progress and setting realistic goals, being continually on the lookout for new productivity improvement techniques, and developing a schedule for implementing the productivity program and committing the necessary resources.

2. Operations management is the process of designing, operating, and controlling a production system that transforms physical resources and human effort into goods and services. This is done through the production/operations process, which has three basic phases: input, transformation process, and output. The inputs are the materials and human talents used to produce the output. The transformation process consists of the production activities that take the inputs and combine

---

[40] Fein, "Improved Productivity," 13.
[41] Reported in Fein, "Improved Productivity," 6.

them in some special way so as to produce the outputs. The outputs are the final results of the transformation process.

3. There have been many technological breakthroughs over the last decade. Some of these are being used to automate the workplace. One of the most important is flexible manufacturing systems that allow companies to produce a small amount of output with the same efficiency previously reserved only for large production runs. Such advances are also helping American firms meet the productivity challenge.

4. One of the major dimensions of operations management is design of a production system. This process usually begins with research designed to generate product or service ideas. Then the organization selects the ideas that are feasible, marketable, and compatible with its strategy. The last stage is the actual design of the product or service. In improving quality and reducing product problems, many firms use value engineering and value analysis. Value engineering is the analysis of new products and the application of research and development concepts to these products for the purpose of designing the most efficient, lowest cost, highest quality output. Value analysis is the analysis of existing production products, specifications, and requirements demanded by production documents and purchase requests. Other commonly used tools and techniques include computer-aided design and computer-aided manufacturing.

5. Production planning is the process whereby management meshes demand forecasts for goods and services with scheduled resource outputs. Production planning often involves the use of master production schedules and careful consideration of product life cycles.

6. Two other major areas of operations management are purchasing and inventory control. Purchasing practices and organizational arrangements are commonly drawn up to ensure the most efficient purchasing possible. Inventory control procedures often make wide use of material requirements planning and JIT production.

7. Another critical area of operations management is work flow layout. There are three basic layout formats. One is product layout in which the personnel are arranged according to the progressive steps used in building the product. A second is process layout in which all components are grouped on the basis of the functions they perform. The third is fixed-position layout in which the workers come to the work.

8. Quality control is the process of ensuring that goods and services are produced according to predetermined specifications. In this process, management typically makes use of both feedforward and feedback control. Many firms are also beginning to emulate Japanese approaches by encouraging personnel to do the job right the first time and by giving them authority and responsibility for quality control, as opposed to assigning this function to a special department.

9. The implementation of operations management concepts depends more on monetary rewards than it does on psychological satisfaction brought about by job enrichment. Today a growing number of firms are opting for productivity plans in which gains are shared by the employees and the management.

KEY TERMS

Feedforward control   A control system that is used to help avoid problems rather than to deal with them after they have occurred.

Fixed-position layout   A layout in which the workers come to the work.

Flexible manufacturing systems   Computer-controlled systems that allow companies to produce desired outputs at low price and high quality.

Inputs   Materials and human inputs used in the production process.

JIT production   The purchase or production or both of small quantities just in time for use.

Material requirements planning   A systematic, comprehensive manufacturing and controlling technique used to increase the efficiency both of material handling and of inventory control.

Operations management   The process of designing, operating, and controlling a production system that transforms physical resources and human effort into goods and services.

Outputs   The final result of the transformation process, these goods or services are sold to customers or used in the creation of other goods or services.

Process layout   A layout in which all components are grouped on the basis of the functions they perform.

Product design   A phase of operations during which management decides the specific physical dimensions of the goods or services to be produced.

Production planning   The process whereby management meshes demand forecasts for goods and services with scheduled resource outputs.

Productivity   A performance measure determined by dividing output by input.

Product layout   The arrangement of machines, equipment, and personnel according to the progressive steps used in building the product.

Quality control   The process of ensuring that goods and services are produced according to predetermined specifications.

Rucker plan   A gain sharing productivity plan in which a company establishes the relationship between the total earnings of hourly rated employees and the production value created by the company in determining productivity gains to be shared by the employees and managers.

Scanlon plan   A gain sharing productivity plan that compares total payroll dollars to dollar sales value of production in determining productivity gains, which are then shared by the employees and managers on a 75/25 basis.

Transformation process   The production activities that take inputs and combine them in some special way so as to produce the desired outputs.

Value analysis   The analysis of existing products, specifications, and requirements demanded by production documents and purchase requests.

Value engineering   The analysis of new products and the application of research and development concepts to these products for the purpose of designing the most efficient, lowest cost, highest quality output.

Work flow layout   The process of determining the physical arrangement of the production system.

QUESTIONS FOR ANALYSIS AND DISCUSSION

1. What is meant by the term productivity? What do managers need to know regarding how they can achieve increased productivity in their operations? In your answer, cite at least four of the findings reported by Y. K. Shetty.

2. What is meant by the term operations management? Put the definition in your own words, being sure to include a discussion of the production/operations process in your answer.

3. Is the production/operations process confined to the manufacture of products or can it be used by nongoods-producing organizations as well? Explain your answer.

4. How has technology invaded the factory? Cite some examples and explain how this development is leading managers to redirect their attention to the factory floor.

5. What is meant by the term design of a production system? What importance do value engineering and value analysis have to product design/redesign? How can CAD and CAM be of value in product design?

6. What is production planning all about? In your answer be sure to discuss the importance of master production schedules and product life cycles.

7. Of what value are purchasing practices to effective operations management? What role does material requirements planning play in helping organizations control their inventory? What role does JIT production play? Be specific in your answers.

8. There are three basic work flow layouts and all others are simply variations of these three. What are these three basic work flow layouts and when would each be used? Use examples in your answer.

9. In your own words, what is meant by the term quality control? What roles are played by feedforward and feedback control in helping ensure the best quality?

10. You have just been asked to tell a group of business people how American firms can meet the Japanese challenge. What would you tell them? Identify and describe the three main points you would make to the group.

11. How important are reward systems to operations management? Explain your answer, being sure to incorporate a general discussion of productivity plans and their value for personnel motivation.

CASE

Problems on the Line

Shelling Products is a medium-sized manufacturing firm located on the West Coast. Founded by George Shelling, the company has always been run by family members. The firm specializes in the production of high tech components that are used in aircraft, computers, and telecommunications satellites.

Last year the president of the firm, Margaret Shelling, was reviewing new product ideas with her top engineers. They pointed out to her that with the company's current experience, it could profitably produce modern technology consumer products. At the top of their list of suggestions was the portable telephone. Margaret had her marketing people check out the idea and found there were only a handful of firms that manufactured these portable phones, although the industry consensus was that by the end of the 1990s there would be many more competitors.

A month later Margaret contacted one of the nation's largest retail stores and asked them if they would be interested in a portable phone. Shelling Products would design, develop, and manufacture the unit, and the retailer would sell it. The idea sounded fine to the other company, especially since Shelling would be underwriting all design, development, and manufacturing costs.

It took Margaret's engineers two months to strip down competitive models, study them, design the Shelling offering, and get it into production. Then it was but six months until Shelling was ready to make its first shipment of the phones. The retailer mounted a vigorous advertising campaign to accompany the announcement that these phones could be purchased at any of its outlets around the country. Thanks to its high technology and efficient production system, Shelling's price was quite low and the retailer offered the phones for 25 percent less than the amount they could be purchased for from the competition. Best of all, the first phones arrived at the stores on December 1, just in time for Christmas. By the end of December, the retailer had sold most of the 25,000 units and placed an order for another 25,000 to be delivered by the end of January. Things could not have looked brighter for Shelling. Then the bottom fell out.

On January 15, Margaret received a call from the retailer's headquarters. The firm was being deluged with complaints from customers who were experiencing difficulty using the phone. The biggest problem was that the phone would suddenly cut off in the middle of a call. The second most common complaint was that the reception was extremely poor and people were unable to hear the other party. Based on the number of calls it has received, the retailer estimates that approximately 20 percent of all the phones have quality problems. It is urging customers to return the phones to the store in exchange for new ones. In turn the phones will be shipped back to Shelling for repairs. If the estimate of 20 percent defects is accurate, Shelling will just break even on the product. If any more than 20 percent are returned, the firm will lose money on the venture.

Margaret called a meeting of her engineers and design people earlier today to tell them the problem. "The first shipment of defective phones should be arriving later this week," she said. "We'll have to strip them down, find out what went wrong, and then repair them as soon as possible. I want this problem given first priority. Put all of your other work on hold." The head of engineering told her, "I'm going to personally head up this project. I'll get back to you with my findings within 72 hours of the time we receive the first shipment."

1. From your reading of the case, what went wrong? Why are so many of the phones defective?
2. Could this problem have been avoided or lessened through the use of better product design? Could value engineering and value analysis have helped? Explain.
3. What lessons should Shelling Products learn from this problem? Identify and discuss three.

YOU BE THE CONSULTANT

The Quality "Rules"?

Edgar A. Baskins, vice president for quality control and productivity at the Coreland Machine Design Corporation, has introduced a new program to improve production quality. In the past, the factory has tried "quick-fix" approaches. These were unsuccessful and Mr. Baskins is determined not to make those mistakes again. He wants to promote a long-term commitment to quality by all of the 160 workers at Coreland.

In his pursuit of the most effective program, Mr. Baskins read the 14 key points of Edward Deming, the noted quality expert, as well as articles and books by other experts in the field. Drawing together all of this information, Mr. Baskins has developed a 10-point quality control program which he has had posted throughout the factory. It is as follows:

Coreland's 10 Points for Quality

1. We must continually strive to provide the best quality products. This means a willingness to change and adapt our production processes and procedures.
2. We must eliminate the need to inspect every product by building quality into the goods we produce.
3. We must stop purchasing on the basis of price alone and award our contracts to suppliers who provide us the best quality inputs.
4. Purchasing must be combined with the design and manufacture of our products. There must be interdepartmental cooperation between these three areas.
5. Supervisory training must be given a higher priority. Only when our line managers learn how to blend a concern for both the people and the work will our efficiency reach its highest level.
6. There must be ongoing training and education for all workers. Unless we provide our people with the most up-to-date tools and techniques, we will not be as efficient as we should.
7. We must eliminate slogans, exhortations, and similar production-related concepts such as "zero defects." These cause adversarial relationships and our objective should be to create teamwork.
8. Work standards that prescribe numerical daily quotas should be eliminated. A well-motivated work force does not need these standards.
9. Annual merit ratings and management by objectives programs should be abolished. These rob people of pride in their work and establish artificial barriers that diminish quality production.
10. Greater attention must be given to increasing people's responsibility for product quality. Everyone should view herself/himself as a quality control individual rather than relying on the quality control department to handle this function.

After reviewing these 10 points, many of the employees have begun to raise doubts. They are concerned that these points will increase their work responsibilities and cause interdepartmental problems. They have called a special meeting with Mr. Baskins to discuss the implementation of this 10-point program.

Your Consultation

Assume that you have been called in by Mr. Baskins for advice on how to explain and institute his new 10-point program. What would you tell Mr. Baskins? How should he handle the situation? Be as helpful as possible in your consultation.

17

Performance Appraisal and Organizational Development

Effective managers need to control not only organizational performance but personnel performance as well. When people are not doing well, the manager needs to identify the problem and then work to correct it. This chapter studies the ways in which modern organizations evaluate personnel performance and change organizational behavior. It examines the performance appraisal process, highlighting common appraisal problems that must be overcome. It also explores organizational climate and shows how organizational development techniques help management control personnel performance. When you have finished reading all of the material in this chapter, you will be able to:

1. Explain how the performance appraisal process works and describe four of the most popular techniques for appraising performance.
2. Identify and describe some of the most common problems associated with performance appraisal and tell how these problems can be dealt with.
3. Discuss how conflict and change can be controlled by management.
4. Identify and describe some of the properties of organizational climate and the ways in which this climate can be measured.
5. Define the term organizational development and describe how some of the traditional approaches to organizational development work.
6. Answer the question: Does organizational development really pay off?

601

PERFORMANCE APPRAISAL

Performance appraisal provides employee feedback

Performance appraisal is one of the most common procedures used to control an organization's personnel. Analogous to the general control process, it consists of comparing desired and actual personnel performance. Using the results, management can take corrective action and make decisions regarding future performance objectives. A good overall example is provided in "Management in Practice: Avoiding The Family Feud At Johnson Wax."

Nature of the Appraisal System

The purpose of performance appraisal is to provide both managers and subordinates with feedback on how well the subordinates are doing. These appraisals, as seen in Table 17-1, are used to determine such things as merit pay increases, promotions, training, transfer, and discharge. In large measure, performance appraisal is the primary process used for evaluating and developing organizational personnel.

Characteristics of a well-designed system

A well-designed appraisal system has five basic characteristics: (1) it is tied directly to the person's job and measures the individual's ability to successfully carry out the requirements of the position; (2) it is comprehensive,

TABLE 17-1   Primary Uses of Performance Appraisals

Use	Small Organizations Percent	Large Organizations Percent	All Percent
Compensation	80.6	62.2	71.3
Performance Improvement	49.7	60.6	55.2
Feedback	20.6	37.8	29.3
Promotion	29.1	21.1	25.1
Documentation	11.4	10.0	10.7
Training	8.0	9.4	8.7
Transfer	7.4	8.3	7.9
Manpower Planning	6.3	6.1	6.2
Discharge	2.3	2.2	2.3
Research	2.9	0.0	1.4
Layoff	0.6	0.0	0.3

Source: Alan H. Locher and Kenneth S. Teel, "Performance Appraisal—A Survey of Current Practices," *Personnel Journal* (May 1977):246. Reprinted by permission of Personnel Journal, Inc., Costa Mesa, CA. All rights reserved.

MANAGEMENT IN PRACTICE

Avoiding the Family Feud at Johnson Wax

*T*he late Herbert Fisk Johnson, Jr. had one last request of his son Sam—to keep the Johnson Wax Co. in the family. Holding onto his father's belief that private is better, Sam Johnson is working hard to preserve a family dynasty and avoid the "feuds" that have destroyed so many others including these:

Pulitzer Publishing
Dissident family members were bought out and forced a public offering of 18 percent of the company.

Getty Oil
After years of bickering, the son Gordon engineered a sale of the family's 40 percent interest to Texaco.

U-Haul
Heirs of Leonard Schoen, the company's founder, are feuding over control and may end up selling the company.

Louisville-Courier Journal
Years of bickering by family members resulted in a sale of the company's holdings, including its flagship newspaper.

With these family feuds apparent, Sam Johnson has all four of his children, ages 29 to 33, involved in the family business. Curt, the eldest son, is operating a new venture capital unit; Fisk, the younger son, is a marketing associate for a new laundry products firm owned by the family; daughter Helen is involved in marketing operations; and daughter Winifred,

the youngest of all, works part-time in public affairs. However, the involvement of the children is only one major portion of a family firm. The other is protecting the estate upon the death of the owner from taxes that could force executives to liquidate assets or go public with the stock. With an estimated personal worth of $500 million, Sam Johnson needed to plan carefully.

Taking the leisure products group public (Johnson Worldwide Associates Inc.), Johnson raised $26.7 million and through a second stock offering raised an additional $27.4 million. By doing this Sam Johnson hopes family shares can be traded or sold publicly to pay estate taxes and thus avoid a panic or feud over settling the estate.

The plan appears to be a solid effort of going public to remain private. The family still controls 35 percent of the publicly traded class A stock and 92 percent of the closely held class B shares which confer the voting rights to elect 75 percent of the board of directors. In addition, Wall Street seems unaffected by this family control. Johnson's stock price has doubled to $21 a share and analysts predict it may climb higher. In any event, Johnson's momentum is on the rise and the family is working hard to structure a dynasty that avoids the feuds of other family firms.

Source: James E. Ellis, "Sam Johnson is Going Public to Stay Private," *Business Week* (December 5, 1989):58–60.

measuring all of the important aspects of the job rather than just one or two; (3) it is objective, measuring task performance rather than the interpersonal relationship of the rater and the ratee; (4) it is based on standards of desired performance that were explained to the personnel in advance; and (5) it is designed to pinpoint the strong points and shortcomings of the personnel and

FIGURE 17-1   A System of Managing and Appraising by Objectives

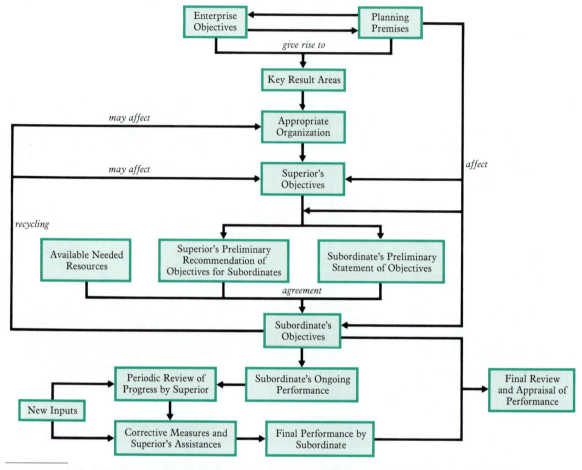

Source: Harold Koontz, "Making Managerial Appraisal Effective," *California Management Review* (Winter 1972):49. Copyright © 1972 by the Regents of the University of California. Reprinted from *California Management Review,* 46–55 by permission of the Regents.

provide a basis for explaining why these shortcomings exist and what can be done about them.[1]

There are many ways to design and implement a performance appraisal system so that it will have these characteristics. One of the most useful is to tie the appraisal closely to the objectives of the position. Figure 17-1 illustrates one way of doing this. A close comparison of this figure with Figure 6-9 shows that this method is based on the management by objectives (MBO) approach. Not

---

[1] Beverly Kaye and Shelly Krantz, "Performance Appraisal: A Win/Win Approach," *Training and Development Journal* (March 1983):32–35.

all performance appraisal systems are so closely tied to MBO, however. In fact, researchers such as Alan Locher and Kenneth Teel report that, on the average, only about 13 percent of all organizations use MBO for performance appraisals.[2] Nevertheless, the basic concept is useful in linking job performance and appraisal.

Value Behind Performance Appraisals

Formal performance appraisals provide value in several different ways. All effective managers believe that appraisal systems can be a beneficial tool for improving employee performance, attendance behavior, and job satisfaction.[3] More specifically, the following purposes can be served through effective appraisal systems:

- personal development
- reward
- motivation
- personnel planning
- communication[4]

A number of organizations are finding that close monitoring of the appraisal system can redefine, evaluate, and improve the appraisal system. Xerox, for example, discovered various areas of dissatisfaction with its system and worked carefully to remove barriers to employee teamwork and reworked its rating system. This improvement, along with the use of the manager as a coach and the addition of developmental objectives, significantly improved the performance appraisal system.[5]

The values of an appraisal system are tied closely with the norms and beliefs of the organization itself. Thus, the culture or climate of the organization will help determine equitable and useful appraisal systems. Figure 17-2 depicts this sequence.[6]

Techniques for Appraising Performance

A number of different techniques can be used in conducting performance appraisals, and most organizations design their own techniques. Four of the

---

[2] Alan H. Locher and Kenneth S. Teel, "Performance Appraisal—A Survey of Current Practices," *Personnel Journal* (May 1977):247.

[3] Mark A. Mallinger and Tom G. Cummings, "Improving the Value of Performance Appraisals," *Advanced Management Journal* (Spring 1986):19.

[4] Mallinger and Cummings, "Performance Appraisals," 19.

[5] Norman R. Deets and D. Timothy Tyler, "How Xerox Improved Its Performance Appraisals," *Personnel Journal* (April 1986):50–52.

[6] Roy Serpa, "Why Many Organizations—Despite Good Intentions—Often Fail to Give Employees Fair and Useful Performance Reviews," *Management Review* (July 1984):44.

FIGURE 17-2

Cultural Norms in
Organizations
Claiming to Value
Performance

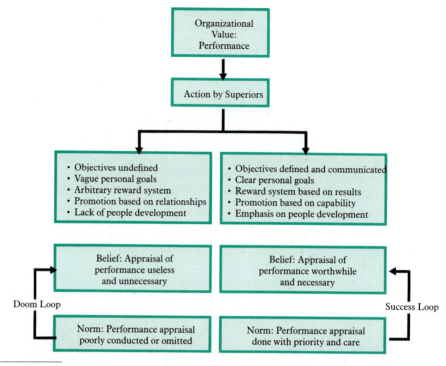

Source: Roy Serpa, "Why Many Organizations—Despite Good Intentions—Fail to Give
Employees Fair and Useful Performance Reviews," *Management Review* (July 1984):44.
Reprinted by permission.

most popular are graphic rating scales, paired comparison, critical incidents,
and behaviorally anchored rating scales.

Graphic Rating Scales

Graphic rating
scales are easy to
fill out

Graphic rating scales are the most widely used method of performance appraisal. They are also easy to fill out. Figure 17-3 illustrates one such scale.
Regardless of the way these scales are constructed, however, it is common to
find the category or factor listed on the left and the varying degrees of the
category or factor listed along a continuum to the right. The form often contains
a description of each category. Quality of work, for example, may be defined as
"the caliber of work produced or accomplished in comparison to accepted
quality standards." In some cases, as in Figure 17-3, degrees of the factor are
also described. If the results of the evaluation are going to be used to compare
people within the same unit or department, some sort of weight usually is given
to each factor, such as a 1 for a marginal rating, 2 for below average, 3 for
average, 4 for above average, and 5 for outstanding.

FIGURE 17-3   Illustration of a Graphic Rating Scale

Name *(Last)*	*(First)*	*(Initial)*	Period Covered From	To
Pay Title	Social Security Nr.	Status		If Prob, Date Ends
Department	Division		Unit	

CHECK ITEMS ⊞ Strong ⊟ Weak ☑ Satisfactory ⊡ Not applicable	INDICATE FACTOR RATING BY "X"			
	UNSATISFACTORY	NEEDS ATTENTION	SATISFACTORY	OUTSTANDING
1. QUANTITY OF WORK ☐ Amount of work performed ☐ Completion of work on schedule	Seldom produces enough work or meets deadlines.	Does not always complete an acceptable amount of work.	Consistently completes an acceptable amount of work.	Amount of work produced is consistently outstanding.
2. QUALITY OF WORK ☐ Accuracy ☐ Effectiveness ☐ Compliance with instructions ☐ Use of tools & equipment ☐ Neatness of work product ☐ Reports & correspondence ☐ Thoroughness	Too poor to retain in job without improvement.	Quality below acceptable standards	Performs assigned duties in a satisfactory manner.	Performs all duties in an outstanding manner. Exceptional accuracy, skill or effectiveness.
3. WORK HABITS ☐ Attendance ☐ Observance of working hours ☐ Observance of rules ☐ Safety practices ☐ Personal Appearance	Too poor to retain in job without improvement.	Work habits need improvement.	Work habits satisfactory.	Exceptional work habits. Always observes rules and safe practices.
4. PERSONAL RELATIONS ☐ With fellow employees and supervisors ☐ With public	Too poor to retain in job without improvement.	Personal relations need improvement.	Maintains satisfactory work relations with others.	Exceptionally co-operative with public, co-workers and supervisors.
(FOR SUPERVISORS ONLY) 5. SUPERVISORY ABILITY ☐ Planning & assigning ☐ Training & instructing ☐ Disciplinary control ☐ Evaluating performance ☐ Delegating ☐ Making decisions ☐ Fairness & impartiality ☐ Unit morale	Poor supervisory ability. Work of unit frequently unsatisfactory.	Supervisory ability inadequate in some respects. Works results of unit below par at times.	Obtains good results from subordinates. Controls unit efficiently.	Outstanding ability to get maximum from unit and available resources.

RATER'S COMMENTS: *(attach additional sheets if needed)*

RATER'S RECOMMENDATION (for employees under consideration for a merit raise or permanent status) This is to certify that the overall performance of the subject employee ☐ is ☐ is not satisfactory. The employee ☐ is ☐ is not recommended for ☐ a merit raise ☐ permanent status. This report is based on my observation and knowledge. It represents my best judgment of the employee's performance. RATER_____ Date_____	I have reviewed this report. It represents the facts to the best of my knowledge. I concur in the recommendation, if any, as to merit raise or permanent status. REVIEWER_____ Date_____ In signing this report I do not necessarily agree with the conclusions of the rater. I understand that I may write my comments on the reverse side. I have received a copy of this report. EMPLOYEE'S SIGNATURE_____ Date_____

Paired Comparison

Paired comparison is a ranking method in which each individual in a unit or department is compared with all of the others. Sometimes this comparison is done on an overall basis. For example, the manager ranks the five people in the unit from "best" to "poorest," mentally combining all of the important evaluation factors and using them to arrive at a final ranking. More often, the manager is given a series of job-related factors such as work quantity, work quality, job knowledge, dependability, and initiative and asked to rank each person on each factor. When ranked using this kind of paired comparison, Mr. A may be the best on work quantity and work quality, third on job knowledge and dependability, and last on cooperation and initiative. After all of the individual rankings are completed, the supervisor totals them up, averages them out, and determines who is the best worker.

Paired comparison
uses forced
rankings

In paired comparison a forced ranking choice is used so that only one person can be the "best." If a number of factors are used for evaluation purposes and two or more people come out with identical average scores, a further comparison is made. For example, if two people are tied for the best ranking in the unit, the manager goes back to the factor considered most important, such as work quantity. The worker who ranked highest on this factor gets the best rating in the unit. Remember that since no two people can get the same ranking on a particular factor, this comparison separates the best person in the unit from the second best worker.

One of the things that many organizations like about the paired comparison is that it eliminates the possibility that a supervisor will give all the workers an excellent rating, something that is possible when the graphic rating scale is used. On the other hand, while it is often possible for the manager to distinguish easily between the best and poorest performers, it can be difficult to distinguish or rank those in the middle. So the paired comparison approach is not without its shortcomings.

Critical Incidents

The **critical incidents** method requires the manager to record incidents in which the subordinate did something that was unusually effective or ineffective. For example, a sales supervisor may record: "When told by a customer that the piece of machinery was too inefficient for his company's needs, this salesperson immediately switched the customer to the top-of-the-line model and quickly closed the sale." Or a police sergeant may note: "This officer withheld his fire in a situation calling for the use of weapons because innocent bystanders might have been endangered in the process."

Effective and
ineffective
behavior is
recorded

These critical incidents are recorded in a daily or weekly log. The book generally has predesignated categories such as planning, decision making, interpersonal relations, and controlling, so the entry can be made quickly.

Commenting on the value of the critical incident, Wayne Cascio, a personnel psychologist and noted expert on performance evaluation, has written:

> These little anecdotes force attention on the situational determinants of job behavior and also on ways of doing the job successfully that may be unique to the person described . . . supervisors can focus on actual job behavior rather than on vaguely defined traits. Ratees receive meaningful feedback and they can see what changes in their job behavior will be necessary in order for them to improve. . . . In addition, when a large number of critical incidents are collected, abstracted, and categorized, they can provide a rich storehouse of information about job and organizational problems in general and are particularly well-suited for establishing objectives for training programs.[7]

Behaviorally Anchored Rating Scales

BARS are job related

Behaviorally anchored rating scales, BARS for short, require a great deal of effort to construct. If the job is done properly, however, performance ratings are likely to be both accurate and reliable. The construction of the rating scales involves a number of distinct procedures. First, a group of employees or managers or both meets to identify and define the important dimensions of effective job performance. Next, another group takes each of these dimensions and develops critical incidents for each of them. These incidents are chosen to illustrate effective, average, and ineffective performance. Then a third group is given a list of the dimensions and the accompanying definitions and critical incidents used to illustrate them. This group is charged with eliminating the critical incidents that do not illustrate effective, average, or ineffective behavior in that dimension. A fourth group is then used to place a scale value on each incident associated with a dimension. Typically, a seven- to nine-point scale is used.

Figure 17-4 illustrates a BARS scale used to evaluate the organizational ability of checkstand workers in a supermarket. Using this scale, the supervisor can quickly and easily evaluate the grocery checker's organizational ability. Other scales would also be developed to address such dimensions as conscientiousness, knowledge and judgment, human relations skills, skill in operation of the register, and skill in bagging.[8] The scales are then pilot-tested.

A number of advantages are ascribed to BARS. One is that the appraisal instrument is job related, measuring the worker's ability to carry out or exhibit task performance behavior. Moreover, both workers and management participate in developing the instrument, and the steps involved in this process and in testing the instrument help ensure that it is both valid and reliable.

---

[7] Wayne F. Cascio, *Applied Psychology in Personnel Management,* 3rd ed. (Reston, VA: Reston Publishing Co., 1987), p. 88.

[8] Lawrence Fogli, Charles L. Hulin, and Milton R. Blood, "Development of First-Level Behavioral Job Criteria," *Journal of Applied Psychology* (February 1971):7.

FIGURE 17-4 A Behaviorally Anchored Rating Scale for Measuring the Organizational Ability of a Checkstand Worker

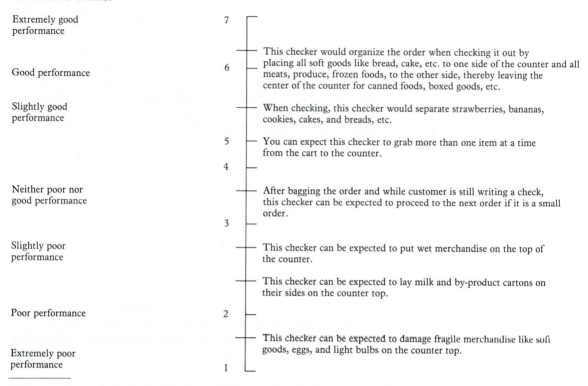

Extremely good performance	7	
Good performance	6	This checker would organize the order when checking it out by placing all soft goods like bread, cake, etc. to one side of the counter and all meats, produce, frozen foods, to the other side, thereby leaving the center of the counter for canned foods, boxed goods, etc.
Slightly good performance		When checking, this checker would separate strawberries, bananas, cookies, cakes, and breads, etc.
	5	You can expect this checker to grab more than one item at a time from the cart to the counter.
	4	
Neither poor nor good performance		After bagging the order and while customer is still writing a check, this checker can be expected to proceed to the next order if it is a small order.
	3	
Slightly poor performance		This checker can be expected to put wet merchandise on the top of the counter.
		This checker can be expected to lay milk and by-product cartons on their sides on the counter top.
Poor performance	2	
Extremely poor performance	1	This checker can be expected to damage fragile merchandise like soft goods, eggs, and light bulbs on the counter top.

Source: Lawrence Fogli, Charles L. Hulin, and Milton R. Blood, "Development of First-Level Behavioral Job Criteria," *Journal of Applied Psychology* (February 1971):7. Copyright 1971 by the American Psychological Association. Reprinted by permission of the publisher and author.

Problems with Performance Appraisals

A number of problems can threaten the value of performance appraisal techniques. Most of these relate to the appraisal instrument's validity or reliability. **Validity** is the extent to which the instrument measures what it is supposed to measure. **Reliability** is the extent to which the instrument consistently yields the same results. In the case of an assembly-line worker, for example, a valid performance evaluation instrument is one that measures such performance-related dimensions as manual dexterity, speed, and ability to keep up with the line. If the instrument is reliable, assuming that the person's work performance does not change much, each time the individual is evaluated he or she should receive approximately the same rating. Unfortunately, in many instances performance appraisals lack validity or reliability. Specifically, some of the most common problems include central tendency, leniency or strictness errors, the halo effect, recency error, and personal biases.

Central Tendency

Some evaluators give everyone an average rating

Central tendency occurs when the evaluator gives average ratings to just about everyone. No matter how good or bad their performance, the individuals are all given evaluations within a narrow range such as from low average to high average. Naturally, this tendency rewards the poorest workers and penalizes the best ones.

Leniency or Strictness Errors

Others are overly lenient or strict

Leniency or **strictness errors** occur when the manager is either too easy or too hard on the employees. Leniency rewards the low and average producers by giving them more than they deserve. Strictness punishes the average and above-average producers by putting them in the same basic category as the low producers.

Halo Effect

Evaluators may be overly influenced by one or two factors . . .

The **halo effect** exists whenever a rater allows an individual's performance on one or two factors to influence how the person is rated on all factors. For example, a supervisor is supposed to rate an assembly-line worker on work quantity, work quality, attitude, perseverance, work habits, and interpersonal relations. The only factor that is measured quantitatively in the plant is work quantity, and on this factor the individual is high. Allowing this fact to influence the rating, the supervisor gives the worker the highest rating on all other factors as well. The supervisor has allowed performance in one area to influence the overall assessment.

Recency Error

overly influenced by the most recent performance . . .

Recency errors are related to employees' most recent behavior. Quite often, supervisors remember what an employee did last week but not what the individual did three months ago. As a result, the most recent behavior has a greater impact on the performance evaluation than does more remote behavior. When this error is present, an average worker who does excellent work in the month prior to the annual evaluation will get a better evaluation than an excellent worker who does poor work during this month.

Personal Biases

or influenced by personal bias

Another common cause of evaluation error is personal bias on the part of the individual conducting the performance evaluation. One of these biases is called **similarity**. When this bias is present, a subordinate who has the same values, attitudes, and habits as the supervisor is given a higher rating; conversely, a subordinate who does not seem to have these traits is given a lower rating. A second typical personal bias is a result of the amount of interaction that occurs between the manager and the employee. Some managers give a higher rating if they interact quite a bit with the individual; others give a lower rating in their effort not to be influenced by such interpersonal relationships.[9]

Legal Considerations in Performance Appraisal

A great deal has been written in recent years about the legal problems of performance appraisal systems and the ways to deal with them. One of the most common recommendations is to tie the appraisal directly to job-related behavior.[10] A second is always to use at least two appraisers, such as the direct supervisor and this person's boss.[11] This check is particularly important when a substandard evaluation is being given.[12] A third is to use objective factors in the appraisal whenever possible so that it is possible to pinpoint job performance more accurately and follow up later on by showing the employee where and how such performance can be improved.[13] Finally, the performance appraisal system should be clearly communicated to every employee to avoid any misunderstanding in the forms, factors, or interpretation of results. Table 17-2 provides a list of prescriptions for legally defensible appraisal systems.

CONTROLLING CONFLICT AND CHANGE

In addition to appraising performance, managers often find it necessary to control conflict and change. **Conflict** is opposition or antagonistic interaction between two or more parties.[14] **Change** is an altering of the status quo.[15] Conflict brings about change but the reverse is not always true. As a result, in the

---

[9] Clinton O. Longenecker, Henry P. Sims, Jr., and Dennis A. Gioia, "Behind the Mask: The Politics of Employee Appraisal," *Academy of Management Executive* (August 1987):183–193.
[10] William H. Holley and Hubert S. Field, "Will Your Performance Appraisal System Hold Up in Court?" *Personnel* (January–February 1982):59–64.
[11] Ed Yager, "A Critique of Performance Appraisal Systems," *Personnel Journal* (February 1981):129–33; John D. McMillan and Hoyo W. Doyal, "Performance Appraisal: Match the Tool to the Task," *Personnel* (July–August 1978):12–20.
[12] Patricia Linenberger and Timothy J. Keaveny, "Performance Appraisal Standards Used by the Courts," *Personnel Administrator* (May 1981):89–94.
[13] Marvin G. Dertien, "The Accuracy of Job Evaluation Plans," *Personnel Journal* (July 1981):566–70. See also: George S. Odiorne, "Measuring the Unmeasurable: Setting Standards for Management Performance," *Business Horizons* (July–August 1987):69–75.
[14] Stephen P. Robbins, "'Conflict Management' and 'Conflict Resolution' Are Not Synonymous Terms," *California Management Review* (Winter 1978):67.
[15] Richard M. Hodgetts, *Modern Human Relations,* 2nd ed. (Hinsdale, IL.: Dryden Press, 1984), 392.

TABLE 17-2   Prescriptions for Legally Defensible Appraisal Systems

1. Procedures for personnel decisions must not differ as a function of the race, sex, national origin, religion, or age of those affected by such decisions.

2. Objective type, non-rated, and uncontaminated data should be used whenever they are available.

3. A formal system of review or appeal should be available for appraisal disagreements.

4. More than one independent evaluator of performance should be used.

5. A formal, standardized system for the personnel decision should be used.

6. Evaluators should have ample opportunity to observe the performance of the rated employee (if ratings must be made).

7. Ratings on traits such as dependability, drive, aptitude, or attitude should be avoided.

8. Performance appraisal data should be empirically validated.

9. Specific performance standards should be communicated to employees.

10. Evaluators should be provided with written instructions on how to complete the performance evaluations.

11. Employees should be evaluated on specific work dimensions rather than a single overall or global measure.

12. Behavioral documentation should be required for extreme ratings (for example, critical incidents).

13. The content of the appraisal form should be based on a job analysis.

14. Employees should be provided with an opportunity to review their appraisals.

15. Personnel decision makers should be trained on laws regarding discrimination.

Source: J. Bernardin and W. Cascio, "Performance Appraisal and the Law," in R. S. Schuler, S. A. Youngblood, and V. Huber, eds., *Readings in Personnel and Human Resource Management,* 3rd ed. (St. Paul: West, 1988), p. 239.

controlling of human resources, the manager may sometimes deal with one of these conditions and at other times with both.

Conflict Management

For a long time, management believed that all conflict was inherently bad. Today that view has changed as managers have come to realize that conflict can bring about necessary changes. As Stephen Robbins, a well-known writer on the subject, has noted:

> Conflict is the catalyst of change. If we do not adapt our products and services to the changing needs of our customers, actions of our competitors, and new technological developments, our organizations will become sick and eventually die. Is it not possible that more organizations fail because of too little conflict rather than too much?" [16]

---

[16] Robbins, " 'Conflict Management' and 'Conflict Resolution,' " 69.

TABLE 17-3   Contingency Approaches for Dealing with Conflict

Technique	Brief Definition	Strengths	Weaknesses
Problem-solving (also known as confrontations or collaboration)	Seeks resolution through face-to-face confrontation of the conflicting parties. Parties seek mutual problem definition, assessment, and solution.	Effective with conflicts stemming from semantic misunderstandings. Brings doubts and misperceptions to surface.	Can be time consuming. Inappropriate for most noncommunicative conflicts, especially those based on different value systems.
Subordinate Goals	Common goals that two or more conflicting parties each desire and cannot be reached without cooperation of those involved. Goals must be highly valued, unattainable without the help of all parties involved in the conflict, and commonly sought.	When used cumulatively and reinforced, develops "peace-making" potential, emphasizing interdependency and cooperation.	Difficult to devise.
Expansion of Resources	Make more of the scarce resource available.	Each conflicting party can be victorious.	Resources rarely exist in such quantities as to easily expanded.
Avoidance	Includes withdrawal and suppression.	Easy to do. Natural reaction to conflict.	No effective resolution. Conflict not eliminated. Temporary.
Smoothing	Play down differences while emphasizing common interests.	All conflict situations have points of commonality within them. Cooperative effects are reinforced.	Differences are not confronted and remain under the surface. Temporary.

Conflict can be caused by distrust, threats to status, or misperceptions

On the other hand, conflict can be a result of distrust, fear, anxiety, tension, and other potentially dysfunctional causes. For example, when resources are being allocated it is not unusual to find individuals vying with each other for their share of the money or units competing for increased budget allocations. In such cases, given the fact that there are usually limited resources, when one party wins, others lose.

Status is another common cause of conflict. The production people may resent having to accept product modifications initiated by the Engineering

Technique	Brief Definition	Strengths	Weaknesses
Compromise	Each party is required to give up something of value. Includes external or third-party interventions, negotiation, and voting.	No clear loser. Consistent with democratic values.	No clear winner. Power-oriented—influenced heavily by relative strength of parties. Temporary.
Authoritative Command	Solution imposed from a superior holding formal positional authority.	Very effective in organizations since members recognize and accept authority of superiors.	Cause of conflict is not treated. Does not necessarily bring *agreement*. Temporary.
Altering the Human Variable	Changing the attitudes and behavior of one or more of the conflicting parties. Includes use of education, sensitivity and awareness training, and human relations training.	Results can be substantial and permanent. Has potential to alleviate the source of conflict.	Most difficult to achieve. Slow and costly.
Altering Structural Variables	Change structural variables. Includes transferring and exchanging group members, creating coordinating positions, developing an appeals system, and expanding the group or organization's boundaries.	Can be permanent. Usually within the authority of a manager.	Often expensive. Forces organization to be designed for specific individuals and thus requires continual adjustment as people join or leave the organization.

Source: Stephen P. Robbins, " 'Conflict Management' and 'Conflict Resolution' Are Not Synonymous Terms," *California Management Review* (Winter 1978):73. Copyright © 1978 by the Regents of the University of California. Reprinted from *California Management Review,* vol. 21, no. 2. By permission of The Regents.

Department; the marketing research people may be angry over having to submit weekly budget expenditures to the Finance Department; the Personnel Department may not like having to comply with EEO guidelines developed by the Legal Department.

A third common cause of conflict is misperception. Individuals or groups misinterpret what others are doing or why they are doing it. This problem may be caused by differences in age, education, background, or values, or it may be a result of communication breakdown.

In any event, the manager must work to control the conflict by either guiding it along constructive lines or seeking to resolve it. How can this be done? Robbins, using a contingency approach, has presented some major resolution techniques along with the strengths and weaknesses of each (see Table 17-3). Depending on the specifics of the situation, the manager can choose the technique that offers the greatest chance of managing the conflict constructively.

Dealing with Change

Change is inevitable, particularly in modern organizations.[17] Work rules are revised, new equipment is introduced, product lines are dropped and added. As internal and external conditions change, the workforce has to adjust. (See, for example, "Management in Practice: College Football Goes Worldwide.") Quite often it does this easily, but sometimes there is resistance to change. To deal with this situation, the manager must understand how the change process works.

The change process consists of three phases: unfreezing, introduction of the actual change, and refreezing. During the **unfreezing** phase the manager must analyze why the change is needed and the possible reasons for resistance to it. Many of the reasons for resistance can be traced directly to the manager. Typical ones include the following:

Typical reasons for resisting change

1. Failure to be specific about the change.
2. Failure to show why the change is necessary.
3. Failure to allow people affected by the change to have a say in planning it.
4. Failure to consider the work group's habit patterns.
5. Failure to keep employees informed about the change.
6. The creation of excessive work pressures during the change.
7. Failure to deal with employee anxiety regarding job security.[18]

Whatever the specific reasons for resistance, one of the most helpful ways to view the situation is in terms of **force field analysis**. On the one hand there are forces pushing for the change. On the other hand there are forces pushing against the change. The manager has to (a) increase the strength of the pressures pushing for the change, (b) decrease the strength of the forces resisting the change, (c) change a resisting force into one supporting the change, or (d) do a combination of these. Some of the ways in which this can be done include:

---

[17] Nobel McKay and Serge Lashutka, "The Basics of Organization Change: An Eclectic Model," *Training and Development Journal* (April 1983):64–69.

[18] Jack N. Wismer, "Organizational Change: How to Understand It and Deal with It," *Training/HRD* (May 1979):31.

MANAGEMENT IN PRACTICE

College Football Goes Worldwide

*A*thletic directors in major universities across America have a tremendous challenge in managing and controlling the athletic programs. Now they are confronted with a new opportunity for their football programs that also provides a whole new set of problems. Sports promoters in Europe and Asia have been anxious to match up American college football teams for appearances in their respective foreign countries. Here are some of the matchups that were made and their overseas site for the game.

Teams/Site

Pittsburgh vs. Rutgers/*Dublin, Ireland*
Syracuse vs. Louisville/*Tokyo, Japan*
Senior All-Stars/*Yokohama, Japan*
Duke vs. South Carolina/*Manchester, England*
Houston vs. Arizona State/*Tokyo, Japan*

The money is the lure for most colleges and universities. For example, Pittsburgh and Rutgers each received $200,000 for their appearance in Dublin, while Duke and South Carolina each got $400,000 for appearing in Manchester. In addition, all expenses are paid for by the sport's promotion group in that country and the players receive some international exposure with cultural experience. And, the fans *are* enthusiastic. In 1989, 50,000 fans paid $69 per ticket to see the Louisville-Syracuse game in Tokyo. The Rutgers-Pittsburgh matchup in England drew 40,000 people paying $30 per seat. Promoters are already lining up a "Miami Hurricanes vs. Arkansas Razorbacks" matchup for 1991 in England with an expectation of $1 million profit.

However, the idea is not without risk. In 1989 promoters worked to organize the first "Glasnost Bowl" in Moscow. Not only had they lined up Illinois vs. USC but also they arranged for ABC to televise the game. However, contract problems with the Soviet Union eventually led to cancellation of the event. Despite the risks, promoters around the world are currently working on other deals to lure major university football teams to their country. Athletic directors now must consider travel plans for the teams, the coaches, the cheerleaders, and the entire band. So, while new markets and new revenues for universities are clearly evident, so are new problems as college football goes worldwide.

Source: Gregory L. Miles, "These Players Are Really Going Long," *Business Week* (December 11, 1989):138.

Ways to reduce resistance

1. Involving the employees in the planning of the change.
2. Providing accurate and complete information regarding the change.
3. Giving employees a chance to air their objections.
4. Taking group norms and habits into account.
5. Making only essential changes.
6. Learning to use proper problem-solving techniques.[19]

---

[19] Wismer, "Organizational Change," 31.

Applying Creativity to Change

Another way to effectively deal with change is to apply creativity. Using a systematic approach, the idea of creativity can be implemented to move the change towards a "vision." The following steps are suggested as a guideline in applying the systematic application of creativity:

- Principle 1: Challenge the limits
- Principle 2: Clarify the intention
- Principle 3: Create a vision
- Principle 4: Define the "purpose"
- Principle 5: Deal with the corporate condition
- Principle 6: Commit to expanded levels of integrity, trust, and responsibility[20]

Figure 17-5 illustrates the eight stages of commitment involved in change. The preparation phase includes contact with, and then awareness of, the change. The acceptance phase introduces an understanding of the change with the beginnings of positive perception. Finally, the commitment stage covers installation, adoption, institutionalization, and internalization of the change. When managers follow the course of creativity and change, these "stages of commitment" could be of value for an effective understanding of the process. More importantly, the manager gains insight into the progress of commitment involved with the introduction of change. This is an important step towards establishing the desired organizational culture.

ORGANIZATIONAL CLIMATE/CULTURE

Performance appraisal, conflict, and change are personnel control issues that the manager faces on a periodic basis. If the organization is a good place in which to work, however, it is likely to have few problems related to conflict and change. On the other hand, if the environment is characterized by a great deal of distrust, anxiety, and fear, the organization probably will have many of these problems. That is why modern organizations are so interested in the topic of organizational climate, also referred to as culture.

---

[20] James Selman and Vincent F. DiBianca, "Contextual Management: Applying the Art of Dealing Creatively with Change," *Management Review* (September 1983):13–19. See also: Frank J. Sabatine, "Rediscovering Creativity—Unlearning Old Habits," *Mid-American Journal of Business* (Fall 1989):11–15.

FIGURE 17-5
Stages of Change
Commitment

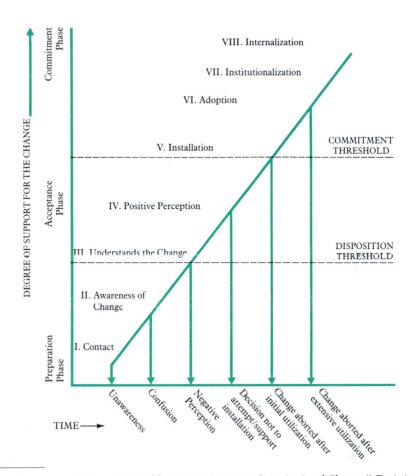

Measuring the Climate/Culture

Factors influencing overall climate   It is difficult to define the term organizational climate, or organizational culture, because there are so many properties in the work environment that serve to influence job behavior. Four of the most common include:

■ Decision-making practices—Are the personnel allowed to participate in the decision-making process, or are most important decisions made by the top managers?

■ Communication flows—Are the personnel informed about what is going on, or is the channel of communication basically one of orders flowing down from the top and progress reports flowing up from the bottom?

■ Motivation—Do the people who work the hardest and do the best work get the greatest rewards, or is everyone treated the same regardless of contribution?

■ Concern for the people—Does the organization try to improve working conditions and show that it is interested in the personnel, or is the enterprise most concerned with getting the work out regardless of human resource cost?

By designing questionnaires that provide answers to questions such as these, the organization can obtain feedback on its climate. Then it can develop programs to address the many problems that have been uncovered. Depending on what the management would like to know, all sorts of data feedback can be obtained. Figure 17-6 illustrates the results of a multilevel management survey conducted among units with the highest turnover. Both managers and nonmanagers in these units were asked to rate their superiors on a host of different organizational characteristics, from clarification of goals and objectives to feedback, delegation of authority, and the recognizing and reinforcing of good performance. The 50 percent line in the figure represents the average score received by all managers who were rated. Notice from the figure that in the units with the highest turnover a number of responses were significantly different from the norm (for example, goal clarification, goal pressure, delegation, and approachability). It is to these areas that management must direct its attention.

Feelings and attitudes must be measured

One of the most important things to remember about measuring the organizational climate is that the information being collected provides insights into organizational behavior and feelings that are not readily available to management. In fact, many managers, upon finding how the workers in their unit feel about various conditions, remark, "I didn't know that. I thought things were a lot better than this." Without some form of instrument to measure organizational climate, management typically does not know how the personnel really feel about many things. This is as true at the worker level as at the management level. For this reason, Figure 17-6 could be used to collect information at all levels of the hierarchy.

Organizational climate is like an iceberg

Another thing to remember about organizational climate is that it is very much like an iceberg. Part of an iceberg is visible (the ice above the water) and part of it is not (the ice below the water). An organization's climate is similar in that there are aspects that can be readily observed and others that are hidden. In the readily observed category are such things as the goals of the organization, its financial resources, its technological state and performance standards, and the skills and abilities of the personnel. In the hidden category are the attitudes, feelings, values, norms, supportiveness, and satisfaction of the personnel.

FIGURE 17-6 Multilevel Management Survey Results Concerning Managers in the Unit of an Organization with the Highest Turnover

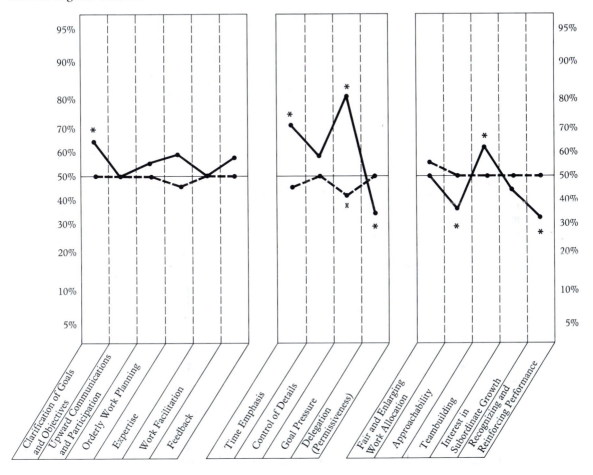

19 Managers Rating Their Superiors
65 Non-Managers Rating Their First-Line Superiors
*   Significantly Different from Norm

Source: Clark W. Wilson, "Assessing Management and OD Needs," *Training and Development Journal* (April 1980):73. Copyright 1980. *Training and Development Journal,* American Society for Training and Development. Reprinted with permission. All rights reserved.

When these hidden characteristics require attention, it can be provided through the use of organizational development techniques.

ORGANIZATIONAL DEVELOPMENT

When an organization uses a planned, systematic approach to effect change, it is said to be using **organizational development** (OD) efforts. Wendell L. French and Cecil H. Bell, two leading OD authorities, define the term this way:

OD defined

> Organization[al] development is a long-range effort to improve an organization's problem-solving and renewal processes, particularly through a more effective and collaborative management of organization culture — with special emphasis on the culture of formal work teams — with the assistance of a change agent, or a catalyst, and the use of the theory and technology of applied behavioral science, including action research.[21]

OD not only emphasizes solving behavior problems, but also focuses on ensuring that they do not recur. It often requires changes in the attitudes, feelings, and perceptions of the people involved. For this reason, many OD efforts make use of an outside expert called a change agent, or catalyst. This person enters the organization, analyzes the situation, and then helps bring about a solution.[22]

Regardless of whether the organization uses an outside change agent or relies upon people within the hierarchy to play this role, OD efforts share some basic characteristics:

Basic characteristics of OD

1. The emphasis is not on a one-shot solution to organizational problems but on an ongoing process in which organizational members learn how to interact successfully with others in solving these problems.
2. Intact work groups are used in the sense that everyone stays in his or her current work unit and remains in it throughout the OD change.
3. The change agent uses applied behavioral science principles, not theoretical, abstract concepts.
4. The objective of the OD effort is to change the values and behavior of the employees so as to improve intra- and intergroup harmony.
5. The analysis and recommended changes are based on data collected within the organization rather than ideas or recommendations that have worked in other enterprises.

---

[21] Wendell L. French and Cecil H. Bell, Jr., *Organization Development* (Englewood Cliffs, NJ: Prentice-Hall, 1978), 14.
[22] Laurie Weiss, "Revisiting the Basics of Conflict Intervention," *Training and Development Journal* (November 1983):68–70.

6. The efforts of the OD process are directed toward dealing with current problems and deciding how the personnel can solve them, working as a unit.

At the heart of the OD process are three basic components: diagnosis, action, and process maintenance. In the diagnostic component, information is gathered on characteristics of the organizational climate, including decision-making processes, communication patterns and styles, relationships between interfacing groups, the management of conflict, the setting of goals, and planning methods.[23]

The action stage is characterized by what are called OD interventions. This is a catchall term used to describe the structured activity in which individuals, groups, or units engage in accomplishing task goals that are related to organizational improvement. These interventions typically focus on problems central to the needs of the organization, rather than on hypothetical, abstract problems that may be peripheral to the members' needs.

> The dual aspect of OD interventions can be clarified with an illustration. Let us say that the top executives of an organization spend three days together in a workshop in which they do the following things: (1) explore the need for and desirability of a long-range strategy plan for the organization; (2) learn how to formulate such a strategy by analyzing other strategies, determining what the strategic variables are, being shown a sequence of steps for preparing a comprehensive plan, and so forth; and (3) actually make a three-year strategy plan for the organization. This intervention combines the dual features of learning and action: the executives engaged in activities in which they learned about strategy planning, and they then generated a strategy.[24]

After the action stage is complete, the OD practitioner monitors feedback and ensures that everything is going according to plan. Are the interventions proving to be timely and relevant? Are the activities producing the intended results? This phase is known as **process-maintenance**. During this phase the change agent ensures that there is continued involvement, commitment, and investment in the program by the members.

What specific type of OD intervention will the change agent use? It depends on the nature of the problem.[25] There are a number of traditional approaches, however, that can provide insights into the question. The following discussion examines some of these.

---

[23] Richard Beckhard, *Organization Development: Strategies and Models* (Reading, MA: Addison-Wesley, 1969), 26.

[24] French and Bell, *Organization Development,* 64.

[25] Robert R. Blake and Jane S. Mouton, "Out of the Past: How to Use Your Organization's History to Shape a Better Future," *Training and Development Journal* (November 1983):58–65.

Traditional Approaches to OD

A number of traditional OD approaches are used in modern organizations. While there are far too many to address all of them here, three will be given consideration: sensitivity training, survey feedback, and grid training.

Sensitivity Training

The **sensitivity training** or T (training)-group approach has been used since 1946. The objectives of T-group sessions include one or more of the following:

Objectives of T-groups

1. To make participants increasingly aware of, and sensitive to, emotional reactions and expressions in themselves and others.
2. To increase the ability of participants to perceive, and to learn from, the consequences of their actions through attention to their own and others' feelings.
3. To stimulate the clarification and development of personal values and goals consonant with a democratic and scientific approach to problems of social and personal decision and action.
4. To develop concepts and theoretical insights that will serve as tools in linking personal values, goals, and intentions to actions consistent with these inner factors and with the requirements of the situation.
5. To foster the achievement of behavioral effectiveness in transactions with the participants' environments.[26]

T-groups all function in about the same way. The participants are placed in an unstructured setting in which the leader of the group provides no direction. There are no agendas or rules. Gradually, they begin to focus attention on each other and on what is happening to them. Finally, the focus turns inward and the members begin to analyze each other.

Is T-group training of any real value? This approach has supporters as well as critics. For example, Jerry Porras and P. O. Berg found that positive results were reported by people who used it.[27] On the other hand, there is evidence that practitioners are not highly enthusiastic about sensitivity training, as seen by the fact that when personnel directors of large firms were surveyed, twice as many said they would not recommend its use as would recommend it.[28] Thus, newer approaches are now replacing the T-group method.

---

[26] Fred Luthans, *Organizational Behavior,* 3rd ed. (New York: McGraw-Hill, 1981), 614–15. See also Leslie This and Gordon Lippitt, "Managerial Guidelines to Sensitivity Training," *Training and Development Journal* (June 1981):144–50.

[27] Jerry I. Porras and P. O. Berg, "The Impact of Organization Development," *Academy of Management Review* (April 1978):259–60.

[28] William J. Kearney and Desmond D. Martin, "Sensitivity Training: An Established Management Development Tool," *Academy of Management Journal* (December 1974):755–60.

Survey Feedback

Survey feedback is a comprehensive OD intervention in that it draws survey data from all levels of the hierarchy and then feeds this information back to the personnel who provided it. These personnel then analyze, interpret, and act upon this data. An employee attitude form similar to the one in Figure 17-7 typically is used in collecting this data.

Research at the Institute for Social Research at the University of Michigan reveals that the following four steps are necessary if the survey feedback approach is to be optimally useful:

Steps in survey feedback

1. Organization members at the top of the hierarchy are involved in the preliminary planning.
2. Data are collected from all organization members.
3. Data are fed back to the top executive team and then down the hierarchy in functional teams.
4. Each superior presides at a meeting with his or her subordinates in which the data are discussed and in which: (a) subordinates are asked to help interpret the data, (b) plans are made for making constructive changes, and (c) plans are made for the introduction of the data at the next lower level.[29]

As the information is made available at each level, action plans are created for dealing with the necessary changes. In this process, the social, structural, goal, and task subsystems of the organization are changed. What makes this OD technique so valuable is that the personnel who are going to be affected by any changes help shape them. Also, the information being fed back to them is data they themselves helped generate. How successful has this technique been? French and Bell report that:

> Survey feedback has been shown to be an effective change technique in OD. In a longitudinal study evaluating the effects of different change techniques in 23 different organizations, survey feedback was found to be the most effective change strategy. . . . Survey feedback is a cost-effective means of implementing a comprehensive program, thus making it a highly desirable change technique.[30]

Grid Training

Grid training is an outgrowth of the managerial grid approach to leadership, a topic that was introduced in Chapter 13. When used for OD purposes, grid training has a pre-phase and six major follow-up phases. In the pre-phase,

---

[29] French and Bell, *Organization Development,* 154.
[30] French and Bell, *Organization Development,* 156.

FIGURE 17-7   Employee Attitude Survey

Describe working conditions in your unit by placing an "X" along each of the following continua.

Objectives are very vague.	1 2 3 4 5 6 7 8 9 10	Objectives are extremely clear.
Goal setting is done by a few who are often unaffected by the goals.	1 2 3 4 5 6 7 8 9 10	Goal setting is done by all persons who are affected by these goals.
Motivation is low.	1 2 3 4 5 6 7 8 9 10	Motivation is high.
Personal goals are suppressed for the "good of the organization."	1 2 3 4 5 6 7 8 9 10	Personal and organizational goals are integrated.
Communications are guarded.	1 2 3 4 5 6 7 8 9 10	Communications are open.
Relevant feelings are withheld.	1 2 3 4 5 6 7 8 9 10	Relevant feelings are shared.
Conflict is repressed or ignored.	1 2 3 4 5 6 7 8 9 10	Conflict is handled constructively.
Mutual support is low.	1 2 3 4 5 6 7 8 9 10	Mutual support is high.
Personal responsibility is low.	1 2 3 4 5 6 7 8 9 10	Personal responsibility is high.
The trust level is low.	1 2 3 4 5 6 7 8 9 10	The trust level is high.
Concern is mainly for work output.	1 2 3 4 5 6 7 8 9 10	Concern is mainly for people.
Procedures are inflexible.	1 2 3 4 5 6 7 8 9 10	Procedures are flexible.
Performance standards are low.	1 2 3 4 5 6 7 8 9 10	Performance standards are high.
Rewards are few.	1 2 3 4 5 6 7 8 9 10	Rewards are many.
Controls are imposed.	1 2 3 4 5 6 7 8 9 10	Controls are jointly determined.
Conformity is high.	1 2 3 4 5 6 7 8 9 10	Conformity is low.
The organizational climate is restrictive and tight.	1 2 3 4 5 6 7 8 9 10	The organizational climate is supportive and casual.
There is centralized leadership.	1 2 3 4 5 6 7 8 9 10	There is shared leadership.
There are many competitive relationships in the unit.	1 2 3 4 5 6 7 8 9 10	There are many collaborative relationships in the unit.
The superior's interpersonal skills are low.	1 2 3 4 5 6 7 8 9 10	The superior's interpersonal skills are high.

selected key managers who will later be instructors in the program attend a seminar where they learn about the managerial grid. In this week-long seminar, they are taught about grid concepts, have a chance to assess their own leadership styles using the managerial grid questionnaire, develop team action skills, are taught problem-solving and critiquing skills, and learn how to analyze an organization at work. The participants are then put through the six major phases of the grid OD seminar. Here they learn what grid training is all about and how to conduct it in their own organization. With this knowledge the initial participants are in an ideal position to evaluate the program and determine whether or not it is a good idea for their own enterprise. If they decide to go ahead with grid training for everyone else in the organization, the first major phase can begin. The six phases in this comprehensive OD effort, briefly described, are the following:

Major phases in grid training

- *Phase 1: The Managerial Grid* In this phase a grid seminar is conducted by the in-house managers who have already been trained in the grid approach. During this phase attention is focused on the leadership styles of the participating managers and on how they go about solving problems, critiquing, and communicating with subordinates. During this phase, the trainees also learn to become 9,9 managers.
- *Phase 2: Teamwork Development* The objective of this phase is to perfect teamwork. This is done through an analysis of team traditions and culture and the development of planning, problem-solving, and objective-setting skills. The participants are given actual work problems to solve and are provided with feedback on how well they function in a team setting.
- *Phase 3: Intergroup Development* The focus now moves to developing intergroup relations and getting work groups away from believing that they can attain their objectives and succeed only at the expense of other groups in the organization. The dynamics of intergroup cooperation and competition are explored.
- *Phase 4: Developing an Ideal Strategic Corporate Model* Now the focus switches to strategic planning, with the major goal being to learn the concepts and skills of corporate logic necessary to achieving excellence for the enterprise. The participants contribute to, and agree upon, important objectives for the organization. They are also encouraged to develop a sense of commitment to these objectives.
- *Phase 5: Implementing the Ideal Strategic Model* The participants now work on implementing the corporate model that has been developed. Emphasis is given to organizing and developing planning teams whose job is to examine every phase of the enterprise's operations in seeing how the organization can be moved more in line with the ideal model.

■ *Phase 6: Systematic Critique* In this final phase, the results of the program are evaluated. Progress is determined, barriers and problems are pinpointed, and plans for future action are determined. This last phase serves to ensure that the organization does not slip back into its old way of doing things. The best of the present is saved, while efforts are made to improve the areas of performance that are below par.

Quite obviously grid OD is a comprehensive program. In fact, it takes from three to five years to fully implement grid training throughout an organization. Given the time and expense required to implement this program, an organization must be fully committed to the effort before embarking on phase one, or the end result is likely to be a waste of valuable resources. On the other hand, many organizations that have employed grid training have been quite pleased with the results. French and Bell, summarizing Blake and Mouton's OD approach, report:

> Grid organization development is an approach to organization improvements that is complete and systematic and difficult. Does it work? Blake, Mouton, Barnes, and Greiner evaluated the results of a Grid OD program conducted in a large plant that was part of a very large multiplant company. The eight hundred managers and staff personnel of the four-thousand-person work force at the plant were all given training in the Managerial Grid and Grid OD concepts. Significant organizational improvements showed up on such "bottom-line" measures as greater profits, lower costs, and less waste. Managers, themselves, when asked about their own effectiveness and that of their corporation, likewise declared that changes for the better had resulted from the program.[31]

Does OD Really Pay Off?

Do OD programs really help organizations?[32] Research shows that they do. In particular, by developing teamwork, opening lines of communication, and creating bases for trust, enterprises often are able to reduce such undesirable behavior as absenteeism and turnover and the cost of replacing and training staff personnel.

One of the most interesting studies measuring the savings to an organization for eliminating human behavior problems was conducted by Philip Mirvis and Edward Lawler.[33] Using the branch system of a midwestern banking organization, they surveyed 160 tellers from 20 branches. These individuals were cashiers handling customer deposits, withdrawals, and other transactions. Mirvis and Lawler then calculated the loss to the bank caused by cashier absenteeism and turnover. Their results are presented in Table 17-4.

---

[31] French and Bell, *Organization Development,* 161.

[32] Elizabeth S. Gorovitz, "Looking Beyond the OD Mystique," *Training and Development Journal* (April 1983):12–14.

[33] Philip H. Mirvis and Edward E. Lawler, III, "Measuring the Financial Impact of Employee Attitudes," *Journal of Applied Psychology* (February 1977):1–8.

TABLE 17-4	Cost Per Incident of Absenteeism and Turnover		
Variable	**Cost (in dollars)**	**Cost Variable**	**(in dollars)**
Absenteeism		*Turnover*	
Absent employee		Replacement acquisition	
Salary	$23.04	Direct hiring costs	$ 293.95
Benefits	6.40	Other hiring costs	185.55
Replacement employee		Replacement training	
Training and Staff time	2.13	Preassignment	758.84
		—Learning curve	212.98
Unabsorbed burden	15.71	Unabsorbed burden	682.44
Lost profit contribution	19.17	Lost profit contribution	388.27
Total variable cost	23.04	Total variable cost	293.95
Total cost per employee	$66.45	Total cost per employee	$2,522.03

Source: Phillip H. Mirvis and Edward E. Lawler, III, "Measuring the Financial Impact of Employee Attitudes," *Journal of Applied Psychology* (February 1977):4. Copyright 1977 by the American Psychological Association. Reprinted by permission of the publisher and author.

OD interventions can increase efficiency

OD change agents quickly note that their behavioral interventions deal with problems such as absenteeism and turnover and can reduce the types of cost reported in Table 17-4. Mirvis and Lawler support these arguments. After measuring the intrinsic satisfaction (How satisfied are you with your job?), job involvement (How important to you is what happens in the bank?), and intrinsic motivation (Do you get a feeling of personal satisfaction from doing your job well?) of the tellers, they reported the data in Table 17-5. Notice from the data

TABLE 17-5	Dollars Saved Through Improved Job-Related Attitudes				
		Cost (in dollars) Per Teller Per Month			
Attitude	*Change*	*Absenteeism*	*Turnover*	*Shortage*	*Total*
Intrinsic	Increase	2.40	10.17	25.98	38.55
Satisfaction	Remain the same	5.44	17.04	25.27	47.75
	Decrease	8.48	23.93	24.55	56.96
Job	Increase	5.74	7.08	23.62	36.44
Involvement	Remain the same	5.44	17.04	25.27	47.75
	Decrease	5.14	27.01	26.91	59.06
Intrinsic	Increase	4.45	11.55	24.41	40.41
Motivation	Remain the same	5.44	17.04	25.27	47.75
	Decrease	6.43	22.54	26.13	55.10

Source: Philip H. Mirvis and Edward E. Lawler, III, "Measuring the Financial Impact of Employee Attitudes," *Journal of Applied Psychology* (February 1977):6. Copyright 1977 by the American Psychological Association. Reprinted with permission of the publisher and author.

that as attitudinal measures increase, the costs associated with absenteeism, turnover, and teller shortages (errors caused by incorrect cash outlays) go down.

The results of studies such as these are important in evaluating OD efforts. In particular, they point out the dollar-and-cents benefits associated with maintaining a favorable organizational climate. This is why organizational development is so important and useful in helping management control personnel performance.[34]

SUMMARY

1. Performance appraisal is an evaluation system that provides managers and subordinates with feedback on the subordinates' performance. A well-designed system has five basic characteristics: it is tied directly to the person's job; it is comprehensive; it is objective; it is based on standards of desired performance; and it is designed to provide the personnel with feedback on their strong points and shortcomings.

2. Performance appraisals provide value in several different ways, including personal development, rewards, motivation, personnel planning, and communication.

3. There are a number of popular techniques for appraising performance. One is the graphic rating scale, which allows the appraiser to easily evaluate a person by checking off his or her performance in a number of different categories. A second is the paired comparison, in which each individual in a unit or department is compared with all of the others. A third is the critical incidents method, in which effective or ineffective behavior is noted and used as a basis for evaluation. A fourth is the behaviorally anchored rating scale, in which employees and managers join together to identify and define dimensions of effective job performance and develop rating scales from their results.

4. A number of problems are associated with performance appraisals. Some of the most important include central tendency, leniency, strictness, the halo effect, the recency error, and personal biases. How can these problems be reduced? A number of suggestions were provided in the text, including the need to make performance evaluation as job related as possible.

5. In addition to appraising performance, managers often find it necessary to control conflict and change. Conflict is opposition or antagonistic interaction between two or more parties. Change is an altering of the status quo. Conflict management can be handled in many different ways.

---

[34] See, for example, Barry A. Mace and Philip H. Mirvis, "A Methodology for Assessment of Quality of Work Life and Organizational Effectiveness In Behavioral-Economic Terms," *Administrative Science Quarterly* (June 1976):212–26.

Some of the most effective were presented in Table 17-3. In dealing with change, the manager often must work to overcome resistance. This has to be done in a three-stage process: unfreezing old behaviors, introducing the desired change, and refreezing the new behaviors. Managers also may utilize systematic application of creativity in dealing with change.

6. To control personnel performance, an organization should know what the organizational climate is like. There are many properties in this climate including decision-making practices, communication flows, motivation, and concern for people. These properties are often measured through such techniques as attitude surveys.

7. When an organization uses a planned, systematic approach to effect change, it is said to be using organizational development (OD). At the heart of the OD process are three basic components: diagnosis, action, and maintenance.

8. A number of traditional OD approaches are used in modern organizations. Three of the most common are sensitivity training, survey feedback, and grid training.

9. Does OD really pay off? Research shows that it does. By helping develop teamwork, open lines of communication, and create bases for trust, the enterprise often is able to reduce undesirable behavior such as absenteeism and turnover and increase bottom-line performance.

KEY TERMS

Behaviorally anchored rating scales A performance appraisal system consisting of rating scales, designed by employees or managers or both, that are anchored to job-related behaviors and are used to help managers distinguish between effective, average, and ineffective job performance.

Central tendency A performance appraisal error in which an evaluator gives average ratings to almost everyone.

Change An altering of the status quo.

Conflict Opposition or antagonistic interaction between two or more parties.

Critical incidents A performance appraisal method in which the manager records unusually effective or ineffective subordinate behavior and uses this information for evaluation purposes.

Force field analysis The analysis of change through a consideration of the forces pushing for the change and of those pushing against it.

Graphic rating scales Performance appraisal instruments that contain factors, and degrees of each, on which individuals are evaluated by their superior.

Grid training A comprehensive OD intervention in which grid concepts are introduced, intra- and intergroup teamwork is developed, a strategic planning model is formulated and implemented, and a systematic critique is carried out.

Halo effect   The perception of an individual on the basis of one particular trait, such as intelligence, appearance, or dependability.

Leniency   A performance appraisal error in which an evaluator gives very high ratings to almost everyone.

Organizational development (OD)   A long-range effort to improve an organization's problem-solving and renewal processes with the assistance of a change agent or catalyst.

Paired comparison   A performance appraisal method in which each individual in the unit or department is compared with all of the others.

Performance appraisal   An evaluation system that provides both managers and subordinates with feedback on the subordinates' performance.

Process-maintenance   The stage of an OD effort in which the change agent ensures that there is continued involvement, commitment, and investment in the program by the members.

Recency error   A performance appraisal error brought about when a rater allows an individual's most recent behavior to have a greater impact on the evaluation than the individual's overall behavior.

Refreezing   The final phase of the change process, in which the manager rewards workers who are going along with the change and encourages other employees to do the same.

Reliability   The extent to which an instrument consistently yields the same results.

Sensitivity training (T-group approach)   An OD technique designed to help participants become more aware of their own feelings and those of others.

Similarity   A performance appraisal error in which an evaluator gives higher ratings to subordinates who are viewed as having the same values, habits, and attitudes as the evaluator.

Strictness   A performance appraisal error in which an evaluator gives very low ratings to just about everyone.

Survey feedback   A comprehensive OD intervention that draws survey data from all levels of the hierarchy and then feeds the information back to the personnel who provided it.

Unfreezing   The first phase of the change process, in which the manager analyzes why change is needed and the possible reasons for resistance to it.

Validity   The extent to which an instrument measures what it is supposed to measure.

QUESTIONS FOR ANALYSIS AND DISCUSSION

1. In your own words, how does the performance appraisal process work?
2. How are each of the following techniques used in the performance

appraisal process: graphic rating scales, paired comparison, critical incidents, behaviorally anchored rating scales? Be complete in your answer.

3. What are some of the most common problems associated with performance appraisal? How can these problems be dealt with? Explain.

4. What is meant by the term conflict? How can conflict be managed effectively?

5. In what way does force field analysis help explain the change process? Be complete in your answer.

6. The change process consists of three phases. What are these phases and what occurs in each?

7. Why do people resist change? How can such resistance be overcome? Be complete in your answer.

8. What are the key stages of commitment involved in change?

9. In your own words, what is meant by the term organizational climate? How can this climate be measured? What will the results tell management?

10. What is meant by the term organizational development (OD)? Be complete in your definition and description.

11. At the heart of the OD process are three basic components. What are they? Identify and describe each.

12. Of what value is sensitivity training? Does it have any drawbacks? Explain.

13. How does survey feedback work? Of what value is it to modern organizations?

14. When would an organization use grid training? How does this OD intervention work? What benefits does it offer? Be complete in your answer.

15. Does OD really pay off? Defend your answer.

CASE

Getting a Fair Shake

Clare Wickline is not happy. For the past seven weeks she has been the new supervisor of a work unit in a large West Coast enterprise. When Clare took over the unit, she was told that most of the workers were "okay" but she would have trouble with some of them. The departing manager, who was taking a job in an unrelated business, gave her the latest performance appraisals on all of the 23 employees. Four of them were rated excellent, four were rated good, 12 were rated average, and the last three were rated poor.

In this company the workers are briefly shown their performance evaluations. The boss then has a general discussion with each employee and tells the individual what he or she is doing well and what the person can do better. This short talk is used to measure and discuss progress and offer suggestions for future personnel development. When the salary raises come out, they are tied directly to the evaluation.

Initially, Clare used the most recent appraisals to help her in supervising the work group. She is now beginning to feel, however, that the ratings do not reflect the true potential and contribution of the individuals. For example, of the three who were rated poor, Clare has found that one of them is an excellent worker, one is good, and the other is average. On the other hand, of the four rated excellent, one of them is good and the others are either average or poor. The same pattern holds for most of the other workers. In each case the employee's attitude, performance, and contribution to the unit are not reflected by the performance appraisal.

The form used for the appraisal was a graphic rating scale that evaluated five factors: work quantity, work quality, appearance, attitude, and job knowledge; Clare is unsure about the way her predecessor arrived at his evaluations. She is beginning to get the impression, however, mostly from some of the workers, that he spent very little time finding out what everyone was doing. For the most part he relied on four informal group leaders to get things done. These were the employees who had the highest ratings. The three who were rated poor were those who had turned out the lowest work quantity during the one week in which a team of management consultants came by to review overall output in the unit.

Clare has talked to her boss and learned that the company has had very good success with its current graphic rating scale. She can use another form of appraisal technique if she prefers, however. The boss has told Clare that her predecessor was fired because he was highly ineffective in terms of his own work quantity, work quality, appearance, attitude, and job knowledge. "I wouldn't pay much attention to those performance evaluations he left behind," the boss told her. "They are probably highly biased and based strictly on non-job-related performance." Clare is currently putting together her quarterly review of each person's performance. She hopes to overcome many of the previous problems. "For once," she told her boss, "I'm going to see that these people get a fair shake."

1. If Clare did not choose to use a graphic rating scale in evaluating the performance of her people, what would you suggest she use? Defend your answer.
2. What particular problems were there with the way the previous supervisor evaluated the personnel?
3. How can Clare sidestep making these errors? What recommendations would you give her?

YOU BE THE CONSULTANT

Looking into the Grid

Carbrough Research and Development has just gone through some major changes, and it looks like there will be more in the near future. The company originally was a research and development (R&D) firm that specialized in making models and mockups for hard-to build equipment. Jacques Carbrough, who founded the firm in 1939, gathered around him the best designers and research people he could find. As the firm's reputation began to spread, the company slowly but surely began to move into manufacturing. "Since we know so much about how to design complex equipment, why not manufacture the product as well?" was the way the founder's son, Jean, explained why the company moved into the production area.

During the 1950s and 1960s the company did extremely well. About this time the top management also began to notice that the firm was being divided into two distinct groups: the R&D-oriented people and the manufacturing people. The two worked independently of each other for the most part and there were no real problems. Given the fact that the top management consisted mostly of R&D types, however, some underlying feelings were beginning to cause friction.

During the 1970s the company began to expand its holdings. Taking a conglomerate approach, it started purchasing firms in diversified fields. The acquired companies included a plastics manufacturer, a chemical firm, a real estate development firm, a small but profitable insurance company, and a well-known, although modest, New England publisher.

Last week Jean Carbrough's son Paul was installed as the chief executive officer of the conglomerate. Since then he has been working hard to get a handle on things. Having come up the ranks through the R&D side of operations, he is somewhat at a loss regarding how to manage and control the enterprise's farflung acquisitions. In particular, Paul has noticed that while ROI and profit are up to expectations, something is lacking. When he was just starting out in the firm 20 years ago, there was greater esprit de corps. People seemed to trust each other more. There was an attitude of "Let's get together and do this as a team." That now seems to be gone. In its place is a rather stuffy bureaucracy in which people do what they are told to do and not much more. There seem to be distinct lines between "us" and "them" among the major divisions of the original company and between the company and its newly acquired subsidiaries.

Paul is convinced that this attitude and value system will affect operations negatively. It is only a matter of time. As a result, he has been thinking about what can be done to improve things. A few years ago he attended a training program designed to familiarize the participants with some basic OD interventions and their value to organizational efforts. Although he does not know a great deal about the managerial grid, he was impressed with what he heard and believes it might well be ideal in dealing with the problems he sees. In particular, Paul would like an OD technique that would bring all of the units together. He knows that other techniques can be used in dealing with more limited issues such as interpersonal conflict or team dissension. These, however, can be incorporated into the process along the way.

Paul's greatest concern is that the conglomerate is changing too quickly.

The industries in which the company's diversified firms operate are extremely competitive, and they will have to hurry to keep up. Their basic nature may change and their relationship with the organization at large may become strained. In order to prevent this problem and maintain overall control of personnel performance, Paul would like to look seriously into employing the grid approach.

Your Consultation

Assume that you have just been called in by Paul to act as his consultant. First, describe to him how the grid OD approach works. Be as complete as possible in your answer. Then explain the benefits that this approach can have in terms of dealing with conflict and change, improving organizational climate, and improving bottomline performance in the enterprise. Finally, discuss some of the responsibilities and problems that Paul's organization will encounter if it chooses the grid approach.

Integrative Case Study
PRESSURE IN THE PARTS DIVISION

The Situation

The company has been manufacturing a wide variety of electronics systems for many years. It sells commercial systems, retail products, and government systems. It is widely recognized for the quality of its management and recently has received acclaim for the quality and reliability of its products. It has a reputation as being a good place to work. There are pressures and challenges. Today most of them arise from the internationalization of the electronics industry.

In the 1970s electronic manufacturing firms came under heavy international competitive forces. No matter how good they were in the past, they have had to change to survive. U.S. firms had to dramatically increase reliability, shorten delivery times, and reduce prices. This has meant taking wholly new approaches to design, to manufacturing processes, to procurement, to inventory of parts and finished goods, to order processing: in short, to every aspect of the business.

The company has to be able to provide repair parts for equipment it sold in the past. While new models may come out and old ones be discontinued, the repair parts are still needed. It is financially impractical and physically impossible to keep all possible parts in stock. The parts division is responsible for building repair parts to fill market predictions or as ordered by customers. With good management, sales of manufactured parts can be pleasingly profitable.

Ten years ago the company mounted a major campaign to reduce defects. It meant major education efforts, changes in managing, and changes in attitudes. The ongoing campaign has been successful. But not only was there pressure to reduce defects and mistakes, even in service activities, to impossibly low levels — "impossible" in 1970s thinking — there was constant pressure to reduce costs. Two key programs were JIT (Just-In-Time delivery from parts vendors and from manufacturing to shipping) and cycle time reduction.

Cycle time is the time it takes to complete one manufacturing cycle; i.e., to get one complete item through assembly. It is much more than just the time people spend working on an item for it includes all the waiting time to go from one stage to the next. Many different events can cause delays in manufacturing.

April — Pressure on the Parts Division

The manufacturing manager of the parts division, Tom,* was pleased with the latest operations report. They were hitting their targets. Ninety-six% of orders

---

* Only first names are used, since that is the way everyone in the plant spoke of or to each other. This case was prepared by Charles F. Douds of DePaul University. The names of the individuals and the firm have been disguised to preserve the firm's request for anonymity. Presented and accepted by the referred Midwest Society for Case Research. All rights reserved to the author and the MSCR. Copyright © 1989 by Charles F. Douds.

were shipping within one day of completion—over 10,000 items/day. A year and a half ago they had $1,200,000 of work in process. The cycle time reduction plan had reduced it to $200,000. Great! They were able to be more responsive to their customers, too. A short cycle time meant quick delivery. But it wasn't easy.

What wasn't obvious in the figures was the pressure this put on parts manufacturing. With the new productivity pressure they couldn't just build parts for inventory months or years before they might be needed the way they used to. Everything had to be scheduled very tightly. The scheduling and planning people had to be closely tied into sales and marketing had to be right on the nose with the numbers they gave to production control.

Now scheduling was giving them many more work orders each for smaller quantities than before the push for cycle time reduction. Each one of his five assembly departments would typically have 30 work orders in process, except unit fabrication would usually have 90. The smaller quantities and frequent changes meant they had to be fast and flexible or setup costs would eat them alive.

Tom had been feeling the heat to get units produced on schedule: and produced with virtually no errors. He and Walt, his key associate, had many discussions on how to improve shop productivity and reduce the cycle time. Just last month he had started having weekly meetings with the supervisors and schedulers. It was helping.

FIGURE 1   Parts Manufacturing Division

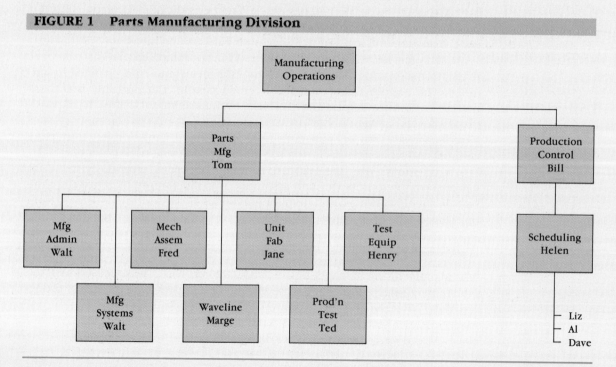

Organization Structure

Parallel to parts manufacturing were distribution, production scheduling, overseas parts manufacturing, and marketing, selling, and accounting functions. Production operations had five units on the shop floor and two office groups.

Walt is responsible for both office groups (Figure 1). His manufacturing systems group, four people, mostly did process design work, and manufacturing administration, also four people, handled the department's paperwork. Walt is Tom's general idea man and troubleshooter. In each of his functions he has a small group of talented and flexible people with lots of good connections to other parts of the corporation important to parts manufacturing, such as MIS and plant engineering.

Mechanical assembly was the one that bent and punched metal sheets to make chassis and boxes. It dealt with a smaller number of kits because many assemblies did not need metal parts. Fred had a simple work flow (Figure 2). His department always gave its output to other departments. Rarely did it depend upon another department for its parts. It also depended upon a much smaller number of vendors than the other fabricating departments.

FIGURE 2   Some Parts Production Workflows

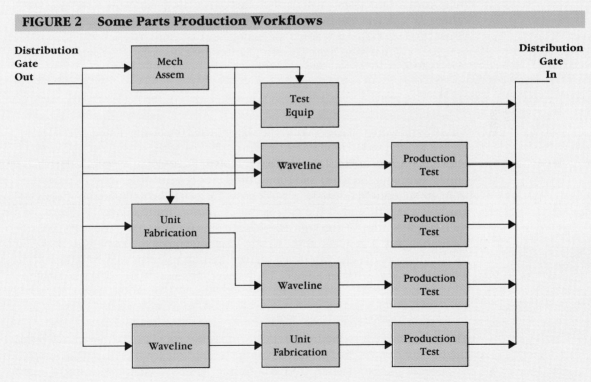

Note: Quality control done by work groups

The waveline fabricated printed circuits by inserting components into circuit boards and using a "wave solder" machine to fasten them in place. Its output could go to other fabricating departments, production test, or "the gate" where completed items were accepted for shipment.

The test equipment department built complete assemblies for the company's line of test equipment. Some were very old designs; some were very complex; some very rugged. Its output usually went directly to the gate.

The unit fabrication department handled the widest variety of kits and assemblies and built the greatest number of units. It could receive items from any department. Its output could go to other fabricating departments, production test, or the gate.

Production test did no fabricating, so it was dependent upon all other departments for finished assemblies to test. They also did the electronic "alignment" of receivers and transmitter assemblies. When they discovered errors most often they returned the units to the department that built them. That was never good news.

There is no separate quality control unit. It was eliminated about a year ago when the error-reduction program became fully successful. Everyone does their own inspections, which includes inspecting what they receive from others. An extensive training program is ongoing. Managers, secretaries, supervisors, marketers, team leaders, salesmen, and assemblers — everyone — is expected to regularly go back for refresher training sessions. Customer feedback is the ultimate criterion. Six Sigma has been working well.

The Work Flow

Kits of parts were put together in the warehouse area by the distribution department and released to manufacturing through "the gate" — the gate in the fence between the two areas of the building. Finished goods were returned to distribution (through the gate) and then stored if necessary until shipped. The time from the scheduled release of a work order for a kit to be manufactured until it is finished and returned to the gate is the *cycle time* for that job.

Work can move through manufacturing in many different ways as indicated in Figure 2. A given item is always manufactured the same way, so when the supervisors or schedulers see a given part number they know who will be working on it in what sequence. They never make drawings of the work flow.

The Build Report from Accounting

The report that everyone in manufacturing relies on to plan their daily work is the weekly *build report* produced on the mainframe by MIS from data entered by accounting, purchasing, and scheduling. It shows what kits were released from the gate each week. A kit is the raw parts needed to manufacture a batch of assemblies. These kit releases drive everything in manufacturing. All subsequent operations depend upon what kits are to be built. For the last six months the report also shows the cycle time for each completed work order. Their present target was a maximum of 16 days.

The build report shows each and every kit scheduled, released, and finished. Work orders that have been released but not yet finished are only shown as released. (If some of the kits in a work order have been finished, that partial completion will be shown.) It does not show anything whatsoever about the progress of kits through the various production departments. Note particularly that the build report comes out only *once a week.*

The finished goods figures in the build report show the dollar payments credited to each supervisor's area for finished work orders. Actually these are only internal transfer payments, but they are the basis for accolades—or frowns—from above.

The Future Manufacturing Control System from MIS

All the competitive pressures for enhanced reliability and productivity had lead top management to authorize a major project called the Manufacturing Control System (MCS). It included not only major new software, but also an entirely new mainframe computer as well. It is supposed to integrate the corporation's operations. It cuts across all departments from the lowest levels up and provides comprehensive reports to everyone. It is intended to serve all levels of management and supervision. It is designed to provide extensive decentralization with simultaneous oversight available from the top. It's an ambitious undertaking based on contemporary management theory and contemporary principles of MIS.

All levels of management and supervision provided extensive input during its design. Development started two years ago and was continuing.

May—Cycle Time Task Force

At a weekly meeting in April Tom and Walt had proposed setting up a task force to make their daily scheduling easier and more effective. They were beginning to realize that the scheduling method they had been using for so many years was not good enough any more—"gate-to-gate" scheduling, explained below. They needed something better.

At the first meeting Walt clearly was in charge by mutual agreement of the other members—Bill, Helen, Art, and Jane. Bill was Tom's counterpart—manager of production scheduling. Helen worked for him as supervisor of the schedulers. Art, a former assembly technician, was now doing PC work for Walt. Jane was the production supervisor with the heaviest load of work orders and the largest staff. She was quick to mention that she hadn't volunteered. They were a task force, but no one had dignified them with such a title—titles weren't that important around here. They felt such things as organization charts were for the bureaucratic types elsewhere.

Walt summarized the situation. They all knew that scheduling was getting more difficult, especially for the supervisors on the shop floor. The time to manufacture was getting shorter and shorter. They were meeting and exceeding their cycle time goals, but it was getting more and more difficult to manage.

Walt noted that the MCS — Manufacturing Control System — being created by MIS theoretically would help. It was no news when Walt said that they needed to do something now since MCS wasn't scheduled for completion for another two years.

Everyone knew that the build report was always out of date by Monday afternoon, even though it came out Monday morning and so they all had to mark it up with changes and corrections. Jane had brought her copy of last week's build report to show how she scheduled her people. She had the largest group of assemblers (24) and probably built the widest range of assemblies. While all her people were encouraged and rewarded to have multiple skills, not everyone could do everything so they had to be scheduled carefully. Given the wide variety of things to be built, this was the case for all the supervisors, for variety is fundamental in parts manufacturing.

Jane's copy of the weekly build report was black with penciled-in data. She often spent five hours a day working on it, part of that time at home. While Jane was an extreme case, the other supervisors used the report in much the same way.

Although her people did their own inspection, electronic testing and alignment were done by the technicians in production test supervised by Henry. Much of her production went to his group. Improving the cycle time figures for the plant had focussed a lot of attention on the two of them.

The group looked at these details in this and subsequent meetings, trying to figure out why a system that had worked well in the past was now having problems. These were the major changes that had occurred:

1. The reliability program had been instituted nearly 10 years ago. It was and remained successful here as long as they kept having education sessions and kept everyone going back for refreshers — managers and workers alike.
2. Four years ago all of their long-run work had been shifted to a new plant in Puerto Rico. It's a typical assembly line operation building spare parts for more recent, high-volume equipment. They have enough time to train low-skilled workers in each assembly step. They don't need the high level of skill needed by the workers here in the States.
3. Two layers of management were removed (without layoffs). The communication lines had been shortened. Tom was now having weekly meetings with all the supervisors, some of the schedulers, and other staff. Now there were no insulating layers of foremen or managers.

With it all laid out clearly they slowly came to realize that there was no reasonable "something different" to blame. All the changes, at least in terms of the task force's issue, were neutral or helpful. The problem lay in the gate-to-gate loop. Simply shortening that time made everything more complex. As they sped up, the old methods based on accounting's build report was creaking and groaning. They were to the point where something better was needed. Perhaps MCS could provide it; but it looked like it would be a long time coming.

The Problem Defined by the Task Group

In retrospect their problem seems pretty obvious. They needed more information than the build report could provide. They needed daily information on the status of all the work in process. Their understanding developed along the following lines.

The build report was needed to provide the data on how well they were doing financially and how well on cycle time. Upper level managers were especially concerned about these figures. It was useful to the supervisors in managing the process because it gave the specific work orders that were being released. This was of less concern to division managers, but the line supervisors found it invaluable in scheduling their work and their people. It was the key to decreasing the cycle time from weeks to days. As cycle time shortens, experience was showing them that management becomes more demanding—more dynamic and complex.

With the continuing pressure to decrease cycle time—from 16 days to eight—the management problem was moving to a new level of complexity. What the task force had come to really appreciate was that details on what was scheduled into manufacturing and what had been completed were not enough. The build report provided only the times out of and into distribution's gate. It had been adequate at one time but now more data was needed to manage the shorter cycle times.

The task force specifically realized they now needed data on how the jobs, that is, the work orders, were progressing through their shop from one department to another. They needed data each day (if not more often) on the status of each work order in each department. They needed to know the job status on a daily basis, rather than a weekly basis. They needed to work out the timing among the various steps in completing each job in various departments. More importantly, no longer could they think about the jobs one at a time: they had to find ways to squeeze tasks in around each other. In other words, they had to think about the interactions among all the tasks in the work orders. It was even further complicated by the short cycle times they were now achieving. They couldn't just think about the work in their department. They had to look at other departments to see what would be coming and when. Especially different from the past, they also had to look at their output. If the next department wasn't ready, the goods would sit waiting, hurting your cycle time until the next department was ready. They had to figure out how other's work would affect each of their own jobs. It wasn't enough to plan their own work any more—they had to plan it interdependently with other departments!

In the past scheduling did most of this coordinating. The scheduler, who was in a position to have an overview of the whole situation, acted as the communication link. This was still important and they were still doing it, but no longer was it enough and they couldn't do it all. The supervisors had to be actively planning and making decisions.

In academic terms, the problem the supervisors and schedulers faced was that they had become dynamically interdependent upon each other. They needed current detailed data about the work flow as it moved through the production floor. They needed it on a daily basis, sometimes even an hourly basis.

June — The Auto Scheduling System Plan

Essentially what they needed was a way to match the amount of time needed to build all the work orders released to the production line capacity — that is, the number of people with the right skills available and the amount of work hours required. Release too much and overtime is needed; release too little and good people are sitting on their hands. Because overtime is costly, it was not easy to get it authorized. Skilled supervisors were expected to avoid using it.

There were many complicating factors. Some kits could be totally built within one group, but most involved two or three groups.

Coordinating the activity for any one work order was no problem. Coordinating a half dozen wasn't bad. But most supervisors usually had 20 or 30 active work orders. Exceptions and problems could involve a given work order or individual units within a work order. Each work order might be for anywhere from one to a hundred units.

Then there were always unusual things. A kit might be released with a few components missing, so most of the order gets finished on time but two or three units do not. A vendor might be late with a part and so half-finished units stack up. Some units failing in circuit testing turn out to have a part marked correctly, or so it seems, but the part actually has the wrong value. The vendor is at fault but it still takes time to get the right part. Customers sometimes cancel orders. All in all there are dozens of reasons for changes and exceptions.

Then there were the problems involving people. For instance, missing parts finally arrive but the supervisor can't find the units that were set aside someplace in the shop. Maria is on vacation so Ruth, the only other one with the skill for this particular unit, has to do it. Only she is in the middle of making units that have to be tested. If those units don't get to production test this afternoon, they will be delayed past their cycle time limit since a high priority job is scheduled into production test tomorrow. Given time, all of these interactions can be worked out. Time is what they no longer have.

Cycle time reduction makes managing an ever-more-demanding job. The task force plan was to build their own production scheduling data system. It would provide several reports tailored to their needs. They called them:

cycle time report
hours roll-up report
scheduled hours report

Others were available as needed. Each of these would help the supervisors and schedulers make their day-to-day decisions. All the reports came from actual data from the shop floor. At least once a day each shop supervisor would enter data about which releases were started and units completed on each work order. Notes could be added about special problems. Scheduling would also enter information that affected what was currently being built. In practice, the schedulers were frequently in contact with the supervisors, helping them solve problems about missing or improper parts or giving them information about in-coming goods or such things.

The data could be processed in various ways. It could show where everything was, how much had been finished, how long it took, and for unfinished units, how long since they had been released. Those getting close to their cycle time limit would be highlighted in a special "hot potato" report. Anyone could get a copy of any report at any time. It would be up-to the minute.

They called this the *automatic scheduling system.* Actually, there was nothing automatic about it. Its design should allow them to do a better job making their own scheduling decisions. It would provide daily updated information in formats tailored to the needs of each decision maker. It would help them visualize the whole situation or examine any aspect or detail. It would run on PCs tied together in a network and use the data base program dBase III. A year or so ago the company had installed a local area network (LAN), tying together a half dozen PCs in manufacturing and scheduling. With the cables in place for the network it would be easy to add the few more PCs needed.

This system would duplicate functions that were to be in the manufacturing control system. They were treading on MIS turf, although the system would be used totally within their own group, in their own building. Walt's people had done their missionary work well. They described the plan to MIS and there was no objection.

July — Initial Development

Art had gotten into PCs a number of years ago. He was a technician in the production test group. Building boards for old equipment didn't give much opportunity to do programming. He enjoyed learning it on his own.

Walt had learned of his interest and so, wearing his hat as manager of administrative services, had Art do some programming for him from time to time. Most often it was to build a little data base or to fix up a new report. Recently, wearing his hat of manager of manufacturing systems, he added Art to his group on a full-time basis. Art was delighted with the opportunity, the new job title, and the challenge of the programming.

Dave began working closely with Art on the specifics of the reports. Dave had majored in systems analysis. He had enjoyed his summer work at the company and joined them full time after graduation a year ago. He had spent a couple of summers with scheduling and now, after a year in another unit, he had been transferred back to them. The cycle time project was like a magnet to him. His supervisor, Helen, and Walt were pleased to see this. He had products that he was responsible for scheduling, but he gradually got or was given — it never was too clear which — more responsibility on the auto scheduling project.

Art talked to the supervisors, schedulers, and managers to identify more exactly the data needed. Reports could be tailored later on relatively easily since they were doing their own work using a standard PC data base program. However, it was important to ensure that they were collecting all the data needed.

Most of Art's time was spent on developing the data base and the complications introduced by using the LAN. The new version of the product he wanted to use would be the first version of it designed to be used with a LAN. For several months the publisher had been using that famous line of the software industry. "It's due out any day now."

August — First Trial in Mechanical Assembly

The program would be brought on line one department at a time. It would be easier to find and fix problems that way. Fred's mechanical assembly department was going to be the one to test the program.

He had his group leader keep the old manual system going. That is, he made the usual pencil annotations in the weekly build report. Fred didn't mind too much having to put up with all the errors. In fact, he seemed to rather enjoy catching Art and Dave with them. What he didn't like was the way the items were appearing on the list. The build report was all alphabetical. Now they were grouped by type.

Art was working very hard on the more fundamental programming problems they were uncovering. He, Dave, and often Fred had many sessions together. Dave felt he was really getting his teeth into systems analysis work, and he was.

September — Waveline on Line

Marge's group, the waveline, was the second one on the auto scheduling system. She had been looking forward to it. Here was a practical use for a PC. She and her husband had a PC at home, but she had never done much with it. She had taken a course at the junior college and used it some. She really didn't do much letter writing. She enjoyed figuring out how to keep her recipes on the PC, but once done it didn't seem too practical.

Marge believed in education. She had started out on the line as an assembler. She liked learning new tasks but, "When you did 1,000 of the same unit, it got boring." She wanted her workers to be versatile, especially now that they were doing their own testing. Now all newly hired assemblers had to have at least seventh grade English and math. She was glad her workers could go to class in the building after work. The company paid fifty % of the tuition.

She liked the auto scheduling system. She really liked not having so much paperwork to deal with. The data you got was only your data: it didn't include everyone else's. Only your current work was there. She didn't have to lug around a pile of 17-inch fanfold paper. There was a lot less data to write down: you didn't have to recopy part numbers and other entries. You only had to enter the data that had changed. Instead of dealing with a report that was out of date almost as soon as you got it, now she could get an accurate report every day. Right now it only had Fred's and her groups' data.

She entered her data every day—except when they were having trouble with the system, of course. Her group leader kept the manual system going so they wouldn't be in trouble when they didn't get the new report because the system was down.

It was after they got more groups on the system that the bickering began.

October — Overloaded Hardware

They began having lots of trouble with the hardware as more people began to use it. Before they put the auto scheduling system on it the LAN had never been used by more than one person at a time and even then not too often. The system would work in fits and starts. Neither the local dealer nor the LAN manufacturer were able to find all the problems. Evidently this was the first installation to really challenge this brand of LAN with a heavy load. Repeatedly, Art was the one who proved to the dealer's or the manufacturer's experts that the LAN software had one particular problem or another.

With the system going down so often, there were many errors in the data. Dave was kept more than busy running around to get missing data, to check that data was right, to go over the reports, and to calm frazzled tempers. His pleasant disposition and always cheery face made him just the right sort of person for the job.

Actually, some days they were getting enough data so that the supervisors could really begin to work with it. It used to be that Marge would get her cycle time numbers when she already had a good idea that they were bad. The system provided a new report so now she could see delays in the making. She was learning how to interpret the numbers.

They gave her ammunition to go after Ted in production test. She knew all along that they were putting her off. Ted could usually pull off a wisecrack or smooth things over. But the last few months the pressure for meeting cycle time had been getting more intense and she was sure they were putting her off more often. Her cycle times were never as good as Jane's. Now she was beginning to see the reason, although Jane wasn't on the system yet.

Ted had mixed feelings. Like everyone else, he felt secure with the old familiar way. Jane kept calling the build report her "security blanket" and that appealed to Ted, too. Dave kept after him, showing him things about the reports. Eventually, after Dave saw what was bothering him, he and Art created a new report for Ted. With it, Ted could see what was coming and plan ahead. It showed what the cycle times would be when the kits got there—useful information. It wasn't too useful yet without Jane's information, but he didn't mind at all that the menu screen showed his name on his own special report.

The problem for everybody was that too often the useful information was wrong. There were still surprises happening on the floor. Things that weren't on the schedule would suddenly show up to be worked on—usually with the plea to "get on it" so the cycle time target wouldn't be missed.

November—Advantages Seen with Complications

In November they had all the departments on the system except Jane's. The supervisors were becoming accustomed to using the reports at least to the extent they could read and interpret the data for their own departments.

They were finding that the data had all the detail they wanted. As they worked with it they could begin to see the implications for how one thing could affect another. This was true for both the schedulers and the supervisors but as yet they were not always willing to admit it.

Henry, responsible for building test equipment, was the latest one to go on line. New to the job in the last year, he was quite flexible. He liked the way the data was sorted for him. Fred, in mechanical assembly and the first one on, still said he liked having everything alphabetical but seemed to be adapting. Except for parts coming from Fred, Henry's products were usually independent of the other departments. Dave, as usual, helped him get started on the system. After the first couple of weeks Henry, with Dave's help, learned that errors in his data were caused by what he typed in or failed to type in.

The others were not especially aware of Henry's success, for they didn't work with him that closely. They were finding some of the data useful, but they didn't trust it because of past experience.

Marge had a good experience, but she didn't talk about it much. She began to see why her cycle times were always longer than Jane's. Her output spent more time waiting for production test. Many work orders from either her group or Jane's moved through with no delay, but when you sorted out all the data carefully and did some calculations you could see how the waiting time hurt her statistics more than Jane's. Never before had she been able to really figure out the reason. When she had needled Ted about it in the past, he always denied favoring Jane. Probably he wasn't doing it consciously, but now with new daily data she could negotiate better with him.

In prior weeks the system had lost data as more people put more into the system. Tracking down the problem had caused Art many sleepless nights. There had been a succession of hardware problems. Some were solved but some were inherent. He finally developed a scheme that did an end run around the problem. Every night he stayed late and ran a special program that corrected the difficulties. He knew that since the middle of October no data had been lost because of hardware (and related operating system software) problems.

Then there were the people problems that messed up the data and sometimes lost it. Marge, without telling anyone, had tried creating her own report. In her explorations some data was changed and deleted. It was a while before someone noticed it. Of course, once noticed and the cause found, it was easy to restore a backup copy and only tedious to update the new data entered. Art was doing a good job on the backups, but still the schedulers and the supervisors had several days of planning disrupted by the bad data.

There were other times that the supervisors or their group leaders made mistakes that ended up creating problems with the data. Sometimes it was due to carelessness. Sometimes it was due to not following instructions. Sometimes it came from the risk inherent in the design philosophy of allowing the system to be flexible for the eventual benefit of everyone.

Then there was the data that was not there because Jane's unit fabrication department was not yet on line. Given that her work orders had the greatest interaction with other departments, this legitimately missing data had the greatest psychological as well as technical impact.

Everyone had learned to not fully trust the data. Everyone had bad experiences. This negativity was reinforced by the continuing slow response from the system as data was entered. Art had consulted widely with many people about the technical problems of the system and had done everything possible to speed up the response time. It was better now — especially if they did not all get on at the same time — but the basic problem could only be solved with money. Art now knew there was a fundamental problem with the LAN. It needed to be replaced. They needed a bigger hard disk, too; they were generating so much data. Top management would not budget the money until the Parts department could show that the system was helping them. Art was confident it could help, but as yet the others were not.

It was difficult to overcome the biases. Many problems were blamed on the hardware. Sometimes it was true, sometimes not. Many problems were blamed on the software. At one time that was true and an occasional one would still crop up. Problems were blamed on the users. That didn't make anyone feel good. The user in question preferred to blame the hardware or software. Was it the frustration with the automatic scheduling system, the stress of cycle time reduction, or something else? Maybe they didn't even notice it but now there certainly was an attitude of blaming that didn't exist before.

They had enough information and enough success to get a real sense of what the automatic scheduling system could do for them, but they were all frustrated. Now they could begin to really see in ways they had never seen before the scope of the day-to-day scene (except for unit production's missing data). Now they had the ammunition to argue pointedly and constructively with each other, but the arguments were often upset and made useless by missing data that one person had and another did not. This often made tempers rise.

The Schedulers and the Automatic Scheduling System

The schedulers in the production scheduling department worked closely with the manufacturing supervisors. The division was proud of this relationship, for in many companies there is tension between the two. Neither the JIT program nor the cycle time reduction effort could have been so successful without a productive relationship. The schedulers were production's link to purchasing, marketing, and even the customer. Changes, and there were many, were cleared through scheduling—they buffered manufacturing from many surprises and uncertainties.

Each department supervisor had a scheduler who was responsible for scheduling the release of work orders that originated in that particular department. The schedulers were on the second floor along with various other support groups; manufacturing was on the first floor. Each person had their own little cubicle with desk, chair, file cabinet, computer terminal, and no room left over. The terminals were tied into the data system that provided the weekly build report from accounting.

The scheduling group had been represented on the task force by Dave. As we have seen, he became a kingpin in the automatic scheduling system development and support. In general, the schedulers had supported the idea. However, as each department went on line the scheduler for that department had to enter the detailed work order release data every day into the local PC system. This was an exact duplicate, only in a different format, of what they entered into the mainframe terminal. With the terminal on their desk they could enter data when ready or look things up as needed. They shared one PC. To use it they had to go to the cubicle where it was located.

As data began to be available from the automatic scheduling system the schedulers began to make some use of it. Gradually they found some of it to be useful, most often as they worked with the supervisors working out adjustments to changes. They had less use for it in working out original release schedules.

What really did get to them was having to enter all their data twice. They complained to Walt and Art repeatedly about this but here parts production was totally dependent upon MIS and MIS was unyielding. They would not tie parts production's local area network into the accounting data base on the older mainframe computer.

The work order schedule data was only a small part of what was in the data base. Most of it was vital cost and financial data. MIS felt too many things could go wrong patching the LAN into the older mainframe. It was part of an older system that did not have good provisions for external access. If parts manufacturing was to have access to the data base, new hardware would have to be added. But of greater concern, MIS could not be sure of the integrity of the accounting data base if other systems could access it. This would not be a problem with new systems such as the MCS, but it was with the old one.

In December Helen had a meeting with her people in Bill's office. Bill, Helen's boss, had been on the original task force. Now there was so much dissatisfaction he was concerned. They felt they were wasting time when the system was supposed to save time and improve scheduling. Bill asked some pointed questions but they couldn't come up with numbers for answers. Managers do like hard data. They decided they would keep track of their time hour by hour for the next month. Then they would have the figures to show to Walt and Tom. While Dave, attending this meeting as a scheduler, still believed in the system's potential, he did agree that having numbers would clarify the issue.

December — The Last Department

By December it was time to bring Jane's unit production department onto the system — the last one and the one with the most difficult scheduling problems. It was surely the biggest one in terms of total number of work orders released. Unit fabrication accounted for fifty % of the total. Jane was still taking her build report home every night to update it and plan the next day's work. This kept her in control of her many problems. She usually had about 90 orders in process, with about 60 new ones each week. It was difficult to count them because changes — cancellations, rush orders, etc. — affected her more often than the others. That made control quite a challenge.

It was amazing that she met the cycle time goals as well as she did. It took a lot of devotion and flexibility. In the old days they used to be able to get overtime approved for their people, but no more. Only for a full blown crisis! Now you couldn't use overtime to keep control, but that didn't mean you couldn't look outside your own group. Part of the secret to her ability was the way she was able to get Ted to keep the priority up on her units going through production test. Yes, Ted had always accommodated her well.

Dave and Art had made the arrangements for Jane to start on the system. She was not at all keen about it. Even though it took a lot of time, her own way worked. The time she spent didn't hurt anyone else. She had everything under control.

Liz did all the production control work for Jane. The volume in Jane's unit fabrication department kept her more than busy. Despite the load she liked the challenge and variety. She regularly came to work between 6:30 and 7:00 A.M. and left at 4:00 P.M. At least that is what it was before Dave showed her how to use the system on the PC. That looked okay, but it was annoying to have to leave her desk and be away from her phone.

It was only after she started seriously using it that she really began to understand what others had been talking about—how slow the system was. After entering a line she had to wait and wait before it came back ready for the next entry. Putting the initial data on the system for unit fabrication—two weeks worth—took her a full day. She didn't get anything else done. The next day it took her two hours. After a few days it became clear the system was adding one to two hours to her work day. Jane was supposed to be entering her data, too, but after the first few days it wasn't happening regularly. Now Liz had to work with both Jane's manual entries in the build report and the new work.

She wasn't the only one getting irritated. The rest of the schedulers, except for Dave, of course, had been complaining for some time. Al, who always saw the world through a dour eye, had some choice phrases for the system. Even Helen, who had been behind the original idea, was cooling off. They all now had more work to do and they had to work with two different systems—the new one and the pencil annotations in the supervisors' build reports. Not to mention that they had to enter much of the same data into the mainframe terminals at their desk as well as into the new automatic scheduling system.

Jane's attitude wasn't helped when she found cycle times getting worse on some of her work orders. She always kept everything in such good control, but now she was having difficulty with Ted more often. She couldn't figure out why.

Jane wasn't entering data yet. She had all kinds of reasons. She called her laboriously marked up build report her "security blanket." None of the other supervisors made fun of her. Sometimes they used the "security blanket" phrase themselves. Just recently a lot of data kept coming out wrong. That did nothing to increase her belief that she could use the system to control her more difficult area. She didn't want to hear the successful conclusion of the latest bad data story.

Dave and Art tracked it down to Marge's area. Rather than entering data herself Marge now had her group leader entering the data daily. The group leader never seemed to have a problem when Dave or Marge were there. Even though Dave explained several times and wrote out the procedures, problems persisted. It took a while for it to come out that she had never learned to read English! She was trying to deal with the menu screens, the job tickets, and other paper entirely from memory.

Liz, Jane's scheduler, faithfully entered her data, staying late to get it done. It was two weeks before she had to take a close look at the daily report. She hadn't had any reason to look at the reports in detail because Jane still wasn't entering her data. She found that the hours scheduled were off by a full day. That could really foul up scheduling 24 people! She showed it to Helen, then took off downstairs to find Art.

Art, then Dave, then Walt went over the data and questioned her. Yes, there were items missing. Was she sure she had keyed them in? Yes. Had she been interrupted and started up at the wrong spot? No. Through the years she had developed her own routines so she didn't make those mistakes any more. They asked so many questions, they made her feel dumb. She didn't like that.

The next meeting was not a calm one. As a matter of fact, it was almost raucous. They had never been ones to hide their emotions all the time. They all knew that anyone had to let off steam every once in a while, but the once-in-a-whiles were becoming more frequent since fall.

The supervisors had been getting a lot of lectures in the meetings about entering their data every day. To a greater or lesser extent they were doing it. Except, of course, for Jane. Supposedly all the problems with the LAN had been solved except for its miserably slow response part of the time. But now the system was eating their data! They really came down on Art. And he couldn't say much.

It was too bad that it had to happen so close to Christmas. They had another heated Monday meeting with the supervisors—Tom, Walt, and Art. The arguments were the same, only hotter. They felt they couldn't depend upon the data. When they release work orders they have to show up as really released. Scheduled items have to appear. It was taking forever for the system to respond.

The responses were the same platitudes: "We're trying to improve." "We've all got to work with each other." "You've got to put your data in every day." "Be more patient, the system's not really that slow." Even Art, big, calm, cool, collected Art had some hot things to say. Everyone felt maybe he was beginning to take the criticism personally.

The schedulers didn't mention the time data for they had only been collecting it for a few days. Already it looked like it wouldn't prove their point —they weren't actually spending as much time with the system as they thought they were. Liz had to put in a good bit of time, but part of that was dealing with Jane's continuing use of her security blanket. (But could you really blame Jane?) They had to admit that various aspects of the new reports were useful. However, they would have to continue entering the same data into the auto scheduling system and the mainframe terminal.

If nothing else the meeting showed that for a variety of reasons there was a lot of aggravation coming out of the system and the pressure to further improve their cycle time.

Friday, January 13th

Bill was the one who officially called the meeting for Friday—the 13th, as it happened.

Enough had been invested in the system. It wasn't the money. The company encouraged trying things out.

They had successfully adapted to other changes in the organization. The reliability program had been a major challenge they had conquered. The Just-In-Time inventory program had been another big challenge they had met. The next major challenge had been cycle time reduction and they had brought their average down to almost half the goal. All these had challenged their management skills and they had responded successfully. Now they needed to further improve the cycle time—to make it even shorter.

Last summer everyone agreed they had figured out the problem and had a good solution. What was going on? Why was it that the daily reports were so seldom correct? Was there something intrinsically wrong with the approach? How much animosity was the system worth? Enough was enough.

Bill, Tom, and Helen came downstairs together. Walt and Art joined them from their offices near the conference room . . . and closed the door for the afternoon or as long as it would take. Enough was enough. A decision must emerge.

Discussion Questions

1. What is unique about the parts division production process?
2. What was the effect of Just-In-Time and cycle time reduction on their production process?
3. What lead to the creation of the task force?
4. The group called the system they installed the automatic scheduler. In what sense is this title appropriate? Inappropriate?
5. Was the automatic scheduler actually needed?
6. What was limiting the auto scheduler in January?
7. Until two years ago there were two levels of managers between the supervisors and the plant manager, Tom. Are these midlevel managers actually needed in this situation?
8. Everyone in this organization refers to others (including the CEO) by their first name. What does this suggest about their culture and this case?
9. In recent years has the complexity of the organization changed?

SIX

MANAGING THE ENTERPRISE IN A CONTEMPORARY ENVIRONMENT

Part Six is designed to provide insights regarding the changes that are likely to take place in management during the next decade and the challenges and opportunities that await you should you choose a career in this field.

Chapter 18 deals with the ethical standards and social responsibility of enterprises. Attention is focused on ethical practices as well as the debate over the social responsibility that companies have today.

Chapter 19 introduces the concept of corporate entrepreneurship. Venture teams working within corporate boundaries are shaping the future innovations for the next century; and the ability to manage this entrepreneurial spirit will be a key factor for the 1990s and beyond.

Chapter 20 addresses the future trends that you can expect to face as a manager. Employee values and attitudes, women in management, quality of work life, and social values impacting the workplace, including the disease AIDS, are all presented as factors shaping the world of management.

Chapter 21 focuses on management career planning and you. It provides a profile of currently successful executives, explains the six career phases through which most managers pass, and presents the typical problems faced by managers as they begin their careers. The latter part of the chapter focuses on the nature and effects of organizational stress, and offering guidelines for managing stress to ensure a long, healthy career.

When you have finished reading the material in this part of the book, you will be better able to put everything you have learned in this book into an overall framework and see how it applies to you. Most importantly, you will have learned about some of the important challenges and opportunities that await you should you choose a career in the field of management.

18

Ethical Standards and Social Responsibility

Every enterprise seeking to operate in contemporary society is faced with the challenge of ethical practices and social responsibility. These issues have been coming to the forefront during the last few decades. Today managers must realize their importance and be prepared to take the necessary actions.

The first objective of this chapter is to examine the nature of ethics and values among today's managers. The second objective is to discuss the topic of social responsibility, including the debate for and against business playing an active role. The third objective is to examine the nature and role of a social audit.

When you have finished studying the material in this chapter, you will be able to:

1. Describe ethical behavior in corporations.
2. Define codes of conduct and give some examples of them.
3. Define the term ethics and discuss managerial values.
4. Explain the importance of top management support for social responsibility.
5. Identify the benefits associated with assuming social responsibility.
6. Explain what a social audit is.
7. List the 10 commandments of social responsibility.

ETHICS IN BUSINESS

How could top-level executives at the Manville Corporation have suppressed evidence for decades that proved that asbestos inhalation was killing their own employees? What could have driven the managers of Continental Illinois Bank to pursue a course of action that threatened to bankrupt the institution, ruin its reputation, and cost thousands of innocent employees and investors their jobs and their savings? Why did managers at E. F. Hutton find themselves pleading guilty to 2,000 counts of mail and wire fraud, accepting a fine of $2 million, and putting up an $8 million fund for restitution to the 400 banks that the company had systematically bilked?[1] These questions illustrate the degree of illegal or unethical conduct in corporations today. Amitai Etzioni, renowned professor of sociology, has reported that in the last 10 years, roughly two-thirds of America's 500 largest corporations have been involved, in varying degrees, in some form of illegal behavior.

As the foundations of ethics and codes of conduct are examined, keep in mind that illegal practices are commonplace in some industries and among some managers. One reason is accounted for by rationalization. A *Harvard Business Review* survey found the following four to be the most common:

1. A belief that the activity is within reasonable ethical and legal limits, that is, that it is not "really" illegal or immoral.
2. A belief that the activity is in the individual's or the corporation's best interests, that is, that the individual would somehow be expected to undertake the activity.
3. A belief that the activity is "safe," that it will never be found out or publicized.
4. A belief that, because the activity helps the company, the company will condone it and even protect the person who engages in it, that is, that no one will be punished.

Ethics

Ethics refers to right and wrong conduct

The word **"ethics"** refers to right and wrong conduct. In recent years, like social responsibility, business ethics have become a focal point of public atten-

---

[1] Saul W. Gellerman, "Why Good Managers Make Bad Ethical Choices," *Harvard Business Review* (July–August 1986):85. For more on this subject, see James A. Waters and Frederick Bird, "Attending to Ethics in Management," *Journal of Business Ethics* (August 1989):493–97; and Kenneth R. Andrews, "Ethics In Practice," *Harvard Business Review* (September–October 1989):99–104.

tion. That is true not only for national firms but for MNCs as well. Elkins and Callaghan have noted that:

> Illegal and questionable political payoffs, bribes, and "grease payments" abroad by U.S.-based multinationals have unfolded as matters of grave concern. Over a short period of time, over 250 firms have disclosed such payments totaling in excess of $300 million. Such corporate stalwarts (heretofore) as Gulf Oil, Lockheed, 3M, United Brands (Chiquita Bananas), Phillips Petroleum, Goodyear, and Exxon have joined the flock, disclosing payments under the decree by the Securities and Exchange Commission. Exxon alone, for example, has admitted to more than $46 million in illicit and questionable payments made between 1963 and 1972. United Brands' activity ultimately led to the suicide of its chairman. And the SEC is pressuring for still further disclosure by these and other multinationals.[2]

Are business ethics really on the decline? While newspaper stories might suggest that they are, the facts do not support such a bleak finding. Actually, most business executives feel that their ethics are good and getting better. Furthermore, most say that their ethical conduct is higher than that of the average business executive.[3]

What will influence ethical standards in the future? A survey conducted among practicing executives by Steven Brenner and Earl Molander produced the lists provided in Table 18-1.[4]

Many factors affect ethical standards

Notice from the table that public disclosure, publicity, and the fear of people finding out about ethics violations are of primary importance. Other considerations such as a code of professional ethics, social pressures, and business's sense of social responsibility are also important. On the other hand, business executives blame society's low standards, social decay, and the rise of materialism for causing low standards in business.

Two other factors, mentioned only indirectly in this study, will most influence ethical standards during the 1990s: the manager's own standards and those of the organization. The two reinforce each other. Corporations that demand the highest ethical codes will get them. Those managers whose personal codes do not meet the standards of the organization will either leave or be forced out. Competition plays a key role in this process. When one business firm offers kickbacks to its customers, it is difficult for others not to follow suit.

---

[2] Arthur Elkins and Dennis W. Callaghan, *A Managerial Odyssey,* 3rd ed. (Reading, MA: Addison-Wesley, 1980): 61–62.
[3] Steven N. Brenner and Earl Molander, "Is the Ethics of Business Changing?" *Harvard Business Review* (January–February 1977):57–71. See also Idalene F. Kesner, Bart Victor, and Bruce T. Lamont, "Board Composition and the Commission of Illegal Acts: An Investigation of Fortune 500 Companies," *Academy of Management Journal* (December 1986):789–99.
[4] Brenner and Molander, "Is the Ethics of Business Changing?" 55–71.

TABLE 18-1 Factors That Influence Ethical Standards	Percentage of Respondents Listing Factor
Factors Causing Higher Standards	
Public disclosure; publicity; media coverage; better communication	31
Increased public concern; public awareness, consciousness, and scrutiny; better-informed public; societal pressures	20
Government regulation, legislation, and intervention; federal courts	10
Education of business managers; increase in manager professionalism and education	9
New social expectations for the role business is to play in society; young adults' attitudes; consumerism	5
Business's greater sense of social responsibility and greater awareness of the implications of its acts; business responsiveness; corporate policy changes; top management emphasis on ethical action	5
Other	20
Factors Causing Lower Standards	
Society's standards are lower; social decay; more permissive society; materialism and hedonism have grown; loss of church and home influence; less quality, more quantity desires	34
Competition; pace of life; stress to succeed; current economic conditions; costs of doing business; more businesses compete for less	13
Political corruption; loss of confidence in government; Watergate; politics; political ethics and climate	9
People more aware of unethical acts; constant media coverage; TV; communications create atmosphere for crime	9
Greed; desire for gain; worship of the dollar as measure of success; selfishness of the individual; lack of personal integrity and moral fiber	8
Pressure for profit from within the organization from superiors, from stockholders; corporate influences on managers; corporate policies	7
Other	21

Note: Some respondents listed more than one factor, so there were 353 factors in all listed as causing higher standards and 411 in all listed as causing lower ones.

Source: Reprinted by permission of the *Harvard Business Review*. The exhibit is from "Is the Ethics of Business Changing?" by Steven N. Brenner and Earl A. Molander (January–February 1977):63. Copyright © 1977 by the President and Fellows of Harvard College; all rights reserved.

They stand to lose business if they do not match the competition. This is the reason why public disclosure and government regulation will continue to be important. As long as everyone is playing the game according to the same rules, there is equity.[5] If some are acting unethically, however, they have an unfair

---

[5] Patrick E. Murphy, "Creating Ethical Corporate Structures," *Sloan Management Review* (Winter 1989):81–87; and Jeffrey Gandz and Frederick G. Bird, "Designing Ethical Organizations," *Business Quarterly* (Autumn 1989):108–112.

advantage. For this reason we are likely to see continued public attention directed to the area of business ethics.[6] People want to know when business managers are acting unethically. So do ethical managers, who feel that this public spotlight will keep other managers on the straight and narrow path.

With these ideas in mind, see if your ethical values rank high or low. The ethics test presented in Table 18-2 will provide some insight into your own ethical position.

Codes of Conduct and Ethical Practices

Areas covered by codes of conduct A **code of conduct** is a statement of ethical practices or guidelines to which an enterprise adheres. There are many such codes, some related to industry at large and others related directly to corporate conduct. These codes cover a multitude of subjects, ranging from misuse of corporate assets, conflict of interest, and use of inside information, to equal employment practices, falsification of books and records, and antitrust violations.

During the 1960s a number of codes of conduct were discussed in the business literature.[7] During the 1970s the revelations about the Watergate break-in and illegal or questionable payoffs at home and abroad resulted in a public outcry regarding codes of conduct and ethical practices.

How prevalent are codes of conduct today? Bernard J. White and B. Ruth Montgomery recently conducted a national survey and found that of the 673 chief executive officers who responded, more than 75 percent reported having such a code. (See Table 18-3.) White and Montgomery's findings are significantly different from the findings of S. Mathes and G. Thompson who conducted a similar survey during the 1960s. In the earlier survey only 60 percent of the respondents said that they had a code of conduct. More recently, in 1988, a survey of executives by *Personnel Journal* revealed that 72 percent of the organizations had published codes of ethics.[8]

What, specifically, do typical codes of conduct contain? Table 18-4 provides the general content of codes of 30 business firms randomly selected by White and Montgomery. Commenting on the overall nature of these codes, the authors noted:

> Most of the codes provide some "context," a general statement about the code of ethical issues in the company's management philosophy, and the

---

[6] Charles R. Stoner, "The Foundation of Business Ethics: Exploring the Relationship Between Organization Culture, Moral Values, and Actions," *SAM Advanced Management Journal* (Summer 1989):38–43.

[7] See, for example, Robert W. Austin, "Codes of Conduct for Executives," *Harvard Business Review* (September–October 1961):53–61.

[8] S. Mathes and G. Thompson, "Ensuring Ethical Conduct in Business," *The Conference Board Record* (December 1964):17–27; and James Court, "A Question of Corporate Ethics," *Personnel Journal* (September 1988):37–38.

TABLE 18-2   An Ethics Test

Many situations in day-to-day business are not simple right-or-wrong questions, but rather fall into a gray area. To demonstrate the perplexing array of moral dilemmas faced by 20th-century Americans, I've prepared a "nonscientific" test for slippage. An appropriate use of this instrument would be in the moral development workshops suggested in the article. Don't expect to score high. That is not the purpose. But give it a try, and see how you stack up.

Put your value system to the test in the following situations:

Scoring Code: Strongly Agree = SA
Agree   = A
Disagree   = D
Strongly Disagree = SD

	SA	A	D	SD
1) Employees should not be expected to inform on their peers for wrongdoings.	—	—	—	—
2) There are times when a manager must overlook contract and safety violations in order to get on with the job.	—	—	—	—
3) It is not always possible to keep accurate expense account records; therefore, it is sometimes necessary to give approximate figures.	—	—	—	—
4) There are times when it is necessary to withhold embarrassing information from one's superior.	—	—	—	—
5) We should do what our managers suggest, though we may have doubts about its being the right thing to do.	—	—	—	—
6) It is sometimes necessary to conduct personal business on company time.	—	—	—	—
7) Sometimes it is good psychology to set goals somewhat above normal if it will help to obtain a greater effort from the sales force.	—	—	—	—

	SA	A	D	SD
8) I would quote a "hopeful" shipping date in order to get the order.	—	—	—	—
9) It is proper to use the company WATS line for personal calls as long as it's not in company use.	—	—	—	—
10) Management must be goal-oriented; therefore, the end usually justifies the means.	—	—	—	—
11) If it takes heavy entertainment and twisting a bit of company policy to win a large contract, I would authorize it.	—	—	—	—
12) Exceptions to company policy and procedures is a way of life.	—	—	—	—
13) Inventory controls should be designed to report "underages" rather than "overages" in goods received.	—	—	—	—
14) Occasional use of the company's copier for personal or community activities is acceptable.	—	—	—	—
15) Taking home company property (pencils, paper, tape, etc.) for personal use is an accepted fringe benefit.	—	—	—	—

Score Key: (0) for Strongly Disagree   (1) for Disagree
(2) for Agree   (3) for Strongly Agree

If your score is:

0	Prepare for canonization ceremony
1–5	Bishop material
6–10	High ethical values
11–15	Good ethical values
16–25	Average ethical values
26–35	Need moral development
36–44	Slipping fast
45	Leave valuables with warden

Source: Lowell G. Rein, "Is Your (Ethical) Slippage Showing?" *Personnel Journal* (September 1980):743. Reprinted with permission of Personnel Journal, Inc., Costa Mesa, CA; all rights reserved.

TABLE 18-3 Percentage of Companies (Overall and by Size) Reporting Various Practices Related to Corporate Codes of Conduct											
		Size Categories*									
Question	Overall Response	1	2	3	4	5	6	7	8	9	10
Does your company have a code of conduct?	(N = 611)										
■ yes	77%	40%	57%	74%	75%	72%	90%	85%	87%	92%	97%
Who receives a copy?	(N = 486)										
■ officers/key employees	97%	83	97	94	98	100	100	98	96	100	100
■ other employees	55%	46	60	35	54	58	42	60	46	70	68
Who signs it periodically?	(N = 481)										
■ offices/key employees	85%	75	62	80	87	80	85	91	86	91	90
■ other employees	(N = 451) 27%	23	27	12	17	30	25	23	31	47	39
Are procedures specified for handling violations of the code's provisions?	(N = 478)										
■ yes	63%	41	46	38	54	58	55	66	75	85	83
Have procedures been enforced in the last several years?	(N = 463)										
■ yes	62%	42	43	30	48	48	64	63	77	83	91

* The overall sample of 673 was broken into deciles by size. Category 1 is $0–60 million; category 2 is $60-132 million; category 3 is $132–201 million; category 4 is $201–300 million; category 5 is $300–467 million; category 6 is $467-717 million; category 7 is $717–1,150 million; category 8 is $1,150-1,900 million; category 9 is $1,900–4,000 million; category 10 is $4,000 million and above.
Source: Bernard J. White and B. Ruth Montgomery, "Corporate Codes of Conduct," *California Management Review* (Winter 1980):82. Copyright © 1980 by the Regents of the University of California. Reprinted from *California Management Review,* vol. 23, no. 2. By permission of The Regents.

role of the code in capturing and communicating rules and guidelines on such matters. Two-thirds include a blanket statement on the employee's responsibility for "compliance with all applicable laws and regulations." Beyond these general statements, the most frequently treated subject is conflict of interest. Nearly 65 percent of the codes made a statement about employees' responsibility to avoid conflict-of-interest situations. About half of all the codes detail the types of conflict of interest specifically prohibited:

TABLE 18-4   Codes of Conduct: Content analysis (n = 30)

Subject	Percentage in which Subject is Addressed
A. Date on code of conduct	77%
B. General statement of ethics and philosophy	80
C. Compliance with applicable laws	67
D. Observance of moral and ethical standards of society	20
E. Specific reference to Foreign Corrupt Practices Act	17
F. False entries in books and records	50
G. Misuse of corporate assets (general)	50
1. Political contributions	67
a. Acceptable under certain conditions if legal	37
b. All banned	30
2. Facilitating payments	20
3. Payments to government officials/political parties	63
4. Gifts, favors, entertainment	57
5. Secret payments	23
6. Undisclosed or unrecorded funds or assets	53
7. False, misleading support documents	37
H. Conflict of interest (general)	73
1. Interest in competition	50
2. Interest in suppliers	57
3. Interest in customer	50
4. Relatives or associates	50
5. Acceptance of gifts	77
6. Membership on boards of directors	30
I. Arrangements with dealers and agents	23
1. Foreign or third party payments	13
2. Responsibility for dealers' actions	43
3. Commission levels	33
J. Antitrust compliance	40
1. Relations with competitors	30
2. Relations with customers	30
3. Relations with suppliers	30
4. International transactions	13
K. International trade boycotts	10
L. Inside information	63
M. Relations with shareholders and security analysts	7
N. Confidential information	40
O. Equal employment opportunity	30
P. Partisan versus issue political activity	13
Q. Implementation/administrative procedures (for the code)	83

Source: Bernard J. White and B. Ruth Montgomery, "Corporate Codes of Conduct," *California Management Review* (Winter 1980):84. Copyright © 1980 by the Regents of the University of California. Reprinted from *California Management Review*, vol. 23, no. 2. By permission of The Regents.

interests in competitors, suppliers, or customers, and conflicts created by relatives' or associates' interests.[9]

Based on the results of such research, two important conclusions can be reached. First, codes of conduct are becoming more prevalent in industry. Management is not just giving lip services to ethics and moral behavior; it is putting its ideas into writing and distributing these guidelines for everyone in the organization to read and follow. Second, in contrast to earlier codes, the more recent ones are proving to be more meaningful in terms of external legal and social development, more comprehensive in terms of their coverage, and easier to implement in terms of the administrative procedures that are being used to enforce them.[10]

Of course, the most important question still remains to be answered: Will management really adhere to a high moral code? Many managers would respond to this question by answering "Yes." Why? The main reason is that it is good business. One top executive put the idea this way:

> Singly or in combination, [unethical] practices have a corrosive effect on free markets and free trade, which are fundamental to the survival of the free enterprise system. They subvert the laws of supply and demand, and they shortcircuit competition based on classical ideas of product quality, service, and price. Free markets are replaced by contrived markets. The need for constant improvement in products or services is removed.[11]

A second, related reason is that by improving the moral climate of the enterprise, the corporation can eventually win back the confidence of the public. (See "Management in Practice: Companies Attack the Ethics Issue.") This would mark a turnaround in that many people today question the moral and ethical integrity of companies and believe that businesspeople try to get away with everything they can. Only time will tell whether codes of conduct will serve to improve business practices. Current trends indicate, however, that the business community is working hard toward this objective.[12]

---

[9] Bernard J. White and B. Ruth Montgomery, "Corporate Codes of Conduct," *California Management Review* (Winter 1980):85.

[10] White and Montgomery, "Corporate Codes of Conduct," 86. For more on this topic, see Donald R. Cressey and Charles A. Moore, "Managerial Values and Corporate Codes of Conduct," *California Management Review* (Summer 1983):121–27; and Steven Weller, "The Effectiveness of Corporate Codes of Ethics," *Journal of Business Ethics* (July 1988):389–95.

[11] Reported in Darrell J. Fashing, "A Case for Corporate and Management Ethics," *California Management Review* (Spring 1981):84.

[12] Amitai Etzioni, "Do Good Ethics Ensure Good Profits?" *Business and Society Review* (Summer 1989):4–10; and also L. J. Brooks, "Corporate Ethical Performance: Trends, Forecasts, and Outlooks," *Journal of Business Ethics* no. 8 (1989):31–38.

MANAGEMENT IN PRACTICE

Companies Attack the Ethics Issue

The concern over corporate ethics has been growing in recent years. And why not? Consider the following scandals:

- Rockwell International Corp. has been indicted by a federal grand jury for defrauding the Air Force.
- Hertz Corp. has overcharged consumers and insurers $13 million for repairs to damaged rental cars.
- Ocean Spray Cranberries Inc. has been indicted by a federal grand jury for pollution in Middleboro, MA.

In light of these types of questionable activities, corporate executives are attempting to attack the issue with training, education, and followup.

The Business Roundtable, composed of chief executives from 200 major corporations, conducted a study of 10 major corporations that were implementing ethical practices. Some of the key findings included the following companies' efforts:

- **BOEING**   CEO involvement; line managers lead training sessions; ethics committee reports to board; toll-free number for employees to report violations.
- **GENERAL MILLS**   Guidelines for dealing with vendors, competitors, customers; seeks recruits who share company's values; emphasizes open decision making.
- **JOHNSON & JOHNSON**   A 'credo' of corporate values integral to J&J culture, companywide meetings to challenge the credo's tenets, and surveys to ascertain compliance.
- **XEROX**   Handbooks, policy statements emphasize integrity, concern for people; orientation on values and policies; ombudsman reports to CEO.

Overall, companies are realizing that top management commitment to an ethics program is a critical factor. In addition, written codes of conduct that clearly communicate the intentions of management must be published and distributed to all employees. And, finally, there must be a careful monitoring of the program to ensure compliance by all personnel. Understanding these guidelines used by some corporations is helping others to implement stronger programs.

Source: Ken Kerbs, ''Businesses Are Signing Up for Ethics 101,'' *Business Week* (February 15, 1988):56–57.

Managerial Values

Managers are sometimes confronted with difficult decisions because of their values and ethics. To some degree these values and ethics are encouraged and developed through organizational influence. Industry codes of conduct establish levels of acceptable behavior. To a greater degree, however, these values are personal. Managers bring them to the job and use them in decision making.

TABLE 18-5   Comparison of Managerial Values

Phase I Profit Maximizing Management	Phase II Trusteeship Management	Phase III Quality of Life Management
Economic Values		
1. Raw self-interest	1. Self-interest 2. Contributors' interests	1. Enlightened self-interest 2. Contributors' interests 3. Society's interests
What's good for me is good for my country.	What's good for GM is good for our country.	What is good for society is good for our company.
Profit maximizer	Profit satisficer	Profit is necessary, but . . .
Money and wealth are most important.	Money is important, but so are people.	People are more important than money.
Let the buyer beware *(caveat emptor).*	Let us not cheat the customer.	Let the seller beware *(caveat venditor).*
Labor is a commodity to be bought and sold.	Labor has certain rights which must be recognized	Employee dignity has to be satisfied.
Accountability of management is to the owners.	Accountability of management is to the owners, customers, employees, suppliers, and other contributors.	Accountability of management is to the owners, contributors, and society.
Technology Values		
Technology is very important.	Technology is important but so are people.	People are more important than technology.
Social Values		
Employee personal problems must be left at home.	We recognize that employees have needs beyond their economic needs.	We hire the whole person.
I am a rugged individualist, and I will manage my business as I please.	I am an individualist, but I recognize the value of group participation.	Group participation is fundamental to our success.
Minority groups are inferior to whites. They must be treated accordingly.	Minority groups have their place in society, and their place is inferior to mine.	Minority group members are people as you and I are.
Political Values		
That government is best which governs least.	Government is a necessary evil.	Business and government must cooperate to solve society's problems.
Environmental Values		
The nature environment controls the destiny of man.	Man can control and manipulate the environment.	We must preserve the environment in order to lead a quality life.
Aesthetic Values		
Aesthetic values? What are they?	Aesthetic values are okay, but not for us.	We must preserve our aesthetic values, and we will do our part.

Source: Robert Hay and Ed Gray, "Social Responsibilities of Business Managers," *Academy of Management Journal* (March 1974):142. Reprinted by permission.

TABLE 18-6   Twelve Questions for Examining the Ethics of a Business Decision

1. Have you defined the problem accurately?
2. How would you define the problem if you stood on the other side of the fence?
3. How did this situation occur in the first place?
4. To whom and to what do you give your loyalty as a person and as a member of the corporation?
5. What is your intention in making this decision?
6. How does this intention compare with the probable results?
7. Whom could your decision or action injure?
8. Can you discuss the problem with the affected parties before you make your decision?
9. Are you confident that your position will be as valid over a long period of time as it seems now?
10. Could you disclose without qualm your decision or action to your boss, your CEO, the board of directors, your family, society as a whole?
11. What is the symbolic potential of your action if understood? if misunderstood?
12. Under what conditions would you allow exceptions to your stand?

Source: Reprinted by permission of the *Harvard Business Review.* Exhibit from "Ethics Without the Sermon," by Laura L. Nash (November–December 1981). Copyright © 1981 by the President and Fellows of Harvard College; all rights reserved.

Values

There are a number of ways of examining managerial values. One is to study those set forth by Edward Spranger and measured by the Allport-Vernon-Lindzey *Study of Values*.[13] This approach looks at six specific kinds of values:

There are six specific kinds of managerial values

- **theoretical:** values showing a concern for order, system, and logic
- **economic:** values showing a concern for usefulness and practicality
- **aesthetic:** values showing a concern for art and beauty
- **social:** values showing a concern for people and their welfare
- **political:** values showing a concern for power over people and things
- **religious:** values showing a concern for unity and harmony in things

Research reveals that businesspeople and top managers have the highest concern for economic and political values. If these values are not very high when the manager joins the organization, they become so or the person does not do well in the management ranks. These values are essential for success.[14]

---

[13] Gordon W. Allport, Phillip E. Vernon, and Gardner Lindzey, *Study of Values* (Boston: Houghton Mifflin, 1960).

[14] Richard M. Hodgetts, et al., "A Profile of the Successful Executive," *National Academy of Management Proceedings* (1978):378.

Changes in
managerial values
have occurred in
three phases

Another way to examine **managerial values** is to look at the way these values have changed over time. Many of the changes have been influenced by society at large, as is evident from close analysis. One of the most popular comparative models is that by Robert Hay and Ed Gray, who have described the three phases through which many businesses have progressed.[15] The model is presented in Table 18-5.

Phase I was in vogue 50 years ago. Except in small firms, however, it no longer accurately describes the values of managers. Phase II is most representative today. The manager is a trustee of the organization's resources and views the job as one requiring a balance between concern for profit and concern for people. Phase III, quality of life management, is not representative of most organizations. However, many people feel that managerial values are shifting in this direction. Perhaps the cliché that best describes Phase III is "we worry about the people and let profits take care of themselves." In any event, values certainly do affect internal organizational operations.

How will you decide the ethics of each business decision as a manager? Table 18-6 provides some insights into how to analyze these decisions from a personal, ethical standpoint.

SOCIAL RESPONSIBILITY IN CORPORATIONS

Over the last three decades, social responsibility has emerged as a major issue. Although it takes different forms for different industries and companies, the basic challenge exists for all.

Social responsibility consists of those obligations a business has to society. These obligations extend to many different areas. Table 18-7 presents some of these.

Stages of Corporate Social Behavior

The diversity of social responsibility opens the door for questions concerning the *extent* to which corporations should be involved.

In examining the stages or levels of social responsibility behavior that corporations exhibit, it becomes apparent that there is a distinct difference in the way corporations respond. S. Prakash Sethi, a frequent contributor to the literature, has established a framework that classifies the social actions of corporations into three distinct categories: **social obligation**, social responsibility, and **social responsiveness** (see Table 18-8). This framework illustrates the

---

[15] Robert Hay and Ed Gray, "Social Responsibilities of Business Managers," *Academy of Management Journal* (March 1974):135–43.

TABLE 18-7 What Is the Nature of Social Responsibility?	
Environment	Pollution control
	Restoration or protection of environment
	Conservation of natural resources
	Recycling efforts
Energy	Conservation of energy in production and marketing operations
	Efforts to increase energy efficiency of products
	Other energy-saving programs (for example, company-sponsored car pools)
Fair business practices	Employment and advancement of women and minorities
	Employment and advancement of disadvantaged individuals (handicapped, Vietnam veterans, ex-offenders, former drug addicts, mentally retarded, and hardcore unemployed)
	Support for minority-owned businesses
Human resources	Promotion of employee health and safety
	Employee training and development
	Remedial education programs for disadvantaged employees
	Alcohol and drug counseling programs
	Career counseling
	Child day-care facilities for working parents
	Employee physical fitness and stress management programs
Community involvement	Donations of cash, products, services, or employee time
	Sponsorship of public health projects
	Support of education and the arts
	Support of community recreation programs
	Cooperation in community projects (recycling centers, disaster assistance, and urban renewal)
Products	Enhancement of product safety
	Sponsorship of product safety education programs
	Reduction of polluting potential of products
	Improvement in nutritional value of products
	Improvements in packaging and labeling

range of corporate intensity in social issues. Some firms simply react to social issues through obedience of the laws; others make a more active response, accepting responsibility for various programs; still others are highly proactive and are even willing to be evaluated by the public for various activities.

Elizabeth Gatewood and Archie B. Carroll examined specific examples of **corporate response strategies**. Table 18-9 illustrates the four strategies that they found exhibited by the companies: reaction, defense, accommodation, and proaction. These strategies are similar to those described by Sethi in that both illustrate continua of behavior.

Another way to examine this concept is through the use of a social responsibility scale (see Figure 18-1). This scale extends from zero (minimum social responsibility response) to 10 (maximum social responsibility response). One

TABLE 18-8   Classifying Corporate Social Behavior

Dimension of Behavior	Stage One: Social Obligation	Stage Two: Social Responsibility	Stage Three: Social Responsiveness
Response to social pressures	Maintains low public profile, but if attacked, uses PR methods to upgrade its public image; denies any deficiencies; blames public dissatisfaction on ignorance or failure to understand corporate functions; discloses information only where legally required	Accepts responsibility for solving current problems; will admit deficiencies in former practices and attempt to persuade public that its current practices meet social norms; attitude toward critics conciliatory; freer information disclosures than stage one	Willingly discusses activities with outside groups; makes information freely available to public; accepts formal and informal inputs from outside groups in decision making; is willing to be publicly evaluated for its various activities
Philanthropy	Contributes only when direct benefit to it clearly shown; otherwise, views contributions as responsibility of individual employees	Contributes to noncontroversial and established causes; matches employee contributions	Activities of stage two, *plus* support and contributions to new, controversial groups whose needs it sees as unfulfilled and increasingly important

Source: Excerpted from S. Prakash Sethi, "A Conceptual Framework for Environmental Analysis of Social Issues and Evaluation of Business Response Patterns," *Academy of Management Journal* (January 1979):68. Reprinted by permission.

TABLE 18-9   Corporate Response Strategies

Phase	Strategy Action
Reaction	Collected information from state health boards
	Conducted laboratory testing with suspected bacteria
	Assembled a group of outside scientific advisers
Defense	Set up military-type command post
	Refuted and/or questioned several aspects of CDC study
	Prepared news releases
Accommodation	Proposed warning label
	Voluntarily halted production
	Pulled back products from store shelves
Proaction	Offered to buy back all unused products including free promotion samples
	Pledged research expertise for further study
	Agreed to finance and direct an educational program
	Issued a warning to women not to use Rely

Source: Elizabeth Gatewood and Archie B. Carroll, "The Anatomy of Corporate Social Response: The Rely, Firestone 500, and Pinto Cases," *Business Horizons,* 24 (September–October 1981):13. Reprinted with permission.

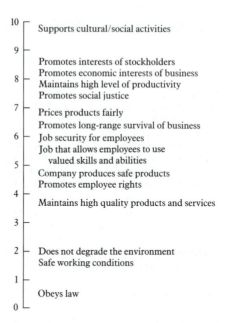

FIGURE 18-1
A Social
Responsibility
Scale

Source: Adapted from Kimberly B. Boal and Newman Peery, "The Cognitive Structure of Corporate Social Responsibility," *Journal of Management* (Fall/Winter 1985):71–82.

represents the reactive form of obedience and 10 the proactive form of social support.

The Social Responsibility Debate

As might be anticipated, there is still a great deal of philosophical debate regarding the involvement of corporations in society's affairs. Some people believe business should assume a strong social responsibility stance. Others believe business's role should be minimal.

Some people feel businesses should exhibit social responsibility

Social responsibility supporters say that business should play an active role in ensuring such things as (1) equal opportunity in employment, especially for minorities and women; (2) protection of the environment from all dangers created by a business's production processes or output; and (3) safe and properly functioning products that provide full value for the purchase dollar.[16]

Others oppose such action

Opponents of active social responsibility argue that business's primary objective is economic, not social. They maintain that pursuit of noneconomic goals results in a less effective organization. Arguments set forth by both groups are provided in Table 18-10.

---

[16] For more on these specific areas, see Fred Luthans, Richard M. Hodgetts, and Kenneth A. Thompson, *Social Issues in Business,* 6th ed. (New York: Macmillan, 1990).

TABLE 18-10   The Social Responsibility Debate

Point	Counterpoint
1. Our economic system works best when businesses pursue stockholder interests.	1. Our economic system works best when businesses pursue the interests of society at large.
2. Businesses are economic institutions and are most efficient when allowed to do what they do best—pursue profit. This is socially preferred behavior.	2. Profit alone no longer implies socially preferred behavior.
3. Businesses are prohibited from engaging in socially responsible behavior by both the law and their corporate charter.	3. The courts have continually upheld the right of businesses to pursue socially responsible behavior even when it reduces overall profits; corporate charters also support such action.
4. Managers are not trained to pursue social goals.	4. Managers may not be trained to pursue social goals, but since their actions have social and political impact, they cannot now claim incompetence as a defense against becoming socially responsible.
5. Social responsibility often leads managers to give away money that rightfully belongs to stockholders.	5. In spending money on social responsibility programs, the company is simply paying society back for the social costs of doing business.
6. Social responsibility is a threat to democracy.	6. Social responsibility is not a threat to democracy. Businesses are social institutions and must live up to society's standards. Moreover, if they do not, the government is likely to step in and make them.

Note: For more on this topic, see Thomas M. Jones, "Corporate Social Responsibility Revisited, Redefined," *California Management Review* (Spring 1980):59–67.

Top Management Support

As indicated earlier, businesses exhibit varying degrees of social responsibility and responsiveness. Some of this is a result of increased government regulation. Examples include the Equal Pay Act, which requires that all workers be given equal pay for equal work, and the Civil Rights Act, which prohibits discrimination on the basis of race, color, creed, sex, or national origin. At the same time, much of the movement towards increased social responsibility can be attributed to the personal values and support of top management.

There are a number of reasons for high-level support. One is **enlightened self-interest**, which holds that by helping society a corporation is actually helping itself in the long term, since it is improving or developing potential customers. A second is **sound investment theory**, which proposes that the stock value of socially responsible corporations rises over time versus those of corporations which have not demonstrated social responsibility. A third is that socially responsible corporations can avoid government regulation or interference; a management commitment to social needs can avert excess government concern and allow the company to direct its own strategies.

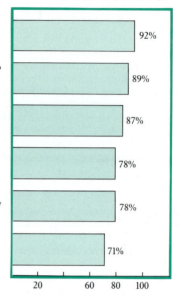

FIGURE 18-2
Top Management
Support for Social
Responsibility

Fundamental Social Responsibility Assumptions

Percent of 116 Corporate Chief Executive Officers Agreeing Mildly or Strongly

• Responsible corporate behavior can be in the best economic interest of the stockholders. — 92%

• Efficient production of goods and services is no longer the only thing society expects from business. — 89%

• Long-run success in business depends on its ability to understand that it is part of a larger society and to behave accordingly. — 87%

• Involvement by business in improving its community's quality of life will also improve long-run profitability. — 78%

• A business that wishes to capture a favorable public image will have to show that it is socially responsible. — 78%

• If business is more socially responsible, it will discourage additional regulation of the economic system by government. — 71%

Source: Data from Robert Ford and Frank McLaughlin, "Perceptions of Socially Responsible Activities and Attitudes: A Comparison of Business School Deans and Corporate Chief Executives," *Academy of Management Journal* (September 1984):670.

These three reasons help explain why many top managers support a proactive social responsibility stance.[17] Figure 18-2 describes still others. All of these points illustrate the dimension of top management support in the area of social responsibility. Figure 18-2, based upon a study of 116 chief executive officers, demonstrates the support now being exhibited by top level managers.

The Benefits of Social Responsibility

Is social responsibility a profit-motivated activity or a sincere act of philanthropy by corporations? The answer is that both statements are correct. Many companies realize the advertising and public image values associated with a socially responsible performance. In addition, companies often act in a sincerely philanthropic manner. (See "Management in Practice: Corporations Invest in Education.") In either case, the mutual benefit realized is far greater than the concern over the true motivation for the activity.

[17] Henry Mintzberg, "The Case for Social Responsibility," *Journal of Business Strategy* (Fall 1983):3–15.

MANAGEMENT IN PRACTICE

Corporations Invest in Education

In February 1987, a new elementary school was opened in the North Lawndale district of Chicago. This school would *not* be a typical innercity elementary school. It was formed through a partnership of sixty corporations—including Sears, Quaker Oats, United Airlines, and Baxter International—for the purpose of experimenting in innovative education and family engineering.

The Corporate Community School was founded by corporations as a no-fee, full curriculum school for ages 2–13 because they realized that unskilled, uneducated, and undisciplined people do not make for a solid class of citizens. Thus, in order to have better prepared employees and more knowledgeable customers in the future, education must improve for innercity schools.

A "laboratory" effort was launched in Chicago in a neighborhood where every child comes from a poor family. Specifically, ten percent are malnourished, seventy-five percent have urgent dental problems, eighty-four percent are from unwed mothers, and sadly, 24 out of 1,000 die before the age of one. The neighborhood is crowded with drunks, drug addicts (and pushers), and muggers. It was exactly this type of environment that Corporate Community Schools of America sought to challenge.

Removing the obstacles to learning became the first priority of the school. Eyecare, dental care, and medical services are provided for students. Family counseling is available and encouraged. Parental involvement is actively pursued by the school's teachers and administrators. In addition, the school is open from 7 A.M. to 7 P.M., with child care provided before and after school hours.

The next priority was enrollment. Although limited to 150 students, the applications were sought from churches and social agencies in order to serve the neediest families. The current cost of the school is approximately $5,000 per student (national average is $4,300) and teachers are paid 10 percent more than public school teachers.

Finally, the learning atmosphere is a priority. Children are encouraged to work at their own pace. Grades and traditional grade levels are not used. The school reports the individual progress of each child to the parents on a quarterly basis. Responsibility, problem solving, and working cooperatively are stressed by the teachers.

To date, the experiment appears to be successful. The children are learning, adapting, and achieving. It will take time and continual support before the project can ever fully be evaluated. However, the corporations have committed themselves to the future of this project.

Source: Steve Weiner, "We Decided to Show How Things Can Work," *Forbes* (September 18, 1989):180–88.

The benefits of social responsibility accrue to both society and the corporation. Society reaps the rewards of actions by the corporation. At the same time, the corporation may realize a number of long-run benefits, including improved public image, retention of talented managers, help in recruiting qualified personnel, improved community living standards for employees, and the attracting of investors.

Whatever the motivation, society and business can mutually benefit from clearly directed, socially responsible activities.

Developing a Social Audit

In order to demonstrate the accountability of social responsibility, many corporations have developed a "social audit." The idea is based upon financial audits that review and report a firm's financial activity. The **social audit** reviews, reports, and evaluates the social responsibility activities of a firm.

Numerous problems have hindered a complete acceptance of the social audit. Primary among these are the areas in which information will be collected and the ways in which the data will be gathered. The following questions illustrate the difficulty in accurately reporting social responsibility:

- Which areas of social responsibility will be measured?
- How are the data to be collected and analyzed?
- What criteria for measurement will be used?
- How can results be measured?
- Who will decide the relative value of the different forms of social responsibility?

As the questions indicate, a social audit is difficult to plan and implement. In doing so, the organization must carefully formulate its approach. The most useful steps in doing so include the following:

1. List all programs with social impact.
2. Explain why the organization is involved in each area, that is, establish the rationale.
3. Clearly state the objective(s) of each program.
4. As the program continues in effect, offer a descriptive account, in nonquantitative terms, of what has been accomplished, keep a progress report.
5. As much as possible, for example, quantify the costs and benefits of each program.[18]

The Ten Commandments of Social Responsibility

In carrying out their social responsibility programs, many firms have adopted rules, policies, and procedures designed to help them effectively integrate

---

[18] For more on this, see Raymond A. Bauer and Dan H. Fenn, Jr., "What Is a Corporate Social Audit?" *Harvard Business Review* (January–February 1973):38; Felix Pomeranz, "Social Measurement Revisited," *Journal of Accountancy* (August 1980):70; David F. Fetyko, "The Company Social Audit," *Management Accounting* (April 1975):31–34; and Raymond A. Bauer, L. Terry Couthorn, and Ranne P. Warner, "Auditing the Management Process for Social Performance," *Business and Society Review* (Fall 1975):39–45.

these programs with the rest of the organization's activities. At the same time, many are developing a social responsibility philosophy that spells out the organization's reasons for social involvement. Some researchers have suggested that a useful guide in this process is the adherence to certain general commandments of social responsibility which help organizations identify and respond to their social commitment. The following is an example of one recommended set.

I. Thou Shall Take Corrective Action Before It Is Required.
II. Thou Shall Work with Affected Constituents to Resolve Mutual Problems.
III. Thou Shall Work to Establish Industrywide Standards and Self-Regulation.
IV. Thou Shall Publicly Admit Your Mistakes.
V. Thou Shall Get Involved in Appropriate Social Programs.
VI. Thou Shall Help Correct Environmental Problems.
VII. Thou Shall Monitor the Changing Social Environment.
VIII. Thou Shall Establish and Enforce a Corporate Code of Conduct.
IX. Thou Shall Take Needed Public Stands on Social Issues.
X. Thou Shall Strive to Make Profits on an Ongoing Basis.

SUMMARY

1. Ethics refers to right and wrong conduct. In recent years this area has become a focal point of public attention.
2. There are a number of reasons that help account for an improvement in ethical standards. These include public disclosure, publicity, media coverage, and better communication. At the same time, there are a number of reasons that help account for a decline in ethical standards. These include social decay, materialism, hedonism, and loss of church and home influence.
3. A code of conduct is a statement of ethical practices or guidelines to which an enterprise adheres. Research shows that codes of conduct are becoming more prevalent in industry. These codes also are proving to be more meaningful in terms of external legal and social development, more comprehensive in terms of their coverage, and easier to implement in terms of the administrative procedures that are being used to enforce them.
4. Managers have six specific kinds of values: theoretical, economic, aesthetic, social, political, and religious. These values have changed over time and today's manager has values different from those of managers 50 years ago. In fact, a comparison of managerial values reveals that the profit maximizing ideas of early managers have now been replaced by trusteeship management or quality of life management.

5. Social responsibility consists of those obligations a business has to society. These obligations can take many different forms from concern for the environment, to fair business practices, to the management of human resources, to product safety.

6. Corporate social behavior has a number of different stages or levels. These range from reacting to social issues to accommodating them to implementing social responsibility programs before the need to do so becomes paramount. These stages or levels also entail the degree of involvement by the enterprise ranging from a minimum concern for social responsibility to a strong involvement in many areas of social concern.

7. There are some people who feel business should not assume a social responsibility posture. Most managers, however, disagree with the philosophy and believe that business can and should be involved. If a company is to be actively involved in the social responsibility area, it is important that the top management strongly support these efforts.

8. In evaluating social responsibility performance, many firms use various forms of social auditing. The social audit reviews, reports, and evaluates the social responsibility activities of a firm. A large number of firms also have developed a basic philosophy regarding social responsibility and, in many cases, adhere to general guidelines such as the 10 commandments that were set forth at the end of this chapter.

KEY TERMS

Aesthetic values   Managerial values showing a concern for art and beauty.

Code of conduct   A statement of ethical practices and guidelines to which an enterprise adheres.

Corporate response strategies   Specific strategies that a corporation may exhibit in response to difficult social situations. These include reaction, defense, accommodation, and proaction.

Economic values   Values showing a concern for usefulness and practicality.

Enlightened self-interest   A theory that holds that by helping society an enterprise is actually helping itself in the long term.

Ethics   A reference to right and wrong conduct.

Managerial values   The values and ethics possessed by managers and executives that are personal, established by industry codes, or developed through organizational influence.

Political values   Managerial values showing a concern for power over people and things.

Religious values   Managerial values showing a concern for unity and harmony in things.

Social audit   An evaluation and report on the social responsibility activities of an enterprise.

Social obligation   Corporation's action regarding social behavior that demonstrates contributions to society only when required or when a direct benefit to the company is shown.

Social responsibility   Corporation's action regarding social behavior that accepts responsibility for solving current problems and contributes to established causes.

Social responsiveness   Corporation's action regarding social behavior that willingly discusses activities with public groups and contributes to new and sometimes controversial groups whose needs are seen as increasingly important.

Social values   Managerial values showing a concern for people and their welfare.

Sound investment theory   A theory that holds that socially responsible corporations' stock values rise over time versus those corporations that are not socially responsible.

Theoretical values   Managerial values showing a concern for order, system, and logic.

QUESTIONS FOR ANALYSIS AND DISCUSSION

1. What is meant by "ethics" and how does it apply to business?
2. What are "codes of conduct"? Are they prevalent in companies today?
3. There are six specific kinds of values described by Edward Spranger. Identify each one.
4. Are managerial values changing? Are managerial ethics improving? In your answers, be sure to include a discussion of the three phases of managerial values and factors that influence ethical standards.
5. What is social responsibility? In your answer, include the levels of social responsibility that corporations exhibit.
6. There is a great deal of debate over the involvement of corporations in society's affairs. Outline a few arguments "for" and "against" the social responsibility of corporations.
7. What is a "social audit" and what steps are involved?
8. In what ways is it beneficial for top management to support social responsibility? In your discussion, include the idea of enlightened self interest and the sound investment theory.

CASE

Who Will Ever Know?

Carpentile, Inc. is a large pharmaceutical company. Six months ago headquarters received a phone call from the aide to a governor of one of the nation's largest states. It seems that this state had been spending hundreds of millions of dollars annually on medical supplies for the elderly and the indigent and wanted to find ways to reduce this bill. One suggestion had been that the state place all of its pharmaceutical orders with one large manufacturer and work out an arrangement that would ensure it the lowest possible costs. Carpentile was very interested in the project and asked the governor's office to supply it with the types and quantities of drugs that it needed.

Most of the items on the list were manufactured by Carpentile and could be directly supplied at large discounts to the various hospitals and medical facilities throughout the governor's state. A small percentage of the pharmaceutical supplies would still have to be purchased from other firms, but Carpentile offered to negotiate the lowest possible price for the state. These arrangements were agreeable to the governor and the key members of the state legislature and a contract was signed last month.

Earlier today one of the people in the Accounting Department came in to see the president of Carpentile. Apparently, there was a mistake in one of the price quotes that was given to the governor's office. One of the largest quantities of medicine was billed at $1.05 a vial. The actual cost should have been 55 cents a vial. The error will lead to the state paying Carpentile $89,300 more than it should. The accountant has left the information with the president for his actions.

The vice president of manufacturing has suggested to the president that nothing be done about the billing error. "Leave it alone. No one will ever know," he told the chief executive officer. However, the vice president of marketing has urged the president to call the governor's office, point out the error, and tell the governor that an adjustment will be made in the final billing. "Why cut corners on a contract where we are making so much money? Besides, what if someone audits our bill and finds out that we charged almost twice the going rate for quantity purchases of that drug? We're going to have egg all over our faces."

1. Does the president have a moral obligation to call the governor? After all, the two parties agreed on this price, did they not?
2. What do you think the president should do? Why?
3. What lesson does this case reinforce regarding the social responsibility of businesses? Explain.

YOU BE THE CONSULTANT

A Changing Environment

Harrington Brothers Inc. has been in business for more than 85 years. The company specializes in replacement parts for industrial machinery. Two years ago the firm patented a replacement part that swept the market. Many manufacturers were hard-pressed for cash, and profits were at a 10-year low. As a result, most manufacturers preferred to repair their machinery rather than to replace it with new models. The Harrington replacement part could be used in any of 65 major industrial machines and, when compared with the replacement parts offered by the competition, it was both cheaper and more efficient. Within eighteen months Harrington had captured almost 75 percent of the replacement part market. In an effort to ensure delivery of the parts, Harrington went to a double shift in its factory and used five suppliers for the needed materials. The company never had a problem with suppliers. If one was unable to provide the required materials, another would.

Six months ago, however, two competitors came out with a replacement part that is slightly more expensive than Harrington's but offers greater efficiency and longer life. This part allows a machine to be run at a speed 10 percent faster than normal while incurring very little wear and tear.

Harrington has purchased a dozen replacement parts from each of the two competitors and has examined what each competitor did to make the parts. After careful analysis, Harrington has realized that the competitors simply took Harrington's patent and figured out a way to improve it. Employing a follow-the-leader strategy, they piggybacked on Harrington's basic concept. In the process, the company violated Harrington's patent. After giving the matter a lot of thought, Harrington has decided not to sue the competition but rather to steal their ideas and improve on them. "If they're going to take our patents, we'll take their improvements," the president told the board of directors last month.

At the same time, the company has run into another problem. Two of its salespeople in Europe have been very successful in selling replacement parts there. The company has now learned, however, that the salespeople have been giving kickbacks to the purchasing managers in some firms. Because kickbacks were paid in the form of "commissions" and charged to Harrington's account, the company thought the salespeople had merely hired additional agents to help with the selling and that the commissions were legitimate expenses. Harrington paid the money directly to the salespeople, who then passed it on to the purchasing managers. Now the Internal Revenue Service has informed Harrington that it wants to make a full audit of the company's books for the last three years. Upon hearing the news, the company president smiled and said, "Oh, brother. It all seems to happen at the same time doesn't it?" The financial officer agreed.

Your Consultation

Assume you are the president's primary advisor. What do you think about the fact that the company is going to steal the competition's ideas and improve on them? What advice would you give to the president? What would you recommend be done about the two salespeople who were giving kickbacks? Be as complete as possible in your answer.

19

Corporate Entrepreneurship: Managing Innovation

The 1990s have brought the spirit of entrepreneurship to existing enterprises. The concept of corporate entrepreneurship, also referred to as intrapreneurship, is creating a new strategy of innovation and new venture development within the organization's structure.

In order to be an effective manager in the 1990s, one must be able to apply the major functions of planning, organizing, leading, and controlling to more innovative project teams. The entrepreneurial success stories from 3-M, Hewlett-Packard, Merck, General Electric, Rubbermaid, and Johnson & Johnson are just some of the latest during the last five years. Today's management challenge is how innovation through corporate entrepreneurship is developed, nurtured, motivated, and rewarded. The entire concept must be understood in the framework of existing management principles.

When you have finished studying this chapter you will be able to:

1. Understand the concept of corporate entrepreneurship.
2. Describe specific entrepreneurial strategies for organizations.
3. Illustrate the climate/structure needed for corporate entrepreneurs to exist.
4. Discuss ways to motivate individuals toward innovative activities.
5. Compare the characteristics of traditional managers and corporate entrepreneurs.
6. Describe the most effective ways to manage the process of corporate entrepreneuring.

INTRODUCTION

Today's corporate strategies focus heavily on innovation.

The current decade is seeing corporate strategies focused heavily on innovation. This new emphasis on entrepreneurial thinking developed during the "entrepreneurial economy" of the 1980s.[1] Peter Drucker, the renowned management expert, described four major developments that explain the emergence of this economy. First, the rapid evolution of knowledge and technology promoted the use of high-tech entrepreneurial start-ups. Second, demographic trends, such as two-wage-earner families, continuing education of adults, and the aging population, added fuel to the proliferation of newly developing ventures. Third, the venture capital market became an effective funding mechanism for entrepreneurial ventures. Fourth, and most importantly, American industry began to learn *how to manage entrepreneurship.*[2]

The contemporary thrust in entrepreneurship as the major force in American business has led to a desire for this type of activity *inside* enterprises. While some researchers conclude that entrepreneurship and bureaucracies are mutually exclusive and cannot coexist,[3] others have described entrepreneurial ventures within the enterprise framework.[4] Successful corporate ventures have been undertaken in many different companies including 3-M, IBM, Hewlett-Packard, General Electric, and Polaroid. Today there is a wealth of popular business literature describing a new "corporate revolution" taking place, thanks to the infusion of entrepreneurial thinking into larger bureaucratic structures.[5] This infusion is called "corporate entrepreneurship"[6] or "intrapreneurship."[7] Steven Brandt described management's role in taking on the new challenges that corporations are confronting when he stated:

> The challenge is relatively straightforward. The United States must upgrade its innovative prowess. To do so, U.S. companies must tap into the creative power of their members. Ideas come from people. Innovation is a capability of the many. That capability is utilized when people give commitment to the mission and life of the enterprise and have the power to do something with

---

[1] Peter F. Drucker, "Our Entrepreneurial Economy," *Harvard Business Review* (January–February 1984):59–64.

[2] Ibid., 60–61.

[3] See for example: Zenas Block, "Some Major Issues in Internal Corporate Venturing," *Frontiers of Entrepreneurship Research,* J. Hornaday, J. Timmons, K. Vesper, eds. (Wellesley, MA: Babson College, 1983), pp. 382–89.

[4] John S. DeMott, "Here Come the Intrapreneurs," *Time* (February 4, 1985):36–37.

[5] See for example: Peter F. Drucker, *Innovation and Entrepreneurship* (New York: Harper & Row, 1985); John Naisbitt and Patricia Aburdene, *Reinventing the Corporation* (New York: Warner Books, 1985); and Thomas J. Peters and Nancy Austin, *A Passion for Excellence* (New York: Random House, 1985).

[6] Steven C. Brandt, *Entrepreneuring in Established Companies* (Homewood, IL: Dow Jones/Irwin Co., 1986).

[7] Gifford Pinchott, III, *Intrapreneuring* (New York: Harper & Row, 1985).

TABLE 19-1   Ten Considerations in Reinventing the Corporation

1. The corporations that promote personal growth will attract the best people.
2. The challenge of the 1990s is to retrain managers to be coach, teacher, and mentor.
3. The best people seek ownership and the best companies will provide it with bonus plans, stock inventive plans, employee stock option plans, profit sharing, and even employee ownership *per se.*
4. Third-party contractors of labor will be used increasingly.
5. Authoritarian management is being replaced by a networking, people style of management, characterized by horizontal coordination and support.
6. Intrapreneurship within the corporation allows an employee to get the satisfaction of developing his or her idea without the risk of leaving the company.
7. Quality will be paramount, producing a shift from mass to information in goods and services.
8. Intuition is superseding the numbers used in business and, because of the vast amount of information, this better serves the needs of the new corporation.
9. Large companies are taking lessons from small businesses and learning how to be flexible, to promote innovation, and to create spirit.
10. Rather than considering just infrastructure (water supply, transportation, proximity to markets, etc.), companies must locate where creative people want to live, where there is "ambience" or quality of life factors (good climate, schools, and cultural and recreational opportunities).

Source: John Naisbitt and Patricia Aburdene, *Reinventing the Corporation* (New York: Warner Books, 1985), pp. 45–46.

their capabilities. Noncommitment is the price of obsolete managing practices, not the lack of talent or desire.

Commitment is most freely given when the members of an enterprise play a part in defining the purposes and plans of the entity. Commitment carries with it a de facto approval of, and support for, the management. Managing by consent is a useful managing philosophy if more entrepreneurial behavior is desired.[8]

This new philosophy of management by consent must permeate enterprises seeking to achieve success in the 1990s and beyond. In order to implement such a philosophy, organizations need to recognize and respond to the specific strategies (planning), the proper climate (organizing), the needed motivation (motivating), and the most effective rewards (controlling). Thus, again, the functions of management are present, but in newer, more innovative ways than previously.

STRATEGIES FOR CORPORATE ENTREPRENEURING

There are a number of approaches an organization can take in creating corporate entrepreneuring. In doing so, it is helpful to keep in mind ten considerations in reinventing the corporation which are presented in Table 19-1. When

---

[8] Brandt, *Entrepreneuring,* p. 54.

FIGURE 19-1
Achieving
Uncommon
Performance
Begins by Sharing
the Vision

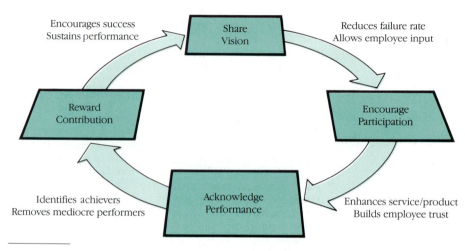

Source: John W. Alexander, "Sharing the Vision," *Business Horizons* (May–June 1989):57.

an entrepreneurial environment is created, the ethos of the original enterprise often changes dramatically. Traditions are set aside in favor of new processes and procedures. Some people, unaccustomed to operating in this environment, will leave; the others will discover a new motivation system that encourages creativity, ingenuity, risk taking, teamwork, and informal networking, all designed to increase productivity and make the organization more viable. Some people thrive in an entrepreneurial environment; others dislike it intensely.

Vision and Objectives

Vision is required.

The first step in planning the direction for the enterprise is sharing the vision of innovation that executives wish to achieve. Since corporate entrepreneuring results in the creative talents of people in the organization, then employees need to know and understand this vision. Figure 19-1 illustrates the importance of shared vision within a strategy that seeks high achievement.

The next step in the planning phase is to identify specific objectives for corporate entrepreneuring strategies and the programs needed to achieve those objectives. Rosabeth Moss Kanter, a noted researcher on innovation, has described three major objectives and their respective programs designed for innovation.[9]

Specific objectives must be set.

The first objective is making sure that current systems, structures, and practices do not present insurmountable roadblocks to the flexibility and fast action needed for innovation. To implement this objective:

[9] Rosabeth Moss Kanter, "Supporting Innovation and Venture Development in Established Companies," *Journal of Business Venturing* (Winter 1985):56–59.

- reduce unnecessary bureaucracy.
- reduce segmentalism and encourage communication across department and functions.
- change internal budgeting and accounting procedures.

The second objective is to provide incentives and tools for innovative projects to be established. Programs designed specifically for this objective are:

- Use of internal venture capital and special project budgets. (This has been termed *intracapital* to signify a special fund for intrapreneurial projects).
- discretionary funds set aside to allow for expansion of projects.
- discretionary time allowed for projects (sometimes referred to as "bootlegging" time).
- performance view and compensation established for intrapreneuring. This means that newer forms of rewards and bonuses must be set up to encourage and support intrapreneurial activity.

The third objective is to seek synergies across business areas so that new opportunities are discovered in new combinations while at the same time business units retain operating autonomy. For this objective to be carried out:

- encourage joint projects and ventures among divisions, departments, and companies.
- use conferences and idea changes to foster the communication and information flow across company boundaries and allow and encourage employees to discuss and brainstorm new ideas.

Specific entrepreneurship strategies will vary from firm to firm. However, they all have similar patterns, seeking a proactive change of the status quo and a new, flexible approach to management of operations. The objectives of these strategies also tend to be similar. (See "Management In Practice: Innovative Persistence at Merck.")

Developing an Innovative Climate

The major thrust of intrapreneuring is to develop entrepreneurial spirit.

Most agree that the term intrapreneur refers to entrepreneurial activities that receive organizational sanction and resource commitments for the purpose of innovative results.[10] The major thrust of intrapreneuring is to develop the entrepreneurial spirit within organizational boundaries, thus allowing an atmosphere of innovation to prosper.

---

[10] See Robert A. Burgelman, "Designs for Corporate Entrepreneurship," *California Management Review* (1984):154–66. Kanter, op. cit.

MANAGEMENT IN PRACTICE

Innovative Persistence at Merck

Merck & Co., one of the nation's leading pharmaceutical firms, invests nearly $21,000 per employee annually on new research. The industry average is $12,700 per employee. This type of financial investment has paid off for Merck. However, the money is only part of the firm's innovative success. Persistence is the other part.

Take the example of Alfred Alberts, a researcher at Merck, who spent ten years working on a new drug called Mevacor. This new chemical could block cholesterol formation in the human system. Its introduction has resulted in a $430 million a year blockbuster. Yet, Mevacor was actually the result of three full decades of research and an investment of $125 million. Says researcher Alberts, "There's a tradition of innovation here. It's not something you can build overnight."

At Merck, a team leader is assigned to each new project team. The leader acts as the corporate entrepreneur by nurturing the entire project from early research to final government approval. It is this person's responsibility to search out the needed scientists and professionals from other areas in the company and convince them to commit time and effort to the project. This builds a true sense of investment for the project leader in the sense that he or she feels committed to the effort.

Since developing a new drug can take ten years or more and, since nine out of every ten attempts usually fail, it is obvious that persistence is a key to successful innovation. And success has been the result of Merck's formula for innovation. The last eleven drugs introduced since 1978 have each produced annual sales of $100 million or better. Vasoter, a drug developed for lowering blood pressure, has produced over $1 billion in revenues during the last three years. As a result, the firm's growth in earnings has been 22 percent annually for the past five years. Obviously, innovative persistence pays off at Merck!

Source: Joseph Weber, "A Culture That Just Keeps Dishing Up Success," *Business Week* (June 16, 1989):120.

In reestablishing the drive to achieve inside today's corporations, one strategy is to invest heavily in "entrepreneurial ways."[11] This concept, when coupled with other specific strategies for innovation and research, can enhance the potential for inventors and venture developers. In fact, one researcher, after profiling inventors as a potential employee source for corporations, found that companies need to provide more nurturing and information sharing in order to attract and develop these individuals.[12]

These characteristics help establish climate.

In conjunction with establishing entrepreneurial ways and nurturing inventors, there is a need to develop a climate that will help innovative people to aspire to their full potential. Four of the characteristics critical in establishing this climate are:

[11] Robert W. Goddard, "Recharge the Power Shortage in Corporate America," *Personnel Journal* (March 1987):39–42.

[12] Roberts D. Hisrich, "The Inventor: A Potential Source for New Products," *Mid-Atlantic Journal of Business* (Winter 1985–1986):67–79.

1. The presence of explicit goals—these need to be mutually agreed upon by worker and management so specific steps are achieved.
2. A system of feedback and positive reinforcement—this is necessary in order for potential inventors, creators, or intrapreneurs to realize there is acceptance and reward.
3. An emphasis on individual responsibility—confidence, trust, and accountability are key features to the success of any innovative program.
4. Rewards based upon results—a reward system that enhances and encourages others to risk and to achieve must be established.[13]

In order to establish corporate entrepreneuring, companies need to provide the freedom and encouragement that intrapreneurs require to develop their ideas. This is a problem in many enterprises because top managers do not believe that entrepreneurial ideas can be nurtured and developed in their environment. They also find it hard to implement policies that encourage freedom and unstructured activity. What can a corporation do to foster the intrapreneurial process? First, the organization needs to examine and/or revise its philosophy of management. Many enterprises have obsolete ideas about cooperative cultures, management techniques, and the values of managers and employees; "You see what you are programmed to see, and you restrict your seeing to the signals that favor your expertise." [14] Unfortunately, doing old tasks more efficiently is not the answer to new challenges; a new culture with new values has to be developed. Table 19-2 illustrates the differences between new venture units and historical operating units in corporations. It is important for managers to recognize the differences in these dimensions if corporate entrepreneuring is to flourish in their enterprise. Bureaucrats and controllers must learn to coexist with, or give way to, the designer and entrepreneur. Unfortunately, this is easier said than done. However, there are some steps that organizations can take to help restructure corporate thinking and encourage an intrapreneurial environment. These include:

1. An early identification of potential intrapreneurs.
2. Top management sponsorship of intrapreneurial projects.
3. A creation of both diversity and order in strategic activities.
4. Promotion of intrapreneurship through experimentation.
5. Development of collaboration between entrepreneurial participants and the organization at large.[15]

[13] Burt K. Scanlan, "Creating a Climate for Achievement," *Business Horizons* (March–April 1981):5–9.
[14] Gustaf Delin, "Rewiring Corporate Thinking," *Public Relations Journal* (August 1983):12.
[15] Robert A. Burgelman, "Corporate Entrepreneurship and Strategic Management: Insights From a Process Study," *Management Science* (December 1983):1349–63; and William E. Souder, "Encouraging Entrepreneurship in the Large Corporation," *Research Management* (May 1981):18–22.

TABLE 19-2   Some of the Differences Between New Venture Units and Historical Operating Units

Dimension	New Venture Unit	Historical Operating Unit
Environment	Dynamic	Stable
Formality	Low	High
Innovation	High	Low
Control method	Face-to-face	Rules & SOPs
Autonomy	High	Low
Experimentation	High	Low
Span of control	Wide	Narrow
Planning frequency	Frequent	Infrequent
Planning detail	Low	High
Performance criteria	Innovation and risk taking	Current profits
Compensation	Deferred	Current
Size of reward	Large	Small

Source: Christopher K. Bart, "Organizing for New Product Development," *Journal of Business Strategy* (July–August 1988):35.

Motivating for Corporate Entrepreneuring

In order to motivate individuals towards the corporate venturing process, managers need to understand the obstacles to corporate entrepreneuring that employees perceive, as well as the differences between corporate entrepreneurs and traditional managers.[16]

Corporate Venturing Obstacles

The obstacles to corporate entrepreneuring are usually based on the ineffectiveness of traditional management techniques applied to new venture development. Although it is unintentional, the adverse impact of a particular traditional management technique can be so destructive that the individuals within an enterprise will tend to avoid corporate entrepreneurial behavior. Table 19-3 provides a list of traditional management techniques, their adverse effects (when the technique is rigidly enforced), and the recommended actions to change or adjust the practice.

Understanding these obstacles is critical in fostering corporate entrepreneuring because they are the foundation points for all other motivation efforts.

---

[16] Donald F. Kuratko and Ray V. Montagno, "The Intrapreneurial Spirit," *Training and Development Journal* (October 1989):83–87.

TABLE 19-3   Sources of and Solutions to Obstacles in Corporate Venturing

Traditional Management Practices	Adverse Effects	Recommended Actions
Enforce standard procedures to avoid mistakes	Innovative solutions blocked, funds misspent	Make ground rules specific to each situation
Manage resources for efficiency and ROI	Competitive lead lost, low market penetration	Focus effort on critical issues; e.g., market share
Control against plan	Facts ignored that should replace assumptions	Change plan to reflect new learning
Plan long term	Nonviable goals locked in, high failure costs	Envision a goal, then set interim milestones, reassess after each
Manage functionally	Entrepreneur failure and/or venture failure	Support entrepreneur with managerial and multidiscipline skills
Avoid moves that risk the base business	Missed opportunities	Take small steps, build out from strengths
Protect the base business at all costs	Venturing dumped when base business threatened	Make venturing mainstream, take affordable risks
Judge new steps from prior experience	Wrong decisions about competition and markets	Use learning strategies, test assumptions
Compensate uniformly	Low motivation and inefficient operations	Balance risk and reward, employ special compensation
Promote compatible individuals	Loss of innovators	Accommodate "boat rockers" and "doers"

Source: Hollister B. Sykes and Zenas Block, "Corporate Venturing Obstacles: Sources and Solutions," *Journal of Business Venturing* (Winter 1989):161.

In order to gain support and foster excitement for new venture development, managers must remove the perceived obstacles and seek alternative management actions to support corporate entrepreneurs.[17]

After recognizing the obstacles, managers need to adapt to the principles of successful innovative companies. James Brian Quinn, an expert in the field of innovation, established the following factors that are apparent in large corporations that are successful innovators.

---

[17] See: Hollister B. Sykes and Zenas Block, "Corporate Venturing Obstacles: Sources and Solutions," *Journal of Business Venturing* (Winter 1989):159–67 and also Ian C. McMillan, Zenas Block, and P. M. Subba Narasimha, "Corporate Venturing: Alternatives, Obstacles Encountered, and Experience Effects," *Journal of Business Venturing* (Spring 1986):177–91.

Here are some
principles
followed by
successful
innovative
companies.

- **Atmosphere and vision.** Innovative companies have a clear-cut vision for an innovative company and the recognized support for an innovative atmosphere.
- **Orientation to the market.** Innovative companies tie their visions to the realities of the marketplace.
- **Small flat organizations.** Most innovative companies keep the total organization flat and project teams small.
- **Multiple approaches.** Innovative managers encourage several projects to proceed in parallel development.
- **Interactive learning.** Within an innovative environment, learning and investigation of idea cuts across traditional functional lines in the organization.
- **Skunkworks.** Every highly innovative enterprise uses groups that function outside traditional lines of authority. This eliminates bureaucracy, permits rapid turnaround, and instills a high level of group identity and loyalty.[18]

Understanding Corporate Entrepreneurs

Initially, the corporate entrepreneur is the general manager of a new business that does not yet exist. In the beginning the individual may be specialized in one area, such as marketing or research and development, but once the individual starts an intraprise, he or she quickly begins to learn all facets of the project. The corporate entrepreneur soon becomes a generalist with multiple skills.

Corporate
entrepreneurs are
action-oriented.

Corporate entrepreneurs tend to be action-oriented. They are able to act quickly. They are also goal-oriented, willing to do whatever it takes to achieve their objectives. They are also a combination of thinker and doer, planner and worker. They combine vision and action. Dedication to the new idea is paramount. As a result, corporate entrepreneurs often expect the impossible from themselves, and consider no setback too great to make their venture successful. They are self-determined goal setters who go beyond the call of duty in achieving their goals.

Corporate
entrepreneurs are
optimistic.

When faced with failure or setback, corporate entrepreneurs employ an optimistic approach. First, they do not admit that they are beaten; they view failure as a temporary setback to be learned from and dealt with. It is not seen as a reason to quit. Second, they view themselves as responsible for their own destiny. They do not blame their failure on others, but rather focus on learning how they might have done better. By objectively dealing with their own mistakes and failures, they learn to avoid making the same mistake again, and this, in turn, is part of what helps make them successful.

One of the best ways to motivate employees towards entrepreneurial

---

[18] James Brian Quinn, "Managing Innovation: Controlled Chaos," *Harvard Business Review* (May–June 1985):73–84.

Entrepreneurs have different motivations and attitudes from traditional managers.

activity is to understand the differences between traditional managers and entrepreneurs. Gifford Pinchott III compared managers, entrepreneurs, and intrapreneurs (another name for corporate entrepreneurs) on specific organizational and project dimensions. Table 19-4 provides a complete breakdown of these comparisons.

For managers, the key factors to understand are the primary motivations of freedom to access resources and response to corporate recognition as well as the similarity of many skills and elements with the entrepreneur. Thus, managers must be prepared to handle a corporate entrepreneur differently than a traditional manager. However, understanding the critical differences in action, status, decisions, and problem solving provide insight into developing procedures and policies that motivate rather than inhibit the development of corporate entrepreneurs; and corporate entrepreneurs can be developed. Peter F. Drucker noted that entrepreneurship operates through the tool of innovation.[19] Thus, it is a discipline that can be learned and developed. In addition, two researchers, Donald F. Kuratko and Ray V. Montagno, have established a training program for corporate managers to develop entrepreneurial skills.[20] Their research has lead to specific factors that organizations and managers can concentrate on in helping individuals within the system develop more entrepreneurial behavior.[21] Some of these factors—top management support, time, resources, and rewards—are within the domain of managers and, thus, become the primary areas to utilize in order to motivate corporate entrepreneurs.

Managing and Evaluating Corporate Entrepreneurship

The final stage for managers to concentrate on is the control function, the managing and evaluation of corporate entrepreneurship activities. As with the traditional functions of management, the overall evaluation, feedback, and reward of entrepreneurial projects will be the measuring tool for the planning, organizing, and motivating of corporate entrepreneurship.

Rewards are important.

One researcher, Vijay Sathe, has suggested a number of areas that management must focus upon if the organization is going to successfully facilitate entrepreneurial behavior. The first is to encourage, not mandate, entrepreneurial activity. Managers should use financial rewards and strong company recognition rather than rules or strict procedures to encourage corporate entrepreneurship. This is actually a stronger internal control and direction method than traditional parameters.

---

[19] Drucker, *Innovation and Entrepreneurship,* op. cit.

[20] Donald F. Kuratko and Ray V. Montagno, "The Intrapreneurial Spirit," *Training and Development Journal* (October 1989):83–87.

[21] Donald F. Kuratko, Ray V. Montagno, and Jeffrey S. Hornsby, "Developing an Intrapreneurial Instrument for an Effective Corporate Entrepreneurial Environment," *Strategic Management Journal* (Summer 1990):49–58.

TABLE 19-4   Comparison of Managers, Entrepreneurs, and Intrapreneurs

	Traditional Manager	Entrepreneur	Intrapreneur
Primary motives	Wants promotion and other traditional corporate rewards. Power-motivated.	Wants freedom. Goal-oriented, self-reliant, and self-motivated.	Wants freedom and access to corporate resources. Goal-oriented and self-motivated, but also responds to corporate rewards and recognition.
Time orientation	Responds to quotas and budgets, weekly, monthly, quarterly, annual planning horizons, the next promotion or transfer.	Uses end goals of 5- to 10-year growth of the business as guides. Takes action now to move to next step along way.	End goals of 3 to 15 years, depending on the type of venture. Urgency to meet self-imposed and corporate timetables.
Action	Delegates action. Supervising and reporting take most of one's energy.	Gets hands dirty. May upset employees by suddenly doing their work.	Get hands dirty. May know how to delegate, but when necessary does that needs to be done.
Skills	Professional management. Often business-school trained. Uses abstract analytical tools, people management, and political skills.	Knows business intimately. More business acumen than managerial or political skill. Often technically trained if in technical business. May have had formal profit and loss responsibility in the company.	Very much like the entrepreneur, but the situation demands greater ability to prosper within the organization. Needs help with this.
Courage and destiny	Sees others in charge of his or her destiny. Can be forceful and ambitious, but may be fearful of others' ability to do him or her in.	Self-confident, optimistic, courageous.	Self-confident and courageous. Many intrapreneurs are cynical about the system, but optimistic about their ability to outwit it.
Risk	Careful.	Likes moderate risk. Invests heavily, but expects to succeed.	Likes moderate risk. Generally not afraid of being fired so sees little personal risk.

Control of entrepreneurial behavior is important.

Another area is the proper control of human resource policies. Managers need to remain in positions long enough to allow them to learn an industry and a particular division. Rather than move managers around in positions, as is the case in many companies, Sathe suggests "selected rotation" where managers are exposed to different but related territories. This assists managers in gaining sufficient knowledge for new venture development.

A third factor is for management to sustain a long enough commitment to

	Traditional Manager	Entrepreneur	Intrapreneur
Market research	Has market studies done to discover needs and guide product conceptualization.	Creates needs. Creates products that often cannot be tested with market research—potential customers do not yet understand them. Talks to customers and forms own opinions.	Does own market research and intuitive market evaluation like the entrepreneur.
Status	Cares about status symbols (corner office, etc.).	Happy sitting on an orange crate if job is getting done.	Considers traditional status symbols a joke; treasures symbols of freedom.
Failure and mistakes	Strives to avoid mistakes and surprises. Postpones recognizing failure.	Deals with mistakes and failures as learning experience.	Sensitive to need to appear orderly. Attempts to hide risky projects from view so can learn from mistakes without political cost of public failure.
Decisions	Agrees with those in power. Delays decision until a feel of what bosses want is obtained.	Follows private vision. Decisive, action-oriented.	Adept at getting others to agree to private vision. Somewhat more patient and willing to compromise than the entrepreneur but still a doer.
Attitude toward the system	Sees system as nurturing and protective, seeks position within it.	May rapidly advance in a system, then, when frustrated, reject the system and form his or her own company.	Dislikes the system but learns to manipulate it.
Problem-solving style	Works out problems within the system.	Escapes problems in large and formal structures by leaving and starting over on one's own.	Works out problems within the system, or bypasses it without leaving.

Source: Adapted from Gifford Pinchott, *Intrapreneuring* (New York: Harper & Row, 1985) pp. 54–56.

entrepreneurial projects for momentum to occur. There will be inevitable failures (see "Management In Practice: 3-M — Tolerating Failure/Mastering Innovation") and learning must be the key to the aftermath of those failures. Thus, sustained commitment is an important element in managing corporate entrepreneurship.

A final element mentioned by Sathe is to bet on people, *not* on analysis. While analysis is always important to judge the progression of a project, it

MANAGEMENT IN PRACTICE

3-M—Tolerating Failure/Mastering Innovation

At the turn of the century, a doctor, a lawyer, two railroad executives, and a meat market manager became partners in a business venture in northern Minnesota. They purchased land on the shores of Lake Superior where they planned on mining corundum, an abrasive used by sandpaper manufacturers. After buying machinery, hiring workers, and bringing in new investors, the five entrepreneurs found out that there was no corundum in their mine. Their idea was doomed to failure. That was the beginning of the Minnesota Mining & Manufacturing Co., now known as 3-M.

The company founders realized that they must invent some new ideas in order to salvage their company. So, new ideas began to percolate among the owners, such as Francis G. Okie's idea to replace razor blades with sandpaper. That's right. He believed that men could rub sandpaper on their face rather than use a sharp razor. He was wrong and the idea failed. But, his ideas continued until he developed a waterproof sandpaper for the auto industry; it was a blockbuster success.

Thus, 3-M's philosophy was born. Innovation is a numbers game; the more ideas you have, the better the chances for a successful innovation. In other words, to master innovation there must be a toleration for failure. This philosophy has paid off for 3-M. Antistatic videotape, translucent dental braces, synthetic ligaments for knee surgery, heavy-duty reflective sheeting for construction signs, and of course, Post-it notes, are just some of the great innovations developed at 3-M. Overall, the company has a catalogue of 60,000 products that contributed to a record $10.6 billion in sales and $1.15 billion in earnings in 1988. More impressively, 32 percent of the sales came from products introduced in the previous five years.

It appears as though 3-M is spinning out new products faster and better than any other company. Their original creative spirit is alive and well. It is fostered through a set of short, simple rules that the company truly believes in and operates upon. They may represent the key factors for today's companies needing to innovate. Here are the rules:

- **Keep divisions small.** Division managers must know each staffer's first name. When a division gets too big, perhaps reaching $250 to $300 million in sales, it is split up.
- **Tolerate failure.** By encouraging plenty of experimentation and risk taking, there are more chances for a new product hit. The goal: divisions must derive 25 percent of sales from products introduced in the past five years. The target may be boosted to 30 percent.
- **Motivate the champions.** When a 3-M employee comes up with a product idea, he or she recruits an action team to develop it. Salaries and promotions are tied to the product's progress. The champion has a chance to someday run his or her own product group or division.
- **Stay close to the customer.** Researchers, marketers, and managers visit with customers and routinely invite them to help brainstorm product ideas.
- **Share the wealth.** Technology, wherever it's developed, belongs to everyone.
- **Don't kill a project.** If an idea can't find a home in one of 3-M's divisions, a staffer can devote 15 percent of his or her time to prove it is workable. For those who need seed money, as many as 90 "genesis grants" of $50,000 are awarded each year.

Source: Russell Mitchell, "Masters of Innovation," *Business Week* (April 10, 1989):58–63.

should be done in a supportive style rather than an imposed style. The supportive challenge can help the entrepreneur realize errors, test their convictions, and accomplish a self-analysis.[22]

Overall, the concept of relying on people is a major managerial task for corporate entrepreneurship to prosper. In this vein, it is important to reward employees effectively for their risk taking on these projects. In one study of typical employees the following were cited as factors to improve productivity:[23]

Job enables them to develop abilities 61%
Pay tied to performance 59%
Recognition for good work 58%
Job requires creativity 55%
Job allows them to think for themselves 54%
Interesting work 54%
Challenging job 53%
A great deal of responsibility 50%

While these are not new factors only to corporate entrepreneurs, they do reinforce the belief that employees are willing to work on new projects and challenging teams *if* the rewards are apparent. It should be mentioned that the exact rewards for corporate entrepreneuring are not yet agreed upon by most researchers.[24] Some believe that allowing the inventive to be in charge of the new venture is the best reward. Others say it is allowing the corporate entrepreneur more discretionary time to work on future projects. Still others insist that special capital, called intracapital, should be set aside for the corporate entrepreneur to use whenever investment money is needed for further research ideas.

Although each enterprise must develop an evaluation and reward system that is most appropriate for its own entrepreneurial process, there are a number of key questions that assist in establishing the type of process an organization has. The following presents seven questions that managers can use to assess their enterprise. Only through the application of these questions can a manager respond to the planning function discussed earlier. The questions are these:

There are a series of key questions that should be answered.

- *Are people in your company permitted to do the job in their own way, or are they constantly stopping to explain their actions and ask for permission?* Some organizations push decisions up through a multilevel approval processes so the doers and the deciders never even meet.
- *Has your company evolved quick and informal ways to access the*

---

[22] Vijay Sathe, "From Surface to Deep Corporate Entrepreneurship," *Human Resource Management* (Winter 1988):389–411.

[23] Robert W. Goddard, "How to Reward the 80s Employee," *Personnel Management* (April 1989):7–10.

[24] See: Zenas Block and O. Ornati, "Compensating Corporate Venture Managers," *Journal of Business Venturing* (Spring 1987):41–51.

resources to try new ideas? Intrapreneurs need discretionary resources to explore and develop new ideas. Some companies give employees the freedom to use a percentage of their time on projects of their own choosing, and set aside funds to explore new ideas when they occur. Others control resources so tightly that nothing is available for the new and unexpected. The result is nothing new.

■ *Has your company developed ways to manage many small and experimental products and businesses?* Today's corporate cultures favor a few well-studied, well-planned attempts to hit a home run. In fact, nobody bats 1000, and it is better to try more times with less careful and expensive preparation for each.

■ *Is your system set up to encourage risk taking and to tolerate mistakes?* Innovation cannot be achieved without risk and mistakes. Even successful innovation generally begins with blunders and false starts.

■ *Can your company decide to try something and stick with the experiment long enough to see if it will work, even when that may take years and several false starts?* Innovation takes years, even decades, but the rhythm of corporations is annual planning.

■ *Are people in your company more concerned with new ideas or with defending their turf?* Because new ideas almost always cross the boundaries of existing patterns of organizations, a jealous tendency to territorial behavior blocks innovation.

■ *How easy is it to form functionally complete, autonomous teams in your corporate environment?* Small teams with full responsibility for developing an intraprise solve many of the basic problems of innovation, but some companies resist their formation.[25]

SUMMARY

1. Corporate strategies are now being focused heavily on innovation. This new emphasis is resulting in an entrepreneurial economy.

2. There are a number of approaches an organization can take in creating corporate entrepreneuring. One is to create a vision of innovation for the organization. A second is to set specific objectives that are attainable, provide rewards for accomplishments, and seek synergies across business areas.

3. The major thrust of intrapreneuring is to develop the entrepreneurial spirit within organizational boundaries, thus allowing an atmosphere of innovation to prosper. Some of the ways that this is done is through the use of explicit goals, feedback, and positive reinforcement; an emphasis on individual responsibility; and rewards based on results.

4. There are a variety of obstacles to corporate entrepreneuring. These are

---

[25] Adapted from: Gifford Pinchott, *Intrapreneuring* (New York: Harper & Row, 1985), pp. 198–99.

usually based on the ineffectiveness of traditional management techniques applied to new venture development. Some of the principles that help remove such obstacles include vision, market orientation, small flat organizations, interactive learning, and skunkworks.

5. Corporate entrepreneurs tend to be action-oriented and optimistic. Other differences between them and traditional managers are provided in Table 19-4.

6. Managers also need to focus on the control function in managing and evaluating corporate entrepreneurship activities. This involves encouraging entrepreneurial activity, maintaining proper control of human resource policies, sustaining a long-term commitment to entrepreneurial projects, and betting on people rather than on analysis. It also involves asking key questions that help tie together the controlling and planning functions.

KEY TERMS

Corporate entrepreneurship   The creation of a new strategy of innovation and new venture development within an organization's structure.

Innovative climate   The atmosphere in a corporation that encourages freedom and responsibility for individuals to develop their ideas.

Intracapital   An internal venture capital used for special projects.

Intrapreneurship   The infusion of entrepreneurial thinking inside of larger bureaucratic structures.

Multiple approaches   Several innovative projects proceeding in parallel development.

Skunkworks   Highly innovative groups that function outside traditional lines of authority.

QUESTIONS FOR ANALYSIS AND DISCUSSION

1. In your own words, what is corporate entrepreneurship?
2. Why has there been such a strong desire in recent years to develop corporate entrepreneurs? Identify and describe two reasons.
3. Why would a firm like General Motors be interested in developing in-house intrapreneurs? Explain your reasoning.
4. What types of strategies have to be created in order to establish an entrepreneurial approach? Identify and describe three of them.
5. A number of corporations today are working to change organizational thinking and encourage a more entrepreneurial environment. What steps would you recommend? Offer at least three and explain each.
6. What are some of the advantages of developing an intrapreneurial environment? Identify and describe three.
7. What are specific obstacles to corporate venturing? Identify and describe four of them with recommended solutions.

8. From the research of innovation expert James Brian Quinn, what are four factors that are apparent in large organizations that successfully innovate? Explain each.
9. How does a corporate entrepreneur differ from a traditional manager? Compare and contrast the two. (Use Table 19-4 for your answer).
10. Of the key corporate considerations presented in the chapter, which are most critical to practicing managers? Explain your reasoning.

CASE

Unlocking the Potential

The Crellback Corporation is a medium-size retailing firm that is well-established in a five-state midwest region. Six weeks ago the owners sold their interest to a small manufacturing firm, Creative Products, that is well known for its innovative product development. Creative Products had sales of $12 million last year and a net profit of $2.1 million. Its primary success is a result of three new products that it has introduced in the last 18 months. As the head of Creative recently said, "The American consumer is continually looking for new goods that will make his or her life easier. These goods need to be easy to use, incorporate new technology and, if possible, not be too expensive. We have managed to build a multi-million dollar firm by using these three guidelines."

Creative would like to use many of its creative ideas at Crellback. Although Creative is a manufacturing firm, it also engages in selling to the extent that it must persuade wholesalers and retailers to carry its product lines. Now, with some of the middlemen cut out of the picture, Creative is looking forward to selling more of its output through the Crellback outlets. However, this is only one aspect of its overall strategy. Creative is also interested in using its creative ideas to develop more entrepreneurial spirit within the Crellback chain. "Many of these people have long regarded themselves as nothing more than clerks or retail personnel," noted the president of Creative. "What we need to do is show them how they can become more entrepreneurial. They need to start thinking of themselves as individuals who are able to generate creative ideas that will increase retail sales. There is not one person in the chain who does not have the ability to do this. Our job will be to unlock this potential and get these people to act like in-house entrepreneurs. My plan right now is to decide the steps that must be taken to get us on this road."

1. What are two steps that Creative should take in beginning to develop intrapreneurial skills among its Crellback personnel? Identify and describe both.
2. If the company is successful in its efforts, what will be some of the differences in the behavior of Crellback managers when comparing the way they now manage with the way they will be managing?

3. What are potential roadblocks that might prevent Creative from carrying out its plan? Identify and describe two of them.

Hiring the Right Manager

For the last five months, Aerodyne, Inc. has been slowly increasing the entrepreneurship climate in the company. During this period it has created three project teams to develop and sell new products/services. One of these is working on a new, highly durable plastic container for use with laptop portable computers. Annual sales for laptops have been increasing for the last three years and an improved portable case could be a major sales item in the industry.

Another of the project teams is developing new packaging for microwave ovens. This new container could withstand the extreme cold of the freezer and the extreme heat of the microwave. If the package is found to be effective, there is an excellent chance that the product could be marketed nationwide. This could result in sales of over $6 million in an 18-month period. The cost of developing the package will be approximately $180,000.

A third project team is working on a material for filling potholes on our highway system. This would strengthen the infrastructure of roads and allow work crews to operate more efficiently. While this material for the highways is still highly speculative, Aerodyne feels that it has developed state-of-the-art technology that will revolutionize the current highway repair system.

Aerodyne currently is in the process of hiring a project manager to head all three projects. It has narrowed the list to two people, Paul Richards and Monica Dailey. Paul is currently a production manager with a medium-size manufacturing firm. He has been in this position for five years, having worked his way up the ranks from machinist. He supervises a department of 117 people and has been responsible for increasing productivity in the department by 37 percent over the last two years. He is considered a very capable manager who works extremely well with others. Monica is a product manager with a large consumer goods firm. She has personally developed and brought to market a very successful consumer good that currently accounts for over 1 percent of her corporation's gross sales. Monica directly supervises a marketing group of 27 people who are responsible for covering the entire U.S. market, including Alaska and Hawaii.

Your Consultation

In your own words, how would you describe Paul and Monica? Are they traditional, entrepreneurial, or intrapreneurial managers? (Use Table 19-4 to help formulate your answer). Based on the information provided about Aerodyne, Inc. and the direction in which it is headed, which of the two people would you recommend be hired? Why? Be complete in your answer.

20

Management in the Future

During the next decade the world of management is going to change significantly. This chapter examines some of the major changes that will occur and presents a picture of the effect these changes will have on the way modern managers do their jobs. As you will see, many of these developments relate to changing values on the part of management, the employee, and society at large. The chapter examines the ways in which management values, attitudes, and interests will change during the next 10 years; it explores employee values, attitudes, and work life; and it analyzes the impact of social values in the workplace. When you have finished studying all of the material in this chapter, you will be able to:

1. Explain the current status of women in top management positions and what their future looks like.
2. Tell why there has been an increased interest in strategic planning among top managers.
3. Discuss the values and attitudes that today's workers have regarding their company and their job.
4. Explain how the quality of work life movement and modern technology will change the way workers do their jobs.
5. Identify and discuss how social values in the workplace are helping shape the world of management, giving particular attention in your discussion to employee assistance programs, the hiring of the handicapped, the elimination of sexual harassment, the changing work ethic, and AIDS in the workplace.

CONTINUING MANAGEMENT TRENDS

Before examining the specific changes taking place in the world of management, it is important to analyze two trends that started a number of years ago. These trends are of continuing interest for managers of the future and need to be discussed. Two growing trends in recent years have included an upsurge of women in executive-level positions as well as the emphasis placed by managers upon strategic planning.

Women in Top Management Positions

During the last decade the number of women in top management has increased steadily. The Bureau of Labor reported in 1989 that 39.3 percent of the 14.2 million executive, administrative, and management jobs were held by women. More significantly, 52% of all managers and professionals under the age of 35 were women.[1] (Also see "Management in Practice: Women Executives in the Upper Echelons.")

Table 20-1 illustrates the increases in women executives by title.[2] The consensus is that women are entering high-level management positions in greater numbers, and at younger ages, than ever before. Identifying women in executive positions as a continued future trend for the year 2000, John Naisbitt and Patricia Aburdene recently wrote:

> Women make up 49.6 percent of accountants, compared with 21.7 percent in 1972. About one quarter of Wall Street's financial professionals are women.
>
> More dramatic is the remarkable increase in the percentage of women graduating from law and medical schools. In 1966, fewer than 7 percent of MDs were granted to women. By 1987 it had reached 32.3 percent, nearly one third. In 1966 women were awarded an even tinier proportion of law degrees (LLB and JD), a mere 3.5 percent. But by 1987, women were taking home 40 percent of all law degrees.
>
> In the 1990s, the ranks of women doctors and lawyers will increase substantially, as will their influence.[3]

Some women are not academically prepared for careers in business

One reason for women's previous underrepresentation in the executive ranks is that in the past most women did not seek careers in management.[4] In college most majored in education or the liberal arts. That is now changing as women

---

[1] "Youth, College Narrow Pay Gap for Women," *Wall Street Journal,* November 17, 1989, p. B-4.
[2] J. Benjamin Forbes, James E. Piercy, and Thomas L. Hayes, "Women Executives: Breaking Down Barriers," *Business Horizons* (November–December 1988):6–9.
[3] John Naisbitt and Patricia Aburdene, *Megatrends 2000: Ten New Directions for the 1990s* (New York: William Morrow & Co., 1990), pp. 224–25.
[4] Lloyd D. Elgart, "Women on Fortune 500 Boards," *California Management Review* (Summer 1983):121–27.

MANAGEMENT IN PRACTICE

Women Executives in the Upper Echelons

The barriers for women in executive positions are slowly diminishing. A new generation of women executives, many with MBAs or Ph.D.s, are advancing into the highest levels of technical organizations. For example, in 1984 Digital Equipment Corporation established the Technology Executive Roundtable for executives representing computer companies with less than $30 million in revenues. There were no women executives. Today 5 percent of the 1,500 companies in the roundtable are headed by women. At Hewlett-Packard, 21 percent of all engineers are female and at AT&T 10 percent of all managers earning over $100,000 a year are women. These women are making their mark and they stand as role models for the up-and-coming managers.

One such model is Iva M. Wilson, president of Philips Display Components Co., a TV picture tube maker that had $300 million in revenues. As a Ph.D. in electrical engineering, she built an international reputation in vacuum tube research. She rose through various positions at Zenith Electronics during her 12 year tenure there. Then, in 1983 she joined Philips as chief engineer, managing a staff of 140. Three years later she became president.

Another role model is Adele Goldberg, a former group manager at Xerox Corp.'s Palo Alto Research Center. She persuaded Xerox to allow her to create a spin-off business, Parc-Place Systems Inc. She raised $4 million in seed money from venture capitalists and launched her business in March 1988. Goldberg illustrates the other growing avenue for women executives—establishing their own new venture.

Other examples of successful women executives include:

Cari M. Grim: President, Word-Star International

Ilene H. Lang: President, Marketing Software Division of AT&T.

Deb Wexler: Founder/President, Microcomputer Power. Started in 1982 with $5,000; 1988 sales $31 million.

Joanna L. Jaddson: Founder/President, Physical Optics, 1989 revenues—$4.5 million.

Maria S. Ligeti: Founder/President, Qronos Technology, 1988 revenues—$10 million.

These are just a few examples of the new generation of women executives, a generation setting the trend for the composition of executive positions in the 1990s.

Source: Emily T. Smith, "The Women Who Are Scaling High Tech's Heights," *Business Week* (August 28, 1989):86–88.

---

are flocking not only to undergraduate business schools but into MBA (Master of Business Administration) programs as well. The Department of Education reported in 1986 that the number of women earning MBAs had increased 344 percent in ten years compared to an increase of only 25 percent for men.[5] This kind of education is bound to help their chances for breaking into the executive ranks.

---

[5] Eleanor H. Raynolds, "Management Women in the Corporate Workplace: Possibilities for the Year 2000," *Human Resource Management* (Summer 1987):267.

TABLE 20-1 Women Executives by Title (Percentages)			
Title	**1982**	**1987**	**Changes**
President	15.1	16.2	+1.1
Executive Vice President	6.9	13.1	+6.2
Vice President	27.2	37.5	+10.3
Manager	9.0	4.8	−4.2
Counsel	0.8	1.4	+0.6
Secretary-Treasurer	9.9	4.1	−3.6
Treasurer	6.2	4.1	−2.1
Secretary	24.9	16.5	−8.4

Source: J. Benjamin Forbes, James E. Piercy, and Thomas L. Hayes, "Women Executives: Breaking Down Barriers," *Business Horizons* (November–December 1988):7.

Some women are taught not to be competitive

Another reason for the small percentage of women in top management is cultural. Women have been taught not to be competitive, so when they get into the world of business they are unprepared for the politics and pressures that go with the job. In an effort to deal with these problems, business firms, as well as universities, are beginning to offer courses for women desiring management positions. In these courses the participants are provided with information and training designed to help them maneuver their way through the corporate jungle.

How does the future look? The answer is, good and getting better. Three major factors can be cited to illustrate that the future for women is becoming brighter. First, more women are staying on the job than in the past. In past years, women left the workforce when they reached childbearing age. Today, the trend is changing. As seen in Figure 20-1, as of 1985, 72 percent of women aged 20–24, 71 percent of women aged 25–34, and 72 percent of women aged

FIGURE 20-1
Staying on the Job

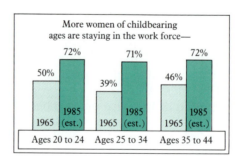

Source: USN&WR—Basic data: U.S. Dept. of Labor. After Beth Brophy and Nancy Linnon, "Why Women Execs Stop Before the Top," *U.S. News & World Report* (December 29, 1986):72–73. © 1986. U.S. News & World Report. Reprinted from issue of Dec. 29, 1986/Jan. 5, 1987.

35–44 remained in the workforce. This represents significant gains in numbers since 1965, underscoring a major cultural change.

Another factor illustrating the positive trend of women into top management is the continuous reduction of the wage gap. It's true that only approximately 1 percent of working women earn over $50,000. However, as seen in Figure 20-2, as of 1985 the median income of women workers demonstrated that they were earning 65 percent of their male counterparts' salaries, up from 59 percent in 1970. The trend in closing the wage gap is continuing from year to year.

Finally, women are seeking new opportunities in increased numbers. As detailed in Figure 20-3, more women continue to enter the professional areas of law, management, and securities as well as the technical fields of computers and engineering. This increase from 1972 to 1985 is another demonstration of the bright future for women executives.

In a study of attitudes about women, for example, Alma Baron questioned approximately 8,000 male respondents, 85 percent of whom were middle or upper-middle managers, regarding their image of women in business The purpose of the survey was (1) to find out how rapidly acceptance of women in management was occurring, and (2) to identify trends that could be useful for a company committed to moving women into the higher management levels. Some of her major findings included the following:

FIGURE 20-2
The Wage Gap

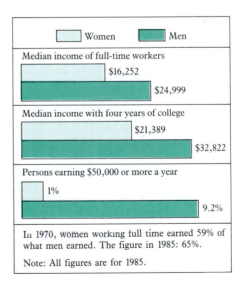

Women   Men

Median income of full-time workers
$16,252
$24,999

Median income with four years of college
$21,389
$32,822

Persons earning $50,000 or more a year
1%
9.2%

In 1970, women working full time earned 59% of what men earned. The figure in 1985: 65%.

Note: All figures are for 1985.

Note: All figures are for 1985.
Source: USN&WR—Basic data: U.S. Census Bureau. After Beth Brophy and Nancy Linnon, ''Why Women Execs Stop Before the Top,'' *U.S. News & World Report* (December 29, 1986):72–73.
© 1986. U.S. News & World Report. Reprinted from issue of Dec. 29, 1986/Jan. 5, 1987.

FIGURE 20-3
New Opportunities

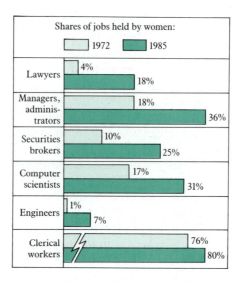

Source: USN&WR—Basic data: U.S. Dept. of Labor. After Beth Brophy and Nancy Linnon, "Why Women Execs Stop Before the Top," *U.S. News & World Report* (December 29, 1986):72–73. © 1986. U.S. News & World Report. Reprinted from issue of Dec. 29, 1986/Jan. 5, 1987.

1. Half of the respondents accepted women in managerial roles and less than 5 percent were negative toward women in these roles.
2. The higher the level of the executive's education, the more likely it was that he approved of women in managerial positions.
3. Men who work for women are more likely to accept them as managers, while men who do not work for women have a more negative opinion of them as managers.[6]

The survey confirms what we have been saying about women in management. The old stereotypes are fading. There is evidence that biases against women in business have lessened considerably in the last decade. This trend should continue in the foreseeable future.[7]

Continued Interest in Strategic Planning

During the next 10 years we will also see a change in the way management plans for the future. A true administrative science approach is emerging. This is due,

---

[6] Alma S. Baron, "What Men Are Saying About Women in Business," *Business Horizons* (January–February 1982):10–11.
[7] For more on this, see Geraldine Spruell, "Making It, Big Time—Is it Really Tougher for Women?" *Training and Development Journal* (July 1985):30–33 and Eleanor H. Raynolds, "Management Women in the Corporate Workplace: Possibilities for the Year 2000," *Human Resource Management* (Summer 1987):265–76.

in particular, to recent developments involving the collection and analysis of inter- and intra-industry business performance data on such key planning issues as strategy formulation, performance and its relationship to return on investment (ROI), the impact of product quality on ROI, the effect of modern technology on profit, and strategy implementation. Ten years ago, management scientists and behavioral scientists were chastising administrative scientists for their overreliance on intuition, gut feeling, hunch, and other less than scientific approaches. Progress since then shows that a more scientific approach is being taken, especially in the case of the strategic decision making used by top management.

Profit Impact of Marketing Strategy

The profit impact of marketing strategy (PIMS) is not the only example of the way administrative science evolved in the 1980s, but it provides an excellent illustration of the way the process is occurring. PIMS originated as an internal project at General Electric, where it was used as a tool in both corporate and division-level planning. In the early 1970s the PIMS program was established as a developmental project at the Harvard Business School and was located at the Marketing Science Institute, a research organization affiliated with that business school. In the mid-1970s the program was organized as an autonomous institute known as the Strategic Planning Institute (SPI). Business firms that become members of the institute provide information describing the characteristics of their market environment, the state of their competition, the strategy being pursued by their various divisions, and the operating results obtained for each. This data is then analyzed for the purpose of determining answers to questions such as the following:

Important questions are being answered

- What profit rate is "normal" for a given business, considering its particular market, competitive position, technology, cost structure and so forth?
- If the business continues on its current track, what will its future operating results be?
- What strategic changes in the business give promise of improving these results?
- Given a specific contemplated future strategy for the business how will profitability or cash flow change, short-term and long-term?[8]

Results to Date

Findings regarding business strategy

Information from the SPI has proven extremely useful to the member firms. In particular the institute has been able to generate a number of important findings

---

[8] *PIMS: The PIMS Program* (Cambridge, MA: The Strategic Planning Institute, 1980), 5.

FIGURE 20-4
Product Quality,
Market Share, and
Return on
Investment

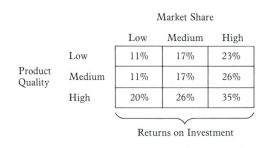

	Market Share		
	Low	Medium	High
Low	11%	17%	23%
Medium	11%	17%	26%
High	20%	26%	35%

Product Quality

Returns on Investment

regarding business strategy. One of the most interesting is that as business firms increase their levels of intensity per dollar of sales revenue (as in the case of airlines, bulk chemical-processing plants, and distributors of consumer goods requiring large inventories), their ROI declines. Why does this occur? The answer is that as firms invest more money in such things as capital equipment and plant, each becomes eager to produce at capacity. The results are frequent price wars, marketing wars, and other intensely competitive measures that collectively reduce revenue and increase costs. What should a firm do if the technology of its business clearly requires a high level of investment in plant, equipment and working capital? The SPI recommends that (a) the firm should not automatically assume that more is better in terms of investment intensity; (b) in evaluating a proposed investment that is clearly larger rather than merely proportional to an increase in capacity, the firm should consider the strategic effect as carefully as the cost effect of the project; and (c) it should adopt a market strategy that minimizes the profit-damaging effect of capital-intensive technology.

Another interesting finding reported by the SPI relates to product quality, market share, and ROI. The SPI puts the idea this way:

> The combined experience of the approximately 1,200 businesses now represented in the PIMS data pool indicates that *businesses selling high-quality products and services are generally more profitable than those with lower-quality offerings.* . . . Both return on investment and net profit as a percentage of sales rise as relative quality increases. Note, however, that the impact of differences in quality is greatest at the extremes of very low and high quality.[9]

Figure 20-4 illustrates PIMS research data related to product quality, market share, and ROI. Notice from the future that higher product quality is positively related to ROI *independently* of market share. Firms with high product quality have greater returns than those with low product quality. If these compa-

[9] Robert D. Buzzell, *Product Quality: The PIMSLETTER on Business Strategy,* no. 4 (Cambridge, MA: The Strategic Planning Institute, 1978), 2.

nies also enjoy large market shares, so much the better in terms of ROI. Additionally, quality seems to be an important influence on profit in virtually all kinds of markets and competitive positions. This finding is illustrated in Table 20-2. Notice from the data that, on average, the higher the quality of the product, the greater the return on investment.

Overall Strategy Findings

Drawing upon its results to date, most of which have been from manufacturing firms, the SPI has begun reporting its findings on business strategy. Five of these are the following:

Strategy-related conclusions

1. Business situations generally behave in a regular and predictable manner. In most cases, it is possible to measure the approximate results (within three to five points of after-tax ROI) of most businesses (almost 90 percent) over a moderately long period of time (three to five years) on the basis of observable characteristics of the market and the strategies being used by both the business itself and the competition. Since business situations can be understood by using an empirical scientific approach, the process of formulating strategy is now becoming an applied science.

2. All business situations are basically alike in following the same "laws of the marketplace." Despite differences in product line, profitability, and company culture, all business firms seem to be governed by the laws of supply and demand.

3. The laws of the marketplace determine about 80 percent of the observed variance in operating results across different businesses. Simply put, this

TABLE 20-2	Quality and Return on Investment by Type of Business				
	Quality Level				
Type of Business	*Lowest*	*Below Average*	*Average*	*Above Average*	*Highest*
	Average Return on Investment				
Consumer durables	16%	18%	18%	26%	32%
Consumer nondurables	15	21	17	23	32
Capital goods	10	8	13	20	21
Raw materials	13	21	21	21	35
Components	12	20	20	22	36
Supplies	16	13	19	25	36

Source: Robert D. Buzzell, *Product Quality: The PIMSLETTER on Business Strategy,* no. 4 (Cambridge, Mass.: The Strategic Planning Institute, 1978), 5. Reprinted by permission.

finding means that the characteristics of the served market, the business itself, and the competition make up about 80 percent of the reasons for success or failure. Operating skill or luck of the management constitutes the other 20 percent.

4. The expected impacts of strategic business characteristics tend to assert themselves over time. This finding has two major parts. First, if the fundamentals of a business change over time, for example when there is a decrease in the quality of the product line or the amount of vertical integration increases, profitability and net cash flow will move in the direction of the norm for the new position. Second, if a business's realized performance deviates from the expected norm, based on the laws of the marketplace, it will tend to move back toward that norm.

5. Business strategies are successful if their "fundamentals" are sound, unsuccessful if they are unsound. Simply put, if a business uses a strategy that is based on the empirical laws of the marketplace, it will tend to do better than a competitor that formulates strategy based solely on hunch, intuition, gut feeling, and personal opinion.

Quite obviously, findings such as these are very helpful to businesses that want to improve their strategy. These results also point out the value of systematic analysis of market conditions and reinforce many of the key ideas presented in Chapter 7.

During the next 10 years, we are going to be seeing even more attention focused on ways to analyze market conditions and formulate (and reformulate) strategic response. The approach that has been examined here is only one of a number that are beginning to gain popularity with business firms interested in learning how to become more effective in long-range planning and market strategy. It is, however, an important beginning.

EMPLOYEE VALUES, ATTITUDES, AND WORK LIFE

Management's world will also change as a result of employee attitudes, values, and work life—all of which are in a state of transition.

Changing Values and Attitudes

The values and attitudes of workers have been in a state of flux for many years. Research data show that over the last quarter of a century there has been a major shift in these attitudes. This shift is occurring throughout industry and reflects employees' basic attitude changes toward both their companies and their jobs.

At the present time there is a marked difference in the satisfaction of employees at the upper levels of the organization and those at the other levels.

This difference, commonly referred to as the **hierarchy gap**, exists in virtually every organization and in regard to just about every substantive issue, from pay and promotion to quality of work life. The following discussion, drawn from a major *Harvard Business Review* study, examines some of the most important developments that are occurring.

Views Toward the Company and the Job

During the last 25 years there has been a continuing decline in the attitudes of employees toward the company as a place in which to work. Managers still rate their firm higher than do clerical or hourly employees, but there is far less positive attitude on the part of all the personnel than there was back in the 1950s. The same basic pattern appears when employees are asked to rate (1) their company as a place to work when compared with what it was when they started, (2) their department in terms of a "good" place in which to work, and (3) how much they like the type of work they are doing currently.[10] Commenting on the situation at large, Harvard University researchers have noted:

Attitudes are less positive

> It is the gap and the downward trend in hourly and clerical employees' satisfaction that we find so disturbing. Certainly, dissatisfaction is not new. To many, work may never be anything other than an unpleasant, inescapable fact of life; at best—a way to pay bills, associate with other people, and have scheduled things to do. Rapid advancement in technology and automation, the increasing impersonality of work and large organizations, and the instability of time-honored values and traditions are certainly prime contributors to dissatisfaction. The impact of these forces on the working world is not yet as visible as was the dissent in colleges during the late 1960s, but discontent among hourly and clerical employees is every bit as pervasive and seems to be growing.[11]

When taken as a whole these findings, drawn from more than 75,000 workers in a wide array of industries ranging in size from less than 500 to more than 200,000 employees, present an ominous picture for the manager of the 1990s. There is decreasing satisfaction among both hourly and clerical employees. Additionally, while managers are more positive about the entire situation, they too agree with the hourly and clerical employees that their firms are not as good a place to work as they were once.

Extrinsic Motivators: Security and Pay

If the personnel are dissatisfied with the organization, the initial conclusion is that security and pay are poor. Surprisingly, perhaps, this latest *Harvard Busi-*

---

[10] These findings can be found in M. R. Cooper et al., "Changing Employee Values: Deepening Discontent," *Harvard Business Review* (January–February 1979):117–25.
[11] Cooper et al., "Changing Employee Values," 122.

ness Review study found just the opposite. By the mid- to late-1970s employees were reporting that they were basically satisfied with these extrinsic motivators. (Of course, the recession of the early 1980s may have changed these attitudes somewhat.) While there has been a general decline in the satisfaction of the workforce, it cannot be traced solely to insecurity and low pay, the most commonly cited culprits.

Security and pay are adequate . . .

Attitudes Toward Management and Supervision

as is supervision

Also positive are the attitudes of the personnel toward management and supervision. In fact, researchers have found these attitudes improving. Apparently, efforts in recent years to upgrade management and supervision have been successful. On the other hand, these upgrading efforts, often accomplished through human relations training, have not been able to increase job satisfaction among many of the personnel.

Feeling Toward Esteem-Related Factors

But feelings of self-esteem are low

In the domain of esteem-related factors, employees are particularly negative. These factors include opportunity for advancement, willingness of the organization to listen to problems and complaints, the respect with which one is treated, and company response to employee problems and complaints.

> These attitudes suggest that there are strong disincentives to perform well on a job, since some of the major rewards for good performance are missing, and employees perceive that management makes many decisions arbitrarily. It is here, in the area of providing opportunities for individual growth and challenge and of developing ways to recognize and respond equitably to the needs of the workforce, that efforts to change need to be focused. It appears clear that current changes in extrinsic areas such as pay and job security will be less likely to improve job satisfaction.[12]

Management Response

What should management do about these findings? The first thing is not to argue over their validity. There are many reasons to explain the current attitude trend. One is that today's newer workforce has different values from the workforce of a generation ago. A second is that the older segment of the workforce has changed what it believes. A third is that the workforce is just beginning to articulate what it has always valued. Whatever the reason, one thing is clear: the changes that have been reported here are representative of those in industry at large, and any change in them is unlikely in the foreseeable future. The goal of management during the next 10 years must be to become aware of and prepare

---

[12] Cooper et al., "Changing Employee Values," 124.

for employee needs via a pragmatic response. Many of the concepts discussed in Chapter 11 provide viable strategies for dealing with the changing attitudes of the workforce. In particular, the use of survey feedback and the development of two-way communication channels must become a reality in modern organizations.

Two-way communication must be promoted

> Although such findings may seem to paint a bleak picture of the outlook for effective employee relations, this is not necessarily the case. What is undeniably required, however, is that corporations recognize the new realities within which they must function. The crucial issues then become the degree to which management can successfully identify, anticipate, and address these changing values as they surface, or before they surface, in their own organizations. But, make no mistake about it, changing employee values are not myth. They will be the realities that companies must face in the 1980s.[13]

Changing Work Life

Life *at* work is also going to be changing during the next 10 years as the quality of work life movement gains momentum and as modern technology alters the workplace.

Quality of Work Life Movement

The quality of work life (QWL) movement was initially discussed in Chapter 10, where concepts like flexitime were introduced. As seen in Table 20-3, this QWL idea is being used by many different types of firms, and while not all companies have attained positive results, it remains a popular concept.[14]

Flextime and flexiweek are becoming popular

Another work-related idea is that of flexiweek. **Flexiweek** is a working schedule in which employees have alternating four-day and six-day work weeks. As with flextime, the results are mixed: some firms have had very good success with the concept, others have not.

One research study, conducted by David A. Ralston,[15] demonstrated the key factors that are recognized as benefits of flexitime: improved commuting, decreased tardiness, decreased leave time, improved coordination of on- and off-job responsibilities, improved employer-employee relationships, increased job satisfaction, and improved productivity were all demonstrated as benefits from the use of flexitime. Commenting on the future application of flexitime, Ralston notes:

---

[13] Cooper et al., "Changing Employee Values," 125.

[14] Donald J. Petersen, "Flexitime in the United States: The Lessons of Experience," *Personnel* (January–February 1980):21–31. See also Jean B. McGuire and Joseph R. Liro, "Flexible Work Schedules, Work Attitudes, and Perceptions of Productivity," *Public Personnel Management* (Spring 1986):65–73.

[15] David A. Ralston, "The Benefits of Flexitime: Real or Imagined?" *Journal of Organizational Behavior* (October 1989):369–73.

TABLE 20-3   Selected Examples of Flextime in Industry

Banking

State Street Bank of Boston wanted to increase productivity, get better attendance, reduce overtime, and increase employee morale and job satisfaction.

Research design: Longitudinal attitude study, conducted one year after pilot study (1974–75).

Sample: 127 employees (mainly clerical) in corporate accounting, benefits, Bank Americard collection, and trust operations.

Research results:
1. Hard data:
   - Average sick-day leave went down in two departments and up in two.
   - Overtime costs declined from $38,258 to $21,115 over the study period.
   - Turnover dropped in three out of four departments. It also dropped faster than the bank's overall rate.
   - Efficiency dropped in two out of three departments.
2. Soft (attitude) data: Virtually all departments wanted to retain flexitime, but in two departments support for the program dropped slightly during the one-year study period.

Insurance

Metropolitan Life Insurance was aiming for a better coordination of work schedules and a way for employees to avoid rush-hour crowds and traffic.

Research design: A three-month pilot study.

Sample: 400 employees (jobs not specified, but presumed clerical).

Research results:
- Tardiness was eliminated.
- Employee morale improved.
- Need for personal time off declined.
- Employees tended to select the hours corresponding to those times when they were needed the most.

Manufacturing

Control Data Corporation had goals of maximizing employees' choice in establishing work hours, and ensuring that business needs as well as employee needs would be satisfied.

Research design: Pilot study, longitudinal over a three-year period, measuring attitudes. Also, hard data were monitored for such factors as absenteeism and sick leave.

Sample: 100 managers and 286 nonmanagerial personnel from the Aerospace and Microcircuit divisions.

1. Hard data: turnover, productivity, and sick leave showed slightly favorable trends.
2. Nonsupervisory personnel:
   - 85 percent felt morale improved under flexitime.
   - 73 percent felt that the pressure of getting to work on time had decreased.
   - 57 percent felt that driving time had decreased.
   - 66 percent felt that productivity had increased, while 11 percent felt it had decreased.
3. Managers: Felt that flexitime had a positive effect or, at worst, did not have a detrimental effect.

Source: Reprinted from "Flexitime in the United States: The Lessons of Experience," Donald J. Peterson, *Personnel,* January–February 1980, pp. 24–26. © 1980 by American Management Associates, New York. All rights reserved.

A majority of all women are now in the work force, and the number of working mothers is increasing rapidly each year. Likewise, dual career couples are also on the increase. For these rapidly growing segments of the work force, flexitime is a truly viable, and almost necessary approach to work scheduling. For employers, flexitime means they can increase the size and quality of their labor pool by being able to include individuals who might otherwise be forced out of the full-time labor market or who might find it more advantageous to seek employment elsewhere. [16]

Yet there is more to the QWL movement than flextime and flexiweek. Throughout this decade we are going to see an increase in union–management cooperation for the purpose of developing QWL approaches. Work design programs are now out of the theory stage and into the application stage. This is an important development because of the tremendous increases taking place in technology in the workplace.

Modern Technology

Modern technology is going to continue to change life at work. Years ago, when working conditions were less than ideal, employees adjusted to the trials and tribulations of the workplace. Alvin Toffler, internationally known for his analysis of social change, recalled his own early experience in a factory this way:

> I swallowed the dust, the sweat and smoke of the foundry. My ears were split by the hiss of steam, the clank of chains, the roar of pug mills. I felt the heat as the white-hot steel poured. Acetylene sparks left burn marks on my legs. I turned out thousands of pieces a shift on a press, repeating identical movements until my mind and muscles shrieked. I watched the managers who kept the workers in their place, white-shirted men themselves endlessly pursued and harried by higher-ups. I helped lift a sixty-five-year old woman out of the bloody machine that had just torn four fingers off her hand, and I still hear her cries — "Jesus and Mary, I won't be able to work again!" [17]

What the future holds   To a large degree, all of this is changing. The workers of the 1990s will be operating under very different conditions. In particular, we are going to see the use of increased technology, with people learning new skills so that they can use these new developments. On the assembly line there will be more robots employed for welding and for ensuring quality control. In office work, computers will be used to provide and process information. These developments will not come at the expense of worker freedom or autonomy, however. Many of the latest developments in QWL will remain, and we will see even more, for two

[16] Ibid., p. 372.
[17] Alvin Toffler, *The Third Wave* (New York: William Morrow, 1980), 118.

reasons. First, workers will not put up with a "back to the old days" movement because at that time they were mere adjuncts of the machine. Their values are far different from those of their fathers and grandfathers. Second, in order to make technology work, a new approach will be needed. A recent *Fortune* magazine study on life at work puts the idea this way:

> Bosses will have to change the way they handle the workforce. The old "kick ass and take names" school of running a plant isn't effective with today's more educated workforce. Nor is reductionism, or Taylorism, which simplifies and narrows tasks down to the most elementary (and boring) functions. "Western civilization built itself by subdividing science and work, but reductionism has run its streak," says Paul Strassman, a Xerox vice-president for strategic planning. The principles of organizing laid out by Frederick Taylor, a turn-of-the-century mechanical engineer, become less applicable as technology evolves. Workers in the office and factory . . . need more knowledge and autonomy.[18]

As organizations begin to adapt to the needs of the employees, we will see dramatic changes in the way work is done. AT&T is an excellent example. When it was faced with becoming a competitor in a deregulated communications business, the firm changed the way some of its workers carried out their tasks. Today many telephone installers and repairmen (now known as systems technicians) no longer go to work in jeans carrying a sagging belt of loaded tools around their waist. They dress in slacks, shirt, and tie and have their tools stowed in a brief case. Instead of driving around in a van, they have a company sedan. The new appearance symbolizes a change in the status of these blue-collar technicians. The changes have been accompanied by increased training so that these people now cannot only solder a wire or bring a line into a building but, in many cases, can also reprogram a computer-controlled office switchboard. In this regard training is becoming a high-priority item for management.

Over the past couple of decades, major attention has been focused on training young and disadvantaged workers. "Now," notes Pat Choate, senior policy analyst for TRW, Inc. and a nationally known economist, "it is absolutely necessary to focus our attention on the whole workforce."[19] (Also see "Management in Practice: Kodak's Investment in the Future.")

Training will become important

The overall effect of such training on American output will be positive. At Westinghouse Electric, for example, both secretaries and their bosses have been trained to use computer terminals on which they can write and send memos, edit letters, store and recall information, design charts, and perform various other communication functions. In short, technology is beginning to accommodate the desire of employees for meaningful jobs while simulta-

[18] Jeremy Main, "Work Won't Be the Same Again," *Fortune* (June 28, 1982):59.
[19] Main, "Work Won't Be the Same," 60.

Kodak's Investment in the Future

George Eastman, the founder of Kodak, had always been a strong supporter of education. At the turn of the century, he emphasized that education was an investment as opposed to an expense. Throughout the years Kodak followed through on Eastman's approach and spent resources on college and graduate education for its work force. However, a new development by Kodak changes the traditional view of investing in education.

The current president of Kodak, Kay Whitmore, found a report by the National Alliance of Business most disturbing. The report stated that the number of available jobs will increase by 15.6 million from 1985 to 1995, yet the number of people in the labor force will increase by only 13.7 million. This indicated to Whitmore that the labor gap would have to be filled through increasing the number of employable high school graduates; a tough challenge considering the problems in public school systems indicated by the lack of basic skills among high school graduates.

In 1985 a task force of executives from Kodak, Xerox, Bausch & Lomb, and Wegman's, along with educators from the University of Rochester, studied the Rochester, New York, school system. Their recommendations included the following: better job placement for students; increased opportunities for partnerships between businesses and the schools; increased awareness of education as a key to the community's future; better access to better resources for school districts; and development of managerial skills of school administrators.

Since Kodak employs nearly 50,000 people in the Rochester area, Whitmore realized the importance of responding to these recommendations. The future of Kodak's workforce was tied directly to the future of Rochester, and the core of this response was education. Thus, the birth of "Rochester Brainpower."

The project is a cooperative effort of Kodak, the chamber of commerce, social service agencies, and the city schools. The goal is to improve the quality of education in the public schools in order to provide Rochester with a stronger workforce for the 1990s and beyond. The results are impressive already—over 1,700 students placed in jobs and over 77 school/business partnerships formed. In one case, Kodak's Corporate Information System Division sponsored a Computer Science Club at one of the high schools. Within 14 months, 60 students joined to have the opportunity to work with Kodak employees. The club has generated projects on robotics, artificial intelligence, programming, and electronic messaging.

In May 1989 the program's early successes were recognized by President Bush, who presented it The Presidents' Award for Private Sector Initiatives. When doing so, the president noted, "Like a wise man planting a tree for a future generation, Kodak is planting its own seeds."

Source: Ronald Tanner, "Kodak Brainpower," *Intrepreneur* (September–October 1989):25–27.

neously meeting the desire of organizations for increased productivity. The result will mean a better work life for employees at all levels of the hierarchy.[20]

SOCIAL VALUES IN THE WORKPLACE

In addition to changing management and worker values and attitudes, social values will help shape the world of management during the upcoming decade. These values are a result of changes in both the external and internal environment. One change is the attention given to employees with personal problems such as alcoholism or drug addiction. At the present time employee assistance programs are beginning to spring up in larger organizations to deal with these problems. Before the decade is over this development will probably spread to medium-sized and smaller enterprises as well. Other major socially oriented developments will include the continued emphasis on hiring the handicapped and on developing policies and programs for eliminating sexual harassment in the workplace.

Employee Assistance Programs

In the past, employees who had alcoholism or drug addiction problems could expect to be fired by their employer. Individuals who suffered excessive degrees of stress found they either had to cope with the situation or get out. Today, in many firms, this is no longer true. Thanks to the rise of **employee assistance programs (EAPs),** many companies are helping their people cope with a multitude of personal problems.[21] One of the major reasons why firms are developing such plans is economic. The cost of personal problems, in terms of absenteeism, poor workmanship, lost productivity, and related factors, is now running over $10 billion annually. Something has to be done.

An EAP is designed to help employees deal with many of the problems common to modern society: alcoholism, drug abuse, stress, mental exhaustion. At the present time there are approximately 2,000 EAPs nationwide. The pattern used in setting up these plans is typically the following:

Pattern for setting up an EAP

1. A policy statement is issued indicating that management is supportive of the program. The statement also points out that employees may sometimes need this type of personal assistance because of factors beyond their control, and the assistance will be available to them.

---

[20] For more on this see Naisbitt and Aburdene, op. cit., pp. 298–99.
[21] See Keith McClellan, "The Changing Nature of EAP Practice: EAPs Have a Bright Future," *Personnel Administrator* (August 1985):29(6), and Richard T. Hellan, "An EAP Update: A Perspective for the 80s," *Personnel Journal* (June 1986):51–53.

2. If there is a union in the organization, representation and support of the program are secured from this group.
3. Qualified counselors and other skilled personnel are retained and are used to help in diagnosis and referral to appropriate agencies where the individual can receive professional assistance.
4. A comprehensive insurance benefit package covering this assistance is provided to all employees.
5. A comprehensive approach for evaluating the effectiveness and impact of the EAP is developed.[22]

When does someone need the types of services provided by an EAP? This is not easy to say. Usually there are visible signs that something is wrong. For example, in the case of an alcoholic employee, attendance, general behavior, and job performance begin to decline, as illustrated in Figure 20-5. At this point the boss usually calls in the subordinate to discuss some of the job-related symptoms: poor work, exhausted appearance, and absenteeism. If the employee realizes that these symptoms are a result of alcohol, drugs, exhaustion, or some other personal problem and decides to straighten out immediately, the problem is on its way to being resolved. If things continue to deteriorate, however, the superior discusses the situation again, this time in the presence of a counselor. The superior then leaves the subordinate with the counselor so that they can discuss the situation privately. Quite often the subordinate admits to the counselor that there is a problem and agrees to join an employee assistance program. In other cases management has found that employees simply come in and ask for assistance without any prodding at all. Commenting on the way two of the most common problems, alcohol and drugs, are dealt with, Keith Davis, the noted human relationist, has written:

Procedure for handling problems

> Successful employer programs treat alcoholism as an illness, focus on the job behavior caused by alcoholism, and provide both medical help and psychological support for alcoholics. . . . The company demonstrates to alcoholics that it wants to help them and is willing to work with them over an extended period of time. A nonthreatening, no-job-loss atmosphere is provided: however, there is always the implied threat that alcohol-induced behavior cannot be treated indefinitely. For example, if an employee refuses treatment and incompetent behavior continues, the employer has little choice other than dismissal. . . .
>
> Company programs for treatment of drug abuse other than alcohol usually follow the same patterns as programs on alcoholism except that hard-drug treatment may be controlled more strictly because of the hard-drug user's greater probability of criminal behavior on the job. Most firms combine

---

[22] Thomas N. McGaffey, "New Horizons in Organizational Stress Prevention Approaches," *Personnel Administrator* (November 1978):26–32.

FIGURE 20-5   How an Alcoholic Employee Behaves

How an Alcoholic Employee Behaves

BEHAVIOR	EFFICIENCY	CRISIS POINTS DURING DETERIORATION	VISIBLE SIGNS
EARLY PHASE Drinks to relieve tension. Alcohol tolerance increases. Blackouts (memory blanks). Lies about drinking habits.	90% 75%	SUPERVISOR'S EVALUATION CRITICISM FROM BOSS	**ATTENDANCE** Late (after lunch). Leaves job early. Absent from office. **GENERAL BEHAVIOR** Fellow workers complain. Overreacts to real or imagined criticism. Complains of not feeling well. Lies. **JOB PERFORMANCE** Misses deadlines. Mistakes through inattention or poor judgment. Decreased efficiency.
MIDDLE PHASE Surreptitious drinks. Guilt about drinking. Tremors during hangovers. Loss of interest.	50%	FAMILY PROBLEMS LOSS OF JOB ADVANCEMENT FINANCIAL PROBLEMS, e.g. WAGE GARNISHMENT WARNING FROM BOSS	**ATTENDANCE** Frequent days off for vague ailments or implausible reasons. **GENERAL BEHAVIOR** Statements become undependable. Begins to avoid associates. Borrows money from co-workers. Exaggerates work accomplishments. Hospitalized more than average. Repeated minor injuries on and off job. Unreasonable resentment. **JOB PERFORMANCE** General deterioration. Spasmodic work pace. Attention wanders, lack of concentration.
LATE MIDDLE PHASE Avoids discussion of problem. Fails in efforts at control. Neglects food. Prefers to drink alone.	25%	IN TROUBLE WITH LAW TYPICAL CRISIS PUNITIVE DISCIPLINARY ACTION SERIOUS FAMILY PROBLEMS–SEPARATION	**ATTENDANCE** Frequent time off, sometimes for several days. Fails to return from lunch. **GENERAL BEHAVIOR** Grandiose, aggressive or belligerent. Domestic problems interfere with work. Apparent loss of ethical values. Money problems, garnishment of salary. Hospitalization increases. Refuses to discuss problems. Trouble with the law. **JOB PERFORMANCE** Far below expected level.
LATE PHASE Believes that other activities interfere with his drinking.		SERIOUS FINANCIAL PROBLEMS FINAL WARNING FROM BOSS AREA OF GREATEST COVERUP TERMINATION HOSPITALIZATION	**ATTENDANCE** Prolonged unpredictable absences. **GENERAL BEHAVIOR** Drinking on job. Totally undependable. Repeated hospitalization. Visible physical deterioration. Money problems worse. Serious family problems and/or divorce. **JOB PERFORMANCE** Uneven and generally incompetent.

INCREASING DEPENDENCY OVER TIME

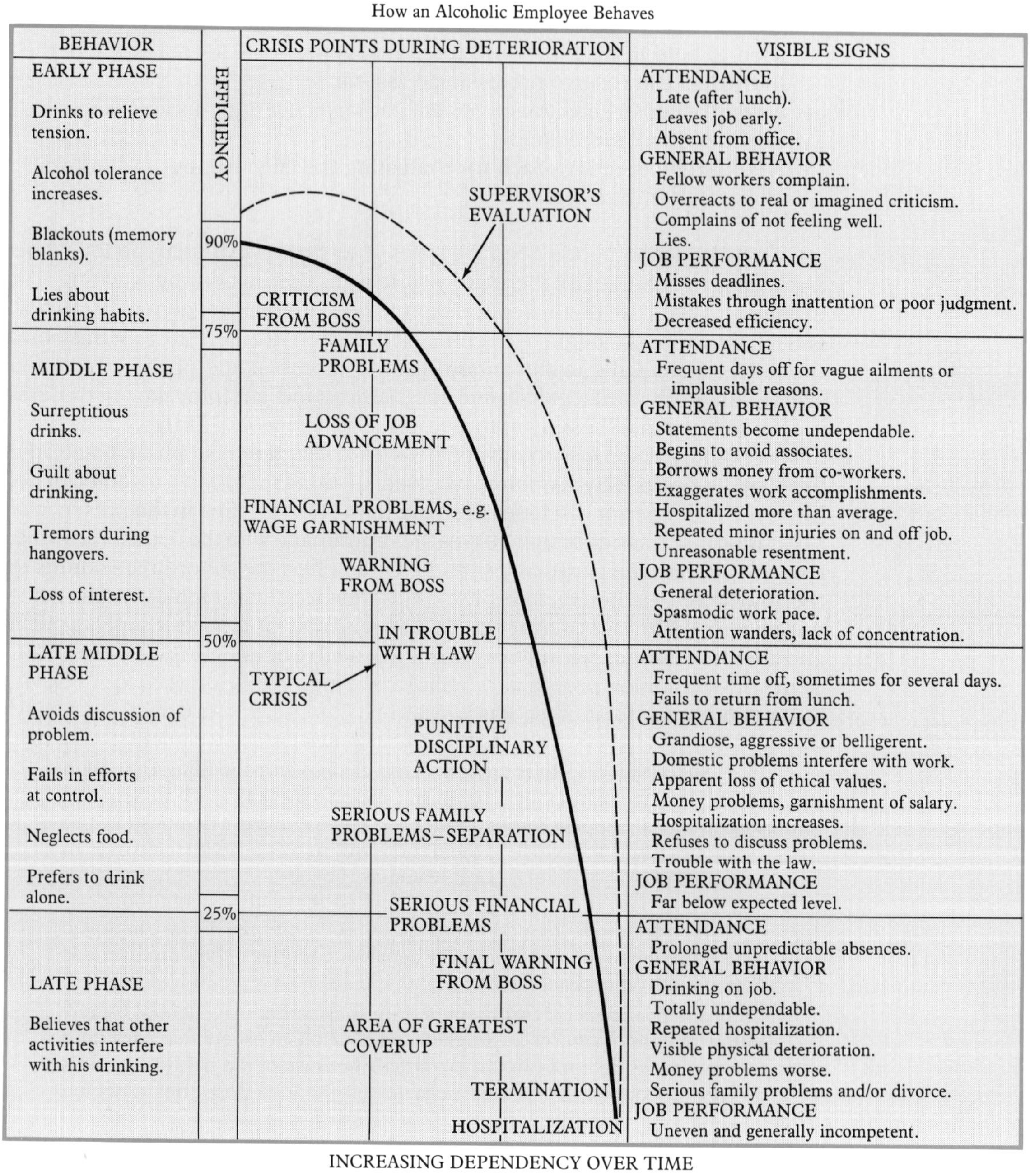

Source: *The Miami Herald* (May 31, 1981):1F. Reprinted with permission of the Miami Herald.

treatment of alcoholism, drug abuse, and related difficulties into one program for the treatment of people with behavioral-medical problems. Normally the program focuses on both prevention and treatment.[23]

How well have EAPs been working out? Psychologist Andrew DuBrin reports:

> EAP has proved to be both humanitarian and cost effective. . . . One successful application . . . is the Kennecott Copper Company facility in Ogden, Utah. Data are available for 150 male employees who averaged 12.7 months in treatment for conditions such as alcoholism. . . . A comparison of before and after treatment showed a 52 percent decrease in absenteeism, a 74.6 percent decrease in worker compensation payments, and a 55.3 percent decrease in direct medical costs after treatment in the program.
>
> More comprehensive research evidence is provided by a study of 11 major EAP programs conducted by the Human Ecology Institute. The general finding was that 57 percent of the cases referred for alcoholism were recovered or noticeably improved after treatment. Supervisory ratings and other means of performance assessment revealed that there was an associated positive change in work performance.[24]

Employee assistance programs help illustrate the impact of social values on the world of management. Twenty years ago these programs would have been viewed by management as unjustified costs, and employees suffering these types of problems simply would have been fired. Employees, for their part, would have viewed suggestions by management that counseling and other assistance were needed as an invasion of privacy or a meddling in private matters. Today, these social problems are out of the closet and both sides appear willing to deal with them. Over the next decade we should see the continued growth of EAPs. In particular, organizations can profit from their use in helping personnel at all levels, including the top, deal with personal problems that affect work performance.

Hiring the Handicapped

Another major social development will be an increased emphasis on hiring the handicapped. Efforts to encourage this trend have already been promoted through legislation such as the Rehabilitation Act of 1973 and the Vietnam era Veterans' Readjustment Assistance Act of 1974. The Rehabilitation Act has been

---

[23] Keith Davis and John W. Newstrom, *Human Behavior at Work: Organizational Behavior,* 7th ed. (New York: McGraw-Hill, 1985), 361, 363.

[24] Andrew J. DuBrin, *Contemporary Applied Management* (Plano, TX: Business Publications, Inc., 1982), 218. See also Susan Hurley, "Measuring the Value of Employee Assistance Programs," *Risk Management* (June 1986):56(2).

Definition of
handicapped

particularly important because of its definition of a handicapped individual as anyone who (1) has a physical or mental impairment that substantially limits one or more major life activities, (2) has a record of such impairment, or (3) is regarded as having such an impairment. More specifically, the term **handicapped** has been used in referring to individuals who are visually or hearing impaired, partially paralyzed, missing a limb, or mentally retarded.

Research Findings

In the past, a number of employer beliefs have served to limit the chances of equal opportunities for the handicapped. Some of the most common of these beliefs are that (1) insurance and workers' compensation costs will rise because the handicapped will have a higher accident rate than the workforce in general; (2) these workers will have high absenteeism and tardiness; (3) the quality and quantity of their work output will be lower than that of the average worker; (4) the physical layout of the workplace will have to be modified at great expense to accommodate these workers; (5) coworkers will not accept them on an equal basis; and (6) the handicapped have to be treated differently from other workers. Research reveals that these beliefs are incorrect. For example, after conducting a systematic analysis of the literature on this subject, Sara Freedman and Robert Keller report:

Research findings
regarding the
handicapped

> Research on efforts to hire the handicapped has indicated positive consequences for both the individual and the company. DuPont . . . has released a study of 1,452 employees with a variety of disabilities that included orthopedic difficulties, blindness, visual impairment, heart disease, amputation, paralysis, epilepsy, hearing impairment and total deafness. The types of positions held included machine operators, craftsmen, professionals, and managers, to name just a few. A job performance survey rated 91 percent of the disabled employees as average or better than average to the regular workforce.[25]

The DuPont study also found that employee morale did not suffer. There was no significant morale differences between the handicapped workers and the rest of the workforce. Additionally, 96 percent of the handicapped had average or better than average safety records, and 79 percent were rated average or above on dependability.[26]

Findings at other firms support this general pattern. For example, Gopal Pati, a frequent contributor to the literature, conducted a study of 16 corpora-

[25] Sara M. Freedman and Robert T. Keller, "The Handicapped In the Workforce," *Academy of Management Review* (July 1981):452–53.

[26] Robert B. Nathanson, "The Disabled Employee: Separating Myth from Fact," *Harvard Business Review* (May–June 1977):6–8. See also William G. Johnson and James Lambrinos, "Wage Discrimination Against Handicapped Men and Women," *Journal of Human Resources* (Spring 1985):264–77.

tions employing approximately 800 handicapped workers. He found lower turnover and absenteeism and average or above-average performance among the handicapped. He also reported that insurance costs were not affected and that expenditures for accommodations were minor or nonexistent.[27] The California Governor's Committee also found support for hiring the handicapped.[28] Preliminary findings of a pilot study conducted at the Lockheed Missile and Space Company examined three cost indices: (1) days of sick leave, (2) dollar costs of claims under one insurance plan, and (3) number of medical care opportunities kept under a second insurance plan. The results indicated that handicapped persons had lower costs than the average employee. Numerous other studies also support the value of hiring the handicapped.[29]

Why have the handicapped performed so well? There are two basic reasons. First, as found by a number of research studies, many handicapped workers are more intelligent, more motivated, better qualified, and have higher educational levels than their nonhandicapped counterparts. Second, these results may also be a reflection of the fact that handicapped people have to be overqualified in order to get and hold a job. To the extent that the latter is true, handicapped people may well be kept in lower-level jobs long after similarly qualified, nonhandicapped personnel have been promoted.[30]

The Future of the Handicapped

During the next decade, we will see an increase in the employment opportunities provided for the handicapped. One reason is that, to a large degree, these individuals are an untapped source of personnel manpower for modern organizations. Second, we are likely to see more of them rise into the ranks of management as enterprises begin to realize that they have been approaching the hiring of the handicapped from the wrong point of view.[31] As Robert B. Nathanson and Jeffrey Lambert, compliance planning specialists, have noted:

> No matter how well-trained, sensitive, well-meaning, or objective they may be, supervisory and managerial personnel, line workers, and other professional and nonprofessional staff are not immune to holding biases, beliefs or prejudices about persons who are disabled. These feelings and thoughts, deeply and often subconsciously rooted, are carried into daily interaction with disabled employees and can have a profound effect on their social and vocational integration into the business community.[32]

[27] Gopal C. Pati, "Countdown on Hiring the Handicapped," *Personnel Journal* (March 1978):144–53.

[28] Freedman and Keller, "Handicapped In the Workforce," 453.

[29] Ibid., 453–54.

[30] Ibid., 453.

[31] Frank Bowe, "Intercompany Action to Adapt Jobs for the Handicapped," *Harvard Business Review* (January–February 1985):166.

[32] Robert B. Nathanson and Jeffrey Lambert, "Integrating Disabled Employees into the Workplace," *Personnel Journal* (February 1981):110.

These attitudes take many different forms. Some of the most common include the following:

Typical attitudes
toward the
handicapped

1. Feeling sorry for the individual because he or she is disabled.
2. Classifying all handicapped people on the basis of their deficiency, for example, thinking that all blind people have the same interests, abilities, and needs.
3. Adopting an attitude of "Don't worry about anything; I'll protect you."
4. Feeling that handicapped people should not be hired because they will present too many problems for the organization to handle.
5. Realizing that the individual has the capacity to do the job but hoping not to have to come into personal contact with the individual because of feelings such as "He gives me the creeps" or "Why does she have to be assigned to my area?"
6. Expressing amazement at the individual's ambition and referring to the person as courageous, remarkable, or brave.
7. Encountering a feeling of anxiousness or tension in having to face those with physical disabilities.[33]

As organizations begin to gain experience regarding the values and attitudes of handicapped people and come to understand them better, attitudes like these will diminish. At the same time, management will begin to understand more clearly how to tap this labor source effectively. Attention will be focused on the individual characteristics of the handicapped and the best ways to train, place, and employ these people. In the process, both sides will find themselves making adjustments. For the present, management will find this area to be both a challenge and a problem requiring its time and resources; but the payoffs will prove worthwhile for both sides.[34]

Dealing with Sexual Harassment

During the last decade, the issue of **sexual harassment** has become an important employer consideration. Particularly because of the legal obligations created under Title VII of the Civil Rights Act, management is finding itself having to pay closer attention to this type of behavior. While there is no uniform definition of the term sexual harassment, the following definitions are three attempts by official organizations to explain what it means.

What constitutes
sexual harassment?

[Sexual harassment includes a]ny repeated or unwarranted verbal or physical sexual advances (or) sexually explicit discriminatory remarks made by someone in the workplace which are offensive or objectionable to the recip-

---

[33] Nathanson and Lambert, "Integrating Disabled Employees," 110–13.
[34] Susan F. Jarvis, "For Employers of Handicapped Workers: Obligations and Ideas," *Personnel* (July 1985):42–44.

ient or which cause the recipient discomfort or humiliation or which interfere with the recipient's job performance. (*Continental Can Co. v. Minnesota,* 22 FEP cases 1808 [Minnesota, 1980])

Sexual harassment is any unwanted physical or emotional contact between workers or supervisors and workers which makes one uncomfortable and/or interferes with the recipient's job performance or carries with it either an implicit or explicit threat of adverse employment consequences. (Hearings before the House Committee on Post Office and Civil Services, 96th Congress, 1st Session [1979])

Sexual harassment includes . . . continual or repeated verbal abuse of a sexual nature including, but not limited to, graphic commentaries on the victim's body, sexually suggestive objectives or pictures in the workplace, sexually degrading words used to describe the victim, or propositions of a sexual nature. Sexual harassment also includes the threat of insinuation that lack of sexual submission will adversely affect the victim's employment, wages, advancement, assigned duties or shifts, academic standing, or other conditions that affect the victim's "livelihood." (Michigan Task Force on Sexual Harassment in the Workplace).[35]

When is management liable for sexual harassment in the workplace? Recent guidelines echo the sentiments of court decisions that hold that the employer has an affirmative duty to maintain a workplace that is free of sexual harassment and intimidation. More specifically, these guidelines hold that the organization is guilty if it knew or should have known of the harassment, or knowingly or constructively allowed the harassment to occur. On the other hand, if the enterprise moves to take immediate and corrective action to end the harassment, liability can be avoided.

Harassment and the Courts

When is the employer responsible?

A number of important questions about harassment and employer responsibility have been addressed in court decisions. Two of the most important of these are: Under what circumstances is the employer responsible for employee actions? Does the person filing the harassment charge have to demonstrate that the organization has a policy or practice of such harassment?

In reference to the first question, there is no uniformity of decision. Some court cases have held that an employer is not liable for acts unrelated to the performance of the supervisors' jobs, while others have held the employer strictly liable for supervisors' actions. After a thorough review of harassment cases, Patricia Linenberger and Timothy Keaveny report that the trend appears to be that an employer is indeed responsible for discriminatory practices by supervisory personnel. The reasoning is that if the organization wants to

---

[35] Patricia Linenberger and Timothy J. Keaveny, "Sexual Harassment: The Employer's Legal Obligations," *Personnel* (November–December 1981):61–62.

delegate its duties, it must remain responsible for the way in which these duties are carried out.[36]

In reference to the second question, again there have been mixed decisions by the courts. One of the most recent, by the Ninth Circuit Court of Appeals, held that an employer was liable under Title VII when the action complained of was committed by a superior, even though the superior's behavior was in clear violation of company policy. This court ruling represents the broadest interpretation of employer liability. It is unlikely that in the future the courts will hold employers to such broad liability. The ruling does show, however, how great the employer's responsibility can be. How can organizations work to protect themselves against such action? A number of important steps should be carried out.

Taking Proper Action

Steps an employer should take to control sexual harassment

Most experts believe that the first step in controlling sexual harassment is a strong policy statement from top management condemning such behavior. This policy should contain a workable definition of the term sexual harassment. In particular, the definition should be as objective as possible. The policy statement should spell out possible sanctions against those who are guilty of such harassment and offer protection for those who make such charges. It should make it clear that retaliatory action against an employee who makes charges will not be tolerated. The employer also should establish an effective grievance procedure.

> The complement to a strong sexual harassment policy statement is an effective grievance procedure. The court cases highlight the need for such a mechanism by stating that employers *are* liable for the sexual harassment of employees or supervisors if management become aware of the problem and does nothing, or if management should have been aware of the harassment. Thus, it is clear that a procedure that provides the means by which employees can bring such complaints out into the open is necessary.[37]

The employer should also conduct a prompt and thorough investigation when made aware of a complaint. Finally, if someone is found guilty, disciplinary action must be taken.

Sexual harassment is not a new issue. As many organizations are learning, however, its consequences are. As a result, during the upcoming decade more

---

[36] Linenberger and Keaveny, "Sexual Harrassment," 64–65. For further ideas see David E. Terpstra and Douglas D. Baker, "Relationship of Nature of Sexual Harassment, Evidence, and Pre-Filing Actions to Sexual Harassment Charge Outcomes," *Academy of Management Proceedings* (50th Anniversary Meeting: Chicago, IL 1986), 342–46.

[37] Linenberger and Keaveny, "Sexual Harrassment," 67.

of them will be thinking through the steps that must be taken to protect their employees from harassment and themselves from legal action.[38]

Work Ethic

The **work ethic** consists of the beliefs people have about their jobs and about carrying them out. This ethic may have religious overtones, as in the case of the individual who believes a life of hard work will be rewarded in the hereafter. Or it may simply be reflected in the belief that work is desirable because it helps society. Both of these philosophies, as seen in Figure 20-6, are forms of the work ethic.

Figure 20-6 also identifies some other common attitudes toward work. Some people work long hours, bring tasks home with them, and never seem able to slow up. These people are **workaholics** who represent an extreme form of the work ethic. Other people believe in the **worth ethic** either because work provides them satisfying feelings of competence, job mastery, or self-esteem or because it offers personal rewards such as money and a feeling of accomplishment. One final attitude toward work can be defined as the **leisure ethic.** People who subscribe to this ethic fall into two groups. For the first, work is an unfortunate obligation, although people in this group manage to find satisfaction in the money they earn. For the second, work is regarded as totally undesirable. People in this group work only to survive.

Work Values

Research shows that the work ethic in some degree is still accepted by most workers. There are differences, however, between the age groups. Some of these are shown in the following table.[39]

More Important to Younger Workers	More Important to Older Workers
Money and fringe benefits	Pride in craftsmanship
Quick promotions	Hard work
Enriching jobs	Commitment to the organization
Friendship of coworkers	Service to others
Leisure and free time	Organization's role in the community

[38] Jeanne Bosson Driscoll, "Sexual Attraction and Harassment: Management's New Problems," *Personnel Journal* (January 1981):33–36, 56; Oliver L. Niehouse and Joanne Ross Doades, "Sexual Harassment: An Old Issue—A New Problem," *Supervisory Management* (April 1980):10–14; Patricia Linenberger and Timothy J. Keaveny, "Sexual Harassment in Employment," *Human Resource Management* (Spring 1981):11–17.
[39] David J. Cherrington, *The Work Ethic* (New York: AMACOM, 1980), 65–71.

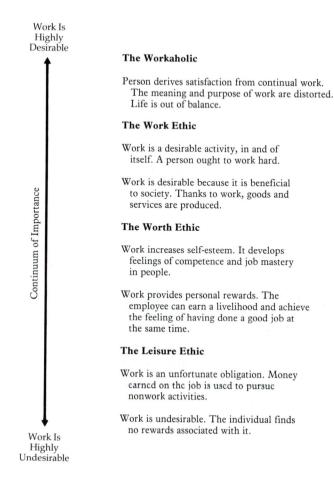

FIGURE 20-6
The Meanings of Work

Work Is Highly Desirable

Continuum of Importance

The Workaholic

Person derives satisfaction from continual work. The meaning and purpose of work are distorted. Life is out of balance.

The Work Ethic

Work is a desirable activity, in and of itself. A person ought to work hard.

Work is desirable because it is beneficial to society. Thanks to work, goods and services are produced.

The Worth Ethic

Work increases self-esteem. It develops feelings of competence and job mastery in people.

Work provides personal rewards. The employee can earn a livelihood and achieve the feeling of having done a good job at the same time.

The Leisure Ethic

Work is an unfortunate obligation. Money earned on the job is used to pursue nonwork activities.

Work is undesirable. The individual finds no rewards associated with it.

Work Is Highly Undesirable

Younger workers are more interested in money, fringe benefits, and rewards. Older employees are more concerned with work pride, service, and commitment to the organization. These attitudes represent internal environmental forces that managers must confront. How can a modern organization develop desirable work values among its people? Researchers have suggested that managers should:

Principles for developing desirable work values

1. Establish an organizational climate that fosters positive work values and a commitment to excellence.
2. Communicate clear expectations about productivity and high-quality craftsmanship.
3. Teach and explain the value of work, the dignity of labor, and the joy of service.
4. Establish individual accountability through effective delegation.

5. Develop personal commitment and involvement through individual choice and participation.
6. Provide feedback on performance through effective performance appraisals.
7. Reward effective performance with pay and other social reinforcements.
8. Continually encourage employees in their personal growth and skill development.[40]

AIDS IN THE WORKPLACE

During the last few years, **AIDS** — Acquired Immune Deficiency Syndrome — has become one of the most troublesome and misunderstood problems of the 1980s. The number of diagnosed cases has doubled every year since 1981, when the disease was first discovered.

Congress has spent hundreds of millions of dollars for research into the causes and cures for AIDS. Despite this medical research, a vaccine to control or cure the virus is yet to be found. Thus, an emotional fear has developed concerning a disease that many believe is out of control. This fear is derived from many causes, including the fact that the disease has been universally fatal, it is associated with sex and drug use, and very little is understood about the virus itself.

From a managerial perspective, the disease presents a formidable challenge to decision makers in organizations. There are specific questions that now face managers, such as:

1. What are the legal issues regarding AIDS at work?
2. Should we enact policies concerning applicants or employees who have AIDS?
3. Should we educate workers about AIDS? If so, how?
4. Should employers test applicants for AIDS?[41]

The managerial dilemma was perhaps best summarized by Mary Rowe and Michael Baker in the following:

> While the latest epidemiological facts may help managers dispel some of their own fears, most managers will never before have confronted an epidemic that upsets themselves and others so much. As a result, managers

---

[40] Cherrington, *Work Ethic,* 181–82.
[41] Frank E. Kuzmits and Lyle Sussman, "Twenty Questions About AIDS in the Workplace," *Business Horizons* (July–August 1986):36.

dealing with AIDS may doubt their own capacity to make rational, responsible decisions. In light of this fear, managers must stay well informed and must talk with colleagues about what they can do to cope with their own fears of AIDS; about the legal climate, to avoid discrimination claims and liability; and about helping their companies plan for managing fearful employees.[42]

SUMMARY

1. Over the last decade the number of women in top management has increased. At present, 39.3 percent of all working women hold managerial positions. Some of the reasons holding back their progress include the failure of women to choose business careers, and cultural factors discouraging women from being competitive. Today this is beginning to change, and the future for women in the executive suite looks brighter than ever before.

2. During the next 10 years there will be a major change in the way management plans for the future. A true administrative science approach is emerging thanks to progress by organizations like the Strategic Planning Institute. Through the analysis of business-related data, it is becoming possible to draw conclusions regarding how to formulate strategy and how to make strategic changes in the business plan when things go awry.

3. Management's world also will change as a result of employee attitudes, values, and work life. Today employees are not satisfied with their companies or their jobs. This dissatisfaction is not tied to security, pay, and supervision but to esteem-related factors such as the way employees are treated, their opportunity for advancement, the willingness of the organization to listen to their problems and complaints, and the respect with which they are treated.

4. Life at work is also changing. This is happening for two major reasons. The first is the quality of work life (QWL) movement. QWL concepts such as flextime and flexiweek are becoming more popular. At the same time organizations are finding that they have to adjust to modern technology by changing the way workers do their jobs. During the next 10 years we will see a change in management's philosophy of handling the workforce as well as an increased emphasis on training and retraining workers to ensure a harmonious blending of the workforce and modern technology.

---

[42] Mary P. Rowe, Malcolm Russell-Einhorn, and Michael A. Baker, "The Fear of AIDS," *Harvard Business Review* (July–August 1986):28.

5. As a result of society's changing values, many employers now offer Employee Assistance Programs, which treat drug- and alcohol-dependent employees. Additional changes include the number of handicapped workers hired, as well as their assessed performance on the job; an awareness of sexual harassment in the workplace and the need to quickly address and resolve this problem should it occur; and the problem of AIDS in the workplace – the newest and potentially most devastating problem of the 90s. During the next 10 years we will see increased attention focused on these and other issues.

KEY TERMS

AIDS   A disease known as Acquired Immune Deficiency Syndrome.

Code of conduct   A statement of ethical practices or guidelines to which an enterprise adheres.

Employee assistance programs   Programs designed to help employees deal with social problems such as alcoholism, drug addiction, and excessive stress.

Flexiweek   A working schedule in which employees have alternating four-day and six-day work weeks.

Handicapped employees   Individuals who are visually or hearing impaired, partially paralyzed, missing a limb, or mentally retarded.

Hierarchy gap   The difference in perceived satisfaction between employees at the upper levels of the organization and those at the other levels.

Leisure ethic   To regard work as totally undesirable and work only to survive.

Sexual harassment   Any unwanted physical or emotional contact between workers or between supervisors and workers which makes one uncomfortable or interferes with the recipient's job performance.

Workaholic   One who works long hours and never seems to slow down; thus, they represent an extreme form of the work ethic.

Work ethic   The beliefs that people have about their jobs and about carrying them out.

QUESTIONS FOR ANALYSIS AND DISCUSSION

1. Why are there not more women in top management positions? What does women's future in the executive suite look like? Defend your answer.
2. Why is management becoming more interested in strategic planning? What new developments have occurred that are encouraging greater attention in this area? Explain.

3. How do workers feel about their company? Their job? Their pay? Supervision? Esteem-related factors? Discuss each separately and then draw overall conclusions about the values of modern workers.

4. In what way can we expect the quality of work life movement to affect the way work is done during the 1990s? Will technology also play a role? Explain.

5. What is an employee assistance program? How does it work? Do you think we will see more of them during the next decade? Why or why not?

6. What have researchers learned about the abilities and performance of handicapped workers? In light of your answer, how likely is it that more attention will be devoted to hiring the handicapped? Support your answer with as many facts as you can muster.

7. What is meant by the term sexual harassment? Put the definition in your own words.

8. Is management liable for sexual harassment in the workplace? If management has an expressed policy forbidding such harassment, does this policy reduce or eliminate its liability for such actions?

9. How can management ensure that it is taking proper action to prevent or discourage sexual harassment? Be complete in your answer.

10. What is meant by the work ethic? Explain the differences between a workaholic and the leisure ethic.

11. Explain some of the differences in work values based upon age groups.

12. What is AIDS and why has it become such an emotional issue? Include the challenges that managers must now confront.

CASE

The AIDS Dilemma

George Harris is the senior manager of a large production division at Intertech Corporation. He has just finished a conference with Bill, who is one of the top foremen in the division. Bill has told George that he needs a hospital leave starting immediately. At the hospital, Bill will be undergoing tests for an "unknown disease," but there is a possibility it may be AIDS.

After Bill leaves the office, George feels ill at the thought of AIDS spreading throughout his factory division. In a motion of disgust, George carefully covers Bill's coffee cup with a napkin and drops it in the garbage. Then, he begins to wonder what if Bill really does have AIDS.

Later that day George is in the company cafeteria and is confronted by one of the longtime employees of the division. The worker is angered and scared about the rumors being spread throughout the division concerning Bill having AIDS. George attempts to explain that nothing has been diagnosed for sure yet;

however, the employee interrupts and tells George that workers are threatening absenteeism, boycott, or even resignation, unless "something" is done to protect everyone.

Walking back to his office, George is met by his secretary who explains that near-hysterical workers and family members of the workers are flooding the office with questions and demanding answers. George sits back in his chair and ponders this unbelievable situation. The company has no policy that governs this new disease. George realizes he knows very little about it himself, and never before have the employees reacted like this.

1. What do you think George Harris should do? Why?
2. What lessons can be learned from this situation? Be specific.
3. What exactly is AIDS and why would it spread such fear throughout the production division at Intertech?

YOU BE THE CONSULTANT

Carl's Dilemma

Carl Bettenhouse is the CEO of a major consumer goods firm headquartered in New York City. Quite a bit of Carl's time is spent outside the office. Not all of his work is business, however. Because of the position he occupies, Carl is also very active in community activities. He serves on a number of boards of charitable organizations, is active in the theater league, and is currently involved in efforts to raise money for the restoration of historical buildings in the Washington, D.C., area.

Despite his involvement in nonbusiness activities, Carl makes it a point to know what is going on around the company. Every Monday morning two aides bring him up to date on everything that has happened during the week. He is given sales figures, cost data, and profit results. This information is useful in making organizational decisions; it also helps Carl answer questions asked by people he meets in social settings. Typical examples include: What business are you in? What products or services do you provide? Do you think your stock is a good investment? Carl likes questions like these because they give him a chance to break the ice and talk about a subject he knows quite well.

The other day, however, Carl found himself in a quandary. He was at a charity dinner designed to raise funds for an orphanage. Carl was enjoying himself, mixing with the guests, and discussing a variety of topics. In the process he happened upon a news reporter who was covering the dinner. The two began to talk and Carl learned that the reporter seldom covered such events. Usually she was assigned to business and industry stories. When she learned that Carl was a CEO her face lit up. For the next half hour the two talked about Carl's company. The news reporter was quite knowledgeable regarding business activity and some of the latest developments in Carl's industry. As the two talked, the topic eventually turned to social values and the way modern organizations are meeting their social obligations. Carl was well informed on what his company was doing in many different areas, including hiring the handicapped and setting up employee assistance programs. He expressed pride in the fact that his firm was the first one in its industry to have an EAP in place.

As the two continued talking about other things his company was doing, the conversation moved to women in top management. "How many female executives do you have in your organization?" the reporter asked Carl. Carl admitted that off the top of his head he did not know. This is when the reporter's attitude suddenly changed. "Well, Carl, it can't be very many," she said. "If there were you would have those statistics right at your fingertips. Every single thing I have asked you, you were able to answer with specific numbers and factual data. But when we get into the subject of women in the executive suite, you suddenly draw a blank. Apparently this is an area where your firm is not doing very much."

Carl was taken aback by this line of reasoning. He assured the reporter that she was quite mistaken. In fact, he invited her to come by his headquarters the next afternoon to meet with him and the vice president of personnel and discuss the progress of women in top management at his firm. He offered her an exclusive story using his company as an example. "If we are not doing our job properly, tell your readers this. We have nothing to hide. The fact that I don't know as much about this area as I do about a lot of others should not be taken as an indication that our organization is lax in meeting its responsibilities to promote women into the upper ranks of management." The reporter told Carl she was delighted to hear this and agreed to meet with him at 3:00 P.M. the next day.

Later that evening, Carl placed a call to the vice president of personnel and told him what had happened. "I want you in my office first thing in the morning," he told the vice president. "Have with you all of the statistics you can gather regarding the total number of personnel employed by us, the number of women in this group, and the percentage of them who hold executive management positions. You and I had better review some of the questions she is likely to ask us and have data available to back up anything we say. This woman is very sharp and I don't want us to make any mistakes. If we do, we are likely to read about them in the newspaper later this week." The vice president said he would have all of the information Carl needed and would be in his office at 10:00 A.M. sharp. He also told Carl that he was bringing along a new in-house consultant who knew quite a bit about the role and scope of women in the workforce in general and might be very helpful in providing information for answering some of the reporter's questions.

Your Consultation

Assume that you are the in-house consultant and have been asked to gather information about the current status of women in the executive suite. After a careful review of the material in this chapter, what would you tell Carl regarding the equal opportunities for women in top management? What is holding them back? What particular benefits do they offer to modern organizations? How many of them are there in the top ranks? Also, what information would you like to have about Carl's organization so that you could make the best possible case for the company's offering women opportunities equal to those of men? Be as complete as possible in your answer, using as many statistics and other facts as you can gather.

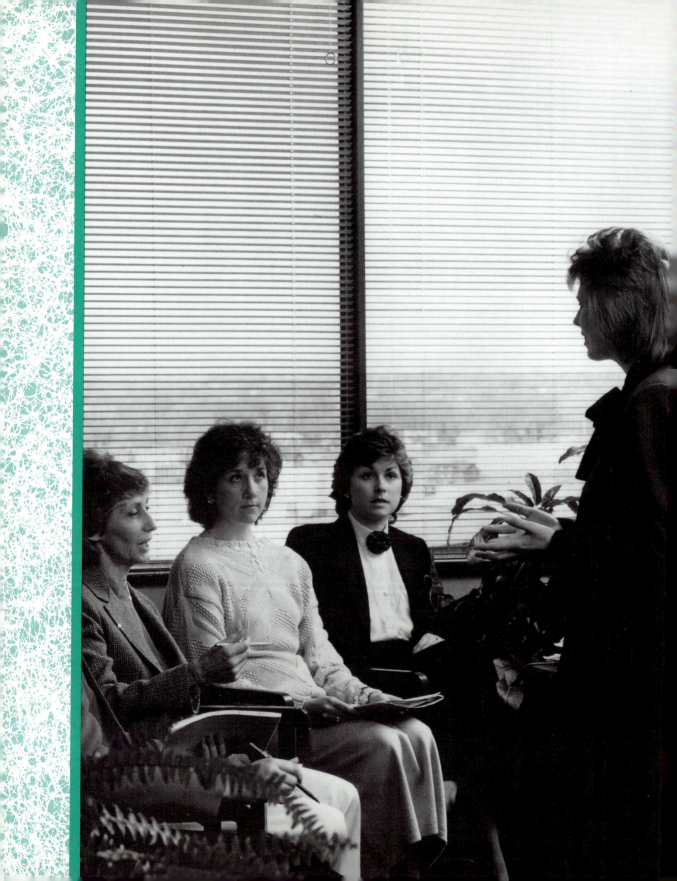

21

Management Career Planning And You

Now that you have completed your study of what management is all about, it is time to turn to one last, crucial area: management career planning. This chapter looks at management as a career, examines a profile of successful managers, and suggests guidelines that can be useful to you in planning a management career of your own. When you have finished studying the material in this chapter, you will be able to:

1. Describe a profile of currently successful executives.
2. Explain the six career phases that most managers go through.
3. Discuss typical career problems faced by managers when they start out and later in their careers.
4. Describe useful strategies in terms of career self-evaluation, career tactics, and career development planning.
5. Describe the nature and effects of organizational stress.
6. Tell how a Type A person works and why this person is highly susceptible to coronary heart disease.
7. List specific steps that will help you manage stress, avoid burnout, and ensure a long, healthy career.

A PROFILE OF SUCCESS

Before we begin a systematic analysis of how to manage a career effectively, let us examine a profile of some successful business leaders to find out who seems to succeed and why.

Functional Background

A few years ago, *Fortune,* the prestigious business journal, conducted an investigation of the backgrounds of the nation's top 512 chief executives.[1] The results of this study are shown in Table 21-1. Notice from the table that in the 1980s more chief executives came from business than from any other area. Does this mean that business majors have the best chance of reaching the top? Not necessarily. David L. Kurtz and Louis E. Boone, who researched the subject of functional background, reported these conclusions:

No particular background is essential

A study that used 20 years of data from each of 239 companies found that a new president had the same functional background as the previous chief executive in only 25 percent of the cases. The obvious lesson is that candidates for entry-level jobs should not select a functional area on the basis of the CEO's specialty. No particular functional background is essential for a chief executive in most industries today.[2]

Compensation

How well are these executives compensated? In answering this question, we must note that many top managers receive the bulk of their annual compensation in bonuses, stock options, and other perquisites. Economic and competitive developments greatly influence this total package. In some years executives make very large amounts, while in other years, because of small bonuses or a depressed stock market, total compensation is much less. Nevertheless, speaking in very broad terms, executive compensation over the last decade has been quite good.

Compensation is quite good

In 1990, Dave Stewart of the Oakland Athletics baseball team and "Most Valuable Player" in the 1989 World Series, received a two-year contract extension worth $7 million. He received a $2 million signing bonus, and salaries of $2.5 million for 1991 and 1992. Top executives also received large compensa-

---

[1] Maggie McComas, "Atop the *Fortune* 500: A Survey of the CEOs," *Fortune* (April 28, 1986): 26–31.
[2] David L. Kurtz and Louis E. Boone, "A Profile of Business Leadership," *Business Horizons,* (September–October 1981):30.

TABLE 21-1   The Functional Backgrounds of Chief Executives

Main Field of Study	Undergraduate % of CEOs	Graduate % of CEOs
Business	33.3%	56.3%
Engineering	24.0%	10.8%
Economics	17.5%	4.6%
Humanities	15.3%	6.9%
Physical Sciences	5.8%	3.1%
Social Sciences	5.6%	1.5%
Law	1.4%	21.4%
Other	4.8%	2.8%

Source: Maggie McComas, "Atop the *Fortune* 500: A Survey of the CEOs," *Fortune* (April 28, 1986), 26–31. Reprinted by permission of *Fortune* Magazine: © 1986 by Time Inc. All rights reserved.

tion packages. Michael Eisner, CEO of Walt Disney, earned $32.6 million in 1988; and *Forbes* magazine reported that the top 800 CEOs of the nation's largest corporations earned $782 million collectively. Almost one-half of them were paid over $1 million in total compensation. The critical difference between executives and athletes may be in the structure of the total package. Table 21-2 shows how compensation has changed for executives with salary, bonus, and stock gains. Table 21-2 shows how compensation has changed for executives with salary, bonus, and long-term compensation.

Executive Roots

Birthplace makes no difference . . .

Does it make any difference where one is born? In the main, the answer is no. For example, the *Fortune* survey of top executives revealed that 33.1 percent were from the Midwest, 32.3 percent were from the Northeast, 21.8 percent were from the South, 9.9 percent were from the West (Southwest), and another 2.9 percent were foreign born (from countries such as Canada, France, Italy, England, Germany, and Ireland). Foreign-born executives have, in the past, headed such well-known firms as Dow Chemical, General Electric, H. J. Heinz, Revlon, and NCR. The only pattern that does emerge when examining U.S. born executives is that many of them came from industrialized areas. Only 9.5 percent of the *Fortune* study reported being from a rural area. Thus, overall, very little emphasis can be placed on one's birthplace (see Figure 21-1).

but enterprise and economic background do

However, the economic backgrounds of executives demonstrated that the majority came from middle-class to wealthy families as opposed to lower class (poor) backgrounds. Over 50 percent reported the occupation of their father as executive, manager, or small business owner. Thus, the economic background and occupation of their father apparently did influence the career track of today's executives.

TABLE 21-2   The 25 Highest Paid Executives

Ranked below are the 25 chief executives who earned the most cash—salary and bonus—compensation last year. Notice how the realization of large stock gains tends to be an infrequent event.

Company	Chief Executive	Salary + Bonus* (000)			Stock Gains (000)		
		1987	1988	% increase 1988/1987	1987	1988	% change 1988/1987
Reebok International	Paul B. Fireman	$15,424	$11,439	−26%	0	0	
Walt Disney	Michael D. Eisner	6,730	7,506	12	0	$32,588	
Reliance Group	Saul P. Steinberg	4,272	4,498	5	0	0	
Warner Commun	Steven J. Ross	3,125	4,481	43	0	8,822	
Toys "R" Us	Charles Lazarus	3,594	4,429	23	$56,410	0	
Morgan Stanley	S. Parker Gilbert	3,000	4,425	48	0	0	
Salomon	John H. Gutfreund	1,253	4,000	219	0	0	
Columbia S&L Assn	Thomas Spiegel	3,860	3,960	3	0	4,106	
Hewlett-Packard	John A. Young	1,099	3,749	241	256	1,988	676.6%
American Family	John B. Amos	2,957	3,700	25	0	749	
Gulf & Western	Martin S. Davis	2,299	3,673	60	0	0	
Leslie Fay Cos	John J. Pomerantz	NA	3,442	NA	0	0	
Ford Motor	Donald E. Petersen	3,730	3,285	−12	0	7,151	
American Express	James D. Robinson III	1,973	2,764	40	989	6,419	549.0
Tyson Foods	Don Tyson	3,447	2,568	−25	0	0	
Merrill Lynch	William A. Schreyer	1,902	2,500	31	0	0	
Apple Computer	John Sculley	2,140	2,479	16	0	7,013	
Occidental Petroleum	Armand Hammer	1,938	2,455	27	0	0	
Bear Stearns Cos	Alan C. Greenberg	5,712	2,448	−57	0	0	
General Electric	John F. Welch Jr	2,057	2,352	14	0	0	
ITT	Rand V. Araskog	1,840	2,234	21	1,027	617	−39.9
Intl Minerals & Chem	George D. Kennedy	1,100	2,188	99	0	0	
Coca-Cola	Roberto C. Goizueta	1,823	2,164	19	969	0	
Textron	Beverly F. Dolan	1,855	2,066	11	657	0	
Ogden	Ralph E. Ablon	1,389	2,058	48	3,651	2,282	−37.5

* Excludes "other" compensation: see tables, pages 192ff. NA: Not available.
Source: Susan Chin, "The Power and the Pay: The 800 Best Paid Executives in America," *Forbes* (May 29, 1989):160.

Career Factors

The *Fortune* study also revealed some interesting points concerning top executives' career backgrounds. Sales and marketing were atop the career emphasis listing with financial falling second and legal third (see Table 21-3).

The educational attainment, in terms of degrees, by executives was quite accomplished. Only 14 percent of the *Fortune* survey never went beyond high school while 65 percent reported continuing their studies beyond a bachelors degree. Twenty-two percent of all executives reported having an MBA or Master of Science in Business degree (see Figure 21-2).

Experience in the current company was an overwhelming factor in the *Fortune* survey, as 72.5 percent reported previous experience with their current

FIGURE 21-1
Executive Roots

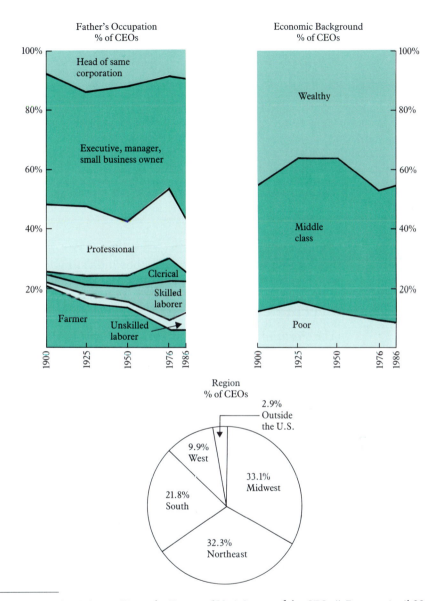

Father's Occupation
% of CEOs

Economic Background
% of CEOs

Region
% of CEOs

enterprise while 38.3 percent reported experience in another company (see Table 21-4). Almost 63 percent indicated having worked for their company 10 years or more before becoming the CEO. In addition, 33.2 percent worked for only that one company while 47.3 percent indicated experience with one or two other companies. More than 61 percent of CEOs had worked for the same

TABLE 21-3   Career Backgrounds of Top Executives

Main Career Emphasis	% of CEOs
Sales, marketing, distribution	31.6%
Financial	27.0%
Production, operations	19.5%
Legal	9.2%
Engineering, design, R&D	9.0%
General management	3.5%
Personnel	0.2%

Source: Maggie McComas, ''Atop the *Fortune* 500: A Survey of the CEOs,'' *Fortune* (April 28, 1986):27. Reprinted by permission of *Fortune* Magazine; © 1986 Time Inc. All rights reserved.

company more than 10 years (see Table 21-5). Only 19 percent reported working for four or more companies, thus indicating loyalty, longevity and experience with a firm are important career factors (see Table 21-6).

Executive Concerns

The *Fortune* survey also brought out some of the issues of great concern to contemporary executives. Table 21-7 depicts the responses from the executives

FIGURE 21-2
CEO Education

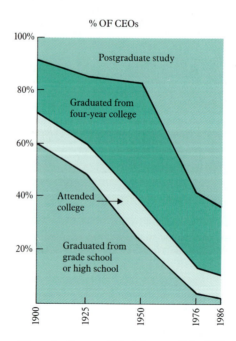

Source: Maggie McComas, ''Atop the Fortune 500: A Survey of the CEOs,'' *Fortune,* April 28, 1986. © 1986 Time Inc. All rights reserved.

TABLE 21-4   CEO Career Factors

Factors	% of CEOs
Experience in current company	72.5%
Experience in another company	38.3%
Initiative in organizing company	20.3%
Inheritance or family influence	10.2%
Investment in company	6.6%
Executive recruitment firm	6.6%
Result of takeover	2.5%

Source: Maggie McComas, "Atop the *Fortune* 500: A Survey of the CEOs," *Fortune* (April 28, 1986):30. Reprinted by permission of *Fortune* Magazine; © 1986 Time Inc. All rights reserved.

with cost containment, productivity, and training and motivating employees being the key concerns. New product development and government regulation were also reported by almost one-half of the executives surveyed.

A look at these issues provides you with a better insight into many of the topics covered throughout our text. (See "Management in Practice: '10 Out of 10' at Celanese.") Many of the issues that appear on the executive list are also topics within our text and for good reason. It allows you to examine these issues closer as a student and, thus, prepare for the types of problems executives confront.

Overall Findings

Overall, the major factors presented illustrate that the key to executive success is competence. You must know what you are doing. It also helps to attain a college degree, especially in business. Experience is then vital as your drive and determination move you up in an organization. You must want to succeed and be prepared to pay the price. One of the most effective ways to rise in the ranks

TABLE 21-5   Years with Company before Becoming C.E.O.

Number of Years	% of CEOs	
	1976	*1986*
Less than 1	9.5%	17.0%
1–2	5.5%	6.2%
3–5	6.5%	7.2%
6–9	7.4%	7.9%
10–14	12.9%	13.3%
15 or more	57.7%	48.2%

Source: Maggie McComas, "Atop the *Fortune* 500: A Survey of the CEOs," *Fortune* (April 28, 1986):30. Reprinted by permission of *Fortune* Magazine: © 1986 by Time Inc. All rights reserved.

TABLE 21-6   Number of Companies Worked for before Becoming a CEO

Number of Companies	% of CEOs
1	33.2%
2	24.4%
3	22.9%
4	11.1%
5 or more	8.3%

Source: Maggie McComas, "Atop the *Fortune* 500: A Survey of the CEOs," *Fortune* (April 28, 1986):30. Reprinted by permission of *Fortune* Magazine: © 1986 by Time Inc. All rights reserved.

is with a well-developed career plan. As this plan is implemented, you will find yourself going through what are called career phases.

CAREER PHASES

In general terms, most people go through a series of career phases or stages. These phases do not last the same amount of time for everyone, and some people seem to have more difficulty at one (or two) phases than do most others. Nevertheless, six distinct career phases can be identified.

TABLE 21-7   Executive Concerns

Issues of Great Concern	% of CEOs Citing[1]
Cost containment	78.7%
Productivity	77.7%
Training & motivating employees	70.1%
New product development	46.3%
Government regulation	43.9%
Global competition	35.5%
Short-term earnings	26.0%
High taxes	24.4%
High corporate debt	11.1%
Litigation against company	9.4%
Takeover threats	9.0%
Labor problems	5.1%

[1] Totals more than 100% because of multiple citations.
Source: Maggie McComas, "Atop the *Fortune* 500: A Survey of the CEOs," *Fortune* (April 28, 1986):29. Reprinted by permission of *Fortune* Magazine: © 1986 by Time Inc. All rights reserved.

MANAGEMENT IN PRACTICE

"10 Out of 10" at Celanese

Celanese is a $3 billion-a-year chemical firm, employing 15,000 people, that wanted to be a perfect company. In order to achieve such a lofty goal, the company management sought to institute a quality mentality in the corporate culture. Taking a cue from the Olympics, Celanese's chairman John Macomber characterized the effort as achieving a "10 out of 10." Specific management goals were devised. These included:

Work Environment

- Respect for individuals and contributions each can make
- Openness and trust prevail
- Communication based on trust
- Freedom to innovate and take risks
- Diversity accepted and valued
- Short-term actions consistent with long-term goals
- Desire for continual improvement
- Dedication to understanding and meeting customer requirements

Quality Reputation

- Recognized quality leader
- Employee pride
- Customer preference
- Shareholders value
- Business/financial community respect

Employee Involvement

- Clear understanding of mission and objectives
- Everyone participating with enthusiasm
- Participative goal setting and measurement
- Teamwork and problem solving at all levels
- Full participation in decision making
- Recognition of quality performance

Products, Processes and Systems

- Consistently superior to competition
- Equal emphasis on human administrative and technical resources
- Quality the key element in planning and decision-making
- Cost of quality less than 5 percent, zero failure cost

To ensure the development of these goals into their culture, Celanese created the General Management Development Program. This program takes people through two years of part-time training to prepare them as future managers. In addition, a Quality Action Team was devised with representation from all parts of the company—secretarial, maintenance, managers, workers, etc. This team meets periodically to bring problems to the surface. Communication is the key to this team, so that management's awareness is improved. Also, group dynamics is stressed for team problem solving, and the evaluation of managers has been changed from bottom line performance to openness, communication, and participation of subordinates.

Overall, this companywide effort to achieve the perfect "10" has made progress according to Art Nichols, director of quality at Celanese. There is now lower absenteeism, higher quality control, more satisfied customers, and fewer transfer requests, and thus has resulted in a $60–70 million improvement in annual operating income. It may not be perfect yet, but it's a start.

Source: Dale Johnson, "Reaching for the Perfect 10 in Business," *Intrapreneur* (September 1989):48–51.

Phase 1: Breaking Away (Ages 16–22)

A job initially is viewed as a means of self-support

During the phase of **breaking away**, the person begins to establish independence and autonomy from the parents. The person strives to demonstrate that he or she is capable of managing in life. Most people finish their schooling during this period and take their first full-time job. Far from being interested in a career, at this stage most people view their job basically as a means of income and self-support. It helps them accomplish their objective of breaking away.

Phase 2: Initial Adulthood (Ages 22–29)

Then a career plan begins to emerge . . .

During the phase of **initial adulthood**, individuals begin to become adults in the truest sense of the word. One of the primary objectives during this phase is the development of social and intimate relationships with members of the opposite sex. Many people marry during this age period. They also begin to develop organizational and professional ties. A career plan now begins to emerge. This is true for both women and men. In fact, recent research reveals that both groups go into management for the same reasons.[3]

Phase 3: Transition Period (Ages 29–32)

followed by a personal evaluation period

During the **transition period**, people often become uneasy about their career progress. Key questions people ask themselves include: Am I moving ahead fast enough? Should I change jobs or move to another organization? Many people do move to another firm during this period. They know they will not always be mobile, and they decide to take advantage of the situation while they can.

Phase 4: Settling Down (Ages 32–39)

Next comes a drive to succeed . . .

During the phase of **settling down**, individuals are likely to have chosen a career and to be spending their time trying to get ahead. Social contacts are greatly reduced, for most people now have little time for cultivating friendships. Most of their energies are devoted to career-oriented objectives and to their immediate family. During this time they establish the groundwork for career advancement. If a person is not labeled "a winner" or "up-and-coming" by the time he or she is 40, the executive suite may be out of bounds.

Phase 5: Possible Mid-Life Crisis (Ages 39–43)

followed by another in-depth evaluation period

During the period of **mid-life crisis**, people realize that some youthful ambitions will never be fulfilled. It becomes clear that the social or financial position once dreamed of will not materialize. The person may never get to be the CEO. He or she may have to settle for being a good, but not the best, salesperson in the

---

[3] Benson Rosen, Mary Ellen Templeton, and Karen Kichline, "The First Few Years on the Job: Women in Management," *Business Horizons* (November–December 1981):26–29.

firm. For many people, the recognition that many of their dreams will go unrealized comes as a crushing blow. If they are unable to cope with this situation, they face mid-life crisis. This term refers to a psychological state in which individuals feel that they have failed and that there is no way for them to bounce back. These feelings are typical when individuals review their careers and conclude that they are too old to change careers but do not want to continue with things the way they are. During this phase it is not uncommon to find people quitting their jobs or doing foolish things such as wearing outlandish clothes to a conservative job or going out and buying a boat that is beyond their means and trying to live a different lifestyle. Still others turn to excessive drinking or make a spectacular break with the past, one that hurts their careers. Of course, not everyone behaves this way. In fact, the more realistic people are about their careers, where they are going, how they are going to get there, and what they are willing to settle for, the more likely it is that they will not suffer mid-life crisis.

Phase 6: Establishment of Equilibrium (Ages 43–50)

Then things often return to normal

During the phase of **establishment of equilibrium**, things return to normal. The person is likely to review career progress, find that things are going along pretty well, and be basically pleased with the results. There is a large degree of contentment, optimism, and stability. If the person is not going to become an executive vice president, he or she has come to realize and accept this fact. If the person is not able to afford a million-dollar house in the suburbs, he or she finds comfort in a more modest residence.

As you can see, as an individual moves through these phases, his or her attitudes, values, opinions, and even lifestyles change. The person matures and grows in different ways. The important thing to draw from an understanding of these career phases is the different types of changes that people confront during their careers. By having an idea of what you are likely to encounter, you are in a better position to deal with career problems, and there are many of them. The next section examines some of the most typical ones.

CAREER PROBLEMS

It will not always be smooth sailing for you. You will occasionally find yourself facing career problems. Two crucial periods come when you first start out and again later on when you may face a career plateau.

Starting Out

When you begin your career, you are likely to have a great deal of drive and determination. You will want to do well and succeed. Unfortunately, in many cases you will find that your initial view of work is quite different from reality.

Simple and Boring

One of the first things you will learn is that, except in rare cases, the work will be simple and perhaps even boring. You will be eager to apply the specific tools and techniques that you learned in college. You will be seeking opportunity and challenge, but there will be little of either. Most of your time will be spent on routine, basic assignments. You may find yourself asking, "Is this it? Doesn't this job have any meaningful aspects? Do I really want to do this for the next year or two?" If you stay with the organization, things should get better. At first, however, you are just going to have to suffer through.[4]

Initial jobs are usually routine

Organizational Politics

A second early problem relates to organizational politics. When you are new to the enterprise, you are unaware of the power relationships that exist. You do not know whom to cultivate, what to say, or with which groups to associate. You are likely to believe that if you do a good job, everything else will take care of itself. However, if you and your boss have a good relationship but your boss is considered to be a maverick or good in his present position but not promotable, you and your boss may both find yourself eventually having to look for jobs elsewhere. Or, if you write a report showing how the enterprise can cut its workforce by 5 percent and save $500,000 and the cuts are to come from the department of a powerful manager, your promotion path to the top may be blocked. There are many mistakes you can make because you do not know the politics of the organization.

You may not know the power relationships that exist . . .

Knowing What Counts

Perhaps the basic rule of success for young managers is, "Keep your boss pleased with your performance." Unfortunately, the way to do this is not always clear. Some young people believe they should be as efficient and businesslike as possible. Such behavior sometimes results in their being labeled as lacking in human relations skills, however. Others are extremely personable but are viewed as lacking drive or determination to succeed. Whatever the reason, early evaluations count; and if you are rated as average or below average by your first boss, regardless of how tough an evaluator he or she is, this is likely to hurt your future with the organization. For this reason, you have to learn early on how you are going to be evaluated and then act accordingly.[5]

or how your performance will be measured

---

[4] See Marcia A. Manter and Janice Y. Benjamin, "How To Hold On To First Careerists," *Personnel Administrator* (September 1989):44–48.

[5] Betsy Jacobson and Beverly L. Kaye, "Career Development and Performance Appraisal: It Takes Two to Tango," *Personnel* (January 1986):26–27.

Loyalty Issues

Loyalty means different things to different people

Loyalty means different things to different people. Some managers view it in terms of obedience: do as I tell you to do. Others view it in terms of effort: come early, stay late, work hard. Other common interpretations relate to (1) success, as found among managers who want their subordinates to do whatever it takes to get the job done, even if the activities are shady; (2) protection, as found among managers who want their people to shield them from ridicule and remember that it is "us against them"; and (3) honesty, as found among managers who want their subordinates to convey to them both good and bad news. The first challenge for the young manager is to determine which of these interpretations is expected. The second challenge is to decide whether the conduct it calls for is personally acceptable.

Ethical Problems

Ethics may prove to be an issue for you

Sometimes, loyalty problems are also ethical problems. **Ethics**, however, which can be defined as principles that determine right and wrong conduct, extend far beyond simple loyalty. Many members of the general public believe businesspeople are willing to carry out unethical practices in order to succeed. When viewed from a broad perspective, ethics apply to a number of different subjects, ranging from legal issues to economic self-interest to the impact of one person's actions on other people. Young managers have to decide how far they are prepared to go in order to succeed in their careers. For some, the pressure to conform to less than personally acceptable levels of conduct can be quite great. In some organizations failure to cross this line can cost you a promotion; in other organizations you will be fired if you do. The real issue is finding out what particular ethical problem will confront you, deciding whether your values and those of the organization are in agreement, and being willing to move on to another enterprise if ethical dilemmas cannot be resolved to your satisfaction.

Later On

As your career progresses, you will face still other problems. One of these, discussed earlier, is mid-life crisis. Another more common problem is the career plateau.

The Career Plateau

Upward progress may be halted

Few individuals find their careers to be a continuous climb to the top. Most discover that there is a career plateau after which further promotions come either infrequently or not at all. Some people reach their career plateau more quickly than others, but it is a problem for just about everyone.

Priscilla M. Elsass and David A. Ralston, after studying the career plateau's causes and effects, have reported that the career plateau has been commonly defined as that point at which future hierarchical mobility seems unlikely. The pyramidal structure of organizations, which dictates that less than 1 percent of all employees will reach the highest level, has always made career plateauing inevitable for most employees. Recently declining rates of corporate growth and a rapidly expanding work force have made plateauing even more likely.

Unfortunately, being plateaued is often seen by the individual as tantamount to career failure. For employees who desire career growth, plateauing leads to stress. Even for those individuals who choose security and stability as career priorities, a sense of failure and guilt is often associated with not being more ambitious. Consequently, the career plateau has been cited as a factor leading to a number of stress-related, undesirable outcomes that have a strong impact on both individual and organizational well-being.[6]

Personal and organizational factors are the causes

What causes the career plateau? In Near's survey, 80 percent of the managers partially attributed it to personal factors such as motivation effort, and ability. These managers plateaued because they lacked sufficient desire, drive, or talent. She also found that 60 percent of the managers partially attributed their plateau to organizational factors such as the competition for promotions and a belief on the part of the enterprise that the person was too valuable in his or her present position to be moved to a higher level.[7]

Whatever the reason, the plateau takes three typical patterns. Some people continue up the line until they reach a position where they are unable to progress any further because they lack the ability to go on. These individuals tend to stay in their jobs either until retirement or until they are forced out

Some people are terminated

because the organization labels them as deadwood and terminates their employment. A second pattern is that in which people become obsolete after they plateau because they are unwilling to keep up with the latest developments in their field. They, too, are eventually terminated. The typical pattern is one in which the individual maintains a successful plateau status. Whether this plateau occurs for organizational or personal reasons, the employee's performance remains high and the organization keeps the person on.

Early in your career you are not likely to be very concerned with career plateauing. It will become a concern as you move into middle management, however, or reach your mid-30s. Will you be able to deal with it? Will the organization be willing to help out? The first question can be answered only by

---

[6] Priscilla M. Elsass and David A. Ralston, "Individual Responses to the Stress of Career Plateauing," *Journal of Management* (January 1989):35–36.

[7] Janet P. Near, "The Career Plateua: Causes and Effects," *Business Horizons* (October 1980):54 and Walter L. Polsky and Loretta D. Foxman, "Professional Answers to Career Questions: Advice to a 15-year Personnel Manager Seeking Employment Following a Layoff," *Personnel Journal* (September 1986):36(2).

you. If you maintain a strong desire to succeed and are determined to keep moving up the ladder, the chance of overcoming personal plateau causes is fairly good. In answering the second question, you need to look at the career development programs offered by the firm. There are numerous ways in which management can avoid practices leading to ineffective plateauing and the need to fire deadwood. Some of these are discussed in the next section.

There are ways to overcome the plateau

CAREER STRATEGIES

Before you begin a career in management, you need to evaluate your own needs, desires, and ambitions.[8] What type of career do you want? You also need to understand career tactics that can help you sidestep problems and take advantage of opportunities. Finally, you must be aware that career development can help you formulate a long-term plan that will take you to retirement. These three areas constitute career strategy.

Self-Evaluation

Make a self-examination

The best way to begin a career strategy plan is with a self-examination. What do you do well? What do you do poorly? What would you like to do in terms of a career? The answers to questions like these will help you balance ability (what you do well) with interests (what you would like to do) while sidestepping areas where you are not likely to succeed (what you do poorly). One of the most effective ways to obtain a profile of your work personality is to formulate a series of questions such as those presented in Figure 21-3. These are not designed to be comprehensive, but they do indicate what we are talking about. The purpose of such questions is to help you describe yourself. There are no right and wrong answers; the questions are designed for descriptive purposes only. As you begin to formulate in your mind the type of work you would like to do, you will not find any job that is perfect in terms of demands, pressures, hours, financial reimbursements, and so forth. You will be able to use this type of self-evaluation checklist, however, as a guide in identifying the type of career or job that is best for you.

Focus on the future

A supplemental way to obtain personal insights is through the use of time continua. Your life consists of three time periods: past, present, and future. Most people concentrate their attention only on the present. If they do look in any other direction, it is usually to the past for the purpose of reminiscing. The

---

[8] For another view of this process, see William L. Mihal, Patricia A. Sorce, and Thomas M. Conte, "A Process Model of Individual Career Decision Making," *Academy of Management Review* (January 1984):95–103.

FIGURE 21-3

Types of Questions
for Obtaining
Personal Insights
Useful in Career
Planning

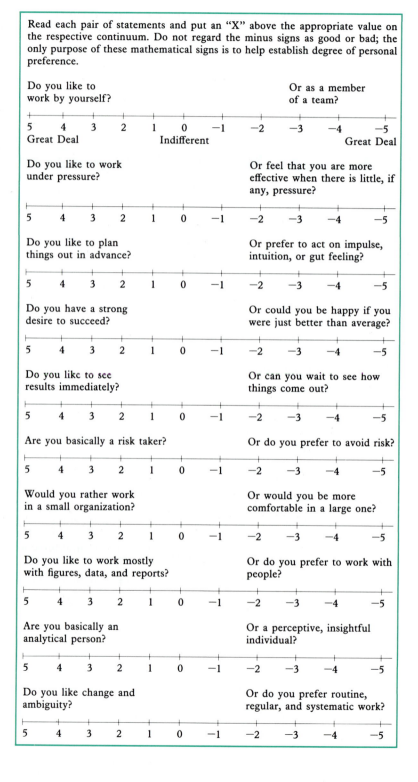

FIGURE 21-3

Types of Questions
for Obtaining
Personal Insights
Useful in Career
Planning

Read each pair of statements and put an "X" above the appropriate value on the respective continuum. Do not regard the minus signs as good or bad; the only purpose of these mathematical signs is to help establish degree of personal preference.

Do you like to work by yourself?   Or as a member of a team?

5   4   3   2   1   0   −1   −2   −3   −4   −5
Great Deal   Indifferent   Great Deal

Do you like to work under pressure?   Or feel that you are more effective when there is little, if any, pressure?

5   4   3   2   1   0   −1   −2   −3   −4   −5

Do you like to plan things out in advance?   Or prefer to act on impulse, intuition, or gut feeling?

5   4   3   2   1   0   −1   −2   −3   −4   −5

Do you have a strong desire to succeed?   Or could you be happy if you were just better than average?

5   4   3   2   1   0   −1   −2   −3   −4   −5

Do you like to see results immediately?   Or can you wait to see how things come out?

5   4   3   2   1   0   −1   −2   −3   −4   −5

Are you basically a risk taker?   Or do you prefer to avoid risk?

5   4   3   2   1   0   −1   −2   −3   −4   −5

Would you rather work in a small organization?   Or would you be more comfortable in a large one?

5   4   3   2   1   0   −1   −2   −3   −4   −5

Do you like to work mostly with figures, data, and reports?   Or do you prefer to work with people?

5   4   3   2   1   0   −1   −2   −3   −4   −5

Are you basically an analytical person?   Or a perceptive, insightful individual?

5   4   3   2   1   0   −1   −2   −3   −4   −5

Do you like change and ambiguity?   Or do you prefer routine, regular, and systematic work?

5   4   3   2   1   0   −1   −2   −3   −4   −5

future is where you will spend your career, however, and you should devote your attention to this time period when examining who you are and what you want to do.

There are two popular ways of focusing on the future. The easiest, although sometimes most threatening, way is for you to write your own obituary. What do you want people to write about you after you are gone? As you write this obituary, you are actually identifying things you have done (or would like to do) before you die.

<aside>Note meaningful job-related events you want to have happen</aside>

A second way is to go back into the past and identify and describe important or meaningful events that have happened to you in your life. Perhaps you remember winning a special prize at school. Or perhaps there was a big birthday party for you and you received a very special present from your favorite aunt and uncle. Whatever these events were, write them down. The reason for this is to get you thinking about what important things have already happened to you. Now continue your list into the future and write down all of the important or meaningful job-related events you would like to experience during your career. By examining this list, you can obtain an idea of what you want to do. You have, albeit indirectly, set some objectives for yourself. Now you need to determine how you can achieve them, and career tactics can help.

Career Tactics

Regardless of the career you choose, you should know some of the ways to increase your chances of success. Every organization has its own set of rules (see "*Management-in-Practice: J. Crew — Dream Merchants*"), but there are some general guidelines that are helpful in virtually every enterprise.

<aside>Strive for high performance</aside>

One of these is: be a high performer. Nothing will help you succeed faster than proving you are competent. In fact, when you are first starting out, there will usually be very little management can use to differentiate you from others at your level. All of you may be in your early- to mid-20s, have college degrees, and exude a great amount of enthusiasm and company loyalty. Since all of you cannot be promoted at the same time, management will look for the highest performers. Who does the best job? This is the individual who will be promoted, and that is why it is so important for you to choose a job at which you can succeed. First results really do count!

<aside>Be prepared to blow your own horn</aside>

A second rule is: keep a hero file. When you do something well and the boss sends you a memo telling you about your success, save the memo. If you are charged with writing a special report or preparing a document, keep a copy of it. If you are given an award, make a note of it. In this way, if you ever decide to change jobs you have a file of evidence that shows how effective you have been. This is as useful within the firm as it will be if you should be interviewing for a position with another organization.

<aside>Start managing others as soon as possible</aside>

A third rule is: get into a management position as quickly as possible. The sooner you are managing people, the more likely it is you will be given the chance to increase your responsibility and manage even larger groups and

MANAGEMENT IN PRACTICE

J. Crew—Dream Merchants

J. Crew is a $130 million-a-year catalog company offering classic American sportswear. The president, Emily Cinader, took the lead from her father, Arthur, and planned the company's direction for a distinctive niche. In attempting to differentiate the company from competitors such as L.L. Bean or Land's End, Emily designed clothing that was more mainstream, outdoor sportswear as opposed to the rugged outdoor look.

The J. Crew idea is simplicity and conservatism. It has been described as a cross between Ralph Lauren and Calvin Klein. Yet, Cinader has worked hard to create an image from this design: a polo shirt from J. Crew should represent an image of a relaxed east coast lifestyle rather than just another polo shirt. Additionally, the catalog layout, copy, and design must be superb at conveying this image to prospective customers.

Cinader keeps this development in perspective with the marketing trend of shopping. In 1983, 57 million people shopped by mail or phone, while in 1989, 91 million people moved into this arena. Yet, according to the Direct Marketing Association, there are approximately 10,000 different catalogs now being published. Cinader's careful attention to the development and layout of J. Crew's catalog is one major key to reaching this emerging volume of customers amidst the increasing competition for catalog readership.

In short, it appears that J. Crew's desire to create an imaginary world through the mailbox is working. And Emily Cinader is firmly at the helm.

Source: Tim Appelo, ''She's Got the Look,'' *Savvy Women* (January 1990):49–51.

departments. Remember that when it is time to choose someone for a management opening, the person who currently has the next greatest amount of managerial responsibility and scope of authority is often given the nod. All things considered, a manager of a 15-person unit is more likely to be promoted head of a department of 25 people than is a manager of a 10-person unit.

Get yourself a sponsor

A fourth rule is: find a sponsor. A sponsor is someone who will help move you along in the organization. This individual will note your accomplishments to the right people, see that you are given a fair shake when it comes to promotion and salary, and ensure that your career is not sidetracked. The most common sponsor is one's boss, although it sometimes is an individual higher up the ranks who becomes aware of your work and decides to look after you because you are a talent the organization needs. For example, you may serve on a management committee with people from all levels of the hierarchy, and one of these individuals may take a liking to you. Or you may write an industry analysis that is read by a senior vice president who concludes that you have real talent. Whoever they are, sponsors are important people and in career planning it is very helpful to develop one. This is particularly true for women, many of whom admit that sponsors have been very helpful to them in their careers.

Help your boss get ahead

A fifth rule is: help your boss succeed. Remember that unless you move to another department or unit, your only way up the ranks is by assuming the position of your boss. You cannot do this if the boss remains. So by helping this person, you help yourself at the same time. There are a number of useful approaches in following this rule. One is to help your boss overcome any weaknesses he or she might have; for example, if the person is poor at report writing, help out by offering to write or rewrite these reports. A second way is to help the boss become better at things he or she likes. For example, if your superior likes to spend time visiting with the staff and building a public image in the community, work to free up the individual from desk routine. Help the boss become what he or she wants to become. Remember that when someone is promoted (or moves to another organization), that person will have to recommend a replacement. If you are out to help the boss succeed, you may well be tapped for that promotion.

Put opportunity ahead of money

A sixth rule is: seek opportunity before money. Many young people will change jobs if more money is offered to them. This is a mistake. In your early years on the job, you should be interested in building a track record for good performance. Very few young managers, except for sales managers or others whose compensation package is tied directly to performance, receive bonuses or other financial incentives. During your first two to three years on the job, you are going to be making about what everyone else does who started with you. Anyone who makes more does so for a reason. The most common reason is that the person has agreed to take a difficult, technical, time-consuming or dead-end job. In any event, such people often find that after they have been in this job for a couple of years, they are unable to move back into the mainstream quickly. There are no openings or the salaries are too low to entice them back. What they fail to realize is that they have accepted a staff or highly technical position that has taken them out of the running for line positions and top executive jobs. They have opted for money, but in the process have given up promotion opportunities. A second part of this picture is that as managers begin to move up the line, two values vie with each other. One is economic (money) and the other is power (authority). We know from research that managers whose highest value is political do the best of all. Research findings show that when confronted with the choice, a person is better off opting for power (promotion, authority, responsibility) because this is the best way to get ahead. Moreover, if you do succeed in moving up, the money will follow. *(Again see Table 21-2.)*

Maintain your mobility

A seventh rule is: keep yourself mobile. It is possible that you will not be able to succeed in your first (or second or third) organization. You may find your route blocked by a manager who does not like you. Or your boss may be someone who is out of favor with the upper-level management, with the result that everyone who works for this person is considered in the same light. How do you know when to stay and when to move? Here are some helpful guidelines:

1. If your boss is not considered promotable, move to another department or organization; there is no way you are going to overcome this problem unless he or she is fired—an uncommon event in many firms.
2. Look over the people at the same level of the hierarchy as yourself and estimate when they are most likely to be promoted; if you are not promoted at about the same time, consider going elsewhere.
3. By the time you are 30, you should be in a managerial position. If you are not, the firm may have designated you as lacking management timber. It may be time for you to move on.
4. Set some financial goals for yourself, such as earning $40,000 annually by the time you are 30 years old. Check to be sure that this figure is competitive in the industry. Then, if you have not made it, ask yourself why. If the answer is that the firm simply does not pay competitively at your level, look into your opportunities with other companies.
5. If you do exercise your mobility and go to another firm, never say anything bad about your old organization. Leave on good terms and give the impression that your decision was strictly a career move, nothing personal. If you do talk down your old employer, this can hurt you with your new one. Remember that people may smile when they hear you rip up the other firm, but they will be thinking, "I wonder what this person will say about us when he (or she) leaves here." You will get an image as someone who is quick to tear down others, and this reputation can hurt you.

Career Development Plan

A self-examination can help you formulate a short-range career plan.[9] An understanding of career tactics can help you develop an intermediate-range plan. Consideration of career development can help you with long-range planning; but career development does not always depend exclusively on you. Over the last decade organizations have come to realize that career development is a problem not only for the manager but for the organization as well. Why do some enterprises have a great deal of deadwood (ineffective plateauees)? Part of the answer is found in some of the organization's potentially harmful career development failures, such as:

Career development failures

1. Failure to accurately appraise marginal or poor performance and to initiate corrective action. Long-run problems can be fostered by avoiding the short-run unpleasantness of negative appraisal, thus allowing possibly correctable behavior to become entrenched habit, which later becomes "someone else's problems."

---

[9] For a more indepth analysis, see Barbara J. Feitler-Karchin, *Job Search Strategies* (Continuing Education Systems, Inc. Hinsdak, IL, 1986).

TABLE 21-8   Specific Career Activities

Career Counseling

Career counseling during the employment interview.
Career counseling during the performance appraisal session.
Psychological assessment and career alternative planning.
Career counseling as part of the day-to-day supervisor/subordinate relationship.
Special career counseling for high-potential employees.
Counseling for downward transfers.

Career Pathing

Planned job progression for new employees.
Career pathing to help managers acquire the necessary experience for future jobs.
Committee performs an annual review of management personnel's strengths and weaknesses and then develops a five-year career plan for each.
Plan job moves for high-potential employees to place them in a particular target job.
Rotate first-level supervisors through various departments to prepare them for upper-management positions.

Human Resources

Computerized inventory of backgrounds and skills to help identify replacements.
Succession planning or replacement charts at all levels of management.

Career Information Systems

Job posting for all nonofficer positions; individual can bid to be considered.
Job posting for hourly employees and career counseling for salaried employees.

Management or Supervisory Development

Special program for those moving from hourly employment to management.
Responsibility of the department head to develop managers.
Management development committee to look after the career development of management groups.
In-house advanced management program.

Training

In-house supervisory training.
Technical skills training for lower levels.
Outside management seminars.
Formalized job rotation programs.
Intern programs.
Responsibility of manager for on-the-job training.
Tuition reimbursement program.

Special Groups

Outplacement programs.
Minority indoctrination training program.
Career management seminar for women.
Preretirement counseling.
Career counseling and job rotation for women and minorities.
Refresher courses for midcareer managers.
Presupervisory training program for women and minorities.

Source: Marilyn A. Morgan, Douglas T. Hall, and Alison Martier, "Career Development Strategies in Industry—Where Are We and Where Should We Be?" *Personnel* (March–April 1979):16. Copyright © 1979 by American Management Association, New York. All rights reserved.

TABLE 21-9   Career Negotiation Scenarios

Organizational Position	Nature of Transaction	Individual Position
"You stay with us now and in return we can offer some exciting challenges in the future." →	1. Both parties agree to increase career options within organization. ←	"I can accept the current job for a while longer if you can help me get into an executive career track."
"We will provide options for outside professional opportunities such as a sabbatical or study, or travel to professional conferences." →	2. Side payments are made.	← "I'll remain in this organization if you provide outside professional opportunities to offset lack of career opportunities in the organization."
"We can only offer long-term benefits as compensation for lack of work challenge or on chances of increased responsibility. We will give a good vacation and retirement package." →	3. Side payments are made (career is not a negotiating issue).	← "I will accept limited job projects if I can get an early retirement package."
"If you stay with us for the short term, we will help place you in another attractive organization." →	4. Compromises are made to make use of individual's current talents and to facilitate a future move to another organization.	← "My career in this organization will not last long, so why don't you agree to help me move into another organization in a few years or so."
"Let's get what we can until he or she is no longer useful." →	5. Both parties engage in cynical manipulation.	← "I'm going to get mine and get out."

Source: James F. Wolf and Robert N. Bacher, "Career Negotiation: Trading Off Employee and Organizational Needs," *Personnel* (March–April 1981):53. Copyright © 1981 by American Management Association, New York. All rights reserved.

2. Failure to provide training, skill upgrading, and development of [high performers]. This tends to assure that performance will slip as the requirements of a given position change, even if the incumbent's motivation remains high.
3. Failure to appraise, counsel, and develop career paths in the context of an individual's total life situation, and the parallel tendency to promote people beyond their current ability, leading to ineffectiveness and psychological stress.
4. Failure to monitor the attitudes and aspirations of individual managers. Many organizations depend upon informal observations and interpretations of superiors. Conditions maintaining individual performance vary among individuals as a function of particular goals and values.[10]

How can people ensure that these failures do not exist in their firm? One way is to find out the career programs that are currently in use. Some of the most common include career counseling, career pathing, human resources planning, career information systems, management or supervisor development, training, and programs for special groups. Table 21-8 spells out each of these activities in more detail.

---

[10] Thomas P. Ference, James A. F. Stoner, and E. Kirby Warren, "Managing the Career Plateau," *Academy of Management Review* (October 1977):608.

Negotiate for
yourself

In addition to investigating career development programs, you must learn how to negotiate for yourself. Using the tactics described in the previous section, as well as your own experience and judgment, you must work out an arrangement that is as beneficial to you as it is to the enterprise. These negotiations can take numerous forms. Table 21-9 illustrates five typical career negotiation scenarios. Remember that these negotiations are designed to supplement the organizations' career development programs. The enterprise may offer you assistance in pathing out your career, but you have the responsibility to look out for your own interests. This responsibility is vital to every career development plan.

Formulate a
long-range plan for
yourself

The other important step in career development planning is to bring together your job-related needs and personal needs and align them with your career stages. Table 21-10 shows how this can be done. Notice from the table that as you move through your career, your strategies have to change. You must

TABLE 21-10	Career Planning and Career Stages	
Career Stage	**Job-Related Needs**	**Personal Needs**
Just starting out	A variety of job activities. An examination of abilities, desires, and goals.	Determination of preliminary job choices.
		Settling down to work.
Early career	Development of competence in specialty areas.	Dealing with rivalry and competition at work.
	Development of creativity and innovation.	Dealing with work—family conflicts.
	Job rotation into new areas for purpose of increased job experience.	Obtaining support for career choices.
		Establishment of autonomy.
Mid-career	Updating of technical knowledge and skills.	Dealing with mid-life crisis.
	Development of skills in training and coaching younger employees.	Reorganizing thinking about oneself in regard to work, family, and the community.
	Rotation into new jobs for acquiring new skills.	Reducing self-indulgence and competitiveness.
	Development of a broader view of work and personal roles in the organization.	
Late career	Planning for retirement.	Support and counseling of others in the organization.
	Shifting from a power role to one of guidance and consultation.	Development of a sense of identity in extraorganizational activities.
	Identification and development of successors.	
	Starting of activities outside the organization.	

match your work life with your personal life. If either is out of step with the other, your career can suffer. Remember that your career success depends, to a large extent, on your ability to formulate a well-designed strategy that meets your particular needs.[11]

EXECUTIVE HEALTH

Before concluding our discussion of management as a career, we need to consider the topic of executive health. In the last 10 years this has become a very important issue in modern organizations. After all, every time an executive dies the organization loses one of its most important assets. Who will replace this person? Will the new executive have the same degree of judgment, skill, intelligence, and insight? If not, the organization will have suffered a tremendous blow because of the executive's death.

If you want to make it to the top and become a key executive, you have to know more than just how to manage your career. You have to know something about managing your health. This subject has a number of important dimensions, including (1) organizational stress and its effect on the executive's well-being; (2) managerial personality and the differences between those most likely to have heart attacks and those least likely to suffer this fate; (3) excessive stress, namely burnout; and (4) ways to cope with stress and lead a long and fruitful management life.

Organizational Stress

Every year more than 650,000 Americans die from heart attacks. Another 29 million have some form of heart and blood vessel disease.[12] One of the most important causes of coronary heart disease (CHD) is stress. In organizational settings there are many factors or stressors that can cause CHD. Figure 21-4 provides a model for understanding the relationship between stress and CHD.

Stressors are both intra- and extraorganizational

Notice from the figure that **stressors** can be categorized as intraorganizational and extraorganizational. Intraorganizational stressors occur at three levels: individual, group, and the organization at large, while extraorganizational stressors are heavily influenced by personal factors. When stress is examined as a composite, three major types are perceived: job, career, and life. How serious are the outcomes of such stress? The answer is that it depends on the person. Some people are better able to adjust to stress because of such things as

[11] For more on careers, see Harry Levinson, "A Second Career: The Possible Dream," *Harvard Business Review* (May–June 1983):122–29.
[12] American Heart Association, *Heart Facts* (Dallas: American Heart Association, 1977).

FIGURE 21-4 A Model for Organizational Stress Research

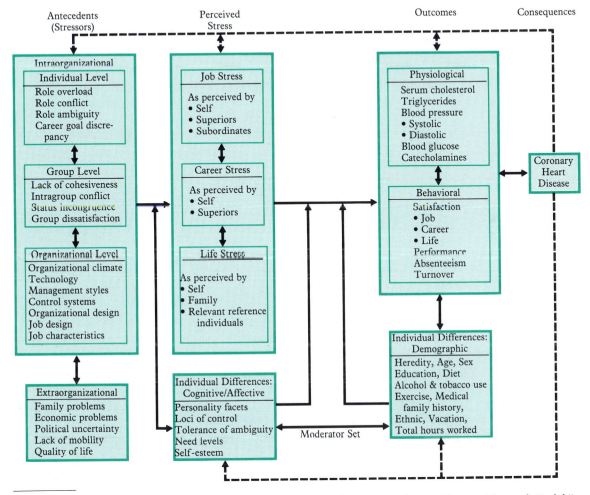

Source: Michael T. Matteson and John M. Ivancevich, "Organizational Stressors and Heart Disease: A Research Model," *Academy of Management Review* (October 1979):350. Reprinted by permission.

heredity (their bodies can withstand more stress), education (better educated people tend to be able to take more stressful situations than less well-educated people), exercise (they work it off by playing tennis or jogging), and vacation (they get away from the stress by going on a five-day cruise). Other people cannot deal with stress very well. These people are becoming the focus of attention.

What implications does the study or organizational stressors have for modern management? Michael T. Matteson and John M. Ivancevich, well known for their studies on stress and executive health, have noted the following management and organizational implications:

1. Accumulated evidence places the organization at the center of any discussion of stressors and coronary heart disease.
2. Behavioral factors and organizational stressors should be considered in developing coronary preventive medicine programs in much the same way that traditional risk factors such as blood pressure, cigarette smoking, and diet are considered.
3. Available research suggests that three levels of intraorganizational stressors and various or extraorganizational stressors should be viewed as interacting, including family circumstances, organizational climate, intragroup conflict, and role ambiguity.
4. The importance of individual differences in reactions to stressors must not be underestimated because for some people, organizational stressors are not harmful emotionally, physiologically, or psychologically while for others they are.
5. Managerial activities are not restricted to improving performance or increasing profitability; in the larger context of managerial accountability it rests in the implicit obligation to improve the quality of organizational life for subordinates.[13]

How can management address this area of stress and its effect on executive CHD? By creating and maintaining a work environment that contributes to the reduction of CHD and increases both general health and longevity. The important thing for you to realize is that in your career there will be times when stress is extremely great and you will have to learn to cope with it, if only for limited periods of time. One of the best ways to prepare yourself is to find out the type of person you are when it comes to stress. There are two basic personality patterns: Type A and Type B.

Type A and Type B Behaviors

In 1974, after a decade of medical research, two cardiologists wrote a book that has provided a wealth of information regarding the ability of individuals to cope with stress.[14] In their book they coined two terms that have become part of the literature of stress management: Type A and Type B behaviors. Of the two, Type A has received the greatest amount of attention because it is characteristic of individuals who suffer from CHD. Friedman and Rosenman described **Type A behavior** as an action-emotion complex that can be observed in any person

---

[13] Michael T. Matteson and John M. Ivancevich, "Organizational Stressors and Heart Disease: A Research Model," *Academy of Management Review* (October 1979):354–55.
[14] Meyer Friedman and Ray Rosenman, *Type A Behavior and Your Heart* (New York: Knopf, 1974).

who is aggressively involved in a chronic, incessant struggle to achieve more and more in less and less time and, if required to do so, against the opposing efforts of other things or other persons. In contrast, the Type B person is rarely harried by desires to obtain a wildly increasing number of things or participate in an endlessly growing series of events in an ever-decreasing amount of time. In particular, the main characteristics of Type A individuals include (1) a sense of time urgency (they try to get more and more done in less and less time), (2) a quest for numbers (they try to quantify things in terms of dollars or other measurable terms), (3) insecurity of status (they are outwardly confident and self-assured but are often insecure underneath and constantly struggling for recognition through the number of achievements and the rate at which their current status improves) and (4) aggression and hostility (they are extremely competitive and trend always to challenge other people in sports, games, work, and general discussions).[15]

Are you a Type A person? Or do you have some of the main characteristics of such people? The quiz in Table 21-11 provides some insights into this question. The important thing to remember is that if you are a Type A person (or have fairly similar characteristics), you are more prone to CHD than the average person. Additionally, even if you avoid coronary problems, you are still subject to burnout.[16]

Stress and Burnout

Individuals subjected to prolonged degrees of stress can suffer what is called **burnout**. In the beginning the person may actually increase performance and efficiency. This fact is sometimes referred to as the **Yerkes-Dodson** law, first described by Drs. Robert M. Yerkes and John D. Dodson of the Harvard Physiologic Laboratory. They showed that as stress increases, efficiency and performance also go up to a certain level. If the stress continues, however, performance and efficiency decrease.[17] The result of excessive stress is burnout.[18]

There are numerous symptoms of burnout

There are many symptoms of burnout. Some of the most common include chronic fatigue, job boredom, cynicism, impatience, irritability, and an unfulfilled need for recognition. How can you tell if you are a potential burnout victim? One way is to answer questions like those in Table 21-11, since Type A persons are most likely to suffer burnout. Another way is to realize that burnout

---

[15] Philip Goldberg, *Executive Health* (New York: McGraw-Hill, 1978), 103.

[16] See Jacqueline N. Hood and Leonard H. Chusmir, "Factors Determining Type A Behavior among Employed Women and Men," *Academy of Management Proceedings* (50th Anniversary Meeting: Chicago, IL, 1986), 332–36.

[17] Herbert Benson and Robert L. Allen, "How Much Stress Is Too Much?" *Harvard Business Review* (September–October 1980):88.

[18] See Ayala Pines and Elliot Aronson, "Why Managers Burn Out," *Sales and Marketing Management* (February 1989):34–38.

TABLE 21-11   Are You A Type A Person?

Read each of the following description and ask yourself, in each case, if the statement is descriptive of you. Note the number of times you answer yes.

1. Think of doing two or more things at the same time.
2. Schedule more and more activities into less and less time.
3. Fail to notice or be interested in your environment or things of beauty.
4. Hurry the speech of others.
5. Become unduly irritated when forced to wait in line.
6. Become unduly irritated when driving behind a car you think is moving too slowly.
7. Believe that if you want something done well, you have to do it yourself.
8. Gesticulate when you talk.
9. Frequently jiggle your knee or rapidly tap your fingers.
10. Use explosive speech patterns or frequent use of obscenities.
11. Have a fetish of always being on time.
12. Have difficulty sitting quietly or doing nothing.
13. Play nearly every game to win—even when you are playing against children.
14. Measure your own, and others' successes in quantitative terms (number of sales made, patients seen, books read)
15. Use head nodding, fist-clenching, table pounding or sucking in of air when speaking.
16. Become impatient when watching others do things you feel you can do better yourself.
17. Use rapid eye-blinking or tic-like eyebrow lifting.
18. Feel guilty when relaxing.
19. Have a tendency to dominate conversations and change the subject to topics that interest you.
20. Constantly find yourself having to move, walk, and eat rapidly.
21. Have great difficulty finding time to improve yourself or explore new and interesting things.
22. Evidence a great fear of slowing down because you feel your success is due to your ability to do things faster than others.
23. Create deadlines even if none exist currently.
24. Have few hobbies or diversions outside of your work.
25. Often try to do two things at the same time such as drive your car and read the morning newspaper.

If your answer to more than 15 of these is yes, you have Type A characteristics. If your answer to 20 or more is yes, you are undoubtedly a Type A person.

candidates have three distinguishing characteristics. One characteristic is that their problem is predominantly job related. Oliver Niehouse, a personnel development adviser, explains the idea this way:

> In many respects, individual worker problems . . . can contribute to a stressful environment. Some people thrive on stress; but even for them, there is a limit . . . The potential to exceed that limit can occur whenever a significant change in job responsibility takes place. For example, your organization absorbs another company and suddenly your human resources have doubled; you're trying to ferret out the human resources problems underlying a drop in productivity on an assembly line; or, like a manager at one computer firm who was given an opportunity, you dive into a heavy

schedule of organization and management development programs and workshops that tax your own resources.[19]

Idealists are subject to burnout . . .

A second distinguishing characteristic is excessive idealism or extremely high self-motivation or both. It is often the maverick executive with the "I've got to succeed" attitude who suffers the ill effects of burnout. Another typical victim of burnout is the manager whose entire objective is to win and who never looks closely at the end result. Upon reaching the goal the person asks, "Is this all there is?" Unsatisfied with the objective, the individual pushes on to new goals, never satisfied with current accomplishments and always looking toward new ones.

as are those who never slow down

A third distinguishing characteristic of burnout candidates is that they set goals that are often too difficult to reach. As a result, they are in a continual battle that can never be won. No matter how long or hard the person works, the goal is beyond his or her abilities. Should it become possible, the individual will revise the objective so that it again becomes unattainable. No wonder, then, that some experts define burnout as the "total depletion of one's physical and mental resources caused by excessive striving to reach some unrealistic, job-related goal(s).[20]

Learning to Cope

How can you manage stress, avoid burnout, and assure yourself a long, healthy career? The answer is by combining a moderate amount of work-related stress with a good diet and a regular schedule of exercise and relaxation.[21] Primary in this prescription is your diet. What nutritional experts say is true — you are what you eat. Americans typically consume unhealthy amounts of cholesterol, white flour, sugar, and salt. The U.S. Senate Select Committee on Nutrition and Human Needs has recommended the following dietary goals:

Set dietary goals

1. Increase consumption of fruits and vegetables and whole grains.
2. Decrease consumption of meat.
3. Increase consumption of poultry and fish.
4. Decrease consumption of foods high in fat.
5. Partially substitute polyunsaturated fat for saturated fat.
6. Substitute nonfat milk for whole milk.
7. Decrease consumption of butterfat, eggs, and other high-cholesterol sources.

---

[19] Oliver L. Niehouse, "Burnout: A Real Threat to Human Resources Managers," *Personnel* (September–October 1981):28.

[20] Niehouse, "Burnout," 29.

[21] Isabel Walker, "Getting In Shape for Business: Physical Fitness for Executives," *Management Today* (May 1985):99.

8. Decrease consumption of sugar and foods high in sugar content.
9. Decrease consumption of salt and foods high in salt content.[22]

Start a physical
fitness program
A second important way to cope is to develop a physical fitness program. By exercising regularly (jogging, playing tennis or racquetball, swimming, lifting weights, or doing calisthenics two to three times a week) you can keep yourself in good physical shape. Robert Kreitner, a management researcher, has noted that these physical fitness programs are now taking on organizational dimensions:

> Company-sponsored fitness programs have sprung up by the hundreds in recent years and represent a tremendous wellness resource. They can help counter the unhealthy side effects of the typical sedentary life/workstyle. Recent studies have begun to document the long-pro-claimed administrative and economic benefits of company fitness pro-grams. Among the documented benefits are lower absenteeism and turn-over and a positive impact on productivity. Employees who are encouraged in their pursuit of fitness by convenient access to quality facilities and sup-portive organizational climate will much more likely stick with a workout program than those with less supportive circumstances.[23]

How can you bring together the three important aspects of executive health: coping with stress, proper diet, and regular exercise? By making them a part of your own daily routine. You must systematically formulate a program that incorporates them into your daily life. Some of the key parts of such a program should be the following:

Coping with Stress

1. Avoid unrealistic deadlines.
2. Pace yourself.
3. Determine when you work best during the day and schedule the most difficult or complex work for those time periods; during the rest of the day carry out assignments requiring average or less-than-average demands.
4. Plan your work day in advance so you know what is supposed to be happening and you can get mentally prepared to meet these challenges.

---

[22] U.S. Senate, Report of the Select Committee on Nutrition and Human Needs, *Eating in America: Dietary Goals for the United States* (Cambridge, MA: MIT Press, 1977), 13.
[23] Robert Kreitner, "Personal Wellness: It's Just Good Business," *Business Horizons* (May–June 1982):34. Also see "Health Risk Assessment: The Neglected First Step is Corporate Wellness Programs," *Management Review* (June 1984):42, and Marc Leepson, "Does Wellness Really Work?" *Nations Business* (August 1988):46–49.

Diet

Develop an overall strategy for maintaining your health

1. Do not eat too much.
2. If you have to lose some weight, cut down on supper because there is less time to burn off these calories before you go to bed.
3. Keep your alcohol intake to one to two drinks a day maximum.
4. In addition to the earlier suggestions on diet, stay away from desserts and other fattening foods unless you are on a regular exercise program and can work off these calories.

Exercise

1. Engage in a regular physical activity every day and, if you can have the time (and ability) look into semi rigorous activity such as swimming, jogging, handball, or racquetball on a regular basis (two to three times a week). Be sure to have a physical exam before starting any of these programs
2. When you exercise, work on relaxing your mind by thinking about something that makes you happy and helps you develop a positive mental attitude.
3. If you find yourself getting nervous or tense during the day, sit comfortably in a quiet location and with your eyes closed, and work to calm yourself mentally. Examine what is bothering you and gently try to reestablish a psychological equilibrium.[24]

SUMMARY

1. Successful executives have very similar profiles. Perhaps the most important profile characteristic is their competence. They know their jobs. These individuals also tend to be long-time employees of the firms they head. Recent research shows that these executives come from many different functional areas and that they are well compensated for their efforts.
2. Most people go through a series of career phases or stages. The six most common are breaking away, initial adulthood, a transition period, settling down, possible mid-life crisis, and an establishment of equilibrium.
3. Many people encounter career problems. Some of the most common for people just starting out include simple and boring work, organizational

---

[24] See Kenneth J. Smith, G. Timothy Haight, and George S. Everly, Jr.,"Evaluating Corporate Wellness Investments," *The Internal Auditor* (February 1986):28–34.

politics, knowing what counts, loyalty issues, and ethical problems. Later on the most common problem is the career plateau.

4. Numerous career strategies can help you succeed. One of these is a sound self-evaluation. By determining what you are good at and what you like, you can help identify an initial career path. A complementary approach is to write an obituary or describe meaningful job events you would like to have happen to you during your career.

5. A second career strategy is the effective use of career tactics. You should be a high performer, keep a hero file, get into a management position as quickly as possible, find a sponsor, help your boss succeed, seek opportunity before money, and keep yourself mobile.

6. A third career strategy is to formulate a career development plan. This involves investigating organizational efforts designed to assist in career pathing, learning to negotiate for yourself, and aligning your job-related and personal needs with your career stages.

7. Another important part of career planning is executive health. Millions of Americans suffer from heart and blood vessel disease, which is partially attributable to stress. Type A people are most likely to suffer coronary heart disease. Three interdependent steps people can take to deal with this problem are to cope with stress, follow a proper diet, and exercise regularly.

KEY TERMS

Breaking away   The first career phase. During this period individuals begin establishing independence and autonomy from their parents.

Burnout   A total depletion of one's physical and mental resources caused by excessive striving to reach some unrealistic, job-related goals.

Career plateau   A period during which individuals find that their upward progress is halted and, in many cases, their climb to the top is over.

Establishment of equilibrium   A career phase during which individuals reevaluate their progress, find that things are going along pretty well, and feel a large degree of contentment, optimism, and stability.

Ethics   Principles that determine right and wrong conduct.

Initial adulthood   The second career phase. During this period many people begin developing organizational and professional ties and formulating a career plan.

Mid-life crisis   A career phase during which individuals evaluate their work progress, determine that things are not going well for them, and encounter strong psychological stress which can result in their doing foolish or bizarre things.

Settling down   The fourth career phase. During this period most people begin working hard to establish the groundwork for their career advancement.

Stressor   A factor, intraorganizational or extraorganizational in nature, that results in tension, anxiety, nervousness, or other forms of stress.

Transition period   The third career phase. During this period people evaluate their career progress and sometimes, if things are not going according to their plan, move to another organization.

Type A behavior   Behavior that is characterized by an action-emotion complex that can be observed in any person who is aggressively involved in a chronic, incessant struggle to achieve more and more in less and less time.

Yerkes-Dodson law   A law of physiology that holds that as stress increases, efficiency and performance initially increase and then decrease.

QUESTIONS FOR ANALYSIS AND DISCUSSION

1. If the current president of a firm is a finance person, how likely is it that the next president will also be a finance person? Explain.
2. How well are executives compensated? Cite some data to support your conclusion.
3. What is the major factor that accounts for executive success? Be complete in your answer.
4. In general terms, most people go through a series of career phases or stages. What are these phases or stages? Identify and describe each in detail.
5. Do the career motivations of young men differ from those of young women? Explain, being sure to cite statistics to back up your answer.
6. Are there any particular problems that you are likely to encounter when starting out your career? Identify and describe three.
7. What is a career plateau? What causes such a plateau? How can such a problem be overcome? Explain.
8. In making a self-evaluation, what are some of the most important questions you should ask? State and describe four.
9. Of what value is writing an obituary to an individual interested in career planning? How can writing down a list of important or meaningful job-related events that you would like to have happen to you during your career help your plan for the future? Explain.
10. Are there any career tactics that can help you increase your chances of success? Identify and describe four.
11. Of what value is a career development plan? What would be included in such a plan? Be as complete as possible in your description.
12. In what way is stress related to coronary heart disease? Explain, being sure to include information from Figure 21-4 in your answer.
13. How does a Type A person act? In what way is this kind of behavior likely to lead to coronary heart disease?
14. How are stress and burnout related? If a person suffers from stress, will he or she also suffer burnout? Explain.

15. How can you manage stress, avoid burnout, and assure yourself a long, healthy career? Be sure to include in your answer a discussion of diet and physical fitness.

CASE

While The Quitting's Good

Sally Cabrera is not happy. For the last year, ever since she was graduated from college, she has worked for a utility firm in the Midwest. During this time she has found herself disillusioned, frustrated, angry, and exhausted.

When Sally first started her job, she had a great amount of enthusiasm and drive. She was looking forward to using all of the tools and techniques she had studied in college. That is not what happened, however. Within a few weeks it was obvious to her that she could do the job with just a high school diploma. Everything was highly routine and simple. Before long Sally found herself becoming bored with the work. Mostly she just read reports, checked data, and kept her boss informed.

In the beginning her boss asked her questions about what the data meant. Sally liked this because it gave her a chance to make a systematic analysis of the information. It soon became evident, however, that the boss was simply trying to get a better personal understanding of the data; it was not to give Sally a chance for analytical experience. In fact, on occasion Sally asked her boss if he would like her to work up some special types of reports or data comparisons, but he always said no.

Sally attributed a great deal of her boss's lack of concern to the fact that rigorous data analysis was not vital to the work. She concluded that the boss had plenty to do without getting into other projects.

Three weeks ago Sally received her annual performance evaluation. She was ranked low/average. Her boss wrote on her evaluation that she had average drive, was only marginally competent in her work, and did not show a great deal of interest or enthusiasm for the job. Sally was shocked. She felt that she had gone out of her way to do a good job. If anything, she thought she would get a superior rating.

After talking with three other people who started at the same time she did, Sally learned that her performance rating was the lowest of all. Additionally, one of these people told her that he had learned he was going to be promoted within a week. Given her performance evaluation, Sally knows that there is no chance of her being promoted. In fact, she thinks it may be time to start looking around for employment elsewhere. "I might as well move while I'm mobile," she told her mom. "I've only been with this firm for a year and already I've fallen behind those who started when I did. If I wait another year, I might not be able to find anything. After all, if I got a low/average rating when I was really trying, what kind of rating will I get now that I've finally given up? I think I'd better quit while the quitting's good."

1. What typical problems did Sally run into on her first job? Identify and describe them.
2. Drawing upon your understanding of career tactics, what would you recommend that Sally do now? Explain.
3. Before she decides to accept another job offer, what should Sally do to prevent running into the same problem again? Explain.

YOU BE THE CONSULTANT

A Matter of Life Or Death

No one ever gave Josh Adams anything for nothing. He earned it all. So when he was elected chief executive officer (CEO) of his corporation at the age of 43, he openly admitted that he got where he was through drive, determination, and hard work. In fact, he loved to recount some of his trials and tribulations to young managers in the firm, urging them to keep their noses to the grindstone. "Maybe someday you'll replace me," he told them. "Remember, you're never too young to succeed."

When he assumed the CEO position, Josh began to work even harder. He increased the number of people in his office by 50 percent, and the amount of work that the office generated more than doubled. At the same time, Josh was gone almost half the time. Four months ago his schedule had him in Saudi Arabia the first week of the month; Paris, London, and Brussels the second week; back at the home office the third week; and in Tokyo the fourth week.

Three months ago he was in Los Angeles to break ground for a new office building the firm was constructing there. As usual his schedule was hectic. As he was heading back to the airport Josh became ill. His assistant ordered the driver to head for the UCLA Medical Center. Josh was lucky. Within an hour he was admitted and initial tests had been run. Josh had suffered a mild heart attack. "If you had been in the air winging your way back to New York," the doctor told him, "you might have wound up in the hospital for three months. As it is, you'll be with us for three weeks."

Josh was relieved, "I'm glad it's not going to be any longer than that," he told the doctor. "I've got a million things to do back at the office." It was then that the doctor pulled his chair up close to Josh's bed and started talking in a hushed, serious tone. The essence of what he said was the following:

> Listen, forget all of this stuff about a lot of work back at the office. You're darned lucky not to have had your entire career terminated. You are a very sick man. Oh sure, I know how hard you work. I've read your comments in

the newspaper. You're a national celebrity. And you're also going to be the youngest CEO in the cemetery this month. Who do you think you are? Do you think your body is going to last forever? Look at how far you've come in your short lifetime. You're one of the most famous businesspeople in the country. But everything has its price. I've heard you quoted as saying just that. So apply your own philosophy to yourself. Look at how fast you work, how fast you live. You've lived more in 43 years than most people have in their entire lifetime. Now it's catching up with you. Do you exercise? Do you watch what you eat? Do you take time to relax? Undoubtedly not. So think about it, Josh. You're going to have to change your lifestyle or you're going to die.

The doctor's words shocked Josh. He had never really thought much about his health. He was always able to get by on four or five hours of sleep a night. Oh sure, he did not eat very healthful foods but he took a vitamin pill every day. And as far as exercise was concerned, while he did not follow any formal program, he felt that he got more than enough exercise running for planes and taxis. Now he thinks that the doctor might be right. Perhaps he has neglected his health in his never-ending quest for the top. Yet he still finds himself caught in a dilemma.

On the one hand, Josh believes he probably should slow down. He needs a better plan for coping with stress. A good diet and a regular exercise program would also help. On the other hand, he has gotten where he is because of his incessant drive. He has developed a lifestyle which, while it is different from that of most other people, has allowed him to succeed where just about everyone else has failed. He has risen far above the crowd. If he changes his habits, he is afraid that he will fall back into the group of "average" individuals found in every organization. How can he protect his unique character and philosophy if he allows himself to adopt a slower lifestyle? The answer to this question still evades him, but Josh knows that he has to do something. At the moment, his doctor's parting words are still ringing inside of his head, "If you don't slow down, you'll kill yourself. Only you can make that decision, Josh. Do you want to live or do you want to die?"

Your Consultation

Assume that you are Josh's closest friend and that he has shared his dilemma with you. What would you advise him to do? Explain, being sure to incorporate into your answer a discussion of executive health, Type A behavior, stress and burnout, diet, and exercise. Phrase your answer so that it will help Josh cope with the stresses of a CEO's job while still helping him lead a long, healthy life.

Integrative Case Study

MARY KAY COSMETICS, INC. — CORPORATE PLANNING IN AN ERA OF UNCERTAINTY

Mary Kay Cosmetics, Inc. of Dallas, Texas, is an international manufacturer and distributor of skin care products, makeup items, toiletry items, accessories, and hair care products. Founded in 1963 by Mary Kay Ash, a highly motivated entrepreneur, the firm experienced spectacular sales growth in its early years. As a direct selling organization, much of its success was based on motivating and constantly replenishing its over 170,000-member sales force. Mary Kay had planned to become "the finest and largest skin care teaching organization in the world."

Senior management recognized in early 1989 that the firm was suffering from some of the same problems which were affecting the whole direct sales industry. The company was suddenly having problems attracting new recruits who would become beauty consultants and sales directors as well as consumers of the firm's product line. Management was evaluating a corporate strategy which had been developed by the firm's founder. The organization was repositioning itself for future growth. The question was now, "What do we need to do to get us where we want to go, to reach the kind of customer we want to reach, to recruit the kind of consultant we want to recruit?"

Background Information

Mary Kay Cosmetics was founded on September 13, 1963 in Dallas, Texas, by Mary Kay (now Mary Kay Ash). The company had an initial working capital of $5,000, the right to use a skin care formula that had been created by a hide tanner, and nine saleswomen. The first headquarters was a 500-square-foot storefront in Exchange Park, a large bank and office building complex in Dallas.

The first basic line of cosmetics was manufactured to specification under the label of "Beauty by Mary Kay" by another firm. It included what was called the "Basic Skin Care Set." It consisted of a limited number of basic items which when used as the company suggested provided a balanced program of skin care. The firm also sold custom wigs. Wigs were styled at the headquarters location and at skin care shows and were originally used as a traffic generator. They were discontinued in 1965. Management believed that it could achieve corporate success in direct sales by establishing a "dream company" which would be based on the personal philosophies of the founder. The Mary Kay philosophy

This case was prepared by James W. Camerius of Northern Michigan University. Presented to the Midwest Society for Case Research Workshop, 1989. All rights reserved to the author and to the Midwest Society for Case Research. Copyright © 1989 by James W. Camerius.

suggested that every person associated with the company, from the chairman of the board to the newest recruit, live by the golden rule, "Do unto others as you would have them do unto you," and the priorities of God first, family second, and career third.

Initial corporate strategies included heavy emphasis on personal relationships, opportunities for women to fully utilize their skills and talents, no geographical restrictions on sales territories, and a sales presentation in the home for no more than five or six women. Merchandise was available for immediate delivery from stock. All products were sold on a cash basis. Every Mary Kay representative was considered an independent businessperson to be remunerated in the form of commission. Pink was selected as the corporate color.

By 1989, Mary Kay Cosmetics, Inc. had again become a private corporation after going public in 1968. It had sales in 1988 of $405,730,000, a sales staff of 170,000 beauty consultants and sales directors, a compensation structure to allow women to earn commensurate with their individual abilities and efforts, and total brand awareness of ninety percent of all American women. Mary Kay was ranked by the *Wall Street Journal* as an industry leader in basic skin care research and in product development. The company had a new production facility, a new warehouse, and a new corporate headquarters in Dallas, all of which were internally financed. The product line was distributed throughout the United States and through wholly owned subsidiaries in Australia, Canada, Argentina, and West Germany. The average number of beauty consultants, their average productivity, and net sales for the years 1984–1988 are shown in Figure 1.

The Mary Kay Mystique

Much of the initial and continuing success of the firm was attributed to the entrepreneurial spirit of its founder and chairperson emeritus, Mary Kay Ash. Mary Kay traced her strong-willed, competitive spirit to the constant, positive reinforcement her mother gave her while growing up in Texas. "I was taught to put my best effort into everything I did, and I can honestly say that I've always

---

FIGURE 1   Analysis of Mary Kay Independent Beauty Consultants

1984–1988

Year	Average Number of Consultants	Average Productivity	Net Sales ($000)
1988	170,316	$2,382	$405,730
1987	148,080	$2,199	$325,647
1986	141,113	$1,807	$255,016
1985	145,493	$1,711	$248,970
1984	173,101	$1,603	$277,500

done that," Mary Kay said. "I competed with myself and strove to excel." Her "you can do it" philosophy guided the company through the challenges and setbacks of its early years.

Mary Kay spent 13 years of her professional direct sales career with Stanley Home Products, Inc. She became one of the firm's leading salespersons and was promoted to management. She also worked for another 11 years in a similar position with a company in Houston called World Gift. After becoming its national training director for 43 states, she left the organization. Later, upon deciding that retirement did not satisfy her, she developed a strategy and philosophy that was to become Mary Kay Cosmetics. She became its first president. A son, Richard Rogers, joined her upon the death of her second husband. Another son, Ben, and a daughter, Marilyn, eventually became part of the organization.

As president, Mary Kay became a walking showcase for the company's products. Her values and motivational incentives became the basis for the firm's marketing program. Her definitions of happiness brought women to the firm as beauty consultants, sales directors and users of the product line. "Under her 'frills and lace' is a high-powered businesswoman who has built a skin care empire, and in a pioneering style," suggested *Marketing and Media Decisions,* a trade magazine. The color pink, her favorite color, was found in her attire, her office, her home, and every facet of corporate life.

A unique and idealistic individual, Mary Kay Ash was called "one of the most influential and respected personalities in business and philanthropic circles" by *Executive Female,* a respected magazine among entrepreneurs. She also received many of the most distinguished cosmetic, direct sales, and professional awards, including "Cosmetic Career Woman of the Year," "Direct Selling Hall of Fame," and the 1978 "Horatio Alger Award." She was the cover feature on several magazines, including the *Saturday Evening Post; Business Week* named her one of America's top corporate women, and *Time* cited her in its economy and business section. She also appeared on such television shows as "Sixty Minutes," "Phil Donahue," and "Good Morning America."

"Far from being an employer," indicated Nicole Woolsey Biggart in a recent book on direct selling organization leadership, "Mary Kay Ash . . . is mother, sister, guardian angel, and patron saint to the women who sell her products." In this context a national sales director maintained, "We don't adore Mary Kay, we admire her, and we would want to emulate her." In the belief that "adore" versus "admire" was a good distinction, management felt that Mary Kay had positioned the company for the day when "she no longer would be here." As president, Mary Kay had maintained, "Although Mary Kay Cosmetics was created as the dream of one woman, it has long since achieved independent existence. And because our company is grounded in a solid foundation of specific values and principles, its continuance no longer depends upon any single person."

A number of programs were in place to cushion the eventual departure of

Mary Kay from active management. Initially, her philosophy was captured on film, in books, and in articles written about her. Also, a national sales director program, made up of the firm's top saleswomen, was established to emphasize continuing the Mary Kay spirit in the company. Mary Kay was developed as an entity as opposed to an individual by perpetuating all of the ideas that she felt should be part of her dream company. "This is important," indicated Richard C. Bartlett, the current president in an interview, "here we are talking about philosophical beliefs which traditionally, in business and religion and other organizations, do continue on if the organization is imbued with them."

On November 10, 1987, Mary Kay Ash was named chairman emeritus. Richard R. Rogers, her son, was named chairman. Richard C. Bartlett, whose initial experience in direct selling was with Tupperware and later as vice president of marketing at Mary Kay, was named president and chief operating officer. "I plan to remain active in the firm on a continuing basis, working with salespeople," indicated Mary Kay. "Our sales force now consists of tens of thousands of skilled sales professionals, and they are supported by an experienced management team."

The Corporate Concept

The original corporate strategy of the firm was based on the "Mary Kay Marketing Plan." In the plan the sales force or beauty consultants sold the company's skin care products at home demonstration shows. They were supervised and motivated by sales directors who also were responsible for replenishing the sales force on a continuing basis with new recruits. The plan was a corporate strategy designed to include the best features and avoid the mistakes Mary Kay had previously encountered in her twenty years with direct selling companies.

As a part of the plan, the marketing program was intended to foster retail sales to ultimate consumers. Commissions were earned by beauty consultants on products sold at retail prices to ultimate consumers. All products were purchased directly from the company and were based on the same discount schedule. All sales directors were once beauty consultants, thus avoiding the multilevel practice of selling franchises or distributorships.

In the plan there were no territories to limit where consultants could sell or recruit. The consultant was required to purchase a showcase of basic products and carry an inventory. Consultants were encouraged to sell only Mary Kay products during their skin care classes to avoid creating trademark confusion and divided effort.

Consultants were considered to be self-employed. The marketing plan was intended to support the independent contractor status. At the corporate level, management was expected to manufacture quality cosmetics, plan product and market development, provide for discounts and commissions, advertise, plan for working capital for corporate growth, and offer incentive awards and prizes for beauty consultants who excelled in sales, recruiting, or leadership.

One of the most unique aspects of the marketing plan was the use of national and regional seminars, career conferences, and management conferences which individuals could attend on a voluntary basis for inspiration, training, and general professional upgrading. At the national level, this strategy manifested itself annually in what the company called "Seminar." Seminar was an elaborately produced series of four consecutive three-day sessions which attracted a total of 24,000 sales participants to the Dallas Convention Center.

The highly motivational event had a tradition of recognition, education, and entertainment. It included hours of classes on product knowledge, marketing and sales techniques, and other business management topics. It culminated in an awards night in which thousands of glamorous, elegantly dressed, bejeweled women received extravagant recognition as achievers in the organization. Mary Kay traditionally presided over the event. She appeared on stage, sometimes emerging at the top of a series of lighted stairs, sometimes arriving in a carriage drawn by white horses and surrounded by footmen.

Typically, participants would proceed to the stage to claim expensive prizes such as mink coats, gold and diamond jewelry, trips to places like Acapulco, and use of new pale pink Cadillacs, Buicks, and Oldsmobiles. "So in our company, we eliminated practical gifts," indicated Mary Kay, "I would try to choose prizes that would excite and thrill the recipient. I thought that the best prizes were things a woman wanted but probably wouldn't buy for herself." The legendary pink Cadillac, for many, became a symbol of Mary Kay Cosmetics and its incentive programs.

The Changing External Environment

All of the firm's products were sold on the principal bases of price and quality in highly competitive markets. On the basis of information available to it from industry sources, management believed there were some 13,000 companies (including both direct sales and manufacturing companies) that had products that competed with Mary Kay. The firm competed directly with direct sales companies in sales of cosmetics products and indirectly with firms which manufactured cosmetics and toiletry items which were sold in retail or department stores. It also competed in the recruiting of independent sales persons from other direct selling organizations whose product lines may or may not have competed with those of Mary Kay.

The direct selling industry consisted of a few well-established companies and many smaller firms which sold about every product imaginable, including toys, animal food, plant care products, clothing, computer software, and financial services. Among the dominant companies were Avon (cosmetics), Amway Corp. (home cleaning products), Shaklee Corp. (vitamins and health foods), Encyclopedia Britannica, Tupperware (plastic dishes and food containers), Consolidated Foods, Electrolux (vacuum cleaners), and the Fuller Brush Co. (household products). Avon Products, Inc., was substantially larger than Mary Kay in terms of total independent sales people, sales volume, and resources.

Several other competitors, such as Revlon, Inc., a firm that sold cosmetics primarily through retail stores, were larger than Mary Kay in terms of sales and had more resources.

By the late 1980s corporate management at Mary Kay considered the direct selling industry and the cosmetics industry to be at maturity. The spectacular sales growth characteristic of the 1960s and 1970s had given way to a pattern of stagnant revenue and profit growth. The industry was having difficulty attracting new sales people who generated much of its sales growth and provided a return to sales directors. Competition for the customer was great, as there were not as many users coming into the market. Industry problems were blamed on a number of factors: the increasing number of working women, which cut into both the number of available recruits and sales targets; the improvement in the economy, which encouraged women to avoid involvement in part-time sales and to shop for more expensive beauty products; shorter product life cycles, which forced new products, new innovations, and twists of existing products which were getting old; and the growing competition from firms selling similar products. There were also hostile takeovers, such as the 1989 bid of Amway Corporation for Avon Products, Inc., and leveraged buyouts, such as the December 1985, LBO of Mary Kay by its founders. According to President Bartlett, senior management would have to "react by being much more flexible, by being able to come out with new products, by introducing new innovations, and by developing new strategies for existing products that were getting old."

Industry research had identified Avon, a direct competitor, as having products which were used by older people who wanted a less expensive product. Noxell, the manufacturer of Cover Girl products, was viewed as the creator of a moderately upscale product line that appealed to a younger market. Estée Lauder was a product line that was more upscale and appealed to an older market segment. In product image, Estée Lauder had been historically in an enviable position. The firm cultivated this in all of its literature, all of its packaging, and in all of its product formulas. Revlon, whose image varied by product line, was sold through department stores and mass merchandisers. It built a multi-billion dollar business by buying out old established lines like Max Factor, Charles of the Ritz, Germain Monte, Diane VonFurstenberg, and Almae.

Although maturity was sometimes looked on with disfavor, Mary Kay executives felt that this did not mean a lack of opportunity for increased profitability or lack of opportunity to increase sales. The changing nature of competition in the cosmetics market was identified as one of the strategic concerns in the design of the Mary Kay product line. Both the mass market and upscale segments of the skin care marketplace were perceived to be changing rapidly. In both cases a plethora of new entries emerged, some from well-established American firms such as Estée Lauder, some from innovative American firms such as S. C. Johnson, and some from European or Japanese firms. One example was an entry from L'Oreal, a European firm. The skin care line, Plentitude, was sold through mass market outlets. An example of a Japanese firm was the Kao

Safina line which was introduced through Kao's American acquisition, Jergens Skin Care.

The changing nature of science and technology was also identified as a strategic concern in an analysis of the external environment. Management felt that the period of the late 1980s and the early 1990s would see the debut of several new "cosmeceuticals"—products marketed as drugs and capable of making drug claims, but with wide impact on the pharmaceutical and cosmetics markets. Upjohn's Rogaine and Ortho Laboratories' Retin-A, treatments for acne which doubled as antiwrinkle creams, were predicted to become over-the-counter drugs within the next two to three years. New drug applications for six to eight other retinoids were known to be under way with antiaging claims. At the same time, greater understanding of skin physiology enabled the development of more advanced traditional skin care products, including those which could legitimately make counterirritant claims and those which could protect users from environmental damage, such as from the sun.

The decade also saw a proliferation of regulatory activity affecting the cosmetics industry. In the United States such activity was seen from the Food and Drug Administration (FDA), the Federal Trade Commission (FTC), Congress, and various state legislatures. At the same time, cosmetics regulations were changing in the European Economic Community (EEC) countries and Argentina, Canada, and Australia. Prospects for expansion into Mexico and Thailand presented the challenge of learning to deal with regulations in markets that were new to Mary Kay. It was clear that a new wave of regulatory activity affecting the industry had commenced. Ingredients, claims, packaging, testing, advertising, and other activities of the cosmetics industry were being closely scrutinized by regulators and legislators with a view toward regulatory control. A series of hearings held by Congressman Ron Wyden (D-OR) during 1988 were predicted to produce new cosmetics legislation in Congress.

Corporate research revealed that the Mary Kay customer was primarily identified by its beauty consultants. The company did very little direct customer prospecting. Beauty consultants found their customers one by one or in small groups through referrals, and by holding skin care classes where they might know one person but not the other members of the group. The typical Mary Kay customer was a female, in her late thirties, married, and caucasian. Geographically, she lived in all fifty states as well as in those countries where Mary Kay had operations. Most customers were rural and suburban as opposed to urban. The Mary Kay method of selling was perceived by management to be more disposed to the woman who might not have easy access to a store and also appeared to lend itself on the supply side of mobility by automobile. By occupation, customers were white collar, and professional with moderate incomes and a high school education with some college. In practice, the upper and lower ends of a market segmented by social stratification variables tended to be neglected. Consultants were perceived to be slightly more upscale than their typical customer and customarily sold down to lower levels of social stratification.

The senior vice president of Mary Kay, Barbara Beasley, had hoped to expand the customer base through greater penetration in three key segments: blacks, hispanics, and mature women. In a corporate analysis of the changing consumer, she concluded that because of greater education and disposable income, many more women were becoming regular users of product lines used previously by only a few consumers. Increased consumer sophistication meant that high performance products would be required that had meaningful claims and would fit within the Mary Kay context of a teaching orientation. The market was identified as becoming increasingly segmented by usage as consumers gravitated toward brand positions such as those formulated for sensitive skin, for contact lens wearers, for mature skin, and for ethnic consumers.

Marketing Strategies

Several marketing strategies emerged as the result of an overall reexamination of existing corporate strategies. The area receiving initial attention was the product line. The lines, as reviewed in Figure 2, consisted of skin care products for women and for men, glamour items, toiletry items for women and for men, accessories, and hair care products. Skin care products, in various formulas related to skin type, included cleansers, skin fresheners, facial masks, moisturizers and foundation makeup, and were sold in sets as a five-step beauty program. Glamour items or cosmetics included lip and eye colors, mascaras, blushers, eye liners, face powder, and lip gloss. Toiletry items included hand and body lotions, bath products, and colognes. Hair care products consisted of shampoo, conditioners, and hair spray. Accessories such as samples, makeup mirrors, cosmetics bags, and travel kits were sold primarily as hostess gifts, business supplies, or sales aids.

FIGURE 2   Product Line by Sales Percentage

	Year Ended December 31,			
	1988	1987	1986	1985
Skin Care Products for Women	38%	40%	46%	41%
Skin Care Products for Men	1	2	1	1
Glamour Items	28	32	24	31
Nail Care Products	7	—	—	—
Toiletry Items for Women	13	13	15	13
Toiletry Items for Men	3	3	3	2
Hair Care Products	1	1	2	2
Accessories	9	9	9	10
Total	100%	100%	100%	100%

The Product Lines

There had been no significant additions to the product line in the first thirteen years of the company. Mary Kay had purchased the rights to a line that she had been using personally for about ten years. Initially, the line consisted of only ten products focused on skin care. Although management evaluated the product line on an ongoing basis, adjustments were kept to a minimum. Corporate policy had been to purposely limit the line to a minimum number of essential skin care and glamour items. Each company consultant was encouraged to carry a basic inventory. With a product line of no more than fifty items, inventory could be kept at a manageable level, products could be delivered immediately, and product information could be kept at a manageable level (see Figure 2).

The Mary Kay product strategy was to offer "preeminent" products to customers. According to management definition, each product sold was "to be outstanding; to stand above others; to have paramount rank, dignity, or importance." This was to mean products would be of excellent quality, be competitively priced, and be safe to use. As the product line was limited, compared to competition, each individual product had to appeal to a reasonably large segment of consumers. New product introductions were made in the cosmetics, skin care, fragrances, and toiletries markets. The five-year product plan was to focus on three major areas: (1) update, enhance, and improve current product lines, formulations, and packaging; (2) introduce significant new products in the treatment/skin care category; and (3) introduce a completely updated glamour line which would include a new system for recommending and using color, new product formulations, new packaging, and updated shades. The value-added provided by the consultant would be enhanced by offering consumer-oriented videos, brochures, profiles, packaging inserts, and other educational material.

The Mary Kay Color Awareness program was introduced to update the glamour line. Its intent was to simplify the selection of glamour makeup shades by guiding women in their own color decisions and was based on three key principles: skin tone, personal preference, and wardrobe. With the program, the sales force had the ability to help customers make color choices in these areas. A line of color-coordinated eye shadows, lip colors, and blushers was introduced to support the program.

A reformulated skin care line specifically designed for men was introduced in 1987 as part of the strategy to update the skin care line. It consisted of a cleansing bar, toner, facial conditioner and oil absorber, sunscreen, moisturizer, and shave cream. It replaced a product the company called "Mr. K" skin care which was the women's products repackaged in brown tubes. Management made its appeal to women who bought the product for men by saying, "Don't you care about your husband's skin? Look what it did for you. Look what it can do for him." Management predicted that this would be a growth area as more and more men started to care about their skin.

A skin care program called "skin wellness" was introduced as an education program for consumers on awareness of the factors that would impact the skin, particularly what sunlight was going to do. It was considered a natural fit for Mary Kay because of the teaching orientation of the sales process. It educated the consumer on how to identify certain kinds of skin cancers in the early stages. It advised a monthly program of skin self-examination in which the consumer would literally look over her body from head to toes in a mirror. Irregularities would be checked again in a month to see if they had changed. There was no mention of Mary Kay products in the program. Although perceived as a consumer affairs, goodwill, and trust-building program, the consumer could buy products from Mary Kay which would help with protection from the sun.

Packaging

Pink was selected as the corporate color because Mary Kay thought that attractive pink packages would be left out on display in the white bathrooms in vogue in 1963. The entire product line, however, had recently been repackaged. Every item was changed to make graphics consistent, to be up-to-date, and to have individual identity but still look like it was part of the Mary Kay family of products. A new corporate logo, a mix of gold and hot yellow to symbolize the heat of the sun and its eclipse, was featured on the new packages. A new shade of pink, one which was more mauve and less yellow, was selected to complement the logo. It was considered to be more subtle, more current, more upscale than the shade of pink that had become the corporate color. It was part of the quality and value image that the company wanted to convey. The new pink would ultimately find its way onto company trucks, uniforms, promotional material, and ultimately the Cadillacs.

Advertising and Promotion

In the early 1980s, when the company was growing at a very fast rate, management experimented with consumer advertising. The program was initiated in the sales division, not marketing. The advertising campaign involved magazines as well as television advertisements. Although no great change in consumer demand was documented, the reaction from the sales force was very positive. Management had concluded that if it were to use advertising in the future, it would want to impart a message to the consumer that would improve the corporate image and support the field sales force in the form of recognition and compensation.

Management justified its lack of interest in consumer advertising by claiming that it spent what its competitors spent on advertising in compensating the sales force. About thirty-three percent of total dollar income of the firm was estimated to go back to the field sales force in terms of commission and rewards. Promotional efforts were concentrated on rewarding the field sales force for their accomplishments. In seminars, for example, thousands of consultants and sales directors were presented with more than $5 million in selected prizes for their outstanding performance.

The firm had an active public relations and publicity program which centered on Mary Kay Ash, launching new products in fashion magazines, and publicizing the activities and accomplishments of the field sales force. Press releases in the form of corporate publicity and financial information were a part of this program.

Direct Support

A direct support program was introduced as part of a program to "build a company of substance, to create a product line of high quality, and to provide a service of value to the consumer." The program involved direct mail. Consultants sent the names of their customers to corporate headquarters. Management then did a mailing to the customer that appeared to come from the beauty consultant. An upscale, four-color brochure plus a personal letter was included that identified both the consultant and consumer by name. The beauty consultant would then follow up by telephone to the consumer to inquire if the information had been received. Initially, the program created some suspicion from the field sales force. Sales people thought that management was going to take these customer names and create a house account and service customers directly. "So we worked on that for a while," contended Barbara Beasley, senior vice president for marketing, "and I think we were able to prove to them that our objective was not to bypass the consultant in starting up this direct mail program, but rather to support the consultant, which is why it's called direct support." The direct support program was based on the consultant's contacts. If the consultant did not make the follow-up telephone call, if the consultant didn't deliver the products to the consumer, then no sale was ever made. All products always were sold through the sales force.

Beauty consultants were offered products at wholesale discounts from suggested retail prices, for resale to retail customers. At retail, the Mary Kay product line was priced competitively, just below brands which were distributed through department stores and generally well above direct retail store/mass distributed brands. Company literature included suggested retail prices, but the ultimate retail price was determined by the consultant who could charge less than the suggested retail by running her own promotions. "She can ultimately set the retail," said Curran Croskeys, vice president of product marketing at Mary Kay. "She buys it at a discount off retail, so it's up to her as to how much profit she wants to make."

Planning in a Marketing-Orientated Firm

Philosophically, corporate planning at Mary Kay Cosmetics was based on the golden rule, "Do unto others as you would have them do unto you," and the priorities of God first, family second, and career third. Mary Kay maintained, "I've found when you just let go and place yourself in God's hands, everything in your life goes right. I believe we have success because God has led us all the way." In this context she identified her son, Richard Rogers, chairman of the board and chief executive officer, as a "brilliant administrator and outstanding corporate planner [who] is recognized as one of today's bright, young financial geniuses." "Yet," she noted, "not even he can look at computer printouts or market surveys and truly predict the future."

On a more operational basis, the management team was led by Bartlett as president and chief operating officer. The organization, in Bartlett's experience, was really focused on celebrating the achievements of the sales force. In a typical organization chart, he maintained, the board chairman, the president, vice presidents, and managers were ordered down to the sales organization. At Mary Kay the situation was thought of in the reverse. The sales force was perceived to be at the top. The president's job was to support the executive team, who in turn supported other people, who in turn supported the sales force. "The program was based upon," as Bartlett suggested, "loyalty to the people involved, loyalty to the product, and loyalty to the plan." There was a loyalty to the people, such as the director who brought the consultant into the business. There was product brand loyalty, built up because the company found that it's a rare woman who could effectively sell the company's products who didn't believe in them. And there was loyalty to the plan in the form of compensation, recognition, and incentive contests that recognized sales people as individuals for their achievements.

The mission statement of the firm ("To achieve preeminence in the manufacturing and marketing of personal care products by providing personalized service, value, and convenience to Mary Kay customers through our independent sales force") summarized the attitudes of management towards people in field sales as well as customers. It was considered an all-exclusive statement of what the company wanted to be. As President Bartlett indicated, "We used to have financial goals as part of the mission statement, and we have gone away from that. That didn't work as well for us." Having a flexible, philosophically-oriented statement yielded some clearly delineated objectives for the corporation. Division and department objectives supported the mission statement.

To emphasize the importance of the corporate mission statement, President Bartlett had it printed up on small tent cards. These were distributed to all of the employees to remind them of the fundamental social and economic purpose of the firm. On the other side of the tent card were three words: "listen, listen, listen."

Manufacturing was emphasized in the first statement of preeminence because management felt that consumer driven organizations needed to have competitive products and excellence in manufacturing to survive. As part of the changing focus at Mary Kay, the senior vice president of research and development/quality assurance reported directly to the president. Previously, the R&D and quality assurance programs reported inside the manufacturing group. "I wanted, frankly," indicated President Bartlett, "to draw the manufacturing group into this mission so that they were not feeling separate from it; they are a part of it."

The use of the phrase personal care products in the mission statement was a revision of an older mission statement that included the phrase: "being the leading teaching-oriented skin care cosmetic company." This was a narrow statement that tended to focus on skin care only. The personalized service phrase was a continuation of what the firm had done well at for twenty-five years. Management did not want this area to be neglected by other changes in the mission. Convenience was included because the strength of the firm was thought to be in the consultant. When the customer lost the consultant it became inconvenient to buy Mary Kay products. Included was the phrase, "through our independent sales force." The sales force was thought to "drive" the objectives of the company.

There was no formal planning department at Mary Kay Cosmetics. The emphasis was placed on having a corporate mission that would be flexible and could be looked back on from time to time, as opposed to a strategy that said the firm was expected to reach certain goals in a specific year. Management felt that, as a basic strategy, a team of flexible, hard-hitting, and adaptable executives would be better able to handle the major changes that were occurring in the external environment. A recent appointment of Dr. Myra Barker as senior vice president of research & development/quality assurance and chief scientific officer reflected this strategy. "This reflects our concern for being in harmony with what might hit us scientifically in the cosmetic marketing world," indicated President Bartlett. "Good strategy is implementation strategy—where you don't get off with a planning group and say, 'This is where we're going to arrive at an X time in the future.' . . . but you're flexible enough, and you have the intellectual muscle to adapt to change."

"I fear a rigidly-in-place plan" and "I fear formal planning departments" were responses of President Bartlett when asked in his Dallas office if Mary Kay Cosmetics had a formal plan for looking ahead. Bartlett had concluded that "we have a overriding mission which we can look back on, and I'd rather view the mission we have, as opposed to a locked-in-concrete strategy that says we will come out at such and such a place in the year 2000. While I say that," he maintained, "there is no way that we can really anticipate all the major changes coming at us now, the geometric progression of information, governmental interference, regulation, and all the myriad of factors that we have to face."

Although there was not a formal strategic planning department at Mary Kay Cosmetics, the product line was planned out for five years. Each year key executives, such as the president, department heads, directors and all who might be involved in implementing the strategy, would meet to brainstorm sociological, consumer, industry, and scientific trends. Out of this meeting would emerge a product plan. For three years out it was very detailed, showing what the firm was doing every month. President Bartlett felt that such planning was necessary to anticipate the changes that they knew were going to happen.

"You gain flexibility by having this type of plan," suggested Curran Croskeys, vice president of product marketing. "By having a track to follow you accomplish the plan in a routine way. You use brainpower and other resources to change if you have to."

The Contemporary Challenge

One era ended and another began when Mary Kay Cosmetics experienced its first sales decline in 1984. The early era is a case study in entrepreneurship. The latter era is a study in the efforts of an established organization attempting to achieve its objectives in a changed business environment. Mary Kay's initial objective was "to establish a company that would give unlimited opportunity to women." In the late 1980s there was an increase in full-time job opportunities for women elsewhere. Not only were they not available to sell the product, but they were not at home to buy it.

Mary Kay Cosmetics, Inc. had for over twenty-five years focused on celebrating the achievements of its sales force. Much of the forward momentum in that sales force had come from the entrepreneurial spirit of Mary Kay Ash, the founder of the company. Mary Kay had been elevated to the position of chairman emeritus. A new management team was in place. The firm had repositioned itself to meet the challenges of a new decade. The question now is, can the firm accomplish its corporate mission and objectives in this changing environment?

DISCUSSION QUESTIONS

1. Evaluate and justify the personal selling strategy of Mary Kay Cosmetics. What factors should a manufacturer consider before choosing to include personal selling as a form of promotion in the marketing mix?
2. What evidence is there to conclude that the marketing concept is understood and applied by Mary Kay management?
3. Evaluate the strategies that Mary Kay management has introduced as part of its positioning strategy. How much impact will these strategies have in the competitive environment as the firm seeks profitable growth in the marketplace?
4. How important is a mission statement in giving direction to strategy development in a marketing-orientated organization?
5. How much importance is placed on the planning function at Mary Kay Cosmetics?
6. What conclusions can you draw from a review of the financial performance of Mary Kay Cosmetics, Inc. from the years 1978–1988?
7. Discuss the importance of changes in the external environment. How much impact do they have on strategic planning in organizations like Mary Kay Cosmetics?

APPENDIX A   Consolidated Statements of Cash Flows Years Ended December 31, 1988, 1987

	1988	1987
Cash flows from operating activities:		
Net loss	$ (8,998,000)	$ (20,888,000)
Adjustments to reconcile net loss to net cash provided by operating activities:		
Depreciation	8,288,000	9,180,000
Amortization	6,410,000	7,052,000
Defined benefit retirement program expense	3,598,000	—
Accretion expense	17,493,000	14,834,000
Deferred tax provision	(7,522,000)	(106,000)
Write down of assets	11,000,000	4,696,000
Loss on disposition of assets	27,000	325,000
Extraordinary expenses	1,245,000	10,923,000
Changes in assets and liabilities:		
Decrease (increase) in:		
Accounts receivable	(1,806,000)	(125,000)
Inventories	(15,870,000)	(12,767,000)
Income tax receivable	—	6,206,000
Other current assets	(895,000)	(464,000)
Goodwill	—	—
Other assets	(392,000)	(195,000)
Increase (decrease) in:		
Accounts payable	2,984,000	589,000
Accrued liabilities	11,283,000	8,817,000
Deferred sales	1,858,000	(1,996,000)
Other liabilities	(458,000)	(343,000)
Federal income tax refund	3,986,000	10,164,000
Other, net	729,000	754,000
Net cash provided by operating act.	32,960,000	36,656,000
Cash flows from investing activities:		
Purchase of investment	(15,541,000)	—
Capital expenditures	(6,025,000)	(2,576,000)
Proceeds from sales of assets	383,000	1,130,000
Net cash provided by (used in) investing activities	(21,183,000)	(1,446,000)
Cash flows from financing activities:		
Principal payment of long-term debt	(90,000,000)	(125,733,000)
Increase in long-term debt	(82,535,000)	90,000,000
Cost of refinancing debt	(1,569,000)	(8,596,000)
Proceeds from loans from life insurance policies	796,000	—
Net cash used in financing act	(8,238,000)	(44,329,000)
Net increase (decrease) in cash and cash equivalents	3,539,000	(9,119,000)
Cash and cash equivalents at beginning of year	11,500,000	20,619,000
Cash and cash equivalents at end of year	$ 15,039,000	$ 11,500,000

(continued)

APPENDIX A   Consolidated Statements of Cash Flows Years Ended December 31, 1988, 1987 *(continued)*

	1988	1987
Additional information:		
Cash payments (refunds) for:		
Interest (net of amounts capitalized)	17,290,000	29,107,000
Income taxes	4,755,000	(15,235,000)
Noncash financing activities:		
Restructuring an existing note receivable		
Decrease in note receivable	$ 17,267,000	—
Decrease in accounts receivable	1,000,000	—
Increase in note receivable	(11,000,000)	—
Increase in assets held for sale	(10,000,000)	—
Increase in deferred taxes	2,733,000	—
Restructuring an existing note payable:		
Decrease in long-term debt	(16,000,000)	—
Decrease in accrued liabilities	(862,000)	—
Increase in long-term debt	16,500,000	—
Increase in deferred taxes	362,000	—

APPENDIX B   Mary Kay Cosmetics, Inc., Dallas, Texas Financial Performance
1978–1988

Year	Net Sales (000)	Net Profit (000)	Total Assets (000)	Net Worth (000)
1988	$405,730	$(8,998)	$289,043	$(100,757)
1987	325,647	(20,888)	261,568	(90,324)
1986	255,016	(55,502)	284,180	(69,351)
1985	13,457[1]	(1,306)	328,922	(13,647)
	235,513[2]	21,286	272,166	183,304
1984	277,500	33,781	217,554	163,746
1983	323,758	36,654	180,683	131,725
1982	304,275	35,372	152,457	95,316
1981	235,296	24,155	100,976	61,952
1980	166,938	15,135	74,431	38,633
1979	91,400	9,632	50,916	24,618
1978	53,746	4,873	36,305	25,947

Source: Company annual reports
[1] Period from December 5 to December 31, 1985
[2] Period Ended December 4, 1985

APPENDIX C   Avon Products Inc., New York Financial Performance 1978–1986

Year	Net Sales (000)	Net Profit (000)	Total Assets (000)	Net Worth (000)
1986	$2,883.10	$158.70	$2,296.30	$ 681.30
1985	2,470.10	(59.90)	2,289.00	926.40
1984	2,605.30	181.70	2.287.50	1,157.10
1983	2,607.60	172.90	2,256.80	1,273.10
1982	2,710.10	186.60	2,227.60	1,245.10
1981	2,725.20	216.50	1,611.90	930.50
1980	2,569.10	242.10	1,583.10	928.30
1979	2,377.50	244.00	1,417.00	866.30
1978	2,086.30	233.60	1,282.40	770.70

Source: Company annual reports

APPENDIX D   Direct Selling Industry 1980–1988

Year	Retail Sales (000)	Salespeople
1988	$9,695,556	3,996,000
1987	8,789,415	3,614,000
1986	N/A	N/A
1985	8,360,000	5,129,994
1984	8,640,000	5,808,928
1983	8,575,000	5,114,276
1982	8,500,000	4,933,413
1981	N/A	N/A
1980	7,500,000	4,908,947

Source: Direct Selling Association–1988

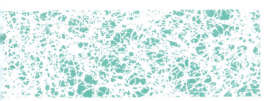

NAME INDEX

SUBJECT INDEX